THIRD EDITION

Cuisine *and* Culture

A HISTORY OF FOOD AND PEOPLE

Linda Civitello

WILEY

JOHN WILEY & SONS, INC.

Library of Congress Cataloging-in-Publication Data:

Civitello, Linda.
Cuisine and culture : a history of food and people/Linda Civitello—3rd ed.
    p. cm.
Includes bibliographical references and index.
ISBN 978-0-470-40371-6 (pbk.); 978-0-470-41195-7 (ebk.)
  1. Food—History. 2. Food—Social aspects. 3. Food habits—History. I. Title.
TX353.C565 2011
641.3—dc22

                        2010016916

Printed in the United States of America

V10013015_082219

CONTENTS

Recipes, Menus, and Ingredients

Food Fables

Crossing Cultures

Culinary Confusion

Holiday Histories

Charts/Boxes

FOOD FOR THOUGHT

"We are what our ancestors ate and drank."

—Ethnobotanist Gary Nabhan[1]

This book is the short version of the long story of the greatest predator on planet Earth—humans. It examines cuisines and cultures from the African savanna to the kitchens of California.

What Does Food Mean?

From prehistory, humans have given meaning to everything connected with food: who is allowed to fish for it, farm it, kill it, or mill it; what vessels and utensils are used in the preparation; what time of day the meal is eaten; who sits where at the table (if you're eating at a table)—how close to an important person, a certain food, the salt, a person of another gender, race, or class; what order the food is served in; who serves it; whether it is hot or cold, cooked in water or by direct fire. In European and American cultures, serving a whole boiled chicken at an important occasion would be an insult, while in Taiwan, it is the centerpiece of a banquet. There is no one food that is consumed by everyone on Earth.

A look at average households in two cultures that seem the same can reveal profound differences in attitudes to food, nature, and the environment. Both cultures spend a great deal of money on plants and take great pride in their landscaping. Both cultures keep animals. Both cultures create habitats for fish. But in the first culture, everything is for food. The plants and animals are edible and the artificial ponds are stocked with fish for eating. In the second culture, everything is for show. The plants are ornamental, the animals are pets, and the fish in the aquariums are expensive, exotic, and inedible. The first culture is ancient Rome; the second is the United States. The Romans had words for meadow and grass *(herba)*, because those were places where sheep could graze. But a lawn, good land where no food is grown, would have made no sense to them.

Identity—religious, ethnic, national—is intensely bound up with food. Every group thinks of itself as special and uses food to show it: "We eat this. They [religion, ethnic group, country] eat that." Whether you take your tea with cream, sugar, and small sandwiches in the afternoon; green in a special ceremony; ice cold; spiced and called *chai;* or use the leaves to smoke foods or tell your fortune depends on whether you're in England, Japan, the United States, India, China, or Turkey.

Alcohol, too, is used differently in different cultures. For Jews and Christians, wine has always been a crucial part of the religion. In ancient Greece, wine was consumed after the meal at a symposium, a religious and political ritual attended only by men. In ancient Rome, men and women drank wine with the meal. Impatient Americans couldn't wait for the meal and invented the cocktail.

What Makes a Meal?

What defines a meal varies throughout the world. In the United States and England, meat makes the meal, usually beef. The more important the meal, the bigger the beef: the thicker the steak, the larger the roast. In ancient Rome, roast pig was the banquet centerpiece. In Italy now, pasta will usually put in an appearance. In Medieval Europe, bread was the staple food, meaning that there was bread and often not much else; most of the day's calories came from just bread. In Asia, the staple food is rice, and to be considered a meal, there must also be vegetables.

War and Food

Cuisine and Culture also examines the connection between war and food. During a war, the work force, usually the farmers, goes off to fight, leaving the fields to women; boundaries change; the food supply is interrupted. Or food is used outright as a weapon: control the food supply and win the war. The wars have been numerous, including nine world wars (see Appendix C), while the periods of peace have been so few that historians have named them: Pax Romana, Pax Mongolica, Pax Turkica, Pax Americana. Overcoming the traditions and prejudices of cuisine and culture can be difficult or impossible, even when survival is at stake. During WWII, starving American servicemen could not bring themselves to eat nutritious insects, although they ate Spam in enormous quantities.

The Chef and Cookbooks in History

The role of the chef has changed profoundly, too, from the anonymous cooks of ancient times to the celebrity chefs of today. The duties and status of other people involved in food preparation have also changed. Originally, butchers killed animals. With industrialization, butchers now cut the already killed animals into pieces. In some cultures, like ancient India, butchers were considered "unclean" and were of very low status. But in Jewish communities in Eastern Europe in the nineteenth century, butchers were valued because they had food. Parents were happy to have their daughter marry a butcher, because she would never starve.

Printed cookbooks have existed for only about 500 years, but didn't have specific amounts and instructions until about 250 years ago. Cooking schools began a little more than 100 years ago, in France. Although throughout history most cooking in the home was done by women, women chefs are recent arrivals, from the middle of the twentieth century.

Historiography: A Brief History of Food History

Food history is a new field. The first comprehensive work, British author Reay Tannahill's *Food in History*, was not published until 1973. Maguelonne Toussaint-Samat's *A History of Food* appeared in 1987, but her book was not translated into English (by Anthea Bell) until 1992. The anthology *Food: A Culinary History from Antiquity to the Present*, edited by Jean-Louis Flandrin and Massimo Montanari, was published in 1996. Three years and seven translators later, the English version was published. The focus of all of these books is European; the editors of the latter two are Renaissance and Medieval specialists, respectively.

In the years since the first edition of this book, there has been an explosion of serious books about food. Chief among them is *The Oxford Companion to Food and Drink in America*, edited by Andrew Smith and with many entries written by him, in addition to all of his other books. I incorporate as much of the new research as possible, but there are still gaps in our knowledge either because sources are missing or because they haven't been translated yet.

Food historians have spent great portions of their lives studying one subject— Charles Perry's astounding knowledge of medieval Arab and Mongol cuisine, and twentieth-century California cuisine; Clifford Wright on the Mediterranean; Claudia Roden on Arab food; Najmieh Batmanglij's beautiful books about Persian food and the Silk Road; Betty Fussell on corn; the numerous books by Andy Smith, Warren Belasco, Roger Horowitz, and so many more. This book cannot go into that kind of depth, but I hope it will whet your appetite to look further into these works and others. This entire book is an appetizer, a broad overview to put food in historical, political, social, economic, anthropological, and linguistic context.

What's New in the Third Edition of *Cuisine and Culture*

This edition of *Cuisine and Culture* differs from the first two editions in several important ways. It is longer, so there is more information. Some is new, some expanded. There are more recipes and more primary source quotes. More cuisines and cultures are included, among them Norwegian, Ethiopian, Canadian, and Maya.

The chapters have been reorganized. The greatest changes are in the Fourth Course, which covers Inca, Maya, Aztec, and Southwestern American cuisines and cultures in much more depth. The Ninth Course deals exclusively with the cuisines and cultures of Africa and Asia. It explores the Arab influence in Africa since the Middle Ages, and differences in regional African cuisines. There is an African Spices Chart, as well as specifics on the European colonization of Africa. The regional cuisines of India are examined; a chart compares various curries: *vindaloo, garam masala, rogan josh,* and others. There is much more on Japanese cuisine, including umami.

A taste of what's new in the other chapters: the Second Course has additional information about Greek and Roman cuisines, including attitudes toward drinking wine, a Drunkenness Chart, and a comparison of the Greek symposium and the Roman *convivium.* The Third Course has more information about the Arab Agricultural Revolution and the invention of distilled liquor. Information about Asia that was in this chapter has been moved to the Ninth Course.

The Fifth Course on the Columbian Exchange has more on the cross-cultural exchange of foods and on the Renaissance. The Sixth Course deals with only America, from its founding through 1850; the Seventh Course covers seventeenth- and eighteenth-century France. The Eighth Course now covers the Civil War and Industrial Revolution in the United States, from 1850 to 1900, and Europe in the nineteenth century.

More information on industrialization is presented in the Tenth through Twelfth courses, including a section on Depression Innovation—how the food industry dealt with the Depression in the 1930s; a chart of multinational food providers; and a chart of the largest food sellers in the United States.

Forbidden Fruit

We humans are restless creatures, curious and greedy. We want to see what's on the other side of the hill, down the river, in the cave. How else to explain that the Latin word for bread—*panis*—ended up in Japanese crumbs—*panko*—courtesy of the Portuguese; why the name for a favorite Swedish food, stuffed cabbage, is half the Swedish word for cabbage—*kål*—and half the Greco-Turkish word for stuffed vegetables—*dolmar;* or why the word for tomato is the same in Italian—*pomodoro*—and in Polish—*pomidory?*

What we believe about food has changed over time. Once people knew for sure that potatoes caused leprosy and sugar cured toothaches. Romans believed that cinnamon grew in swamps guarded by giant killer bats. Americans thought beer was a really good drink for children. A princess was laughed out of town because she dared to use a fork. And Italian food was very, very bad for you. It's all true, and it's all here.

Keep reading.

Acknowledgments

This book would not have been possible without the depth and breadth of the Wiley bench. JoAnna Turtletaub gave me the initial good news that Wiley wanted this book; Julie Kerr shepherded it through the first two editions. This third edition benefited from the calm guidance of Christine DiComo McKnight, always available to bounce an idea around or suggest a solution. I would also like to thank Abby Saul for shepherding the book through production; copyeditor Doreen Russo, for the second time; and Nick Anderson, the designer. I thank the reviewers of this and the previous editions for their suggestions: Dr. Michael T. Adessa of the Scottsdale Culinary Institute; John Bandman of the Art Institute, New York (and also for his photographs); and Bryan Flower of Robert Morris College.

This book is possible because I live in a world-class city between two world-class library systems: the UCLA libraries and the Los Angeles Public Library. Unfortunately, because of budget cuts, each is now closed one day a week: UCLA on Saturday, LAPL on Sunday. The Culinary Historians of Southern California—especially Nancy Zaslavsky, Charles Perry, Richard Foss, and Carol Penn-Romine—and their lecture series provided stimulation and fundraising for the LAPL's superb collection of food books. Andrea Rademan's peripatetic food group provided degustation. I am extremely grateful to Nina Diamond for allowing me to record a food and art audio tour for the Getty Museum.

The indefatigable Thomasine Howlett keeps finding wonderful students for me to teach at St. Joseph's Table in Venice, California. The Association for the Study of Food and Society was and is a constant source of amazing information, especially Ken Albala, Rachel Laudan, and Nancy Harmon Jenkins. And, of course, Andy Smith.

I have so many guardian angels looking out for me, providing me with humor, support, and food. My family: my dear Aunt Yolanda, 94 years young; my Uncle Charlie, who died while I was finishing this book; my brothers Mike and Joe; my sister-in-law Sue; my niece Dana; and my 100+ cousins, including the new-found Sandy. My family of friends: Pamala Ferron; Barbara Hartley; Ellen and Kelly Hill; Juanita Lewis (usually carrying a roast chicken); Melinda and Jack Arnold; Ralph and Kelli Kenol; Carol Lynch; Marilyn Moss; the Orringer family; Mary Ann Milano Picardi; Rod Pinks; Mary Ryan; Randi Sunshine and Dan Sherkow; Mary Connor; Marco Filippi and Gaia Guidi of Olio & Olive, who keep me supplied with olive oil; Alberto and Ursula Vera of Sorrento Italian Market; and Dr. Solomon Hamburg and his wonderful nurses for being real life-savers. I thank my students, current and former, for giving me more of a boost than they can ever imagine.

Most of all, I thank my ancestors for having the foresight to be Italian.

From Raw to Cooked

Prehistory

Animals don't cook. The ability to use fire is one of the crucial things that separates us from them. Scientists used to think that humans were different from animals because we use tools and have language. Then we discovered that animals use tools and can communicate with each other and sometimes even with us, like Koko, the gorilla who learned sign language. As Stephen Pyne, the world's leading authority on fire, points out, there may be "elements of combustion" on other planets, but so far, "We are uniquely fire creatures on a uniquely fire planet."[1] Fire enabled humans to cook. In 2009, in a book called *Catching Fire: How Cooking Made Us Human*, anthropologist Richard Wrangham theorized that "Our ancestors were able to evolve because cooked foods were richer, healthier and required less eating time."[2]

Humans Learn to Find Foods: Hunting and Gathering

The oldest fossil of human ancestors that has been excavated so far was approximately 12 million years old.[3] It was found in Spain in 2009, and dubbed *Anoiapithecus brevirostris*. The oldest fossils discovered before that were in Africa; they were between six and seven million years old.[4] From the jaws and teeth of these hominids—human-like creatures—scientists deduce that they were primarily plant

1

eaters—herbivores. Our back teeth, the molars, are flat like stones for grinding grain and plants, and that is what we still use them for when we chew. Scientists think that over millions of years, early humans developed two survival advantages: (1) between four million and one million B.C., human brain size tripled, growing to what it is today, approximately 1,400 cubic centimeters; and (2) they stood upright on two feet—became bipedal—which allowed them to see farther and left their hands free to use weapons for protection and to kill animal food. Food historians speculate that early humans learned to like the taste of meat from small mammals and animals that could be caught and killed easily, like lizards and tortoises, and from scavenging the leftover carcasses of large animals killed by other large animals.[5]

These early humans were hunter-gatherers, nomads who followed the food wherever it wandered or grew. Work related to food was divided by gender. Men left the home to hunt animals by following them to where they went for food, especially salt. Women gathered fruits, nuts, berries, and grasses because their lives revolved around a cycle of pregnancy, birth, and child rearing.[6] Gathering was more reliable than hunting. Becoming carnivores—meat eaters—probably helped humans survive, too. In case of a shortage of plants, there was an alternate food source. Now we were omnivores—we ate everything. We still have the front or canine teeth, sharp like a dog's for tearing meat, to prove it. However, human teeth weren't sharp enough to pierce animal hides. For that, something else was necessary—tools.

Scientists believe that humans invented tools about 1.9 million to 1.6 million years ago. Early humans butchered animal meat, even elephants, with blades made out of stone, which is why this period is called the Stone Age (as opposed to the Bronze Age and the Iron Age, which came later). Archaeologists call these people *Homo habilis*—"handy man." Then, approximately 1.5 million to 500,000 years ago, another group appeared called *Homo erectus*—"upright man." These people migrated north from Africa to Europe and east to India, China, and Southeast Asia. They had better tools than any of the other groups. And for the first time, they had fire.

Humans Learn to Use Fire: Cooking vs. Cuisine

Scientists believe that humans evolved for millions of years before they learned to use fire between 500,000 and one million years ago. Scientists speculate that fires started by accident, either by lightning or when hunters were pounding meat with stone hammers on stone slabs and sparks flew. In whatever way the fire started, humans figured out how to keep it going by appointing somebody keeper of the flame day and night, perhaps the first specialized job. For the first time, humans had a tremendous tool with which to control the environment. It kept night terrors and animals away. It was also sacred, "the only substance which humans can kill and revive at will."[7] The god who controlled lightning was usually the most powerful god in early religions. Most cultures have creation myths of how humans stole or were given fire by the gods and how they were punished and suffered for this divine knowledge. Fire completely transformed food from raw to cooked, which allowed humans to eat otherwise indigestible foods and made food preservation possible. Control of fire gave humans control of their food supply—a huge survival advantage.

Once humans had fire, how did cooking begin? Perhaps by accident, although anthropologists are still arguing about this. One theory is that an out-of-control fire burned down a hut and accidentally cooked some pigs. People wandered in, tried the cooked meat, and liked it. Another theory is that a forest fire first roasted meat; still others think that cooking was a more deliberate, controlled act by humans.[8] In any case, now there were more options than raw bar and tartare.

It was cooking, but was it cuisine? Historian Michael Freeman's definition of cuisine is "a self–conscious tradition of cooking and eating . . . with a set of attitudes about food and its place in the life of man."[9] So, cuisine requires not just a style of cooking, but an *awareness* about how the food is prepared and consumed. It must also involve a wide variety of ingredients, more than are locally available, and cooks and diners willing to experiment, which means they are not constricted by tradition. Since early humans were still eating to survive, and had no control over their food supply, their cooking during this period was not cuisine.

We might never know exactly how people mastered fire and started cooking their food; we only know when—between 500,000 and one million years ago. Roasting over an open fire was probably the first cooking method. Pit roasting—putting food; in a pit with burning embers and covering it—might have come next. Then spit roasting, when hunters came home with the animal already on a spear and decided to cook it by hanging it over the fire and turning it. With sharp stone tools, meat could be cut into smaller pieces to make it cook faster. Food could be boiled in large mollusk or turtle shells where they were available, or even in animal skins,[10] but pots were not invented until around 10,000 B.C. and there were no sturdy clay boiling pots until about 5000 B.C.[11] Cooking in any of these vessels probably would have produced bacterial contamination, since there was no soap and no effective way to clean them. Finally, scientists believe that *Homo sapiens sapiens*—"wise man," the direct ancestor of humans—appeared between one million and 100,000 years ago.

Humans Learn to Communicate: Dance, Speech, Art—Culture

Before language was invented, early humans spoke with actions. They danced, which dance historian Joan Cass defines as "the making of rhythmical steps and movements for their own sake (as against steps and movements done in order to go somewhere, to do work, or to dress oneself)."[12] They danced together in religious ceremonies to ensure fertility of humans and crops, for rain, for a successful hunt. If the dance produced the result they wanted, they kept doing it exactly the same way again and again, turning it into a ritual. Music was added—beans or small stones in a pouch shaken or rattled, animal bones with holes drilled in them like a flute, maybe an animal skin stretched over a cooking pot to make a drum.[13] Then, about 100,000 years ago, we developed language. This, too, helped humans to survive. We could warn our tribe of danger, tell them where there was food, plan ahead and cooperate in work, name things and places, and generally organize the world, which is a step to controlling it.

Early art, too, was often communication connected to fertility and food. Small figures, women with exaggerated breasts and hips, were carved out of rock. Animals were painted on cave walls. A mask "changes your actual identity and merges you with the spirit that the mask represents."[14] This is called sympathetic magic. As Sir James Frazer points out in *The Golden Bough: A Study in Magic and Religion*, the principle at work is that "like produces like": if you make a symbol of what you want, it will happen. The woman will have a child, the hunt will be successful, the animal your mask represents will be found. You have control over these things because you have, in a sense, created them.[15] The animals most commonly represented in prehistoric cave paintings found in France and Spain are horses, followed by bison, deer and reindeer, oxen, the ibex, then elephants and mammoths.[16] So food, art, and religion have been connected in these regions since the earliest human times.

PREHISTORIC HUMAN ACHIEVEMENTS

WHEN–B.C.	WHERE	WHAT
65 million		Dinosaurs become extinct
12 million	Spain	Oldest hominid fossil
1 million – 500,000		Fire
before 100,000		Dance
100,000		Speech
33,000	Chauvet, France	Cave paintings and other art
25,000–20,000	Willendorf, Germany	Stone sculpture—fertility goddesses
18,000; 15,000	Lascaux, France; Altamira, Spain	Cave paintings and other art
14,000	Middle East	Dogs domesticated from wolves
before 10,000	Japan	Pottery
8000		Ice Age ends—agricultural revolution begins in the Middle East

Corpses, Middens, and Coprolites

How do archaeologists know what happened before written history? How accurate is the information? The same scientific tools that solve crimes today, such as DNA and microscopic analysis, can solve ancient mysteries. Much of what we know about early humans comes from three sources: corpses—their preserved bodies; middens—their garbage piles; and coprolites—their fossilized feces. Bodies have been found all over the world, preserved by drying in hot climates, by freezing in cold climates, and by bogs in wet climates. Overdeveloped bones in the right forearm tell us that these people threw spears.[17] Analyzing their intestinal tracts reveals what these people ate, and also that many of them had the same intestinal parasites that we still have today.[18]

From middens, archaeologists know that in some ways the eating habits of early humans were not that different from ours: they smashed or broke bones to get to the marrow, too. And they did it for the same reason—because they liked it, not because there was nothing else to eat.[19] Today, this is called osso buco, Italian for "bone with a hole." The difference is that early humans ate bone marrow with their hands while squatting around a fire, while osso buco is eaten with a silver marrow spoon. Many of the recipes in French master chef Escoffier's cookbook *Le guide culinaire* have marrow as an ingredient, even sweet puddings like his Pouding à l'Américaine (#4438) and Pouding à la Moelle (#4439). Broken jaw bones and pierced skulls indicate that early humans savored the taste of animal tongues and brains. The shells of shellfish like mussels and limpets also survive in middens, telling us that humans ate these as far back as 60,000 to 120,000 years ago.[20]

From coprolites, we know what foods early humans ate because we can see what they excreted. Seeds, fibers, and other indigestible matter ended up in the coprolite. In this way, the human digestive tract was also part of the food chain, helping plants to spread. From these methods, we know that wild crab apples were consumed 750,000 years ago in Kazakhstan, just north of modern Afghanistan.

Dating the items found in corpses, middens, and coprolites is done by several methods. Carbon dating measures the amount of radioactive decay in a life form. Tree ring analysis—dendrochronology—can reveal what the climate was like and how much rainfall occurred at certain times. Analysis of pollens can also help decipher ancient dates.

The Ancient Agricultural Revolution

Geography and climate are the two most important factors that determine where life is hospitable to plants and animals, including humans. Scientists believe that the Ice Age, some time between 40,000 B.C. and 12,000 B.C., made it possible for Asian peoples to migrate east and cross into North and South America. The Ice Age had dried up the seas, creating dry land between Asia and Alaska, making it possible to walk from one continent to the other.

When the Ice Age ended around 10,000 years ago, the last of the glaciers receded and the planet warmed up. This was the first of three major climate changes planet Earth has experienced. The other two were the Medieval Warm Period (A.D. 950–1300) followed by the Little Ice Age, which ended about 100 years ago. Some scientists think that we are in a new period of global warming caused by pollution from gases produced by car engines and machinery (the "greenhouse effect") and that we have to do something about it fast. Others think it is just part of a natural cycle. Still others think that climate is random and that a catastrophic change could occur suddenly for no reason and be completely out of the control of humans.

Humans Learn to Domesticate Foods: Sheep and Goats

Gathering nuts and seeds and grasses and hunting wild game was unreliable, inefficient, and could support only a limited population. Humans wanted more control over their environment and a guaranteed supply of food, especially food they liked. So about 10,000 years ago, humans began to tame wild plants and animals. From the earliest times, food was bred to taste better, be hardier, and yield more—in other words, it was genetically modified. This was a time-consuming and difficult process, because all plants and animals have ways to defend themselves—husks and tusks, shells and spines. The first domesticated animals were sheep and goats, then pigs and cows.

After domestication came farming. Fire was a force here, too. Slash-and-burn agriculture is one of the oldest and simplest ways to clear the land of trees. Once used extensively by primitive tribes, it is still used today in some places, like Borneo. The process: slash the bark on the tree, which stops the sap from flowing and eventually kills the tree. The leaves die and fall off, allowing sunlight to filter onto the forest floor, where the fallen leaves decompose into fertilizer. Then crops are planted. In two or three years, when the soil starts to show signs of being depleted of nutrients, the dead trees are burned, the ash provides fertilizer, and more crops are planted. Unfortunately, this requires constantly moving into new areas and destroying the forests.

Humans Learn to Cultivate Foods: Barley and Wheat

The first cultivated plants were barley, then wheat *(Triticum)* from wild grasses. There are about 30,000 varieties of wheat.[21] Ancient wheats—emmer, spelt, einkorn—had several layers of protection, including a very hard inedible outer covering called chaff, which had to be roasted to be removed. Then friction had to be applied to the wheat to separate it from the chaff, a process called threshing. This was done by having oxen walk on the wheat, or by hitting it. The chaff was lighter than the wheat, so it could be blown or fanned away. Then the wheat had to be ground to make flour. This was done by hand until animals began to be used around 800 B.C. These flours were stone ground and coarse ground, and most likely still contained bits of chaff or fine particles of stone. The problem was that heating the wheat to remove the chaff killed what makes it rise—gluten. So the earliest breads were flat, more like crackers. Some examples that still exist are Indian chapatis—flour and water baked on a hot griddle; pooris—also flour and water, but quick fried; and Jewish matzoh, which is baked. A very important change occurred about 7000 B.C., when wheat with a weaker chaff began to be grown, so the roasting step could be removed and the gluten was free to rise.[22] Leavened bread was probably first made in Egypt, and it was probably an accident.

Did domestication and cultivation occur only once or more than once in different places? Some plants like barley, lentils, and rice seem to have been domesticated in multiple places. There is also evidence that pigs were kept around 7000 B.C. in the city of Jericho in the Near East and thousands of miles away on the island of New Guinea in the South Pacific.[23] Domestication altered some plants and animals so much that they became dependent on humans for reproduction. Maize, native to the Americas and what we call corn, is an example. The seeds, which are the kernels, no longer fall off by themselves, but have to be removed from the cob.

THE ANCIENT AGRICULTURAL REVOLUTION

WHEN–B.C.	WHERE	WHAT
10,000	Southwest Asia	Wheat, barley, sheep, goats domesticated
8000	Mexico	Chiles and squash domesticated
8000	Peru	Lima beans domesticated
7000	Southwest Asia	Bread wheat developed; flax for fabric
7000	Southwest Asia and New Guinea	Pigs domesticated
6000	Northern China (first agriculture in China)	Millet domesticated
6000	Middle East[24]	Apples cultivated
6000–5000	Southwest Asia	Cattle, chickpeas, lentils domesticated
6000–4000	Southwest Asia (modern Armenia)[25]	Grapes cultivated for wine
5000	Yangtze River Delta, China; Central India	Rice domesticated
4000	Southwest Asia	Olives domesticated
3000	Southwest Asia	Cities, irrigation, wheel, plow, sail
2686–2181	Egypt	Pyramid building
2500	China	Water buffalo domesticated

Fermented Beverages: Mead, Wine, Ale

Settling down and farming allowed humans to have some foods and beverages it is impossible to have if you are a nomad. Mead—fermented honey—was probably the first fermented drink, perhaps another food accident. Maybe honey was left out, rain fell, yeast settled on the mixture. In both Greece and Rome, before winemaking, mead was offered to the gods.[26] Honey was a mysterious substance to ancient people. Greeks knew bees were connected to it, but not exactly how. Romans thought honey fell from heaven and landed on leaves, "the saliva of the stars."[27] Honey is produced from the nectar in flowers gathered by bees to feed young bees. Most of the water in the nectar evaporates, resulting in honey, which is 35 to 40 percent fructose, 30 to 35 percent dextrose, 17 to 20 percent water, and contains small amounts of enzymes, etc.[28]

Humans also started drinking wine very early. Maybe winemaking was done deliberately. Or perhaps wine was another culinary coincidence: grapes left at room temperature fermented naturally. Maybe crushed grapes and their juice left in the bottom of an animal skin fermented. Animal skins are all right for short-term transport of wine, but they aren't an efficient way to store it. Pottery is, and by about 6000 B.C. clay jugs were being used. A clay jug with a narrow mouth can be stoppered to prevent the oxidation that will turn wine to vinegar, while animal pouches can't. It is from the wine residue, tartaric acid, in these clay vessels that we know how long ago humans were drinking wine.

It takes two years before vines bear fruit, and there is a very short time frame, just a few days, during which the grapes have to be picked and crushed—until recently, by stomping on them. Then they must be kept at a temperature that will allow them to ferment, and stored. It is impossible to wander around and to make wine, too. So, two of the earliest professions were growing vines and making wine.

From the beginning, wine was an upper-class drink. Beer was the beverage of the masses, and it, too, might have been the result of an accident. The housewives who were responsible for food preparation malted their grain—they let it sprout because it tasted better and it was easier to mill and bake into bread. Somehow, the malted grain fermented into an alcoholic beverage and began to be produced on its own, and women became the brewers.

Early Human Settlements

The early human settlements were small villages, extended family groups organized like a tribe or clan of 200 to 300 people, with an elder male as the final authority in disputes. Perhaps he was also a sort of spiritual leader or medicine man. Nothing was written, no laws were needed, because everyone was in agreement about what was right and wrong, and everyone was engaged primarily in the same occupation—procuring and preparing food. People who had special skills, like weaving, carving, or making baskets or pottery, would have done it *after* their duties connected to food were completed. But that changed as the advantages of farming and domestication became apparent. The settlements became larger, the land was irrigated with complicated systems of canals that required organization and cooperation, and governments arose.

Advanced Civilization: Cooking Becomes Cuisine

An *advanced* civilization then had all the elements that our civilizations have now: cities with thousands of people doing specialized labor, advanced technology, structure and institutions like government, and a way to keep records. These advanced civilizations were possible because there was a surplus of food, so not everyone had to farm all the time. Specialized labor became possible—like artisans, priests, warriors, chefs, teachers, and government officials to keep records of the population so they could collect taxes and raise an army. Advanced civilizations are where cooking for survival changes to cuisine—cooking with awareness, for a purpose other than just to make food edible.

Some historians think that cities were started for the purpose of worship. Could one feeble voice raised in prayer reach the gods? Thousands would have a better chance of being heard. For whatever reason they began, cities became centers of trade.

Salt: "White Gold"

One of the most valuable trade items from earliest times was salt. It is not a condiment like pepper or mustard or ketchup, but a mineral, NaCl, sodium chloride. Humans need it to live. Our nervous systems can't function without it. Its prevalence shows in the many phrases connected with salt: a valuable person is the "salt of the earth," which is how Christ referred to his apostles; a useless person is "not worth his salt." One of the oldest ways of obtaining salt was by boiling or evaporating seawater. This was done in ancient Egypt; in ancient Gaul—the Romans' name for France; in France in the eighteenth century, to avoid paying the salt tax; and in India in the twentieth century as a way to gain independence from England and the British salt monopoly. This is a very expensive and labor-intensive way to get salt compared to mining rock salt.

Currently in the United States, between two and three million tons of salt are mined each year from a mine that runs under the center of the United States, from Detroit and Cleveland south to Louisiana. This salt mountain is as big as Mt. Everest, the tallest mountain on earth. Only 4 percent of the salt that is mined is consumed; the other 96 percent is used to de-ice roads and by the chemical industry, which breaks it down into sodium and chloride. America also has the Great Salt Desert in Utah and the Bonneville Salt Flats, where cars are test raced.

In addition to salt, humans need fresh water to survive, so it is not surprising that the earliest civilizations began around rivers: the Tigris and Euphrates in southwest Asia, the Nile in Egypt, the Yellow (Huang He) in China, and the Indus in India.

The Fertile Crescent

The Fertile Crescent is an area of land that runs from the Mediterranean on its western end, then curves to the east in a crescent shape to the Tigris and

Euphrates rivers in modern Iraq, down to the Persian Gulf. It was in this part of the world, the land called Mesopotamia, which means "between the rivers," that scientists believe an advanced civilization began approximately 5,000 years ago—around 3000 B.C.

The Tigris and Euphrates Rivers

The cities in Mesopotamia were surrounded by walls for defense. Inside the walled city was another walled mini-city, the temple. Inside the temple was the most important building, the granary, where the city stored its food. Priests and priestesses honored the gods full-time by preparing food for them and celebrating with feasts on their special days. So, from the earliest civilizations, food, religion, and government were connected.

As thousands of unrelated humans came to live together in cities, they needed organization. A leader named Hammurabi became known as "the lawgiver." The Code of Hammurabi consisted of laws governing every aspect of life in Mesopotamia: the management of the irrigation canals, marriage, divorce, adoption, farming, construction, and so on. The punishment in many cases was literally "an eye for an eye" or a broken bone for a broken bone. Punishments were worse for crimes against the state than for crimes against other citizens. For example, the fine for stealing a sheep, pig, or ox from a temple was triple the fine for stealing from another citizen. The code also governed the wine trade and taverns. Tavern owners, usually women, had to report any talk they heard about plots to overthrow the government. And they were warned about serving watered-down wine. The punishment fit the crime—death by drowning.[29]

We know this because writing was invented in Mesopotamia, too. It was called cuneiform, which means "wedge-shaped," after the symbols that were pressed onto blocks of wet clay with an instrument called a stylus. After the clay hardened, the symbols became permanent records. Writing gives historians more information than just corpses, middens, and coprolites. Some of the written sources for information about food are recipes, correspondence, songs, poems, and other literature; laws; business records; and household lists from temples, palaces, and the homes of the wealthy.

Cuneiform went out of use in the first century B.C., and over the next several hundred years the tablets disappeared. In the 1840s, British archaeologists discovered 30,000 tablets and pieces of tablets.[30] Among them they discovered the world's first recipe for ale.[31] Sumerians brewed "eight barley beers, eight emmer beers, and three mixed beers."[32] Hops were not added until almost 4,000 years later in the Middle Ages in Europe. Today in Sudan, a beer called *buza is* still brewed in this ancient way without hops.[33]

"Let the gods eat roasted meat, roasted meat, roasted meat!"[34]

The abundance of food in Mesopotamia is evident in the records of what was presented to the gods and goddesses, who needed to eat four times a day. Their mainstay was bread, as it was for humans. The main god, Anu, and three main goddesses, Antu, Ishtar, and Nanaya, got 30 loaves a day—each. They also got "top quality dates," figs, and grapes.[35] There was also much meat given every day to them and to other minor divinities, about 10 total, at the four meals:

> 21 top-grade sheep, fattened and without flaw, fed on barley for two years; 4 specially raised sheep, fed on milk; 25 second-grade sheep not fed on milk; 2 large steers; 1 milk-fed calf; 8 lambs; 30 . . . birds; 20 turtledoves(?); 3 mash-fed geese; 5 ducks fed on flour mash; 2 second-grade ducks; 4 dormice; 3 ostrich eggs and 3 duck eggs.[36]

This was sacred food, ritually prepared. The millers, bakers, and butchers had to recite prayers of thanks to the gods and goddesses as they ground the grain, kneaded the bread, and slaughtered the animals. Then the priests placed the food on golden platters and set it before the gods, perhaps on a table. Historians don't know what happened then, but they speculate that the priests ate the food themselves or sold it if the temple needed money.[37]

In addition to lists like these for religious purposes, we have 40 recipes from Mesopotamia, from three different sources. They are typical of the way recipes were written until about 400 years ago: ingredients without amounts, and only a hint at technique. For example: "Meat is used. Prepare water; add fat [ ], milk(?); cypress(?) as desired, and mashed leek and garlic. It is ready to serve."[38] The brackets indicate that the translator cannot understand the words; the question marks indicate that the translator is not sure. One set of recipes is for 25 broths made with venison, gazelle, kid, lamb, ram, spleen, pigeon, mutton, and "meat" not further identified. There is one for turnip broth. The aromatics are usually onion, leek, garlic, and sometimes mint; the spices are cumin and coriander, which might be sprinkled on top just before serving. Sometimes the soup is strained; sometimes crumbs or flour are thickeners. Another set of recipes is more elaborate, giving instructions on how to slaughter various birds for religious ceremonies. One recipe is for small birds cooked in a fatty aromatic broth, served *en croûte*—in a crust. The birds are washed in cold water before they are put in the kettle, and again after they are heated in the broth, just as modern cooks skim the scum.[39]

In Mesopotamia, foods were preserved by drying, salting, covering them in oil, or in the case of dairy, by turning it into clarified butter and cheese. Ingredients mentioned in other sources are pomegranates, arugula, fish, pistachios, cherries, plums, lentils, anise seed, grasshoppers, eggplant, jujubes (a kind of date), vetch (legumes), honey, turtles, sesame seeds, and pork. They did not eat horses, dogs, or snakes.[40]

Such culinary creations call for great skill, so cooks were a highly regarded professional class who served apprenticeships to learn their trade. They were specialized, with cooks separate from bakers and pastry cooks. Their services were affordable only by the wealthy. A royal household might have 400 cooks and 400 pastry chefs.[41] The gods mirrored this: a major god like Marduk might have a minor god, who would be known as Cook of Marduk.[42]

How Humans Eat Together

By the first millennium B.C., Mesopotamians were giving elaborate banquets to display the power and wealth of the government. One was a 10-day feast to celebrate the building of the king's palace:

> . . . 69,574 guests were invited . . . Dozens of items were served in enormous quantities: 1,000 plump oxen, 14,000 sheep, 1,000 lambs, several hundred deer of various kinds, 20,000 pigeons as well as other birds, 10,000 fish, 1,000 jerboa [a rodent], 10,000 eggs, plus thousands of jugs of beer and skins full of wine.[43]

Oil was also used at banquets, but not in the food—it was perfumed and used in the guests' hair.[44]

In contrast to these public spectacles with vast amounts of food, people in Mesopotamia, like people everywhere, also had ceremonies that were more modest and personal.

HOLIDAY HISTORY:

Kispu

Kispu was a memorial meal that took place once a month on the last day of the Mesopotamian lunar calendar, during the dark of the moon. It was observed by all members of a family, living and dead. Kispu—from the word meaning "to break in pieces and distribute"—reinforced two important Mesopotamian beliefs: that your family was always with you, even after death, and that just because people were dead didn't mean they didn't need to eat. They just didn't need to eat as much. It also reinforced the wider family of the community, because the king also observed kispu. He honored the dead of his dynasty, the rulers before him, and all those who had died fighting for their country. Even the gods celebrated kispu, proof that breaking bread transcends time.[45]

Inventions That Aid in Trade: Wheel, Plow, Sail

Three extremely important inventions came out of Mesopotamia: the wheel, the plow, and the sailboat. The wheel and the plow were possible because of the availability of animal labor. Wheeled carts pulled by oxen or horses could transport more goods to market more quickly. They also made waging war with chariots possible. Animals pulling plows to turn the earth over for planting were far more efficient than humans. The sail made it possible to trade with countries that could be reached only by sea, or could be reached more quickly by sea, like India. All three inventions made the cities of Mesopotamia powerful trading centers with as many as 30,000 people each.

The wheel was put to use for one special food. A special breed of sheep produced especially delicious fat in its four-and-a-half-foot-long tail. But the tail was heavy and dragged on the ground, so humans made a little wheeled cart so the sheep could carry its tail around. Tail fat from this sheep is still highly prized today.[46]

Even after thousands of years of domestication and farming, of the tens of thousands of edible plant species on earth, only about 600 are raised for food now. Many were first grown in the Fertile Crescent. Now, because the Tigris and Euphrates rivers have been dammed, only about 10 percent of the fertile Mesopotamian marshlands still survive. The other 90 percent is now desert.[47]

Egypt: The Nile River

The Nile is the longest river in the world, its headwaters 4,160 miles upstream from where it empties into the Mediterranean Sea. The Nile was the giver of life for the ancient Egyptians. Water to drink and fish like carp, mullet, and sturgeon came from it. Every spring it overflowed its banks, bringing rich, fertile soil down from the mountains into the valley to grow food. There were three seasons in Egypt, all connected to the Nile and to planting: flooding was from the middle of June to the middle of October, when the floodwaters receded; sowing and growing lasted until the end of February; and harvesting continued until mid-June or July when the cycle began all over again. Humans scattered barley and wheat seeds by hand, then sent goats into the fields to walk on them and push them down into the soil so birds couldn't eat them before they had a chance to germinate.[48] By 1300 B.C., apple orchards were planted along the Nile.[49] Like the Mesopotamians, Egyptians irrigated. However, sometimes the water stagnated and became hospitable to mosquitoes and flies. Other vermin like mice and rats were also a problem because they chewed or burrowed their way into the granaries. Cats were domesticated in Egypt and worshipped because they kept the rodent population down.

One ancient food still eaten in Egypt is beans: "Beans have satisfied even the Pharaohs."[50] Most popular were and are fava beans—*ful nabed*; and brown beans—*ful medames*, the national dish of Egypt.

....

INGREDIENTS:

Egyptian *Ful Medames*[51]

2 pounds *ful medames,* soaked overnight

2–4 cloves garlic, crushed

6 *hamine* eggs (simmered in water with onion skins for at least 6 hours)

finely chopped parsley

olive oil

quartered lemons

salt and pepper

....

Ancient Egyptian culture revolved around a cycle of death and rebirth connected to the Nile. Many of the Egyptian gods and goddesses were related to death, but Osiris, who had triumphed over death, was also the god of resurrection and good. Egyptians believed that if they led good and orderly lives, they would be united with Osiris after death. On judgment day, when their hearts were weighed to see if they were heavy with sin, Egyptians made a "negative confession" to prove they had not violated the laws, many of which dealt with food and farming:

> I have not mistreated cattle.
> I have not cut down on the food or income in the temples.
> I have not taken the loaves of the blessed dead.
> I have not taken milk from the mouths of children.
> I have not built a dam against running water.[52]

The pharaoh was equated with the Nile as the giver of life. The people expected the pharaoh, like the river, to reappear after his death. To rule properly in the afterlife, he would need two things: an impressive tomb—a pyramid; and his body.

The Embalmers: Cinnamon and Salt

The Egyptians salted human bodies to preserve them so the spirit would be able to find its home again after death. First the brain was removed by drawing it out through the nose. Then the torso was cut open and the bowels and internal organs were removed. The cavity was stuffed with pungent-smelling spices like myrrh and cinnamon, then sewed back up. The corpse was submerged in a mineral salt called natron for 70 days. Then the salt was washed off and the body was wrapped in bandages. Now it was a mummy.

Mummification was done by the high priests, who had their heads shaved to be pure. Before the invention of insecticides in the twentieth century, shaving was the only way to guarantee that the servants of the gods would not have lice that could spread to the pharaoh. As a result of embalming, the priests knew a great deal about human anatomy. They used this knowledge to set bones; they also performed the first known brain surgery around 2500 B.C. They treated wounds with honey and moldy bread. This makes medical sense: the high sugar content of the honey draws moisture out of the cells, killing any bacteria,[53] and penicillin, which was discovered by British scientist Dr. Arthur Fleming in 1928, comes from mold.[54]

The Book of the Dead: Food in the Afterlife

The great pyramids were built during a period known as the Old Kingdom, which lasted from 2686 B.C. to 2181 B.C. The pyramids were packed with everything a king would need to live and rule properly in the afterlife, including his wife and servants, who were killed when he died. This custom worked to protect the pharaoh from assassination by those close to him; they knew that if the pharaoh died, they died, too. Sometimes even pets were mummified. Foodstuffs

Sphinx and Pyramid of Khafre at Giza, Egypt. Built ca. 2558–2532 B.C. The Sphinx, carved from a single mass of limestone, is 187 feet long and 66 feet high. The pyramid is 471 feet high. *Courtesy Corbis Digital Stock.*

found in pyramids include butter and cheese. Artwork and artifacts in pyramids reveal that the pharaohs ate well: a variety of meats, fish, dairy, fruits, vegetables, ostrich eggs, pastries.[55] Even beer making is depicted on pyramid walls.

Fermented Food: Bread

If the Nile was the giver of life, then bread *was* life. In ancient Egyptian, the word for bread was the same as the word for life.[56] In the beginning, bread was simple: grain and water patted into a flat circle with the hands, laid on a hot rock next to the fire to cook. This produced a flat bread. As far as food historians know, Egypt produced the first leavened bread, perhaps by accident. One theory is that yeast landed on some dough left out; another is that ale was mixed with the flour instead of water. In any case, the gluten in the flour went to work and the bread puffed up—still an awe-inspiring event. A piece of the fermented dough from the previous batch could be kept to guarantee that the next loaf would rise, and sourdough was born. Or you could just take the head off the beer or what was left in the bottom of the container after brewing, and add it to the flour. New technologies developed around leavened bread, such as closed ovens and molds shaped like triangles and long loaves. Commercial bakeries produced at least 40 different kinds of bread and pastries.[57] Commercial bakeries were necessary to provide for feasts the pharaohs gave:

10,000 biscuits . . . 1,200 Asiatic loaves, 100 baskets of dried meat, 300 cuts of meat . . . 250 handfuls of beef offal, 10 plucked geese, 40 cooked ducks, 70 sheep, 12 kinds of fish, fat quails, summer pigeons, 60 measures of milk, 90 measures of cream, 30 jars of carob seeds . . . 100 heads of lettuce, 50 bunches of ordinary grapes and 1,000 bunches of oasis grapes, 300 strings of figs, 50 jars of honeycomb, 50 jars of cucumbers, and 50 small baskets of leek bulbs.[58]

These foods were eaten with the hands. In early Egypt, upper-class diners reclined on mats or cushions on the floor in front of low tables, but over the years, chairs and standard-height tables came into use. Servants brought the food. The wealthy had a separate room just for cooking, instead of doing it on the roof or in the back of the building. But there was a vast underclass that had completely different eating habits.

Pyramid-Builder Food: The Jewish Diet

One of the earliest types of human relationships was slavery. In ancient societies, slavery was based on being in the wrong place at the wrong time: if you lost a war, you became the property of the winners. So the Jews became the slaves of the Egyptians. The Jews were the first people to believe in one god. This type of belief—monotheism—made their religion portable. Their one god was not connected to a particular place, but was everywhere, unlike the many gods in polytheistic religions that were attached to sacred groves or rivers or mountains. For example, many of the gods of the ancient Egyptians were connected to the Nile, so worshipping them anywhere else would have been impossible.

The Jews have many dietary laws. One of the most important is kosher butchering. The purpose is to inflict as little pain as possible on the animal, one of god's living creatures. The animal is hung upside down; then its throat is cut quickly with an extremely sharp blade. This has benefits for the animal and for humans. It is humane because the animal loses consciousness quickly and doesn't suffer. The advantage to humans is that gravity drains the blood away, so the butcher can easily see any tissue that is white, which means it is toxic to humans. Any animal that is not killed in this ritual religious fashion, for instance if it dies from disease or an accident, is considered impure—*treyf* (trafe)—and is forbidden. The koshering process continues in the kitchen, where the meat must be soaked, salted, and rinsed to remove all traces of blood.[59] The words *kosher* and *treyf* crossed over into English to refer to things that had nothing to do with food. For example, a person or deal that is kosher is aboveboard, honest, decent. *Treyf* is trash.

Other Jewish dietary laws prohibit eating the flesh of four-legged animals that don't ruminate—that is, chew their cud—or that have cloven hooves. Chief among these is the pig. Also forbidden: rodents, reptiles, and fish that do not swim or have scales—shellfish. Jews must not "boil the kid in the milk of its mother," which prohibits eating meat and dairy foods at the same meal or even within several hours of each other. Orthodox Jews must wait six hours after eating meat to have milk.[60] They also keep kosher kitchens so that meat and dairy never touch each other. The kosher kitchen has two preparation tables, two sets of pots and dishes kept in separate cabinets, and two sets of cooking and eating utensils. Traditionally, red dishes are for meat; blue are for dairy. Some modern kosher kitchens have separate sinks and dishwashers.

There is a large third class of foods, neither meat nor dairy, that is safe to eat with anything. These are called *parveh*—neutral—and include plant foods like flour, fruits, vegetables, and sugar; salt; some beverages; and fish. However, there are some restrictions on these foods, too. For example, fruit must not be eaten until a tree has been bearing for at least three years.

While the Jews were enslaved, Moses went to Pharaoh and told him that god had said, "Let my people go, that they may hold a feast to me in the wilderness." But Pharaoh wouldn't let the Jews go. They prayed to their god for freedom; he answered with a series of plagues that were intended to starve and hurt the Egyptians while saving the Hebrews. The plagues turned the Nile to blood so that the water wasn't drinkable and the fish died; covered the land with frogs that got into the ovens and the kneading bowls; filled the air with gnats and flies; killed the livestock of the Egyptians but let the Hebrews' animals live; covered humans and beasts with sores; caused it to hail so hard that the plants and the trees died; sent swarms of locusts to eat what was left of the crops and fruit; and covered Egypt with a thick darkness for three days.[61] The final punishment was the worst: their god would send the angel of death to kill the first-born son in every house unless people did as he commanded. This is the origin of Passover, one of the most sacred celebrations in Judaism.

HOLIDAY HISTORY:

Passover

The Jews did as god commanded: they slaughtered a one-year-old lamb, dipped a bunch of the herb hyssop in the blood, and touched the doorposts and the lintel, the beam above the door, as a sign of where they were. Then they roasted the lamb and ate it with unleavened bread and bitter herbs. The angel of death saw the sign and passed over the houses of the Jews, but did take the first-born sons of the Egyptians and the first-born of their cattle. There was a great cry of grief throughout Egypt and Pharaoh finally let the Jews go.

God told the Jews when to celebrate Passover and what to eat. Passover begins in the "first month [of the lunar calendar], on the fourteenth day of the month at evening [and continues] until the twenty-first day of the month at evening." Ritual foods for the Passover dinner, called a *seder*, include *harosset*, a mixture of chopped apples and nuts that symbolizes the bricks the Israelites were forced to make when they were building the pyramids; horseradish represents the bitterness of slavery; a hard–boiled egg dipped in salt water is the tears the slaves cried. Unleavened bread—*matzoh*—is eaten for seven days because the Jews left Egypt so quickly that there was no time to take leavening.[62]

The Christian holiday of Easter is connected to Passover. (See Chapter 2.)

According to the Old Testament, that is how the Jews finally gained their freedom. The leader in their exodus from Egypt was Moses, who parted the Red Sea and led them to Canaan (although he was not allowed to enter), the "land of milk and honey," foods that represent a place of plenty.

China: The Yellow (Huang He) River

China has some of the most dramatic geography on earth, and plant and animal life to match. In Tibet, on its western border, are the Himalayan mountains and the highest peak on earth. At almost 30,000 feet, Mt. Everest is nearly twice as high as the tallest peak in the lower 48 states, California's Mt. Whitney. China's lowest point, approximately 900 feet below sea level, is more than three times lower than California's Death Valley. China has climate extremes, too, from tropical rain forest to permanent ice caps. It has no Mediterranean climate, but has drenching monsoon rains followed by drought. It also has an enormous population: by A.D. 2, 60 million people.[63]

Historians believe that agriculture arose independently in China and Mesopotamia, because the Chinese cultivated millet, a grain that was unknown in the Middle East, at approximately the same time that wheat was domesticated in the Middle East. The earliest Chinese civilization, from approximately 6000 B.C., was the village of Ban Po in the floodplain of the Yellow or Huang He River in north central China. The village's defense was not a wall, but a moat. The people lived in huts with plaster walls and thatched roofs made of straw. Pigs and dogs were raised. Communal grain—millet—was buried in hundreds of pits scattered in the village. In 2005, archaeologists made an astounding find: millet noodles, perfectly preserved. This brought up the old rivalry between China and Italy over who invented noodles first. This "contest" began with the writings of Marco Polo (see Chapter 3), but each country still claims that it was making noodles first. The Italian response is that these are noodles, but they're not pasta, which is made from wheat.

At around the same time in northern China, salt was harvested when lake waters dried up during the summer. Salt production, either by harvesting or evaporation, predates what is usually used as a source of salt in China—soy sauce. Salt production dates from almost 2000 B.C., soy from around 1300 B.C. Soy sauce began as fish fermented in salt. Then soybeans were added, and finally, the fish was omitted, leaving just soybeans and salt. Soybeans are extremely nutritious legumes: they nourish the humans who eat them and the soil in which they are planted.[64] One of the earliest spices known in China is cinnamon. It is mentioned in the first herbal, in 2700 B.C.[65]

Chinese New Year is one of the oldest festivals observed anywhere. Around 2600 B.C., the Emperor Huang Ti began keeping records based on a lunar month and the twelve signs of the Chinese zodiac. Just as we have Sagittarius, Capricorn, and Scorpio, the Chinese have the Rat, the Tiger, the Rabbit, and other animals.

Chinese New Year

The Chinese New Year celebration is called Spring Festival and is deeply connected to China's ancient farming culture and to the moon. It begins at the new moon closest to the beginning of spring, usually the second new moon after the winter solstice. It always falls between January 21 and February 21, and lasts 15 days.[66]

New Year's Eve dinner is a feast of traditional foods that are supposed to bring good luck and prosperity in the coming year. Each region of China has its own specialties. Near the sea, it might be prawns, dried oysters (*ho xi*), raw fish salad (*yu sheng*), angel-hair seaweed (*fai-hai*), and "sleep together and have sons"—dumplings boiled in water (*jiaozi*).[67] In the south, rice in pudding and wrapped in leaves are favorite foods, while in the north, it's steamed dumplings made of wheat. A whole animal represents abundance, but fresh bean curd is avoided because it is white, the color of death. And don't cut your noodles—long noodles mean long life.

The Festival of Lanterns is the last night of Chinese New Year, when lights and firecrackers drive away demons and promise a good year ahead. New Year's Day is when *Hong Bao* (Red Packet) takes place. Presents and money wrapped in red paper—the color of good luck—are exchanged, along with greetings to relatives and neighbors.[68] Our year 2012 is 4709 in China. *Gong hai fat choy!* (May prosperity be with you!)

CHINESE ZODIAC YEARS

2011	Year of the Rabbit	2014	Year of the Horse
2012	Year of the Dragon	2015	Year of the Sheep
2013	Year of the Snake	2016	Year of the Monkey

Some Asian cultures celebrate New Year when China does. But around the world, New Year's festivals are celebrated at many different times of the year, in many different ways. For some, it is a religious ceremony and a time of cleansing. For others, it is a time for partying. For Great Britain, the new year used to begin in March. Then, in 1752, they adjusted the calendar to make it conform to the solar year. They added 11 days. They also shifted the beginning of the year to January. All of England's colonies around the world, including the ones in America, also adopted this New Calendar.[69]

Confucius and the *I Ching*

The Chinese philosopher known to the West as Confucius (551–479 B.C.) declared that everything on Earth would run smoothly if subjects respected rulers, younger brothers respected older brothers, wives respected husbands, and friends respected friends. He also supposedly assembled the *I Ching* (the *Book of Changes*) and the *Book of Songs*, a combination of court and peasant songs that

CROSSING CULTURES:

NEW YEAR CELEBRATIONS

COUNTRY/ RELIGION	NAME	DAY	HOW CELEBRATED
African-American	New Year's Day	January 1	Hoppin' John (red beans and rice)
Cambodia	Chaul Chnam Thmey	April 12, 13, or 14	House cleaning, visiting Buddhist monasteries
Denmark	New Year's Eve	December 31	Boiled cod with mustard sauce
Greece	New Year's Day	January 1	Pass out *vasilopita* (St. Basil's sweet bread w/lucky coin inside) in church
India/ Hindu	Diwali	October or November	Victory of good over evil; fireworks, oil lamps
Iran	Nowruz	Spring Equinox	Purification with bonfires and spring cleaning; fish and herbed rice
Ancient Ireland	Samhain	October 31 / November 1	(now Halloween) Bonfires, bobbing for symbolic magic apples
Italy	Capo d'Anno	December 31	Fireworks, lentils, sparkling wine
Japan	Shogatsu	January 1–3	Cleansing to start new, view sunrise, soba (buckwheat noodles = long life)
Judaism	Rosh Hashanah	162 days after first day of Passover	Holy day; cleansing; sweet foods
Korea	Sol-nal	January 1	Rice cake soup—*ttokkuk*
Russia	Novyi God	January 1	Roast goose or chicken, sweet cookies, vodka
Thailand	Songkrahn	April 13	Cleansing with water
U.S.	New Year's Eve / New Year's Day	December 31 / January 1	Party and drink champagne; watch football on January 1
Vietnam	Tet Nguyen Dan	Lunar (Chinese)	Red envelopes with money; fireworks

reveals much about the cuisine and culture of the time. It mentions 44 vegetables and herbs, including bamboo, Chinese cabbage, and celery; peaches, plums, and apricots; and pine and hazel nuts. Confucianism was the basis for government in China for many centuries. In the fifteenth century A.D., the Confucian scholars who ruled China made the decision that China would not trade with the rest of the world, which eventually proved damaging to China.

The Wall That Salt Built

In 221 B.C., Shi Huangdi, which means "first emperor," decided to build a Great Wall to protect China from attacks by the Mongols to the north. It was an expensive project, paid for with taxes from the state monopoly on salt—the first such monopoly in history.[70] The wall, 25 feet high and thousands of miles long, was built by more than one million men. It is one of only a few man-made structures on earth that can be seen from space. Like the pharaohs before him or the Roman emperors after him, Shi Huangdi began other massive public works projects, including a palace that held 40,000 people. Convinced that he was such a great emperor that he would rule China even after his death, he had 6,000 life-size warriors and horses and 1,400 chariots sculpted out of clay and put in his tomb. Shi Huangdi also standardized written Chinese, which helped to unify China. However, taxed beyond endurance, and with a shortage of crops because farmers were working on the emperor's grandiose projects, the empire collapsed.

India: The Indus River

Like the civilizations in Mesopotamia, Egypt, and China, early civilizations in India were centered around a river, the Indus, in the western part of the country. Because of its location at the junction of Asia and the Middle East, India has been the site of a great deal of cultural exchange through many overlapping migrations. The first of these occurred approximately 65,000 years ago. Then, around 6000 B.C., people from the Middle East migrated east into India, bringing domesticated cattle, sheep, goats, and their experience growing wheat. Other people migrated west from China, bringing rice and, later, tea. By 750 B.C., Indo-Europeans had come south into India from the flat, dry grasslands called the steppes. They contributed the horse and their knowledge of iron. Other Indo-European-speaking people migrated into eastern Europe. Today, most of the languages spoken in Europe, India, Iran, and North and South America are based on this common Indo-European parent language. In math, India gave the world the zero and the decimal system.

Some important food firsts came from India: the first plowed field in the world, before 2800 B.C., and the chicken.[71] The technology for turning sugar cane into granulated sugar existed at least as early as 800 B.C. in India; the word *sugar* comes from the Indian word *sharkar*. Many words for food come from ancient Indo-European or other Indian languages, even though the food might have originated somewhere else. The words for a rice dish with spices and meat—*pilaf, pilav,* or *pulao* in Persian and Arabic—come from the much earlier

Indian *pallāo* or *pulāo*. English words for rice *(arisi)*, pepper *(pippali)*, mango *(mānggā)*, orange *(nāgarangā)*, curry *(kari)*, and chutney all originated in India. *Tamarind* means "fruit of India" in Arabic.[72] Pulses consumed were peas, chickpeas, and lentils. Fruits included coconuts, pomegranates, dates, lemons, some melons, and possibly bananas.[73] In the beginning, India was not a heavily vegetarian country. The sacred cow came later (see page 23).

Hinduism

India gave the world two major religions, Hinduism and Buddhism. Hinduism arose some time between 750 B.C. and 550 B.C. after Aryans (people "of noble birth") arrived from the north. It has a body of sacred literature called the Vedas, but unlike the other great religions of the world, no one person was the founder. The Vedas mention barley, but not wheat or rice; sugar, distilled liquor, grinding stones, and the mortar and pestle.[74] They also give instructions on how to carve beef for the priests who ate it at feasts. The fundamental belief of Hinduism is a rigid caste or class system that determines everything about a person's life, including what and with whom he or she can eat. There was a racial component to the caste system: those at the top were Aryans, more likely to be wealthy and educated, while those at the bottom were darker-skinned, poorer non-Aryans. The highest caste is the Brahmins, who are often also the priests. Lower down are warriors, then peasants. At the bottom are the untouchables, manual laborers and people in trades the Hindus considered necessary but less desirable or "unclean," like butcher and garbage collector. The "untouchable" was meant literally; the slightest physical contact with an untouchable *or even his shadow* would contaminate a Brahmin physically and spiritually so much that he would have to undergo ritual purification. One of the means of purification involved ghee, clarified butter. By heating butter to remove the milk solids—the part that would cause butter to become rancid—the butter could be preserved for a long time, even in the hot climate of India. Hindus cannot change the caste they were born into during their life on Earth. They can, however, move up in the next life. Through a series of reincarnations (rebirths), they can work out bad karma— past wrongs—and eventually achieve divine peace, one of the four goals of Hinduism. The other goals are wealth and power, responsibility, and physical pleasure, which is celebrated in temple carvings of many people having sex in a great variety of ways. The caste system persists today in India in thousands of complex social relationships that determine everything about daily life.

In ancient India, one drink, soma, was sacred to the priests, who used it in their offerings to the gods, particularly the goddess of the moon, who gave her name to the drink. This was a controlled substance, far beyond mere alcohol. All-powerful, it produced superhuman feelings and supposedly healed all diseases. It was made by grinding the plant, then "The ground mass was collected on a cowhide, strained through a cloth of sheep's wool, and the sparkling tawny filtered liquid mixed for consumption with milk, curds or flour."[75] There are several candidates for the plant that could have produced these effects, but Indian food historian K. T. Achaya settles on the fly agaric mushroom, *Amanita muscarita*, a hallucinogen.

Buddhism

India's second great religion, Buddhism, arose in the fifth century B.C. Unlike Hinduism, it does have a founder, Siddhartha Gautama, known as the Buddha, who sought to understand the cause of suffering in the world. Fasting by eating only six grains of rice a day didn't help. Wandering didn't help. Finally, he sat under a fig tree and meditated for 49 days and reached the wisdom of enlightenment. Buddhism rejected the caste system of Hinduism, so it appealed more to the lower classes. It also rejected the many gods of Hinduism but kept the belief in reincarnation as a way to change and achieve perfect peace without pain, which Buddhists call nirvana. The Buddha declared that the flesh of many animals, in addition to humans, should not be eaten: elephants, dogs, horses, hyenas, bears, and the big cats—lions, tigers, panthers. But he never said that cattle should not be eaten. That happened around 2,000 years ago, after an ecological disaster in India made it culturally suicidal to raise cattle for food, and long after the Buddha was dead.

CULINARY CONFUSION:
The Death of Buddha

The Buddha died around 486 B.C. at the age of 80, after eating a meal that supposedly brought on an attack of dysentery. What did he eat? As food historian Achaya points out, it depends on how one word, *shukaramaddava*, is translated. It could be connected to "boar." Or it could mean sprouts softened by boars, or mushrooms that grow where boars have softened the ground. Scholars are still debating.[76]

The Sacred Cow

A word about the sacred cow. In India, cows are sacred because they produce oxen, castrated male cows. It takes a wealthy culture to support large animals for their meat alone. Sheep and goats give milk and hair repeatedly and are killed for food only when they have outlived their other functions. But an ox eats a great deal of food, takes up a great deal of space, and gives no milk. Killing it for food would mean that it has no life as a work animal, which is what cattle are used for in India. They pull plows in the fields and carts on the roads. Their dung is fuel, fertilizer, and free. An Indian farmer who owns an ox can feed his family; if his ox dies, they might starve or be forced to move to the city. He can't borrow oxen from his farmer neighbors, because the cycle of heavy rain then no rain means that all the fields have to be plowed at the same time. The zebu cattle native to India survived because they were able to adapt to these rain-drought cycles.

They have humps like camels where they store water and food, and they are resistant to tropical diseases. Cattle are so important to the economy that when India became an independent nation after World War II, it wrote a bill of rights for cattle into its constitution.[77] In India's neighbor, Tibet, its native cow—the yak—provides the same functions today as the cow in India: labor in the fields, transportation, fuel, and manure.[78]

In the ancient worlds of Africa, the Middle East, the Indian subcontinent, and Asia, as humans evolved, so did human interaction. Over millions of years, humans had become bipedal; developed bigger brains; made tools and weapons out of stone, then bronze, then iron; progressed from herbivores to carnivores and omnivores; mastered fire and learned to cook; invented dance, language, art, and religion; domesticated hundreds of species of plants and animals; and created complex systems of irrigation, government, and law. In the first millennium B.C., as merchants from all of these areas traveled the trade routes, so did their food, language, beliefs, and customs. The knowledge of wine making from the Near East, sheep and goat herding from the Fertile Crescent, olive oil from Egypt, and spices from India, especially black pepper, extended farther west and north than they had before, along the Mediterranean Sea, to another continent—Europe. All of these cuisines and cultures converged on a small, new country that would lay the foundations for Western civilization—Greece.

Grain, Grape, Olive

The Mediterranean Sea

The Mediterranean Sea was the center of cuisine and culture for the Greeks and Romans. The word *Mediterranean* means "middle (medi) of the earth (terra)," and the sea connected the earth of three continents: Europe to the north, Africa to the south, and Asia to the east. To the west was the Atlantic Ocean and the unknown, so to ancient people, the lands surrounding the Mediterranean were the known world. The Mediterranean climate is subtropical, with dry, sunny summers and mild, wet winters. This climate is found between 30 and 40 degrees north and south latitude: central and southern California, South Africa, central Chile, and southwestern Australia—the world's wine-producing areas.

The ancient cuisine of the Mediterranean was based on the trinity of grain, grape, and olive. These were not just the basic foods of everyday life—they were also sacred. The gods and goddesses who provided these foods were worshipped, and the foods themselves were the substance of religious ceremonies—both polytheistic Greek and Roman, and monotheistic Jewish and Christian ones.

Greece

Geography

The geography of Greece strongly influenced its culture and cuisine. Greece is a rocky, mountainous country surrounded by the sea on three sides. Since only 15 to 20 percent of the land was flat enough or fertile enough to farm, they couldn't grow enough grain to feed themselves. When a country is faced with this situation, it has three choices: (1) trade, (2) colonize, or (3) conquer. Greece did all three. It traded its staple crops, olive oil and wine. It founded colonies like Sicily to produce grain. But when it tried to conquer other territories, it was defeated and was conquered itself.

Geography affected government in Greece by keeping it small and local, because travel over steep peaks and down deep valleys was difficult and time consuming. Each city was like a small country and ruled itself. It is from the Greek word for these city-states—*polis*—that we get our word *politics*. The city-state of Athens was the birthplace of democracy. However, Greece was no political paradise: only free males were allowed to be citizens and to vote. Women had no say in the government and neither did much of the labor force, which was slaves.

Geography also influenced human relationships in Greece. Because the land made travel so difficult, the guest-host relationship was sacred. If a stranger, even a poor man, appeared at your door, it was your duty to be a good host, to take him in and share your food and wine with him. "We do not sit at table only to eat, but to eat together," said the Greek author Plutarch.[1] Dining was a sign of the human community and differentiated men from beasts. In return, the guest had obligations to his host. These included not abusing his host's hospitality by staying too long, usually not more than three days. A violation of this relationship by either side brought justified human and divine wrath, as shown in Homer's epic poem, *The Odyssey*. After the Trojan War, which lasted almost 10 years, Odysseus, King of Ithaca, wandered for almost another 10 years trying to return to his home. In his absence, his house was filled with men who pressured his wife to choose one of them as her new husband. While they waited, they ate the roasted meat of his animals; the fruit from his orchards of fig, pomegranate, apple, and pear; and they drank his wine. When Odysseus finally arrived home disguised as a lowly swineherd, the suitors refused to give him food or shelter. Then Odysseus revealed himself and justifiably killed them all.

Nectar, Ambrosia, Aphrodisiacs

To the Greeks, the stories about the gods were their religion. Christian writers who came later called them myths. There were 12 major Greek gods, called the Olympians because they lived on Mt. Olympus. They were immortal and ate mysterious food that was forbidden to humans—the sweet drink called nectar and the heavenly food named ambrosia—not to be confused with the twentieth-century fruit salad made with orange sections, sliced bananas, and shredded coconut in an orange juice and confectioners' sugar sauce.

Even though the gods did not eat human food, they were human in their behavior. They fought among themselves, lied, cheated on their spouses, got angry, and were not above disguising themselves to get what they wanted, frequently a beautiful young girl. The husband-and-wife team of Zeus and Hera headed up the gods. Both a goddess and a god were connected to fire. Hestia, the Goddess of the Hearth, the only sister of Zeus and a virgin, was worshipped in public and in private every day because every city had a sacred fire that was kept burning constantly. In this case, the goddess paralleled what the humans did, since the daughter of the household was responsible for keeping the fire going. There could be no cooking or heat without it. Hestia also received offerings at the beginning and end of every meal. One of the rituals of founding a new colony was to take fire from the old city to the new one to guarantee continuity. It survives today in the ceremony of the Olympic torch, which has to be carried by hand from Athens to the site of the Olympic games every four years.

The god connected with fire was Haephestus. Like many Greek gods, he had both a positive and a negative side. On the positive side, he was a blacksmith, which showed the power of fire to create and be useful to mankind, as in cooking. The negative was that he also represented the power of fire to destroy, because he lived in a volcano (his Latin name is Vulcan). In another typically Greek contrast, Haephestus, the only god who was not beautiful and physically perfect, was married to beautiful Aphrodite, the goddess of love. She gave her name to foods that are thought to be sexual stimulants—aphrodisiacs. Some foods that we consider aphrodisiacs: oysters, caviar, champagne, chocolate, and snails.

The gods used hunger as a punishment for cannibalism. Tantalus, the only mortal who had ever dined with the gods on nectar and ambrosia, then invited the gods to a banquet and fed them his son, boiled. The gods figured it out before they started eating (except for one bite of his shoulder) and gave Tantalus a punishment to fit his crime—eternal agonizing hunger and thirst. He was forced to stand in a pool of water, but every time he bent down to take a drink, it disappeared. He reached up to pluck the ripe apples, pomegranates, pears, and figs dangling just over his head, but the wind blew the branches out of his reach. It is from Tantalus that we get our word *tantalize*—to drive somebody crazy with desire.

Demeter, Goddess of Grain: The "Good Goddess"

One of the most powerful goddesses was Demeter [duh-MEE-ter], the goddess of all growing things—who was Mother Earth or Mother Nature, with hair the color of wheat:

. . . beauty spread round about her and a lovely fragrance was wafted from her sweet-smelling robes, and from the divine body of the goddess a light shone afar, while golden tresses spread down over her shoulders, so that the strong house was filled with brightness as with lightning.[2]

The *meter* part of her name is related to *mater*, the word for mother. She was also identified with the Egyptian goddess Isis.

Demeter was often pictured holding stalks of wheat, as in the constellation Virgo, which represented her.[3] Its brightest star is Spica, which means "sheaf of wheat." Sometimes Demeter carried a cornucopia—a horn of plenty—filled with fresh fruit. She was also known as The Lady of the Golden Blade because she usually wore a crown and carried a golden sword, either for fighting battles or for harvesting crops. Sometimes she carried a torch. This represented her search through the underworld for her daughter, when she disguised herself as a human, an old woman.

FOOD FABLE:

Where Winter Comes From

Demeter had a beautiful daughter named Persephone [purr-SEH-fuh-nee[4]], whom she kept hidden from the roving eyes of the male gods. One day, the thing Demeter feared the most happened: Persephone let out a scream that shook heaven and Earth and vanished. Demeter was devastated. She left Mt. Olympus and wandered the Earth disguised as an ordinary human, looking for her daughter. She would not eat or drink the food of the gods, only the little bit of food the reapers ate: barley-water with mint; or water, meal, and pennyroyal.[5]

Finally, the Sun told her that Hades, the god of the dark kingdom of the dead, had seen Persephone picking flowers and thought she was so beautiful that he opened the Earth and captured her. Demeter grieved so much when she heard this that everything on Earth stopped growing. Zeus finally stepped in to negotiate a compromise because all the humans were going to starve. Persephone could be with her mother, but only part of the year. She had eaten a pomegranate seed that Hades had given her, which meant that she had to return to the underworld to be with him.

That is how Persephone came to be both the goddess of springtime and of the dead. During Persephone's eight months above ground, joyous Demeter lets things grow and flourish. But when Persephone is in the world of the dead for four months every year, Demeter mourns and nothing grows.

And that is where winter comes from.

The Greeks viewed the growing of grain as a sexual union between the sky and the ground: "Rain, fallen from the amorous heaven, impregnates the Earth, and it bringeth forth for mankind the food of flocks and herds and Demeter's gifts."[6]

In ancient Greece, the most widely consumed of Demeter's gifts was barley, which grew better than wheat in Greece. She declined wine and was worshipped instead with a sacred drink made from barley: Demeter "bade them mix [barley] meal and water with soft mint and give her to drink . . . to observe the sacrament."[7] Mint was also sacred to Demeter, as were the poppies that her priestesses wore. Among fish, the red mullet was sacred to Demeter. The animal most sacred to her—a pair of them drew her chariot—was the serpent, a symbol of rebirth.

Symbols of animal and vegetable fertility and sweet things were sacrificed to Demeter: pigs, bulls, honey-cakes, and fruit. Barley was sprinkled around her temple as an offering to ensure that the Earth would be fertile. As time passed, the barley was replaced by wheat, then rice. The custom of scattering rice spread from the temple to the wedding ceremony to guarantee fertility in marriage.

Barley and wheat, the two main grains, were consumed in many ways. The easiest and cheapest was simply to mix the whole grain with water and cook it into a porridge. Barley or wheat flour could also be mixed with water and cooked into a porridge, or it could be patted flat with the hands and cooked on a rock or in an oven as a small unleavened bread. The addition of yeast created leavened bread, but not by much—barley is low in gluten, so it makes a dense bread. Adding wheat flour, rich in gluten, to the barley results in a lighter bread. Baking it into dry, twice-cooked biscuits allowed the grains to be preserved. These biscuits, called *paximadia* or *paximathia*, are still made in Greece today. More than any other food, bread represented civilization to the Greeks because it was a completely human product, controlled by humans every step of the way.

Dionysus, God of the Grape

The goddess Demeter—she is the earth; . . . she nourishes mortals with dry food; but he who came afterwards . . . discovered a match to it, the liquid drink of the grape, and introduced it to mortals. . . . He who is a god is poured out in offerings to the gods, so that by his means men may have good things.

Euripides, Bacchae 275

Each winter in Greece, grapevines seemed to die, only to be miraculously reborn in the springtime. Just as the Nile represented resurrection to the Egyptians, Dionysus [die-uh-NIGH-sus], the god of the vine, was the sacred symbol of resurrection and immortality to the Greeks. He was believed to be the son of a mortal woman and Zeus, king of the gods. In Greek mythology, just as Prometheus brought the gift of fire to humans, Dionysus discovered the grapevine and taught humans how to cultivate it and to make wine. He is often represented wearing a garland of grape leaves and vines laden with grapes in his long, flowing hair.

Dionysus shows up in Greek mythology later than Demeter and appears to have arrived in Greece after traveling throughout the Mediterranean south to Egypt, as far west as the Iberian peninsula (today's Spain and Portugal), and east to India. In many places he was met with hostility because the rulers did not want their people to drink wine. Sometimes people who drank wine for the first time thought they had been poisoned.[8] Eventually, however, Dionysus overcame them and taught them the cultivation of the vine, which was regarded as sacred to him and a symbol of civilization.

Dionysus had two sides. Through mild intoxication, he could lift men out of their ordinary state of mind, inspire them to creativity, and bring them closer to the gods. Poetry written to celebrate the festival of Dionysus grew into one of the great symbols of civilization, Greek tragedy. So Dionysus is also the god of the theater. Wine was used as a medicine and mixed with medicine, so Dionysus is also referred to as Physician or Health Giver.[9]

However, extreme intoxication brings men closer to beasts. For this reason, women were rarely allowed to have wine; public banquets were usually restricted to men. On the rare occasions when women were invited, they didn't get the good, strong, aged wine the men drank. They were served "sweet wine or barely fermented grape juice."[10] In Greek mythology, the pack of women who followed Dionysus were in a wild sexual frenzy. Dionysus was sometimes accompanied by satyrs, male creatures with insatiable sexual appetites, indicated by the goat horns on their heads. This is where we get the term *horny*. He is also often riding on or driving a chariot pulled by wild cats—tigers, lynxes, panthers—because that is how men become when they are drunk.[11] Sometimes Dionysus is shown drunk, spilling wine that a wild cat cub laps up.

DRUNKENNESS SCALE
according to Athenaeus, an Egyptian Greek, ca. A.D. 200[12]

NUMBER OF BOWLS OF WINE	EFFECT
1	Health
2	Love and pleasure
3	Sleep
AFTER THE THIRD BOWL OF WINE IS CONSUMED, "WISE GUESTS GO HOME."	
4	Violence
5	Uproar
6	Drunken revel
7	Black eyes
8	Brings the police
9	Biliousness
10	Madness and hurling the furniture

Grapes grew well in Greece and were plentiful; Greek wine production from grapes began by 1500 B.C.[13] The Greeks drank their wine sweetened with honey because the amphorae—the ceramic vessels they used to store wine—were waterproofed with resin, a sticky secretion from trees that tasted like turpentine, also a resin. The taste persists today in the Greek alcohol retsina. At one of the most sacred Greek ceremonies, wine was not consumed with dinner as a beverage, but after, at what the Greeks called a symposium.

The Symposium—Drinking Together

The symposium was an elaborate ceremony, "a meeting of men that only took place following a meal" to consecrate a special public or private event like a wedding or to thank the gods for a victory in games or to make a political decision.[14] By the seventh century B.C. the symposium was an accustomed practice. It usually took place in a public building, often a temple, or in a special symposium room in the home of a prominent citizen. Slaves served the guests, who took their sandals off and reclined on couches propped up on one arm. Small tables were set up in front of each couch. The size of the symposium room was measured by how many couches were in it—five to seven were the norm—the way that the Japanese describe the size of a room by the number of tatami mats that fit on the floor.

The meeting began with a blood sacrifice, a religious offering to the gods of an animal, usually a young lamb or goat, that had been ritually killed. The animal was a substitute for the human that had been sacrificed in earlier times. "The slaughter of animals in sacrifice and the butchering of the meat was the task of the *mageiros* (the Greek word for chef, butcher, and sacrificer of animals): he divided the meat between the worshippers."[15] After the gods got the best portion—thigh meat and fat—the humans ate.

The food served at a basic symposium was divided into three categories. The "first table" service was staple foods—lentils, barley, and wheat—along with their side dishes or accompaniments—vegetables, cheeses, eggs, fish, meat. After the first-table food was eaten, the small tables in front of each couch were cleared. Then hands were washed with warm water, soap, and perfumed oils; floors were cleansed of the scraps thrown on them during dinner. The men were given garlands to put on their heads and chests.

Then began the "second table" course. This is when the wine appeared, and food to eat with it—dried fruit, nuts, sweets. Poetry was recited, flutes played, decisions made. The sense of community was further reinforced because all the men drank wine from the same cup.[16] Some of these cups still exist; they are excellent sources, pictorial representations of what took place at the symposium. The wine in the cup was diluted, often at the ratio of one part wine to two or three parts water. The altar where Dionysus was worshipped often had an altar to the freshwater nymphs nearby, to remind men to drink wine diluted with water.[17] The Greeks regarded diluted wine as a symbol of civilization; it helped to avoid drunkenness. The "third table" was a drinking party.

How to Drink and Not Get Drunk

The ancient Greeks loved wine and were always searching for ways to drink without getting drunk. Creative thinking led them to what they thought was the antidote to the downside of Dionysus: drinking purple wine from a purple vessel made of semi-precious stone would cause the two purples to cancel each other out and negate whatever was in the wine that caused drunkenness. In Greek, the prefix *a* means "not," *methyein* means drunk (from *methy*—wine), so the Greek word for "not drunk" became the name of the purple stone the vessel was made out of—amethyst.[18]

In their excellent book *The Classical Cookbook*, historian Andrew Dalby and chef Sally Grainger have re-created many meals from ancient Greece and Rome, with recipes that work in modern kitchens. They describe one symposium in 400 B.C., where the guests were served the first table of many substantial and elaborate dishes: eel in mulberry sauce, honey-glazed shrimp, squid with sea salt, baby birds in flaky pastry, and a huge tuna baked and cut into steaks.[19] Bread was there, too, of course, in the form of barley rolls. For the second table, the guests got "sweet pastry shells, crispy flapjacks, toasted sesame cakes drenched in honey sauce, cheesecake made with milk and honey, a sweet that was baked like a pie; cheese-and-sesame sweetmeats fried in hottest oil and rolled in sesame seeds."[20] Raisins also appeared only on the second tables.

Grapes were consumed in other ways besides as wine: eaten fresh out of hand; as must—Latin *mustum*, new wine—the unfermented juice pressed from wine grapes; boiled down into must syrup; dried into raisins; as raisin syrup and raisin wine. The seeds were pressed into grapeseed oil; the leaves were cooked and eaten.

Athena, Goddess of the Olive

To the Greeks, the olive was the symbol of the goddess Athena, who created it. She was the warrior goddess, sprung full grown and fully armed—helmet, shield, spear—from the brow of Zeus. She protected the city named after her— Athens—but she was worshipped throughout Greece and helped the Greeks win the Trojan War described in Homer's epic poem *The Iliad*. However, her symbol the owl shows that she also represented peace and wisdom. She was also the goddess of crafts like weaving and pottery, and she invented the rake and the plow, which benefited all humankind.

Olives, the fruit of the *Olea europaea* tree, had been cultivated and pressed for their oil in the eastern Mediterranean by Palestinians and Syrians since about 5000 B.C. Olive oil was like liquid gold in Greece. Prized for cooking, as medicine, and as fuel, olive oil was one of the basics of trade in the ancient Mediterranean. It was also used as a body lotion, sometimes scented with perfume. For example, in the Olympics, which began in 776 B.C., naked men greased with olive oil competed in the earliest sports: running, the long jump, the discus and javelin throws, wrestling, boxing, and a combination of five events called the pentathlon—all still part of the modern Olympics, which began in 1896. (The winner wasn't totally naked: he was crowned with a wreath of laurel leaves from the god Apollo's sacred tree.)

Unripe green olives and even ripe black ones are bitter. Before they can be eaten they must be dried in salt or cured in brine, water, or oil. If they are going to be crushed to extract the oil, it must be done carefully with just the right amount of pressure to force the oil out of the olive, but not smash the bitter pit into it. In ancient times:

> The olives were first crushed in basins. The resulting mash was then transferred to straw baskets for the actual pressing to be done. Several baskets were stacked in a press. Various methods of producing a graduated pressure were developed over the early centuries, chiefly a long, extremely heavy beam counterpoised with weights. The crushed fruit yielded a liquid comprised of water and oil. It had to be allowed to settle before oil could be skimmed off at successive intervals.[21]

Ancient people didn't have the levels of labeling that came into existence at the end of the twentieth century, but "virgin" means first pressing; "extra virgin" means less than 1 percent acidity; "cold-pressed" means that heat, which would alter the chemical composition and taste of the oil, was not used.[22]

The dusty gray-green trees are slow growing but live to be hundreds of years old. When it was discovered that olive trees, which are very sensitive to cold, grew well in Greece's mild climate, they became a staple crop. However, their deep roots let the topsoil wash away, finishing off the erosion that had begun centuries earlier when the Greeks started chopping down trees to build houses and ships.

The olive tree is highly symbolic in Western culture. Jews and Christians know it from the Old Testament story of Noah's ark and the flood. When the dove that Noah sent out to see if the world was still flooded flew back to the ark with an olive branch in its mouth, everyone knew that the flood waters had receded and that there was peace again. The dove and the olive have symbolized peace ever since.

At harvest times throughout ancient Greece, people celebrated the harvests with festivals. Mothers wearing white robes carried the first-harvested wheat to the altar of Demeter, the goddess of grain, as offerings. Dionysus, the god of the grape, received the first grapes harvested; and to Athena, the goddess of the olive, went the first olives. In addition, thanks were offered to Athena before spring planting.

OLIVE CHRONOLOGY[23]

??	Olive trees perhaps domesticated in Iran and Turkestan
3500 B.C.	Olive trees cultivated in islands near Greece and Turkey
15th century B.C.	Phoenician traders bring olive trees to Cyprus and Crete
8th century B.C.	Greek colonists take olive trees to Sicily, southern France, Spain, Thrace, Black Sea area
8th century B.C.	Ekron (modern Israel) produced more than 1,000 tons of olive oil/year
ca. 175 B.C.	Rome—Cato writes *On Farming*, much of it about olives and oil
A.D. 2nd century	Rome—Columella writes about difficulty of harvesting olives
1497	Olive trees from Spain arrive in Caribbean and Mexico
ca. 1775	"Mission olive" trees planted at Spanish missions in California
1803	First record of olive oil pressed in California
1899	Ripe—not green—olives canned
1933	California man invents mechanical olive pitter; martini fans rejoice[24]
21st century	European Union, especially Spain (Andalusian region) and Italy, produces three-fourths of world's olive oil

For the ancient Greeks, grain, grape, and olive came together in many ways. Baked goods often consisted of barley flour and wheat flour, with must or wine as the liquid that also provided sugar for the yeast, and olive oil as the fat. Proportions of ingredients, shapes of the baked goods, and seasonings and additions like herbs, raisins, cinnamon, or nuts determined whether the finished product was savory or sweet. Without animal products like butter or eggs that go rancid, these breads, rolls, and biscuits could keep for months. Even today in Greece, foods savory and sweet are often made the same way. If you are looking for authentic recipes, beware of recipes that contain sugar or baking powder; they are modern additions.

Food from the Sea

The Greeks were also a nation of sailors who ate the abundant variety the sea provided: fish like mullet, turbot, grouper, and sea bream, as well as eels, octopus, and squid. The measure of an ancient Greek cook was what he could do with fish.[25] The first chef we know by name in history was a Greek man named Mithekos, from the polis of Syracuse, in Sicily. His book of recipes—ingredients and instructions—mostly for fish, has disappeared. We know about it only because mention of it survives in other writings.

Especially popular was the dark-fleshed bluefin tuna, *Thunnus thynnus*, native to the Mediterranean. These large fish—they can weigh almost a ton—were preserved in salt or olive oil, as they still are today in the Mediterranean. Bonito, the bluefin's 10-pound relative, was wrapped in fig leaves and slow-cooked in the ashes.

CULINARY CONFUSION:

Tuna

Americans are most familiar with white-fleshed tuna, known as albacore (*alba* means "white" in Latin), marketed as "chicken of the sea." This is really the longfin tuna, *Thunnus alalunga* (*ala*=fin, *lunga*=long), which is found in the Atlantic and Pacific oceans, but not in the Mediterranean. However, what the French call albacore is the red-fleshed yellowfin, *Thunnus albacares*. This tuna is not found in the Mediterranean either, but is found in tropical and subtropical waters, and is prized by Japanese sushi and sashimi chefs, who call it yellowtail. In Hawaii, it is known as ahi.

The Golden Age of Greece

Food was democratic in Greece, at least until the fifth century B.C. Everyone ate the same modest meals based on barley or wheat as a paste, porridge, or unleavened bread; olives; vegetables like lettuce, cabbage, and onions; and herbs like basil and oregano, which is still common in Greek cuisine. Sometimes these were supplemented with fish or meat from goats and sheep. Vinegar was a favorite ingredient of the Greeks. Black pepper was not used in cooking, but as a medicine. They also ate fruit, especially grapes, and figs, which the philosopher Aristotle observed caused their teeth to rot: "Why do figs, which are soft and sweet, damage the teeth?"[26]

Cows were not common because of the shortage of pasture land, so a man who owned oxen was considered rich.[27] However, he didn't kill them because he needed them to plow his fields and for transportation. Goats and sheep were kept; the young ones were reserved for ritual blood sacrifice to the gods. It was a matter of economics, too. Goats and sheep produced mohair and wool, and milk to drink and preserve as cheese, so they were killed when they were old and had outlived all their other purposes.

That was the diet in Athens, in northern Greece. In the southern part of Greece was the rigid militaristic society of Sparta. Infants that were not born healthy and physically perfect were tossed off a cliff. Girls and boys ran and played rigorous sports to toughen them up. When they were seven years old, the boys were sent away for military training. They lived in barracks and slept on hard wooden benches. Spartan food matched the Spartan life. Although cheese, barley, and figs were food fundamentals in Sparta, the staple food was a black broth made from pork stock, vinegar, and salt.[28] It is from their denial of what they considered luxury that we get the word *spartan*.

In the fifth century B.C., Athens and Sparta allied and defeated the Persian Empire in a series of wars. At one battle, Thermopylae, 300 Spartan warriors died, but their sacrifice, which was shown in the movie *300*, was crucial to the Greek defeat of Persia. The peacetime that followed was the Golden Age of Greece. Athens grew to between 300,000 and 500,000 people and created the buildings, paintings, and sculptures that are the hallmarks of Greece and Western civilization, like the Parthenon, a hilltop temple with a 40-foot statue of Athena. The Golden Age was the great age of theater in Greece, the comedies of Aristophanes and the tragedies of Aeschylus, Sophocles, and Euripides that are still performed today.

The Parthenon in Athens, Greece. *PhotoDisc, Inc.*

The Professional Chef

The Golden Age was also the beginning of a wealthy class and a split in the culture between rich and poor, which was reflected in Greek cuisine. The poor continued to subsist on barley heated up to remove the chaff and ground into cakes called *maza*, wheat pastes or unleavened bread, some sheep or goat cheese, and olive oil.[29] The wealthy had more elaborate meals, with more variety in diet. They consumed legumes like chickpeas, lentils, and vetch, and seeds from flax, sesame, and poppies. They also ate the meat of domesticated animals, including dogs, after observing sacrificial rituals. The forests provided large and small game: boar, deer, hare, and fox. The vegetables commonly eaten were turnips, leeks, watercress, onions, garlic, and purslane.[30] The new profession of beekeeping made honey more available.[31]

The rise in urbanization, wealth, and trade produced a need for more than the free guest-host hospitality of earlier times. City-run inns provided professional hospitality for traveling merchants and businessmen throughout the Greek world, often in waterfront areas.[32] All of these people needed food, so cooking became a profession. In addition to being able to afford chefs, the wealthy could afford to buy imported wines. They also drank much more wine than the poor. Cuisine was not as elaborate as it later became in Rome, but some of the chefs became known by name. One, Archestratus, from Sicily, wrote much about food but not in a cookbook. He wrote food poetry, parodies that made fun of epic poems like *The Iliad* or *The Odyssey*, which were recited—sung to a lyre, a kind of harp—as entertainment at a symposium. Guests expecting a song about heroic deeds must have been surprised when instead they got verses about fish. Only fragments survive, partly because Greek philosophers like Plato didn't think cooking was an art, or that food writing was worth preserving in libraries.

Another Greek, Athenaeus, tells the story of a man named Philoxenus who had some unusual cooking and eating habits:

> Philoxenus, having first taken a bath, would go round among the houses in his own city and others as well, followed by slaves carrying oil, wine, fish-paste, vinegar, and other relishes, then he would enter a [stranger's] house, and season whatever was cooking for the rest of the company. . . . When all was ready, he would . . . greedily enjoy the feast.[33]

Thousands of years later, there is a show like this on the Food Network—*Food 911* hosted by chef Tyler Florence. He goes into people's homes and fixes whatever is wrong with what they are cooking. But he doesn't stay to "greedily enjoy the feast."

The Golden Age of Athens ended when it waged a 27-year war with Sparta for control of the Greek peninsula. Much of Sparta's strategy was to cut Athens off from its food supply. Knowing this, Athens tried to invade Sicily in 415 B.C. to turn it into a grain-producing colony. Two disastrous years later, the Sicilians emerged victorious after destroying Athens's navy and one-third of its total military force.[34] The war finally ended in 404 B.C. when Sparta blocked Athens's sea route to its grain supply. Without food, Athens was forced to surrender. The Golden Age of Greek civilization was over.

Alexander the Great and the Magic Apples

A new conqueror appeared, from Macedonia, just north of Greece. Alexander was not Greek but he loved Greek culture. His tutor was the philosopher Aristotle, who had been the student of Plato, who had been the student of Socrates. Alexander's goal was to conquer the known world, and he did. His empire stretched east from Greece through Persia (modern-day Iran) and Iraq to the

Indus River on the western border of India, north through what are now Afghanistan and Pakistan, and south into Africa. His conquering created a new culture, Hellenistic, that was a combination of four cultures: Greek, Persian, Indian, and Egyptian.

This had an impact on the cuisine of Greece, because new methods of food preparation and new foods were introduced. One writer bemoaned all the changes that were occurring with food:

> Do you see what things have come to? Bread, garlic, cheese, *maza*—those are healthy foods, but not these salted fish, these lamb chops sprinkled with spices, these sweet confections, and these corrupting pot roasts. And by Zeus, if they aren't simmering cabbage in olive oil and eating it with pureed peas![35]

Alexander established cities everywhere he conquered and named at least 15 after himself. The center of learning in the world shifted from Athens to Alexandria, Egypt. It had a library with 700,000 volumes of Greek writing, a zoo, a botanical garden, an observatory, and a great lighthouse more than 400 feet high to keep the ships safe, many of them carrying wheat from the Nile River valley to feed the Mediterranean world.

Alexander was on a quest for immortality—the legendary Water of Life or the magic Golden Apples. He didn't find either one, but he did find other apples that were supposed to let him live to be 400 years old.[36] He didn't live to be 40. He died of a fever, maybe malaria, one month short of his thirty-third birthday. Still seeking immortality, he arranged to have himself preserved in honey and placed in a glass coffin in Alexandria, Egypt. After his death in 323 B.C., as usual after the death of a powerful leader, there were wars of succession and his empire was split up into smaller areas ruled by several generals.

But Alexander's vast empire would soon appear small. Power in the Mediterranean was shifting to a fast-rising country located west of Greece on a peninsula shaped like a boot—Italy.

Rome

The Founding of Rome, 753 B.C.: Suckled by a Wolf

Every country has myths about its founders. In the United States, these myths are about honesty. As a boy, George Washington supposedly chopped down a cherry tree and "couldn't tell a lie" when his father asked him about it. Abraham Lincoln's nickname was "Honest Abe." The myth of the founding of Rome is that Romulus and Remus, twin boys, were born under an olive tree, which symbolized that they were descended from a god—in this case, Mars, the god of war—and a Latin princess. They were abandoned at birth, but a she-wolf saved them by nursing them. When they grew up, Romulus murdered Remus and founded the city of Rome.[37] What we know for sure is that Rome was founded in the eighth century B.C. on seven hills, 20 miles up the Tiber River for defense—all the better to see invaders' ships coming. There was also a natural harbor there. Salt deposits along the banks and at the mouth of the Tiber provided a valuable item to trade.[38] One of the first roads in Rome was the Via Salaria—the Salt Road.

Roman Culture: Gods and Goddesses

Rome absorbed much of its culture from Greece, via the Greek colonies in Sicily. These included the idea that the mind and the body were connected and affected each other—"a healthy mind in a healthy body" *("mens sana in corpore sano").* Greek slaves who were prized for their learning as tutors and their skill as cooks brought their customs and beliefs to Rome with them. Many of the Roman gods are Greek gods with name changes. Jupiter and his wife Juno presided over the Roman gods just as Zeus and Hera presided over the Greek gods. The Roman goddess of the harvest, Ceres, counterpart of the Greeks' Demeter, gave her name to our word for grain—*cereal.* The Romans believed that Ceres was the mother of many things: "Ceres first turned the earth with the curved plough; she first gave corn and crops to bless the land; she first gave laws; all things are Ceres's gift."[39] Dionysus, the Greek god of wine, became Bacchus and gave his name to a wild, drunken orgy, the bacchanalia. The Romans transferred one of the Greek beliefs about wine into a saying that is still with us today: *In vino veritas*—"In wine there is truth"—meaning that after a few drinks, people reveal their true feelings. The major Greek goddess Athena changed into the major Roman goddess Minerva, still the goddess of the olive and of wisdom. Her festival was in mid-March and was celebrated with gladiatorial combat. Aphrodite, the goddess of love, became Venus, accompanied by the little winged love god with the arrow, Eros—Cupid to the Romans. Venus/Aphrodite still cheated on her husband, the hunchbacked blacksmith who still lived under Mt. Aetna in Sicily. His Latin name, Vulcan, became our word for erupting mountains—*volcano.* One of the most important gods in the military Roman culture was Mars, the god of war.

The Grain Wars: The Punic Wars

From 264 to 146 B.C., Rome and the Phoenicians, whose capital city was Carthage in what is now Tunisia in northern Africa, were locked in a series of wars to the death for control of trade in the western Mediterranean, especially the grain fields of Sicily. To aid them in trade, the Phoenicians had invented a system of writing that is the basis of our alphabet. In the second of these wars, called Punic Wars, a Carthaginian general named Hannibal made one of the boldest moves in military history. Instead of sailing across the Mediterranean and attacking Italy from the south, which they expected, he marched thousands of soldiers and 60 elephants over the Alps and attacked Italy from the north, taking them by surprise. For more than 10 years, Hannibal's soldiers and elephant(s) (historians think that perhaps all the elephants died except one) ate their way up and down the Italian peninsula, through fields of wheat and barley, through orchards of apples, pears, and lemons, and through the vineyards. They devastated the country's farms and economy, especially the rich agricultural areas of northern Italy, so badly that the damage to the fields could not be repaired for many years. Rome eventually won by attacking the city of Carthage, but 50 years later when it looked like Carthage might make a comeback, Rome finished the Phoenicians off. After a three-year siege, Carthage was burned and razed. The 50,000 Carthaginians who were not killed outright were sold into slavery. Then the ground was spread with salt so that nothing would ever grow there again.[40] Rome now controlled the western Mediterranean Sea. Mediterranean means "middle of the land" in Latin, but after Rome gained control of the eastern part of the sea, too, they called it simply *mare nostrum*—"our sea."

Hannibal had long-lasting effects on the Roman economy. Small farmers couldn't afford to replant or repair the damage. They also couldn't afford to compete with the slave labor on the *latifundia*, the large plantations. So they sold their farms to the wealthy landowners and then either roamed the countryside looking for work as laborers or moved to the cities where they were poor or homeless. Soon, one-third of the population of Rome was slaves and another one-quarter was poor.

The Roman Republic

Rome began as a monarchy but by the third century B.C. it was a republic with a three-part government: 300 senators who made the laws and served for life; two co-consuls who commanded the army and administered the laws; and a court system. Almost 2,000 years later, the Founding Fathers of the United States, fluent in Latin and familiar with the history of Rome, patterned parts of the American government on the Roman Republic and used Rome to justify slavery. The young United States even referred to itself as a republic. We still use Latin words for legal terminology and government positions: *governor, senator.*

The Roman Republic ended when Julius Caesar gained too much power as a general, defied the senate's order to disband his army, and proclaimed himself dictator for life. The senators agreed that he could be dictator for life, then stabbed him to death in the senate in 44 B.C., on March 15, which the Romans called the Ides [EYE-dz] of March. This plunged the country into 17 years of civil wars during which Roman general Marc Antony and his ally, Cleopatra, the queen of Egypt, committed suicide after they lost a decisive naval battle to Octavian, Julius Caesar's grandnephew and adopted son.

The Roman Empire

In 27 B.C., Octavian emerged victorious as Rome's sole ruler and first emperor with the title of Augustus—majestic. The reign of Augustus initiated 213 years of the *Pax Romana*—Roman Peace—for the simple reason that Rome had no enemies left to defeat and no one to stop its expansion. The empire Augustus controlled sprawled across three continents. In Europe, it reached north through

Gaul (present-day France) to the island of Britannia (England) and its most important city, Londinium, and west to present-day Spain, Portugal, and the Atlantic Ocean. In Asia to the east, it extended into Armenia, Syria, Judaea, and Arabia. It also controlled grain-rich north Africa, the breadbasket of the empire, Egypt's rich Nile Valley, and modern-day Libya, Morocco, and Tunisia. Tunisia was the source of most of the olive oil for the Roman Empire. Olive oil was so important to the Roman economy that planting enough olive trees excused a farmer from military service. Through trade with countries outside the empire, Romans now had access to exotic foods and spices, animals, fabrics, and people.

Trade Routes: The Silk Road and Cinnamon Land

Much of Rome's trade with other countries centered around spices. These were acquired over the Silk Road to China and the sea routes to India and Africa. The Silk Road was not a paved road like the other Roman roads, but a series of caravans that traveled through deserts and over mountains to the end of the road— the international marketplace in the capital city of Chang'an in northeastern China, where traders from many countries came to buy and sell. What the Romans wanted most, in addition to spices like ginger, turmeric, and galangal, was silk. They prized it and liked to wear it to banquets, where they protected it with large aprons. However, the Romans could only buy silk, not produce it, because silk production was a Chinese monopoly and a closely guarded state secret. Silk was literally worth its weight in gold.

By sea from India and Africa to warehouses in the Spice Quarter in Rome came spices for cooking, for perfume and incense, and for medicine. Cinnamon was the most valuable. It was one of several spices, including white pepper, ginger, and cardamom, that were extremely expensive not only because of the shipping costs, but because a 25 percent tariff—an import tax—was added. The nobles, frequent targets of poisoning, often by their relatives, believed that if you combined almost every spice known to mankind, it would make an antidote that could counteract even the most powerful poison. Cinnamon was also used to mask the "smell of burning flesh at special cremation ceremonies."[41] Black pepper was not on the list of luxury items because the Romans considered it a necessity. Other luxury items subject to the tariff were silk, wool, and cotton; purple cloth (reserved for the upper class); lions, lionesses, leopards, panthers; and jewels—diamonds, emeralds, pearls, turquoise.[42] In 301, the emperor Diocletian set maximum prices for many of these goods to try to stop the runaway inflation that was making them cost increasingly more while Roman money became increasingly worth less.

Arab traders had a monopoly on cinnamon and told the Romans fantastic stories to keep their sources secret. They claimed it grew in remote swamps, high up in trees, where killer bats swarmed. We know now that the Arabs got it from Indonesia, sailed to Madagascar and then to Somalia on the east coast of Africa, which was called Cinnamon Land. From there it went up the Red Sea, overland to the Nile, and by ship across the Mediterranean.

The culture of Rome—its food, laws, customs, and language—spread on the roads with the governor, the army, and the merchants, and displaced existing cuisines and cultures. Rome dominated trade so completely that some countries, like the Kush area of northern India in what is now Afghanistan and Pakistan, were forced to develop metal money in order to do business with Rome. In the provinces, Romans replaced local kinds of apple trees with ones they preferred. As early as 200 B.C., the Romans planted apple orchards in Britannia.[43] Roman knowledge of gardening, grafting, and pruning spread, too. Italian wines reached into the provinces and replaced Greek wines, not just because the taste of Italian wines like Opimian and Falernian was preferred, but also because at 1,600 gallons per acre, Italian vineyards produced a volume that Greeks couldn't match.[44]

WINE CHRONOLOGY—ANCIENT

WHEN	WHERE	WHAT
8500–4000 B.C.	Zagros Mts. (Iran)	Earliest traces of wine
4000	Persia (Iran)	Rose petal wine exported[45]
3150	Egypt	Wine jars in ruler's burial chamber
2750	Mesopotamia	First written mention of wine
2340	Mesopotamia	First written mention of wine cellar
1750	Mesopotamia	Code of Hammurabi regulates taverns
1330s	Egypt	Wine labeled with year of vintage, name of vineyard, and vintner in King Tut's tomb
1000	Mediterranean	Phoenicians trade wine, spread viticulture
5th century	Greece	Greek wine found in France, Egypt, Black Sea, Danube
3rd century	Greece	Thriving wine industry; export 10 million liters/year to Gaul[46]
c. 200	Rome	First Latin writing about viticulture, *De agricultura* by Cato[47]
A.D. 1st century	Greece	Wooden barrels replace pottery amphoras
65	Spain	Columella writes down "principles of viticulture"[48]
92	Rome	Emperor Domitian decrees that no new vines can be planted; he is ignored
280	Rome	Domitian's law repealed

To glorify Rome, the emperors embarked on a massive campaign of public building based on the discovery of a new kind of sand—concrete—that made it possible to create stronger buildings using arches to distribute the weight. It was during this time that many of the greatest buildings of ancient Rome were built: the Forum; the Colosseum, which opened in A.D. 80; the Pantheon, temple of all the Roman gods; and the aqueducts that brought water into Rome. The Forum, four levels high, was the business, political, religious, and market center of Rome, like a giant mall. If all roads led to Rome, all roads in Rome led to the Forum. Spacious, open plazas were surrounded by multicolored marble columns and luxurious public baths and public toilets also made of marble. It contained markets for local and imported produce, restaurants that sold fast food, and small boutique-type stores that sold expensive imported spices and other luxury goods under armed guard. It was the location of religious festivals, sacrifices, and offerings of rare, scented oils and incense to the warrior god, Mars—and behind the temples, of dirty deals and prostitution. Government administrators and bureaucrats, the equivalent of the Internal Revenue Service and Social Security, also worked at the Forum.[49]

Upper-Class Cuisine and Culture—The *Convivium*

For the 10 percent of Rome's population who were the wealthy upper class—called patricians—breakfast in the morning and dinner in the evening were the main meals, eaten at home. Lunch was lighter, often bought from a street vendor. Breakfast was mostly leftover cheese, olives, and bread. Lunch was called *prandia* and might be followed by a visit to the public baths. Dinner was *cena* if it was only family; if there were guests and it was more elaborate with additional courses like appetizers and desserts, it was called a *convivium*.

Like the Greeks, the Romans believed strongly in the guest-host relationship. In Latin, the word for guest and the word for host are the same—*hospes*. It is where we get our word *hospitality*. However, the Roman ritual meal, the *convivium*, differed from the Greek ritual meal, the symposium, in several ways. First, the Romans ignored the religious rituals that the Greeks had observed regarding meat. They didn't make ritual blood sacrifices before eating meat. Second, the meat that the Greeks consumed was usually lamb or mutton, while the Romans believed that the pig was made for the banquet table. Third, for the Romans, wine was not a controlled substance to be consumed by itself after the food, but a beverage for drinking with food. They drank wine with their meal, a custom that is still observed in Italy today. Fourth, the *convivium* was not restricted to men. Both sexes participated in eating and in drinking wine. Fifth, the Romans didn't ritually purify the dining room after eating and before drinking wine because the wine was not a religious substance, and because they didn't wait until the end of the meal to drink it.

SYMPOSIUM–CONVIVIUM COMPARISON

GREEK SYMPOSIUM	ROMAN CONVIVIUM
Religious	Secular
Blood sacrifice offered to gods before	No blood sacrifice
Lamb or mutton	Pork
Wine after meal	Wine with meal as beverage
Men only	Men and women
Dining area purified before wine	Dining area not purified

But what time did Romans dine? The Romans divided the day into two parts, with the middle of the day, noon—*meridiem*—as the dividing line. Midday was important because Rome was a society of laws, and lawyers had to be in court before noon. The Romans called the part of the day before noon *ante-meridiem*, which we abbreviate "a.m."; *post-meridiem*, "p.m.," was after the middle of the day. They read the time on big sundials in their gardens or on one-and-one-half-inch portable, pocket-sized sundials. Neither worked on cloudy days. Water clocks, which measured the flow of water against lines drawn on a basin, served as a back-up but were not portable, so people were much more casual about time.

Roman dinner would have been in the late afternoon or early evening. Depending on how elaborate the *convivium* was, it could last all night. Since the dining room was where entertaining took place, it was the best room in the house. It was called the *triclinium* [try-CLIN-ee-um], after the couch on which three people could recline while they ate. The dining room was elaborately decorated with paintings on the walls or a mosaic tile floor that might have pictures of food, like fish and baskets of grain.

Dining *Al Fresco*

When the weather was good, wealthy Romans dined outside in the fresh air—*al fresco*. Dining in an elaborate sunken or terraced garden could be just as elegant as dining indoors. They might have ornamental flower gardens as well as food gardens, with separate landscape designers for each. Care was taken to grow special plants for bees—usually rosemary, thyme, and roses.[50] Urns, statues, sundials, shrines, and altars decorated the gardens. Grapevines trained on an arbor or nets that kept birds in provided shade. Water pumped in from the aqueducts splashed in fountains, mosaic-lined pools, and ponds stocked with fish and ducks. The outdoor *triclinium* was built in, made of marble, cement, or stone, with soft pillows on top. A ledge built into the couch served as a cup holder so wine was within easy reach. Sometimes the couches were built around a small pool so the food could float on trays, cooled by the water. Or dinner guests might climb up into a tower and enjoy the view; take a siesta on a sleeping couch in a small outdoor room after the meal; or have dinner in a treehouse.[51]

The Vacation Villa

Some wealthy Romans got out of the city altogether. Like wealthy people today, Romans had vacation houses at the seashore, on a lake, or in the mountains. Their villas (Latin for "farmhouse") were often within 20 miles of Rome so they could visit them easily and oversee their farms. Vacation villas were built for relaxation and to take advantage of the views. Pliny the Younger, a Roman author, had an estate with almost 30 rooms, including quarters for slaves. He called it "my little villa." Eating and entertaining took place in two dining rooms and a banquet room. The main dining room had windows and doors that looked out over the sea on three sides. Glass was very expensive, so windows were usually made of mica or were just holes cut in the walls and closed with shutters. The other dining room and the banquet room were in two separate towers. The second dining room, with eastern and western exposure, faced a vineyard and a garden planted with rosemary bushes, and fig and mulberry trees. The banquet room had ocean vistas.

Pliny was keenly aware of which windows got breezes and sun from which direction, at what time of day, and in which seasons. There was also an herb garden on the grounds, grain storage, and aboveground wine storage purposely placed near the furnace because the Romans thought smoke helped the wine age. The villa had built-in bookcases, a bathing room with two tubs, and a separate room next to it for applying bath oil. In addition, there were three public bathhouses in the small town. State-of-the-art heating in the villa was provided by hot air generated in the furnace room and circulated into the rest of the house through pipes under the floor.[52]

Another Roman with a villa was Cato, who wrote advice on farming, *On Agriculture*, around 175 B.C. Cato covers everything from how to preserve lentils to suggesting that guard dogs be chained during the day to make them sharper at night; to instructions on planting, harvesting, and care of equipment; how to treat farm hands; and more. He has much information about olives, including how to process them into oil.

> When the olives are ripe they should be gathered as soon as possible, and allowed to remain on the ground or the floor as short a time as possible, as they spoil on the ground or the floor. The gatherers want to have as many windfalls as possible, that there may be more of them to gather; and the pressers want them to lie on the floor a long time, so that they will soften and be easier to mill. Do not believe that the oil will be of greater quantity if they lie on the floor. The more quickly you work them up the better the results will be, and you will get more and better oil from a given quantity.[53]

This is still how the best olive oils are processed in Italy today: hand-harvested, not bruised from falling or dirty from being left on the ground, and pressed as soon as possible after picking. Cato also included a recipe for olives. It is simple, easy, and doesn't need any adjusting for today's table.

RECIPE:
Cato's Herbed Olives[54]

Recipe for a confection of green, ripe, and mottled olives. Remove the stones from green, ripe, and mottled olives, and season as follows: chop the flesh, and add oil, vinegar, coriander, cumin, fennel, rue, and mint. Cover with oil in an earthen dish, and serve.

Cato also has extensive instructions on the care and planting of wine grapes; making wine; how to find out if wine has been watered—desirable for Greeks, an insult to Romans; how to use wine as a remedy for gout and as a laxative; how to remove a bad odor from wine; etc. He provides a recipe for cakes made from must.

RECIPE:
Cato's Must Cakes[55]

Moisten 1 modius [approximately 16 cups] of wheat flour with must; add anise, cumin, 2 pounds of lard, 1 pound of cheese, and the bark of a laurel twig. When you have made them into cakes, put bay leaves under them, and bake.

The Farmer's Villa

In the country, a real villa, the house where the farmer lived and worked, was very different from the vacation villas of the rich. Under one roof were the living quarters for the farmer and his family, an underground prison for chained slaves, a kitchen with high ceilings so the beams didn't catch on fire, baths, a bakery, dining room, barn, stable, threshing room, and separate rooms for olive and wine presses and wine fermentation. Again, great care was taken with direction: the grain storage had to be open to the north, because north wind is the coldest and least humid, so the grain would stay dry and not rot.[56]

Garum: Fermented Fish Sauce

In Ancient Rome, the food had to be outstanding to match the stunning surroundings. Underlying much of Roman cooking was a pungent fermented fish sauce called *garum*, a unique combination of salt, sea, and sun. It originated in Greece and was perhaps the ancestor, in a roundabout way, of Worcestershire sauce. The theory is that Romans exported *garum* to India in ancient times and then the British brought it back from India to England 2,000 years later. *Garum* was readily available commercially, made from recipes like these:

RECIPE:

Garum or Liquamen

Garum, also called liquamen, is made in this way. The entrails of fish are placed in a vat and salted. Also used are whole small fish, especially smelts, or tiny mullets, or small sprats, or anchovies, or whatever small fish are available. Salt the whole mixture and place it in the sun. After it has aged in the heat, the garum is extracted in the following manner. A long, thickly woven basket is placed in the vat full of the above-mentioned fish. The garum enters the basket, and the so-called liquamen is thus strained through the basket and retrieved. The remaining sediment is called allec.

The Bithynians make garum in the following manner. They use sprats, large or small, which are the best to use if available. If sprats are not available, they use anchovies, or lizard fish or mackerel, or even old allec, or a mixture of all of these. They put this in a trough which is usually used for kneading dough. They add two Italian sextarii [approximately one quart] of salt to each modius [one peck, a quarter of a bushel] of fish and stir well so that the fish and salt are thoroughly mixed. They let the mixture sit for one night and then transfer it to a clay vat which is placed uncovered in the sun for two or three months, stirring it occasionally with sticks. Then they bottle, seal, and store it. Some people also pour two sextarii of old wine into each sextarius of fish.[57]

To compare: good quality *garum* cost twice as much as vinegar, the same as lower-grade aged wine, and less than half of what top-quality honey or fresh olive oil cost. Approximately one pint of *garum* cost the same as one pound of pork, lamb, goat, or second-quality fish, and twice as much as a pound of beef. The expensive meats were chicken—one pound cost five times as much as one pint of *garum*—and goose, which cost more than 16 times as much.[58]

Apicius and the First Cookbook

The first cookbook dates from the first century A.D. This compilation of recipes divided into 10 books or chapters is only a fragment; baking and pastry are missing, which indicates that these were separate specialties. *De re coquinaria* (*Cooking Matters*) is attributed to a man named Apicius, which means "epicure" or "gourmet."

Who Was Apicius?

Little is known about him; in fact, there are three men named Apicius who might be candidates. One was a high-living man-about-town who loved to eat well and had many dishes named after him, including cheesecakes. He spent a great deal of his wealth on food, endowed a cooking school, and supposedly killed himself when his fortune dropped below a level that could support his expensive habits. Some food historians find this story difficult to digest.[59]

De re coquinaria was translated from Latin into Italian and German after the invention of the printing press in the fifteenth century, but an English translation didn't appear until 1936. Only 530 copies were printed then because culinary history was in its infancy and there wasn't much interest in the subject. Translating the manuscript was a lifelong dream and labor of love for Joseph Dommers Vehling, a world-class chef who grew up in a small town on the German-Dutch border and was trained and worked in the grand hotels of Europe before he became an executive chef planning menus for the railroads in the United States. Vehling loved food and cooking as well as the Latin language and Roman culture. A world traveler, he had visited the Roman ruins. In Pompeii, buried suddenly by a volcanic explosion in A.D. 79, he saw ancient bakeries, ovens, and flour mills, as well as olive oil, figs, lentils, and spices preserved in amphorae [am-FOR-eye].

Pompeii, ovens. *Photo courtesy Nancy Uhrhammer.*

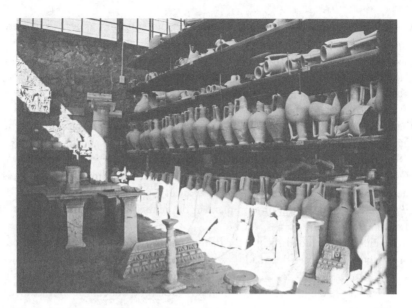

Pompeii, amphorae. *Photo courtesy Nancy Uhrhammer.*

From the recipes of Apicius it is clear that the Romans liked sauces and meat. Food historian Mireille Corbier states that the 10 most common ingredients in Apicius's 468 recipes are black pepper, *garum*, olive oil, honey, lovage, vinegar, wine, cumin, rue, and coriander. Absent is garlic, the seasoning of the poor.[60] For the wealthy, a feast meant meat and meat meant pork: "nature made the pig for the banquet table."[61] Pigs were fattened and their livers enlarged in much the same way geese were prepared for foie gras until recently—force feeding. Pigs were fed dried figs, then guzzled mead. The liquid expanded the figs, which killed the pigs.[62] True omnivores, the Romans ate sow's udders, calf's brains, flamingo tongues, sheep heads, pork sweetbreads, and capon kidneys. Vehling says that the capon—a castrated male bird—was supposedly "invented" by a Roman surgeon in response to a law that made it illegal to fatten hens. So he castrated a rooster, which caused it to fatten naturally.[63] Romans also raised the dormouse *(Glis glis)* commercially, plumping and tenderizing these small mammals by confining them in earthenware vessels that looked like flower pots with ventilation holes and feeding them a high-fat diet of walnuts, chestnuts, and acorns.[64] Rabbits and hares were also raised commercially. Dogs were eaten, too. Milk came from cows and camels. Cheeses, both domestic and imported, were eaten alone with bread or as an ingredient in other dishes.[65] Olive oil was the main fat; butter—salted—was introduced centuries later when the Germanic barbarians invaded.

Vinegar added tang in these recipes in combination with honey or *garum*, while raisin wine and honey were the sweeteners for many main dishes. Honey was also used to preserve fruit and meat. Oregano and mint appear frequently. The use of spices in some of the recipes is eerily modern. A recipe for pears could have come out of California 2,000 years later: "Stew the pears, clean out the center, crush them with pepper, cumin, honey, raisin wine, broth and a little oil; mix with eggs, make a pie [custard] of this, sprinkle with pepper and serve."[66]

Historians have speculated about one common spice, *silphium*. Tannahill says the herb is completely unknown now; others thought it might be laserwort,[67] the *fang feng* of Chinese medicine, used to treat sinus infections and fevers.[68] Some historians think *silphium* was used to extinction because it prevented pregnancy.[69] But the one thing on which they all agree, going back to Pliny (A.D. 24–79), is that *silphium* is extinct. *The Classical Cookbook* offers an acceptable substitute for *silphium:* asafoetida, the resin of a plant in the fennel family so stinky that it is also known as "devil's dung."

Apicius also included recipes for drinks, even floral wines. He gives recipes for rose wine, fake rose wine made with citrus leaves but without roses, and violet wine. *The Classical Cookbook* gives a substitute for *passum*, a poor man's raisin wine that was made in Crete but which now would be the equivalent of expensive *vin santo*.

··

RECIPE:

Raisin Wine[70]

2½ cups red wine
4 ounces raisins

Soak the raisins in the wine for two to three days until they are soft and swollen. Blend or mash the mixture and strain through a fine sieve, pushing through as much as possible of the pulp. Can be used immediately.

··

Most of the recipes in Apicius are based on sauces. One example is this fish sauce: ". . . tak[e] one ounce of pepper, one pint of reduced wine, one pint of spiced wine and two ounces of oil." In Roman cooking, a white sauce is made with white wine, white pepper, and egg yolks: "Put yolks of hard boiled eggs in the mortar with white pepper, nuts, honey, white wine and a little broth." Eggs were frequently used as a thickener or binder, along with bread crumbs, honey, and animal blood. The blood could be either from an animal that had been killed, or from a living animal that had been bled. Favorite fruits included grapes, pomegranates, quinces, figs, mulberries, apples, and pears; and the stone fruits: plums, cherries, and peaches. Like a Roman Martha Stewart, Apicius even provided serving tips: "An expensive silver platter would enhance the appearance of this dish materially," he wrote at the end of a recipe composed of sow's belly and figpecker (a bird) breast seasoned with crushed pepper and lovage, sweetened with raisin wine, layered with thin pancakes, and topped with pine nuts.[71]

There are even some medicinal recipes, like one for spiced salts that can be used "against indigestion, to move the bowels, against all illness, against pestilence as well as for the prevention of colds." Apicius didn't need to include many medicinal recipes in his cookbook because a book explaining in detail the medicinal uses of 600 species of plants also appeared in the first century A.D. The *Materia medica*, written by Dioscorides, was one of the major medical textbooks for over 1,000 years. The first century A.D. also produced Pliny's *Naturalis historia*, which has several sections on the medicinal uses of plants and animals, even imaginary ones like dragons.

Feasts: Trimalchio and Lucullus

"Trimalchio's Feast" makes fun of upper-class Romans who had too much money and too much time and spent both trying to outdo each other with lavish banquets. The "Feast" is one section of the *Satyricon,* which was written approximately A.D. 61 by Petronius, who was Emperor Nero's style adviser. Much of the feast resembles doings at Nero's court. The banquet begins with the guests reclining on couches while slave boys from Alexandria, Egypt, wash their hands in water cooled with snow. The courses become increasingly elaborate. They include exotic imported foods, foods disguised as other foods, over-the-top presentations. There are dormice sprinkled with poppy seeds and honey, hundred-year-old wine, a tray with the signs of the zodiac and food that matches, such as a piece of beef on Taurus (the bull), an African fig on Leo (lions come from Africa), fish on Pisces, and on Libra (the scale), a scale with a tart on one side balanced by a cake on the other. Underneath the zodiac tray is "a hare equipped with wings to resemble Pegasus [a mythical flying horse]."[72]

The dinner is also a show, with a meat carver named Carver, live birds that fly out of the belly of a cooked boar, and party favors like little suckling pigs made out of pastry. The entertainment even extends to the cooks. When a huge cooked hog is brought in, Trimalchio starts yelling that it hasn't been gutted. The cook miserably admits that, yes, he forgot to gut the hog. Trimalchio has the cook stripped naked and calls in two torturers. All the guests immediately start making excuses for the cook, even though they think that he is criminally careless. At this, Trimalchio says to the cook:

> "Since your memory's so short, you can gut [the hog] right here before our eyes!" The cook put on his tunic, snatched up a carving knife . . . and slashed the hog's belly in several places. Sausages and meat-puddings . . . immediately tumbled out. The whole household burst into unanimous applause at this. . . . As for the cook, he was given a drink and a silver crown . . .[73]

Shortly after he wrote the *Satyricon*, Petronius fell out of favor with Emperor Nero and was forced to commit suicide.

Lucullus, unlike the fictitious host Trimalchio, was a real person, a general who lived in the first century B.C. He was so successful on his military campaigns in Asia and Africa that he returned to Rome with phenomenal wealth and treasures of war. He built public gardens and libraries, multiple villas for himself, and became a patron of the arts. He also spared no expense on food. His banquets became legendary in his lifetime, running to the tens of thousands of dollars. Now his name is synonymous with luxurious and lavish, and an invitation to a Lucullan feast is still an honor.

Lower-Class Cuisine: Street Food

At the other end of the food chain were the 90 percent of the population that made up the lower classes in Rome—the plebeians. They lived in poorly built tenement apartments that frequently collapsed or caught on fire. This was due to negligence, not a lack of construction expertise, because the same culture built the Colosseum and the Pantheon, which are still standing. The tenements had no kitchens, so street vendors did a thriving business selling bread and grain pastes. Wheat was the mainstay of the poor. In 122 B.C., reformers lowered the price of grain so the poor could afford it; in 58 B.C., wheat became free to those who qualified. The wheat was usually prepared two ways: mashed and boiled into porridge, or ground and baked into bread.[74] Leavened and unleavened bread; bread with poppy seeds, with pepper, with salt, with cheese, and with honey; square bread and round bread; flat bread and shaped breads could all be produced on a massive scale because the Romans had the technology to produce flour on a massive scale. This required more than human labor—the donkey was harnessed to a grinding stone called a quern and walked around it in endless circles to separate the wheat from the chaff.[75]

For a cold beverage, soldiers and the poor drank *posca*, vinegar diluted with water. *Calda* was wine diluted with hot water. They also had a kind of bread soup with vinegar and mashed cucumber, the forerunner of gazpacho. Indoors at the *taberna* (where we get our word *tavern*), patrons could drink wine and nibble on salted foods, chickpeas, or turnips, the way popcorn and peanuts are served in American bars. The *popina* served simple dinners and alcohol. Both places provided gambling and prostitutes.[76]

Christians: Life and Death in the Colosseum

During the *Pax Romana*, Rome didn't wage war against other countries. It did wage war internally, however, against Christians and Jews, who were considered atheists because they refused to worship Roman gods. They also threatened the power of the state because they were willing to die for their god, not for the state. Christianity was only one of the many religions that arose as a response to the excesses of luxury and cruelty among the upper classes in the Roman Empire. Romans persecuted Christians by, among other things, forcing them into to-the-death combat with other humans or animals in the Colosseum, an arena that could hold up to 50,000 people. After some of the human-animal battles, the animals, like bears, were butchered and became upper-class suppers.[77]

A DAY IN THE LIFE OF THE ROMAN EMPIRE

	PATRICIANS: 10% OF THE POPULATION	PLEBEIANS/SLAVES/FARMERS: 90% OF THE POPULATION
You are	A wealthy landowner, in the military or in the government. You pay for the spectacles at the Colosseum.	Poor or unemployed. You go to free public entertainment at the Colosseum or the Circus Maximus.
You live	In a many-room house with kitchen and dining room, built around a courtyard. You have other homes.	In one room with no kitchen in a poorly built tenement that catches on fire or collapses.
You wear	Imported silk.	Coarse homemade fabric tunic.
You eat	Pork, wine sweetened with honey, food with sauces like *garum* and expensive imported spices prepared by servants; in your home or at friends' villas.	Grain pastes, bread bought from street vendors or made from free government grain, skin from the fish that made the *garum*; in a *taberna* or *popina*.

The emperor Constantine ended the persecution of the Christians in A.D. 313 after he supposedly saw a cross in the sky as a good omen just before he won a battle. In A.D. 325, he convened the Council of Nicaea in Anatolia (modern-day Turkey), which made the cross the official symbol of Christianity and set the date for Easter at the first Sunday after the first full moon following the spring equinox.[78] This is why Easter can fall anywhere between March 22 and April 25.

Easter is preceded by Lent, a 40-day period of fasting (excluding Sundays) that begins on Ash Wednesday, which signifies mourning. The period before

The Colosseum in Rome, Italy. *Courtesy Corbis Digital Stock.*

Ash Wednesday is one last celebration of partying and eating the rich foods like cheese, meat, and eggs that are restricted or forbidden during Lent. This is called Mardi Gras ("fat Tuesday") or Carnevale—literally, "meat good-bye." Lent made a virtue of fasting during a time of scarcity. At the end of winter there was little fresh food for humans or beasts; even dried or salted food was in short supply. Some monks supposedly survived the winter on triple bock beer, very high in vitamins and carbohydrates.

In A.D. 380, the emperor Theodosius decreed that Christianity was the official religion of the Roman Empire.

Jews: Masada and the Diaspora

The *Pax Romana* was not a time of peace for the Jews, either. The Romans killed hundreds of thousands of Jews, most in two separate battles. In A.D. 70, the Romans destroyed the Temple in Jerusalem, leaving only one wall, which is now a holy shrine, the Wailing Wall. In A.D. 132, the Jews decided to take the decision about how they would die away from the Romans: they killed themselves at the rock fortress cliffs of Masada rather than let the Romans kill or enslave them. The rest fled their homeland of Judea for safety, scattered in the Diaspora. The Jews were without a homeland for almost 2,000 years, until 1948, when the United Nations created the country of Israel in the old Jewish homeland, so that Jews all over the world could have a safe haven after the Holocaust of World War II. However, in those 2,000 years, Muslims had occupied the land and considered it their home. The conflict between Muslims and Jews continues to this day.

Bread and Circuses: The Decline of Rome

The *Pax Romana* ended in A.D. 180 when wars with foreign countries resumed. These wars, diseases, loss of loyalty, and economic decline weakened the Roman Empire. The Plague of Antoninus, named after the reigning emperor, was new and terrifying, one of the first zoonoses—diseases that cross over from animals to humans. It began as a disease of cattle but in humans was called smallpox because of the small pus-filled sores that covered the skin. The 15-year epidemic that ended in A.D. 180 killed millions.[79] At one point, 5,000 people a day were dying in the city of Rome alone. Then another plague (some historians think it was measles) struck the empire. Christians stayed with the sick while pagan Romans ran; grateful people converted to Christianity.[80]

The high death tolls created vacancies in many jobs that were crucial to the running of the empire. It killed so many farmers that the empire's food supply was threatened. To remedy this, Rome offered land to people who were not citizens if they promised to farm it, then passed laws forcing people to farm and making farming hereditary.

Easter

Easter is a combination of Jewish, pagan, and Christian rituals. Its name comes from the Jewish Passover, *Pesach* in Hebrew. In Italian, it is *Pasqua*; in French, *Pâque*; in Spanish, *Pascua*; in Swedish, *Påsk;* in Russian, *Paskha*. In English, Easter gets its name from Eostre, the Old English goddess of fertility and dawn. Her festival was during the spring equinox as plants began to grow again and young animals like bunnies, lambs, and chicks were born. The Christian part of Easter is the story of the crucifixion and resurrection of Christ.

Lent ends with the Last Supper, on Holy Thursday, when it is believed that Christ gave the ceremony of communion to his followers, the 12 disciples: "Take of this bread and eat of it, for it is my body. Take of this wine and drink of it, for it is my blood." Then Christ was betrayed by one of the apostles, Judas, who sold him out to the Romans for 30 pieces of silver. The betrayal is portrayed in Leonardo da Vinci's fresco *The Last Supper* by Judas knocking over the salt cellar, a traditional sign of evil.[81] The next day, Good Friday, is the deepest day of mourning in the Christian religion because it is the day Christ was crucified (on a cross made of olive wood), died, and was buried. Christians believe that on Easter Sunday Christ rose again and later ascended into heaven.

Eggs were forbidden during Lent, but were used heavily in ritual foods when the fast was broken on Easter Sunday. They were in special egg breads like Ukrainian *paska* or Russian saffron-scented *kulich*. Sometimes the bread is decorated with dyed hard-boiled eggs or shaped into a cross. For Easter dinner, traditional foods depend on geography. In the Mediterranean, it is lamb; in Northern Europe, ham; in England, beef.

The custom of giving painted eggs for Easter dates to the later Middle Ages. Baskets to hold the eggs represent birds' nests. The Easter Bunny with his basket of painted eggs came to America with German immigrants in the nineteenth century. In Washington, D.C., children used the grounds of the Capitol Building as a playground and for egg hunts until Congress, unhappy with the torn-up lawn and tired of voting money to keep repairing it, passed a law against it. However, in 1878, children from Washington, D.C., went to President Rutherford B. Hayes and asked if they could have an Easter egg hunt. The president and his wife Lucy agreed to let the children use the White House grounds. Easter egg hunts have taken place on the south lawn of the White House ever since. It is the largest public event held at the White House, but it is only for children six years old and under. (See Chapter 10 for Ukrainian Easter eggs and Fabergé eggs, the jeweled eggs made for the Russian royal family.)

There was also an unfavorable balance of trade. More money was going out of the empire to buy spices, silk, and animals for the contests in the Colosseum, the Circus Maximus (which means "biggest circle"), and other arenas than was coming in. By A.D. 250, there were 150 of these spectacles a year, almost one every other day,[82] and the government was giving oil, wine, and pork to 200,000 urban poor in addition to bread.[83] The free food and free admission to the entertainment kept the poor from being hungry and angry and made them grateful to the government instead.

In the Colosseum, completed in A.D. 80, the Circus Maximus, and other arenas, the Roman Empire controlled its underclasses in three ways. Giving the urban poor free bread kept them from revolting because they were hungry. Giving them free entry to these torture-spectacles kept them in one place so they could be managed. It was also a serious warning about the power of the state. In effect, upper-class Romans were telling lower-class Romans, "Watch out, or you could end up down there."

In A.D. 330, Emperor Constantine took a desperate measure to preserve the empire—he split it in half. He made the old city of Byzantium his new capital in the east and named it after himself, Constantine *polis*—Constantinople. The division strengthened the eastern half, which survived; the western didn't. He also stopped the persecution of Christians throughout the empire.

The Fall of Rome, A.D. 408–476: "The funeral of the world" [84]

The fifth century was a time of increasing chaos in the Western Roman Empire, which was cut off from the more powerful Eastern Empire. The military was unable to defend the borders against barbarians—Visigoths, Ostrogoths, and Vandals—illiterate Germanic nomadic tribal people.

You Just Might Be a Barbarian If . . . [85]
(WITH APOLOGIES TO JEFF FOXWORTHY)

✦ You eat your meat raw
✦ You warm your raw meat by putting it between your thighs
✦ You warm your raw meat by putting it between your saddle and your horse
✦ You have never eaten bread
✦ You eat your food without sauce
✦ You drink ale because you think wine is for wimps

Finally, the once invincible Roman army couldn't even protect the city of Rome. In 408, invaders held it for ransom: 3,000 pounds of black pepper.[86] In 410, Visigoths ransacked Rome for three days. Wealthy Romans who had estates and villas outside the cities fled to them and buried their silver dinnerware—knives, spoons, cups, dishes, serving pieces—in the fields, where it was still being unearthed in the twenty-first century. In 452, Attila and his army of Mongol nomads—Huns—appeared outside the city. The emperor of Rome commanded no army and wielded no real power so Pope Leo I negotiated the peace with Attila. This was the beginning of the Christian Church's rise to its position as the most powerful political force in Europe in the Middle Ages.

The barbarian invasion became final in A.D. 476 when the German general Odoacer seized the throne from the last Roman emperor, 14-year-old Romulus Augustulus. The great Roman Empire was broken, its western half destroyed. Rome, the city a million people had called home, was almost a ghost town. Now its entire population—20,000—could fit in the Colosseum two and a half times. Nature took over, obliterating the signs of the great civilization. Wind and weather finished off what the barbarians had left of the architectural master-pieces that Rome built. The magnificent Forum, all the shops empty, offices gutted, temples untended, grew wild. Among fallen marble columns and through abandoned buildings where an empire once ruled the Earth, down roads where great armies had marched, cows wandered and chewed weeds. Descent began into the decentralized, isolated, rural, illiterate life that would characterize west-ern Europe for centuries to come. With the breakdown of the Roman roads came the end of the western empire and the beginning of the end of the Latin language. Communication was cut off, trade expired. No more exotic animals or sexy fabrics or spicy foods. For nearly the next thousand years, almost everything in western Europe would be homegrown, homemade, and homespun.

Crazy Bread, Coffee, and Courtly Manners

CHRISTENDOM AND ISLAM IN THE MIDDLE AGES, 500–1453

The Middle Ages is the time between the fall of the Western Roman Empire at the end of the fifth century and the modern world, which began with the Renaissance in the fourteenth and fifteenth centuries. With the roads no longer safe, western Europe became isolated. Literacy and learning declined. Daily life centered around individual farm-based rural societies. Feudalism, a system based on loyalty to a local lord rather than to a distant king or to a country, determined a person's place in society. However, in the eastern half of the Roman Empire, the Byzantine Empire, with its capital in Constantinople, safeguarded Roman culture and laws, mixed with Greek culture. Thriving markets brought in foods from the eastern Mediterranean and the Black Sea. Farther east, a new religion—Islam—propelled a great trading empire and created cities where goods and ideas flowed and new cuisines were invented. It was inevitable that these great empires would clash. In the eleventh and twelfth centuries, a series of Crusades, which were unsuccessful from a military and religious standpoint, created new cities, reopened trade routes, and spread cuisines and cultures from Asia to Europe and across northern Africa.

Christendom: Western Europe, 500–1000

The early Middle Ages, the period from A.D. 476 to about A.D. 1000, was a time of chaos and attempts at political organization. The Christian church based in Rome and its leader, the bishop of Rome, called "father" in Italian—*il papa*, or the pope—emerged as the most powerful forces in European politics and daily life. The Church controlled every aspect of life in the Middle Ages in Europe, from Spain to eastern Poland, from Italy to England and Ireland. The Church told people what they could eat and when, when to fast, and when to abstain. The Church even controlled time: the bells rang out, signaling to the illiterate when to get up, say morning prayers, go to Mass, say evening prayers, and go to bed.

After the invasions of the Goths in the fifth century, the Church worried that these beer-drinking barbarians would tear up the vineyards or destroy the wine presses or somehow drive wine—necessary to Christian worship—out of existence. But they didn't. Viticulture continued to flourish, maybe because the barbarians had found a use for wine that made sense to them—as armor. Linen saturated with a mixture of wine and salt dried hard as a board.[1] However, the Church's problem wasn't beer-drinking barbarians but wine-drunk priests and monks who made spectacles of themselves. Attempts to control them weren't very successful, even though public drunkenness was against the law.

Gluttony

Drunkenness was part of gluttony—eating or drinking to excess. Gluttony was against the teachings of the Church. It was "the first bodily sin," because eating the apple caused Adam and Eve to lose the Garden of Eden. The sin of gluttony could be committed in three ways: (1) eating before meal time; (2) eating food "choicer than the necessity of the body or his rank and station in life demands"; and (3) "eating or drinking [more] than may benefit his health."[2]

Feudalism

Feudalism was a political, social, economic, military, and legal system based on local, personal relationships and loyalties. It was an extension of the class system that had existed in the Roman Empire, transferred to the countryside, where it preserved the unequal class percentages: 10 percent upper, 90 percent lower. Class divisions in food, clothing, education, and occupation were enforced by law. There was none of the upward mobility that is available to us in modern society through education, changing jobs, or starting over someplace else. People who wanted to be more attractive by decorating their clothes with fur trim or buttons, items reserved for the nobility, attracted the clothes police. Serfs endured this system because the Church told them it was God's will, their lot in life. And because there was nowhere else to go.

There were few cities, and those were small, with only a few thousand people. Little travel or trade was done because the roads were unsafe and in disrepair, so the manors had to be self-sufficient. The lord of the manor provided land for the serfs to farm; in exchange, the serfs would be the army when the lord needed one. The lord also provided bread. Unlike modern English, Old English, the language spoken in England from the middle of the fifth century until the end of the eleventh, divided its words into genders. *Hlaf*—loaf, the staple of life— was a masculine word. "Lord" was *hlaford*—loaf keeper; "lady" was *hlaefdige*— loaf kneader. A servant was a *hlaf-aeta*—loaf eater.[3] The serfs had to pay a fee to use the lord's mill to grind their grain into flour and to use his oven to bake their bread. Sneaking off to do these things somewhere else resulted in a fine because on the medieval manor the lord was also the law.

A DAY IN THE LIFE OF THE MIDDLE AGES

	NOBLES: 10% OF THE POPULATION	SERFS: 90% OF THE POPULATION
You live	In the manor house, the largest and tallest structure on the estate after the church.	In a small, one-room, leaky, thatched-roof hut with your family, your animals, their vermin, and your vermin.
You wear	Fur, velvet; cape, long tunic, buttons.	Homespun flax; short tunic and leggings (or the clothes police come).
You eat	Meat; fine-grained white bread for your delicate health; spices and foods from the Middle East: almonds, dates, sugar; *blancmange*; wine, beer, mead, cider.	Oat gruel; coarse, dark bread that might poison you with ergot; fruits, vegetables, pulses, cheese; beer, cider.
You do	Oversee the farming, collect taxes, administer the law. Anything requiring literacy.	Farm. Farm. Farm. Fight if your earthly or heavenly lord needs you to. You are illiterate.

The Christian Diet and the Theory of Humors

The Great Chain of Being reflected the world view in the Middle Ages: everything and everybody had a place ordained by God. At the top was God; at the bottom were inanimate objects like rocks. Along with this went the theory of the four humors to explain how the human body functioned and how to treat it. This theory was first proposed in ancient Greece by Hippocrates, the father of medicine; refined by another physician, Galen, in the second century A.D.; and turned into rock-solid doctrine by the Church in the Middle Ages. It is a philosophy of food, and attempts to provide balance. Physicians had nowhere else to get information about the human body because the Church imposed an absolute ban on Christians performing autopsies. There was also no experimentation or firsthand observation of disease or the living human body. Scientists didn't know that the blood circulated through the body until the eighteenth century. So food was medicine, and the theory of the four humors was the medical bible. It is important to remember when you look at the chart below that what category a food was in had nothing to do with how it appears, but with the effect it supposedly had on the body. One problem with the chain was that food animals didn't really fit. They were sandwiched in between air and water, because although they lived *on* the earth, they weren't *in* it like carrots, which were only fit for the lower classes. There were also rankings within each category. Chicken, higher in the air element, was served at banquets attended by the nobility. And, of course, cooking it by a hot, dry fire method like roasting made you that much closer to God. Pork, the least valued of the food animals, was fit for peasants. Veal and mutton were in the middle. Fruit, which grew on shrubs and trees, ranked higher than vegetables, which grew in or on the ground, and the higher up in the tree the fruit was, the more it was fit for nobility.[4]

THE GREAT CHAIN OF BEING AND THE FOUR HUMORS[5]

			God			
			Angels			
ELEMENT	**HUMOR**	**EMOTION**	**COLOR**	**TEMPERATURE**		**ANIMAL/PLANT**
fire	yellow bile	choler (anger)	yellow	hot	dry	phoenix (mythical), spices
air	blood	sanguine	red	hot	wet	birds, fowl, meat animals
water	mucus	phlegmatic	clear/ white	cold	wet	whales, fish, crustaceans
earth	black bile	melancholy	black	cold	dry	trees, leafy plants, roots
			Rocks and inanimate objects			

The theory of humors was that one of these four personality types predominated in each person. If you were sick, your body was out of balance because one of the humors had overwhelmed the others. This could result in anything from pale skin and irritability to cowardice, leprosy, and death. It was crucial to restore balance by eating something that represented the opposite element. For example, brains and tongue were cold and moist, so they had to be counteracted by hot, dry spices like pepper, ginger, and cinnamon.[6] Vinegar (*vin aigre*—literally, wine sour) was considered cold and dry, so a vinegar-based sauce had to be balanced with hot spices like mustard, garlic, and rue.[7] So did a sauce based on *verjus* (literally, green juice), the unfermented juice of unripe fruit, usually grapes, but also crabapples.

Foods within each humor were further divided into degrees from one to four, four being the most intense. In the late Middle Ages, after contact with Muslims because of the Crusades, hot spices included cinnamon, clove, pepper, and others from the Middle East. Cinnamon, cumin, and nutmeg were hot and dry in the second degree, so they were very beneficial to health. Black pepper was a fourth-degree spice, so it was dangerous and had to be used sparingly. At the other end of the scale were mushrooms, fourth-degree cold and wet, to be avoided always.[8] As food historian Jean-Louis Flandrin points out, "In medieval recipes . . . hot ingredients played a crucial role. In fact, they dominated the seasoning."[9] Looked at from the point of view of dietetics, the heavy use of spices in medieval cooking makes more sense. It also explains why so many medieval recipes result in food that is spicy, sweet, and sour. It is not to mask food that had gone bad, especially meat. Bad food smelled as bad to people in the Middle Ages as it does to us, and laws forbade selling meat more than one day old.[10] Among the upper classes, the good host played it safe and served a variety of foods to restore the balance of all personality types. Hungry peasants bent the rules and ate a diet heavy in vegetables.

FOOD FABLE:

Feed a Cold, Starve a Fever

"Feed a cold, starve a fever." Have you ever thought that old saying makes no sense because you're supposed to stuff yourself when you're congested? It's a holdover from the Middle Ages in our culture. It does make sense if you look at it from the medieval idea of humors and restoring balance to the system. The theory is that eating will make the stomach work, which will heat it up and counteract a cold. On the other hand, not eating is supposed to make the stomach cool down and counteract a fever.[11] Medieval recipes reflected this—people with fevers had to avoid spices.

The Breakdown of the Latin Language

The learned men of the time, the nobles and the clergy, could understand each other when they talked about dietetics and the humoral theory because they wrote and spoke Latin. But the spoken language of the serfs deteriorated into the vernacular—local languages with less complicated grammar. Italian, French, Spanish, Portuguese, and Romanian are called the Romance languages because they are derived from Latin, the language that was spoken in Rome.

A Latin saying about food was also preserved in the Romance languages. *De gustibus non est disputandum* means "there's no arguing about tastes." In French, this became *chacun à son goût* ("everyone to his own taste"), and in Italian, *tutti i gusti son gusti* ("all tastes are tastes"). English is a blend of about 60 percent Latin and 40 percent German. The chart shows what happened when Latin broke down into the Romance languages, and also the influence of German on English.

THE BREAKDOWN OF LATIN AND THE CREATION OF ENGLISH

ENGLISH	LATIN	ITALIAN	FRENCH	SPANISH	GERMAN
bread	panis	pane	pain	pan	brot
cook (noun)	coquus (cocus)	cuoco	cuisinier	cocinero	koch
cow	va	vacca	vache	vaca	kuh
egg	ovum	uovo	oeuf	huevo	ei
honey	mel	miel	miele	miel	honig
kitchen	culina	cucina	cuisine	cocina	küche
milk	lac	latte	lait	leche	milch
hen	gallina	gallina	poule	gallina	henne
wine	vinum	vino	vin	vino	wein

The Vikings

In the Middle Ages, Europeans and Russians had a common enemy. Down from Scandinavia—now Denmark, Norway, and Sweden in northern Europe—swooped the Vikings. Because they came from the north, the Vikings were also called Northmen, Norsemen, or Normans. The Vikings were extremely skilled sailors. They built ships that were so shallow they could come within a few feet of shore and attack without warning. They raided towns and monasteries to steal food and left terror everywhere they went. Using oars and later sails, their ships went south into Russia and even to Byzantium.

Their greatest raids were against England and northern France, where they influenced the culture, especially the language. Our days of the week are named after Viking gods—the warrior gods Tiwa, Odin or Wodin, and Thor (who had the lightning bolt) are Tuesday, Wednesday, and Thursday, while the love goddess Freya is Friday. The territory the Vikings conquered in northern France is named after them—Normandy. A thousand years later, in 1944, Normandy Beach was where the Allies invaded Europe to retake it from the Nazis in the greatest amphibious military invasion the world has ever seen.

What we know about the Vikings comes from archaeological excavations. Their diet was heavy in meats and animal fats. Milk was turned into butter and cheese and eaten at both meals. The morning or day meal—*dagverther*—added bread and porridge. The evening or night meal—*nattverthr*—added meat. Fresh-killed meats were spit-roasted or pit cooked; older, tougher meats were boiled in soup or stew. Preservation methods were drying, brining, and smoking. The most common animal was pig. Wild land animals were hunted for food, for sport, and to keep them from destroying crops. The Vikings trained hawks to kill wild birds. Saltwater and freshwater fish and mammals were hunted for food and trade. Eel and salmon could also be used to pay rent for property. In Viking settlements in England, the most common fish was cod; in Germany, it was herring. Of less importance in the Viking diet were fruits and vegetables. Wild fruits like apples, pears, and berries—raspberries, blackberries, elderberries, and lingonberries—were gathered, not cultivated. The most common vegetables were cabbage, carrot, turnip, parsnip; the most common grains were barley and rye.[12]

The raids finally stopped because the Vikings were able to grow their own food when the climate changed as Europe entered a time known as the Medieval Warm Period.

The Medieval Warm Period, 950–1300

The years 950 to 1300 were a period of global warming. Icebergs began to retreat. Northern seas that were formerly frozen were now navigable; the growing season was longer so more food could be produced. The Vikings stopped raiding and started exploring. They settled Iceland, then Greenland, which was colder than Iceland. The name was a public relations ploy—they thought it would attract settlers. From Greenland, they went southwest into Newfoundland, in modern Canada. They called it Vinland—Vineland—after what they called grapes but which might have been cranberries they found growing wild there.[13] A Viking settlement has been excavated at the mouth of the St. Lawrence River in Canada.

The Northern European Agricultural Revolution

Around the year 1000, because of the Medieval Warm Period and the longer growing season, advances were made in agriculture that increased food production. Fields were split into thirds and farmed two-thirds at a time instead of one-half. Crop rotation allowed one-third of the field to lie fallow and regain nutrients while the other two-thirds produced food. New technology in the form of a harness that allowed horses to pull plows more efficiently also aided in increasing crops. However, some of the crops that grew were not necessarily healthier.

Crazy Bread

One of the foods that everyone ate during the Middle Ages was bread—when they could get it. Famines occurred twice a year: at the end of winter, when the previous year's crops were all used up, and in the middle of the summer, when the fields were full of crops not yet ready to harvest. Desperate people ate what they could, even if it made them sick. Sometimes they got poisoned by ergot, a fungus that grows on grains, especially rye. Ergot poisoning could cause hallucinations, twitching, and dry gangrene—limbs went numb, turned black, and then fell off but there was no wound. The ergot fungus wasn't destroyed by harvesting, drying, milling, or baking. The loaves that contained the fungus and caused these horrors were called crazy bread. Over the five centuries from the eleventh to the sixteenth century, there were many episodes of ergot poisoning, which people thought of as epidemics of disease. In controlled doses, ergot was used as a medicine, especially to speed up childbirth.[14]

Byzantium: The Eastern Roman Empire

While what had been the Western Roman Empire struggled, the Eastern Roman Empire—Byzantium—in modern-day Turkey, was thriving. It was wealthy, Christian, and Greek. It also preserved Latin culture and Roman foods, like *garum*, which disappeared in the west after the fall of the western empire. Byzantium controlled the Roman Empire in Asia, east as far as the Tigris and Euphrates rivers in modern Iraq, the north coast of Africa, and Egypt inland down the Nile. The empire's capital, Constantinople, was ideally situated for trade where the Black Sea joined the Mediterranean. It had a good natural harbor and an abundance of fish. Constantinople was a city of learning and markets and sports. The main arena in Constantinople, the Hippodrome, could hold 60,000 spectators (10,000 seats more than the Colosseum in Rome), cheering for their favorites in horse races. But because it was a Christian city, there were none of the bloody, to-the-death events like gladiatorial combat that had taken place in the western empire.

Byzantine Cuisine

The markets of Byzantium were flooded with food, including some the Romans never had, like caviar, mace, nutmeg, and something we consider now a staple of the Mediterranean diet—lemons. Other foods introduced into the Mediterranean diet from western Asia were the eggplant, some melons, and oranges. There was one market for cattle and sheep, another for pigs. Every day, 1,600 boats unloaded freshly caught fish at the docks. The craft bazaars were run by artisans and salespeople who were mostly women. All of these markets were closely controlled by government inspectors who enforced the laws and in some cases, like the fish market, set daily prices depending on the size of the catch.[15]

From fragments of Byzantine books on dietetics, recently translated by Andrew Dalby, we know a great deal about their eating habits. The advice in these books is based on the theory of humors first put forth by the Greek Galen, but varies wildly from author to author. In some cases, they completely contradict each other. One author lists foods and their properties: "Wheat has a high proportion of heat and is the best of all grains. It produces healthy, excellent blood"; wine "heats the stomach," while mead "gives a good facial complexion"; "sweet mulberries have a hot and moist nature and move the bowels." Medicinal plants include roses (cold and dry) which "help with overheating of the liver," violets, myrtle, basil, marjoram, water lilies and white lilies, wild chamomile, sandalwood, camphor, saffron (cold and dry), and cloves and nutmeg (both hot and dry). Aphrodisiacs are chickpeas, melons, dates, and rocket (arugula). The author recommends meat because it "is more nourishing than any other food and makes the body healthy," especially "red meat with no fat." The "best and lightest of all meats" is the domestic hen: "Chicken soup cures coldness in the intestines."[16]

A second author arrives at very different conclusions. Leading off in the "foods that are indigestible" category is beef. He lists other categories, including foods that produce good or bad humors, are digestible or slimming, move the bowels, settle the digestive system, and "hurt the head"—among them, mulberries, milk, plums, walnuts, and tarragon. The "least nourishing" line-up contains many foods that we consider extremely nourishing now: fish, beets, grapes, olives, oats, oysters, walnuts. For this author, nothing is an aphrodisiac.[17]

A third self-help book is in the form of a monthly calendar instructing the reader about which foods and activities are right and wrong for each month according to the humoral theory:

> January: sweet phlegm. Take three small doses of fine and very aromatic wine, but not too quickly. Take no food for three hours. Food should be roast lamb served hot, or roast sucking pick, and gravies spiced with pepper, spikenard and cinnamon; . . . also eat pigs' trotters and head, jellied, with vinegar. . . . [Various vegetables] and their cooking liquor, to be drunk flavoured with spices. . . . Four baths in the course of the month. . . . Make a compound skin lotion by mixing [aloe, myrrh, egg yolks]. . . . After washing the ointment off, rub down with cooling wine and egg yolks mixed with hot rose oil, then make love.[18]

March is the month of moderation in food and sex, with a concentration on sweet flavors. In April, the quality of life will be improved by avoiding "all bitter flavours" and inhaling "the scents of violets, roses, lilies, wild chamomile and all aromatic flowers," while in September, "all kinds of bitter food should be eaten." June, the month of "hot blood," requires eight baths but no soup or sex. No baths in November, because it is the month of "watery phlegm." Cabbage is taboo in December, but baths, ointment washed off with wine, and sex are prescribed.[19]

All of these books are addressed to literate, wealthy people. They worry about their weight, they are bathing in luxury items like wine and eggs and scented oils, and the spices, like spikenard, are extremely expensive. Spikenard was an oil used in perfume and sometimes food. It came from an herb that grew high up in the Himalaya mountains.[20] They deal with issues that exist in the twenty-first century, too: what to do with this abundance and variety of food, wine, flowers, spices, methods of cooking. The choices are staggering, and these books provide a way to navigate through them. Again, the search for immortality underlies the advice.

How Food Helped Russia Choose Its Religion

The Byzantine Empire, like the Western Roman Empire, used slave labor. Their slaves came from eastern Europe, what is now Bulgaria, Russia, Poland, Czechoslovakia, and Ukraine. The people from these places were called Slavs, which is where the word *slave* originated. In the tenth century, an Eastern Orthodox clergyman went on a mission to bring Christianity and literacy to the Slavs in Russia. The Russian alphabet still bears the name of this traveling holy man, St. Cyril—the Cyrillic alphabet.

In 988, Prince Vladimir of Kiev felt he had to decide on a religion for himself and for his people. He knew his people, their habits and likes and dislikes (and his own), so he used food to help him decide. Russians liked pork, so that ruled out Judaism and Islam. Islam had a second strike against it because alcohol was forbidden, which was completely unacceptable to Russians: "We Russians like to drink, and there is no way we can live without it."[21] Christians in Rome fasted too much. False rumors reached Vladimir that Hindus ate humans. So Prince Vladimir chose the Eastern Christianity of Byzantium for his country. It had fast days, too, but peasants could still eat caviar, which was fish, during Lent. In 989, he ordered everyone in the city of Kiev down to the river to be baptized.[22]

Some foods that today are considered traditionally Russian didn't appear in Russia until the end of the Middle Ages or later. Sausage—*kolbasy*—appeared in written Russian for the first time in 1292. Vodka came from Poland *(wódka)* after 1500.[23] Sour cream and borscht also didn't appear until contact with the west after 1500. The potato reached Russia around 1700.

Russia's conversion to the Eastern Orthodox religion strengthened the patriarch, the leading bishop of the Christians in the east, and took power away from the pope in the west. After years of sparring through the mail and threatening each other, pope and patriarch both delivered knockout punches in 1054: they excommunicated each other and split into two separate religions. Under the new Eastern Orthodox Church, ministers could marry, people could get divorced, and the government controlled the church, something the Church in Rome would not allow.

However, as much as they disagreed with each other, they had common worries: from the south, a new religion was expanding and gaining strength.

The Muslim Empire

Muslims believe that in the beginning of the seventh century, the Angel Gabriel spoke to Muhammad (also sometimes spelled Mohammed), a 40-year-old Arab from a powerful family from Mecca in present-day Saudi Arabia, and revealed the teachings of god—Allah. These are written in the holy book, the Qur'ān, also sometimes spelled Koran. The people in Mecca had their own polytheistic religion and forced Muhammad and his followers out of Mecca in the year A.D. 622 in the Christian calendar, which is the year 1 in the Islamic calendar. They traveled to Medina, where they regrouped. In 630, Muhammad and 10,000 of his followers returned—armed—and Mecca surrendered. In honor of Muhammad's triumphant return to Mecca, Muslims make a pilgrimage, called a *hajj* [hahj] to Mecca at least once in their lifetime. Muslims must also face Mecca and pray five times a day and fast during the holy month of Ramadan.

The Islamic calendar is lunar, so each year begins about 11 days earlier than the year before. Just as the Christian calendar has "A.D." or *anno domini*, which is Latin for "in the year of our lord," the Islamic calendar has "AH" or *anno hegirae*, Latin for "in the year of Muhammad's exile" to Medina, called the *hejira*. The Islamic 1434 AH corresponds to the western calendar's 2012.

HOLIDAY HISTORY:

Ramadan

Ramadan is the holiest month in the Muslim calendar. It was during Ramadan that the Angel Gabriel appeared to Muhammad and revealed the Qur'ān. Ramadan reminds Muslims that there is more to life than earthly things, and that fasting is not enough. If a Muslim does not "abandon falsehood in words and deeds, Allah has no need for his abandoning of his food and drink."[24]

Ramadan is observed with a month-long fast which shifts every year because of the Muslim lunar calendar. So, unlike the Catholic Lent, which always occurs at the end of winter when food is scarce, Ramadan can occur during harvest or planting time.

Every day during Ramadan, nothing can be eaten from sunup to sundown. Muslims must also abstain from sex and tobacco during this time. Breakfast has to be finished before dawn. After sundown, the day-long fast is broken, traditionally by eating dates and water. Dinner follows. Because the world of Islam is large and spread out through many countries and continents, the foods that break the fast vary from region to region. They often begin with a rich meat soup and end with sweet desserts like baklava or halva.

The end of Ramadan is celebrated with a feast called *Eid il-fitr*.

The Muslim religion helped to create the Muslim Empire and a rich blend of cuisines and cultures. Making a pilgrimage forced Muslims to travel. Muslim merchants trusted other Muslims: they believed in the same god, spoke the same language, had the same beliefs, used the same money. They even trusted each other across long distances, giving written notes of payment—a *saqq*, which came to be pronounced "check." The Muslims also had something very powerful that they had gotten from the Hindus in India: numbers. What the world knows as Arabic numerals—1, 2, 3, 4—were invented by Hindus. So was the zero. These numbers aided business because they made it possible to add, subtract, multiply, and divide in ways that were impossible with Roman numerals.

The Muslims also had a vast literature of poetry, stories, and fables like *Aladdin and the Magic Lamp*, *Ali Baba and the Forty Thieves*, and *The Thousand and One Nights*. Dreams of flying carpets must have seemed like supersonic travel to people who plodded across the desert on camels for months. Another dream involved turning ordinary substances into gold, or finding a way to turn gold into food. This was the pseudoscience of alchemy. People in the Middle Ages believed that gold could cure dangerous diseases and confer immortality. The alchemy craze spread into Europe. If gold couldn't be turned into real food, then maybe the same effect could be achieved by making real food look like gold. This was done with spices like turmeric and saffron, which was grown in England, Spain, and Italy after a British pilgrim smuggled a bulb out of Asia Minor.[25]

The Arab Agricultural Revolution

The Muslims stepped into the vacuum created by the fall of the Western Roman Empire. They carried their cuisine and culture with them across three continents. Their capital city, Baghdad, in present-day Iraq in Asia, became the new Rome, a center of trade with a population of almost one million. Muslim ships sailed across the Mediterranean and Arabian seas and the Indian Ocean; camel caravans traveled the Silk Road into China and across the deserts of Africa. Northern Africa, including the Sahara Desert and the east coast along the Indian Ocean, were in their control.

In Asia, they extended east into what had been the Persian Empire, the modern countries of Iraq and Iran, and into India. To India, they brought melons, pomegranates, grapes and raisins, peaches, almonds, pistachios, cherries, pears, and apricots.[26]

In Europe, they advanced as far north as France, where they were stopped by Charles Martel (Charles the Hammer) at the battle of Tours in 732. They retreated south into Spain. The Muslims introduced spinach, melons, eggplant, and artichokes to Europe. They planted orchards of stone fruits—peaches, cherries, apricots.[27] To Spain, they also introduced sugar, saffron, rice, and the bitter orange—which the British would use later for marmalade. Arab conquerors who controlled Sicily from 827 to 1091 introduced sugar cane cultivation there in the tenth century.[28] The Muslim Middle Eastern influence is apparent, too, in the meat and fruit combined in stews.

The Muslim Meal

Caliphs and sultans had cooking staffs which might be free or slave labor, under the direction of a master chef whose first priority was to make sure that nobody poisoned the food and killed the ruler. The meal began then and still begins now with *mazza* (sometimes spelled *mezze* or *meze*), which is often mistranslated as "appetizer." As food authority Clifford Wright explains in his masterwork, *A Mediterranean Feast*, the concept of appetizer—something to remind your stomach to get excited about eating—is ridiculous to Arabs. You're either hungry or you aren't, and if you are, your stomach doesn't need a warm-up. The only thing *mazza* has in common with appetizers is the small size of the portions. Wright says that since these tidbits can be an entire meal, the correct translation of *mazza* is actually closer to smorgasbord.[29]

The earliest Muslim recipes date from Baghdad in 1226. They were recorded by al-Baghdadi, who "loved eating above all pleasures," as cookbook author Claudia Roden tells us.[30] Many of al-Baghdadi's recipes are for glorious *tagines*—meat and fruit stews simmered for hours over a low flame until the meat is falling-apart-melt-in-your-mouth tender. This complies with the Arab dietary law about not eating blood. An example is *mishmishiya*, made with lamb and dried apricots. It gets its name from the Arab word for apricot, *mishmish*. Cumin, coriander, cinnamon, ginger, and black pepper provide the spice; saffron, the color; ground almonds, the thickening.[31] Stews are perfumed with waters distilled from rose petals or orange blossoms.

Another recipe is for almond-stuffed meatballs shaped into logs, browned in the fat of the fat-tailed sheep and simmered in a sauce of almonds, pistachios, and spices—cumin, coriander, cinnamon, and black pepper—and garnished with "sugar candy dates."[32] As in many early cookbooks, al-Baghdadi provided ingredients and instructions but no amounts. Roden remedies this by including al-Baghdadi's recipes alongside her modern versions—with amounts—in *A Cookbook of Middle Eastern Food*.

Milk, usually from sheep or goats, was made into yogurt or preserved in salty cheeses like feta or kasseri. Vegetables and pulses like eggplant and chickpeas were and still are puréed and mixed with garlic, lemon juice, salt, and sesame paste—tahini—to make baba ganoush and hummus. Spinach was eaten often. Starches included bread cooked by slapping it onto the side of an oven called a *tannur* (like the Indian *tandoor*); rice, an import from Asia, mixed with dried fruit and nuts to make pilaf; and couscous—steamed semolina—which today is the national dish of Morocco, Tunisia, and Algeria in northern Africa.[33] Grape leaves and eggplant were stuffed with mixtures from the less expensive all-rice to the extremely expensive all-meat. Olive oil could be a garnish or an ingredient. In one famous dish, olive oil is used in alarming quantities.

FOOD FABLE:

Imam Bayaldi—"The Holy Man Fainted"

The Turkish dish *imam bayaldi* means "the *imam* (holy man) fainted." According to legend, the *imam* either swooned in ecstasy when he tasted such a heavenly dish or passed out when he got the bill for the olive oil in it. In any case, Claudia Roden's modern version calls for one-half cup of olive oil for six long medium-sized eggplants (not jumbo American ones), with additional olive oil in the stuffing.[34] Clifford Wright's recipe uses 10 tablespoons of extra-virgin olive oil for one-and-one-half pounds of eggplant.[35]

Muslim Desserts

The finale to a Muslim meal was a spectacular dessert made with sugar, which the Arabs had learned how to extract from sugar cane through trade with India. Much of the preparation of sweets was done in convents, perhaps a refuge for Muslim women, used to living in the protection of the harem, who converted to Christianity and joined a convent to maintain their protected status. These are the legendary desserts such as baklava, flaky phyllo pastry layered with butter and ground pistachios and drizzled with sugar syrup scented with orange-flower water, and dates stuffed with sugar and ground almonds and dipped in a rosewater-scented sugar syrup.[36] (Phyllo pastries can also be made savory, like Greece's spinach-cheese turnover, *spanakopita*.)

The Muslim Diet

Many Muslim dietary restrictions correspond to the dietary laws of the Jews. For example, Muslims were also forbidden to eat pork, as well as blood, and any animal that was dead but not killed specifically for food, like roadkill. Animals that were killed for food had to be killed in a ritualistic way. The butcher had to say, "In the name of God, God is most great," and then cut the animal's throat while it was conscious. This is called *halal* meat, and means to Muslims what meat killed by a kosher butcher means to Jews. Any animal killed in the name of another god is prohibited.[37] In the Middle Ages, Muslims preferred mutton and camel hump.

Muslim Beverages

"Drinking fermented beverages was also prohibited in order to keep Muslims from praying while intoxicated."[38] Muhammad did not like the violence that followed drinking. Wine could be a reward in paradise, where it wouldn't be abused, but it was forbidden on Earth. However, a new food that was becoming popular in the Muslim empire was welcomed by the religion: coffee.

Coffee: Red Berries and Dancing Goats

FOOD FABLE:

Where Coffee Comes From

The goats were behaving strangely. Instead of calmly foraging for food, they were running around, leaping up in the air, butting heads. The shepherd boy, named Kaldi, in eighth century Ethiopia, on the east coast of Africa, was worried. What could have caused this? When it continued the next day, he watched them closely and saw that they had found something new to eat: the small red berries and glossy green leaves of a strange tree. After they ate the berries, they started dancing and doing what for goats passes for singing—bleating. When the goats showed no other effects from eating this strange new food (like falling over dead, which the boy was afraid of), he tried some, too. He liked the way they made him feel.[39]

The truth: coffee does grow on a tree with glossy green leaves and small red berries, called "cherries." As for the dancing goats—anybody's guess. At first, people got their coffee just the way the goats and the goatherd did: by chewing the leaves and berries. Then the leaves and berries were steeped in water, like tea. The cherries were also ground into a paste and mixed with animal fat and eaten. It was not until the sixteenth century that the berries were roasted, ground into a powder, and mixed with water to produce the beverage we know as coffee. It was accepted by Muslim monks because it kept them alert through their prayers.[40] It was also advertised as a medicine that could "aid digestion, cure headaches, coughs, consumption, dropsy, gout, and scurvy, and prevent miscarriages."[41]

So coffee began as a special drink, used in ritual ways in ritual spaces. Wealthy people had a separate room in their home for taking coffee.[42] The lower classes went to public coffeehouses. Coffee soon became an international commodity. And, until almost 1900, it was all Arabica beans.

COFFEE CHRONOLOGY [43]

8th century	Ethiopia—legend of the dancing goats
900s	Coffee first appears in writing, by Arab physician Rhazes
by 1500	Muslim pilgrims spread coffee to Persia, Egypt, Turkey, North Africa
1511	Governor of Mecca says the Koran forbids coffee and closes coffeehouses because people gather there and make fun of him
1536	Coffee exported through city of Mocha in Yemen; called "Mocha"
1600s	India begins cultivation from seeds smuggled in by a Muslim
1650–1690	Coffeehouses open in England (and banned briefly), Germany, Venice, Paris, Vienna
1696	Paris doctor prescribes coffee enemas
1699	Dutch transplant trees to Java in Indonesia; coffee becomes known as "java"
1710	French invent infusion method of brewing coffee
1723	French begin growing coffee on Martinique in the Caribbean; later Haiti, too
1727	Coffee smuggled into Brazil
1773	Boston Tea Party—Americans stop drinking tea as a political protest
1788	Santo Domingo grows half the coffee in the world

1820	Caffeine ($C_8H_{10}N_4O_2$) isolated from green coffee beans
1832	Coffee replaces rum as official drink of U.S. Army
1833	First commercial coffee roaster imported to U.S., to New York City
1850	Jim Folger sells preroasted coffee to California gold miners
1869	Coffee leaf rust *(Hemileia vastatrix)* destroys East Indies coffee industry; *robusta* from central Africa emerges as resistant alternative
1878	*The Spice Mill*, first U.S. trade publication for coffee (and tea and spices)
1878–1880	São Paulo, Brazil, coffee floods world markets, price drops, market collapses
1881	Coffee Exchange opens in New York to regulate prices
by 1900	Americans drink 50% of the coffee in the world
1900	Hills Bros. invent vacuum-packed coffee can
WWII	American GI Joes drink so much coffee it becomes known as "a cuppa Joe"
1966	Alfred Peet opens specialty coffee shop in Berkeley, California
1971	Starbucks opens in Seattle, sells fresh roasted beans

Culture Clash: The Crusades

In 1093, the Emperor Alexius in Constantinople was worried because a new group of barbarian nomads, the Turks, were pressing in on Constantinople from the east. In Rome, Pope Urban II decided to send an army of Christians to rescue Constantinople, then continue to the Holy Land and reclaim it from the Muslims. The pope guaranteed that for anyone who went on a crusade all earthly sins would be forgiven—a ticket to heaven. Between 1096 and 1204, there were four major crusades to the Holy Land, followed by a Children's Crusade in 1212. Other crusaders went to North Africa, and the Spanish Inquisition began its own crusade against the Muslims in Spain. After the initial victory by surprise in the First Crusade, the Christians lost all the others.

The Crusades caused profound changes in the world and helped to bring about the end of the Middle Ages. They weakened the system of feudalism in Europe because the ruling class—lords and knights—spent their fortunes on crusades and many were killed in battle. Crusaders who did return to their estates found that many of the serfs, left alone, had taken off to find a better earthly life. They had gone to the new cities that arose along the routes to the Holy Land to provide food and supplies for the crusaders.

Christendom: The Late Middle Ages in Europe

When a serf moved to the cities where there were thousands of people, he needed something he had not needed on the manor: a last name. Everyone had a first name, called a Christian name, received at baptism, but no last name. Many simply made their profession their name: Cook; Miller; Smith, shortened from blacksmith, goldsmith, silversmith, or tinsmith; Wright, as in cartwright or wheelwright, the people who made carts or wheels; Cooper, the people who made barrels; or Baker.

As the cities grew, there was increasing specialization in the professions. They subdivided into narrower and narrower groups. For example, the definition of baker was very strict: the person who kneaded the dough and shaped it into a loaf. The person who tended the fire to make sure the bread cooked at just the right temperature was a different profession. When work was scarce, the two clashed over where one job ended and the other began. Pastry makers made pies, but if the pie had poultry inside, the poulterers wanted control of it. In Paris, bakers controlled pâtés until the pastry guild was formed in 1440, and then patissiers had the right to make both sweet and savory tartes. These conflicts sometimes ended in lawsuits.

Two of the first food laws were also passed around this time. In 1210, King John of England fixed the price of bread; in 1266, the Assize of Bread regulated the quality. The function of these laws was to prevent bakers from overcharging and from stretching the loaf with things not fit for human consumption, like dirt and stones, and to punish bakers who did.[44]

Guilds: The Butcher, the Baker, and the Wafer Maker

One of the ways people could have a better life in the cities was by getting a profession, like the food professions. The way to get into any trade or craft was to join a guild, which was like a union. The purpose of the guilds was twofold: to control prices and to control wages. The guild created a monopoly on a certain product, which controlled its quality; and limited the number of people in the profession so that there would not be a glut, which would cause the price people could charge for their goods and services to drop.

There were three stages in guild membership: apprentice, journeyman, and master. Children were sent into apprenticeship as soon as they were able to function by themselves, usually around six or seven years old. They performed tasks like sweeping up and running errands. They learned at first by observing. When they got older, they began to learn by doing—hands-on. The apprenticeship lasted until the late teen years, when the journeyman stage began. In this phase, the craftsperson was given increasingly complex projects and responsibility, which could include supervising apprentices. The final stage was becoming a master. To do this, the journeyman had to complete a project entirely on his own, to the satisfaction of the master and the requirements of the guild. Only then could he call himself a master craftsman and set up his own shop. For example, the requirements of a journeyman wafer maker were to produce a minimum of 800 wafers, in three different sizes, per day.[45] Not everyone attained master status; many remained journeymen all their lives, just as today not everyone becomes an executive chef.

Advertising

One way guilds promoted themselves was by advertising. They donated money for stained glass windows in the new churches that were being built. Rising sometimes more than 100 feet, these cathedrals dwarfed every other building in the area and could be seen for miles: Notre Dame and Chartres in France; Canterbury, Westminster, and Durham in England; Dresden in Germany. The cathedrals used new architecture that had narrow stone supports inside leading up to the characteristic pointed Gothic arch.

Notre Dame—Our Lady—Paris, France. Construction on this Gothic Catholic cathedral began in 1163 and ended in 1345. *Courtesy Robert Pierce.*

The large spaces between the arches were adorned with something new: glorious stained-glass windows that flooded the cathedral with multicolored, heavenly light. However, the glass could be made only in small pieces, not large sheets, so all the windows were mosaics. In these windows, in color, we can still see people in the food professions—butchers, bakers, fishmongers, grocers, and tavern keepers—engaging in the daily activities of their professions.[46] Tavern owners also advertised by having criers walk the streets banging on a bowl of the wine special for the day and calling out to entice people to have a taste.[47]

The cathedrals were centers of life for the community. The faithful attended Mass every Sunday (preferably every day); the open space in front of the church was the marketplace; the bells tolled time. One of the bells was at night, to remind people that it was time to attend to the fires in their fireplaces and go to bed. Starting a new fire was time-consuming and difficult, so many people chose to keep the fire going at night. The danger was that the house would burn down, so they covered the fire. "Cover the fire" was *couvre-feu* in French, which became *curfew* in English.

Sugar: "White Salt"

New professions—confectioner and pastry chef—were made possible by a new food, one the Arabs had and that the Europeans had never seen before and wanted very much after they were introduced to it. They called it "white salt." Its grains were approximately the same size as those of salt, but it was pure white, unlike salt, which varied from grayish to greenish depending on the minerals it contained. And it was sweet. The Arabs had learned from people in India how to take the sugar cane stalk, remove the juice and leave only the sweet dry crystals. The process was time-consuming and labor-intensive. Sugar—exotic, expensive, tasty—was highly prized by the upper classes in Europe as a medicine. Apothecaries shaved flakes off cones of sugar and sold them by the gram like other drugs. Medieval physicians considered sugar the perfect medicine for treating toothaches.

Cheese

Many cheeses still important today—Emmentaler, Gruyère, Parmigiano—were first produced around the twelfth century. These were formed into huge round wheels, each made of as much as 1,000 liters of milk, so dairy farmers from an entire region would contribute. The Latin word for cheese—*caseus*—is the origin of the English word *cheese* and the Spanish *queso*. The French and Italian words for cheese—*fromage* and *formaggio*, respectively—are also from Latin, but from the word *forma*, because the Romans shaped their cheese by putting it into baskets or forms. Some cheeses like Port-Salut are named after the monasteries that produced them. "The monks of the Benedictine and Cistercian monasteries, thanks to whom the population did not starve to death entirely during the Dark Ages, were the pioneers of the new cheese-making industry of medieval times."[48]

Beer and Wine

One way to preserve grain through the winter was to ferment it and turn it into beer. In the Middle Ages, beer was flavored with an herbal mix called *gruit*. This was herbs like yarrow, wild rosemary, and sweet gale, also called *myrica* gale. They were considered aphrodisiacs and narcotics.[49] By the end of the Middle Ages, hops had become the preferred way to flavor and preserve beer. Although some countries still make beer without hops, this was the beginning of beer as most of the world knows it now.

The commercial wine industry, which had ceased after the fall of the Western Roman Empire, revived again after about 500 years. By the tenth century, the wines of the Champagne region of France had distinguished themselves by vineyard, and were associated with royalty because they were traditionally served at coronations. By the thirteenth and fourteenth centuries, there were vineyards in the German Rhineland and in the Tokay region of Hungary.[50] In 1398, Tuscany in northern Italy produced Chianti for the first time—and it was white.[51]

In 1395, Philip the Bold, the Duke of Burgundy, ordered that only pinot noir grapes were to be grown in Burgundy. Some vintners had begun cultivating gamay vines, which produced more grapes that were hardier and ripened earlier. Philip declared that wine from gamay grapes was foul, bitter, and an offense to the reputation of Burgundy. He ordered the vines torn out. The gamay grape found a home elsewhere and eventually became the basis for beaujolais wines, but Burgundy is still made from pinot noir grapes.[52]

Other wine-growing regions also became known by name to wine connoisseurs. The Church inadvertently helped in this when a political struggle in the fourteenth century resulted in two popes, one in Rome and one in Avignon in southern France. The wine the French pope drank came from a vineyard that was called *Châteauneuf-du-pape*—the pope's new castle. Later, the Crusades helped further the wine industry because nobles who left to fight often donated vineyards to the Church so that the monks would pray for their success. If they died, their families donated vineyards so that the monks would pray for their souls. By the end of the Middle Ages, one order of monks, the Cistercians, a division of the Benedictines, owned the largest vineyards in Europe. They had been helped in France by King Louis VII, who exempted their wines from taxes on shipping and sales.[53] Wine was also used as currency, and soldiers' rations always included wine. In England, it was cheaper than ale by as much as 12 to 24 times, and although they didn't know it at the time, it was also healthier—wine kills typhoid bacteria in contaminated water.[54]

The wine merchants' guilds had a great deal of political power because they were often the city government, and taxes on wine paid for many of the expenses of running medieval cities. In London, the Vintners' Company controlled the wholesale and retail wine trade, and received a charter from the king in 1437. Medieval cities passed laws to control the importation and sale of wine, to standardize weights and measures, and to punish tavern owners who tried to cut corners by adulterating wine or passing cheap or sour wines off as more expensive ones. Punishment included fines, having the barrels of bad wine smashed and dumped in the streets, and being forced to drink your own rancid wine.[55]

Distilled Alcohol

Around the eighth century, alchemists in the Arab world discovered how to make distilled spirits, how to heat wine, for example, and condense it into hard liquor—alcohol.[56] The words *alchemist* and *alcohol* are both Arab in origin. Distillation was used in the making of perfume and was also important because what it produced was flammable, and was used for military fires. They distilled essences from jasmine flowers and orange blossoms and used them as flavoring in foods. They also made distilled rose water, which was used to flavor desserts throughout the Arab world, in Europe, and in the United States until the middle of the nineteenth century, when vanilla became affordable and available.

The knowledge gained by the Arabs spread into Europe, where distilling did take place. The spirits that resulted were referred to as "water of life." In French, this translates to *eau de vie*; in Gaelic, the language in Ireland, it was *uisgebeatha*—whiskey. Later, some of the wine that was heated this way became known by its Dutch name, *brandewijn*, "burned wine"—brandy for short.

Bees

Bees were highly prized for many reasons: for honey; for beeswax, which made sweet-smelling, dripless candles; and for propolis, the bee-glue that kept the honeycomb together and was used as an ointment, like a medieval antibiotic. (The Egyptians had used honey, which completely blocks out air, as an antibiotic, too.) It was not just honey for sweetening and medicine that made bees so valuable; it was also fermented and turned into that ancient alcoholic drink, mead. But bees and honey were difficult to come by, so in medieval England if you saw a bee fly by, you said a quick prayer to get it to stay on your land: *Sit down, sit down, bee! / St. Mary commanded thee!*[57] Calling on St. Mary in this prayer is an example of how the Church adopted native pagan rituals and charms. Rather than constantly fighting (and losing against) local pre-Christian customs, the Church allowed the peasants to keep them, but instructed them to substitute "Christ" or "God" for "Father Heaven" and "Mary" for "Mother Earth."[58] The Church had to neutralize many folk beliefs that had been in existence for thousands of years, including important festivals like Halloween.

The Medieval Meal

The medieval meal began and ended with prayer and the washing of hands. The best linen was used at the start when hands were relatively clean; ordinary napkins were saved for the end, when diners' hands were dirty. The washing bowls were made of silver or gilded—covered with gold. If you were important, your family crest might be engraved in the bottom of the basin.

Halloween, October 31, and All Saints' Day, November 1

Halloween and All Saints' Day are examples of how the medieval Catholic Church used a pagan festival to reinforce Christianity. Halloween began in Ireland as Samhain, a celebration of the New Year. This ancient festival was based on folk beliefs that the souls of the dead come back to wander the Earth until they are put to rest. The best way to counteract these ghosts, goblins, skeletons, and monsters is to make yourself look like them, a form of sympathetic magic. Christians renamed it All Hallows' Eve. *Hallow* is from the Old English word *halig* and means "holy," as in the Lord's Prayer: "Hallowed be Thy name." The "een" part of Halloween is short for "evening."

Centuries later, in America, the symbol most often associated with Halloween became a squash native to the Americas—the pumpkin. Huge, round, and orange, it ripens in October. Hollowed out, with scary shapes carved into the shell, and a lighted candle inside, it becomes Jack O'Lantern, a phantom wandering across the marshes waving a light.

Children roam at night, ringing doorbells, playing pranks like covering the houses and shrubbery of unsuspecting neighbors with toilet paper, and demanding candy and other treats or they'll play more tricks—"Trick or treat." In 1922, candy corn, the triangular-shaped, orange, yellow, and white striped candy, was first manufactured. Increasingly, Halloween celebrations in the United States are private parties because crazy people plant razor blades in apples or toxic substances in candy.

Some Christians do not celebrate Halloween because of its pagan origins. In Catholic countries, the day after Halloween, All Saints' Day, is a holy day. In Mexico November 2 is called Day of the Dead *(Dia de los Muertos)*.

Where you sat at the table also indicated how important you were. If you sat at the head of the table or were the guest of honor, you sat in a chair by yourself and you were "above the salt." You got better bread—made of light wheat flour—more of it, and it was served to you. The farther down the social scale you were, the darker the bread. You also got less of it and had to reach across the table to serve yourself. If you found yourself eating one small roll of stale, dark, rye bread, sitting on a bench, far away from the salt, you were in social Siberia and no serving person would waste his time on you.[59]

There was no separate dining room, just a room where boards were set up on trestles and draped with cloths for as long as the dinner lasted, then taken down. The permanent piece of furniture in the room was the buffet, where the host displayed his wealth, maybe expensive gold and silver serving pieces, bowls, and so forth. The kitchen was separate from the main house because of the danger of fire, so the food was probably not warm when it arrived at the table accompanied by an armed guard, even though it was covered.

The Poison Taster

Foods were checked for poison in the most elaborate and unsanitary way possible.

"Unicorn [a mythical beast] horn, which was thought to bleed in the presence of impurity, was much favored. Agate was in more frequent use, being easier to obtain, as were various objects alleged to be toadstone—that (nonexistent) precious jewel believed to be hidden in the head of the toad. Salt was tested with serpent's tongue, known more prosaically now to be the tooth of a shark."[60]

While everybody was busy looking for exotic poisons, they were missing the bacterial cross-contamination that was right in front of them in the handling of poultry and eggs and the fingers or spoons dipped repeatedly into pots; and the metal poisoning from pots made of lead or tinned copper with the tin worn off.

Trencher and *Nef*

At the table, there were serving platters but no plates. Whole-wheat bread, several days old and cut into rectangles, was used as plates called trenchers. Liquids were put into a small bowl that two diners shared. No forks—you ate with your hands. When you reached into the communal dish for one of the various kinds of meat, you were careful in case somebody else was reaching for something by stabbing it with his knife. (This later came to be known as *service en confusion*.[61]) Wine was served diluted with water. One of the most expensive and elaborate pieces on the table was the *nef*, the salt cellar in the shape of a ship, perhaps silver or gilt.

Food was usually fresh in season. Otherwise, meat was preserved by salting or smoking and drying, vegetables were pickled in brine or stored in a root cellar, herbs and fruits were dried. Anybody could present a feast in the summer, but to have a feast in the winter indicated great wealth. So did gold, at any time of the year.

Gold Food: Endoré

In Europe, as in the Middle East, one color was prized above all others: gold. Humans persisted in their search for two things: gold and eternal life, and they believed one guaranteed the other. While alchemists were looking for a way to turn various substances into gold, cooks took a shortcut and made food look gold. This is called gilded or "endoré" [en-door-AY] from the French word for gold—*or*. Spices from the Middle East like saffron and turmeric turned food a beautiful golden color, a practice that continues today in dishes like risotto, even though in the Middle Ages, "one pound of saffron cost as much as a horse" (and a pound of nutmeg cost as much as seven oxen).[62] Food could also be covered in gold leaf. Most of the real gold came from Africa, carried in caravans by Muslim traders.

White Food: Blancmange

Almonds were extremely popular in Europe. They spread across Europe in one dish with different names and different forms. In Italy it was called *bianco mangiare*; in France, *blanc manger*; in Spain, *manjar blanco*; in England, *blanchet manchet*, later, *blancmange* [blah-MANZH]. All meant the same thing: white food, even though in England blancmange came in colors and flavors.

Blancmange was based on almond milk and was thought to be the perfect food: it balanced the four humors; it was smooth, so it was easy to swallow; it was easy to digest; and it was white and therefore very refined and suitable for the upper classes. Blancmange was expensive because it was labor-intensive—the almonds had to be ground by hand. Today, Spain and Italy are among the leading producers of almonds, but more than 50 percent of the almonds grown in the world come from California.[63]

By the middle of the nineteenth century, in American cookbooks, blancmange had become just another pudding, along with rice pudding and custard, which was sometimes suggested as an accompaniment. The main ingredient—almonds—had disappeared from the recipes, replaced by convenient foods as thickeners. Catherine Beecher's *Domestic Receipt-Book* had five recipes for blancmange. One even suggests adding almonds: "Three ounces of almonds pounded to a paste and added while boiling is an improvement."[64] Blancmange was popular until the 1970s when, according to *The Joy of Cooking*, "after a run of nearly a thousand years, the term vanished."[65] A modern Afghan version, called *firnee*, is a cornstarch pudding with chopped almonds, saffron seasoning, and a pistachio garnish.

INGREDIENTS: BLANCMANGE COMPARISON

MIDDLE AGES (RECIPES: WHEATON AND WILLAN)	19TH CENTURY U.S. (RECIPES: BEECHER, CHILD, HALE, RANDOLPH[66])
Almonds, finely ground	Rice, arrowroot, isinglass or calves' foot jelly
Capon breast	—
Chicken stock	Water, milk, cream
—	Salt
Optional ginger and cardamom	Mace, nutmeg, cinnamon, vanilla, orange, lemon peel, orange water, or rose water; in the South, wine
Sugar sprinkled on top	¼ pound of sugar
	Garnish: fruit or marmalade

In the Middle Ages, almond milk—almonds soaked in water and pressed until the water is the thickness of milk (or cream or cheese)—was a useful food during Lent, when any animal products, including eggs and dairy, were forbidden. Now we call this vegan. Almond milk is also one of the mainstays of the current raw food movement.

For the upper classes, after the white food, the other courses could be as many colors as the rainbow of fruit and vegetable dyes could make them. Red grapes or cherries tinted garlic sauce pink; blackberries and mulberries made anything deep blue or purple; parsley turned it green.

Presentation

Presentation was extremely important in the Middle Ages, sometimes more important than taste, because the intent was to show off wealth. At a medieval banquet, a feast for the stomach was not a guarantee, but a feast for the eyes was. The most elaborate dishes were peacock and swan, which arrived at the table cooked and dead looking better than they ever had in life. The birds were killed and skinned carefully to keep the feathers intact. Then the meat was cooked and stuffed back into the skins. The beaks and feet were gilded—covered in gold. Completing the presentation was a beautiful young upper-class woman as server.[67]

Pies were another elegant presentation, and also functional. Before plastic, the crust—called a "coffin"—contained and preserved the filling. Sweet or savory pies had their lids put back on and were stashed in a cold cellar until the next time they were served.

The King's Court: Table Manners

These new foods, new meals and the rise of the king's court created new ways of interacting—manners. People became self-conscious because for the first time there was a right way and a wrong way to behave in social situations, especially at the table. Many words having to do with the new manners came from the king's *court*, which originally meant *courtyard* or farmyard or any enclosed space; *courtly*, which meant having upper-class manners; *courtesy*, the acts of politeness toward others that were shown by a *courtier*, someone at court; a woman showed her respect when she made a *curtsy*; a young man and woman were on their best behavior when they were *courting* each other; *courteous*, having respectful, pleasant manners fit for the king's court. Just what had people been doing that needed changing? Here are some of the new rules for upper-class *adults* at the medieval table:

Le Viandier: Cooking with Spices

These new ingredients and new style of cooking were written down by a Frenchman called Taillevent (real name: Gillaume Tirel; ca. 1312–1395). It was the first European cookbook, although in the days before copyright laws, some sections of his book bore a close resemblance to a book written before he was born. Tirel is an inspiration to anyone in the cooking profession. He began at the bottom of the kitchen ladder as a spit-roaster, endlessly turning the meats on the spit in front of an open fire, but he worked his way up and became master cook to King Charles VI of France. The king was so grateful that he gave Tirel a house, a title, travel allowances, and a coat of arms—three little cooking pots. *Le Viandier* reveals the influence of the Middle East on the cooking of the later Middle Ages in Europe, especially the spices: cinnamon, ginger, cumin, coriander, cardamom. In the following recipe for wassail, substitute honey for the dark brown sugar, and it is straight from the Middle Ages. A Christmas carol from the Middle Ages is about "Now we go a-wassailing." In England, the songs were sung in the apple orchard, to the trees, or the following year the harvest would be bad.[69]

. . . .

RECIPE:

Wassail[70]

FROM THE ANGLO-SAXON *WES HAL*, OR "BE IN GOOD HEALTH"

4 large McIntosh apples
¼ cup plus 2 tablespoons dark brown sugar
¼ cup apple juice or cider
3 12-ounce bottles of ale
1 cup sherry
1 cinnamon stick

(continues)

½ teaspoon ground ginger
½ teaspoon freshly grated nutmeg
Zest of 1 lemon

1 Preheat oven to 350°F.

2 Slit the skins of the apples horizontally about halfway down. Place in a greased baking dish and sprinkle with ¼ cup of the brown sugar and the apple juice. Bake, basting frequently, for about 40 minutes, until apples are soft; remove from oven.

3 Pour the ale and sherry into a saucepan; add the 2 tablespoons brown sugar, cinnamon, ginger, nutmeg, and lemon zest; simmer for 5 minutes. Add the baked apples and their juice, stir thoroughly, and serve hot.

Excerpted from the book The Apple Cookbook *by Olwen Woodier. Copyright © 2001, used with permission from Storey Publishing, LLC.*

The reopening of the trade routes created new classes of prosperous people in Europe. But much more than food and gold was exchanged. Stories traveled on the trade routes, too. Some of the most outrageous stories came from a Venetian trader named Marco Polo. The book about his travels was hugely popular throughout Europe, but some called it *Il Milione*—a million lies—because it seemed so fantastic. Polo claimed he had been to a place the Europeans called Cathay then, China now.

FOOD FABLE:
Marco Polo and Pasta

For hundreds of years, it was accepted "fact" that Marco Polo discovered noodles in China and brought them back to Europe. Now, in his masterwork, *A Mediterranean Feast*, food historian Clifford Wright states flatly that there is no truth to the story of Polo and pasta. Wright unravels the tangled strands of the origin of pasta and takes it down to its basic ingredient: hard semolina or durum (Latin for "hard") wheat. The Chinese did not have durum wheat. Wright places the origins of "true macaroni"— pasta made from durum wheat and dried, which gives it a long shelf life—"at the juncture of medieval Sicilian, Italian, and Arab cultures."[71]

The Little Ice Age: 1300–1900

The Medieval Warm Period in Europe was followed by the Little Ice Age, a period of cooling from about 1300 until about 100 years ago. The temperature change wasn't dramatic, perhaps one to one-and-a-half degrees Centigrade cooler than today. However, the impact on agriculture and shipping ranged from serious to disastrous. Glaciers crept down into valleys, obliterating farms. In some places the land disappeared—the topsoil literally washed away, down to rock. The growing season became shorter, food grew scarcer. Wheat did not grow and ripen normally, could not be dried, and rotted. Grapes covered with mildew made sour wine or none. In England, the temperature drop was enough that grapes could no longer be grown at all. It destroyed a commercial wine industry that was so good France was trying to pass laws to keep British wines out. When the vines died, northern Europeans turned to alcohol brewed from grain: beer, whiskey, vodka.

Fewer ships sailed the seas because of dangerous ice floes, which also kept them from sailing close to shore. Greenland, colonized by Denmark hundreds of years earlier, the oldest colony of any European country, was isolated by the climate change. The European Greenlanders could have learned much from the native people, the Inuit (formerly called Eskimos), about how to survive and where to get food in the increasingly cold environment. But the Europeans considered themselves civilized and regarded the Inuit, who were not Christian, as uncivilized, and refused to associate with them. Unable to overcome their cultural prejudices, unsupplied by Europe, and unequipped for Greenland, the Europeans starved to death; the colony disappeared.[72]

In Europe, hungry people left the land and wandered homeless into the cities, begging for food or stealing it. Thousands died and were left to rot, buried in mass graves, or eaten. The living, suffering from deficiency diseases like anemia, their bodies bloated from lack of protein, were too weak to work, to farm, or to cook. Animals suffered from malnutrition, too. This human and animal malnutrition was passed into the next generation in the form of sickly babies. Their weakened state made them prone to intestinal parasites, diarrhea, and deadly diseases.

Plague: The Black Death, 1348–1350

The newly reopened trade routes to Asia brought more than silk and spices to Europe. In 1348, rats covered with fleas spread plague quickly by land and by sea, aided by poor nutrition and the absence of personal hygiene and public sanitation. In two years the plague killed one-third of the population of Europe, about 25 million people. Another four million died in Southwest Asia; in China the death toll was 35 million. A vicious cycle began. With farmers dead and much of the surviving population weakened, famine followed plague. Then malnourished people were susceptible to disease. Within 100 years, the population of Europe had dropped drastically, from 62.5 million people in 1340 to 43.5 million in 1450.[73] (Now, tetracycline kills plague quickly and easily.)

Some people tried to escape the plague by running away from the cities. *The Decameron* by Giovanni Boccaccio is a series of stories about young Italians hiding out at a villa in the hills above Tuscany, where they make up stories to pass the time. One is a fantasy about a place called Bengodi, a paradise for people who love food: it is built on a mountain of grated Parmigiano cheese, and vines drip sausages. People make macaroni and ravioli all day and cook them in capon broth. Through it all runs a stream of white wine. There is an endless supply of food because as fast as it gets eaten, more gets made.[74]

CHRONOLOGY—FAMINES AND ERGOTISM EPIDEMICS, 750–1800

WHEN	NUMBER	WHAT	WHERE
750–800	6	General famine	Throughout Europe
800–900	12	General famine	Throughout Europe
900–950	3	General famine	Throughout Europe
900–1000	Frequent	Ergotism	Throughout Europe
1000–1100	8	General famine	Throughout Europe
1000–1100	26	Famine	France
1000–1100, esp. 1042, 1076, 1089, 1094	Frequent	Ergotism	Throughout Europe
1250	Period of relative prosperity		
1315–1317		Worst famine of Middle Ages[75]	Throughout Europe
1348–1350	BUBONIC PLAGUE—BLACK DEATH		
1556–1557		Famine	Throughout Europe
1590–1593		Famine	Throughout Europe
1630, 1648, 1652–1654, 1660s, 1680–1685, 1693–1695	Frequent	Famine	Throughout Europe
1700–1800	16	Famine	France (1789–Revolution)

In an age when nothing about germs was understood, blame had to lie elsewhere. Rumors sprang up that the Jews were poisoning the wells in a plot to kill Christians. The solution: kill Jews. And they did, with a vengeance. As a result of these attacks, a great Jewish migration began from the more heavily populated cities of western Europe to the less populated areas of eastern Europe. The Jews felt they would be safe there, especially in Poland. They were relatively safe for 600 years, until the middle of the twentieth century when a small town in southern Poland called Oswiecim became known to the world by its German name: Auschwitz.

The severe drop in population caused massive changes in European life. With people in crucial occupations dead, those left alive could command higher wages. Since whatever they produced—bread, barrels, or wagons—was in short supply, they could charge higher prices. One of the long-lasting effects of the plague was that the populations on the sugar-producing islands like Cyprus and Sicily were severely reduced and slow to increase, so sugar production dropped. It was centuries before sugar production rose to its old levels again, and it would not be in the Mediterranean, but on islands halfway around the world in what came to be called the West Indies—the Caribbean.

In some places in Europe, there was chaos. If all the members of a noble landowning family were dead, there was no one left to inherit their land legally. Squatters moved in and fought over it. Serfs fled to the cities as they had after the Crusades. And like the Crusades, the plague, too, weakened the Church because it couldn't explain what was happening or stop it. People in cities began to ignore the Church's prohibition on doing business and just went and did it anyway. Then the Church and Christians in Europe received another serious blow that also impacted their food.

Turkey: The Fall of the Eastern Roman Empire

In 1453, a thousand years after the fall of the Western Roman Empire, the Christian Eastern Roman Empire also fell. After three-and-a-half centuries of trying, the Ottoman Turks, who were Muslim warriors, finally succeeded in conquering Constantinople. Their leader, Sultan Mehmet, known as "The Conqueror," renamed the city Istanbul and converted the Christian churches to Islamic mosques. He expanded the empire east to the Euphrates River and north to Europe's Danube River. He also began to build the Topkapi Palace and its enormous kitchen. Following sultans added 10 more kitchen sections.

Turkish Cuisine

Turkish cuisine is one of the great cuisines of the world, elaborate and specialized. Although Istanbul is in Europe, the rest of Turkey—the Anatolian Plain—is in Asia, and the Byzantine Empire that it conquered was Greek-influenced. So Turkish cuisine has all of those influences, and more. Turkish pocket bread, called *pita* in other parts of the Middle East, is *pide;* other staples are yogurt, a Turkish invention that preserves dairy; kebabs; pilaf; soup *(çorba); dolmas* (stuffed vegetables); *manti* (filled savory dumplings); and *börek* (filled savory pastry). The flat bread called *lavaş* (lavash) is baked in a *tandir*, a clay-lined pit, related to the *tannur* of Persia and the *tandoor* of India. There was a separate building for *helva* (or halvah), a confection made of nuts—as paste, chopped, or whole—and sometimes dried fruit.[76] The halvah Americans know is made from sesame. By the eighteenth century, "each of six varieties of *helva* was assigned to a separate master chef, with a hundred apprentices working under him."[77] The palace kitchens had to feed sometimes 10,000 people each day, much of it meat: in 1723, "30,000 head of beef, 60,000 of mutton, 20,000 of veal, 10,000 of kid, 200,000 fowl, 100,000 pigeons, and 3,000 turkeys."[78] They also made trays of baklava for the military on the fifteenth day of Ramadan. Like France's King Louis XIV, Sultan Mehmet was above dining with anyone.

The Spice Bazaar that is famous in Istanbul today did not begin until the middle of the seventeenth century. But the Ottomans gave their name to the low, round, padded stool that has revived in the twenty-first century as a combination seat/coffee table.

A New Spice Route

The fall of the Christian Eastern Roman Empire to Muslim Turks in 1453 sent Christian western Europe into a panic that was economic as well as religious. Now the Ottoman Empire controlled the eastern Mediterranean Sea and the trade coming into it from Asia—including the spice routes. Europeans wanted a sea route shortcut to spices, one that would cut out the Muslim middlemen and drive down the prices. It would be worth a fortune to the man who discovered it and to the country that paid for it. A sea captain known to the Italians in Genoa where he was born as Cristoforo Colombo, to the Spanish as Cristóbal Colón, and to the English as Christopher Columbus, had been reading a book written 200 years before he was born by another Italian, Marco Polo. Columbus believed what he read about Asia, and he had an idea about how to get there. He went to see the queen of Spain.

New World Food

POTATO, CORN, CHILE, CHOCOLATE

The Search for Spices

In the beginning of the fifteenth century, Europe's westernmost country took the lead in exploring new routes to find spices. Portugal's Prince Henry the Navigator set up a sailing school. Just as three important technological developments—the wheel, the plow, and the sail—had helped the Sumerians trade 4,500 years earlier, three new technological developments helped the Europeans. The magnetic compass, invented by the Chinese, always pointed north and helped captains get their bearings on the open sea; the astrolabe, an Arab invention, made navigation using the stars possible; and the new triangular sails allowed ships to sail against the wind, not just with it. The Portuguese were the first Europeans to sail south down the west coast of Africa, around the Cape of Good Hope, and up the east coast of Africa.

The Chinese, who sold spices, were also looking for a shorter alternative to the Silk Road caravans that took years to make the profitable trip to the Middle East and the Mediterranean. They sought a sea route. From 1405 to 1433, China sent Admiral Zheng He on seven voyages. He explored the South Pacific and reached the Persian Gulf and Africa. The 300-ship fleet must have been an impressive sight, nine-masted ships 400 feet long, flying red silk sails. They could have kept on going all the way to America, but they stopped. A shift in political power forced the great fleet to retire. The conservative Confucian scholars who were running China didn't want the country to be "polluted" by engaging in business with foreigners, or any business at all. They declared it illegal to build a ship with more than two masts, which made long-distance voyages impossible. Then they taxed businesses and gave tax breaks to farmers to discourage business and encourage farming.

At the same time that the Catholic Church in Europe was loosening its restrictions on engaging in business, China was tightening them. It was a decision that would protect and strengthen China in the short run, but make it vulnerable in the long run. Its merchant class left; many went to Indonesia. For the next 400 years, wealthy, self-sufficient China closed itself off from the world, disdaining to do business with the West except through one port, Canton (Guanghzou). During that time, the West made technological advances that would completely overwhelm China. The next time Europeans came knocking on China's door, they would be carrying new technology made possible by a Chinese invention: guns.

While the Portuguese sailed east searching for spices, some Europeans thought that going west would be the fastest route to the Spice Islands in the Indies. Columbus was an experienced sea captain familiar with maps of the world. They had three continents: Europe, Asia, and Africa. At the center of the map was Jerusalem, the Christian Holy Land. But in Germany, a man named Behaim was building a globe, a round world.[1] Columbus trusted his own observations that the horizon never got closer no matter how long he sailed toward it, and that he was not going to fall off the Earth.

Columbus was petitioning the royalty of Europe to finance his trip to look for spices in the east by sailing west, but he wasn't having much success. In Italy, the Medici weren't interested because if he did find a new route, it would cut out their money-making position as middlemen. The situation in Spain was tense, as the new king and queen revived the Inquisition as part of their campaign to purify Spain and save its soul.

Spain: The Inquisition and Jewish Cooking

In 1474, the same year that in Italy the first cookbook was printed on a printing press, King Ferdinand and Queen Isabella began their reign in Spain. Ferdinand was king of Aragon, and Isabella was queen of Castile, the wealthier, more powerful part of Spain. Their marriage in 1469 brought the two kingdoms together but did not fully unify Spain. In response to the wave of panic that surged through Europe after the fall of Constantinople to the Muslim Turks in 1453, Ferdinand and Isabella decided to reclaim and purify their country for Christianity. To achieve this reconquering or *reconquista*, they had to cleanse the country of two segments of the population that had been living there peacefully for hundreds of years, the Islamic Moors from northern Africa, and the Jews.

The Spanish waged war against the Moors, but they used food to get rid of the Jews. The Inquisition knew that it was possible for people to hide their religious books and lie about their beliefs, but it was impossible for them to hide their food customs. There were already laws against Jews in place. In 1412, Spain had passed laws that forbade Jews to work at certain trades, including grocer and butcher. They could not employ Christians; eat, drink, bathe with, or talk to Christians; and they had to wear only coarse clothes.[2] In 1476, by law Jews had to wear a distinctive symbol. In 1480, Ferdinand and Isabella reconvened the Inquisition. In 1484, Jews were not allowed to sell food. By 1492, the Spanish had driven many of the Moors out of the country after the battle for the city of Granada, and they had issued an order that all Jews must be baptized Christian or leave the country.

The Inquisition, under Torquemada, its famous leader whose name has become synonymous with torture, was thorough and specific. Inquisitors went from town to town, called all the people together in the town square—the *plaza*—and announced what they were looking for: anyone who cooked food on Friday night but didn't eat it until Saturday, because Jews didn't cook on Saturday, their Sabbath; anyone who didn't eat pork; anyone who washed blood off meat before they cooked it; anyone who ate foods the Church had forbidden during Lent, like cheese. Disgruntled servants turned in masters and mistresses; neighbors betrayed neighbors. People who were found guilty were marched through the streets to the plaza, then burned at the stake over a slow, agonizing fire, as a lesson to others to be good Christians or they would burn in the fires of hell. Some Jews "passed" for Christian by pretending to eat like Christians. They made a great show of cooking pork and sharing it with their neighbors; perhaps the neighbors were so overwhelmed by the generosity that they didn't notice that the people who cooked the pork didn't eat any themselves.

Even conversion wasn't a guarantee of safety. Eventually, the Inquisition went after the *conversos*, Jews whose families had converted to Christianity generations earlier but who the Inquisition felt might still be practicing Judaism secretly. In order to survive, the Jews left Spain. Some went west to Portugal, but a great many went much farther away from the Inquisition and from Catholicism altogether: they went north to the only country in Europe that practiced religious toleration, the Netherlands. They took their knowledge of banking and business with them. Ferdinand and Isabella were aware of the economic and intellectual drain on their country but insisted that they had to persevere with their religious cleansing to save the souls of the Christians in Spain.

Waiting to see Queen Isabella was Christopher Columbus, and waiting for Columbus were two new continents—North and South America—and unimaginable mineral, vegetable, and animal wealth. There was nothing in the teachings of the Catholic Church, nothing in the writings of the ancient philosophers, nothing in their scholarly literature or popular folklore or fables to prepare Europeans for the amazing world they were about to encounter.

Map of the western hemisphere, 1572. *Courtesy Corbis Digital Stock.*

The American Empires

Before Columbus arrived in 1492, not one person in North or South America had ever had the common cold. No one had ever gotten measles or been scarred by smallpox. No one had ever suffered through those great child-killer diseases, diphtheria and whooping cough. They had never had mosquito-borne malaria or typhus, which is spread by lice. Those diseases didn't exist in the western hemisphere. There were no weeds like crabgrass or dandelion or kudzu. There were no black rats, no brown rats. American bees buzzed and made honey but they had no stingers.

The people native to North and South America had arrived between 40,000 B.C. and 12,000 B.C. by walking across the Bering Strait between northern Asia and Alaska when the glaciers receded and dried up the Bering Sea, creating a land bridge. These people, relatives of the Mongols, spread from Alaska down to Tierra del Fuego at the tip of South America. They became the Inuit in what is now Alaska, who ate seal meat; the Kwakiutl along the Pacific Northwest coast, who carved totem poles; the Maliwoo, who lived a laid-back life on the Pacific Ocean at what is now Malibu; the Iroquois in the American northeast, with a sophisticated system of government; and many other tribes.

Before Columbus arrived, South America, Central America, and North America each had one dominant culture: (1) the Inca, with their capital city at Cuzco in the Andes Mountains of what is now Peru; (2) the Aztec, whose great capital city, Tenochtitlan, was built on landfill in a lake where Mexico City rises now; and (3) Cahokia, located near present-day St. Louis on the Mississippi River. Although these three cultures were thousands of miles apart, they had several things in common.

First, all were at the center of complex trade routes. Cahokia used the Mississippi River for transportation and trade, along with its thousands of miles of tributaries, including the Ohio and Missouri rivers. The Inca and Aztec built roads.

Second, none of these three civilizations used the wheel except as a child's toy or in games, so no goods were transported by cart. Another reason they didn't have carts was because they didn't have draft animals to pull them. There were no oxen, a prehistoric horse had become extinct, and the animals native to the Americas couldn't be domesticated: polar, grizzly, brown, and black bears; jaguars; and wolves. So everything on these trade routes was carried on boats, on pack animals, or on the backs or heads of people—porters.

Third, in spite of the lack of large domesticated animals or easy means of transportation, all three civilizations built enormous pyramids, some larger than the pyramids of Egypt. The pyramids had religious significance. Some were aligned with the sun at the solstice; some were used for human sacrifice.

Fourth, although there were few domesticated animals, an agricultural revolution had taken place independently in the Americas. The American civilizations had developed new ways of farming and preserving to deal with foods that were beyond the wildest dreams of the people in Europe, Africa, and Asia.

South America: The Inca Empire

The Inca Empire was the largest empire in the Americas. Its 2,500 miles of territory stretched along the Pacific coast of South America from the present-day countries of Ecuador at the equator (which is what *Ecuador* means), south through Peru, Bolivia, and western Argentina to approximately where Santiago, the capital of Chile, is now. The Inca called their empire Tahuantinsuyu—the Kingdom of the Four Corners.

This is a territory of geographical extremes. From desert at the Pacific Ocean in the west, the land rises steeply almost 20,000 feet through rain forest and plateau to the snow-covered peaks of the Andes Mountains. The Altiplano (high plain) sits thousands of feet up in the Andes between two parallel mountain ranges. Like the ancient Romans, the Inca built roads and bridges—14,000 miles of them—to connect their empire. Just as in the Roman Empire all roads led to Rome, in the Inca Empire all roads led to the capital city of Cuzco in what is now Peru, 11,444 feet above sea level. *Cuzco* means "navel of the earth."[3]

Like the Egyptians, the Inca mummified their dead. Like the Europeans, they had sumptuary laws, which forbade excesses in everyday food and dress.[4] To transport food and drink, they used pack animals like llamas. Or they walked on the roads, carrying food and drink on their backs in special large ceramic jars.

They adorned their pottery with geometric designs in black, red, brown, yellow, and white. The Inca then, and their descendants now, also wove brilliantly colored textiles from the wool of alpacas and llamas, both related to camels and both domesticated, as well as wild vicuñas. Inca music featured woodwinds, which included flutes and panpipes made of ceramics or shells, and drums for percussion.

The Inca constructed a mysterious city one-and-one-half miles up in the Andes. Called Machu Picchu, it could be reached only by walking over a log bridge with a steep drop below. It is so remote that it wasn't discovered by the outside world until 1912. For almost a century, archaeologists tried to determine how the Inca used Machu Picchu. In 2009, an Italian professor of archaeo-astronomy theorized that Machu Picchu was not a real, functioning city but a religious pilgrimage site.[5]

The Inca insisted that people they conquered convert to the Inca religion and speak Quechua, the Inca language. They worshipped Inti, the god of the sun, at their most sacred shrine, the Temple of the Sun in Cuzco. They were highly skilled at working with the material they called "the sweat of the sun"—gold. In Cuzco, the walls of buildings were covered in sheets of gold. Very little is left of Inca gold art because it was melted down by the Spanish, as was the gold of the Aztecs. The Inca Empire ended when the Emperor Atahualpa was killed by Spanish conquistadores in 1533.

Communal Land and Eating

Much in the Inca Empire was communal. For example, there was no private ownership of land. The government controlled land and the economy and decided which crops would be grown where. Under government direction, farmers built irrigation systems and terraced the hillsides. Unlike farming in the Fertile Crescent, China, Sicily, or Africa, which was done on broad, flat plains, "Andean peoples grew their crops on millions of tiny plots scattered over a length of thousands of kilometers and perched one above another up mountainsides rising thousands of meters."[6] They were like staircases with stone retaining walls. This method was extremely efficient. At the time of the Spanish conquest, the Inca cultivated almost as many species of plants as the farmers in all of Asia or Europe.[7]

Eating was communal, too. The Inca ate twice a day. The morning meal was the main meal and was communal, because the emperor had decreed that everyone had to eat in the plaza, the town square. He ate there, too. This meant that the women, who were the food preparers, had to make the food at home and pack it. Husbands and wives ate sitting back to back, husbands first. People invited each other to share what they had brought. They did not drink anything until they finished eating, and then they shared the beverages they had brought, too. This provided for equitable distribution of food and meant that even people who didn't have much got at least one good meal, at the beginning of the day. The evening meal was eaten in the home in private.

Machu Picchu. *Photo by Juanita Lewis.*

Quinoa

Planting season for the Inca began with a religious ritual. The emperor took a golden spade and dug the earth for the first planting of the most important Inca crop, the sacred "mother grain," quinoa [KEEN-wah]. Native to the Andes, quinoa is so rich in high-quality protein that it is a substitute for meat even today.[8] Approximately 200 years ago, the German scientist Alexander von Humboldt went to the Andes and said that in South America, quinoa was what "wine was to the Greeks, wheat to the Romans, cotton to the Arabs."[9] The cooked grains are like small transparent pearls and have a bland, neutral taste like rice. (Quinoa is one of the "Foods That Start with the Letter Q" that Rosie Perez studies to prepare for her stint on *Jeopardy* in the movie *White Men Can't Jump*.)

Cuy and *Charque*

In addition to quinoa, another source of protein for much of the population then and now is *cuy*—guinea pig *(Cavia porcellus)*—which the Inca had domesticated by 2000 B.C. The taste has been described as fishy pork. The *cuy* is a small mammal that reproduces rapidly. It was—and sometimes still is—roasted whole, hair off, skin on, seasoned with chile, gutted, and the cavity filled with hot stones.[10] Modern chefs sometimes cook *cuy* by splitting it open and grilling it. Other Inca meats were deer and an animal called a *vizcacha*, which had a body like a rabbit and a tail like a fox. The Inca did not allow cannibalism or the eating of dogs.[11] They strictly controlled hunting for wild animals, which was the privilege of the nobles.

The Inca preserved foods, especially by drying. Our "jerky" comes from the Inca practice of leaving meat out to dry in the desert air and their word for it—*charque*.[12] The difference is that their *charque* was made from llama meat, while ours is more likely to be beef or turkey.

Fish from the coast was dried to feed the army. However, the Inca rulers in Cuzco liked their fish fresh from the ocean, approximately 200 to 300 miles away. Runners brought the fish "alive and twitching, which seems incredible over such a long distance over such rough and craggy roads."[13]

Potato: "A dainty dish even for the Spaniards"[14]

Another source of protein in the Inca diet was the potato. The Inca cultivated more than 3,000 varieties of potato *(Solanum tuberosum)*, which they domesticated between 3700 and 3000 B.C.[15] The Spanish conquistadores saw them in 1535, in southern Peru near Lake Titicaca:

> [T]he roots . . . are the size of an egg, more or less, some round, some elongated; they are white and purple and yellow, floury roots of good flavor, a delicacy to the Indians and a dainty dish even for the Spaniards.[16]

According to Inca law, potatoes could not be peeled "because if they had understanding they would weep while being peeled, therefore do not peel them, on pain of punishment."[17] Whatever religious or cultural reasons the Inca had for passing this law, it served two practical purposes: it meant that people had to eat the nutritious peel, and it kept tons of peels out of garbage piles.

The Inca preserved the potatoes by freeze-drying. Since they were in the Altiplano, a desert at high elevations, the weather was hot and dry during the day and freezing at night. During the day, they squeezed the moisture out of the potatoes with their feet, like crushing grapes for wine, and left them out to dry.

Then the dry potatoes froze at night. The freeze-dried potatoes, called *chuños*, could be stored indefinitely in huge public warehouses in case there was a shortage.[18] The Inca government also kept storehouses of quinoa, fruits, greens, legumes, sun-dried meat and fish, salted meat and fish, and water. These supplies provided food for ill, elderly, and other-abled people.[19]

In the centuries before the Spanish conquistadores arrived, native peoples in the Andes domesticated more root crops rich in carbohydrates than any other people. Most of them, roots like "achira, ahipa, arracacha, maca, mashua mauka, oca, ulluco, and yacon," have yet to catch on outside the Andes.[20] Of all the Andean root crops, only the potato has become a star on the world's dining table.

POTATO CHRONOLOGY

DATE	PLACE	EVENT
3700–3000 B.C.	Peru	Inca domesticate more than 3,000 varieties of potato
1535	Peru	Spanish conquistadores see potatoes for the first time[21]
1550s	Spain	Returning conquistadores introduce potato
1586	England	Queen Elizabeth I's chef cooks potato leaves, throws potatoes away[22]
1590	Italy	Pope gives potatoes to botanist Clusius, who paints first pictures of them[23]
1651	Germany	Government forces people to cultivate potatoes[24]
1660–1688	Ireland	Potato cultivation spreads rapidly; population from 500,000 to 1.5 million[25]
1662	England	Britain's Royal Society sponsors cultivation of potatoes[26]
ca. 1700	Russia	Czar Peter the Great introduces the potato[27]
1719	N. America	Scotch-Irish settlers bring first potatoes to New Hampshire from Europe[28]
1748	France	Parliament declares potatoes cause leprosy, forbids growing them[29]
ca. 1760	Poland	Potatoes reach Poland during Seven Years' War[30]
1760–1840	Ireland	Population increases 600%, 1.5 million to nine million, subsists on potatoes[31]
1763	France	Parmentier promotes potatoes after eating them while prisoner in Germany during Seven Years' War[32]

(continues)

DATE	PLACE	EVENT
1764	Sweden	Government promotes potato growing[33]
1770	Australasia	Captain Cook introduces potato[34]
1780s	France	King Louis XVI grows potatoes in Neuilly. Parmentier sends guards to make potatoes seem valuable; peasants steal the potatoes and plant them, which was Parmentier's goal.
1793	France	*La cuisine républicaine,* first French cookbook written by a woman, Mme Méridot, is all potato recipes[35]
1830	Belgium	Potato fungus—*Phytophthora infestans*—originates[36]
1835	France	Carême includes recipe for English-style potatoes—mashed—in *The Art of French Cooking*
1837	France	Soufflé potatoes created by accident when chef fries potato slices twice[37]
1845	Ireland	Potato fungus wipes out crops; one million Irish die, one million leave
1850s	U.S.	Legend: potato chips invented in Saratoga, NY, by African–Native American cook
1873	U.S.	Luther Burbank "builds" a better potato; becomes Idaho potato
1920s	U.S.	Soldiers return from WWI with a taste for french fries
1960	U.S.	Gil Lamb invents potato water gun knife, revolutionizes potato industry[38]
1986	World	Potato is one of four most important food crops; staple for 200 million people[39]
2001	U.S.	Lamb Weston debuts sweet potato fries[40]

Cooking Techniques

While altitude helped the Inca who lived in the Andes to preserve potatoes, it also made cooking by boiling difficult. At sea level, water boils at 212°F or 100°C. The higher the altitude, the lower the pressure in the atmosphere. This means that water boils at a lower temperature, so food will take longer to cook. The cooking fire will also need more fuel, which will be in shorter supply at higher elevations where trees are scarcer. So for the people in the Inca Empire who lived at higher altitudes, cooking was more by frying than by boiling.

Frying some foods, like beans, produced interesting results. Beans were a staple food throughout the Americas, but the Andean Inca had a bean that burst its shell when heated in oil, like popcorn. These beans are called *nuñas* [NOON-yahz] now and belong to the family known as the common bean *(Phaseolus vulgaris)*. Even today, they are still grown mostly for home use, not commercially. The taste has been described as resembling roasted peanuts.[41]

Corn

Corn, which traveled south from Mexico, was another staple of the Inca diet. To Americans, corn means corn on the cob, with kernels. But the word was in use in Europe long before there was corn on the cob. This has led to some confusion, especially with ancient texts.

CULINARY CONFUSION:
Corn and Maize

The word *corn* was first used to describe any grain, like barley or wheat—even salt, as in corned beef. It also means the "small, hard seed or fruit of a plant," as in peppercorn.[42] The word *maize*—what Americans mean by *corn*, like corn on the cob—came from the Spanish, who learned it from the Arawak Indians of the Caribbean, where *mahiz* meant "stuff of life."[43] Maize was domesticated in central Mexico by about 3400 B.C. It quickly became the basic crop and spread north to the cliff dwellers in the American Southwest and to Cahokia, and south to the Inca Empire.[44] So when European writers before Columbus talk about corn, they can mean many things, but maize is not one of them.

There is further confusion. As food historian Raymond Sokolov points out, "The corn of the Andes [*choclo*] is not our corn. The kernels are much bigger, the taste and texture different."[45] And it was used differently, transformed by a unique technique, into a beer called *chicha*.

RECIPE:
Chicha—Corn Beer

The method of making *chicha* is this: "women . . . put [the sprouted corn] into their mouths and gradually chew it; then with an effort they almost cough it out upon a leaf or platter and throw it into the jar with [ground corn and water]." Later it is boiled and strained. In *The Story of Corn*, food historian Betty Fussell says that *chicha* has "a two-inch head of foam and . . . tastes a bit like English barley water mixed with light pilsner."[46]

Squash

The Inca also ate the many types of squash that originated in the Andes in Bolivia and the area around it—southern Peru, northern Chile, and northern Argentina—as early as 500 B.C. These were large squash; their scientific name means "biggest squash"—*Cucurbita maxima.*[47] The *Cucurbita* family are vines that grow along the ground or that can be trained up trellises. They have large leaves and produce vegetables of varying colors, sizes, and shapes. They are found in the Old and New Worlds. Cucumbers and gourds are from the Old World; the most famous of the New World cucurbits is pumpkin.

The Inca used the entire squash efficiently. In addition to the vegetable itself, the blossom is edible. Usually, the male blossoms are eaten because the female blossoms are attached to the small growing squash. The tender tips of the vines are sometimes eaten, as well as the young leaves. The seeds are rich in protein and can be pressed to extract their oil or roasted and salted and eaten. In Spanish, these are called *pepitas.* Scientists believe that it was for the highly nutritious seeds that the plant was originally domesticated.[48]

The squash that most Americans probably know best is the pie pumpkin *(Cucurbita moschata).* This originated in Mexico or Central America but spread widely. In the Andes today, many more varieties of squash are grown than are popular in the rest of the world. Perhaps some of these kinds of squash will spread, too, the way that purple and other kinds of potatoes have been introduced recently to world markets.

Fruit

A wide variety of fruits indigenous to the Andes was available to the Inca. Some of these fruits are recent arrivals in mainstream American supermarkets. Among them are the Cape Gooseberry, also called goldenberry, the pepino, tamarillo, and cherimoya. The cherimoya is also called "custard apple" because the outside is green like an apple (but with scales), while inside, the pulp is creamy, white, and sweet. Also native to the Andes but little known in the rest of the world are members of the family that includes blackberries and raspberries. These include a berry like a loganberry, which produces deep red juice; the wild "blueberry of the Andes" *(Vaccinium floribundum);* and the giant Colombian blackberry *(Rubus macrocarpus)* which can be as big as a chicken egg.[49] Some varieties of passion fruit *(Passiflora edulis)* are also native to the Andes, although the one most familiar to Americans is native to Brazil.[50] The Inca also ate cactus fruit *(tunas)* and plantains. They snacked on inga pods, now called "ice cream beans" because the pulp is sweet and white with a smooth texture almost like cotton candy.[51]

Strawberries

A type of large strawberry *(Fragaria chiloensis)* is native to the coast of Chile. In 1712, a French sea captain in Chile tasted them for the first time and knew that other people would love them as much as he did. He took many berry plants back to France with him and planted them. They grew perfectly well but they failed to produce any berries. No one could figure out why. Thirty years later, another type of strawberry, one from the east coast of North America *(Fragaria virginiana)*, was planted near the Chilean berries. Then the Chilean berries produced fruit. Why? Because the Chilean strawberries were female, and the Virginia berries were male.

Another fruit native to Peru was the tomato. They were used, along with chile peppers, which originated in Bolivia, to spice up Inca cuisine.[52] Just as corn migrated south to Peru, tomatoes and chile peppers migrated north to Mexico. Europeans first encountered them and many other plants in Central America.[53]

Central America: Vanilla

Vanilla originated in the lowland tropical forests of Central America and the northern part of South America. The earliest legends of vanilla domestication are from the Totonac, people who lived in what is now the area near Veracruz, on the Gulf coast in eastern Mexico, about a thousand years ago.[54] They used vanilla to perfume the temples, just as European nobles in the Middle Ages used Asian spices like cinnamon to perfume their surroundings.[55]

Vanilla is the only edible member of one of the oldest plant families on Earth, the orchids. Even after hundreds of years of study, much about vanilla is still a mystery. Scientists cannot explain exactly how these particular orchids create vanillin, the plant's major flavor, out of its 250 to 500 different chemical compounds.[56]

Vanilla grows on vines that climb up tropical trees called "tutor" trees because they help and support the vines. The flowers open in the morning for at most eight hours. To produce vanilla pods, they have to be hand pollinated during those eight hours. Between six and nine months later, the vines produce long green pods, like huge string beans. The pods have to be hand harvested. They are then heated, often by steam, dried, and aged. This makes them shrink and become dark brown and creates the aroma and flavor of vanilla that we prize, which is a defense mechanism to the damage done to the pods. The pods have no flavor of vanilla until after they are processed, which can take from several weeks to several months.

The process of growing, pollinating, harvesting, and drying vanilla is long and labor-intensive. One pound of cured vanilla beans is the reduction of three to five pounds of pods. This puts vanilla second after saffron as the most expensive spice in the world. It is also the reason that 90 percent of the vanilla used in the United States is synthetic, usually made from the wood pulp that is a by-product of making paper.[57]

90 million B.C.	Orchid family evolves[58]
1200s	Totonac ancestors found city of Papantla near modern Vera Cruz, Mexico
1552	Earliest written mention of vanilla, in Florentine Codex
1605	Botanist Clusius describes vanilla in his book *Exoticorum Libri Decem*[59]
early–mid 1600s	Vanilla plantations established in Oaxaca and Tabasco, Mexico; and northern Guatemala[60]
1694	Botanists discover that plants have sexes; important for pollination
by 1759	Vanilla plants arrive at the King's Garden—Jardin du Roi—in Paris[61]
late 1700s	Tahitian Vanilla—*Vanilla tahitensis*—invented in a laboratory in the Philippines[62]
1791	Thomas Jefferson is the first to import vanilla pods to the U.S.[63]
1819	Vanilla arrives on the island of Réunion, aka Bourbon Island, in Indian Ocean[64]
ca. 1840	Vanilla introduced to Madagascar
1841	Réunion: 12-year-old slave Edmond Albius discovers how to hand-pollinate vanilla
1846	Vanilla cultivated on Java
1846	Vanilla introduced to Tahiti; French Catholic missionaries establish commercial production
mid-1800s	Oven-drying processing of vanilla begins
1875	German chemist Ferdinand Tiemann creates synthetic vanillin from pine trees[65]
1886	Mascarene Islands and Java lead world vanilla production, out-producing Mexico
1891	French chemist De Taire creates synthetic vanillin from cloves[66]
1920	Indian Ocean plantations produce 80% of world's vanilla; Mexico, 15%[67]
1920	Prohibition goes into effect in U.S.; alcoholics buy vanilla for the alcohol
1925	Vanilla important in perfumes with Guerlain fragrance Shalimar
1930	Madagascar has monopoly on world vanilla production, more than 80%[68]
1930s	Synthetic lignin vanillin created from wood pulp, by-product of papermaking[69]

1930s	U.S. Food and Drug Administration regulates vanilla and artificial vanilla
1976	Vanilla accounts for 50% of all ice cream sold in the U.S.[70]
1996	USAID (U.S. Agency for International Development) helps farmers in Uganda, Africa, grow vanilla
1996	John Travolta plays an angel who smells like vanilla in the motion picture *Michael*
1998	Vanilla sells for $9/pound or $20/kilogram
1999	Natural disasters destroy vanilla in Madagascar and Mexico; vanilla prices rise
2002	Vanilla sells for $91/pound or $200/kilogram, 10 times more than 4 years earlier[71]
2003	First international congress dealing with vanilla
2009	Vanilla accounts for one-third of all ice cream sold in the U.S.[72]

Vanilla as a flavoring in foods is relatively recent in world cuisine, since about the middle of the nineteenth century. That was when a clever 12-year-old male slave on the island of Réunion in the Indian Ocean figured out how to hand-pollinate vanilla. Before that, people knew that hummingbirds and honeybees were attracted to wild vanilla but couldn't figure out what role they played in pollinating it. Hand pollination gives humans more control over vanilla production, but it is still a very sensitive and time-consuming process, which adds to the expense.

Even with the expense, vanilla is still the most popular ice cream flavor in the United States. This has been consistent for centuries. In the 1780s, President Thomas Jefferson handwrote America's first recipe for ice cream—vanilla. However, its popularity is slipping. From a 50 percent share of the market in 1976, it had dropped to one-third by 2009. The next closest was chocolate, with less than 10 percent.[73]

Central America: Maya Mystery

Much about Maya civilization is still a mystery. At their height, the Maya extended from Mexico's Yucatan peninsula on the Caribbean Sea, south to the state of Chiapas on the Pacific Ocean. They inhabited all of present-day Guatemala and Belize, as well as western Honduras and El Salvador. Their major ceremonial centers were places like Chichen Itza in the Yucatan and Tikal in Guatemala. Tikal was home to about 50,000 people from the third and fourth centuries until about the year 900. Then the majority of the Maya abandoned their cities and their monuments; the civilization faded.

No one knows why—there's the mystery. There are many theories: drought, foreign invaders, internal divisions, disease, famine, earthquakes, hurricanes, or a combination.[74] The final blow to the Maya civilization, though, is no mystery. It came from the Spanish conquistadores, beginning in 1519 when Hernán Cortés destroyed the first Maya religious center he encountered, at Cozumel, and put up a cross instead.

The Madrid Codex

Fortunately, before the Spanish arrived the Maya wrote down some of their important beliefs and customs. They used paper made from the bark of the strangler fig tree. There are four sets of these multiple-volume manuscripts of hieroglyphs. They are called codices, and they are invaluable. Each codex is identified by the name of the city whose library has it; for example, the Madrid Codex. However, scholars originally believed that the hieroglyphs, which also covered Maya buildings, were just pictures—art, not language—and therefore indecipherable.

That changed in 1970, when an art historian named Linda Schele from the University of Texas at Austin went to Mexico on vacation and visited one of the Maya sites at Palenque. The hieroglyphs spoke to her, and not just as art. She saw pictures that told a story and began to decipher them. She revealed that the public buildings contained lists of kings and events that had occurred under each king. The Maya had written their history in plain sight. Through the efforts of Linda Schele and others, we now know much about Maya cuisine and culture. By 1990, so many of the hieroglyphics had been deciphered that scientists were debating whether the glyphs were a true written language, "because they represent the sounds and structure of spoken language."[75]

The *Popul Vuh*

Another of our main sources for information on the Maya is the *Popul vuh*, written in the middle of the sixteenth century, after the Spanish arrived. This Maya record of religious beliefs is a story of creation, war, sacrifice, death, and resurrection. Like the Romans, the Maya believed that twin brothers were central to the founding of their civilization.

Part of the creation myth is about how the creator, named Maker, Modeler, or Hurricane, tries to make "True People." First he makes people out of wood, but they have no souls. So he sends a hurricane to destroy them and they run off into the forest and become monkeys. He is finally successful in creating humans out of maize dough.[76]

The Corn God

Corn was more than the main subsistence food for the Maya. It was also extremely symbolic. Just as the Greeks believed that the grapevine represented resurrection, for the Maya, corn was "the central metaphor of life and death," the cycle of birth, death, decomposition, and rebirth.[77] They made many artistic representations of the maize god Centeotl, sometimes wearing jewelry in the shape of corn kernels. The Maya believed that Centeotl was the source of more than just maize. From his body sprouted other plants. The maize god

> put himself under the ground, and from his hair emerged cotton, and from an eye a very good seed which they eat gladly, called *cacatzli*. . . . From the nose, another seed called *chia*. . . . From the fingers came a fruit called *camotli*. . . . From the fingernails another kind of broad maize, which is the kind they eat today. And from the rest of the body emerged many other fruits, which the men gather and sow.[78]

Maya were buried with drinking vessels for *atolli*, a beverage made with white maize, if they died when it was in season.

Cacao: Cool, Hot, and Alcoholic

One of the most important trees that sprang from the maize god's body was the cacao tree. The maize god is sometimes shown with cacao pods sprouting out of his head.[79] The Maya were drinking chocolate 1,000 years before the Aztecs, and 2,600 years before the Spanish arrived.[80] They drank it cool or sometimes hot. They even made an alcoholic cacao *chicha* out of the white pulp in the cacao pods.

Cacao is by far the most common glyph on Maya ceramics. The inscriptions on their drinking vessels were personalized. The way we have mugs that say, "Grandpa's Coffee" or "Employee of the Month," the Maya bowls and cups said, "His/her cup for *x* drink."[81] They were specific, mentioning pure cacao, new cacao, ripe cacao, sweet cacao, fresh cacao.[82] One cup even had a top that rotated and locked so that the cacao wouldn't spill while you were carrying it. Maya nobles were buried with their ornate vessels for drinking chocolate.

The Maya also used cacao as dye, as medicine, and as payment for other goods.[83] They also made cacao butter by beating the ground cacao beans with water, and drank that or added it to their chocolate to make it even richer. A thousand years later, in the nineteenth century, the Dutch chemist Van Houten got the credit for inventing this process.[84]

The Three Sisters and Family Farming

The Maya farmed efficiently. Instead of having fields that were spread out and time-consuming to get to and tend, they combined their three staple crops—corn, beans, and squash—in a method known as "three sisters farming." The corn stalks grew straight up and acted as a trellis to support the beans that wound around them. At the base of the corn stalks, the big, broad leaves of the squash plants kept moisture in the soil. The people ate the corn, beans, and squash, and the beautiful golden, trumpet-shaped squash blossoms, still widely used in Mexican cooking today and represented in Mexican art.

The Maya lived in clusters of small one- or two-room stucco buildings with thatched roofs made of palm trees. These were family groups in which the males—father and sons—lived next to each other with their families. The families shared the cultivation and the fruits of communal orchards, vegetables, and herbs for healing. Growing wild near the houses might be trees bearing papaya, avocado, and *ramón*—a fruit high in protein that could be stored in underground chambers for more than a year.[85] Gardens might contain sweet potatoes and manioc.

This was slash-and-burn agriculture, in which the land is worked until it is depleted. Then it is abandoned and the cycle begins again on new land. They also built canals for irrigation and terraces up hillsides. The Maya supplemented what they grew with hunting, fishing, and market purchases. As they worked, they chewed the sticky chicle sap of the *zapote* tree just as we chew the gum—like Chiclets—that is made from it.

Jaguar, Crocodile, and Other Proteins

As in many other civilizations, for the Maya, cuisine and culture were connected to religion. The Maya worshipped a sun god, a common practice throughout the world. However, the Maya were unusual because they accounted for what happened when the sun disappeared from the sky: it turned into a jaguar. This ferocious predator, biggest of the big cats in the Americas, can grow more than seven feet long and weigh up to 200 pounds. The Maya hunted jaguars for food; the men drank jaguar blood and ate raw jaguar meat to prepare for a jaguar hunt. The Maya also worshipped the crocodile. They ate crocodile tail meat, and valued the hide.

They also ate the meat of the peccary, a relative of the pig, and turkey. Oyster, conch, and freshwater turtles provided protein, too. Turtle eggs added calcium to the diet. Maya nobles feasted on roasted deer, muscle meat as well as organs—heart, liver, lungs, stomach, brain.[86] Archaeologists think that the deer haunches were sacrificed to the gods. So were iguanas, lizards that can grow up to 15 inches long.

Bees and Allspice

Bee gods appear throughout the codices. One month of the 18-month Maya calendar was named after bees; there was a month of purification before it to prepare for the bee festivals. Beeswax and honey were used in ceremonies and offered to the bee gods. There was also a month named after bats.

Food was seasoned with berries from the allspice tree, which can grow to 80 feet. Native to the Americas, its flavor is like a combination of three of the Asian spices that Columbus was seeking: cinnamon, clove, and nutmeg. The Maya made a paste of the berries to use as a medicine the way that we use Bengay or Tiger Balm. They also used it to cure meats and to embalm the dead, as the ancient Egyptians used cinnamon.[87]

Blood and Stars

The Maya practiced human sacrifice, especially to the rain god. So blood figured prominently in their religious rituals. One of the most sacred rituals of the Maya was drawing blood from the body. In a public ceremony, the male ruler would stick stingray spines through his penis, collect the blood in a special religious bowl, and set the blood on fire. The vision of a rattlesnake—the connection between the human world and the spirit world, which the Maya called the Otherworld—was supposed to appear out of the smoke of the ruler's blood.[88] Women would pierce their tongues.

Sometimes chocolate was colored red with achiote (annatto) so that it resembled blood. Corn and cacao were among the most sacred offerings the Maya made to their gods of magic life-containing substances that they called *itza* [EATS-ah]. Other offerings included honey, beeswax, and live animals.

The Maya saw their sacred rattlesnake in the constellations of the stars, too, where we see the Pleiades. They saw a frog and a bat where we see Leo the Lion and Aquarius the Water Bearer. Interestingly, both of us see a scorpion in the same constellation.

About 400 years after the collapse of the Maya, a new civilization came to prominence, this time in central Mexico.

Central America: The Aztec Empire

Religion and Ritual

In 1325, a people whose legend says that they came from Aztlan in northern Mexico, and who called themselves the Mexica, arrived at a valley 7,000 feet above sea level and ringed by mountains—the site of present-day Mexico City. Known now as Aztecs, these people worshipped many gods on whom their lives and their food depended: the sun god, Huitzilopochtli; the rain god, Tlaloc; mountain gods; corn gods; and others. The Aztecs believed that the gods had created all these forces of nature by sacrificing themselves and that the gods needed "the precious water"—human blood—to continue to exist.

Bloodletting was an essential part of Aztec religious rituals, as it was of Mayan rituals. The Aztecs drew blood from their ears or the calves of their legs. In elaborate sacred festivals, humans captured from neighboring tribes, purchased, or chosen as a special honor were adorned to resemble the gods and sacrificed in ways appropriate to each god. The rain god's sacrifices were drowned; the fire god's were thrown into a fire.[89] Sometimes their beating hearts were cut out while they were alive and offered to the god. On rare occasions, the rest of the body was ritually divided, stewed with maize and salt, and a tiny bit eaten, about half an ounce, as if it were the body of the god.[90] The gods also received offerings of beheaded quail, corn, and amaranth.

Cooking Equipment and Cooks

The Aztec god of fire lived among three other gods, represented by three stones on the hearth where all the cooking was done. Much of today's Mexican cooking equipment and the food cooked on it are directly descended from the Aztecs. Tortillas were cooked on a clay griddle called a *comalli* (today, *comal*); corn was ground on a *metate*, a three-legged grinding stone, with the Aztec equivalent of the pestle, a stone that fit in the hand and was therefore called a *mano*—hand— by the Spanish. In the Aztec civilization, women were usually the cooks. Mothers taught daughters, and by the time a girl was 13 she was expected to be an accomplished cook. The exception was that men handled the barbecue. However, as Sophie Coe points out in *America's First Cuisines*, it is still unclear how many times a day the Aztecs ate. Some sources say two, others say three—at dawn, 9:00, and 3:00.[91]

There was an upside and a downside to being a cook for nobility in a culture that practiced human sacrifice. The upside: you were employed in a wealthy household, so you had food. The higher the noble person's rank, the greater the number of cooks. The downside: when the nobility died, they needed their chefs to cook for them in the afterlife. The serious downside: the nobles were buried dead but the cooks were buried alive.[92]

The Florentine Codex

Much of what we know about the Aztecs comes from a document called the *Florentine Codex*. This is a compilation of information about Aztec culture, written shortly after the Spanish conquistadores arrived in 1521. It was written down by a friar, Bernardino de Sagahun, who arrived in Mexico in 1529, just eight years after the siege of Tenochtitlan. Sagahun taught himself Nahuatl, the Aztec pictographic language. He spent 40 years recording the codex, a book of grammar, and a dictionary in three languages: Nahuatl, Spanish, and Latin. The books were finally finished 40 years later, in 1569.

The codex was prepared at the direction of the Catholic Church and at Church expense because they wanted to know about Aztec culture so that they could decide the best way to convert the Aztecs. But after Sagahun was finished, the Church kept the codex private because they did not want the Aztecs to dwell on their non-Christian past, and because the codex talked about the horrors of the conquest from the Aztec point of view. Instead, Sagahun's 12 volumes were circulated only within the Church and the Spanish government, and then hidden. It was not until 1979 that a facsimile of the codex was published. It was translated into modern Spanish and then other languages and made widely available to the public.

Chinampas: The Aztec Agricultural Revolution

The Aztecs built their capital city, Tenochtitlan [ten-OHCH-teet-lahn], on an island in the middle of a lake because of a spiritual sign: an eagle landed on a heart-shaped cactus fruit. As the Aztecs grew more powerful and dominant over Central America, highly skilled Aztec engineers connected Tenochtitlan to land by roads built above the lake water. Aztec engineers were equally creative in providing ways to drain swamps and use the soil to farm on the water. They invented the system of *chinampas,* a combination of land and irrigation ditches that looked like floating fields. According to historian Jeffrey Pilcher, Aztec engineers "achieved a virtual agricultural revolution" with the *chinampas.*

Large-scale drainage work began at the command of Itzcóatl (1426–1440) and culminated in the reign of Moctezuma the Elder (1440–1467), when almost 100 square kilometers lay under intense cultivation. The use of aquatic plants for fertilizer and a complex rotation of maize, beans, and vegetables yielded high productivity with virtually no fallow.[93]

Corn: History

For the Aztec, food meant corn, up to 80 percent of their daily calories.[94] Everything else was sauces or sides. So it is not surprising that the ancestors of corn and the oldest examples of corn were found in Mexico.

One of modern maize's ancestors is a wild grass called teosinte. It was discovered in 1978 in southwestern Mexico. This grass provided the root and the stalk of our modern corn plant. Another ancestor is Domestic Corn. The earliest cobs found are from about 10,000 years ago in Mexico. The cobs were tiny, about the size of the nail on the little finger of a human hand. From this corn we get the ear and kernels in rows. Domestic Corn crossed with teosinte, but scientists do not know if it was an accident performed by nature or deliberately done by humans.

From this early corn, humans have spent centuries breeding different types of corn. Sweet Corn is what Americans know as corn on the cob. It has a high sugar content and can be eaten raw. Flint Corn and Flour Corn are hard corn for grinding to make into flour. The flour is called masa and is used in tortillas. Dent Corn is a cross of flint and flour corns. The Aztec grew corn in white, black, blue, yellow, and other colors. In the United States today, the most popular variety of corn is Yellow Dent. This is used for corn chips, taco shells, cornmeal, and cornstarch.

One of the oldest types of corn is popcorn. Sometimes it was popped right on the ear. Cobs between 2,000 and 3,000 years old were found in a cave in 1948—they were still able to pop. Popcorn is not just eaten as popcorn; it can also be ground into meal.

Corn: Religion

Many of the rituals recorded in the *Florentine Codex* involve corn—worshipping corn gods like Cinteotl or goddesses like Chicomecoatl, offering food to the gods, or eating it themselves. Sometimes young women carried full ears of maize on their backs to the pyramid temple to have them blessed. The *Florentine Codex* explains the place of corn in Aztec religion and cuisine:

. . . it was indeed this Chicomecoatl who made all our food—white maize, yellow maize, green maize shoots, black maize, black and brown mixed, variously hued; large and wide; round and ball-like; slender maize, thin; long maize; speckled red and white maize as if striped with blood, painted with blood—then the coarse, brown maize . . . popcorn; the after-fruit; double ears; rough ears; and maturing green maize; the small ears of maize beside the main ear; the ripened green maize.[95]

Corn: Tortillas

Tortillas were Aztec essentials, according to the *Florentine Codex*:

For he who eateth no tortillas indeed then fainteth; he falleth down: he droppeth quickly; there is a twittering as of birds in his ears; darkness descendeth upon him.[96]

Tortillas were made from flour ground from corn that went through a process called nixtamalization to remove the outer coating of the kernel. This was done by briefly boiling the kernels in water and ashes, often from juniper wood, then leaving them to soak overnight and washing away the hard outer part of the kernel. The drained corn was then ground into flour. Nixtamalization does two things: (1) the juniper ash imparts flavor to the flour, the way that juniper berries give gin its distinctive woodsy flavor; and (2) it adds vitamin B and calcium, which are not naturally present in corn.[97]

Corn: Tacos

Tortillas had other advantages, as historian Jeffrey Pilcher points out. Because they were thin, they cooked quickly and used very little fuel. Also, filled with meat or vegetables and folded in half, they became tacos. This was efficient because it kept food hot and needed no utensils. These are what we know today as soft tacos, not deep-fried, brittle preshaped taco shells.[98] Also, handmade, freshly cooked tortillas are pliable, elastic, and taste like corn. They bear no resemblance to the piles of cardboard sold in supermarkets.

Corn: Tamales

Tamales were staples of Aztec cuisine, essential at religious festivals. Tamales are corn stuffing inside corn husks. A seasoned corn filling is placed on corn husks, rolled into a small packet, and steamed. Many kinds of tamales were sold in the marketplace in Tenochtitlan:

. . . salted wide tamales, pointed tamales, white tamales . . . roll-shaped tamales, tamales with beans forming a seashell on top, [with] grains of maize thrown in; crumbled, pounded tamales; spotted tamales; white fruit tamales, red fruit tamales, turkey egg tamales; turkey eggs with grains of maize; tamales of tender maize, tamales of green maize, adobe-shaped tamales, braised ones; unleavened tamales, honey tamales, beeswax tamales, tamales with grains of maize, gourd tamales, crumbled tamales, maize flower tamales.[99]

Tamales appear frequently in the *Florentine Codex*. They were distributed by the government at religious festivals. Each person was given as many tamales "as he could hold in one hand." But he was only allowed to do this once. If he tried to cheat and get too many tamales, "they struck him repeatedly, leaving marks on him with a cord made of reeds."[100] Then they took all the tamales away from him and he was left empty-handed.[101]

Corn: *Huitlacoche*

Huitlacoche [wheat-la-COH-chay] is a fungus that is sometimes called "Mexican truffles." However, unlike truffles, which grow underground, or mushrooms, which grow on the ground, *huitlacoche* grows on the ears of corn. It begins white, then turns black. It is considered a delicacy and is prized by diners today. *Huitlacoche* can be used raw or cooked, just like truffles or mushrooms. The young white *huitlacoche* is better for eating raw, while the black is better cooked. Farmers hate it. They consider it a blight because it destroys the corn. To farmers, it is just corn smut.

Amaranth

The amaranth plant was also important in Aztec religious rituals and cuisine. The leaves of this plant are edible only when the plant is very young; later it becomes a tough weed. Amaranth tamales were offered on some festival days. The *Florentine Codex* lists multiple varieties of amaranth:

> . . . the variety of amaranth called *cocotl*, fine red amaranth seed, [common] red amaranth, black amaranth, bright red or chili-red amaranth, fish amaranth, . . . brilliant black amaranth seed, the bird-seed called *petzicatl*.[102]

Amaranth seeds were combined with a sweet syrup like honey from the leaves or sprouts of the agave plant [ah-GAH-vay] to make a dough called *tzoalli*. The agave, also known as the maguey plant [muh-GAY], is native to Mexico. (If the agave sap is fermented it becomes a wine called *pulque* [POOL-kay]. When the *pulque* is distilled, it becomes the hard liquor mezcal, with a worm added to the bottle. Another member of the agave family, the blue agave, is the origin of tequila.) The *tzoalli* dough was shaped into images of Aztec gods or pyramids. These were handed out and eaten with reverence: "They fashioned for [the gods] their teeth of squash seeds, and their eyes of some beans. . . . And then they offered [the gods] their offerings of food, and they worshiped them."[103] Spanish religious authorities put a stop to this by prohibiting the cultivation of amaranth, which they called diabolical.[104]

Chocolatl: Food of the Gods

One of the most important foodstuffs in Aztec cuisine and culture was chocolate. The Aztecs called it *chocolatl*. The Europeans named it *theobroma*, which means "food of the gods." It had much more than culinary significance in the

Aztec culture. It was the beverage of Aztec emperors and warriors. They drank it lukewarm, frothed on top the same way it is done today, by rubbing a swizzle stick or *molinillo* between the palms of the hands. In their book *The True History of Chocolate*, Sophie and Michael Coe discuss at length how the Aztecs flavored chocolate. They used finely ground chile powder, or sometimes maize, honey (there was no sugar yet), a flower related to the custard-apple, another flower related to black pepper, and "black flower"—what they called vanilla because of the color of the pod.[105] They also made a beverage out of unripe green cacao pods.[106]

Even though the Aztecs had *pulque,* an alcoholic beverage made from agave, they didn't consider it fit for men to drink. Old people could drink it, but chocolate was the drink preferred by nobles and warriors and restricted to them. It was part of a warrior's food ration, along with tortillas, beans, dried chiles, and toasted maize.[107] Besides, drunkenness was punishable by death. However, chocolate was not consumed indiscriminately. It was served as a ritual beverage after a banquet, by itself, along with tobacco to smoke, in a male bonding ritual that echoes the Greek symposium, where wine was restricted to men and consumed ritually after the meal.

The cacao beans were stored in the public granaries, along with maize, but they were much more than food. They were also money in the Aztec Empire. They could be used to pay wages and to purchase items. A turkey hen or a rabbit cost 100 cacao beans, an avocado cost three, a large tomato cost one.[108] But cacao, like other forms of money, could be counterfeited: old beans were stuffed with mud or other debris and mixed in with real beans.

Turkey and Other Proteins

Protein in the Aztec diet came from "deer, peccary, rabbits, jackrabbits, mice, armadillos, snakes, gophers, opposums, and iguanas" that were caught, kept in cages, and fattened up. There were dogs in the Americas, but they were not like modern dogs or the ferocious armored war dogs the Spaniards brought with them. The American dogs were hairless, small, and soft, like a little rolled roast with feet. They were bred and raised for food, probably fed mostly maize, along with avocados and other vegetables.[109]

Also on the Aztec menu were foods from the surrounding lakes: water bugs and their eggs, frogs and tadpoles, lake shrimp, and larvae of the *Comadia redtenbacheri* worm that today resides at the bottom of the mezcal bottle.[110] These were cooked in a variety of ways: ground up into balls, roasted and salted, and cooked in maize husks like tamales. The Spaniards found them palatable; they said the water bug eggs tasted like caviar. One lake food the Spanish could not bring themselves to eat was a plant the Aztec called *tecuilatl*—edible seaweed *(Spirulina geitleri)*. It was partially sun-dried, formed into cakes, then completely sun-dried, and used to make tortillas. Supposedly, it tasted like cheese "but less pleasing and with a certain taste of mud."[111]

The Emperor Moctezuma received the best food, of course. The emperor himself got 300 different dishes each day: "spicy stews of turkey, duck, partridge, pheasant, quail, squab, fish, rabbit, and venison."[112] A thousand dishes were prepared for the rest of his household. The turkey was sometimes considered "a sacred sun bird."[113] Images of turkeys were found in the burial crypts under the Aztec pyramids, along with emblems of the sun with rays.

AZTEC–MODERN FOOD WORDS

NAHUATL	SPANISH	ENGLISH
ahuacatl	avocado	avocado
ahuaca-mulli	guacamole	guacamole
atolli (maize beverage)	atole	atole
cacahuatl	cacao	cacao
chilmolli	chile salsa	chile sauce
comalli	comal	griddle
exotl	frijole Latin: phaseolus	bean French: haricot; Italian: fagioli; Neapolitan dialect: fazool
metatl	metate	mortar
molcaxitl (sauce bowl)	molcajete	molcajete
molli/mulli	mole	sauce/mixture
pinolli (sweet maize drink)	pinole	pinole
tamalli	tamale	tamale
nextamalli (maize softened in wood ash)[114]	tamale	tamale
tenextamalli (maize softened in lime)	tamale	tamale
tlaxcalli	tortilla	tortilla
tomatl (plump fruit)	tomate	tomato
tzictli (sticky stuff)	goma	chicle or chewing gum (Chiclets)

The American Southwest: Chile Man

Most of this food culture of corn, beans, squash, and chiles traveled north on the trade routes from the great Aztec civilization into what is now northern Mexico and the southwestern United States. On the edge of the Aztec trade route, native people built communal dwellings, like apartment houses. The largest had perhaps 600 rooms and 1,000 inhabitants. It was an efficient way to conserve resources in the desert climate.

In addition to the three sisters of corn, beans, and squash, they also ate amaranth. The bean of the mesquite tree was an important source of nutrition, too. Every year, the women gathered enormous quantities of them, and pulverized them into flour with mortars or *metates*. They also collected fruit from the tall saguaro cactus *(Cereus giganteus)* and cooked them into a syrup. In earlier times, it was fermented into an alcoholic beverage that was used in rituals.[115]

Farther north, in the Four Corners area where Arizona, New Mexico, Colorado, and Utah meet today, the Hopi, Zuni, and Tewa people cultivated sacred blue corn and made a bread as fine as tissue paper. Called *piki* bread, it is made from blue corn meal mixed with wood ash or lime, not soaked in it and washed off, as was the procedure for nixtamalization. This provides additional nutrition and also preserves the deep blue, almost black color of the cooked food. The dough is patted out by hand until it is extremely thin, then cooked quickly on top of a hot anvil.

Chile Peppers

Like the Inca, Maya, and Aztecs, the native people of what is today the American Southwest seasoned their food with chile peppers. Chile peppers are the number one spice in the world. They originated in what is now central Bolivia about 7,000 years ago, and were domesticated about 4,000 years ago.[116] *Capsicum* is the name for the entire pepper family, sweet bell peppers as well as chile peppers. They are members of the nightshade family like their other American relatives the tomato, the potato, and tobacco, and their Asian relative the eggplant.

Columbus and the other Europeans were looking for spices, especially black pepper. They found something that was even hotter, so they called it pepper—another confusion, like calling the people Indians.

The heat of peppers, from the large, harmless green bell to the tiny hellfire Scotch bonnet, is measured in Scoville units. This test to measure the strength of capsaicin in various peppers is named after its inventor, a chemist named Wilbur Scoville. The grading of the heat in peppers involved humans actually doing the tasting. Today, Scoville units are measured by machine, using high-pressure liquid chromatography.

CHILE PEPPER HEAT SCALE—SCOVILLE UNITS

HEAT LEVEL	TYPE OF PEPPER
0–100	Bell
500–1,000	Anaheim, New Mexican
1,000–1,500	Ancho, Pasilla
1,500–2,500	Sandia, Cascabel, Yellow Wax
2,500–5,000	Jalapeño, Mirasol
5,000–15,000	Serrrano, early Jalapeño, Aji Amarillo
15,000–30,000	Chile de Árbol
30,000–50,000	Aji, Pequín, Tabasco
50,000–100,000	Chiltepin, cayenne, Tabasco
100,000–350,000	Habanero, Scotch Bonnet
1,150,000–2,000,000	Civilian pepper spray[117]
2,500,000–5,300,000	Law enforcement–grade pepper spray[118]
15,000,000–16,000,000	Pure capsaicin

In the Andes, there are still many varieties of chile peppers unknown outside the area. The *rocoto (Capsicum pubescens)* is almost the size of a bell pepper but with the heat of a chile. In the American Southwest even today, as in Mexico, chile peppers figure prominently in the cuisine and the culture. A braid of chiles, called a *ristra*, means good luck to a household and is given as a housewarming gift. There are many stories in Native American mythology, too, about the origin of the chile pepper.

FOOD FABLE:
Where Salt and Chile Peppers Come From

According to the Papago people of southern Arizona and northern Mexico, the creator of the universe invited all the people he had created to a magnificent dinner. Narama (First Man) "was among the last, and he came naked, covered with salt. . . . [He] took salt from his face and sprinkled it upon the foods. Then he reached down, and his testes turned into chile pods. He began to sprinkle their spice onto all of the foods." This offended the other guests until Narama pointed out that all of the foods on the table— fruits and vegetables, fish and fowl—were not complete without salt and chile. The guests tasted the food, and agreed that salt and chile were necessities.[119]

Chiles are nutritious and high in vitamins A, C, and riboflavin, but *capsaicin*, the active ingredient in chile peppers, stimulates pain receptors in the mouth.[120] Interestingly, the chile pepper is chemically similar to another New World plant, vanilla. Perhaps the heat in the chile is a survival adaptation to prevent it from being eaten by the wrong animals, the ones that will not help its seeds spread. For example, small mammals like rabbits destroy the seeds because their bodies digest them. The digestive tracts of birds, on the other hand, remove only the protective outer coating of the seed, which make them the perfect animals to spread seeds.[121]

North America: Cahokia

North and east of the Pima and Papago peoples, in the center of pre-Columbian North America, Cahokia, a city of huge pyramids, rose from the flat lands on the banks of the Mississippi River, just east of where St. Louis is now. More than 100 flat-topped pyramid mounds, aligned with the rising and setting sun and various constellations, spread out over six square miles. Animal images appear on bowls and shells found here, especially the water spider, which some tribes, like the Cherokee, believed brought fire to humans. Other animals represented are fish, deer, rabbits, raccoons, falcons, snakes, eagles, and frogs.[122] Cahokia reached its peak in the 1100s, when its population was about 10,000 to 20,000. In 1250, it was larger than London.[123] Human remains have been found which indicate that the Cahokians practiced human sacrifice. Little is known about the civilization at Cahokia, but historians believe that the entire city was wiped out by European diseases that spread from the Spanish in Mexico into the interior of North America. By the time Americans reached the Mississippi River in the eighteenth century, Cahokia was a ghost town long gone.

What happened to Cahokia was not different from what was about to happen to the Inca, the Aztecs, and the other indigenous peoples in North and South America; it was just first.

Columbus Sets Sail for the Americas: 1492

All of the native peoples in the Americas knew how to farm and preserve their foods efficiently, how to build roads for trade and temples for worship. They knew how to read the heavens and make calendars, how to govern vast empires. Their craftspeople knew how to make objects of great beauty out of gold and silver, and how to cook complex, sophisticated dishes.

But what the Inca, the Aztecs, the Caribes, the Papago, and all the other native peoples in the Americas didn't know was that in Europe, Spain's Queen Isabella and King Ferdinand had finally decided to bankroll Columbus's voyage.

The monarchs debated long and hard about spending so much money on a venture so risky. They didn't know then that spending more than one million *maravedis*—the equivalent of $151,780 in 1991 U.S. dollars—would yield a 200 million percent profit and make Spain a great empire.[124]

On August 2, 1492, Columbus and his crew of 90 men attended Mass at the Church of St. George in Palos, Spain. The next day they set sail in three ships, the *Niña*, the *Pinta*, and the flagship carrying Columbus, the *Santa Maria*.[125] Six days later, they arrived in the Spanish-owned Canary Islands off the northwest coast of Africa, the last stop before heading west with the wind that Columbus hoped would carry them to the East Indies—the Spice Islands.

When they set sail from the Canary Islands off the northwest coast of Africa on Thursday, September 6, 1492, Columbus's men had enough food to last them for one year.[126] They would have packed standard Spanish food that would last, mostly dried or salted: rice and dried chickpeas; beef, pork, anchovies, and sardines preserved in salt. There were surely casks of olive oil and enough wine to provide the one-and-one-half liter ration that each man expected every day. There was also that misery of the sailor's life, the aptly named hardtack—the unleavened, rock-hard flour, water, and salt biscuit that was more hospitable to parasites like weevils than to humans. The sailors would supplement this with whatever fresh fish they could catch. If any dried fruit was on board, it was for the officers, not the crew. Vegetables, except perhaps garlic and onions, were absent in this diet.[127]

There was no cook on board, so crew members took turns at midday preparing the one hot meal a day (at most) on a *fogón*, an open iron box. There was no top and no front, only a bottom filled with sand, a back, and two short, curved sides—just enough to keep the wood fire off the wooden deck.[128] Since the small ships were pitching on the waves nearly all the time, the food would have been a simple, one-pot meal like beans and rice with meat or fish. Below the deck, the hold was packed with food and water, firewood, gunpowder, rope, and other supplies, so the men worked, ate, and slept outside on deck. Rats, roaches, and lice were also standard on ships.

On September 9, when they lost sight of land behind them and there was nothing in front of them but sea and sky, the crew cried. Columbus wrote in the ship's log, "I comforted them with great promises of land and riches."[129] Columbus also led them in prayer several times a day, as Christianity required even on dry land. After other breaks in morale and false sightings of land in the coming weeks, the crew was near mutiny. Finally, land was sighted for real in what is now the eastern Bahamas on October 12, 1492. It was 33 days after they left the Canaries. Columbus named the island San Salvador—Holy Savior.[130]

"We saw naked people" [131]

Ashore, Columbus and his men prayed in thanks, claimed the land for Spain, and put up a cross. Natives came to greet them. Sure that he was in the East Indies, Columbus mistakenly called these people *Indios*—Indians.

The first thing Columbus noticed about these Indians was that they were naked, good-looking, and friendly, which he assumed would make them easy to convert to Christianity. And they had only wooden weapons, which he knew would make them easy to enslave. What he couldn't see was that they had no immunity to European diseases, not even the common cold.

The stage was set for one of the greatest holocausts in human history.

Food Goes Global

The Age of Exploration

Columbus's "discovery" began a land rush to the Americas and all over the world as Europe sent explorers sailing in all directions. It was the Age of Exploration. Within two years, Spain and Portugal were ready to fight over boundaries. The pope mediated, the way the United Nations does now. In 1494, in the Treaty of Tordesillas, the two countries agreed to an imaginary line the pope drew through the New World from north to south. Everything west of the line—Mexico and most of South America—belonged to Spain; everything east—Brazil—was Portugal's.

Columbus's arrival in the Americas and the wealth he found there built Spain into a superpower in the sixteenth century. The Spanish crown got 20 percent—the "royal fifth"—of everything that came out of its colonies in the New World. But mismanagement, overspending, and wars squandered the fortune.

The sixteenth century began with Catholic Spain's rise to power; it ended with Spain starting to decline as the power passed to northern European countries which had converted to a new Christian religion, Protestantism.

119

WHEN	NAME	COUNTRY SPONSORING/ NATIONALITY	WHERE EXPLORED
1003	Leif Eriksson	Vikings	North America
1405–1433	Zheng He	China	Africa; probably South America
1415–1460	Henry the Navigator (Dom Henrique)	Portugal	Africa, west coast
1488	Dias	Portugal	Africa, south and east coast
1492–1503	Columbus	Spain/Italian	Caribbean; South America, north shore
1497	Cabot	England/Italian	Eastern Canada
1498	da Gama	Portugal	India, west coast
1500	Cabral	Portugal	Brazil
1501	Amerigo Vespucci	Portugal/Italian	South America, east coast
1512–1513	Ponce de León	Spain	Florida
1519	Cortés	Spain	Mexico
1519–1522	Magellan	Spain/ Portuguese	First to sail around the world
1530–1533	Pizarro	Spain	Peru, western South America
1534	Cartier	France	Canada
1540–1542	Coronado	Spain	Santa Fe, New Mexico
1609–1610	Hudson	England	Hudson's Bay, Canada; Hudson River, NY

The Columbian Exchange

The collision of the eastern and western hemispheres—Old and New Worlds—and the foods, plants, animals, and diseases that went back and forth is called the Columbian Exchange. The phrase "The Columbian Exchange" was coined by food historian Alfred W. Crosby Jr. in his groundbreaking 1972 book, *The Columbian Exchange: Biological and Cultural Consequences of 1492*. He said that "two worlds [the hemispheres], which were so very different, began on that day [October 12, 1492] to become alike."[1]

During what historians call the Time of Contact, humans overrode millions of years of natural development in life forms on planet Earth by shipping them all around the globe. After only a little more than 500 years, it is too soon to tell what the long-term effects of this exchange will be.

Old World to New

Within 25 years after Columbus arrived in the Caribbean, the American empires were under full attack by Europeans. The conquistador Hernán Cortés arrived on the Caribbean shore of Mexico in 1517. He had heard stories about the fabulous wealth of the Aztecs and he wanted it: "I came to get gold, not to till the soil like a peasant."[2] He had his men burn the ships so they couldn't run away no matter how tough things got. The food that Cortés exchanged with the natives he met was passed on to Motecuhzoma (we call him Montezuma), who did not eat it but took the salt pork, dried meat, and biscuits to the temple of the god Quetzalcoatl as an offering.[3]

When Cortés and his men arrived at the Aztec capital city of Tenochtitlan, they were amazed at its beauty and grandeur; some of them thought it was a dream. It turned into a nightmare for the Aztecs when they discovered that their fierce warriors were no match for the Spaniards' guns or diseases. A smallpox epidemic ravaged the capital and assured Spanish victory. Soon the entire Aztec empire was under the control of Spain. But Montezuma lives on in a slang name for tourist diarrhea: "Montezuma's Revenge."

What happened to the Aztecs was repeated throughout Central and South America.

Plagues: Megadeath

No people native to the Americas had immunity to European diseases. Why not? And why didn't they have diseases of their own, except syphilis, to give to the Europeans? In *Guns, Germs, and Steel*, Jared Diamond advances some theories to answer these questions. One is that New World people didn't have the livestock that Europeans did, which was where a great many of the zoonoses—animal diseases that cross over to infect humans—originated. For example, the smallpox that ravaged ancient Rome came from cows. Another is that the population of the New World was scattered and not concentrated in cities where normal human interaction would have exposed people to a variety of diseases and allowed them to develop immunities.

Whatever the reason, the Time of Contact was fatal to Native Americans. In three-quarters of a century, from 1520 to 1595, there were at least 14 major epidemics of smallpox, plague, measles, typhus, and influenza from Mexico to Panama. The lowest mortality rates were more than 25 percent; the highest, 90 percent.[4]

EPIDEMICS IN CENTRAL AMERICA, 1520–1595[5]

DATE	DISEASE	LOCATION	MORTALITY
1520–1521	Smallpox	Mexico, Guatemala	more than 25%; ⅓ to ½ or more
1527	Smallpox	Panama	
1529	Smallpox(?)	Nicaragua	
1531	Bubonic or pneumonic plague	Honduras, Nicaragua	
1531–1532	Measles and/or smallpox	Mexico	60–90%
1532	Measles	Guatemala	
1533	Measles	Honduras, Nicaragua	
1545	Typhus or pneumonic plague	Guatemala	"three-quarters died"
1545	*Cocolitzli**	Mexico	80%
1558–1562	Measles and influenza	Guatemala	
1576–1577	Smallpox, measles, and typhus	Guatemala	"many children died"
1576–1581	*Cocolitzli**	Mexico	45%
1587–1588	*Cocolitzli**	Mexico	
1595	Measles	Mexico	

*A translation for *cocolitzli* remains elusive.

From descriptions of the disease at the time, *cocolitzli* seems to have been a hemorrhagic fever: blood gushing from the nose, green urine, yellow skin, black tongue. In 2006, a Mexican epidemiologist, Rodolfo Acuña-Soto, theorized that *cocolitzli* was not a European disease but was native to the Americas and was carried by rodents. It was not caused by the Columbian Exchange directly, but became a deadly epidemic because the population was so weakened by other diseases of the conquest.[6]

Ten years after the Spanish arrived in Mexico, the native population had dropped by nearly 10 million.[7] A hundred years later, 90 percent of the native population was dead, a decline from more than 25 million to about one million.

The Spanish *Conquistadores*

The conquistadores conquered the cuisines as well as the cultures of the native people. Spain immediately began to transplant its culture, especially its food-stuffs, to New Spain. Columbus returned to the Americas the following year, 1493, and brought the major Old World livestock with him: cattle, horses, pigs, goats, sheep. All, except the sheep, eventually took to the wild and reverted to their pre-domesticated state. The pigs turned into wild boars; the dogs went from protecting flocks to eating them, like the wolves they originally were; the horses found excellent grazing land and followed it across the plains—the *lla-nos*—in Venezuela, Argentina, and Uruguay, and later in North America.

FROM EUROPE, AFRICA, AND ASIA TO THE AMERICAS

ANIMALS	VEGETABLES, HERBS, SPICES	GRAINS, LEGUMES	FRUITS[†]
Cat	Beet	*Barley	Apple
*Cattle	Broccoli	*Chickpea	Banana
*Chicken	Cabbage	Lentil	Cherry
*Dog	Carrot	Oats	*Grape
Donkey	Celery	Rice	Lemon
*Goat	Cilantro	Rye	*Melons
*Horse	Cinnamon	*Sugar Cane	Orange
*Pig	Coffee—1723, by the French	*Wheat	Peach
Rat, Black	Cucumber		Pear
*Sheep	Eggplant		Plum
	Garlic		Pomegranate
	Ginger		Quince
	Lavender		Watermelon
	Lettuce		
	Mustard		
	Nutmeg		
	Olive		
	*Onion		
	Parsley		
	Pepper—black		
	*Radish		
	Sage		
	*Salad Greens		
	Sesame		
	Soy		
	Turnip		
	Yam		

* Brought to America in 1493 on Columbus's second voyage
† Columbus brought "fruit stones for the founding of orchards," specifics not known[8]

As Alfred Crosby points out, "By 1600 all the most important food plants of the Old World were being cultivated in the Americas."[9] However, the vegetable foods were not readily accepted by the native people. The new animals and the products they yielded were another matter and changed native cuisines profoundly. They also changed the landscape, in some cases causing ecological disasters. Livestock reproduced at phenomenal rates. In three years, 13 pigs produced 700.[10] Cattle grazed on land where natives had grown food plants. In some cases, Indians domesticated livestock themselves.

Stowaways

Some of the plant and animal life that arrived in the western hemisphere from the Old World came as stowaways. Seeds for weeds might get mixed in with grains, dung, or animal feed. Old World dandelions and daisies arrived this way. So did tumbleweed, Kentucky bluegrass, and the black rat that carries plague and typhus. A rat-caused famine occurred in Bermuda. With no natural enemies, the rats burrowed into the earth, took up residence in trees, and ate so much food that the people starved to death. Diseases were stowaways, too, brought by accident.

Mexico: *Mole* and *Carne*

After hundreds of years of European influence, modern Mexican cuisine is very different from pre-Columbian native cuisines. One of the most important changes was that the diet of South American natives went from heavily vegetarian and very low fat to heavily meat-based and high fat. The staple three sisters of corn, beans, and squash were replaced by *carnitas*—dried shredded pork—and *queso*—cheese. *Chili*—beans in a tomato sauce—became *chili con carne*—chili with meat. Mild chile peppers like Anaheims were stuffed with cheese to make *chile rellenos*. Tortillas now came in wheat as well as corn.

Contact with the Spanish changed chocolate, too. Today, Mexican chocolate is a combination of chocolate and two ingredients from Asia, *canela*—cinnamon—and granulated sugar. Chocolate *caliente*—hot—is still frothed by hand with a *molinillo* rolled quickly back and forth between the palms of the hands, as if you were trying to start a fire, just as the Aztecs did. But chocolate historians believe that one chocolate dish considered typically Mexican might not be.

FOOD FABLE:

Mole Myths[11]

As chocolate historians Sophie and Michael Coe point out, there are many myths surrounding the beginnings of *mole* [MO-lay], but it is definitely *not* of Aztec origin. The Aztecs never combined chocolate with food. It was consumed only as a beverage, often ritually after a meal, when they also used tobacco. The Italians, however, experimented wildly with chocolate, beginning in the 1680s. They put it in pasta, in pasta sauce, in polenta, in breading for liver. They fried eggs in cacao butter. Since these recipes predate the earliest recipes for *mole*, the Coes think that perhaps the Italians invented *mole*. Late-seventeenth-century Hispanic stories give different, vague versions of the debut of *mole*: it was created by accident when chocolate fell into a stew—or it was created on purpose. It was made to honor a bishop—no, a Spanish official. The only agreement is that the word *mole* comes from *molli*, the Aztec word for sauce or concoction.

Whatever its origins, *mole poblano* is still the signature dish of Puebla. But many more kinds of *mole* come from Oaxaca [wa-HA-ca]. There are spicy *moles*; red, yellow, and green *moles*; sweet and sour *moles*. American Rick Bayless adds red wine to his *mole*.[12] Recently, a restaurant opened in Oaxaca that serves what could be called *mole nuevo*, lighter because it is made with vegetable or canola oil instead of lard. Traditionalists resisted it.[13]

....

INGREDIENTS:
Pavo in *Mole Poblano*
(TURKEY IN SAUCE)

One of the earliest recipes for *pavo* (turkey) in *mole* comes from the state of Puebla, southeast of Mexico City. It was an Old World–New World fusion food. The main ingredients—turkey, tomatoes, and chocolate—were New World. So were the three different kinds of chile peppers—mulato, ancho, and pasilla. But it was seasoned with Old World herbs and spices—black pepper, cinnamon, sesame, cloves, and anise. Sweetness was provided by Old World raisins and sugar, and Old World garlic made it pungent. And even though it contains a New World legume, peanuts, their use as a thickener is a technique that goes back to the ground almond thickeners Europeans learned from the Arabs in the Middle Ages.

....

Other Mexican uses of Old World animals include *pozole*—pork and hominy stew; oxtail stew, and tripe stew. There are also many Mexican cheeses made from cow's milk, like *queso fresco*, *panela*, and *ranchero seco*, a dried cheese, as its name says.[14] Desserts, too, were made from Old World foods. Eggs and sugar make *flan*, Spanish custard. Wheat treats include *churros* made of dough like *pâte à choux*, extruded through a machine or a pastry bag into their distinctive long rope shape, then deep fried and rolled in cinnamon sugar.

New Mexico: The Pueblo Revolt
In what is now the Four Corners area of the United States, where Utah, Colorado, Arizona, and New Mexico come together, native people lived in villages like apartment buildings—in Spanish, *pueblo*. Around the year 1100, about 1,200 people lived in one of these pueblos, the five-story, 800-room Pueblo Bonito (Beautiful Town) in what is today northwestern New Mexico. It was the

largest apartment building in the world until 1882, when a bigger one was built in New York City. Descendants of the people spread throughout the American Southwest and built pueblos on *mesas*, flat-topped mountains, many along the upper Rio Grande River. Among them were the Zuni and the Hopi—"the Peaceful People."

Pueblo men irrigated the fields and farmed; the women ground corn and cooked in the large, flat common area, the plaza; the adult males retreated to an underground *kiva* for religious and tribal matters. In 1540, a Spanish soldier reported that the people in a typical pueblo were "usually at work." And efficient workers they were, with very clean buildings for grinding corn and preparing food. Three women would prepare corn at one time, each with a *mano* and a *metate*, like an assembly line: "One of them breaks the corn, the next grinds it, and the third grinds it again. . . . A man sits at the door playing on a flute while they grind. They move the stones to the music and sing together."[15] They also ground ripe pods from mesquite trees into meal, added water, and made sun-dried crackers.

But the Spaniards were looking for gold, and the pueblo people had none and also were not Christian. The Spanish soldiers ignored the line of sacred corn meal the people laid out on the ground as their boundary; took whatever they wanted from them; looked for gold and got angry when they found only beans, squash, tortillas, and turkeys, but took them anyway; told the people that if they surrendered they would not be harmed, then butchered thousands of them when they did. Acoma Pueblo was burned to the ground. Everyone in the pueblo— male and female—over the age of 12 was sentenced to 20 years of slavery; all men over 25 also had one foot chopped off. Enslaved and unable to run away, the Indians took care of the cattle, sheep, horses, goats, and pigs, and tended the olive groves and the orchards of peach, pear, fig, date, pomegranate, cherry, quince, lemon, apricot, and orange trees.

In 1610, the Spanish forced the Indians to build the city of Santa Fe (Holy Faith). The pueblo people were willing to accept Christianity, but only along with their own religions, so the Spanish hanged them and then raided the sacred *kivas* and destroyed all the religious items, including the *kachinas*, the masked images of the holy spirits that the native people believed brought rain and taught hunting and farming to humans.

This brutal forced conversion did not last long. Then came drought and tribes of raiders called *apachu nabahu*—"enemies of the cultivated fields"—which sounded like "Apache" and "Navaho" to the Spanish. The raiders stole all the stored food and ran off with the livestock. The Spanish and the Indians tried to survive on boiled or roasted leather and hides. Starvation was widespread, then disease.

The pueblo people believed these disasters had been sent because they had turned their backs on their native religion and stopped worshipping the *kachinas*. They also saw that the Spanish and their god were powerless. Finally, in a masterpiece of planning, on August 10, 1680, all the pueblos throughout New

Mexico revolted at once. They got rid of anything connected with the Spanish, including the food. They killed the priests, demolished the churches, slaughtered the sheep and cattle and pigs, uprooted the orchards, ripped out the grapevines, and turned the horses loose. The horses headed for the Great Plains, where the Kiowa and Comanche, the Sioux and the Cheyenne, from Texas north to the Dakotas, learned to ride them. The Spaniards were forced out of New Mexico entirely, south to El Paso (now Texas). It was a great victory for the native people—temporarily. Fifteen years later, the Spanish returned to stay.

Peru: Lima Beans and New World Wine

Francisco Pizarro was the conquistador who came to Peru in 1532. The nightmare that had occurred with the Aztecs repeated itself for the Inca—the capture and death of the leader, Atahualpa; the demands for gold. The Inca, too, died in horrifying numbers from European diseases. The Inca regrouped and attacked Pizarro. In 1525, he founded the city of Lima, now the capital, so he could defend himself against Inca warriors. The city eventually gave its name to one of the members of the bean family native to South America.

Between 1540 and 1550, Spain transplanted foodstuffs to Peru: wine grapes, figs, pomegranates, quinces, wheat, barley, citrus. This explosion of Spanish food was subsidized by the crown, which offered a huge prize—two bars of silver—to the first person in each town who produced Spanish foods like wine, olive oil, wheat, or barley on a large scale in Peru. There was wealth to be made in cultivating the new foods, but getting them to survive and thrive in the New World wasn't always easy. Of the more than 100 olive-tree cuttings that one man imported to Peru, only three survived. These were so valuable that he planted them on a walled farm in a valley and had them guarded by "more than 100 blacks and 30 dogs," which were either bribed or distracted, because one of the plants was stolen and showed up far away in Chile where it produced numerous trees. Three years later, somebody sneaked back to the farm and replanted the original tree exactly where he had stolen it.[16]

From the early 1520s to the late 1550s, vineyards of European grapes were established in Central and South America, on both sides of the Andes. Wild grapes grew in the Americas, but they were unsuitable for wine. How did viticulture spread so quickly? It was the law. Under the *encomienda* system, Spanish settlers in New Spain were given land and Indians to work it, and were required to plant 1,000 vines "of the best quality" for every 100 Indians they owned. Grapevines didn't thrive in Mexico because of the climate, but they did in Peru, especially in the south in the Moquegua Valley.

There was a ready-made market for wine in Peru, too, because the vineyards were near the silver mines at Potosí and all their enslaved Indian workers. Peruvian wine makers were so successful after they began producing wine in 1551 that Spanish wine makers protested; in 1595 Spain's King Philip II protected Spanish vintners by restricting grapevine planting in the colonies. Peru had a thriving wine industry until it was heavily damaged in the late nineteenth century by an epidemic of *phylloxera*, a yellow louse almost impossible to see with the naked eye, that eats the roots of *vinifera* grapevines.[17]

Peruvians took to the coconut quickly. The word *coco* is Spanish for "monkey," because they are both round, have brown fur, and eyes. Coconut milk is used frequently, replacing water, chicken or beef broth or stock, or tomato sauce or juice in many recipes. In 1991, food historian Raymond Sokolov wrote: "Peru's traditional dishes . . . comprise the last great cuisine undiscovered by a world gone mad for new tastes." However, he conceded that "Roast or stewed guinea pig has no future in the non-Andean world." And probably neither does roasted llama heart on a stick.[18]

Argentina: Cattle Cuisine, Cowboy Culture

European horses running wild on the *pampas*—the prairies—of Argentina reproduced to the point that it took a day for a herd to pass by. Horses preceded humans into the flat plains of the area around what is now the capital, Buenos Aires, because settlers in 1580 found huge wild herds already there.

The Spanish brought their cattle, the ancestors of the Texas longhorns, and those thrived, too. Herds doubled nearly every 15 months.[19] Soon, beef was plentiful and cheap. As Crosby says, "there were probably more cattle in the New World in the seventeenth century than any other type of vertebrate immigrant."[20] Beef provided food for the enslaved Indians working in the mines. But a more important use was for fat—tallow—to make candles, especially to light the mines. Hides, too, were more important uses of cattle than food. They were tanned and turned into armor and containers of all kinds, from trunks to drinking cups.

A beef cuisine grew in Argentina, especially using a technique learned from Caribbean natives—the barbecue. Argentine barbecue is basted with brine. Barbecue sauce is the vinegar-based *chimichurri*.[21] Modern Argentine marinades and salsas are often based on reductions of Argentine wines.[22]

CULINARY CONFUSION:

Barbecue

What Americans refer to as barbecuing usually means grilling, and is done quickly and aboveground. True barbecue is pit roasting. This involves digging a pit or providing some kind of enclosure, and takes hours so the meat can attain a smooth texture and smoky taste. See "Recipe: Los Angeles County Annual Barbecue," in Chapter 11.

Another classic Argentine dish is empanadas, roughly translated as "stuffed turnovers." They, too, would not have been possible without Old World foods.

The dough is made from wheat and lard; the filling usually contains meat. In Argentina, the meat can be mixed with New World potatoes, or sometimes fruit, like Old World peaches.[23]

Along with the cattle and beef cuisine, the Spanish transplanted their cowboy culture. Americans didn't create the cowboy—Spain did, in the Middle Ages. He was a *vaquero*, from *vaca*, the Spanish word for "cow," and he knew how to use a horse to wrangle a herd, how to handle a branding iron, and what to do on a roundup. In Argentina and Uruguay, the *vaquero* is called a *gaucho*. He brought his Spanish cowboy vocabulary with him: mustang, bronco, lasso, rodeo.[24]

Brazil: *Feijoada* and *Farofa*

Brazilian food is heavily influenced by Portugal, its colonial master, and Africa, where a large part of its population originated. Approximately 38 percent of the 10 million slaves shipped from Africa to the New World went to Brazil, mostly to work in the sugar cane fields.[25] Brazil's most famous dish gets its name from the Portuguese word for "bean"—*feijão* [feh-ZHWAH]. It is an elaborate version of *moros y cristianos*—"Moors and Christians"—which was black beans and white rice. *Feijoada* is a fusion of Old and New World foods and shows the influences of slave cooking in the use of pig parts and in the green leafy vegetable accompaniment. The beans and their liquid provide the sauce. The traditional accompaniments include orange slices and a hot sauce with lime juice.

....

INGREDIENTS:

Feijoada[26]

4 pig's ears	1 pound *linguiça* sausage
1 pig's tail	1 pound fresh pork sausages
Salt	2 tablespoons lard or vegetable oil
3 pig's feet, split	2 onions, finely chopped
1-pound piece of *carne sêca*	2 cloves garlic, minced
3-pound smoked beef tongue	2 tomatoes, peeled, seeded, and chopped
½-pound piece of lean bacon	1 fresh hot pepper, seeded and minced, or
4 cups black beans	⅛ teaspoon Tabasco (optional)
1-pound piece of lean beef chuck or bottom round	Salt, freshly ground pepper

....

The province of Bahia ("the Bay") in eastern Brazil has a very long Atlantic coastline, and much shrimp in its cuisine: dried shrimp, shrimp in sauce, fresh shrimp garnish. Sometimes dried ground shrimp, with their intense flavor, are used as a sauce base for a fresh shrimp dish. The signature fat is *dendê*—palm oil—an African import. One of the most famous dishes from Bahia, *vatapá*—chicken in shrimp and almond sauce—combines these ingredients and adds many more from the Old World, including coconut milk; rice flour is the thickener. In *vatapá* and another Bahian dish, *xinxim de galinha*—chicken with shrimp and peanut sauce—the *dendê* oil is added at the end, like a butter enrichment. Hearts of palm are eaten fresh in Brazil, but are brined and canned to be sold commercially. In the United States, they are usually used in salads.

Cassava, a root, was a staple starch in pre-Columbian Brazil. It is the only edible member of the *Euphorbiaceae* family, which includes plants called succulents. Cassava has many other names: manioc and yuca in Central and South America; fu-fu, a type of porridge, in Africa; *farinha* (flour) in Portugal. But most Americans know it as tapioca, which we make into a sweet pudding, often for children and invalids. In the twenty-first century, tapioca, transplanted to Asia, returned to the United States as boba, in beverages that required large-diameter straws to accommodate the tapioca pearls. In Brazil, cassava meal is *farofa*, grains the color of sand and the consistency of coarse talcum powder. It is toasted in *dendê* and sprinkled on top of food as a garnish.

A fruit native to northeast Brazil is the cashew *(Anacardim occidentale)*, one of the edible members of the poison ivy family; the others are pistachios and mangoes. The cashew fruit grows on trees. It is approximately the shape of a Hachiya persimmon, but yellow, with the comma-shaped cashew nut hanging from the bottom. The fruit can be sweetened and preserved or processed and used for juice. Cashew nuts never appear in their shell in a bowl of mixed nuts, like almonds, walnuts, and pecans, because they are doubly protected with a corrosive substance sandwiched between two layers of shell. Human nutcrackers can't get the shell off, but the big beaks of parrots can. So can roasting.[27] The Portuguese were responsible for spreading the cashew from Brazil to their colonies in the East Indies. It also thrives now in India.

Plantains—*plâtanos*—are also found throughout the southern hemisphere and the Caribbean. They are in the banana family, but unlike bananas, they have to be cooked to be eaten. They are usually boiled or fried or both, and served as a sweet, starchy side dish.

One foodstuff that Europeans invented in the Caribbean and that Brazilians took to right away is rum. Brazilians are magicians with alcoholic beverages. Brazilian rum, called *cachaça* [ca-CHA-sah], is used to make a cocktail called a *batida* [ba-CHEE-dah]. It is mixed with lime juice and sugar, or coconut milk, or passion fruit, pineapple, etc.[28] The history of rum begins with the history of sugar, an Old World food that grew extremely well in the New World.

The Caribbean: Sugar

For the most part, European settlers were more interested in seeing if Old World foods with already established markets could be produced more cheaply and in greater quantities in the New World. One food in particular fit the bill. It quickly rose to dominate the international market, created huge fortunes on both sides of the Atlantic, caused millions of people to be enslaved, created new professions, and changed the eating habits of *Homo sapiens* completely. It was sugar, *Saccharum officinarum*.

The introduction of chocolate, coffee, and tea into Europe caused a rise in the demand for sugar, while the availability of sugar increased the demand for chocolate, coffee, and tea. A sugar spiral developed: as sugar became more available, its price dropped; as its price dropped, it became more available to more people. What had been a medicine for the rich in the Middle Ages was a staple for even the poor by the middle of the eighteenth century.

SUGAR CHRONOLOGY[29]

8,000 B.C.	Sugar begins as a grass in New Guinea
1st century A.D.	Indians learn how to crush sugar cane and extract white crystals
8th century	Arabs learn sugar production from India; spread it throughout empire
13th century	Antwerp, Belgium, is European sugar-refining center
1319	First recorded direct shipment of sugar arrives in England
1493	Columbus introduces sugar cane on his second trip to the Caribbean
1493–1625	Spain dominates the Caribbean and sugar production
1500	Portuguese island of Madeira is world's largest producer of sugar[30]
1544	England begins refining sugar, taking over industry from Low Countries, especially Antwerp, Belgium
1585	London is the center of European sugar refining
1588	England defeats Spanish Armada; England colonizes in the Americas
1619	First Africans arrive in Jamestown, Virginia; attempts to grow sugar fail
1625	Europe gets most of its sugar from Portugal (Brazil); first British settlement in Caribbean at St. Kitts
1650	Lemonade invented in Paris because of drop in sugar price[31]
1650–1850	England, France, Denmark, Netherlands in Caribbean sugar production
1655	British invade Jamaica
1660	British sugar imports exceed all other colonial produce *combined*
1701–1810	252,000 African slaves to Barbados; 662,400 African slaves to Jamaica
1733	British Parliament passes Molasses Act to prevent North American colonies from trading with French West Indies

(continues)

1750	In England, sugar is common even among the poor
1764	British Parliament passes Sugar Act to raise revenue to keep troops in North American colonies after French and Indian War
1791	Successful slave revolt on Haiti (St. Domingue) halts sugar production
1813	First sugar beet refinery, in Passy, France, after Napoleon orders its cultivation to make France self-sufficient
1838	England ends slavery
1848	France ends slavery
1876	Slavery ends in Puerto Rico
1884	Slavery ends in Cuba

Sugar growing, harvesting, and processing were extremely labor-intensive, and the labor was slaves from Africa.

The Caribbean: Slavery—The Notorious Middle Passage

The stench that came from the ship was overwhelming: human excrement, urine, vomit, blood, sweat, and misery. Just as early explorers could smell the blooming flowers of America 100 miles out to sea, later sailors could smell a slave ship 100 miles away. This was the notorious Middle Passage, the middle part of the Triangle Trade, the trip from West Africa to the western hemisphere. No one wanted to be downwind of a slave ship.

The Caribbean was one of the points on what historians call the Triangle Trade: sugar and rum from the Caribbean to Europe, goods from Europe to Africa, slaves from Africa to the Caribbean. Portugal had its own Triangle Trade which sold "third-grade tobacco soaked in molasses" for slaves in Africa, shipped them to Brazil, then brought the good tobacco to the European markets.[32] In the American Triangle Trade, molasses was shipped from the Caribbean to New England, where it was processed into rum, then the rum was traded for slaves in Africa, the slaves were sold in the Caribbean, molasses was shipped to New England, and the process was repeated. On all of these trade routes, the Middle Passage was the same horror.

Why slavery? Why not some other form of labor? Native Americans weren't suitable because they died—in some cases became extinct—from European diseases. West coast Africans were kidnapped by slave traders or African tribal enemies who

The European view of Africa, 1650. *Courtesy Corbis Digital Stock.*

had guns and nets. One of the first fears of those captured was that they were going to be eaten by the strange creatures that had captured them, "those white men with horrible looks, red faces, and long hair."[33] Sometimes the captives were forced to drink alcohol, which further added to the bizarreness of the experience. Then they were chained two-by-two and forced to get on the ship.

The hold, the part of the ship below the deck, was five or six feet high at the most. The male slaves were laid on the floor, with another layer on a shelf above them. If the hold was six feet deep, there were two rows of shelves. Each adult

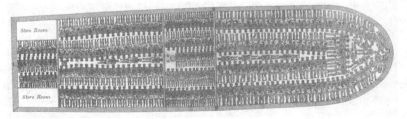

Slaves packed on a ship. *Courtesy National Archives and Research.*

male slave was allowed a space that was *maximum* six feet long and 16 inches wide. If a man were taller than six feet, he would have to spend the entire voyage with his knees bent; if his shoulders were wider than 16 inches, he would have to spend the voyage lying on his side. Sitting upright was impossible because of the shelf above him. Slaves were sick with vomiting and a violent diarrhea known as the "bloody flux." If they were on the top shelf, it dripped down on those below.

Women were not chained so that the sailors could have unlimited access to them. Rape was a standard event for African women on slave ships. But allowing the women to roam freely on the ship backfired. They knew who was drunk on duty and who was passed out; they could find out where the keys to the locked doors and the chains were kept, and sometimes they got them. Women became very important in slave ship revolts.

The most famous revolt was on the *Amistad* in 1839, made into a film by director Steven Spielberg in 1997. For many years, historians assumed that the revolt on the *Amistad* was a rare event, but after the 1960s, when historians were not just white men, but African-Americans, women, and other minorities, their research revealed that mutinies on slave ships were not rare, but common. After all, the slaves had nothing to lose. Unfortunately, the slave revolt on the *Amistad* was rare in its success.

An additional ordeal for the captives on the slave ships was the cheap-as-possible food. They despised the horse beans in slimy sauce they got and threw it around. Sometimes they were fed their native foods like yams, rice, and palm oil. Some tried to commit suicide by refusing to eat. But slaves that weren't eating were valuable cargo in danger of being lost. If whipping or beating didn't get them to eat, forcing their jaws open with a metal device that worked like a car jack usually did. On the other hand, if the voyage took longer than expected and supplies of food or water were running low, slaves were thrown overboard. Ship owners didn't care if part of the cargo was lost this way; it was a business expense and they were insured. The slave trade was very lucrative, producing profits of more than 100 percent.

The nightmare didn't end when the ship arrived in port. There, the slaves were sold at auctions like farm animals and sent to work on the sugar plantations. The tall sugar cane stalks were chopped down with machetes, leaving a razor-sharp stump. It was like working in a field of bayonets. In the tropical climate, before antibiotics, any cut could lead to a life-threatening infection.

Boiling the sugar down to crystallize it was particularly brutal work. Slaves worked in shifts that could last all day and all night; they got Sunday off. They had to stand barefoot on stone floors for the entire shift, which was painful. Tired slaves lost fingers as they fed the cane through the rollers on the grinding machines; "a hatchet was kept in readiness to sever the arm."[34] The majority of the slaves taken from Africa and transported to the Americas—40 percent— went to the Caribbean sugar islands.[35] Life was so harsh the slaves often died within four years, so a new supply was constantly needed. It was cheaper to buy new slaves than to take care of the ones you had. They were disposable.

Slaves on the plantations were fed as cheaply as possible. Their food had to be imported because sugar was grown on all available land. The mainstay of the slave diet was salted beef until the British settled North America; then low-grade salted, dried cod was used. In the eighteenth century, England decided that breadfruit from Tahiti would be a cheap food for its slaves on Jamaica. A relative of mulberry and jackfruit, the melon-sized starchy breadfruit grows on trees and, to some, tastes like Yorkshire pudding or mashed potatoes.

However, the crew of the ship carrying the breadfruit, the *Bounty*, mutinied after Captain Bligh withheld their grog ration, accused them of pilfering from his personal coconut stash, and cut their food rations in half. Set adrift in a small boat, Bligh eventually reached land, was given another ship, and got the bread-fruit to Jamaica, only to discover that the slaves didn't like it. However, it grew well there and still does. It is valued in some countries as feed for livestock, in Trinidad as human food, and in Hawaii as a substitute for taro in poi.[36]

The Caribbean: Rum

One of the by-products of sugar processing resulted in a new alcoholic beverage. The sixteenth century was the beginning of what historian David T. Court-wright calls "the psychoactive revolution." This is the intercontinental traffic in drugs, including sugar and caffeine, that characterizes the modern world. Rum first appeared in the 1640s in the Caribbean. Since sugar production was no longer under the control of Muslims, who forbade alcohol, nothing stood in the way of creating a new type of alcohol from sugar or its by-products. In the hands of the Protestant British, sugar became rum.

There are two different ways of making rum. One, agricultural rum, is made from the fresh-pressed juice of the sugar cane stalk. The other is made from molasses. In both cases, yeast is added to the liquid and allowed to ferment, usually for 24 to 48 hours. It is then distilled and aged in oak barrels that formerly held whiskey or bour-bon. Most rums are blended after they have aged, but some are blended first, then aged together. It is the aging process in the oak that produces rum's rich brown color. A rum must age for at least three years to be called *vieux* (old).

Rum was first distilled on the island of Barbados, where the Mount Gay label has been in existence for more than 300 years. The tiny British colony produced more wealth for England than its tobacco-growing colonies of Virginia and Maryland put together. The River Antoine distillery on Grenada, which makes Rivers Rum, still doesn't use electricity. Water powers the wheel that crushes the cane; *bagasse*, the solid crushed cane left after the juice is extracted, is burned to fuel the still. Today, Demerara, a county in Guyana, is the "largest supplier of bulk rum from the Caribbean."[37]

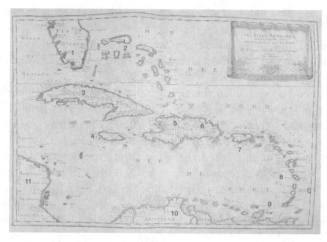

French † British * Spanish

1. * Florida	4. † Jamaica	7. *Puerto Rico	10. *Colombia
2. † Bahamas	5. #Haiti	8. Lesser Antilles (various)	11. *Yucatan
3. * Cuba	6. *Santo Domingo	9. †Trinidad and Tobago	

The Caribbean in 1656, after English and French attacks. Spain is left with only Cuba, Puerto Rico, and Santo Domingo.

Courtesy Corbis Digital Stock.

New World to Old

Spanish, Portuguese, and British transplants of foods, animals, and people had an immediate impact on their colonies in the New World. Using the western hemisphere as a giant plantation for the eastern hemisphere made familiar Old World foods more available to people in the Old World. So there was little incentive for Europeans, especially, to experiment with New World foods.

". . . [I]t being new, I was doubtful whether it might not do me hurt."[38]

So wrote British writer Samuel Pepys in his diary on March 9, 1669. He was talking about a new beverage made from an Asian fruit that had just reached Europe. He thought it "a very fine drink," but still, he was worried about that glass of orange juice. In the years after Columbus's voyages, every country in the world was bombarded with new foodstuffs and new cuisines. But cross-cultural change is difficult; convincing people to eat strange foods from other parts of the world is not always easy. People in Europe hadn't been sitting around for centuries wishing they had a tomato or hoping a pumpkin would appear. It took about 300 years for most of the New World foods to be accepted in Europe. Some, such as maize, still aren't fully accepted as human food, although they are all right for animals.

Sometimes strange new things can only be described by connecting them to familiar old ones. So Columbus's son described cocoa beans as special "almonds"; the explorer Coronado wrote about strange "cows" with horns, which were buffalo; the potato became "earth apple"—in French, *pomme de terre*. In Italy, the tomato became "golden apple"—*pomodoro*—because some of the early tomatoes, which are heirlooms now, were yellow, and because golden apples were familiar from Greek mythology.

Turkey, Tobacco, Beans

Three New World items that did find immediate acceptance throughout the Old World were turkey, tobacco, and beans. Europe, used to eating fowl and accustomed to chicken as a special occasion centerpiece, was ready for a big, new, festive, good-tasting bird. Soon, turkey replaced heron, swan, peacock, and other birds that were nearly inedible but made magnificent presentations.

Tobacco grown in the Chesapeake, the area around the bay in what is now Maryland and Virginia, caught on everywhere it went. Within a hundred years of Columbus's first voyage, tobacco could be found even in the far reaches of Siberia.[39]

Beans were also readily accepted, perhaps because they resembled pulses like chickpeas and lentils. By the middle of the sixteenth century, they appeared in botanical books, and the kidney bean was known throughout Europe as the French bean.

FROM THE AMERICAS TO EUROPE, AFRICA, AND ASIA

ANIMALS	VEGETABLES, SPICES, ETC.	GRAINS, LEGUMES, DRUGS, NUTS	FRUITS
Turkey	Allspice	Beans—Kidney, Lima, Navy	Avocado
Muscovy Duck	Amaranth	Cashew	Blueberry
	Artichoke, Jerusalem	Corn (maize)	Cacao
	Beans—green	Manioc (cassava, tapioca)	Cherimoya
	Jicama	Peanut	Concord Grape
	Peppers—bell	Quinine (anti-malaria drug)	Cranberry
	Peppers—hot	Quinoa	Papaya
	Potatoes—sweet	Tobacco	Pineapple
	Potatoes—white	Wild Rice (a grain, not rice)	Strawberry
	Squash, including pumpkin		Tomato
	Sunflower		
	Vanilla		

Hunger was often the factor that determined whether new foods were accepted. The Chinese, with their huge population that needed to be fed, were quick to accept New World foods, especially peanuts, maize, and sweet potatoes.[40]

In the two-and-a-half centuries after Columbus arrived in the New World, the populations of Africa and Latin America dropped because of the slave trade and disease, respectively. However, foods from the Columbian Exchange caused a huge jump in the populations of Asia, Europe, and Oceania.

WORLD POPULATION IN MILLIONS[41]

	1650	1750	1800	1850	1900	1950	2008[42]
Africa	100	95	90	95	120	198	967
Asia	327	475	597	741	925	1,320	4,052
Europe	103	144	192	274	423	593	736
Latin America	12	11	19	33	63	162	559
North America	1	2	6	26	81	168	329
Oceania	2	2	2	2	6	13	35
Total	545	728	906	1,171	1,608	2,454	6,678

In 2010, China and India both had populations of more than one billion. China's population has been large since antiquity, but the population explosion in India is recent. It dates back to around 1850, when the British arrived, bringing foods from the Americas with them.[43]

Spain: Chocolate and Paella

Although India and other countries did not participate in the Columbian Exchange until hundreds of years after the discovery of the Americas, Spain accepted some of the new foods right away.

Chocolate probably would have caught on sooner in Europe, but the Spanish nobility considered it a powerful aphrodisiac—the Viagra of the sixteenth century—and kept the recipe secret by locking it up in a monastery for almost a century. But something so good couldn't be kept under wraps for long; others eventually got or figured out the recipe and a craze was born. Chocolate was used in different ways in different European countries. Like the Aztecs, the Spanish consumed chocolate as a beverage, but sweetened with sugar. The French confined it to dessert.

The Spanish immediately developed a liking for the wild chile—the *chiltepin* or bird pepper *(Capsicum annuum* var. *aviculare)*—which became known throughout Europe as the "Spanish pepper." It was so highly regarded that they kept it whole in salt cellars on the table. Then each diner took out as much as he wanted and crumbled it into his food.

The traditional dish of Spain is *paella Valenciana*, and it is a mixture of Old and New World foods. *Paella* refers to the pan in which it is cooked; *Valenciana* is the region of Spain where it originated. The classic ingredients are Old World rice, several kinds of meat, olive oil, and saffron, and New World green beans, tomato, and paprika.

Don Quixote: The Peasant Quest for Meat

The upper classes ate chocolate and chiles and meat. The poor were still hungry. This difference in social classes, often shown through food, underlies everything in *Don Quixote* [kee-HO-tay], one of Spain's most famous literary works, written in 1602 by Miguel de Cervantes. This satirical novel, which was the basis for the Broadway musical and movie *The Man of La Mancha*, is about Don Quixote, a man who still believes in knighthood and sets out on his horse to slay dragons—except that they are windmills—and rescue the fair lady—who is really a woman of low repute. He has a trusty sidekick, Sancho Panza. These two—the noble-hearted cowboy and his pudgy, comic-relief sidekick, who, like the court jester, is more philosopher than fool—set the standard for cowboy stories and movies for centuries to come. They are also two halves of the human condition. Quixote is spiritual, a dreamer. Sancho Panza—which means "holy belly"—is the realist who lives in the physical world. From Don Quixote, we get the adjective quixotic [kwik-ZAH-tic]—extremely idealistic, romantic, and impractical.

Don Quixote made a Spanish food famous. The vegetable and meat stew *olla podrida*—literally, "rotten pot"—appears six times. It is mentioned in the second sentence of the book, to show how poor Quixote is and how expensive food is: "An olla of rather more beef than mutton, a salad on most nights, scraps on Saturdays, lentils on Fridays, and a pigeon or so extra on Sundays, made away with three-quarters of his income."[44] This is a difficult life for a man who knows that "veal . . . is better than beef . . . kid . . . is better than goat."[45]

Most of the time Quixote and Sancho have only bread and water to eat. If they are lucky they might get a bit of cheese, an onion, grapes, acorns, or medlars—fruit originally from Persia that even ripe is inedible until it is packed in wet bran or sawdust and ferments internally.[46] A sample of the food at inns explains why upper-class people traveled with their own chefs and cooking staffs. One innkeeper tells Sancho, "all I have is a couple of cow-heels like calves' feet, or a couple of calves' feet like cow-heels; they are boiled with chick-peas, onions, and bacon."[47] At another, on a Friday, Quixote gets stockfish and "a piece of bread as black and mouldy as his own armour."[48] At a low point, Don Quixote says, "I have a mind to let myself die of hunger, the cruelest death of all deaths." But Sancho loves food and life and says, "I'll stretch out my life by eating."[49]

From the point of view of these starving people, upper-class eating habits and the theory of humors are ridiculous. A starving Sancho sits down to a feast only to have each dish yanked away from him by a Hippocrates-quoting physician: "I ordered that plate of fruit to be removed as being too moist, and that other dish

I ordered to be removed as being too hot and containing many spices that stimu-late thirst. . . . Do not eat of those stewed rabbits there, because it is a furry kind of food; if that veal were not roasted and served with pickles, you might try it; but it is out of the question." Sancho points out the obvious—"to deny me food is the way to take my life instead of prolonging it"—and asks for some *olla podrida*, "and the rottener they are the better they smell." When the physician says it is not nourishing, fit only for students and peasants, and that a gentlemen should eat "a hundred or so of wafer cakes and a few thin slices of conserve of quinces," Sancho threatens to kill him.[50]

When Sancho finally gets a major meal to feed his *panza*, it is a starving peas-ant's food fantasy. The wedding of the wealthy Camacho is a utopian exaggera-tion, the Spanish equivalent of the Italian Bengodi, where the vines drip sausages. The first thing Sancho sees is

> . . . a whole ox spitted on a whole elm tree [stuffed with a dozen suckling-pigs] . . . and six stewpots . . . [which] swallowed up whole sheep. . . . Countless . . . hares ready skinned and the plucked fowls; . . . numberless the wildfowl and game of various sorts suspended from the branches that the air might keep them cool. Sancho counted more than sixty wine skins of over six gallons each. . . . There were . . . piles of the whitest bread . . . a wall made of cheeses . . . two cauldrons full of oil . . . for cooking fritters, which when fried were taken out with two mighty shovels, and plunged into another cauldron of prepared honey that stood close by. Of cooks and cook-maids there were over fifty . . .

There are trunks full of spices, too. When Sancho begs to dunk a bit of bread into one of the pots, a cook gladly skims three hens and two geese off the top, to hold him until dinner time.[51] Sancho is able to eat so well here because Camacho is not a member of the upper class with all of its food rules; he is a farmer who has made good and who appreciates food. It is clear that what the peasants want is meat, and the order of food is clear, too, with chickens and geese still the most expensive and desirable. New World foods are entirely absent.

Spain's phenomenal new wealth inspired other European countries to send explorers out, especially its western neighbor, Portugal. Portuguese sweet bread, *pão doce*, went around the world, too. Along the way, it became Hawaiian sweet bread, and ended up in North America in New England.

INGREDIENTS:

Portuguese/Hawaiian Sweet Bread (Pão Doce)

1 pint milk, scalded	1½ tablespoons salt
2 packages yeast, or 2 yeast cakes	4 eggs
¼ cup warm water	1½ cups sugar
8–9 cups flour	⅛ pound melted butter

Italy: The Renaissance

"At no time in European history did spices play as great a role as in the four-teenth, fifteenth, and sixteenth centuries."[52]

Almost 1,000 years after the fall of the Roman Empire, Italians rediscovered the philosophy, art, architecture, and cuisine of the classical Greeks and Romans literally in their own backyards in ancient writings, broken statues, buildings, and pots. The rebirth of civilization now known as the Renaissance began in the fourteenth century in Italy, which was still made up of city-states that did not become a unified country until the nineteenth century. The Renaissance was characterized by an increase in trade and in learning, with an emphasis on humanism and secularism, the importance of the individual, as opposed to the Church or the state. Famous artists of the Renaissance were Michelangelo, Leonardo, Raphael, and Donatello (before they were Ninja Turtles).

Italians rediscovered the cuisine of ancient Rome in 1457 when the Vatican library acquired a manuscript attributed to Apicius. Along with an interest in Roman cooking came a revival of Roman excesses. In the sixteenth century, Italy was wealthy and powerful, at the height of the European world. And the Medici family was at the height of power in the wealthiest, most powerful city-state in Italy, Florence. They had accumulated wealth by being merchants, the middlemen between Arab traders in the east and Europe in the west. They had so much money they started loaning it out and became the bankers of Europe, with branches in major cities like Antwerp, Belgium.

The Medici were the new royalty, although they began as what the French called *bourgeoisie* and the Germans called *burghers*: not born nobles, but merchant city dwellers. This new class of people had money and they wanted to show it off. Fashion and food were two ways to do that. They dressed in layers, all for show: dresses, stockings, shoes, jackets, in great quantities of expensive fabrics like silk, satin, and velvet. Their hair was done into elaborate shapes, increased with fake silk hair and topped with fancy hats in more expensive fabrics and feathers and fur. They used makeup and perfume, and wore jewelry on everything from their hair to their extravagant shoes.

With the growth of cities came an urban population that did not produce its own food. It needed food that was preserved, and for that it needed spices and salt.

FOOD FABLE:

Spices and Rotten Meat

Let's put this one to rest for all time. In the Middle Ages and the Renaissance, people did not use spices to mask the taste of meat that had gone bad. The class of people who could afford spices could also afford meat, which was butchered fresh daily. Also, the laws concerning meat were strict. None of the cookbooks—not in England, France, the Netherlands, Italy, or Spain—talk about what to do with meat that was going bad or "high," or about using spices in this way.[53]

The medieval theory of the humors was partly responsible for the spice increase, because now there were more people who could afford them. But which spices were used changed. The French upper class began to consider spices like black pepper unrefined and lower class. Each class had its own food habits. "Delicate" meats like partridges became increasingly important to the upper classes, who thought they increased intelligence and sensitivity, and that spices made them easier to digest. Cooking "correctly" could mean cooking "with correctives"—opposing elements to counteract an unfavorable humor. For example, oysters, cold and wet, could be "fixed" by roasting them with spices to make them more hot and dry.[54]

At the same time, bread occupied a larger percentage of the diet and budget of the lower classes, which might spend more than half of their income on bread.[55] The bread basket of Europe was Poland and Ukraine in the east, which meant the grain had to be shipped, which created another wealthy class of shippers. The lower classes sent their children, as early as age seven or eight, out to be servants in the homes of the new wealthy classes.[56]

Italy: Martino and the First Printed Cookbook

In the mid-1400s, a German named Johannes Gutenberg invented the printing press. The Chinese had invented movable type centuries earlier but hadn't pursued it because it didn't work with their pictographic alphabet of thousands of characters. But it worked for European languages, which had few letters. The first book Gutenberg printed was the Bible. Then came books for upper-classmen concerned with their health and looking for immortality. The first printing press arrived in Italy in 1465; in 1474, *De honesta voluptate et valetudine (Of Honest Indulgence and Good Health)* was printed in Rome.[57] This combination medical manual and life-advice book also included recipes, which makes it the first printed cookbook.[58] Written in Latin by an Italian named Bartolomeo Sacchi, known as Platina, it was translated into Italian in 1487, into French in 1505, and into English in 1967.[59] Apicius and the customs of ancient Rome influenced Platina's book because he was the Vatican librarian—a new position created by the profusion of books created by the printing press—and since 1457, the Vatican had owned the writings of Apicius.

Chef Joseph Dommers Vehling, the first one to translate Apicius into English, also pointed out that almost all of Platina's recipes were really written by Maestro [MY-strow] (meaning "master") Martino, an Italian from northern Italy.[60] Earlier in the fifteenth century, Martino had written, in Italian, *The Art of Cooking*. Sacchi "borrowed" 250 recipes from *The Art of Cooking* and used them in *De honesta voluptate*. Platina acknowledged Martino's contribution. Before copyright laws, this kind of "borrowing" of other people's work was common. These recipes earned Martino the title Prince of Cooks and caused *De honesta voluptate* to become the first best-selling cookbook.[61] Martino was chef to Cardinal Trevisan, who liked to live very well and threw dinner parties that turned into orgies. Banquets were extremely elaborate, designed to show off the wealth and power of the person giving them, like one held in 1473 in Rome, even though the Church condemned gluttony:

The first service combined pork livers, blancmange, meats with relish, tortes and pies, salt-cured pork loin and sausage, roast veal, kid, squab, chicken, rabbit . . . whole roasted large game, and fowl dressed in their skin or feathers.[62]

Later came fritters in a honey and rose water syrup, lemons wrapped in silver, mutton, venison, suckling pig, capon, duck, and fruits soaked in wine. There were enormous sugar sculptures in the shape of Hercules, castles with towers, and a mountain so big that a man jumped out of it. [63]

Martino was an expert chef. He wrote for other chefs, and addresses them directly: "adding some good spices as suits the common taste or as suits your master's tastes."[64] He does not just list ingredients, but explains techniques in using them: what kind of pot to use, and how long to cook them—"Let the ravioli simmer for the time it takes to say two Lord's Prayers."[65] As historian Luigi Ballerini has pointed out, Martino rehabilitated vegetables, elevating them from their place as lowly peasant food to food fit for the upper classes and food fit to be eaten by itself, without meat.[66] He has recipes for fennel, turnips, fava beans, parsley root, chard, chickpeas, peas, mushrooms, herbs with almond milk, and so on. Fruit recipes include grapes, elderflowers, mulberries, sweet and tart cherries, quince, apples, peach blossom sauce, and prunes.

The Art of Cooking is divided into chapters and begins with "Meats for Boiling and Meats for Roasting"—"Bear meat is good in pies."[67] Italian meats like prosciutto and mortadella are already well established as ingredients, as is Parmigiano cheese. An aspic made from 40 mutton feet, white vinegar, white wine, water, and spices is clarified with 10 egg whites then strained multiple times. Before metal sieves and China caps, it was strained through wool cloth.[68]

....

RECIPE:

Bolognese Torte

FROM *THE ART OF COOKING*, BY MAESTRO MARTINO

"Take [18 ounces] of cheese, and grate. Note that the fatter the cheese, the better; then take some chard, parsley, and marjoram; once cleaned and washed, chop well with a knife and add to the cheese, crushing and mixing it with your hands until well incorporated, adding four eggs and as much pepper as necessary, and a bit of saffron, and likewise, some good rendered lard or fresh butter, mixing and incorporating all these things together as I have said. Place this filling in a pan with a crust below and above, applying medium heat. When it appears to you that it is half-cooked, to give it an even more handsome appearance, make it yellow by brushing it with an egg yolk that has been beaten with a bit of saffron. You can tell that it is done when the crust on top rises and puffs up; it is best to remove it from the flame at this point."[70]

....

Pasta dishes abound—lasagne, macaroni, ravioli, vermicelli. Before tomatoes were introduced from Mexico and became popular in Italian cuisine in the nineteenth century, pasta was boiled and served in broth, or boiled in water and sauced simply with "some good cheese, and butter, and sweet spices," as it still can be today.[69] Or one of the many more elaborate sauces that Martino provides can be used. He has separate chapters on sauces, eggs, fish, fritters, and tortes.

The Perfect Chef

Martino also came to define what a cook should be, as Platina admits in *De honesta voluptate*:

> One should have a trained cook with skill and long experience, patient in his work and wanting above all to be praised for it. He should be absolutely clean of any filth or dirt and rightly know the strength and nature of meats, fish and vegetables so that he may understand what ought to be roasted, boiled or fried. He should be alert enough to discern by taste what is too salty or too flat. He should be as much as possible like [Martino]. . . . He should not be gluttonous or greedy . . . so as not to appropriate and devour food intended for his master.[71]

The passage makes it clear that at this time, cooks were men. It is also clear that some cooks fall short of this ideal and do not know as much about food as their employers expect them to, or are not scrupulously clean, or eat what they cook. Gluttony was still a sin then.

Italy: Scappi's *Opera*

"Bartolomeo Scappi is to cooking as Michelangelo is to the fine arts."[72]

Opera—which means "Works"—is the title of Scappi's High Renaissance cookbook. It was printed in 1570, almost exactly 100 years after Martino's book. Italian cooking had become even more refined by that time, and so had publishing: *Opera* has not just instructions, but illustrations, including a picture of one of the first forks.

Opera has other firsts. As food historian Anne Willan points out, Scappi is "the first European cook to explore the Arab art of pastry-making" in more than 200 sweet and savory recipes. Here, in single- and double-crust pies, are early versions of puff pastry and the Italian standard pie crust, *pasta frolla*.[73]

One of the ways that Scappi's cooking would have been displayed was on something that the Italians had invented to create a beautiful presentation of food, utensils, and glassware. It was called the *credenza*:

> The *credenza* (the word is now used to describe the side table or sideboard) was a course of cold dishes featuring pies, sausages, boiled shellfish, vegetables, salads, and other typical *antipasti*, as well as fruits, sweet cakes, and candies. . . .

The *credenza* was the forerunner of the French cold buffet—apparently introduced to France by Pierre Buffet, a royal cook.[74]

As chef to several cardinals and popes, Scappi set trends at the top of the food chain.

Renaissance Dietetics

"Nothing in the Renaissance mind could be considered more delicious and dangerous than a sweet, ripe, juicy melon."

—Historian Ken Albala[75]

As the Renaissance spread throughout Europe, Martino's book was followed by a flood of books on proper diet and nutrition—approximately 100 books from the 1470s until La Varenne's *Le cuisinier françois* in 1650.[76] All sold well. These books were concerned with balancing the humors to create health and rationality, the system first proposed by the Greek physician Galen in the second century A.D. This was still a diet tailored to the individual, not to entire populations, as our dietary recommendations are now. Humoral theory was strong in the fifteenth century but lost its influence by the middle of the seventeenth, as people began to trust their own tastes—literally and figuratively—more than what some remote authority told them.

As food historian Ken Albala points out in *Eating Right in the Renaissance,* Renaissance dietitians divided taste into eight groups: "sweet, bitter, acute, salty, acidic, styptic [astringent] . . . unctuous [greasy] and insipid [bland]."[77] Some foods were considered dangerous, like fruit. Wet and cold, fruit would drown out the fire of the stomach "engine" and create toxic, putrified fluids of undigested food, rotting the body from the inside out. They were especially afraid of melons, to the point that they might eat them for the thrill and become sick later from the terror. Superfoods—medicines on the side of health—were sugar, saffron, black pepper, wine, and the bland herb borage.[78] Foods that were already perfectly balanced and did not need to be "fixed" were bread and chicken.[79]

Italy Comes to France: Forks and Caterina de' Medici

Cookbooks weren't the only thing that changed during this time. Beginning in the sixteenth century in Italy, a new utensil changed the relationship of humans to food, and to each other at the table. Primitive people had just been discovered in the Americas; civilized people didn't want to eat like them. The fork created a distance between the diner and his dinner. It also distanced the people at the table from each other. No more eating the same food out of the same pot with their fingers as they had in the Middle Ages.

The fork had been known as a serving tool since ancient Rome, used to spear solid food out of the boiling pot. It arrived at the table as a serving tool to keep the hands of all the diners out of the serving dish. Finally, it became an individual utensil. At first, people had to make a serious effort to use it, because it was two-tined, difficult to maneuver, and not as efficient as fingers. Food kept falling off. The fork also cut out one of the sensations that had always been involved with eating: feel. Slowly, it spread from the Italian court to France, then to England, and finally to Germany. It was strictly upper class, crafted from gold, silver, or crystal. One of the means by which the fork began its northward migration was an Italian teenage girl, Caterina de' Medici.

FOOD FABLE:

Caterina de' Medici—Did She or Didn't She?

In 1533, a 14-year-old princess left Florence, Italy, to marry a French prince, in a marriage arranged by the pope. Food historian Luigi Ballerini believes that Caterina de' Medici's marriage brought about crucial changes in European cuisine:

"There is little doubt that she was singlehandedly responsible for changing the course of gastronomic history in France . . . Accompanying her to Paris from her native Florence were . . . celebrated cooks who had perfected such novelties—novel, at least, to the French palate—as aspics, sweetbreads, artichokes, truffles, macaroni, and *zabaglione*."[80]

Food historian Barbara Wheaton disagrees. She says that Caterina didn't have much power or influence at court because she didn't have children for 14 years; because her husband was not supposed to become king, but did because his brother died; and because her husband's mistress set court fashions:[81]

"French *haute cuisine* did not appear until a century later and then showed little Italian influence; and there is no evidence that Catherine's cooks had any impact on French cooking in the early sixteenth century."[82]

So, there is still controversy among food scholars about the role that Caterina de' Medici played in spreading specific foods, cooking techniques, and culinary fashions from Italy to France.

After Caterina's husband died and she ruled through her son, her court was the height of fashion. In 1581, she was responsible for the first real ballet, the *Ballet Comique de la Reine*—the Queen's Comic Ballet. She also helped to popularize a new fashion from the New World—tobacco. The active ingredient in tobacco, nicotine, was named after the French diplomat who sent the seeds to Caterina, Jean Nicot.

Caterina survived and even excelled in the backstabbing world of court intrigue. She was involved in the religious wars between the Catholic majority and the Protestant minority, the Huguenots. On St. Bartholomew's Day, August 24, 1572, French Catholics began a three-day coordinated massacre of 20,000 Huguenots throughout France, after which the pope and King Philip II of Spain celebrated. Caterina was not an innocent bystander.

Italy Comes to Poland: Vegetables

In 1518, another Italian princess, named Bona Sforza (which means "Nice Try"), also entered into a politically arranged marriage. Hers was to Poland's King Sigismund, 24 years older than she. Bona Sforza, like Caterina de' Medici, brought her cooks and gardeners to her new country. Although Polish cuisine already included many vegetables, Bona Sforza brought so many new ones that the Polish word for vegetables is *wloszczyzna*, which means "things from Italy."

POLISH AND ITALIAN FOOD WORDS[83]

ENGLISH	POLISH	ITALIAN
artichokes	karczochy	carciofi
asparagus	szparagi	asparagi
beans	fasola	fagioli
cauliflower	kalafior	calvofiore
chestnut	kasztan	castagna
cutlet	kotlet	cotoletta
marzipan	marzapane	marzapane
meatball	pulpety	polpette
soup	zupy	zuppa
spinach	szpinak	spinaci
tomato	pomidor	pomodoro

Foreign foods incorporated into Polish cuisine later kept their names, too. From France came *sos* (sauce), *krokiety* (croquette), *auszpik* (aspic), and *soufflé*. The Byzantine and Middle Eastern influence shows in *ryż*—rice, and *szaszlyk*—shashlik.

Italy: Indulging and Indulgences

In Italy, the new interest in wealth and indulging the pleasures of the flesh, including lavish Roman banquets, extended to the clergy. Popes and cardinals employed party planners called chamberlains to arrange spectacles and feasts, and chefs to carry out their every wish. One pope had a lavish public wedding and banquet for his daughter and built a huge bull that was a wine-gushing fountain for his own coronation. Catholic clergy are not only forbidden to marry, they are also supposed to be celibate—no sex. Other clergy became wealthy by selling pardons, called "indulgences," even to rapists and murderers. No sin was too horrible to keep a sinner out of heaven if he had enough gold. One cardinal who became wealthy selling indulgences justified his behavior: "It is not God's wish that a sinner should die, but that he should live—and pay."[84] Ordinary pious people protested; reform movements arose. One was led by Savonarola, a monk in Florence, who urged people to return to the teachings of Christ and lead holy lives. He was burned at the stake for criticizing the Church. It was clear that any movement to change the Church would have to come from somewhere that was not in the pope's backyard.

Germany: Martin Luther and the Protestant Reformation

"God doesn't care what you eat."

—Martin Luther[85]

On October 31, 1517, a monk named Martin Luther nailed a list of 95 faults he found with the Church to the door of the cathedral in Wittenberg, Germany. He said that the selling of indulgences had to stop, and that it would cut down on immorality if priests were allowed to marry. After Luther's 95 Theses, as they became known, went to a printer, copies spread like wildfire through Europe. At first the Church ignored its wayward son. But Luther had hit nerves; people began leaving the Church and worshipping Christ in other ways. The pope excommunicated Luther, which meant that he couldn't receive the sacraments so he couldn't get into heaven. Then German princes who sided with the pope declared Luther an outlaw: no one was to give him food or shelter. Other princes shrewdly realized that anything that pulled people away from the Church gave them more power. These princes shielded Luther, who spent the next two years in hiding, translating the Bible from Latin into German so more people could read it. When he went back to Wittenberg, he found that many priests had gotten married and were wearing everyday clothes.

Martin Luther changed not only the way Europeans worshipped, but also the way they ate. The Reformation freed a large part of Europe's population from the Catholic Church's food rules regarding fast days, meatless days (Wednesday and Friday), and saints' days, which accounted for approximately 150 days a year. International trade had brought about a higher standard of living; people wanted to enjoy it without feeling guilty. There was an immediate drop in the number of fishermen in Europe and an increase in meat eating. The English ate so much meat that the Portuguese called them *rosbifes*—roast beefs.[86] Luther also made one of the first mentions of a food new to Europe, the turkey. To this day, Protestants show their contempt for the leader of the Catholic Church by referring to the turkey tail—the "part that goes over the fence last"—as the pope's nose. Catholics retaliate by calling it the parson's nose.

In Geneva, Switzerland, Protestants tried to create a utopia under the leadership of John Calvin. People moved there from all over Europe to practice the new, pure religion. (Calvin's followers in England were called Puritans.) Outlawed under Calvinism: inviting someone to have a drink, being drunk, having a tavern open during the sermon, being in a tavern during the sermon, or having a "great feast." The great feast fine was more than three times as much as the other food fines.[87]

Elizabethan England: Shakespeare and the Dining Room

England, too, became Protestant in 1531 under the rule of Henry VIII, a king of enormous appetites of all kinds. He was a notorious glutton and ended up being married six times. Henry's desire for a son and heir, and the pope's refusal to allow him to remarry, made them enemies. Henry convinced Parliament to pass a law saying that the king was the head of the church in England, and then he seized all the Church's property in England—about 20 percent of all the land in England. Henry finally got his male heir, but ironically, it was the daughter he didn't want who became one of England's greatest rulers.

Queen Elizabeth I of England was born in 1533, the same year that Caterina de' Medici got married. Elizabeth ruled England from 1558 to 1603, and her reign, Elizabethan England, England's Renaissance, was a time of glory for England. Theater and poetry flourished, especially at the Globe Theater in Stratford-on-Avon, where plays by William Shakespeare were performed.

The new sea routes to Africa, India, and Asia brought a rise in the standard of living and a change in cuisine and culture in Elizabethan England. An Elizabethan house might have a separate room for dining, with a table that had leaves under it that could be drawn out to make the table larger—a draw-leaf table. They had pots and pans for boiling and frying, but hollowed-out vegetables made cases for baked puddings. Utensils were silver, but there were only spoons and knives. Real men didn't use forks: "When we have washed our hands . . . we need no little forks . . . to throw our meat into [our mouths]."[88]

The meats they were throwing into their mouths were chicken, capon, goose, turkey, mutton, and steak, as well as game—deer, boar, swan. They ate many birds that we no longer eat, like larks and sparrows. Elizabethans ate all parts of the animal, including sweetbreads, rabbit livers, sheep tongues, pig feet, veal kidneys. Stockfish—dried cod—and eel were common fish. All of these proteins were cooked in sauces that still showed the influence of the Middle East and the Middle Ages: sweet and sour, sugar mixed with vinegar and sometimes mustard.[89] They were spiced with pepper, nutmeg, cinnamon, ginger, and rose water, and sweetened with currants, dates, "raisins of the sun," and white sugar. Sugar was widely used because doctors at the time decreed that sugar was nutritious.[90]

Sometimes these ingredients were made into Elizabethan favorites—puddings and pies. Seasonings were the same for both; the difference was that puddings had an egg binder, while pies were baked into a very stiff, free-standing dough called a "coffin." It was at this time that mincemeat pie became a Christmas standard. Today's mincemeat still contains Middle Eastern spices, but usually not the chopped meat and suet (fat) it had in the sixteenth century. One of the most famous pie presentations is in a nursery rhyme that children still learn today:

Four-and-twenty blackbirds baked in a pie.
When the pie was opened the birds began to sing,
Oh wasn't that a dainty dish to set before the king?

This isn't a fairy tale—they really made pies with live birds. This recipe from England was originally from *The Art of Cooking* by Platina/Maestro Martino, published in Italy in 1474.

....

RECIPE:

Pie with Live Birds

"Make the coffin of a great Pie . . . in the bottome whereof make a hole as big as your fist . . . Let the sides . . . bee somewhat higher than ordinary Pies, which done, put it full of flower and bake it [*i.e.,* bake it blind], and being baked, open the hole in the bottome, and take out the flower." The hole is plugged up with a real pie, and then put "round about the aforesaid Pie as many small live birds as the empty coffin will hold . . ." Then the pie is brought to the table and when the top crust is removed, "all the Birds will flie out, which is to delight and pleasure shew to the company."[91] (So much for sanitation.)

....

Queen Elizabeth I spoke fluent Italian, the language of the European courts and nobility, and Elizabethan food shows the influence of Middle Eastern foods via the Italians: artichokes, spinach, raisins. Another Italian influence was wine glasses, handmade and mouth-blown Murano glass from Venice. The Venetians had also learned to make glass clear *(cristallo)*, in colors, and etched.

Also much in demand were foods cooked "in the French fashion"—usually with broth and wine. The "French fashion" also meant foods that were light on spices, often just a bit of freshly grated nutmeg. This new French cuisine would be written about in 1651 in the ground-breaking cookbook *Le cuisinier françois* by La Varenne.

Elizabeth was a political genius. During her reign, there was no war in England between Catholics and Protestants, although a civil war erupted after her death. Perhaps one of the reasons was that in the sixteenth century, England faced a powerful external enemy: Spain.

And Spain was becoming very angry about British pirates in the Caribbean.

America from Colony to Country

The Mercantile System

Sugar, wine, other foodstuffs, and slavery were part of an economic system called mercantilism. This was based on a country having a favorable balance of trade—more money coming into the treasury than going out. Economically, it was the end of feudalism and the beginning of capitalism, the accumulation of private wealth. Colonies were an important way to achieve this. They provided the home country with cheap raw materials that the home country then sold at a higher price or transformed into finished goods like textiles and sold back to the colony. So in the sixteenth century, hundreds of huge cargo ships, Spanish galleons, sailed across the Atlantic Ocean loaded with sugar, wines, gold, silver, and jewels. The heavily laden, slow-moving galleons were tempting targets and an easy way for other countries to get rich easily. Most of the pirates were in the service of Spain's enemies, especially England. Any country that could hijack or smuggle any valuable commodity did. They were all pirates in the Caribbean.

The piracy reached an intolerable level when sugar cost less in England than it did in Spain or even in the Caribbean. King Philip II of Spain complained repeatedly to England's Queen Elizabeth I, who condemned pirates like Francis Drake in public but rewarded them in private. In addition, Catholic Spain hated

Protestant England. Spain began building a huge armed fleet—in Spanish, an *armada*—to attack England. The pope promised Spain a huge cash bonus when it invaded England and brought it back to the Catholic Church (and restored his property). Spain felt certain of success, because along with Venice and the pope, it had defeated the Ottoman Turks in 1571 at the Battle of Lepanto—"the most spectacular military event in the Mediterranean during the entire sixteenth century"—for control of trade in the Mediterranean.[1]

The Spanish Armada and the Protestant Wind

In July 1588, the Spanish Armada arrived off the coast of England. But the British won. The decisive factor wasn't men or ships; it was nature. A violent wind came up and scattered the Spanish fleet. The British claimed that "the Protestant wind" showed that their god was more powerful than Spain's (just like when the Mongols tried to invade Japan three centuries earlier). The British victory broke the Spanish stranglehold on sailing in the Atlantic Ocean and allowed the British to do something they had wanted to do for a long time: colonize in North America.

Colonial America

The Chesapeake: The Starving Time

England's colonies in North America did not get off to a good start. After one, Roanoke, completely disappeared (historians still don't know what happened to it), British settlers came to the Chesapeake Bay in 1607. They named the colony Virginia in honor of Elizabeth I, the Virgin Queen; they called the capital Jamestown after King James; and they expected to get rich quick—except that the natives refused to be their slaves. In the winter of 1609–1610, when not enough food had been grown, harvested, or preserved, almost all 500 colonists died during what became known as "The Starving Time." Captain John Smith (yes, as in John Smith and Pocahontas) later wrote what he had heard about how the colonists were reduced to eating nuts, berries, acorns, horse hide, and worse:

> And one amongst the rest did kill his wife, powdered [salted] her, and had eaten part of her before it was known, for which he was executed, as he well deserved. Now whether she was better roasted, boiled, or carbonadoed [broiled], I know not; but of such a dish as powdered wife I never heard of.[2]

It was not the last time cannibalism would be resorted to in America.

The Chesapeake: Tobacco

Later Virginians wanted to grow a profitable crop; they tried sugar but the climate was too cold. They settled on a crop native to America: tobacco. Soon, tobacco was bringing in so much money that people planted it on any available land—they ripped up their gardens, grew it between graves. But who would hoe and harvest these thousands of acres of tobacco? The Native Americans who hadn't died of European diseases refused to do it. African slaves were too expensive, although some arrived in 1619. England had the perfect labor force: a surplus of poor, desperate young men in their late teens and early 20s. They signed an indenture—a contract—giving them a free trip to America and free room and board in exchange for four to six years of work. Then they were supposed to get their freedom, tools, corn, and land of their own—something they had zero chance of getting in England. The person who hired the indentured servant and paid for his trip received free labor and 50 acres of land. It was a sweetheart deal all around. Except—most of these young men didn't live four years after they got to America. They died from dysentery, typhoid, malaria. The ones who did live found that there was only one woman for every six men. And soon the best land was in huge plantations owned by a few wealthy men who also had all the political power. In 1676, when ex-indentured servants couldn't get land, women, or the right to vote, which would have allowed them to make their lives better, they went on a rampage. Bacon's Rebellion ended with Jamestown burned and more than 20 ex-indentured servants hanged. Planters wanted a labor force they could control, not these Englishmen who used violence to get their rights. In 1698, England ended the Royal African Company monopoly on the slave trade. Now, anyone with a ship could get into the slave trade. With competition, the price of slaves dropped. Now it was affordable to own Africans and profitable to sell them.

The Carolinas: West African Rice Culture

At about that time, the English established a colony south of Virginia—Carolina, named after King Charles II. Many of the settlers were from Barbados. They intended to grow food for the Caribbean sugar plantations and to grow and export luxury items. After they failed at wine, olive oil, and silk, they decided on rice as their staple crop. Rice requires skilled labor; west Africans, especially from Guinea, had this skill—African women. They also had some immunity to malaria. But most importantly, they weren't Christian, so according to the Christian world at that time, they could be enslaved for the rest of their lives. The white Carolina settlers also imported the Barbados Slave Code, with punishments that escalated from whipping to facial mutilation and sometimes death, which the Code said was the slave's fault for forcing his master to discipline him. Charleston, South Carolina, became the primary port through which slaves entered the United States. By 1710, black slaves outnumbered white settlers in the Carolinas.

In spite of the conditions under which the slaves were brought to America, some of their African cuisine and culture survived. As Judith Carney points out in *Black Rice*, "Rice cultivation in the Americas depended upon the diffusion of an entire cultural system, from production to consumption."[3] And a grueling system it was, with a high mortality rate. There was no off-season; slaves worked year round. First they sowed the seed. Then the fields were flooded, drained, hoed, and weeded. This was repeated four times. Finally, the rice was harvested with a sickle. Then it "required milling, threshing, winnowing, and pounding" *by hand* using a mortar and pestle—millions of pounds. And it had to be done on a tight timetable, because prime season for rice was Lent in Europe. Then the stubble from the harvested rice had to be plowed under and the fields prepared for the next crop.[4]

This influenced how cooking developed in the American South, too, because in the African rice culture, "only women are involved in the processing and cooking of the cereal."[5] African women became cooks in the plantation households. Along with their knowledge of rice cultivation, cooking, and storage, they brought yams, okra, watermelon, and fried food. They also brought back foodstuffs that had been taken from the New World to Africa, like the chile pepper and the peanut, and their word for it—goober. They brought the banjo and the drum and the music that would become jazz. Some of the African cuisine they brought, including the rice itself, had been introduced to Africa by Arab Muslims. As Karen Hess reveals in *The Carolina Rice Kitchen: The African Connection*, many rice dishes in the American South are African versions of *pilau* or pilaf. One of the most famous is Hoppin' John, eaten on New Year's Day to bring good luck. Other versions call for cowpeas, pigeon peas, black-eyed peas, or other peas/beans.

....

RECIPE:

Hopping (or Hoppin') John

"One pint of red peas, one pint of rice, one pound of bacon—let the bacon come to a boil in two quarts of water—skim it—add the peas: boil slowly. When tender, add the rice: let it boil until the rice is well swollen and soft.—Season with red pepper and salt. If liked perfectly dry, it can be steamed, as in boiling rice plain. Serve it with the bacon on top. Salt must be added when nearly done."

—Theresa Brown, in *Modern Domestic Cookery*, Charleston, 1871[6]

....

New England: "Almost beyond believing"[7]

In 1620, Pilgrims—Protestants who wanted to be allowed to worship without being persecuted—landed at Plymouth, Massachusetts. Before they went ashore, the men on the ship entered into an agreement. The Mayflower Compact was the first constitution in America. Only one paragraph long, it set forth an important principle: that all would be equal and work together as a community.

The Pilgrims on Cape Cod, and the Puritans who settled the Massachusetts Bay Colony in Boston 10 years later, had their work cut out for them. These were people used to living in towns. They didn't know how to hunt or fish or farm.

But they didn't like many of the strange plants and animals in North America anyway—those huge quahog clams, the slimy steamers. And the codfish and lobsters were bigger than they were, sometimes six feet long. They wouldn't eat them at first, even after the Indians showed them how.

Maple Syrup: Tapping the Sap of the Sugar Tree

Maple sugar was a primary food in Native American cooking; among some tribes it was the only condiment. It replaced salt, which they did not like, was used to season dried cornmeal porridge, mixed with bear fat as a sauce for roasted venison, sprinkled on boiled fish, and eaten with berries or all by itself, a pound a day.[9] It reconstituted into a sweet drink that was used in ceremonies, along with tobacco smoked in the peace pipe. Women boiled the sap from maple, walnut, hickory, box elder, butternut, birch, and sycamore trees down to sugar crystals, which was difficult because before Europeans came, they had no metal pots. Their vessels were made of birch bark or gourds which held between one and two gallons and could not be placed directly over fire. To boil liquid in these containers, they dropped heated stones into the liquid until it boiled, which involved continuously taking out cool stones and replacing them with hot ones. These small amounts of liquid were then poured into 100-gallon moose-skin vats. It is not surprising that the Indians began to trade for metal pots and utensils as soon as the Europeans introduced them. Another way to process the syrup was to let it freeze at night, then scrape the ice off the top. This required several nights until just syrup was left. Maple sugar that was to be used for gifts was poured into molds that one European described as shaped like "bear's paws, flowers, stars, small animals, and other figures, just like our gingerbread-bakers at fairs."[10]

Maple Moon

Maple Moon was what Native Americans called the time in the spring when the sap started to flow in the sugar maple tree (*Acer saccharum*). Just as the grapevine was a symbol of resurrection for the ancient Greeks, so the maple was for Native Americans. Flowing sap meant the end of winter and the rebirth of nature. The Iroquois performed a religious ritual, a maple dance, to pray for warm weather and plenty of sap. According to legend, an Iroquois chief pulled his tomahawk out of a tree where he had thrown it the night before and went off to hunt. In the meantime, the weather turned warm and sap oozed into a container left by accident at the base of the tree. On her way to get water for cooking, his wife saw the container of liquid and used that instead; everyone agreed it was much better than water.[11]

Seventeenth-century European writers gave Native Americans full credit for knowing how to make maple syrup and sugar, but in the eighteenth century, Europeans started to claim that they had taught the Indians. As maple historians Helen and Scott Nearing have pointed out, language is on the side of the tribes. All their words for maple syrup translate as "drawn from wood," "sap flows fast," "our own tree," while they called white sugar "French snow"—a clear indication of its origin.[12] With the help of the native tribes, the Pilgrims survived their first year and had a celebration.

Thanksgiving Foods

"The turkey is certainly one of the most delightful presents which the New World has made to the Old."

—Brillat-Savarin[13]

Most of the foods Americans eat at Thanksgiving dinner now are native to the Americas: turkey, cranberry sauce, mashed potatoes, sweet potatoes, cornbread stuffing, pumpkin pie. They have additions of butter, flour, sugar, and spices not from the Americas. In French the word for turkey is *dinde*, short for *poulet d'inde*, which means "chicken from India," because the French, like other Europeans, thought the turkey was from the Indies. The turkey was more available than other wild fowl. Geese, ducks, and other wild fowl were abundant in the New World but only in some seasons because they migrated. Turkeys don't migrate, so they were available all year. And they had an instinct that helped humans: when one turkey was shot, the others froze in place. It was easy to kill a dozen turkeys in a morning. Nobody ever called anybody a turkey and meant it as a compliment.

Although Thanksgiving foods are native to the Americas, the style of the food was English. The turkey, transplanted to England from the Americas, was popular in England before the Pilgrims came to Massachusetts in 1620. Potatoes, native to Peru, which was a Spanish colony and England's enemy, went from Peru to Europe and then to New Hampshire with Scotch-Irish settlers in 1719. They probably brought not just potatoes, but also the practice of mashing them with milk or buttermilk. And though pumpkin was not known in other parts of the world, other members of the squash family were. It was natural to use them in pies, a favorite food in England from the Middle Ages.

Cranberries and blueberries, both members of the heather family and both native to New England, were more than food in sauce and pies. Mashed and mixed with sour milk, they were used as paint. That is why the colors most often associated with colonial New England buildings are muted cranberry and milky purple-gray.

Although pumpkin was widely used in the colonies, recipes for the pumpkin pie that Americans are used to on Thanksgiving didn't appear in print until the first American cookbook, written by Amelia Simmons in 1796. She called it "pompkin" and gave two different versions. Both had pumpkin, ginger, and eggs, but one used cream and sugar; the other, milk and molasses. One used the Old World spices mace and nutmeg; the other, New World allspice.[14]

HOLIDAY HISTORY:

Thanksgiving

The first Thanksgiving was in 1621. Fifty-one Pilgrim men, women, and children hosted 90 men of the Wampanoag tribe and their chief, Massasoit. It was in the fall, to celebrate the good harvest of corn (wheat and barley weren't as successful). The celebration lasted three days. There was "wild fowl," and five deer.

The idea of a national day of thanks was raised in the late 1700s with the first president, George Washington, who proposed November 26 as the date. Nothing came of it until the 1850s, when magazine journalist Sarah Josepha Hale rallied the women of America to pressure the president for a national holiday. In 1863, during the Civil War, President Lincoln declared that the last Thursday in November should be a day of giving thanks. It was the same year that Lincoln issued the Emancipation Proclamation freeing the slaves, and made his speech at the battlefield in Gettysburg, Pennsylvania, in which he said the famous words "that government of the people, by the people, for the people, shall not perish from the Earth."

In 1939, President Franklin D. Roosevelt wanted to extend the Christmas shopping season to give the economy a boost and help it recover from the Depression. He moved Thanksgiving one week earlier. Congress objected. The president and Congress did a tug-of-war over the date until 1941 when it was settled: Thanksgiving is the fourth Thursday in November.

In 1970, Wampanoag leader Wampsutta (Anglo name: Frank James) was invited to speak at the Thanksgiving celebration at Plymouth, Massachusetts. When word got out that his speech was about the oppression of Native Americans, the invitation was revoked. He gave his speech anyway, in front of the statue of Massassoit, overlooking the replica of the *Mayflower*. That was the first Native American National Day of Mourning for the culture, the religion, and the lives and lands of their ancestors.

(To find out more about Thanksgiving, log onto www.plimoth.org.)

The Sacred Codfish

The staple "crop" of the Massachusetts Bay Colony was the codfish, *Gadus morhua*. What sugar was to the Caribbean and tobacco was to the Chesapeake, cod was to Massachusetts. There were millions off the coast, north to Newfoundland and Labrador. Once it was salted and dried, cod was stiff as a board and could be stacked and shipped like lumber. It was also almost 80 percent protein. In this form it made its way to Europe: *bacalà* in Italy, *bacalao* in Spain, *bacalhau* in Portugal. According to cod historian Mark Kurlansky, by the middle of the sixteenth century, "60 percent of all fish eaten in Europe was cod."[15] It was the perfect food for Lent. The best grade was sent to Spain; the worst fed the slaves in the West Indies.[16] It could also be bartered for slaves in Africa. Shipbuilders got rich because of cod, too. The cod was so important to the economy of Massachusetts that a large carved wooden codfish hangs in the statehouse in Boston.

Pocket Soup and Johny Cake

American cooking developed along two parallel lines. In the South, where slave labor did the kitchen work, cooking could take more time. Labor-intensive cooking, such as barbecue, could be done by slaves. Barbecue needed a great deal of preparation. Either beef or pork had to be properly butchered and marinated. Then the fire had to reach just the right temperature, and the meat had to be added. The fire had to be carefully watched and the temperature maintained. This required a great deal of labor.

On wealthy southern plantations, meats were hung in a separate smokehouse.

Hogs butchered and curing in the American South. *Courtesy Colonial Williamsburg Foundation.*

However, pit cooking developed differently in New England, in the form of the clambake. There, a fire was allowed to burn down in a pit; then clams, lobsters, and corn were buried under wet seaweed and left to steam for several hours. No labor was necessary to prepare the food before or after it was placed in the pit, except to dig it out.

American cooking in the north arose from the middle-class necessity of doing a great deal of work as quickly as possible. They invented shortcuts and new ways to preserve foods. Two examples are pocket soup and "Johny cake," as it is spelled in the first American cookbook. Travel was not easy in the colonies. Roads were poor or nonexistent and there was no guarantee that travelers would be able to find food when they needed it. Sailors, too, appreciated a bit of home. Pocket soup, also known as portable soup, was the solution. This was an early bouillon cube, soup cooked down until it was a condensed gelatinous mass, then cut into small cubes and dried for 10 days. Dropped into a cup of water, it reconstituted into soup. Johny cake or journey cake was a cornmeal cake that would keep without becoming moldy or disintegrating.

Another example of New England fast food was hasty pudding, made famous in the song "Yankee Doodle" (and in the Harvard University club).[17] This was corn—called Indian or "Injun" meal—or rye meal cooked on top of the stove, not baked, so it was ready in half an hour. This is a long time by today's microwave standards, but the baking times for regular cornmeal pudding recipes in *American Cookery* range from one-and-one-half hours to two-and-one-half hours. Sara Josepha Hale's recipes for cornmeal pudding require three to four hours of cooking, even those that are boiled. What makes hasty pudding hasty is that the meal is soaked first and added a bit at a time, and the pudding is boiled and stirred constantly. In this cooking technique, it resembles polenta.

Technology: Spider, Crane, and Kettle

Early American cooking was open hearth. Cooks had three basic tools: the spider, the crane, and the kettle. The spider was a cast-iron frying pan with three short legs to keep it from tipping over. The crane was a metal swing-arm dripping chains of various lengths so that the kettle height could be varied. Foods that needed more heat could be at the bottom, closer to the fire, while foods that needed lower temperatures would be at the top. The kettle, like the spider, was cast iron with three short legs for stability, because when it was full, it could weigh 40 pounds.

Baking was done in a Dutch oven. This was not the wide pan we call Dutch oven now, but was closer to the *fogon* that Columbus and other sailors used on ships: a metal box that could be placed on the floor of the fireplace. Some fireplaces had an oven built in at eye level—something that would not be available in American homes again until the 1950s. Temperature control was definitely an art, especially for baking. Goods had to be baked sequentially, not simultaneously, with the fire watched closely.

Colonial kitchen with crane in fireplace. *Courtesy Library of Congress, Prints & Photographs Division, Detroit Publishing Company Collection, LC-D4-71183.*

Brown Betty, Sally Lunn, and Anadama

Women, perhaps cooks, have left their names on various foods but not much other information. Brown Betty is a thrifty New England dessert that layers leftover bread with fruit, usually apples, and is baked. It isn't a bread pudding because it lacks eggs to make a custard binder. Sally Lunn is a very light, yeast-risen egg bread. Anadama is supposedly named after Anna, who kept cooking only one thing—a cornmeal and molasses bread—until her husband finally burst out, "Anna, damn her!"

CULINARY CONFUSION:

Cobbler, Slump, Grunt, Dumpling, Crumble, and Crisp

Just as regional cooking developed according to the kind of produce and labor available in each area, different areas had different names for the same food. For example, in most of the country, a cobbler is chopped, sweetened fruit with a sweet biscuit dough baked on top. Except in New England, where it is called a slump, with the further exception of Cape Cod, where it is called a grunt. Other combinations of fruit and dough include dumplings, which are pieces of fruit or a whole fruit, like an apple, wrapped in pastry squares and baked. A crumble is a mixture of flour, butter, sugar, and seasonings like cinnamon and nutmeg crumbled over chopped fruit and then baked. A crumble is different from a crisp because a crisp has more butter, which makes the topping . . . crisper. The topping on a crisp sometimes includes oats.

"Beer is a good family drink"[18]

As food historian John Hull Brown points out in *Early American Beverages*, men, women, and children in colonial America drank alcoholic beverages. Beer, familiar from England, was the earliest drink in the colonies. Women were the brewers; they made beer from nearly anything that grew. They made vegetable beers from corn, tomatoes, potatoes, turnips, pumpkins, and Jerusalem artichokes. They made tree beers from the bark of birch, spruce, and sassafras, and from maple sap. Fruit-based beers were brewed from persimmons, lemons, raisins. There were herb beers using wintergreen, and spice beers made of ginger, allspice, and cinnamon. Even flowers became beer: rose beer. There was molasses beer. They made their ale two barrels at a time, from eight or nine bushels of malt, 12 pounds of hops, five quarts of yeast, and 72 gallons of water.[19] And, of course, just as in ancient Egypt, once they had beer they had leavening for bread, either from the beer itself or from the "leavin's"—the dregs. The beer was bitter until the Germans arrived with new brewing techniques in the nineteenth century.

They also distilled "spirituous waters" and cordials using the stones of apricots, peaches, and cherries; and spices from the Middle East like coriander, cardamom, and anise seed.[20] The spices were kept in a spice cabinet. Wine was made from ginger, currants, and cherries; but sweet wines were imported from the "Wine Islands"—Madeira, the Azores, and the Canaries. Later, the Scots-Irish brewed whiskey from corn, barley, or oats. Colonial Americans drank hard cider distilled from apples, peachy made from peaches, and perry made from pears. The colonists liked to dress up their alcoholic beverages with cream, sugar, eggs, mace, and nutmeg—like eggnog.

"Kill-Devil" Rum, Stonewall, Bogus, and Flip

Rum, distilled in New England after 1670, was cheap and available. It was called by a variety of names—rhum, rumbullion, rumbooze—and used in a variety of mixtures: stonewall, which was cider and rum; bogus, unsweetened beer and rum; blackstrap, molasses and rum; and flip, a popular drink that appears at least as far back as 1690 in New England.

....

RECIPE:
Flip

"An earthen pitcher or huge pewter mug . . . would be filled about two-thirds with strong beer to which would be added molasses, sugar, or dried pumpkin for sweetening, and New England rum, about a gill, for flavor. The bitter, burnt taste was gotten by plunging a red-hot loggerhead, an iron poker-shaped stirrer, into the flip making it bubble and foam."[21]

....

Punch, with its five ingredients of tea, arrack, sugar, lemons, and water, arrived from India via the British East India Company. New Englanders added a sixth ingredient, and rum punch was born. Life was good to New Englanders; they could expect to live 10 years longer than if they had stayed in Old England. But since they attributed their longer life to drinking alcohol, it became difficult to enforce laws restricting its intake.[22]

Life was longer, but food preparation was still difficult and time-consuming. Before the modern stove with a cooktop and an oven was invented in the mid-nineteenth century, most cooking was done with the quadriceps, because it involved long hours of squatting to stir foods in front of the open hearth. A stool or rocking chair could be pulled up next to the fire, but it still involved long hours next to hot open flames.

Cooking in colonial America. *Courtesy Colonial Williamsburg Foundation.*

Benjamin Franklin and Temperance

The eighteenth century was the Enlightenment, also called the Age of Reason. It was supposedly rational and scientific as opposed to the superstitious and ignorant "Dark Ages," as people thought of the Middle Ages then. The Enlightenment was a time of belief in the human mind, and capitalized on the discoveries that had been made in the Scientific Revolution in the seventeenth century.

Benjamin Franklin was a product of the Enlightenment. Born in Boston, he settled as a teenager in Philadelphia where he eventually became a publisher, established circulating libraries, and was one of the founders of the University of Pennsylvania. He also experimented with electricity; taught himself French, Italian, and Spanish; became ambassador to France; and was a strong presence at the conventions that wrote the Declaration of Independence and the Constitution.

Franklin's autobiography contained Enlightenment ideals: his version of the 10 Commandments, which he called the 12 Virtues (he was forced to add a thirteenth, humility). The first virtue was "Temperance: Eat not to dullness; drink not to elevation." He put moderation in food and drink first, he said, because the other virtues would be more easily achieved if you weren't under "the force of perpetual temptations."[23] He also suggested that the way to begin the day was to ask yourself the question "What good shall I do this day?" and end it by asking "What good have I done today?" Franklin didn't always manage to practice what he preached.

Migrations: The Pennsylvania "Dutch"

England's colonies in North America continued to grow in the eighteenth century, partly because England advertised. The mercantile system depended on a large population. The more people in a colony, the more raw materials they could send to the home country and the more manufactured goods they could buy from it. William Penn distributed flyers about how wonderful life was in his new colony of Quakers, people who didn't believe in war or slavery, in Pennsylvania—"Penn's woods." Some of the flyers reached Rhinelanders—Protestant German and Swiss farmers in the Rhine River Valley. A winter of unprecedented brutal cold got them thinking about moving to Pennsylvania. New laws that made it easier for foreigners to become British citizens, and therefore to own land in the colonies, got them on ships headed for Pennsylvania. To the ears of the English settlers already there, *deutsch*, the German

Paul Revere's kitchen, showing the three main occupations of colonial women: cooking, child care, and weaving. *Courtesy Library of Congress, Prints & Photographs Division, LC-USZ620113458.*

word for "German," sounded like "Dutch," and the Rhinelanders have mistakenly been the Pennsylvania Dutch ever since.

A classic Pennsylvania Dutch dish is *schnitz und knepp*, ham stew with dried apples *(schnitz)* and dumplings *(knepp)*. Potatoes also figured prominently in their diet. Mashed potatoes and potato water were in raised breads, cakes, and cinnamon buns—*schnecke*. They made potato fondant candy. On Shrove Tuesday, the day before the beginning of Lent, they made *fastnacht*—doughnuts—with mashed potatoes and potato water. These were solid balls of deep-fried dough; the hole, which allowed the dough to cook faster, was invented later. By 1870, catalogs were selling doughnut cutters with holes.[24]

The Pennsylvania Dutch housewife took pride in her skills at jam making and pickling, her "seven sweets and seven sours." The sweets were fruit butters, conserves, and jams. The sours were pickled vegetables and relishes called chow chow, sweetened with sugar, soured with vinegar, usually seasoned with mustard seed, dry mustard, and celery seed, and colored with turmeric, like chutney. A favorite pickled food still served in bars in Pennsylvania Dutch country is garnet-colored eggs, which go well with beer, along with pretzels.

··

INGREDIENTS:

Pennsylvania Dutch Eggs Pickled in Beet Juice[25]

1 cup beet juice	¼ teaspoon allspice
1 cup vinegar	¼ teaspoon mace
¾ teaspoon salt	1 or 2 small cooked beets
½ teaspoon cloves	Shelled hard-boiled eggs

··

The Pennsylvania Dutch ate pie at all three meals. They filled their pies and tarts with apples, sour cherries, gooseberries, huckleberries, raspberries, blackberries, grapes, raisins, walnuts, or rhubarb. When they had nothing else to put in a pie, they made vinegar pie—water spiced with vinegar and nutmeg, sweetened with sugar, thickened with egg and flour; or cakelike shoofly pie—water, molasses and baking soda with a crumb topping, so sweet you had to shoo the flies away. When the men got together to do serious physical work like building a barn, they also did serious eating. They stacked half a dozen different kinds of pies on top of each other, cut through them all, and chowed down on "stack pie."[26]

The descendants of most of the Rhinelanders moved into mainstream America. But the Amish continue to live a preindustrial life today. They do not have electricity. They drive a horse and buggy, not a car. And they still cook good, solid, abundant food. As Swiss and German food historian Nika Hazelton pointed out, "If you want to see what eighteenth-century rural life in Switzerland was like, you'll do far better in a strict Pennsylvania or Indiana Amish settlement than in present-day Switzerland or Germany."[27]

Hannah Glasse: The Art of Cookery

The first cookbook printed in America was written in England. In 1747, a 39-year-old illegitimate Englishwoman whose half-brother was a knight published *The Art of Cookery Made Plain and Easy*. It was *the* cookbook of the eighteenth century, on both sides of the Atlantic. The author, Hannah Glasse, begins by telling the reader:

> [M]y Intention is to instruct the lower Sort, and therefore must treat them in their own Way. For Example; when I bid them lard a Fowl, if I should bid them lard with large Lardoons, they would not know what I meant: But when I say they must lard with little Pieces of Bacon, they know what I mean. So in many other Things in Cookery, the great Cooks have such a high Way of expressing themselves that the poor Girls are a Loss to know what they mean . . .[28]

Glasse takes a commonsense approach to cooking: why use expensive ingredients when you can get results that are just as good for half the price? Just because something is French doesn't make it better. And be on the lookout for adulterated food. She begins with instructions about how to tell if meat is fresh: for veal, "The loin first taints under the kidney"[29]; in beef, yellowish suet "is not so good."[30] For butter, she tells cooks not to just take what they are given, but to look in the middle. In cheese, they should beware of worms, mites, and maggots.[31] Glasse believes in cooking what is in season, and religious holidays control the calendar: "The buck venison . . . is in high season until All hallows-day [November 1]: the doe is in season from Michaelmas [September 29] to the end of December."[32] Glasse covers everything from basics—literally, how to boil water—to how to brew elderberry wine, turnip wine, white mead, maple beer, and "cyder." Many of her recipes are very modern: "The best way to roast a turkey is to loosen the skin on the breast of the turkey, and fill it with force-meat."[33] She recommends oyster and celery sauce seasoned with mace and lemon, and thickened, as many of her sauces are, with a roux: "some butter rolled in flour."[34] She also includes many of those British favorites: puddings—rice, bread and butter, prune, chestnut, apricot, Seville orange, lemon, almond—still spiced with Middle Eastern ginger, nutmeg, rose water, and orange flower water; custards; cakes; and pies, sweet and savory. There are also recipes for candy, but Glasse later devoted an entire book to it, *The Complete Confectioner*, published around 1770. Some modern food writers have attributed the expression "First catch your hare" to Hannah Glasse, and commented on how humorous it is. But Hannah Glasse never said that. What she said was, "Take your hare when it is cased."[35]

The Earl of Sandwich

In 1762, an English earl's name was used for the first time in print to describe a new food. John Montagu, the fourth Earl of Sandwich, liked to gamble but hated to get up from the table to go eat. The solution: he had cold meat between two slices of bread brought to him. The sandwich caught on around the world.

Sandwich

In the eighteenth century, Sweden's modern *smörgåsbord*—a full-meal elaborate "sandwich table" buffet—began life as the *brännvinsbord* or "aquavit buffet"—appetizers, with the food incidental to multiple flavors of aquavit.[36] In Denmark, it is *smørrebrød*, literally, "bread and butter"; in Norway, *smørbrød*. These are traditional Christmas Eve dinners. The sandwiches are open-faced, a bottom slice of dark rye bread topped with pickled or smoked herring, sardines, salmon, anchovies, cheeses, liver paste, sliced radishes, watercress, chives, onions, pickled beets, cucumbers, dill potatoes. The Swedes add crisp flatbreads and meatballs. A more elaborate sandwich is Danish *rullepølse*—raw meats pounded flat, layered, rolled up, sewn together, simmered for hours in water, then pressed flat and sliced.

The late-nineteenth-century United States produced two meat sandwiches of German origin, the frankfurter, aka hot dog, and the hamburger, both served on buns, and what began as a health food sandwich, the PB&J—peanut butter and jelly. Other American sandwich standards include the BLT—bacon, lettuce, and tomato—and its triple-decker version, the club, with an added layer of chicken or turkey. In the 1930s, the comic strip and movie character Dagwood made the sandwich that bears his name by going vertical with anything in the refrigerator.

There are regional differences and immigrant contributions. New England produced the lobster roll as a lobster salad sandwich, or for purists, just picked lobster chunks in butter on a New England split bun. New York and Nebraska both claim the mid-twentieth-century Jewish-deli Reuben—hot corned beef and Swiss cheese with Thousand Island dressing. New Orleans weighed in with the fried oyster po' (poor) boy, and the muffuletta, Italian cold cuts with olive salad. Italians in Philadelphia created the famous Philly cheese steak, a hot sandwich with grilled onions. Italy's grilled sandwich is the *panino*—"little bread." France's signature sandwich is the *croque monsieur*—grilled ham and cheese.

Other names for sandwich are sub (shaped like a submarine), torpedo, grinder, hoagy, and hero. Sandwich chains include Blimpie and Subway. And of course, there are the burger places: McDonald's, which opened in 1955, Burger King, Jack in the Box, Wendy's, and White Castle, which makes their burgers square and which gained fame when movie characters Harold and Kumar went on a late-night search for one.

In the late twentieth century, immigrants from Caribbean and Asian countries brought their pocket sandwiches to the United States. Trinidadian doubles are two slices of yeast-risen fried bread with a curried chickpea filling. Western Asians put grilled seasoned meat called *shawarma* in pita bread with sauces made of tahini or yogurt or both. Israelis stuff the pita with falafel, fried balls of chickpea batter. Eastern Asian fusion sandwiches called *banh mi* are small French baguettes with fillings like Korean barbecue, Chinese roast pork, Vietnamese lemongrass-marinated beef, and Thai barbecued chicken. Condiments include chiles, fresh herbs, pickled ginger, and lime juice. And although McDonald's is popular in China, cold sandwiches aren't—they're offerings to the dead.

A New People and a New Cuisine

Taxes and Taverns

The struggle between the American colonists and the British Parliament for control of the colonies began in earnest in 1764, the year after the French and Indian War ended, and France lost its colonies in North America except for Haiti in the Caribbean. In an effort to raise money to pay for the war, the British Parliament—where Americans were not represented—taxed sugar. The colonists protested. Parliament lowered that tax, then the next year passed the Stamp Act, which taxed paper, from deeds and wills to newspapers and playing cards. The furious colonists cried "No taxation without representation"—you can't make us pay taxes we didn't vote for—and boycotted British wool. Americans stopped eating mutton to let sheep live and provide Americans with wool. The Sons of Liberty, men recruited from taverns by Samuel Adams, a local brewer (yes, *that* Sam Adams), tarred and feathered the stamp collectors and broke into their houses. The violence forced Parliament to repeal the Stamp Act in 1766, before it went into effect. There were celebrations in taverns throughout the colonies.

Tensions escalated in Boston, a town with fewer than 16,000 people, when the British stationed 4,000 red-coated soldiers—the Bostonians called them "lobsterbacks"—there in 1768 and expected the people to take them into their homes and feed them for nothing. Two years later, after a crowd threw sticks,

England and France in North America, 1755, with disputed land claimed by George Washington for Virginia. *Courtesy Corbis Digital Stock.*

rocks, and snowballs at them, the soldiers opened fire. They killed four Americans, including a black man, Crispus Attucks. Sam Adams began the Committees of Correspondence, a propaganda letter-writing campaign, to report the Boston Massacre and whip all the colonies up against England. Now he would use the Internet, but in colonial America snail mail traveled on the Boston Post Road (highway U.S. 1 on the east coast) through New Haven to New York. Along the way, mail was not delivered to individual houses, but to taverns, where reports of British atrocities inflamed Americans' anger, and strips ripped off dried salted codfish hanging on the wall inflamed their thirst.[37] The Green Dragon Tavern in Boston's North End (now Boston's Little Italy) was where Adams, silversmith Paul Revere (whose name and picture are still on the bottom of the line of cookware named after him), and others got together to plan.

British Prime Minister "Champagne" Charlie Townshend had a new approach: instead of one large tax, many small taxes. The Townshend Acts taxed glass, paint, lead, and tea. The colonists protested. Eventually all the taxes were repealed—except the tea tax. The British East India Company needed the money, so they set the price of the tea *with the tax* lower than what it cost Americans to buy it from smugglers.[38] The Americans were furious—did the British really think they could sucker them into paying a tax they had no part in passing? The tea had to go.

"Boston Harbor a teapot tonight!"

On December 16, 1773, about 150 men in disguise, some dressed like Indians, others with their faces blackened with charcoal, boarded the East India Company ships in Boston Harbor. Hundreds of chests of tea, each weighing 350 pounds, were smashed open with the Indians' tomahawks and thrown into the harbor. In three hours, it was all over. The masterminds of the tea party, John Hancock and Sam Adams, made sure they were seen sitting in a tavern far away. Boston wasn't the only place that protested. In Annapolis, Maryland, colonists burned ships. Other colonies staged public tea burnings.

Parliament retaliated: they shut down the port of Boston until the colonists paid for the tea. Then they came to get the colonists' ammunition and the ringleaders—John Hancock and Sam Adams. But Paul Revere made his famous ride, alerting everyone that "The British are coming! The British are coming!" On April 19, 1775, the American Revolution began. The shot that began the revolution was "the shot heard 'round the world," because it would inspire people in many other countries to fight for their freedom, too.

America "will always have a market while eating is the custom of Europe."—Thomas Paine[39]

However, Americans weren't talking about independence; they still considered themselves Englishmen. Then Thomas Paine published a pamphlet called *Common Sense*, in which he outlined the reasons it would be to America's benefit to break away from England. Paine reassured Americans worried about the financial consequences of breaking away from England that America's food was a necessity to Europe: "Our corn will fetch its price in any market in Europe."[40] He laid his arguments out forcefully: "'TIS TIME TO PART" (uppercase in original).[41] Americans listened. On July 4, 1776, the Declaration of Independence, the document announcing America's freedom from England and using the words *The United States of America* for the first time, was celebrated with fireworks and cheering.

1776 might have been the birth of something else, too. Legend has it that the first cocktail was made in 1776.

FOOD FABLE:

Where the Cocktail Comes From

"[A] barmaid, Betsy Flanagan, at Halls Corners in Elmsford, New York, used a cock's feathers to decorate behind the bar. When one of the imbibers asked for a glass of those 'cocktails,' Betsy served him a mixed drink with a feather stuck in it."[42]

"No meat, no soldier"

Under the eighteenth-century rules of war, fighting was suspended during the winter. In the winter of 1777–1778, British officers were eating and drinking and dancing in New York. British fighting soldiers got rancid, wormy food—rock-hard biscuits that had been captured 15 years earlier in the French and Indian War. They slammed cannonballs down on them to soften them.[43]

Both groups were better off than the 12,000 Americans starving and freezing with General George Washington at Valley Forge, Pennsylvania. They had only animal skulls and hooves that they boiled into thin stews. They had no bread at all for days. Their shoes were worn out or gone; their blankets were threadbare. Some of the men were nearly naked. Limbs froze or became gangrenous and had to be amputated. The near-starvation rations weakened the men's immune systems. More than 2,000 died of typhoid, typhus, smallpox, and pneumonia. Finally, the cry went up from the ranks: "No meat, no soldier." Washington wrote to the Continental Congress and made it clear that if his men did not receive food and supplies, the war would be over.[44] He finally got them.

It is ironic, because before Washington left his estate at Mt. Vernon in Virginia to command the army, he left instructions about running the plantation: "Let the hospitality of the house with respect to the poor be kept up. Let no one go hungry away."[45]

We Couldn't Have Done It without the French

For almost the first two-and-one-half years of the American Revolution, the French provided the Americans, who had few factories, with ammunition, training, and officers like Lafayette. They did it secretly to avoid another war with the British. One of the reasons King Louis XVI aided America was to keep England from winning and then coming after France's lucrative Caribbean sugar property in Haiti. Another was to get revenge on the British, who had beaten them in the French and Indian War.

England's other great enemy, Spain, contributed money to the Americans, but it was a French squeeze play that ended the war. Washington's army had the British army, under General Cornwallis, backed up against the sea at Yorktown, Virginia. Cornwallis wasn't worried—the British fleet would sail down from New York to pluck him and his troops to safety. Except that the French fleet sailed up from Haiti and sandwiched the British in. Game over. General George Washington said farewell to his men at Fraunces Tavern in New York City after the six years of war that changed America from a British colony into the United States.

The Whiskey Rebellion and the BATF

In 1787, the year that British sailors on the HMS *Bounty* mutinied against Captain Bligh as he tried to transport breadfruit from Tahiti to the Caribbean, 55 white, middle-class men, mostly businessmen and lawyers, gathered in Philadelphia, Pennsylvania, to draw up a document that would change the world—the United States Constitution. It went into effect on April 30, 1789, when George Washington was sworn in as the first president in the nation's capital, then New York City. He needed a cook, so he put an ad in newspapers: "No one need apply who is not perfect in the business, and can bring indubitable testimonials of sobriety, honesty and attention to the duties of the station." George and Martha Washington never did get what they needed—their cooks were too extravagant, or they could cook but not bake, which meant that desserts and cakes had to be purchased from commercial bakeries, which cost extra. When the capital moved to Philadelphia, founded by anti-slavery Quakers, one of Washington's slave cooks ran away.[46]

Washington had only three cabinet members: Secretary of State Thomas Jefferson, Secretary of War Henry Knox, and Secretary of the Treasury Alexander Hamilton. One of the first things Hamilton did to stabilize the economy of the new country and ensure that it had good credit with the rest of the world was to raise money by taxing luxury items like imported alcoholic beverages, especially wines and distilled liquors. In the 1790s, Americans drank about six gallons of alcohol per person each year, twice as much as now. Most was beer; about one-third was distilled liquor.[47] Since efforts to grow grapes and make wine had failed in North America in spite of offers of large cash prizes, wine was imported and expensive, so wealthy people would be taxed. Jefferson objected to Hamilton's tax on imported wines for two reasons. First, he thought that it was undemocratic because the tax made wine too expensive for middle-class people to afford. Second, he believed that in countries where good wine was available, there was less drunkenness. Where wine was not available, people turned to hard liquor—"ardent spirits"—and got drunk. Nevertheless, Hamilton's tax on imported spirits proved such a good source of income that

Congress extended it to distilled spirits produced within the United States. This caused problems in 1794.

The farmers in western Pennsylvania who grew corn and rye didn't think the "white lightning" alcohol they made out of it was a luxury. It was a necessity, accepted as payment for goods and services. Transporting bulk grain over bad or nonexistent roads was not profitable. Transporting the grain in its concentrated liquid, alcoholic form, was. They followed their refusal to pay the whiskey tax with boycotts and demonstrations. President Washington knew better than anyone where that could lead. He called up 13,000 militia men to put down the rebellion by a few people. The officers were well fed with "mountains of beef and oceans of whiskey."[48] The organization within the Treasury Department that grew out of the response to this rebellion became the Bureau of Alcohol, Tobacco, and Firearms—the BATF—which still oversees alcohol in the United States today. Jefferson thought that Washington had engaged in overkill. The differences that came to a head over the Whiskey Rebellion were one of the causes of political parties in the United States.

The First American Cookbook

In 1796, a cookbook called *American Cookery* was published in Hartford, the capital of Connecticut. The author was a woman named Amelia Simmons, who described herself as "an American orphan." The book revealed much about Simmons and about the values of the new country. She was a poor woman, but she wrote about meat. The cookbook begins with beef recipes. Continuing the country's tradition of self-betterment, Simmons stated in the first sentence that the book was written "for the improvement of the rising generation of *Females* in America" (italics in original). She hoped that the information in her book would make them "useful members of society." She talked about her own situation— "the orphan must depend solely upon *character*"[49] to make her way in the world (emphasis in original).

On the title page of *American Cookery*, Simmons declared that the recipes were "adapted to this country." Food historian Karen Hess explains the importance of the cookbook: Simmons wrote about the ingredients she knew, many of them New World foods that had been ignored in British cookbooks and appeared in print in Simmons's book for the first time. For example, she published the first recipes for pumpkin and for corn. She used the word cookie, the diminutive of the Dutch word for cake. *Sla* was another borrowing from the Dutch, for salad. "Cabbage salad" became that American favorite "coleslaw."

Simmons also included one very important American first, a leavening shortcut called pearlash, the forerunner of baking powder, which came into use in 1856. The new leavening gave rise to the first baked fast food—quick breads. Before chemical leavening agents, making baked goods rise was time-consuming and expensive. The cook had to either proof yeast and keep it at the right temperature through multiple risings, beat eggs to incorporate air into them, or make pastry with layers of butter that would puff when baked. But baking powder or soda combined with flour and salt produced what Americans called biscuits. American biscuits are not a true biscuit, which is French for "twice cooked" (in Italian, *biscotti*), because American biscuits are cooked only once. But they rise twice now, because of double acting baking powder. This new American way to bake faster and easier caught on immediately in Europe. Simmons's cookbook was so popular that a second, expanded version was published. It included a recipe for Election Cake.

1789 saw the birth of the constitutional government that exists to this day in the United States, and the death of the Bourbon dynasty that had ruled France for hundreds of years. Ideas connected with America's fight for liberty, and the money that helped them succeed—taxes paid by the French people—would topple the monarch who had come to America's aid, King Louis XVI of France. This would have profound repercussions for global politics and cuisine.

Jefferson, the Francophile President

Jefferson was a Francophile—he loved France and all things French. While he was the American ambassador to France from 1784 until the French Revolution began in 1789, he ate and loved Continental food. He traveled widely in Europe, sampling food and wine everywhere he went. He bought a waffle iron in the Netherlands after he tasted waffles, sent a messenger to Naples to buy a "maccaroni mould," learned about wine making in France and Germany, about butter and cheese making in Italy. He took a slave with him to be trained by French chefs. After he returned to America, Jefferson granted the slave his freedom, but only after he trained a replacement. (The slave was his son.) Jefferson also brought crates of pasta and the word *macaroni* back with him. (The word *spaghetti* didn't appear in America until the 1849 edition of *Modern Cookery for Private Families* by Eliza Acton.)

In Washington, Jefferson bemoaned the lack of olive oil, vinegar, *moutarde d'estragon* (tarragon mustard), and other foods he had gotten used to in Europe. He imported food and wine from Europe, engaged in voluminous correspondence with horticulturalists in the United States and Europe, went to the market with his French chef, kept notes on which fruits and vegetables ripened when.

While he was president, Jefferson instituted two new procedures for keeping wait staff out of the presidential dining room, because he didn't want them to overhear what was going on and gossip. One was a "dumb waiter," a small, unmanned elevator with shelves so that food could be sent from the kitchen to the dining room. The other was a special wall with built-in shelves. Used dishes were placed on the shelves in the dining room, Jefferson pressed a button, and the wall turned, sending the used dishes to the butler's pantry and dishes with fresh food into the dining room.

Election Day

The biggest holiday in colonial New England, proud of its democracy, was Election Day, in May; it continued to be a holiday in the New Republic. Thanksgiving and Christmas were not celebrated until the Civil War, but Election Day was a day off from work for everybody. Even blacks joined the parades, singing and dancing to banjo and drum music. In New England, slaves got to vote for leaders in their slave communities: "The Negro 'government' had its 'judges,' 'sheriffs,' and 'magistrates,' and its courts probably tried trivial cases between Negroes as well as petty cases brought by masters against their slaves."[50] Since the tavern was the polling place, it was also an excuse to have an extra drink or let someone buy you one to persuade you to vote for his candidate. But it was almost not necessary to drink to get drunk—there was plenty of liquor in the election cake. At the end of the nineteenth century, reformers campaigned to stop holding elections in taverns and getting voters "liquored up" because it undermined democracy and led to violence and riots. By then, the temperance movement had taken firm hold of cooking, too—the election cake was alcohol-free.

INGREDIENTS: ELECTION CAKE COMPARISON

1796—AMELIA SIMMONS[51]	1918—FANNIE FARMER[52]
30 quarts of flour	1¼ cups flour
1 quart yeast	1 cup bread dough
10 pounds of butter	½ cup butter
14 pounds of sugar	1 cup brown sugar
12 pounds of raisins	⅔ cup raisins
--------	8 finely chopped figs
3 dozen eggs	1 egg
1 pint of wine	--------
1 quart of brandy	--------
4 ounces cinnamon	1 teaspoon cinnamon
4 ounces fine colander [coriander?] seed	--------
3 ounces ground allspice	--------
--------	¼ teaspoon mace
--------	¼ teaspoon nutmeg
--------	¼ teaspoon clove
--------	½ cup sour milk
--------	½ teaspoon soda
--------	1 teaspoon salt

(The finished cake weighed 90 pounds)

Jefferson also brought democracy into international etiquette. Until then, seating at state dinners was rigidly controlled, with great attention given to who sat where. Foreign dignitaries were given the place of honor at the right hand of the ruler of the country they were in. Jefferson declared this undemocratic, and said that seating would be "pell-mell"—sit where you want, without regard to rank. Some were insulted.

In Virginia, Jefferson's plantation, Monticello, had 5,000 acres of orchards, fruit and vegetable gardens, and numerous outbuildings. Although there was a tea room and a dining room, there was no kitchen in the house. On southern plantations, the kitchen was a separate building, to keep the heat out of the main house and also to avoid accidentally burning the main house down.

Jefferson, "The Big Cheese"

The 1,235-pound cheese couldn't be ignored. It arrived in Washington, D.C., on New Year's Day, 1802, a gift to President Thomas Jefferson from the citizens of Cheshire, Massachusetts (and 900 cows). This large food also had a political and religious purpose. The cheese had a motto printed on it: "Rebellion to tyrants is obedience to God."[53] It was the public relations brainchild of a Baptist minister, one of the leaders of the new religious movement that was sweeping America and came to be called the Second Great Awakening, as people everywhere awoke to their inner religious feelings. Americans made pilgrimages to see the big cheese in the White House. And that is how the president of the United States became "the big cheese."

Thomas Jefferson's kitchen at Monticello. *Courtesy of Monticello/Thomas Jefferson Foundation, Inc.*

In 1803, the Big Cheese was worried. President Jefferson had just bought 828,000 square *miles* of land from Napoleon, and his conscience was bothering him. Nowhere did the Constitution say that the president, by himself, could pick up a pen and double the size of the country, not even at the bargain price of three cents an acre. He had authorized the American ambassador to buy New Orleans so the American farmers who were swarming west over the Appalachians into the Ohio River Valley would have a seaport to get their produce to Europe. To trade with other Americans, any foodstuffs from the Ohio River Valley could be floated downriver to where three rivers—the Ohio, the Allegheny, and the Monongahela—met at Pittsburgh. But to trade with Europe, they had to continue down to the mouth of the Mississippi, to New Orleans. The Americans owned Pittsburgh; the French owned New Orleans, which angry Americans were talking about attacking and taking by force. This would throw the new, small United States into a war with a European superpower headed by Napoleon, a military genius. President Jefferson hoped that Napoleon would sell New Orleans to the United States. He was stunned when Napoleon gave the go-ahead to sell everything France owned on the North American mainland. It was one of the greatest real estate deals in history.

But what exactly had America bought? A shortcut to the riches and markets of China and India, they hoped. Maybe this, finally, was the Northwest Passage, the water route through North America to the Pacific Ocean and on to Asia that Columbus, Hudson, Champlain, and the other explorers had not been able to find. Maybe by going north, up the Mississippi River to its headwaters, they would discover a route to Asia. Two years later, Lewis and Clark returned from their exploration with disappointing news—no northwest passage.

New Orleans—Creole Cuisine

New Orleans, however, was not a disappointment. Its Creole cuisine—ruling-class French and Spanish cuisine prepared by African cooks, with some Native American elements—is unique in America. A prime example of this fusion food is gumbo, a sausage and seafood stew. The word is African and so is the use of okra—an African word for an African vegetable—as a thickener. But the roux base is French; the combination of sausage and seafood is southern Mediterranean, like French bouillabaisse; and the seasoning is filé—powdered sassafras leaves obtained from Native Americans. Another New Orleans specialty, jambalaya, comes from *jambon*, French for "ham," and *ya*, an African word for "rice"; *étouffée* means "smothered," but is more like a stuffing for seafood.

Beginning in 1791, New Orleans residents could buy fresh turtles, crabs, vegetables, or slaves at La Halle, the French marketplace. After 1812, travelers, gamblers, and other characters sailed up and down the Mississippi on luxurious steamboats with ballrooms, bars, and casinos.[54] Louisiana bills itself as the

Sportsman's Paradise because of the abundance of deer, quail, duck, and other wildfowl. Prepared meats include everything from sophisticated sausages like boudin, to barbecue, to real fried pork rinds with streaks of pork (nothing like the prepackaged Styrofoam). The Gulf of Mexico provides shrimp, oysters, and crawfish. As elsewhere in the South, corn appears as grits and hominy. Louisiana is also famous for two foods of Asian origin, rice and sugar. Pralines are a pecan, butter, and brown sugar patty. At sidewalk cafés, people snack on beignets—fried pastry puffs dusted with confectioners' sugar—and chicory coffee. It is also the home of Bananas Foster, Oysters Rockefeller, Tabasco sauce, and a very special holiday, Mardi Gras.

HOLIDAY HISTORY:
Mardi Gras and Carnevale

In Christianity, January 6, 12 days after Christmas, is when the three kings who had been searching for the newborn Christ child found him. In Louisiana, it marks the end of the festive Christmas season and the beginning of the festive Mardi Gras season. *Mardi Gras* is French for "Fat Tuesday," the last day of feasting before Lent and its 40 days of fasting begin on Ash Wednesday. The first official Mardi Gras celebration in New Orleans was in 1827, although other celebrations had been occurring in French America since 1718. A fancy dress ball kicks off the series of parades with kings and queens, special Mardi Gras jewelry, and a special King Cake in the official colors of Mardi Gras—purple, gold, and green. Other pre-Lent celebrations occur around the world. One of the largest is in Brazil, where it is called *Carnevale* (which means "goodbye, meat"), and samba clubs practice special dances all year for the festivities.

The King Cake served for Mardi Gras has a tiny plastic baby doll baked inside. Traditionally, the person who gets the piece of cake with the baby in it is king or queen for a day and then has to provide the next party. The custom dates back to the ancient French custom of baking a lucky bean—*fève*—into the bread. The baby refers to the Christ child.

INGREDIENTS:
King Cake—the Cake with a Baby Inside[55]

2 cups sugar	6 egg whites
½ cup butter	½ teaspoon baking soda
2 cups flour	1 teaspoon cream of tartar
½ cup water	juice of 1½ oranges
5 egg yolks	1 tiny plastic baby doll

The End of an Era

Americans and foreigners wanted to meet the Americans who had played such prominent roles in the founding of the country, so they dropped in on them at their homes. Congress provided no funds; the former presidents were expected to pay for these expenses themselves.

After he retired, George Washington complained that visitors to his Virginia home, Mt. Vernon, were turning him into an innkeeper. At Monticello, as many as 50 unannounced guests would drop in at once, stretching the facilities and Jefferson's pocketbook.

John Adams, the second president of the United States, and Thomas Jefferson, the third—one from the North, the other from the South, of different political parties—died on the same day, within a few hours of each other. The day was July 4, 1826—exactly 50 years after the Declaration of Independence was first celebrated.

The United States: Cholera and the Constitution

In 1832, six years after America's fiftieth anniversary, cholera, one of the great sanitation diseases, hit the United States hard. This was a big shock to Americans. They had assured themselves that they were immune to the cholera epidemic that was raging in the rest of the world because they were Christians; "the Asiatic cholera" was a disease of Chinese "heathens." Also, America was the New World, exceptional and clean. No slums, vices, and corruption like the filthy Old World. But cholera was just a disease, and in the nineteenth century, like bubonic plague in the fourteenth, it followed the trade routes. The difference was that in the nineteenth century, the trade routes were global. Americans assumed cholera was the wrath of God. Wealthy Americans, like wealthy Europeans, fled to their homes in the country. Of those who remained in the city, who lived and who died was puzzling: seemingly religious, upstanding members of the community died while ne'er-do-wells lived. The reason: fine, upstanding citizens drank water from wells they didn't know were contaminated, while street people drank germ-free wine, rum, or gin. Americans were terrified; a group of ministers appealed to president Andrew Jackson for a national day of prayer. Jackson declined, citing the separation of church and state. He said that the ministers were free to lead the country in any prayer to any God they wanted, but it wasn't in the president's job description in the Constitution.[56]

Cholera struck the United States again in 1848–1849. It swept through the poor Irish neighborhoods in eastern cities like New York, killing the Irish just after they arrived, already weakened from the potato famine and weeks on the coffin ships. In the west, travelers on the trails added cholera to the list of dangers they faced. In 1866, right after the Civil War, the third and last major cholera epidemic struck the United States. New York City's response was to do what London and Paris had done: create a public health department. In a little more than 30 years, the American attitude toward disease had changed completely.

Disease had gone from being divinely caused to being preventable by science, from a religious problem to a secular one with a solution: clean up the water supply.

"Go west, young man!"

In the 1840s, America was in a fever to head west. "Manifest destiny" was the idea that the restless American people were destined to rule North America "from sea to shining sea." They had already invented technology to connect the country as far west as the Mississippi. In 1807, Robert Fulton's steamboat sailed up the Hudson River, against the current. In 1825, the Erie Canal provided a cheap water route from the Ohio River Valley through Buffalo to New York City in a fraction of the time and cost of land transportation, making more food more affordable. With states in the west functioning almost as its colonies, New York became the Empire State. At the end of the 1820s, the first railroads were built in the United States. In 1844, the wires talked—Samuel Morse invented the telegraph and the code to transmit messages.

But west of the Mississippi was unknown territory until John Fremont—the "Pathfinder"—and his expedition returned in the early 1840s. (Lewis and Clark had gone north, almost to the Canadian border.) Fremont returned with maps, a route—approximately where Interstate 80 runs now—and stories, mostly written by his wife Jessie. The good news was that there was good farm land in California, which was owned by Mexico; and Oregon, which the British claimed.

Going west was not cheap or easy. Each adult needed 400 pounds of provisions, wagons to carry them in, oxen to pull the wagons, and enough money not to have to work for the time it took to go west and to start a business. So the majority of those who went were prosperous white farmers from families who had been in the United States for generations. Few free blacks could afford the trip. Some immigrants went, usually as servants. Inexperienced pioneers packed everything they owned into their wagons and ended up dumping about half of it along the way. The smart ones brought milk cows because there was no dairy industry in California yet and milk was very valuable.[57] Almost everybody walked, because the burden on the valuable farm animals would have been too much, and because it was more comfortable. There were no roads, and the wagons had wooden wheels and no springs. They only had a few months to cross, so they didn't stop for births or deaths. Breadstuff was the staple on the overland trail: wheat flour baked into yeast-risen bread in a Dutch oven when they had the time and the fuel, biscuits, crackers, and cornmeal when they didn't. They supplemented this with coffee, sugar, salt, bacon, and dried fruit.

These farmers from the flat, fertile Midwest had no understanding of the terrain they were heading into. They figured that they could shoot or trap game along the way, as they had at home. Not always. And they found out the hard way what a desert can do to living things and even inanimate objects. They counted on covering about 20 miles a day, but had no idea that the short stretch on the map called "Forty-Mile Desert" in what is now Nevada would take them not two days of walking, but at least five; that many of their oxen would die or go crazy from thirst; and that the curved wood in their covered wagon frames and wheels would dry out, straighten, and splinter. Desperate people ate "bush-trout"—rattlesnakes. People dying of thirst drank their mules' urine or paid $15 for a glass of water when they could get it.

How to Cook a Coyote

The desert wasn't the worst of it. Coming out of the 40-mile crossing exhausted, weak, and low on food, they faced mountains more than 14,000 feet high. The Spanish name—Sierra Nevada—means "snowy peaks," because the snow sometimes stays until July. The famous Donner Party from Illinois, stranded for months in the snow above 6,000 feet during the winter of 1846–1847, butchered their dead. They took great care to label the body parts so no one would accidentally eat a relative. Forty-seven people lived by eating the 40 who died.[58] (Years later, Mormons trapped in the snow without food on their way to Utah chose to die rather than turn cannibal.)

In another case of being stranded in the snow, desperate 18-year-old Moses Schallenberger, who had fallen behind and been left by his wagon train, decided to try to trap something, anything:

> I found in one of [the traps] a starved coyote. I soon had his hide off and his flesh roasted in a Dutch oven. I ate this meat, but it was horrible. I next tried boiling him, but it didn't improve the flavor. I cooked him in every possible manner my imagination, spurred by hunger, could suggest, but couldn't get him into a condition where he could be eaten without revolting my stomach. But for three days this was all I had to eat.[59]

Moses was also able to trap foxes, which he found delicious, though their meat was "entirely devoid of fat," which he craved. He also caught many more coyotes, "but I never got hungry enough to eat one of them again."[60]

The Gold Rush: Feeding the Forty-Niners

After a war with Mexico from 1846 to 1848, the United States owned California and the land reaching to the Pacific Ocean. A treaty with England added Oregon to the United States. In 1848, near what is now Sacramento in northern California, at a sawmill being built on the American River by a Swiss immigrant named Sutter, gold was discovered. The stories were fantastic: men dammed a river and found $75,000 in gold nuggets just lying in the dry riverbed; a man and his two sons picked up more than $9,000 each in a short time.[61] Historian John Holliday described the gold rush in the title of his book: *The World Rushed In*. And it was an almost totally male world. In the first five months of 1850, of the 17,661 people who passed through Ft. Laramie, Wyoming, on their way west, 17,443 were men.[62] They gravitated to taverns, saloons, bars, liquor, and gambling.

No matter where the miners came from or what language they spoke, they all had to eat, and all the food had to be shipped in. Merchants who sold food got rich by mining the miners—they gouged. Five dollars then was the equivalent of about $100 today.

CALIFORNIA GOLD RUSH FOOD PRICE COMPARISON, 1850–2010 (PER POUND)[63]

ITEM	1850—CALIFORNIA GOLD FIELDS	2010—LOS ANGELES SUPERMARKET
sugar	.75	.66
dried beans	1.00	1.07
potatoes	1.00	.30
baking soda	6.00	.90
coffee	.50	3.47
tea	2.50	(in bags) 7.18
vinegar	5.00	2.79

Cooking equipment suffered the same mark-up: tin pans and coffeepots cost $8 each, frying pans, $6. Water in a boarding house cost $20 per week; rent was $500 per month. With saleratus—a leavening agent like sodium bicarbonate— selling for $6 per pound, the men opted for flour and water left out to ferment, leavened with wild yeast that settled from the air. A portion of each batch of this bread could be kept aside and fed to start the next batch. From these bread start- ers, the men became known as "sourdoughs." For those who claim that San Francisco sourdough bread doesn't taste like any other, they're right. The organ- ism in the air there—and only there—is *Lactobacillus sanfrancisco*.[64]

Even when food and equipment were available, everybody was too busy pros- pecting for gold to unload it or get it out of the warehouses. Tons of food rotted, and there was nobody to clean it up. Everything except looking for gold was a waste of time. Even roasting and grinding coffee beans took too long. Folger's stepped in with the first preroasted coffee.[65] When the men complained that their pants kept ripping from all the hard work, a Jewish merchant from Bavaria named Levi Strauss teamed up with a Lithuanian tailor and took out a patent for denim pants held together with metal rivets—"Levi's" blue jeans.[66]

Yes, there was gold "in them thar hills," but there was malnutrition, too. No one who wrote home mentioned dairy or eggs except to note their absence. But- ter from New York arrived brown after a year-long sea voyage around "the Horn"—the tip of South America. Cooks had to sift flour to get rid of weevils and pulled long black worms out by the handful. Gunpowder substituted for salt. A meal usually consisted of "coffee, bacon, beans, and hard bread," eaten standing or sitting on a log.[67] Scurvy killed about 10,000 miners in the 1850s until they started eating winter purslane, which they called "miners' lettuce."[68]

The Native Americans of California, who were described as "timid and friendly," lived on acorns and wild game they shot with bows and arrows. The massive population invasion had the same disastrous effect on them that the arrival of the Spanish had had on the natives of Central America 250 years earlier: they died. Between 1850 and 1860, the native population of California dropped 80 percent, and not from disease; this population had already been exposed to European diseases.[69]

The Gold Rush in California in 1849 was just the first of several mineral rushes. Later, silver was discovered in Nevada; gold in the Black Hills of South Dakota in the 1870s; and gold again in the Alaskan Klondike/Canadian Yukon in 1898. But the sane Canadians sent the RCMP—Royal Canadian Mounted Police or "Mounties"—in first. They turned back anyone who didn't have a six-month supply of food. A year after the Gold Rush began, California had enough people to apply to become a state. When it did, in 1850, it came in as a free state, and began the slide into the Civil War.

While the Americans had been struggling to settle the continent in the seventeenth century, revolting in the eighteenth, and expanding west in the nineteenth, Europeans had made great strides in the world of science. These would change agriculture, cuisines, and cultures throughout the world.

Hutsepot, Stove Potatoes, and Haute Cuisine

SEVENTEENTH- TO EIGHTEENTH-CENTURY DUTCH, RUSSIAN, AND FRENCH CUISINE

The Scientific Revolution

Europe's far-flung colonies were agricultural in the seventeenth century, but in Europe's cities, amateur and professional scientists began to examine everything with a fresh eye, trusting their own observations, as Columbus had done. They, too, were rewarded by discovering new worlds. The telescope allowed them to see Earth's moon for the first time, and to discover Jupiter's moons. A Dutch draper named van Leeuwenhoek looked through the microscope and saw tiny new worlds in water and blood. The universe appeared orderly to physicists like Italy's Galileo and England's Newton, who discovered laws of motion and of gravity; to mathematicians like France's Descartes, who said, "I think, therefore I am"; to Boyle, the founder of chemistry. Sweden's Celsius and the Netherlands' Fahrenheit invented systems for measuring temperature, which would eventually allow cooking with precision. Historians now call this period the Scientific Revolution.

These discoveries challenged the authority of the Catholic Church. In 1633, the Church summoned Galileo before the Inquisition in Rome and found him guilty of heresy—speaking out against the Church—for saying that the Earth revolved around the sun. The Church's position was that the Earth was the center of the universe. Galileo was put under house arrest for the rest of his life. (The Church pardoned him in 1992.) This put serious limits on scientific investigations in the Catholic countries of southern Europe. But in Protestant northern European countries, the Scientific Revolution was supported by the governments and flourished. In 1660, England established the Royal Society to advance science, and would benefit mightily from its discoveries and inventions in the eighteenth century.

The Golden Age of the Netherlands

A small country in northern Europe, the Netherlands, was also prosperous. The Dutch replaced the Italians—the Medici of Florence and the Venetians—as the international bankers, and the world banking center moved to the Netherlands in the seventeenth century. The Dutch dominated or controlled the world shipping trade in spices, sugar, coffee, slaves, precious gems, and grain. Dutch ships also delivered oil, wine, and salt from Portugal, Spain, and France to northern Europe, and gold and silver from New World mines to Old World vaults.

One of the reasons the Netherlands rose to power was that it was unique—a unified, religiously tolerant republic. During the sixteenth century, European monarchs fought with the Church and each other over religion; in some places, religious wars killed a greater percentage of the population than the Black Death had. An exception was the Netherlands, peaceful and open for business. Many of the Jews who had been driven out of Spain by the Inquisition went north to the hospitable Protestant Netherlands and contributed their knowledge of banking and business to an already flourishing economy. The stock exchange, called the Bourse (French for "purse"), was created in Amsterdam in the middle of the sixteenth century. In 1609, the Bank of Amsterdam opened. It had an international money exchange and used the system of writing checks invented by the Arabs in the Middle Ages. The Dutch government guaranteed the safety of deposits—something not available in the United States until 1933. The Dutch *florin* was accepted as payment all over the world, much as the American dollar is today.[1]

"God made the world, but the Dutch made Holland"[2]

Dutch life was tied to the sea and was a constant battle with it. The Dutch invented windmills to pump water out of the fields and reclaim land from the sea, and dikes, walls to hold back the sea. The Dutch fleet of 10,000 ships brought salt, oil, and wine from southern France, Spain, and Portugal to northern Europe and carried grain back. They also carried gold and silver from the Americas. Much of Dutch food and industry centered around the sea. Twenty-five percent of the Dutch population was connected to the herring industry, from fishing to selling, and preserving by smoking, salting, and pickling.[3]

At a time when the economy of other European countries was suffering, the Dutch were extremely prosperous, with a large middle class and a high standard of living. Dutch virtues were cleanliness and thrift. Every morning, Dutch housewives washed not only their own stoops but also the public sidewalks in front of their houses. They lived and ate well. At fish markets, the Dutch bought only live fish. They threw away dead fish, as well as mackerel and red mullet.[4] Even workers could afford meat, cheese, and butter, and the urban poor were provided for in poorhouses that had been recycled from monasteries or convents when the Netherlands converted to Protestantism from Catholicism. Sailors on warships were fed a 4,800-calorie-per-day diet of mutton, beef, pork, smoked ham, bread, beans, peas, and smoked and pickled fish, much of it herring.[5] They were a country that grew no grain and made no wine, but they controlled trade from the breadbasket of Europe, the countries around the Baltic Sea.

Dutch Cuisine: *The Sensible Cook*

In the seventeenth and eighteenth centuries, one Dutch cookbook was predominant in the Netherlands. *The Sensible Cook*, published in 1668, contained 189 recipes and two appendixes, "The Sensible Confectioner" and "The Dutch Butchering Time." The cookbook and a bee-keeping manual were part of the medical section of *The Pleasurable Country Life*, a manual for wealthy bourgeoisie who owned a country house and a garden. It was really a compilation of three books: *The Dutch Gardener*, about ornamental gardens; *The Sensible Gardener*, about medicinal gardens; and *The Medicine Shop or the Experienced Housekeeper*, about the care of humans and animals.

None of the information in *The Sensible Cook* was available to English speakers until 1989, when it was translated by a Dutch woman, food historian Peter G. Rose. As she points out, the gender of the anonymous author of *The Sensible Cook* is unknown, but the book opens with a statement "To all cooks, male and female" and ends with the words "everyone to her own demand."[6]

Before mentioning a word about food, the author tells the reader how to build a stove, one of the rare examples before the nineteenth century of being able to stand up and cook. The recipes are divided into sections: salads, herbs, and vegetables first; then meat, fowl, and fish; followed by baked goods, custards, drinks, and miscellaneous; then a section on tarts; and finally, one on pasties [rhymes with "nasty"], like a savory turnover. The author was an organized person who took the trouble to capitalize the first letters of the main ingredients and to give exact measurements in loot—approximately 14 grams; pint—approximately one-half liter; and pond—approximately 454 grams.[7]

The Dutch ate four times a day—breakfast, the main meal at midday, in the afternoon at 2:00 or 3:00, and in the evening. They ate bread at all four meals: bread and butter, bread and cheese, bread and meat. It was all washed down, any time of day, with beer. Bread was baked by professional bakers in communal ovens even if the dough was made at home, because few people had ovens in their houses. Bread was the mainstay of the Dutch diet until the potato caught on at the end of the eighteenth century.[8] Rice was rare; only a handful of recipes in *The Sensible Cook* use rice. There are also very few foods from the New World. The turkey makes an appearance, as do green beans, called "Turkey beans" because that is where the Dutch got them. But this was a time before the Dutch knew one food that is a staple in their cuisine now: chocolate.

Middle Eastern Influence

The Sensible Cook shows that the Middle East and the Middle Ages were still strong influences on Dutch cuisine. Stews and sauces are thickened with ground nuts, bread, toast, eggs, or—a Dutch innovation—cookies. Sauces of sugar and verjuice or vinegar continue the sweet-sour medieval cooking tradition. The recipe "To make a proper Sauce" shows its Middle Eastern roots: ground almonds are added to the white bread crumb thickener, while sugar and verjuice make it sweet and sour. The only other ingredient is another Middle Eastern spice, ginger. There is little difference in the spices used for meat and for fish. Of the 59 recipes for meat, 30 use nutmeg and/or mace; so do 10 of the 18 fish recipes. For example, sturgeon is studded with cloves, spit-roasted, basted with butter, then stewed with Rhine wine, vinegar, cinnamon, and nutmeg.[9] Bream is also spit-roasted, stuffed with its own roe, chopped egg yolks, parsley, nutmeg, mace, pepper, and butter, sauced with pan drippings, anchovies, and verjuice, and garnished with oregano.[10] Many of the recipes contain a butter enrichment at the end; a recipe for hen stewed with greens reminds: "Especially do not forget the butter."[11] Rose water is still the flavoring of choice for desserts, a holdover from the Middle Ages. The Middle Eastern influence is also apparent in cumin-studded Gouda cheese, and in the lemons, oranges, and ginger in *hutsepot* (hot pot), a seasonal meat and vegetable stew.

RECIPE:

Hutsepot, the Dutch Dish

"Take some mutton or beef; wash it clean and chop it fine. Add thereto some green-stuff or parsnips or some stuffed prunes and the juice of lemons or oranges or citron or a pint of strong, clear vinegar. Mix these together, set the pot on a slow fire (for at least three and a half hours); add some ginger and melted butter."[12]

Santa Claus and Sumptuary Laws

The Dutch displayed their wealth in the furnishings of their homes, their art, their gardens. They had Turkish carpets, Persian silk, Ming china until Delft began producing home-grown Dutch knock-off blue ceramic tiles and tableware, lace, linens by the dozens for bed and table. They also adopted an idea from Topkapi Palace, the residence of the sultan of Turkey: gardens for no purpose except beauty, acres of gardens with not one edible plant in them, just flowers, especially tulips and especially red ones. The buying and selling of tulip bulbs was intense in the Netherlands, where fortunes were made and lost on just a handful of bulbs. Dutch art reflected Dutch life: secular, not religious. The still life paintings celebrated the new, exotic fruits—lemons, oranges, apricots—in settings of abundance and wealth.

All of this abundance presented a dilemma for the Dutch Reformed Church: were the Dutch going to be rich or religious? Were all these spices, sauces, and sugar, these cheeses and meats, all these possessions, the speculating in tulip bulbs, going to cause the Dutch to lose their souls? The response in some cities was sumptuary laws to regulate the sumptuousness—the luxury—of everyday life. For example, in Amsterdam in 1655, no more than 50 guests could be invited to a wedding, the celebration couldn't last longer than two days, and a ceiling was put on how much could be spent on gifts. Some city councils went too far and banned the December 6th festival of food and gift giving in honor of St. Nicholas—Sinter Klaas to the Dutch, Santa Claus to us—along with dolls and gingerbread men. It didn't last—the children rebelled.[13] While the church continued to preach thrift, the Dutch made money and spent it—and consumed it. They never stopped eating their pancakes and waffles sprinkled with sugar or swimming in caramel.

New Netherland

Like other European countries, the Dutch colonized. Between England's colonies in New England and the Chesapeake was the Dutch colony of New Netherland. The Dutch knew that they would have to entice people from other countries to settle New Netherland, because the Dutch people, prosperous and free to practice the religion of their choice, had no reason to leave their own country. The Dutch settlers who did go to New Netherland were amazed by oak trees that grew 70 feet high and made logs that burned hot and bright for hours. As in the Netherlands, bread was a staple in New Netherland, but it was baked at home. The Netherlands was urban, so commercial bakers made bread, but parts of the colony were very sparsely populated so it was necessary for people to have their own brick ovens built into the wall next to the fireplace. American ingredients like corn and pumpkin found their way into standard Dutch recipes like pancakes. Bread was more than food in the Dutch colony; it was a trade item so much sought after by the Native Americans—especially white breads and sweet cakes—that by 1649 there were laws against making bread to trade with the Indians.[14] New Netherland was just a small part of a vast Dutch Empire.

The Spice Islands: Nutmeg vs. New York

Much of the wealth of the Dutch Empire came from its colonies in the Spice Islands, now Indonesia. In 1602, the Dutch East India Company was founded to trade in Asia. Halfway around the world from the Netherlands, but having to make decisions for the good of the empire, the Dutch East India Company became so powerful that it functioned like a state: it could coin money, make treaties, and raise its own army. Within a short time, the Dutch broke the monopoly the Portuguese had held on the nutmeg trade for almost a century.

The British were after the spice trade, too. In 1600, they founded the British East India Company. Like Columbus, they

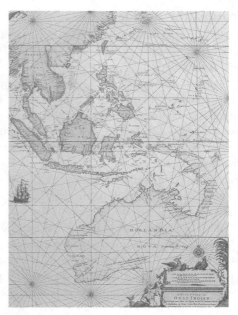

Southeast Asia, Indonesia, and Australia, early 1600s. Note that Australia is called Hollandia Nova—New Holland. *Courtesy Corbis Digital Stock.*

were determined to find their own route to the East Indies. Their quest became more urgent when bubonic plague struck again in the 1660s and physicians believed that nutmeg was the cure. Nutmeg is the seed of the *Myristica fragrans* tree; the shell is mace. The maps of the time showed it was possible to get to the Indies by sailing north of Norway and then east—a northeast passage. Mistake. The crews starved or froze to death.

Determined to get a piece of the East Indies spice trade, the British went to war with the Dutch from 1652 to 1654. They lost, then felt humiliated by the treaty, which gave the Dutch what seemed by far the better deal. The Dutch retained control of the lucrative Spice Islands trade, but all the British got was the puny Dutch colony in North America, New Netherland. The British tried to retain their pride and renamed the colony—New York. The area along the Hudson River where the Dutch settled is now called Dutchess County.

But war wasn't the only deadly danger connected to sailing.

Scurvy, "the plague of the sea"[15]

In 1657, in the sparkling seas off of Acapulco, Mexico, a ship was drifting, bobbing with the waves, shifting with the wind. It was a ghost ship, the entire crew dead from scurvy.

Scurvy is a deficiency of vitamin C—ascorbic acid—which works with iron to make red blood. It also makes collagen, which holds tissue together. Unlike some animals, like horses, humans can't make or store vitamin C, so we have to eat or drink it every day. In the absence of vitamin C, the symptoms of scurvy can appear in little more than a month. They start with tiredness and muscular weakness; then new wounds fester and ulcerate instead of heal; old wounds pull apart; small pinpoint purple spots on the skin indicate internal hemorrhaging; the gums get sore and bleed; the teeth fall out; the eyes and nose drip blood; then death.

The Latin word for scurvy is *scorbutus*, so the foods that fight scurvy are known as anti-scorbutics. Anti-scorbutics are citrus—orange, lemon, lime, grapefruit; cruciferous vegetables—kale, broccoli, cauliflower, cabbage, Brussels sprouts; and the nightshade family—green pepper, potato, tomato. There is the exact same amount of vitamin C in half a cup of broccoli and half a cup of orange juice—62 milligrams. Half a cup of kale has almost 50 percent more than either—93 milligrams.[16] It is not apparent to us now looking at this list of fruits and vegetables that they have anything in common; we know because vitamins were discovered in the 1920s. In the eighteenth and nineteenth centuries, all kinds of theories were put forward: the crew got scurvy because they hadn't been on land in a while; a piece of whale meat tied around a weak arm or leg would cure it; the acidity in certain foods counteracted scurvy. (Asians ate fresh ginger that they grew on their ships and didn't get scurvy.)[17]

In the eighteenth century, the British discovered that limes prevented scurvy—although they didn't know why—and made sure that sailors had them. In foreign ports, British sailors walked around sucking limes and became known, in an unflattering way, as "limeys." But scurvy continued to be a problem on ships even after its cause and cure were known. In the nineteenth century, a shortage of trees for fuel created a demand for whale blubber or fat. Whaling ships from England or New England that sailed for three or four years to the whaling grounds in the Pacific Ocean could never carry enough food and water; they had to rely on what they could pick up along the way. In the Galapagos Islands, west of Ecuador, they got giant 200-pound tortoises, which they somehow hoisted onto the ship, where they spent the time walking around—very slowly—until they were turned into stew. Sometimes sailors were able to buy sheep or other food animals. But the biggest problem, and what the men needed most, were fresh fruits and vegetables, because the greatest killer—"the plague of the sea"—was scurvy.[18]

The Russian Bear

Peter the Great Modernizes Russia

The Netherlands got a special visitor in the eighteenth century. Czar Peter I, known as Peter the Great (1672–1725), realized that if Russia didn't keep pace with Europe, it would be a huge, helpless giant and European countries would come scavenging and pick it apart like vultures. In his program to modernize Russia, Peter visited shipyards in the Netherlands, in disguise, which fooled nobody because he was six feet, eight inches tall and traveled with an entourage. Peter built a navy and upgraded the army. He hired European officers to train his men.

Peter wanted to make Russians behave, look, and eat like Europeans. Europeans read the newspaper, so Peter published Russia's first newspaper, editing it himself. Like the alphabet, which had arrived in 989, the newspaper was late getting to Russia. European men were clean-shaven, so Peter taxed men's beards. But it was cold in Russia. Men were reluctant to part with their face-warmers and paid the tax instead. Peter had more success introducing European foods to Russia. He sent Russian chefs to European countries to learn the latest cooking methods. One of the things Peter found in Europe was the potato. Russia is now the world's leading producer of potatoes. The Russians used distilling techniques they learned from Poland to make potato-based vodka.

But to get a port on the Baltic Sea, Peter would have to go to war with Russia's neighbor, Sweden. Russia won the war, and Peter got his port. He built a magnificent city which he named St. Petersburg, after the first Christian saint, whose name just happened to be the same as his.

Sweden: Land of the Midnight Sun

In the seventeenth century, Sweden was a world power. It was rich in mineral wealth; a majority of the world's copper came from Swedish mines. A series of wars with Denmark had increased Sweden's size. It was becoming urban and had a distinctive cuisine. Rye and barley flour were made into crisp crackerlike breads and served with *gjetost*, a caramelized cheese made from goat milk. The seas provided herring, cod, and Arctic trout. Salmon was marinated and buried in the ground—put in a grave, which is why it is called *gravlaks* or gravlox. Moose hunting was—and still is—a popular sport. The cold climate produced root vegetables like turnips, rutabagas, and kohlrabi. Lingonberries and cloudberries were favorites with humans and with bears. Swedish meatballs perhaps had their origins in Persian kebabs. Dumplings and soups were made of blood—beef, pig, goose. The Swedish version of whiskey is *akvavit*, flavored with caraway seeds.

Sweden had converted to Lutheranism in 1527 during the Protestant Reformation, but like many other European countries, still had saints that were too deeply ingrained in the culture to give them up. St. Nicholas was one. St. Lucia was another.

St. Lucia's Day, December 13

Sweden's St. Lucia's Day—the Feast of Lights—is an example of fusion cuisine and culture: the celebration of a southern Italian Catholic martyr in a Scandinavian Protestant country on a Viking holiday, using Middle Eastern foods, Spanish spice, and Portuguese wine.

According to legend, Lucia was a young woman who fed sick, poor, homeless people in the third century A.D. in the Roman Empire. She fixed candles around her head to light her way when she visited these people in the catacombs—the underground cemeteries. When she was tortured and executed, supposedly on December 13, her legend spread. It caught the imagination of the Vikings and is celebrated now on what was the shortest day in the Viking calendar. Today, young girls wearing long white dresses and a crown of candles get up before dawn and bring food and drink to their families. They also bring much-needed light and festivity to the long, dark Scandinavian winter, which doesn't end until April 30, a day which is celebrated with bonfires and the festival of Walpurgis Night.

The traditional foods are *Lussekatter* (Lucia cats), yeast bread with saffron, raisins, and blanched almonds; and gingersnaps—in Swedish, *pepparkakor*—"pepper cake." The beverage is *glögg,* a Port wine punch with Middle Eastern spices—cinnamon, cloves, cardamom, and ginger—sweetened with orange peel, raisins, and sugar.[19] The *Lussekatter* are formed into elaborate traditional shapes.

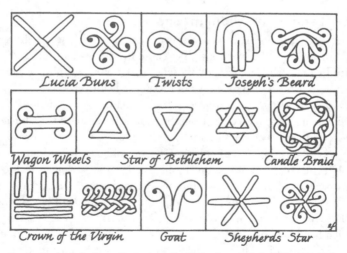

Lusekatter bun designs. *Drawn by Esther Feske, from* Sweden's Regional Recipes, *Penfield Books.*

Norway: "The fish in the seas are our daily bread"[20]

In the eighteenth century, the Swedish Empire controlled most of what are now the independent Scandinavian countries of Norway and Finland. In some parts of Norway, all available land had been cleared by 1666; the only way to get a farm after that was to acquire a piece of an existing farm. This created a new class of people called cotters. They could never own land, only work it, like sharecroppers in the American South.[21] Many spaded the land by hand, not with plows. Life expectancy for men was 45 years at the beginning of the nineteenth century.[22]

Geography and climate shaped life in Norway, with mountains and 15,000 miles of seacoast in multiple fjords or inlets.[23] The Gulf Stream, warm water flowing north from the Gulf of Mexico, warms Norway's west coast and provides more than 200 kinds of edible fish. Fishing was a huge industry; herring was a staple in the Norwegian diet. Lutefisk, fish preserved with lye made from the ash of birch trees, is traditional on Christmas Eve after soaking for several days to remove the lye. In 1854, a Norwegian pharmacist created cod liver oil, high in vitamins A and D, and omega-3.[24] Potatoes arrived in the middle of the eighteenth century; they were often served boiled with the signature Norwegian herb, dill. Other common vegetables are carrots, onions, rutabagas, and cabbage.

Norwegian cuisine has much in common with the other Scandinavian countries. Norwegians eat *rollepølse,* the rolled and pressed sandwich, like the Danes, and meatballs, cloudberries, *gjetost,* and *akvavit* like the Swedes. On their independence day, May 17 (1905), Norwegians eat a beef, pork, corned beef, onion, and potato stew called *lapskaus.* Breads include *lefse,* made with potatoes and sugar, oatmeal flatbread—*havremel flatbrød,* and dark rye bread—*rugbrød.* Christmas specialties are sweet, yeast-risen, cardamom-scented *julekake*—Yule Cake; and gingerbread—*pepperbrød. Kransekake,* which means "wreath cake," is made of almond paste cooked in 18 ring molds, the diameter of each increasingly smaller. Then the individual cakes are piled up and decorated to resemble a Christmas tree. *Kransekake* is also made for weddings. *Krumkakes* are round wafers made in an appliance like a waffle iron or an Italian pizzelle iron. Another Christmas tradition is a small pig made of marzipan (almond paste). This represents the pig that was sacrificed in Viking times to the goddess Freya, who gave us our word for Friday.

Like their Viking ancestors, Norwegians ate (and still eat) two main meals a day: *frokost,* a substantial cold breakfast, and *middag,* a hot meal around 5:00 PM. *Frokost* is like the Swedish smorgasbord, which in Norwegian is *smørbrød.* It includes cured meats and sausages, reindeer, cheese, salmon, pickled herring, fresh berries, waffles, porridge, coffee, and milk. *Middag* might be a stew like *lapskaus.* There might be a snack or light supper before bed. This is called *aftens,* and might be something simple like rice pudding.[25]

Milkmaids

Norwegian farmers engaged in transhumance, which meant moving animals, in this case cows, up and down the mountains with the seasons, in the care of a milkmaid. The milkmaid's day varied with the seasons. In summer, on the mountain, it could begin as early as 4:00 A.M., with milking the animals and sending them out to pasture. The bulk of her day was spent churning butter and making cheese from the milk. At the end of the day, she milked the animals again.

For nineteenth-century Norwegian farmers, winter began on October 14 and lasted until May 20—seven months. In those months, the milkmaid's day began at 6:00 A.M. That was when she went into the darkened barn to shovel manure, give hay to the animals, and milk the cows. Norwegians kept the animals in a closed, dark barn because they believed it reduced the animals' hunger. Then the milkmaid left to eat her own breakfast. She returned to the barn to give twigs or leaves to the animals and water them. The bulk of her day was spent carrying dozens of buckets of water from the stream up to the cookhouse, heating the water, and preparing a mush of leaves and twigs for the animals. Foraging in the forest for animal feed was seasonal work, too.[26]

Butter was a high-value item in the Norwegian barter economy. It was shaped in molds and at weddings was sculpted into a tall centerpiece.

Norwegians Migrate to America

Emigrants from Norway to the United States were few until the second half of the nineteenth century. People were afraid to move because rumors abounded about dangers in the strange new land and on the trip there: ship captains would sell them into slavery, icebergs would crush them, sea monsters or American natives would eat them. However, as they began to receive factual information from reliable sources that wages in America were three to four times as high as in Norway, while the cost of living was half as much, America began to look more attractive.[27] Also, in America, new land was not just available, but affordable. Around 1878 to 1880, when the herring and then jobs in the shipbuilding industry got scarce, Norwegians got "America fever"—the lust for land. They wanted their children to have a better life. They would go where the fields were paved with gold. They would go to America.

Until 1890, Norway sent a greater percentage of its population to the United States than any other European country except Ireland. (After 1890, Italians led the migration to the United States.) More than 20 percent of Norwegians lived outside Norway.[28] There were 565 newspapers and magazines in Norwegian in the United States between 1865 and 1914.[29] In the twenty-first century, there are more Norwegians in the United States than in Norway.[30]

Norwegians bought farmland in the upper Midwest: North and South Dakota, Minnesota, Wisconsin, northern Iowa. At first, they grew the crops that they had grown in Norway, barley and oats. They soon realized that they had to adapt to American farming, and switched to a cash crop—wheat.[31] Norwegians didn't just switch one cold-climate farm for another, their lives changed completely because of geography. America's plains were flat and landlocked; with no mountains or seacoast, there was no transhumance.

Norwegians were shocked by the American attitude toward land. In Norway land was sacred, to be handed down generation after generation, and planting was a holy act. In America land was a source of income, to be sold for profit, and planting was done by machines. Norwegians expected to buy more land so that their children and grandchildren could live near them; Americans hoped to make money by selling the land out from under themselves and moving with no regard for family.[32]

The Sami: Reindeer Cuisine and Culture

Northern Sweden, Norway, Finland, and Russia was the territory of the nomadic Sami people, who used to be called Lapps or Laplanders. Scandinavian population growth in the seventeenth century pushed the Sami farther north, up into the Arctic Circle, so close to the North Pole that the sun barely sets during the summer and barely shines during the winter. Today, there are fewer than 30,000 Sami. The reindeer is central to their lives, the way the buffalo was central to the lives of Native Americans on the Great Plains. The reindeer is what made the Sami nomads—the reindeer roamed the tundra, grazing, and the Sami followed. Reindeer provided food, as well as hides for clothing and shelter. Today, the Sami are still reindeer wranglers and they have reindeer rodeos, but their cuisine now shows foreign influences: reindeer stroganoff and reindeer ragout join reindeer steak. Some Sami are settled in villages, and now modern technology—cell phones, helicopters, snowmobiles—helps them herd the reindeer. Their language has 49 words to describe reindeer in minute detail according to age, gender, head and body color, and what the horns look like.[33] They also have an extensive, specific vocabulary for salmon and for different kinds of snow and ice.

Ukraine: The Breadbasket of Russia

The large, flat plain of Ukraine is like the American Midwest—grain-growing territory, the breadbasket of the country. The peasants there lived harsh lives. Long after the Renaissance, the Reformation, the Scientific Revolution, and many other social and intellectual movements had come and gone, peasants in eastern Europe were still living as they had in the Middle Ages. They were not slaves, but almost. They could not be bought and sold individually, but they were bought and sold with the land. When you bought a farm, you bought the land, the buildings, and the peasants. Laws made it impossible for the serfs to leave the land they worked. They revolted many times, unsuccessfully, until they were finally freed in 1861, the same year America began a Civil War to free its slaves. Until then, the lives of Russian serfs were reduced to the basics: work and try to get enough to eat. The scarcity of food was mirrored in the Russian Orthodox church fast days—up to 200 a year.[34] The staple food was bread—black bread made from rye in the north, wheat bread in the south. It was eaten at every meal. It was sacred to these people and so was the place it was baked.

The Russian Stove

"The stove in the home is like an altar in a church."

—Russian proverb[35]

The stove and the fire in it were treated with the utmost respect. For Americans to understand the Russian stove, we have to get rid of all our ideas about what a stove is. In Russia, where the temperature during the winter routinely drops into double digits below zero, the stove could take up a quarter of the entire hut. It was always built into a corner, made of clay, and functioned as a combination stove, furnace, and fireplace. The stove cooked food, baked bread, and preserved fruits and vegetables by drying. It also kept the temperature just right for fermenting drinks like *beriozovitsa*, made from birch tree sap, and *medovukha*, which was fermented honey like mead, but with hops added. Later, *kvas*—wheat fermented with water and sugar—became popular.

The stove also warmed the house. Beds were built on top of it and around it, like a sleeping loft. In Russia, people who lounged around on the stove—what we call "couch potatoes"—were "stove potatoes."

Tea and Samovar

In the mid–eighteenth century, tea became all the rage in Russia, the only country that invented a separate machine to brew it (until the Mrs. Tea machine arrived to keep Mr. Coffee company in the twentieth century). The samovar was a large metal urn, usually brass, sometimes steel, copper, or silver, with a spigot to drain the hot water. The first technology to heat water for tea (or anything else) was a charcoal-filled tube in the center of the samovar, but today they are also electric. Samovars ran from the plain, water-boiling variety to fancy ones that brewed tea on one side and coffee on the other, or had legs that unscrewed for portability. Some were a complete tea service, including cups and saucers, and creamer and sugar bowl.[36]

Peter the Great had visited England, prowled the shipyards in the Netherlands, and met European heads of state. But the ruler and the country he most admired were King Louis XIV and France. After Louis XIV died, Peter the Great sent a gift of caviar to impress the new king, Louis XV, and it did: he spit it out on the carpet.[37]

France: *Haute* and *Nouvelle* Cuisine

La Varenne and the Beginning of *Haute* Cuisine

One hundred years after Caterina de' Medici's arrival in France, there was a dramatic shift in French cuisine. In the middle of the seventeenth century, in 1651, a French chef named La Varenne published a cookbook called *Le cuisinier françois—The French Cook*. As Anne Willan, who named her cooking school in France after him, pointed out, *Le cuisinier françois* "is a seminal work; it marks the end of medieval cooking and the beginning of *haute cuisine*."[38] Two years after *Le cuisinier françois* appeared, La Varenne published *Le patissier françois— The French Pastry Cook*.

The trademark of most of La Varenne's recipes is subtlety. The hand that sprinkles the spices is light, not heavy like in the Middle Ages. Salt and pepper are the seasonings, with a squeeze of lemon juice and maybe a bouquet garni. Missing are the large doses of cinnamon, mace, clove, ginger. Along with the spices went the reliance on the theory of humors and the idea that food needed to be "fixed" to fit individual temperaments. The use of truffles also shows a break with the medieval theory of humors, because they have to be dug out of the ground, and in the Middle Ages, anything that grew close to the ground, let alone in it, was food for peasants because it was far from heaven. However, the division of *Le cuisinier françois* into meat days and meatless days still shows the influence of the Catholic Church.

People began to appreciate new tastes. And new textures. *Le cuisinier françois* is the beginning of modern sauces—the first roux, the fat and flour thickener. The beginnings of organization in French cuisine are here, also, with two bouillons, one meat, one fish.

More fresh fruits and vegetables appear in these recipes, because they were more readily available and because gardening had advanced considerably, especially among the upper classes. However, there were still not many foods from the New World. La Varenne used the foods that were trendy among the French nobility, like peas, lettuce, and artichokes. People *had* to have peas. Woe to the host who served asparagus instead, although asparagus could be diced and served disguised as peas.

Le patissier is the first thorough pastry cookbook, with precise, clear instructions and definitions of weights and measures, perhaps the influence of the Scientific Revolution that was then taking place in Europe. However, Willan thinks that *Le patissier* was probably not written by La Varenne or was written by him and an anonymous Italian pastry chef, because Italian pastry chefs were the best in the world at that time. Also, cooking and pastry were two separate professions. In any case, it is sophisticated—there are 15 varieties of marzipan. It also has the first cakelike biscuit recipes. La Varenne's books were the beginning of a trend. Forty years later, another chef, Massialot, wrote *Le cuisinier royal et bourgeois*, which continued the style of cuisine La Varenne began.

Vatel: The Frenchman Who Gave His All

Another giant in food history is Vatel. From all accounts, he was a genius in many areas: planning and managing huge festivals, coming up with imaginative ideas for pageants, and menu planning. He impressed all who attended the gala events his employers hosted. Then, in 1671, disaster. As maître d'hotel to the Duke de Condé, Vatel was responsible for planning and executing to perfection a major event for the king, who was coming to visit the duke for several days. The pressure was tremendous. The day a seafood feast and extravaganza was planned, almost no food arrived from the purveyors. Sure that he had destroyed the social and political life of the duke, as well as his own professional life, Vatel committed suicide by falling on his sword. As he was dying, the fishmongers arrived with full carts. But he had left no instructions on how to prepare and present all the food.

Two hundred years later, in 1981, Vatel gave his name to a hotel management school in Paris. It now has seven branches internationally, and in 2000 a movie was made about him starring Gerard Depardieu and Uma Thurman. Thirty-three culinary students from the Instituts Vatel, cutting, chopping, and slicing, made the kitchens and food prep scenes look real.

The Frenchman Who Loved His Coffee (Plant)

Almost everywhere coffee was introduced it met with two responses. The first was overwhelming enthusiasm from the people who drank it. The second was repression by the government. In Mecca, Arabia, the governor ordered the coffeehouses closed when he heard the patrons were making fun of him. King George II did the same in England for the same reason. The French government was going to ban coffee because they were afraid it would replace wine as the national beverage; the Germans feared for their beer. In all of these places, people kept drinking coffee and eventually the bans against it were lifted. An exception was Italy, where coffee was never banned even though Catholic priests appealed to the pope to ban the Muslim beverage. Instead, the pope tried coffee and gave it his blessing.

Coffee changed social and political habits. For the first time, people had a public place and a reason to congregate that did not involve alcohol. Coffee drinking began as a social pastime and became a political one. The rulers who worried about what people in coffeehouses were saying about the government were right to be worried. In France, the ideas that spread through coffeehouse discussions played a real part in the French Revolution. Coffee is also connected with a food fable about the origin of the croissant.

FOOD FABLE:

Where the Croissant Comes From

In 1683, the croissant was supposedly invented after the siege of Vienna. Either (a) a baker working late at night noticed the Turks trying to tunnel under the city and saved Vienna or (b) to celebrate their victory over the Turks, the Viennese bakers invented a new pastry in the shape of a crescent—in French, *croissant*—which was either (a) the symbol on the Turkish flag or (b) the shape of the trenches the Turks had dug and were forced to abandon. That would make the Austrians the first people anywhere to have a cup of coffee and a croissant. Not likely, since the croissant is one of the national foods of France and the earliest recipe is from 1905.[39]

What did happen in 1683 had nothing to do with croissants but did have everything to do with coffee. The Turks attacked Vienna and lost. Pulling up stakes in a hurry, they left carpets, clothing, and 500 huge sacks of strange little round beans. Dark. Hard. Bitter smelling. Maybe camel food? Torch them. But one soldier had been in the Middle East and woke up and smelled the coffee. The beans were saved—so many beans that he opened the first coffeehouse in Vienna with them.[40]

In 1689, an Italian named Procope opened the first coffeehouse in Paris. Ways of consuming coffee had changed drastically from its beginnings in the ninth century, when it was ground into a paste with animal fat and eaten that way. In 1710, the French ground the beans, put them in a cloth bag, poured boiling water over the bag, and invented the infusion method. The French are also credited with adding milk and creating *café au lait*, which moved coffee from an upper-class evening beverage in a public place to a morning luxury indulged in private. Eventually, *café au lait* filtered down into the general population and became the drink of the working class. Grinding coffee into a powder without the bag made it possible to read the grounds at the bottom of the cup, which gave a boost to fortune-tellers.

One Frenchman played a huge role in spreading coffee throughout the world. In 1723, Gabriel Mathieu de Clieu thought coffee would grow well in the Caribbean. He had one plant and nurtured it like a sick baby all the way across the Atlantic Ocean, even giving it his water ration. He was right—the plant loved the Caribbean. A great percentage of the coffee grown in the world today can probably be traced back to that one plant.[41]

Louis XIV: The Sun King

Louis XIV was the most powerful ruler in French history (1643–1715). He was an absolute monarch who claimed his power came from God, which gave him a "divine right" to rule. He said, "I am the state," and was the final and only authority on everything in the French Empire. He grew up under the threat of assassination by the Fronde, nobles plotting against the king. Louis was suspicious for the rest of his life and took safety precautions, including where he lived and how he ate. He built an enormous palace 11 miles southwest of Paris, in Versailles [vair-SIGH], and made the nobles live there so his spies could keep an eye on them.

Dinner at Versailles

The palace at Versailles was like a small city. Originally a hunting lodge, Louis XIV expanded the main building to 2,000 rooms, about 500 yards long, with two 150-yard-long wings. In the center of the U-shaped courtyard, Louis XIV placed a huge statue . . . of Louis XIV. The 15,000 acres of gardens, lawns, and woods included 1,400 fountains. One of the centerpieces was the Gallerie des Glaces—the Hall of Mirrors, a long formal room. A wall of mirrors reflected the gardens outside glass-paned doors—what Americans call French doors. Ten thousand people lived in Versailles; 2,000 worked in the kitchens. Running the palace cost more than half the annual income of France.[42]

Dinner at Versailles was at 10:00 P.M., about the time it gets dark in Paris in the summer. The Sun King took advantage of mealtimes to enforce his power. To guard against poisoning, his food was taken in locked containers from the kitchen to the dining hall, escorted by his private armed guards, the Musketeers. They announced the passage of the king's food through the halls of the palace by calling out, *"Les viandes du roi!"* ("The king's food!"), and everyone had to stop what they were doing and bow. Since he was without equal, Louis dined alone (except sometimes with the queen) in kingly splendor at a huge banquet table high on a platform. Musicians played while he dined; courtiers stood and watched while he ate, hoping for a word of acknowledgment or favor.

The meals Louis XIV ate were legendary. A glutton, he consumed huge amounts of food in no particular order, often against the advice of his physicians.

Once, he ate "four full plates of soup, a whole pheasant, a partridge, a big dish of salad, two big slices of ham, some mutton with *jus* and garlic, a plate of pastry, and then fruit and some hard-boiled eggs."[43] And he ate it all with his hands. Although Caterina de' Medici had brought the fork from Italy more than a century earlier and it was accepted throughout Europe, Louis didn't like it and refused to use it. He did use something else that Caterina had introduced, the handkerchief.

The Orangerie

Sweet oranges became very popular at this time. The first oranges, the ones that the Muslims planted wherever they conquered, were bitter oranges, *Citrus aurantium.* They were called Seville oranges, after the city in Spain where they grew, and were used to make marmalade. The sweet orange tree—*Citrus sinensis* or Chinese orange—traveled through India to the Middle East. It arrived in Lisbon in 1625 and spread quickly all over Europe, replacing bitter oranges in most places.[44] Orange juice and peel were thought to be the antidote to poisons, colic, and tapeworm. Wealthy people gave theme dinners planned around citrus fruit.

MENU:

The Sixteen-Course Citrus Dinner

"In 1529, the Archbishop of Milan gave a 16-course dinner that included:

caviar and oranges fried with sugar and cinnamon

brill and sardines with slices of orange and lemon

one thousand oysters with pepper and oranges

lobster salad with citrons

sturgeon in aspic covered with orange juice

fried sparrows with oranges

individual salads containing citrons into which the coat of arms of the diner
    had been carved

orange fritters

a soufflé full of raisins and pine nuts and covered with sugar and orange
    juice

five hundred fried oysters with lemon slices

candied peels of citrons and oranges"[45]

Louis XIV was an orange *aficionado* because the oranges looked like miniature suns, the symbol of the Sun King. (He also loved sunflowers, new plants from the Americas.) At Versailles, he built an *orangerie*—orange grove—in the shape of a 1,200-foot crescent and used it as a backdrop for the masked balls and entertainments he liked so much, especially dancing and the comedies and satirical plays of Molière. It was the job of the royal gardeners to keep the Sun King supplied with oranges and orange blossoms all year round. The trees were usually kept in wheeled pots so they could be moved in from the cold or just repositioned to take advantage of the sun, like invalids. When fresh oranges weren't available, painters and weavers provided images of oranges throughout the château in paintings and tapestries.[46]

By the time he died in 1715, Louis XIV had turned France into a superpower, a leader in world politics, fashion, and cuisine. But the palaces and the wars and the food were expensive, and Louis left France with a debt equivalent to about $20 billion. Since the nobles paid no taxes, the money would have to be squeezed out of the peasants. Three-quarters of a century later, the peasants would grow tired of paying half their income in taxes so the nobility could feast on luxuries while they starved. They would make the Sun King's descendant, Louis XVI, pay the ultimate tax: his head.

"Wicked Dishes"—*Nouvelle Cuisine*

In eighteenth-century France, a new style of *haute* or upper-class cuisine was brought about by the Enlightenment. It was called *nouvelle cuisine*.[47] As Piero Camporesi points out in *Exotic Brew*, the Enlightenment finished the break from medieval foodways that the Renaissance began. Beef consumption plummeted as heavy meats disappeared from refined tables. Even that last holdover from the Middle Ages, the peacock, was finally retired from the table, replaced by *gibier*—sexy small game like "turtledoves, quails, thrushes, and robins."[48] Aphrodisiacs were the food of the day, most of all raw oysters—"especially when dropped down the front of a dress and then retrieved"[49]—and truffles, not as garnish, but in "a heaping mound . . . tossed simply with a bit of butter or oil."[50] Lamb testicles and stag penis provided stimulation.

Foods that would cause bad breath or gastrointestinal rumblings and interfere with flirting and sex disappeared from fine dining: garlic, onions, cabbage, cheese. The ritual of public hand washing before the meal was discarded, along with the prayer: only people who were dirty needed to wash, and God's presence was not requested at these dinners. The courses were small and delicate, napped in sauce. Chafing dishes placed on "silver boxes filled with hot water which kept the food always hot" meant the servants could be dismissed from the room.[51] Temptation was everywhere: "You are almost always presented with wicked dishes, that is to say with just those dishes that make you eat even when you have no appetite at all."[52] Just in case the exquisite wine made you sleepy, coffee at the end of the meal perked you up—the night was still young.

Large communal banquets in the main hall gave way to intimate, seductive dinners in rooms used only for dining, where mirrored walls reflected firelight from crystal chandeliers. Coarse whole-grain bread trenchers were swapped for delicate china in bright colors and patterns that didn't soak up the new sauce-based cuisine. Chairs, banquettes, and draperies were in silk and satin brocade. So was clothing. No more coarse, loose-fitting fabrics like in the Middle Ages, or heavy velvets that hid the figure as in the Renaissance. Enlightenment clothes were tight fitting, made of slinky fabrics cut to show every curve and bulge: "their clothes . . . clinging to their limbs so that they do not appear covered, . . . their legs visible, . . . their dainty feet in sparkling golden buckles and fine gems like those that . . . used to ornament our hands."[53] And those were the men. Women's dresses were low cut. Both sexes wore enormous wigs. Women's eyes and lips, exaggerated with makeup, peeked out from behind flirtatious hand fans. Witty conversation was added to what was expected at dinner, along with music—something from Mozart, perhaps.

Gardening and Preservation

New gardening techniques pioneered by the chief gardener in France, La Quintinie at Versailles, allowed vegetables to be available longer. Artichokes, once only a spring vegetable, were now fresh three seasons of the year, all except winter. Multiple preservation techniques were included in cookbooks along with recipes. One cookbook has recipes for an Artichoke Fricassee of diced bottoms with cream, nutmeg, egg yolks, and butter; artichoke bottoms with cream, chives, and parsley; artichokes in white sauce, of egg yolks, white pepper, and vinegar; and an Artichoke Pye [Pie] of sliced artichoke bottoms baked with marrow, gooseberries, citron, dates, and butter.

Under the heading "Several Ways of Keeping Artichokes," one recipe describes preservation by boiling, taking out the chokes, brining, then "pouring Oil or Butter on the Top to keep out the Air." Another is for pickling. Two recipes are for dried artichokes: by blanching then baking, or by dredging in flour then baking. In either case, to rehydrate, they should be kept in lukewarm water for two days.[54]

Haute Cuisine and Fine China

Haute cuisine—high cuisine—came out of the large kitchens of France's wealthy nobles. The cooks might be men or women, but the men's salaries were more than triple the women's, and the men were always the managers.[55] Cooking did not include bread, which was bought at the bakery—*boulangerie;* or pastry, which was bought at the *pâtisserie*. In a modest household, the cooking might be done by the woman of the house and a maid. In larger establishments, there would be specialized staffs. In charge of everything was the maître d'hotel, who planned all the meals, hired and fired, managed the accounts, and kept the keys, because the food, wines, linens, and tableware were locked up. In both kinds of households, the day began by putting the stockpot on the fire—*pot au feu*—and throwing yesterday's leftovers and today's new meat into it.

In the eighteenth century in France and throughout Europe, European-made fine china became popular. For centuries, Europeans had been searching for a way to duplicate the delicate, beautiful—and extremely expensive—porcelain plates that came from China. Like the silkworm, this was a closely guarded Chinese state secret. Finally, Europeans found ways to duplicate the Chinese plates closely enough.

CHRONOLOGY: EUROPEAN PORCELAIN (CHINA)[56]

1640–1740	Delft, Netherlands makes glazed earthenware—"poor man's porcelain"
1710	Porcelain patented; Royal Saxon factory at Meissen, Germany; supersecret, all workers are deaf mutes
1713	Porcelain commercially sold at Liepzig, Germany
1719	Porcelain factory in Vienna, Austria
1738	Porcelain factory in Vincennes (later Sèvres), France
1743	Porcelain factory in Naples, Italy
1744	Porcelain factory in Chelsea, England
1756	Porcelain factory moves to Sèvres from Vincennes, France
by 1760	Royal Danish factory at Copenhagen, Denmark
ca. 1794	Josiah Spode II perfects bone china in England

Table Settings: The *Sûrtout*

As dishes of the new cuisine came and went, one item stayed on the table. It was called the *sûrtout* [soor-TOO] because it was above everything else, or the *dormant* [DOOR-mahn] because it remained still or "sleeping" on the table. The *sûrtout*, made of silver, was a tabletop all-in-one with multiple functions. It was a candelabrum; it had cruets for oil and vinegar; it had salt and pepper shakers; it had containers for other condiments; it might have a tray. It also displayed the wealth of the host, although a *sûrtout* could be rented from a *traiteur* [TRAY-tur]—caterer. It was a conversation piece, too. It might have representations of the foods that were going to be served, trendy vegetables like asparagus, artichokes, truffles, and peas.

French Food and Fashions

French food and fashions were spread throughout Europe by French chefs, clothing designers, hairdressers, and nobility. During the Enlightenment, French culture dominated; it displaced Italian and Spanish. Under the reigns of Louis XV and XVI, class differences grew. Bored nobles with too much time on their hands wanted a jolt from new foods and little living toys, so breeders invented lap dogs for them. New foods could be imported, or old foods could be changed to appear to be something else: sky-blue sauce (cream sauce with herbs), veal in the form of donkey droppings (veal birds), asparagus disguised as peas.[57]

This new style, these foods with "lying and peculiar names"[58] were regarded by some as immoral, as was staying up all night in pursuit of earthly delights and sleeping all day instead of working or going to church. These elaborate Enlightenment fashions were called "elegant simplicity," the way that in the twenty-first century, reducing flavors to essences, powders, and foams is called "minimalist." They both require maximum effort from the cook.

While the upper classes feasted on delicacies served on fine china, the lower classes in France had neither plates nor food to put on them.

The French Revolution: "Let Them Eat Cake"

Just as the Seven Years' War was one of the causes of the American Revolution, so the American Revolution was one of the causes of the French Revolution. The French people were inspired by seeing that an underclass could overthrow a monarchy, and they were angry because they had been taxed to the maximum so that people of another country could win freedoms the French themselves did not have.

France was still a feudal society, little different politically and economically from the Middle Ages. The people were divided into three groups, or estates. The first estate was the clergy, which paid about 2 percent of the taxes in France. The second estate was wealthy nobles who paid no taxes. The third estate paid 98 percent of the taxes and was 98 percent of the population: peasant farmers, urban poor, and the bourgeoisie—the merchant class, an educated middle class that took business risks and brought money into France. The third estate paid 50 percent of their income in taxes but couldn't vote, so they couldn't change the tax laws or anything else—like the Americans' cry of "no taxation without representation" that had led to the American Revolution.

"This nation [France] does not have a normal relation to food"[59]

It is impossible to separate food from the French Revolution. More than any other revolution in history, food played a crucial part in the French Revolution, literally and symbolically. At the heart of the issue were two foods essential to the French people: bread and salt. And at the heart of the bread issue were the bakers.

The French have been described as a nation of panivores—bread eaters—and regard their bread as the best in the world. Bread had both literal and symbolic meaning in French cuisine and culture. It was a source of nutrition, providing most of the daily calories, but it also represented health and well-being, the French identity, and the French religion, Catholicism. French bread was supposed to be wheat and white. In 1775, people rioted because they got dark bread.[60] Scientists and chemists claimed that the bakers baked bad bread because they knew nothing about science, so in 1782, a school was established to study bread from milling through distribution, and spread the word to bakers throughout France. Scientist Antoine-Augustin Parmentier was one of the people in charge of the school.

The Bakers and the Bread Police

There was tension between the people and the bakers for almost a century before the French Revolution. Bread was regarded as a public service necessary to keep the people from rioting. Bakers, therefore, were public servants, so the police controlled all aspects of bread production, including making sure that it continued. Bakers had to get permission from the police if they wanted to go into a different profession.[61] Sometimes the police helped the bakers. For example, when merchants hoarded yeast to create an artificial shortage and jack up the price, the bakers' guild had the police search the merchants' homes and shops and confiscate the yeast.[62]

The master bakers exercised very tight control over the journeymen through a certification system. After 1781, every journeyman baker had to register with the guild and get a *livret*—French for "booklet"—which was like their green card or passport. The journeyman had to show the *livret* to rent a room or to get food in a tavern. When he went to work, he gave the *livret* to the master. When he changed jobs, the journeyman had to inform the guild within 24 hours and pay a fee. He also had to show in the *livret* that the master had given permission. Some masters forced journeymen to work for them by keeping the *livret*. If he left without it, the journeyman was like an illegal alien in his own country. Police raided shops where journeymen were working illegally, the way the U.S. Immigration and Customs Enforcement agency—ICE (*La Migra*)—raids shops now. The illegal journeymen could be sent to jail or back to their former masters.[63]

The bakers, like the grain and flour merchants, were presumed to be greedy and selfish. People accused them of numerous crimes: adulterating bread with wood chips, soap, or rotten grain, or baking underweight loaves. They made bitter jokes about it: weigh a dead baker and he'll come up short weight.[64] The bakers complained that it wasn't their fault—it was impossible to get absolutely uniform loaves, what bakers call "scaling." The police knew who was responsible because a baker had to carve his initials into every loaf. Making an anonymous loaf was also a crime, but, of course, harder to prosecute. The police practiced zero tolerance on short weight; loaves even an ounce or half an ounce light were seized. Historian Steven Kaplan, who did an extensive analysis of police archives and other public records for his book, *The Bakers of Paris and the Bread Question, 1700–1775*, did the math on what short weight cost the people of Paris each day: "perhaps between twenty-five hundred and three thousand four-pound loaves . . . enough to feed several thousand families."[65]

The punishments for bakers included fines, having their ovens destroyed or their shops walled up, having their crimes published in the paper or being forced to wear them on a sandwich board and march through the streets. For serious or repeat offenses there was jail time, loss of master status, or even expulsion from the guild. Sometimes the police just looked the other way and let angry customers—often women—beat the bakers up.[66] At the bread market at Les Halles on Wednesdays and Saturdays, the average stall displayed "1,530 pounds of bread distributed as follows: 26 twelve-pound loaves, 40 eight-pound loaves, 101 six-pound loaves (mostly round), and 73 four-pound loaves (mostly long)."[67] Competition for customers was fierce. The bakers, male and female—and sometimes bakers' wives—got into fist or knife fights. Women were also the delivery people—*porteuses*, or female porters. On their backs, they carried baskets with as much as 100 pounds of bread long distances and up four or five flights of stairs.[68]

French bread was made from flour, water, salt, leavening, and massive amounts of human labor. The leavening was a starter that took up to 15 hours to ripen, had to be fed and rested three or four times during kneading, and made a bulky dough that wore the bakers out wrestling with it—they had to knead 200 pounds by hand in 45 minutes. Sometimes they jumped on the dough and kneaded it with their bare feet. As Parmentier knew, this process was brutal on the bakers; the bread got more rest than they did. When some bakers switched to barm—brewer's yeast—because it rose faster and made the dough easier to work with, there was a public outcry. French physicians declared that brewer's yeast "shocked" the flour into rising instead of leading it gently, that it made the bread less white, and that it would have the same toxic effects on the human body as beer—altogether not French.

The Salt Tax—*Gabelle*

Another sore point was salt. French bread needed salt, but because chemistry was in its infancy, they didn't understand what it did besides improve the flavor. It also controls the yeast, stops bacterial growth, makes a finer-grained loaf that looks whiter and has a deeper crust. The salt tax—*gabelle* [GAH-bell]—was levied erratically. The *gabelle* might be high in one village, low in the next. This encouraged smuggling and corruption. Tax collectors were thugs paid to terrorize the peasants to force them to pay. They broke into houses at dawn, searched people in bed, causing pregnant women to miscarry. They took the peasants' property; sometimes they took the peasants and sent them to jail without notifying their families.[69]

Hunger, tension, and street violence mounted. Finally, the king called a meeting of all the classes, the *états generals*. The third estate, which wanted major changes in the government, sat on the left side of the hall; the moderates sat in the middle; and the conservative nobles of the second estate, who wanted nothing to change, sat on the right. This is where politics gets its terms *left wing* and *right wing*. Since the right wing had all the political power, nothing changed—then. In June, Thomas Jefferson, the architect of America's Declaration of Independence, drafted a charter of rights for France, along with Lafayette, who had trained troops and fought in the American Revolution. This document served as the basis for the French Declaration of Rights that Lafayette presented to the National Assembly in July 1789.[70] However, on July 14, 1789, rumors spread through the city that the king had sent armed guards to turn on the people. They stormed the Bastille [BAH-steel], the prison in the center of Paris, to get ammunition.

HOLIDAY HISTORY:

Bastille Day, July 14

July 14, 1789, is French Independence Day. It is to the French what the Fourth of July is to Americans and is celebrated the same way—with fireworks and feasting. In the 1970s, Alice Waters began celebrating Bastille Day at Chez Panisse, her restaurant in Berkeley, California, with an all-garlic menu; the garlic harvest in northern California is at about the same time. This sample menu is from *The Chez Panisse Menu Cookbook*. Every item, including the sherbets, has garlic in it.[71]

Garlic Soufflé

Baked Fish with Garlic Confit

Roast Squab with Garlic-and-Liver Sauce

Fettuccine with Fresh Chestnuts

Romaine and Rocket Salad with Garlic

Two Wine Fruit Sherbets

The Women March: "The baker, the baker's wife, and the baker's boy"

On October 6, 1789, three months after the storming of the Bastille, French women went to market. There was no bread. Their children would starve. No more! The angry women grabbed stones, sticks, pitchforks, and marched to Versailles. It was 12 miles, and it was raining. They were going to get the queen and "fricassee her liver." The people hated the queen because she spent fortunes on clothes and entertainment, did not produce a royal heir for eight years after she married the king (through no fault of hers), and was Austrian. When she was informed that the people were starving because they had no bread, the queen supposedly laughed and said, "Let them eat cake"—really brioche, bread dough enriched with egg and butter.

When the women arrived at Versailles, the palace guard, whose only job was to protect the royal family, joined the women instead. The women got food: they ransacked the kitchens at Versailles. At gunpoint, King Louis XVI, Queen Marie Antoinette, and their son the dauphin (prince) were taken back to Paris and locked up in the Bastille. On the march back, the victorious women chanted that they had gotten "the baker, the baker's wife, and the baker's boy."

On June 21, 1791, the royal family tried to escape to the queen's brother in Austria. They had almost reached the border when a postmaster recognized the king, even though he was disguised as a servant, because his picture was on all the French money. Rumors spread that the king was disguised as a chef. Political cartoons showed the royal family with pig faces, or the king eating pigs' feet. They all implied that the king only cared about "pigging out" and sticking the people of France with the bill while they starved.[72] The royal family was brought back to Paris. The king's head was chopped off by the blade of the guillotine [GHILL-oh-teen], then put on a stick and passed around Paris. Marie Antoinette was beheaded, too, after a light last meal of vermicelli soup. Their son, the dauphin, died in prison.

The Terror

In 1793, the Revolution took a turn toward terror under the rule of Robespierre, a vegetarian. With the nobles executed or out of the country, the Revolution turned on ordinary people and accused them of being enemies of the state. Thousands were sent to the guillotine for trivial reasons like serving bad wine or just knowing a noble person. It was during the Terror that the man who had been the queen's chef for 10 years was executed. On July 27, 1794, the Terror ended when moderates seized control and sent Robespierre where he had sent so many others—on a one-way walk up the guillotine steps. The location where the guillotine stood is now the Place de la Concord.

The Napoleonic Era: 1799–1815

In 1799, a young general named Napoleon Bonaparte seized control of the French government by marching in with the army and declaring he was in charge. The French Revolution and the Napoleonic era that followed brought about cultural changes much more profound than the American Revolution had. The French Revolution created a truly new society with new classes, new values, and new ways of treating people. The first estate, the clergy, was now under the control of the government. The second estate, the nobility, was gone—dead or fled. The third estate—the bourgeoisie, the peasants, and the urban poor—could vote now, which meant they could set reasonable taxes for themselves. And their taxes paid for schools for their children, not for some noble's château or banquet.

"And the restaurants, how many new marvels!"[73]

The changes in the world of cuisine were also profound. The French Revolution changed what, where, and how people ate. The bourgeoisie had more money, since 50 percent of their income wasn't going for taxes, and they wanted to eat well. Out of the ashes of the revolution emerged the modern restaurant, a purely French invention that began in Paris.

The revolution also ended the medieval guild system. The food industry shifted from arguing over which guild controlled which food to which establishment could sell what kind of food to the public. In 1830, a café owner was sued for impersonating a restaurateur because his menu contained 120 items, too many for a café, and he also served lunch.[74]

These new eating habits needed new words to describe them. The words connected with the restaurant are French. Mr. Boulanger had opened the first restaurant in 1765, in Paris, before the Revolution. He served a soup that was supposed to restore the health, called a "restorer"—in French, *restaurant*. Other French words are *restaurateur*, the owner of a restaurant, and *menu*, from the French word for "small," because the menu is a small description of the larger dishes. The eighteenth-century French believed that starting a meal with soup would restore the health, still a custom in twenty-first-century restaurants, and not just in France. Grimod de la Reynière was the world's first restaurant critic; his *Almanach des gourmands* was the world's first restaurant guide, before the brothers Michelin and the husband-and-wife team of Tim and Nina Zagat. The word *gastronomy* appeared for the first time in 1801, as the title of a poem. It referred to the Greek *Gastronomia*, written by Archestratus in the fourth century B.C. This was followed by *gastronome*, a person familiar with good eating.[75]

Brillat-Savarin: "You are what you eat"

Perhaps the first gastronome was Jean-Anthelme Brillat-Savarin [bree-AHT sah-vah-RAN], whose most famous quote was "Tell me what you eat, and I will tell you what you are." Food historian Ken Albala proposes a corollary to Brillat-Savarin's quote: "Tell me what a culture thinks it ought to eat, and I will tell you what it wants to be."[76]

Brillat-Savarin's book of meditations on food, *The Physiology of Taste*, was published in 1825. He also said, "Gastronomy is the intelligent knowledge of whatever concerns man's nourishment."[77] As an upper-class man, he spent two years of the French Revolution hiding out in America, part of the time in Hartford, Connecticut (if he ate Election Cake, he didn't mention it). He also lived in New York City. He had nothing but praise for the American table. The food was absolutely fresh—freshly grown, freshly milked, freshly killed—and there was plenty of it. He knew, because while he was there, he went on a turkey shoot. Brillat-Savarin said that the riches of the Americas were not gold but potatoes, vanilla, and cocoa. He loved the treasures of France, too: "The truffle is the diamond of the art of cookery."[78]

Brillat-Savarin listed the reasons he loved restaurants: you can choose when to eat, how much to spend, what kind of meal to have; you can have the best of what France has to offer, and luxuries imported from all over the world. He was an observer of the wide variety of people who eat in restaurants, too—the ones who eat alone, the country families, married couples, lovers, the "regulars," the foreigners. He points out a pitfall: eating in restaurants is so seductive that it is easy to slip into debt to do it. After all, "A restaurant is Paradise indeed to any gourmand."[79]

Carême: King of Chefs and Chef of Kings

"Antonin Carême is probably the greatest cook of all time."
—Food historian and chef Anne Willan[80]

Antonin Carême was the first celebrity chef, a legend in his own time and a true rags-to-riches story. Carême came to food as a profession not out of love, but out of dire necessity. In 1793, the year Louis XVI and his head parted company via the guillotine, Carême's impoverished parents (they had 24 or 25 children) turned the illiterate 10-year-old boy out into the street to fend for himself and wished him good luck. The boy was no fool—he found work in a kitchen. He rose quickly and became a *pâtissier*. He taught himself to read and in 1815, by the time he was 32, had published two best-selling books, *Le pâtissier royal* and *Le pâtissier pittoresque*. Twelve years later, he had learned everything he could about the other branches of cooking and was one of the best chefs in France. His cooking was legendary even then. One dinner, for the Rothschild family, required an "enormous salmon" and a pound of truffles, shaved and turned and applied to the fish to look like scales.[81] He made Napoleon's wedding cake.

He was also in demand all over Europe. England's prince regent offered Carême a salary he couldn't refuse, about $300,000 in today's money. The prince loved Carême's cooking so much that he even ate in the kitchen once—after a red carpet had been laid on the floor. But homesick Carême returned to Paris after a year. He went to Russia, where he was sometimes invited to dinner as a guest, not as a cook. But it was too cold, with only inferior hothouse vegetables available for six months of the year. Vienna was better, but France was just right for him, and that is where he spent the rest of his life.

Carême brought some Russian cuisine and culture back to Paris with him: the soup, borscht; the elaborate multilayered fish and pilaf *en croûte* called *koulibiac* [coo-LEE-bee-ahk]; decorating the table with fresh flowers instead of porcelain centerpieces; and table *service à la russe*, Russian table service, in which the dishes were presented one after the other instead of all at once, as had been done in Europe since the Middle Ages. *Service à la russe* reflected the enormous wealth of the Russian nobility, because there had to be a vast supply of dinnerware and servers to bring and remove the dishes.[82] Carême also invented many dishes: a chestnut pudding named after the Russian minister to Paris, Nesselrode; veal Prince Orloff (or Orlov), after a Russian nobleman; and the molded dessert charlotte russe, Bavarian cream in a ring of ladyfingers.

Carême Organizes French Cuisine

Carême was a genius at organization. He brought order and consistency to French cuisine. He organized the sauces on which French cuisine is based into a modular system: five leading or mother sauces were the basic building blocks. By adding wine, herbs, cheese, vegetables, etc., to these five basic sauces, hundreds more could be created. These were called small or daughter sauces. The five leading sauces are béchamel, velouté, espagnole, hollandaise, and tomato. Two—espagnole and hollandaise—are named after the countries where they originated, Spain and Holland; béchamel is named after the chef who invented it (or perhaps after an Italian chef, Besciamella); tomato is named after its main ingredient. Only one sauce, velouté, has a name that describes its consistency. In French, *velouté* means "turned into velvet."

Carême also stressed presentation. He believed that "the principal branch of architecture is confectionery." For centerpieces, he re-created the Greek and Roman ruins, Egyptian pyramids, Chinese pagodas, ships and fountains that he had researched in the library. These constructions, several feet high, were called *pièces montées*. Made of spun sugar, marzipan, meringue, and sugar paste, they lasted for years. Carême worked the sugar by immersing his hands in ice water, then straight into the boiling sugar, then back into the ice water.[83]

He also created art in the new branch of cuisine that arose after the French Revolution, the cold buffet with *chaud-froid* (hot-cold) dishes—foods that are cooked first, then coated in aspic and served cold. In 1833, this genius wrote his last book, which would define French cooking throughout the nineteenth century. The king of chefs and chef of kings died the same year.

The Chef's Uniform

The word *chef*, short for *chef de cuisine*—head of the kitchen—also came into use at this time. Earlier, chefs were called cooks or master cooks. With professionalization came the language of the kitchen, names for positions in the profession, and a way to distinguish people in the profession—a uniform patterned after French army uniforms.

The chef's uniform has two practical functions: (1) to protect the chef from the food; and (2) to protect the food from the chef. In the first case, the long sleeves, long pants, and double-breasted jacket are a barrier against burns, spills, and splatters. The black-and-white houndstooth check pattern on the pants is camouflage—try to find the stain. Sturdy shoes guard against falling equipment and knives. Nonskid soles provide traction on floors slippery from spilled food and grease. In the second case, the long sleeves, double-breasted jacket, and neckerchief protect the food from a sweating chef. The *toque blanche*, the tall white chef's hat, keeps the chef's hair out of his eyes and out of the food and also, like the stars on a general's hat or the distinctive hat of an admiral, makes it easy to see who is in charge in a crowded kitchen. Before Carême, the chef's hat was floppy; he put cardboard in his to make it stand tall. The toque is supposed to have 100 pleats, to represent the minimum number of ways a good chef can prepare eggs. (In *The Culinary Guide*, in 1903, master chef Escoffier lists 202 ways to prepare eggs, *excluding* omelettes, which are another 82 recipes, and adds a note that "Using the basic recipe for Omelette Norvégienne it is possible to produce an almost infinite number of variations of this type of omelette [Omelette Surprise].")[84]

The uniform couldn't protect cooks against one serious kitchen hazard: carbon monoxide (chemically, CO) poisoning. Carbon monoxide binds to the hemoglobin in blood, preventing it from carrying oxygen to the body's tissues, including the brain. CO gas is odorless, colorless, and therefore impossible to detect. It is produced by using charcoal fires indoors with inadequate ventilation. CO poisoning was so common among cooks in France that it was called *folie des cuisiniers*—cooks' craziness—because of its symptoms: bizarre behavior, disorientation, and loss of muscle coordination. It also turned the face a bright cherry red, which could make a person suffering from CO poisoning look drunk.[85] This gave cooks a bad reputation. And it probably killed Carême.

"Damn sugar, damn coffee, damn colonies!"—Napoleon[86]

1802. Napoleon was furious. He wanted to recover the land that had been lost in wars with England, rule all of Europe, and restore France's empire. He was becoming frustrated on all counts.

In the Caribbean, Napoleon's troops had failed to retake the sugar- and coffee-producing island of Saint Domingue (Haiti) from rebellious slaves. Now, 20,000 of his troops were dead, killed by Toussaint L'Ouverture, the leader of the slaves, and by yellow fever, a disease spread by mosquitoes. (The Spanish name for the disease is much more descriptive: *vomito negro*.)

In Europe, the powerful British navy blocked ships from French ports. Napoleon tried to make France self-sufficient. If he couldn't get sugar from sugar cane in the Caribbean, then he would grow sugar beets at home. The sugar beet proved to be an excellent source of sugar. Napoleon's decision contributed to the decline of the Caribbean economy and changed the sugar-eating habits of the world.

Napoleon's wars were becoming expensive. How to finance them? He would have to sell some real estate. Fast. But who would buy?

Appert Invents Canned Food

In 1803, armed with the $15 million he got from the United States for the Louisiana Purchase, Napoleon proceeded with his plan to conquer Europe. First, he wanted to make sure his troops had good French food. He was looking for something better than the salted, dried, or smoked food armies usually got. These methods of preservation altered the taste and texture of food, and not for the better. So he offered a prize of 12,000 francs (US$250,000 today) to the first person who could do this.

In 1810, a chef named Nicolas Appert won the prize and published his book, *L'art de conserver pendant plusieurs années toutes les substances animales et végétales—The Art of Conserving for Several Years All Animal and Vegetable Substances.* Appert, born in 1750, grew up in the wine cellars and inns of Champagne, helping his father, an innkeeper. By the time Appert was 22, he was an accomplished chef; by 31, he had his own confectionery shop in Paris. He was also passionate about preserving foods. He wanted to find a new method, one that would preserve the base of French cooking, the sauces.[87] For 10 years, he experimented with ways to preserve food. He finally settled on packing the food in glass bottles—Champagne bottles at first, because he could get so many—and boiling them in a bain marie or water bath.

Appert was killing the germs, but this was before germs were understood. The food tasted good, much better than what other methods produced. Then Appert got lucky. Food critic La Reynière liked what Appert was doing and wrote about him in his food column. However, food packed in glass was not practical in the armed forces. The bottles would be tossed about on the navy's ships, and jostled over bad roads or no roads by the army. The country that ended up getting the patent on Appert's invention and mass-producing it was England, because it was more industrialized than France and had a highly developed tin industry. The cans, made by hand, were flat on top. They had to be opened with a hammer and chisel until the middle of the nineteenth century, when Americans invented the can opener.

Scorched Earth in Russia

Losing his colonies in the Americas increased Napoleon's obsession with conquering Europe. In 1812, he invaded Russia. Russia employed a "scorched earth" policy: they burned their grain and slaughtered their livestock so Napoleon's troops wouldn't be able to live off their land, even though it meant they would starve, too. Napoleon marched into Russia with a Grande Armée of almost 600,000 men, the largest European army up to that time. He limped out with maybe 50,000.

How did the man who believed that "An army marches on its stomach" let hundreds of thousands of his men starve to death? Napoleon's retreat from Moscow is one of the greatest examples in history of how lack of food led to disaster.

After battling his way across Russia, Napoleon arrived in Moscow, the capital. But the city was deserted. Everyone had left, including the czar, who didn't surrender. Fires broke out, men looted. They feasted on luxuries stolen from the palaces of the nobles: figs, liqueurs, jams. Then, just as winter was coming, Napoleon ordered everyone to march back to France. No preparations had been made, except that Napoleon said that small hand mills would be given to each man so he could grind fresh flour for bread. When they marched out of Moscow, the men had sacks of grain, but no mills.

In Napoleon's army, as in nineteenth-century European society, what kind of food you had depended on your social class. Napoleon traveled with a gold dinner service and "always had white bread, linen, . . . good oil, beef or mutton, rice and beans or lentils, his favourite vegetables."[88] The officers had private chefs and carriages stocked with three to four months' worth of food, as one wrote in his diary: "more than 300 bottles of wine, 20–30 bottles of rum and brandy, more than 10 pounds of tea and as much again of coffee, 50–60 pounds of sugar, 3–4 pounds of chocolate, some pounds of candles."[89] But missing were staples: "white bread, fresh meat and *vin ordinaire* I had none," wrote another officer.[90]

Cooks were very valuable. A cook could make stringy horsemeat palatable by turning it into curry or transform horse's blood into blood pudding.[91] With a cook, it was still possible to dine properly:

> . . . a splendid supper, with Madeira and Bordeaux wines, and an abundance of mocha coffee and liqueurs from the isles of the Indies! My cook . . . prepared horsemeat marvellously and all my guests thought I was serving them beef![92]

And you guarded that cook—in one case, six soldiers were assigned to protect one cook. One officer was astounded to find out that the young man who had been cooking for him, driving his carriage, and taking care of his horses was really a 14-year-old girl who had disguised herself to be with the soldier she loved.[93]

However, class differences were fatal: "In the same regiment some companies were dying of hunger while others were living in abundance."[94] The enlisted men had what they could carry in their backpacks. By the time the grain mills Napoleon had promised arrived, the men had long since abandoned the grain because it was too heavy. They abandoned the mills—and their muskets and backpacks—for the same reason. The wagons carrying the heavy guns and ammunition were left by the road, too. But when they abandoned their axes, the men couldn't chop down trees for firewood to melt snow, or break holes in the frozen rivers and ponds to get water. The horses, also dying of thirst, exhausted themselves pawing at the thick ice. Lack of preparation had extended to not putting nails—the equivalent of tire chains—in the bottoms of the horses' shoes. Foraging was dangerous: the Russians were foraging for foragers so they could torture and kill them. This resulted in an ironic justice: luxury items from the houses of the upper classes in Moscow ended up in the hands of Russian peasants, via Napoleon's army.

Winter moved in fast. In sleet, snow, fog, and temperatures down to −18°F (−28°C), wagon wheels sank deep in mud, icicles hung from the men's beards, wine froze: "we had to break our wine by hitting it with a hatchet and putting it over the fire."[95] That was in November. In December it got really cold, down to −34°F.[96]

The men were starving and freezing to death but they looked like they were going to a costume party. This was "The Masquerade" as the men put on whatever clothing they had stolen in Moscow: men's or women's silk opera capes, fancy plumed hats, negligees. Desperate men ate chunks of flesh torn off of living horses too cold and stunned to object, or the bark off trees, or took "some fistfuls of flour dipped in melted snow."[97]

....

RECIPE:

Spartan Broth

"It wasn't always we had some horsemeat or aquavit.... It was then we prepared our thin Spartan broth. Here's the recipe: Melt some snow—and you'll need plenty to get only a little water. Put in some flour. Then, for lack of salt, some gunpowder. Serve up hot and only eat when you're really hungry."[98]

....

Dead men and those too cold or close to death to protest were eaten by flocks of crows and "hordes of dogs." Before the march was over, they had descended to murder, suicide, and cannibalism.

When thousands of these starving men arrived at Vilna, Lithuania, on December 8, 1812, they completely overwhelmed the restaurants in the small town. Men ate and ate and ate—and died, their bodies lacking the enzymes and energy to digest food. Typhus, a disease spread by body lice, killed thousands more.

The Russian people and the Russian winter had been formidable foes and Napoleon had lost. It was an expensive lesson, but not one that another European dictator would learn from. One hundred thirty years later, Hitler, too, would be beaten by the fierce determination of the Russian people and the Russian winter.

But Napoleon wasn't done yet. His final defeat came at the hands of the British and Prussians at Waterloo, Belgium, in 1815 (hence the expression, "Napoleon met his Waterloo"). The British took no chances: they exiled Napoleon to the tiny, remote island of St. Helena in the middle of the Atlantic Ocean, originally founded as a refueling port for the British fleet on its way to the Spice Islands, and in 1821 he died there.

Napoleon and Wellington

The dessert called the Napoleon, also called *millefeuille* [MEEL-foy], because it is made of many (*mille*—a thousand) layers or leaves (*feuille*) of pastry, isn't named after Napoleon. It's named after the city where it was invented—Naples.

The British Duke of Wellington was the man who, along with the Prussians, defeated Napoleon at Waterloo. Beef Wellington is an elegant fillet or chateaubriand spread with foie gras or pâté and duxelles, then rolled and baked in a pastry crust.

Napoleon's Aftermath

America's Second War for Independence

England took advantage of France's preoccupation with Europe to try to retake the United States. In 1815, the same year Napoleon was defeated at Waterloo and Carême published his book, the United States won the last battle in the War of 1812. The treaty that ended the war was signed in December 1814 in Belgium, but news hadn't reached the United States yet. Still, it was fortunate that a ragtag group of American backwoodsmen, last-minute militia, sailors, free blacks, and French pirates, heavily outnumbered, beat the British at the Battle of New Orleans. No land changed hands but the United States was still independent and beginning to gain respect as a power to be dealt with. And the commander at New Orleans, Andrew Jackson, became a hero, which helped elect him to two terms as president. A statue of him on horseback is at the center of Jackson Square in New Orleans.

South America Revolts

Napoleon also caused revolutions throughout Central America and Latin America. When Napoleon invaded Spain in 1808, he placed his brother Joseph on the throne. The Spanish people refused to accept this Frenchman as their king and waged a guerrilla war for years. Spain's colonies felt even less loyalty to a French king. By 1841, all of the New World colonies that had belonged to Spain since the late fifteenth and early sixteenth centuries had formed into the countries that exist today. In 1830, Colombia splintered into modern-day Colombia, Venezuela, and Ecuador. Eleven years later, in 1841, Guatemala, Honduras, El Salvador, Nicaragua, and Costa Rica broke away from Mexico, weakening it. This was of great interest to Mexico's neighbor to the north, the United States, which was expanding rapidly and wanted more land.

Napoleon's invasion of Portugal in 1808 caused the monarchs to leave the country and set up the royal court in Rio de Janeiro, Brazil, for several years. When the monarchs returned to Portugal, Brazilians received their independence.

Europe's Struggle for Democracy

The common people in Europe, inspired by the democratic revolutions in America and France, tried to replace their monarchs with democratic governments. They were repeatedly put down by force. After failed revolutions for democracy in 1848, many Germans wanted to live in a country where they could vote and have a say in how they were governed. They would start over in America.

However, when they got to America, they discovered that although they could be free, four million Americans were enslaved.

Cattle, Coca-Cola, Cholera

From 1850 to 1900, many of the cuisines and cultures of the world as we know it now were formed. The United States changed from a nation of farmers to an urbanized, industrialized world power consuming mass-produced food. In Europe, the industrialization that had begun a century earlier continued. Germany and Italy united the individual city-states of the Middle Ages and became unified countries. Having a unique cuisine was one of the bases of a national culture. This pride in national identity appeared in cookbooks that are still in print today. Many Europeans, especially from southern and eastern Europe, left their home countries and transplanted their cuisines and cultures to the United States.

The American South

Before the Civil War, the slave-owning planter class, the ones who lived in mansions and had overseers, the way of life made famous in movies like *Gone with the Wind*, was about 25 percent of the white population in the South. Of those, according to the census of 1860, only 1,933 families owned more than 100 slaves. The vast majority of whites in the South were subsistence farmers who led difficult, hard-working lives:

By any standards their lives were drab. Their houses more nearly resembled shacks than the mansions of tradition. . . . The produce of their small plantations included meat, grain, and vegetables for subsistence and tobacco, rice or other staples that could be sold for cash.[1]

Slavery and Soul Food: Not Livin' High on the Hog

Still, this was luxury compared to how the slaves lived and ate. Booker T. Washington, who was born into slavery and was the first principal of the Tuskegee Institute in Alabama (opened July 4, 1881; now Tuskegee University), wrote his autobiography, *Up from Slavery*, and described the slave cabin where he grew up. It was one room, 14 by 16 feet, where Washington lived with his mother, brother, and sister. It had a dirt floor, a hole in the center to store sweet potatoes, another hole in the corner to let the cats out, holes in the log walls to let light in, and a door falling off its hinges. There was no stove; his mother did all the cooking over an open fire on the floor. Washington remembers his mother waking the children up in the middle of the night once for a feast, a chicken she had stolen. His father was a white man but Washington never knew who.

In the South, what part of the hog you ate showed your rank in society. The plantation owner's family ate meat from "high on the hog"—roasts, chops, ham. The slaves ate the outer limits—ears, snout, tail, feet or "trotters"; or the inner wasteland—the small intestines, called chitterlings or "chitlins." Chitlins were sometimes used by the whites, but as casings for sausage, not alone as food. Slave cooks prepared the meat from high on the hog but weren't allowed to eat it. They were also not allowed to eat beef, lamb, mutton, chickens, turkey, and geese, which were reserved for the plantation house.[2]

The labor force was not the only difference between kitchens in the North and the South. In the North, the kitchen hearth was the heart of the house. In the South, the plantation kitchen was separate from the house, just another outbuilding along with the dairy, the stable, and the outhouse. On large plantations, supplies were bought and animals slaughtered in bulk—barrels of flour and whiskey, dozens of chickens, thousands of pounds of hogs.[3]

Slave Cooks and Sisters

Fine Southern cooking and legendary Southern hospitality were made possible by the labor of female slaves. Food historian Karen Hess states that in the first half of the nineteenth century, all Southern cookbooks by white women were recipes they got from black cooks.[4] Slave cooks learned by doing, the daughter at her mother's side, using recipes and methods passed on orally and hands-on from earlier generations. The white plantation mistress gave instructions but did not cook, so the black female slave cook reigned supreme in the Southern kitchen. She had a skilled, high-status job; she worked in the house, not the fields, and she was proud of it.[5] Slave owners were afraid of their cooks because the cooks had the power to poison them—and sometimes did.

Slaves had no control of any part of their food supply. If the master allowed, they could supplement their diet with vegetables they grew on their own time on a patch of land near the slave cabin or with fish they caught. Slave women in particular were at the mercy of the masters for food. Slave women who were good breeders and produced many children sometimes got extra food for their families. Often, those who didn't have children were sold.[6]

Some Northern white women began to think they had something in common with slaves, and to agitate for freedom for both. In the first half of the nineteenth century, a man could beat his wife legally as long as he used a stick no thicker than his thumb—the "rule of thumb." In 1848, approximately 100 white women and men gathered at Seneca Falls in upstate New York and wrote the Declaration of Sentiments, a Declaration of Independence for women. It stated that "all men and women are created equal," that women who earned wages were being taxed without representation, and that they should have the right to vote. Just as the Declaration of Independence had a list of grievances against King George III, the women had a list of grievances against men: men prevented women from going to college or into professional careers; passed divorce laws so that women could never get the children; made all property that a woman owned, whether inherited or earned, the property of her husband; and forced different moral standards on women.[7] The people who attended the convention were ridiculed mercilessly in the press. Nevertheless, a powerful movement had been set in motion, and women became more involved in efforts to abolish slavery.

Lydia Maria Child was one. She began as a novelist, then wrote *The American Frugal Housewife*. Published in 1829, it was the only cookbook she wrote and it was an instant best seller. However, her books about rights for slaves and her position as editor of the *National Anti-Slavery Standard* put her on the fringes of American politics; *The American Frugal Housewife* was not reprinted after 1850.

Child's place was taken by Catharine Beecher and her *Treatise on Domestic Economy*, published in 1841. Beecher believed in traditional homemaking for women and opposed the women's movement. She was a practical person and her book explains clearly how to manage a household with few or no servants. She was deeply concerned with all aspects of the health and well-being of everyone in the household, down to what the milk cow was eating.[8] Her *Treatise* provided anatomy lessons and life advice.

Catharine's sister, however, was very involved in the abolition movement, and in 1852, Harriet Beecher Stowe wrote *Uncle Tom's Cabin*, about the horrors of slavery and attempts by the slaves to make a break for freedom. It became the first blockbuster novel in history, electrified Northerners into action, and caught on like wildfire in England. It was banned in the South.

The Quakers, based in Pennsylvania, were actively involved in ending slavery. As far back as 1788 they had promoted maple sugar produced by free labor as a way to end slavery on plantations producing cane sugar. George Washington and Thomas Jefferson tried to grow maple orchards on their plantations, but they were too far south. For a few years, there was a maple sugar "bubble"—an economic rise—as maple sugar sold for half the price of imported cane sugar. Maple sugar and syrup production peaked in 1860, on the eve of the Civil War.[9]

The Taste of Freedom on the Underground Railroad

One of the ways slaves escaped was via the Underground Railroad. This was not a literal railroad. It was a series of "stations"—safe houses where they could hide and get food until they made it to freedom, sometimes in Canada. A famous "conductor" was Harriet Tubman, an illiterate black slave who suffered brain damage at the age of 13 when her white master accidentally smashed her in the head with a lead weight and nearly killed her. Later she escaped from the South, then made 19 trips back into slave territory and smuggled more than 300 slaves out to freedom. The North called her the "Moses" of her people; the South put a bounty on her head.

What some runaway slaves remembered most about their first day away from slavery was the literal taste of freedom: the food, and how it was served. Sometimes they couldn't eat even though they were starving. They couldn't believe they were sitting at a table with white people who treated them not just as equals, but as betters: these white people waited on *them*, encouraging them to eat all the food they wanted. And what food it was!—food they had cooked and smelled and looked at and longed for all their lives but had never been allowed to eat. But once they started eating, they couldn't stop:

> I ate straight on for an entire hour, quite steady. I demolished all the ham and eggs and sausages they placed before me, with their due accompaniment of bread, and then a round of cold salt beef was brought up, from which I was helped abundantly.[10]

Finally free and livin' high on the hog!

Thousands of slaves escaped on the Underground Railroad. But it would take a war to free all four million of them.

The American Civil War: 1850–1865

In April 1861, one month after Abraham Lincoln was inaugurated as president, the Confederacy fired on the United States at Fort Sumter in South Carolina, and the Civil War began. In the beginning, under the command of Robert E. Lee and other brilliant generals, the South was winning. But gradually, the North's greater population, food production, and industrial strength—including two-thirds of the railroad tracks and all the gun factories in the country—began to overpower the South's rural, cotton-based economy. Every major battle of the war except Gettysburg, in Pennsylvania, was fought in the South.

Control of the food supply was crucial to the North's strategy. In *Starving the South*, food historian Andrew F. Smith points out that the North's naval blockade kept salt out of the South, which meant that meat could not be preserved. Hogs rotted at hog-butchering time. Also, "the Confederate government failed to take measures to maximize its agricultural strengths, while it implemented policies, such as impressment and confiscation of goods, that reduced food production, especially in Virginia, where the army most needed provisions."[11]

When the South did have food, it could not ship it because it had not stockpiled parts and equipment to make sure that the railroads could run. Class divisions in the South played a part, too: "The willingness of wealthy Southerners to pay exorbitant prices for scarce items made it more lucrative for blockade runners to carry luxury goods rather than much-needed staple foods."[12]

Scorched Earth in the South: Grant and Sherman

The North's General Ulysses S. Grant, trained at West Point, just as the South's General Robert E. Lee was, knew that a commander can move his troops only as far as he can supply them. And the lesson of Napoleon was not far in the past. Around Christmas in Mississippi in 1862, Confederate troops destroyed all of Grant's food and supplies. The Southerners, filled with "intense joy," came to Grant to gloat, but got a shock when he told them he had given orders to take all of their food for 15 miles around. By May 1863, Grant was employing a scorched-earth policy in Mississippi:

> The country was rich and full of supplies of both food and forage. [The troops were] instructed to take all of it. The cattle were to be driven in for the use of our army, and the food and forage to be consumed by our troops or destroyed by fire . . .[13]

General William Tecumseh Sherman applied the scorched earth policy in 1864 on his six-month march through the South on a front 60 miles wide. Sherman marched south from Atlanta to Savannah and the Atlantic, then north through South Carolina, North Carolina, and Virginia, doing more than $100 million [estimate in 1865 values] in property damage, a great deal of it to railroads.[14] As he started his march, news reached him about the Confederate prison in Andersonville, Georgia, where Union soldiers were being held:

> Inside the camp death stalked on every hand. . . . One-third of the original enclosure was swampy—a mud of liquid filth, voidings from the thousands, seething with maggots in full activity. Through this mass of pollution passed the only water. . . . We could not get away from the stink—we ate it, drank it and slept in it.[15]

"War is all Hell," said Sherman. Southerners in Northern prison camps and in Sherman's path agreed and went one step farther: Sherman was Satan. But the slaves he freed along the way thought he was God.

Florence Nightingale: Cooking for the Troops

When the American Civil War broke out, one of the foremost authorities in the world on military nutrition and sanitation was an upper-class Englishwoman. When England, France, and Turkey went to war against Russia in the Crimean War in 1854, British troops died in horrifying numbers—not in battle, but from disease, a greater percentage than had died in the bubonic plague epidemic in London in 1660. Florence Nightingale went to the front lines and found out why: "Let men be under-fed on salt provisions, imperfectly cooked, and without vegetables or fermented bread"[16] and they'll get scurvy, which will make them susceptible to other illnesses. Nightingale was outraged, as were many in England, because the prevention of scurvy had been known for years. There were also "neither camp kettles nor fuel to cook . . . with."[17] Nightingale and her 38 nurses, against tremendous hostility from male British army doctors, set about procuring better food and clothing for the men, bathing them, and scrubbing the filthy barracks.

In 1861, as the American South prepared for war, they printed a pamphlet called *Directions for Cooking by Troops in Camp and Hospital, Prepared for the Army of Virginia, and Published by Order of the Surgeon General: with Essays on "Taking Food" and "What Food"* by Florence Nightingale. Nightingale's two essays follow recipes for Coffee for One Hundred Men, One Pint Each, and Fresh Beef Soup for One Hundred Men, as well as beef soup, beef tea, thick beef tea, essence of beef, chicken broth, plain boiled rice, rice water, barley water, arrowroot water, and sweetened milk thickened with arrowroot for invalids. Nightingale's philosophy on feeding the sick was based on her observations and broke with tradition. She observed that sick people can't take solid food early in the morning because they have feverish nights and are dehydrated and would do better with "A spoonful of beef-tea, or arrowroot and wine, or egg flip, every hour."[18] She stressed ingenuity, "thinking outside the box" we would call it now, and said "The patients [sic] stomach must be its own chemist"—the stomach was right, the book was wrong.[19]

Nightingale also had the rare ability to see beyond her class. She had a deep respect for "laundresses, mistresses of dairy-farms, head nurses . . . women who unite a good deal of hard manual labor with the head-work necessary for arranging the day's business." Nightingale made nursing a respectable profession for the first time. The sick soldiers in the Crimea called Florence Nightingale, who was often in the hospital wards in the middle of the night, holding a kerosene lamp as she made her way from sick man to sick man, "The Lady with the Lamp."[20]

In the midst of all this death, in 1863, after pressure from women's groups and others, Lincoln declared Thanksgiving a national holiday. Many Americans were also beginning to celebrate Christmas.

Christmas, December 25

Christmas Day, December 25, as it is celebrated in the United States today is a mixture of German, English, and American traditions. It also has remnants of pagan rituals. The Romans had an end-of-the-year festival called the Saturnalia, for which the color red had special significance, especially red hats.

In the mid-1800s, England's Queen Victoria and her husband Prince Albert were photographed in the royal palace celebrating Christmas in the German tradition of Victoria's childhood—with a Christmas tree. The pictures were printed in American magazines and the Christmas tree caught on instantly, along with other German Christmas traditions like singing "O Tannenbaum" (German for "Christmas tree"), the custom of bringing fresh greens like tree boughs into the house in the middle of winter, candy canes, and gingerbread. Plum Pudding became a British Christmas tradition. There are no plums in it; *plummy* means "something wonderful," or "choicest"; also, *plum* sometimes meant raisins. Christmas became commercialized in the nineteenth century when the new department stores used their display windows to tempt people into buying gifts. In the middle of the twentieth century, Irving Berlin wrote the song "White Christmas," sung by Bing Crosby. It became hugely popular after World War II.

In some countries, the Christmas celebration continues until January 6, the twelfth day after Christmas. Twelfth Night or Epiphany is when the three wise men reached the Christ child. In England, the song "The 12 Days of Christmas" with its famous lyrics, "and a partridge in a pear tree," commemorates the observance. In New Orleans, it is the beginning of the celebration that ends with Mardi Gras. In Italy on Twelfth Night, *La Befana*, the good witch, flies in and brings gifts to children. If they are bad, they get only *carbone*—a lump of coal.

Kwanzaa is an African-American holiday that takes place between December 26 and January 1. This celebration of family and culture is a product of the 1960s civil rights movement; Kwanzaa was first celebrated in 1966.

The Civil War ended on April 9, 1865, when General Lee surrendered to General Grant at the courthouse in Appomattox Courthouse, Virginia. Less than a week later, President Lincoln was assassinated. The country immediately plunged into deep mourning.

Reconstruction: 1865–1877

Four million slaves were now free to move, to find family members, to go to school and learn to read, to get married. The United States Constitution was amended to grant rights to the freed people. In 1865, the Thirteenth Amendment granted freedom to all slaves; in 1868, the Fourteenth Amendment guaranteed former slaves the rights of citizens; and in 1870, the Fifteenth Amendment gave black men—but not black or white women—the right to vote.

The First Cookbooks by African-Americans

The first cookbook by an African-American was written in 1866, the year after the Civil War ended. There is only one copy in existence, at the Longone Center at the University of Michigan. A cookbook called *What Mrs. Fisher Knows about Old Southern Cooking* was published in 1881 in San Francisco, but it was not until the 1990s that food historian Dan Strehl discovered that the author, Mrs. Abby Fisher, was a mulatto, born a slave in South Carolina to a slave mother and a French father. She was illiterate, so the book was dictated.

There are 160 numbered recipes in 72 pages. The largest number—58—are for breads, cakes, pies, puddings, and sherbets. Forty-one are for Mrs. Fisher's prize-winning pickles, sauces, and preserves. Her pastry is rolled out "to the thickness of an egg-shell for the top of the fruit, and that for the bottom of fruit must be thin as paper."[21] Compound Tomato Sauce is more like a ketchup, left to stand for 24 hours with onions, allspice, cloves, black and cayenne pepper, then cooked with vinegar.[22] South Carolina was rice country, so rice appears in one of the earliest recipes for jambalaya. Chicken, crab, oysters, and fish are mixed with crackers and turned into croquettes, baked into pies, broiled, fricasseed, stewed with rice in gumbo, or made into chowder. Potatoes are "Irish potatoes." Corn appears in fritters, boiled, in Circuit Hash (succotash), in hoe cake, pudding, and in corn bread with rice. Eggplant, introduced to Africa by the Arabs, is stuffed, as are tomatoes. Tomatoes and milk are used in clam chowder.

HOLIDAY HISTORY:

Juneteenth, June 19

Juneteenth is a special day for African-Americans. It was on June 19, 1865, that the news first reached slaves in Galveston, Texas, that they were free. There was much jubilation then and much speculation now about why they didn't find out sooner. The Civil War had been over since April, and Lincoln had issued the Emancipation Proclamation two-and-a-half years earlier, on January 1, 1863. But then, some masters told their slaves that since Lincoln had freed them and he was dead, they were slaves again.[23]

Frederick Douglass, a famous black leader who escaped from slavery, made a speech in which he told white people that the Fourth of July was their holiday for their country. Juneteenth finally gave the freed slaves something to celebrate, which they did with barbecue and music. Ntozake Shange's book *If I Can Cook/You Know God Can* is this kind of celebration: part cookbook, part memoir, part history of Africans in the western hemisphere, and all soul. It is as if Shange is in the kitchen with you at the prep table, telling stories about the ingredients as you do your mise. The recipe for the traditional good-luck New Year's dish, Hoppin' John (black-eyed peas and rice), ends with: "Yes, mostly West Indians add the coconut, but that probably only upset Charlestonians. Don't take that to heart. Cook your peas and rice to your own likin'."[24] Shange has recipes for every day and for special occasions, like Pig's Tails by Instinct, French-Fried Chitlins, Cousin Eddie's Shark with Breadfruit, and Collard Greens to Bring You Money.

While America was fighting its Civil War, France took advantage of the situation to send troops into the western hemisphere and try to take Mexico. They failed, and Mexicans still celebrate their victory over France.

Cinco de Mayo, May 5

Cinco de Mayo commemorates the day in 1862 when a small group of Mexicans defeated a much larger, better-equipped French force at Puebla and prevented them from taking the capital, Mexico City. (It is *not* when Mexico won its independence from Spain, which was September 16, 1810.) Mexico's default on a loan payment was France's excuse to invade. With aid from the United States, the French were gone by 1867. But the festival lives on in Puebla and in parts of the United States with large Mexican populations. Mariachi music, *folklórico* dancing, parades, and street fairs include traditional foods like margaritas (classic, strawberry, melon, and more), guacamole and chips, green corn tamales at the beginning of the season, and cook-offs of *menudo* (a stew of tripe, hominy, and chile).

The West: Railroad and Indian Wars, 1860s–1886

After the Civil War ended in 1865, Americans resumed moving west. Many of the freed slaves moved to Kansas and became cowboys. One, Bill Pickett, invented steer wrestling—jumping off a horse, grabbing a steer by its horns and wrestling it to the ground, which became (and still is) a major rodeo event. One of the ways he controlled a longhorn was by "bulldogging"—biting its lower lip, which isn't done anymore. Pickett was a rodeo superstar and the first black man elected to the National Cowboy Hall of Fame.

Stagecoach Food

In July 1861, Mark Twain, who later wrote the classic American novels *Tom Sawyer* and *Huckleberry Finn*, went from Missouri to Nevada Territory, which was experiencing a Silver Rush. He traveled by stagecoach and described the food at the stage stops. The cups and plates were tin, the main course was condemned Army bacon, and the breakfast beverage was called slumgullion: "It really pretended to be tea, but there was too much dishrag, and sand, and old bacon rind in it to deceive the intelligent traveler. He had no sugar and no milk—not even a spoon to stir the ingredients with." The manners matched: "Pass the bread, you son of a skunk!"[25] Only once was there real food between the United States and Salt Lake City, a breakfast of "hot biscuits, fresh antelope steaks, and coffee."[26]

European travelers were amazed at how fast Americans ate. They didn't taste their food, they inhaled it. They sat down at the table and were done in five minutes. In boarding houses, service was *à la française*—all the food put on the table at once—but speeded up by an American invention called the Lazy Susan. This was a large platter on ball bearings in the middle of the table, which rotated so that every diner could reach every food.[27] *(Service à la Susan?)*

"I've been workin' on the railroad"

To get to the Pacific Ocean, Americans needed to build a transcontinental rail-road, even though the United States already had almost half of all the railroad tracks in the world. Finding workers wasn't easy; any able-bodied male in California wanted to look for gold, not work for $3 a day. Finally, Leland Stanford (as in Stanford University) had an idea: Chinese. The Chinese were already in California; they had come looking for gold but discrimination by whites had forced them out. Mark Twain visited San Francisco's Chinatown in the 1860s and wrote that the Chinese "are quiet, peaceable, tractable, free from drunkenness, and they are as industrious as the day is long. A disorderly Chinaman is rare, and a lazy one does not exist."[28] Whites said that the Chinese men—on average, under four feet, 10 inches tall—were too small to build a railroad. Stanford shot back, "They built the Great Wall of China, didn't they?"[29]

And like the workers on the Great Wall of China and the pyramids in ancient Egypt, the men who built the railroad had to eat, too. White workers were often sick with intestinal illnesses. Chinese weren't. Diet made the difference. Whites ate what the railroad gave them—boiled beef and potatoes—and drank water from polluted streams. The Chinese got food from Chinese merchants in San Francisco, paid for and cooked it themselves, and drank tea made from germ-free boiled water. They ate:

> Oysters, cuttlefish, . . . abalone meat, [Asian] fruits, and scores of vegetables, including bamboo sprouts, seaweed, and mushrooms, . . . rice, salted cabbage, vermicelli, bacon, and sweet crackers. Very occasionally they had fresh meat, pork being a prime favorite, along with chicken.[30]

Because they didn't get sick, the Chinese were accused of being "devilish." They also bathed daily and didn't drink alcohol. Their only vice was that they smoked opium on Sundays—a habit acquired from the British.

In October 1869, the last spike of the transcontinental railroad—the Golden Spike—was driven in Ogden, Utah, and the east and west coasts of the United States were connected by rail. Food on the trains was considerably better than it had been at the stage stops where Mark Twain ate. The Chicago-based Pullman company manufactured "palace" cars, luxurious "hotels on wheels" with leather seats, brass lamps, and curtains. The dining cars were equally elegant. White linen and solid silver were on the table; champagne, antelope steaks, mountain trout, and fresh fruit were on the plates. The contrast between the wildness of the country outside and the civilization on the train with a chef and a French-influenced menu impressed diners.[31] Also impressive was the excellent service. All the waiters and porters on the Pullman cars were black; until the middle of the twentieth century, these were some of the best jobs black men could get in the United States, and they also provided one of the first labor unions for blacks.

When the transcontinental railroad was finished, the Chinese were 25 percent of the labor force in California. There was not another project that needed as many laborers, so desperate Chinese would work for less than whites. Angry white workers retaliated with mass lynchings of Chinese in Wyoming, San Francisco, and Los Angeles. In 1882, Congress passed the Chinese Exclusion Act to keep the Chinese, the poor, mentally retarded, and prostitutes out of the United States. Particularly hard hit when the Chinese had to leave were the vineyards in northern California. One man remembered watching when they left:

> . . . on foot, on horseback, some riding in laden wagons, others pushing hand-carts; and the parade was lighted by lanterns at the end of poles. . . .

> They weren't the Mongolian Peril to us. They were old Wah Lee with his pigtail who rode me on his shoulders while he bossed the grape pickers. He did the cooking, ran the vegetable garden, and made kites with long tails that went up into the sky. . . . Every farm had its Wah Lee . . .

> The mark of their labor is to be seen everywhere in the [Napa] valley from Yountville to Calistoga where the road begins to wind up the great wooded ramp of Mount St. Helena.[32]

But to the whites moving west, Native Americans were still a problem.

Scorched Earth in the West: Buffalo Culture and the Plains Indians

The United States Army used the same scorched-earth policy on Native Americans that it had used in the Civil War: it wasn't necessary to kill the people, just destroy their food supply. The buffalo was more than just the main source of food for the Plains Indians, it was their entire culture. Buffalo hides made tepees—their homes; clothes, blankets, robes, and moccasins—their shoes. Buffalo horns were used for ceremonial costumes, the bones became sewing needles, the ligaments and sinews were used like rope and wire. Buffalo bladders and stomachs became containers. Approximately 50 million buffalo were killed by the army and by "sportsmen" who rode the new railroads out onto the plains and used long-range repeating rifles to pick off buffalo as if they were in a shooting gallery (with free bullets provided by the army). Sometimes the entire carcass was left to rot except for the tongue, which was prized as food in the eastern United States. Sitting Bull, the chief of the Lakota, said, "A cold wind blew across the prairie when the last buffalo fell—a death wind for my people."[33] But it opened up the land for white people.

The Family Farm Economy

The Midwestern farm economy was a household economy. Everyone participated; the work of women and children was essential. Labor was divided by gender. Because of frequent pregnancies, women stayed closer to the house, but if it became necessary, for example, at harvest time, they worked in the fields, too.

MIDWESTERN FARM FAMILY DUTIES

WOMEN AND CHILDREN	MEN AND BOYS
All food preparation: three meals a day	Chop down trees to clear land
Feed and milk cows	Chop wood for fuel
Feed chickens, gather eggs, clean henhouse	Build and mend fences
Make sausage and prepare hams	Plow and spread manure in fields
Tend domestic garden near house	Sow
Preserve fruits and vegetables	Harvest
Make cheese	Maintain and repair farm equipment
Churn butter	Care for oxen, mules, horses
Clean house	Herd and feed hogs and sheep
Spin wool and flax into yarn	Clean and maintain barnyard
Weave cloth from yarn; dye or bleach it	Slaughter and butcher large farm animals
Cut, sew, mend clothes for entire family	Hunt
Make soap	Make cider
Wash clothes, hang outside to dry	Make maple sugar
Knit socks, mittens, and caps	
Pluck down from geese and ducks, stuff pillows with it	
Make cider and maple sugar	
Bear, nurse, and take care of children	
Make everything look nice	

The Locust Plagues

In spite of the incessant hard work by everyone in the family, nature was still a huge variable. In the Bible, locusts were one of the 10 great plagues the God of the Hebrews sent to force the Egyptians to let the Hebrews go. Locust is another word for grasshopper or cricket and means "burned over place," which is what the land looks like after these insects have been there. A locust can eat as much as 38 pounds in its lifetime, which is only a few months.[34] From 1873 to 1878, grasshoppers descended on Midwestern farms like a Biblical plague. Year after year, they ate everything in sight. First, the large adult grasshoppers swarmed down on the fields with a deafening noise like a million scissors and ate the ripening wheat, oats, barley, and corn. Then they laid eggs. Farmers in Minnesota were sure the tiny eggs wouldn't be able to survive the brutally cold winter or the rainy spring. They survived both and hatched just in time to eat the sprouting wheat, oats, barley, and corn. They repeated this pattern for half a decade. The farmers burned the fields, but the grasshoppers flew away and came back. They covered the crops with sheets and blankets, but the grasshoppers ate them. They invented "hopper dozers," pieces of metal smeared with molasses and dragged through the fields. Not enough grasshoppers stuck to make a difference. Laura Ingalls Wilder, who later wrote the *Little House on the Prairie* books, remembered running home from school and feeling grasshoppers crunch under her bare feet. Finally, unable to control the grasshoppers or make a living, people moved away. In the middle of one of the greatest westward migrations in history, some states lost population.[35]

"Don't fence me in": Cattle Drives and Barbed Wire

The cattle drives began after the Civil War, in 1866, when a surplus of cattle drove the price down to $1 a head in Texas while cities back East were starved for beef. There was no railroad in the South, so Texas cattlemen decided to drive their longhorns north to the railheads, to the legendary tough cow towns—Wichita, Dodge, and Abilene in Kansas; Omaha in Nebraska. These were the towns of lawmen like Wyatt Earp. The trails had names like Chisolm and Goodnight-Loving. By 1885, almost six million head of cattle were driven north to the railheads, and cheap Texas longhorn beef had replaced European breeds.[36]

Each cattle drive had a cook who managed the "chuck" wagon and dished out "grub." After the foreman, the cook was the most important man in the outfit. Other cowboys packed his bedroll and harnessed his team. And they'd better stay out of his way. Cooks were notoriously temperamental. After all, they were cooking for sometimes 100 men, outside, in a different place every day, from the back of a wagon. The cooks spent much time alone, because they had to ride on ahead of the outfit and cook so the food was ready at the end of the day. The pots, Dutch ovens, and frying pans were heavy cast iron. The fare was coffee, beans, coffee, beef, coffee, biscuits, and coffee; nothing raw and green like vegetables, although canned peaches were a favorite, and canned tomatoes provided enough vitamin C to keep scurvy away.[37] Chile was the main spice. With the coffee was the equally essential granulated brown sugar, so dried out that chunks had to be chipped off and then put through a meat grinder. A coffee grinder was on the side of every chuck wagon, too, and coffee in 100-pound sacks. Sometimes they killed one of the cows and made "son of a bitch stew."

Chuck wagon. *Courtesy Security Pacific Collection/Los Angeles Public Library.*

Barbed wire, introduced at the De Kalb, Illinois, County Fair in 1873, began the closing of the open range. As farmers used the new wire to build fences, wars erupted with the cattlemen over who could use the land and in what way. Weather also played a part. In Texas and on the Great Plains, 1886 was the end of the cattle drives. In the blizzards of 1886–1887, the cattle, blinded by snow, instinctively headed south. When the snow cleared, thousands of cattle were found frozen in the fences. It was "The Big Die-Up."

The year 1886 was also the end of the Indian wars—every Indian who had been at war with the United States was dead, in jail, or on a reservation. The last Indian to surrender was Geronimo, son of Cochise and leader of the Chiricahua Apache; he surrendered in Skeleton Canyon in southeastern Arizona, not far from Tombstone. In 1887, Congress passed the Dawes Severalty Act to break up tribal lands and force Indians to dress, speak, worship, and live like Americans.

Unions

Also in 1886, a bombing in Chicago's Haymarket Square killed seven policemen. The Knights of Labor, the major union at that time, was blamed. Membership dropped so drastically that it went out of existence. A new union, the American Federation of Labor (AFL), which still exists today, began later in 1886. Some of the first to join were restaurant workers.

DATE FORMED	LOCATION	ORGANIZATION
1887	New York	Waiters Union
	New York	Bartenders
1888	Brooklyn	Bartenders
	Boston	Bartenders
	St. Louis	German Waiters Union
1890	St. Louis	American Waiters and Bartenders
	St. Paul	Waiters Union
	Chicago	Waiters League (founded 1866 under the Knights of Labor)
	Brooklyn	Waiters Union
1891	Indianapolis	Waiters
	Minneapolis	Waiters
	Denver	Cooks
	St. Louis	Cooks
	Logansport, IN	Bartenders Mutual Aid

The Gilded Age

In the last quarter of nineteenth-century America, everything seemed covered in gold. It was the Gilded Age, after the title of a novel written in 1873 by Mark Twain and Charles Dudley Warner. The Industrial Revolution and America's abundant natural resources were making Americans wealthy and they were showing it off. The word *millionaire* didn't exist before the 1840s; by 1901, America had its first billion-dollar corporation, United States Steel. The wealthy built mansions that rivaled European palaces and often included pieces of real ones that had been dismantled, shipped across the Atlantic, and reassembled. Flatware was gold; dishes were trimmed in gold; ballroom and drawing room ceilings and walls were covered with gold leaf, gold paint, gold draperies.

Shopping and Eating

Galloping consumerism characterized the Gilded Age. Factories produced massive amounts of goods and advertised to get people to buy them. Two new technologies helped Americans to become good shoppers: structural steel and plate glass. The new structural steel was much stronger than the old wrought iron, so less of it was needed to support a building. Like the Gothic cathedrals of the Middle Ages, there was now more space between beams. Into this space went

Silver-plated ware. *From the* American Agriculturist *catalog, October 1884.*

plate-glass windows—one huge piece, six feet high or more. Behind these windows, goods were displayed: the department store was born. At the end of the nineteenth century, when Otis invented the elevator, the skyscraper was born. Going shopping was one of the only excuses a respectable middle-class woman had for leaving the house.

If the shopper couldn't get to the department store, the department store came to the shopper. Catalogs hundreds of pages long from Sears Roebuck & Co. headquarters in Chicago tempted farm families with pictures of stoves, dishes, pots and pans, farm tools, seeds, tractors, hot water heaters, rugs, shoes, ready-made clothes, furniture. All of it could be ordered by mail and delivered by train—even the house to put it in.

Houses were beginning to have indoor plumbing and electricity, and more than one room for eating. The dining room was formal, while there might be a separate, less formal breakfast room for just the family. Middle- and upper-class meals were breakfast, dinner, and supper. There were other meals for women: the "ladies' luncheon" and high tea.

Tin cans and refrigerated railroad cars made this increase in the standard of living possible. Tin cans—Appert's invention, mass produced on American assembly lines by 1876—made previously exotic, out-of-season, or perishable foods affordable and convenient. Canning began in America in the 1820s with lobsters, oysters, and salmon. By 1882, tomatoes, corn, beans, and peas were the most popular canned foods of the at least 51 kinds available.[39] Refrigerated railroad cars made meat, especially beef and pork coming out of the world's largest meat market, the Union Stockyards in Chicago, available throughout the country. In the North, especially, people went to restaurants.

American Restaurants

The Union Oyster House in Boston, Massachusetts, claims to be the oldest continuously operating restaurant in the United States. The building dates back to before 1742 and became the Atwood & Bacon restaurant in 1826. Located in the North End, it is near the wharves and where Paul Revere lived (his house is still standing), and the historic Quincy Market Area (now the Boston Market). The fare was simple.

Oysters were a craze in the nineteenth century, selling for 15 or 20 cents a dozen. Oyster houses and bars sprang up all over the United States. In the middle of the country, with no ocean, there were "prairie oysters"—raw eggs replaced raw oysters, which had a similar consistency. The

Atwood & Bacon restaurant menu, 1826. *Courtesy The Union Oyster House Restaurant.*

condiments were the same: Tabasco, Worcestershire, lemon, vinegar, and ketchup. Farther west, prairie oysters, also called Rocky Mountain oysters, were neither oysters nor eggs, but calf's testicles.

HOLIDAY HISTORY:

Testicle Festivals

Prairie oyster festivals are still held today in the West. Several Montana towns hold festivals in September. They have also been held in Virginia City, Nevada, and in Nebraska. Prairie oysters are also called Montana tendergroin, bulls jewels, and cowboy caviar. Beer is not in short supply at these events.

Boston boasts another "continuously"—the Parker House is the oldest continuously operating hotel in the United States. It was there that Parker House rolls were invented. They claim that Boston cream pie—really a layer cake with a custard filling and chocolate frosting—originated there, too, but this can't be proven.

In New York, Swiss immigrant brothers opened Delmonico's Restaurant at No. 2, South William Street, in 1831. They served Continental cuisine. The restaurant became more than just *the* place to eat for Wall Street financiers. It also served at various times as a telegraph office and a bank. In 1832, President Jackson vetoed the recharter of the Bank of the United States. After 1837, without one central bank in control, any institution with enough credibility to back up its name could issue its own money. Delmonico's and the Parker House did. Here is an example of the currency Delmonico's issued:

Delmonico money. *Courtesy of the Federal Reserve Bank of San Francisco, American Currency Exhibit.*

Other nineteenth-century restaurants were the Pump Room in Chicago, and Antoine's (1840) in New Orleans. Most travelers stayed at hotels, on the

"American Plan"—you paid for room and meals, whether you ate there or not, a *prix fixe* situation. As more European travelers came to the United States, they objected, so hotels switched to the "European Plan"—you paid for your room and only for the meals you ate, like *à la carte*.[40]

Botulism

Modern methods of preservation contributed to some lethal food-borne illnesses (FBIs). One of these is botulism *(Clostridium botulinus)*. Just as yeast is present in the air, botulism is present in the soil. Because it lives deprived of oxygen, it is in a class of organisms called anaerobes (Greek *an*=no, *aero*=air). Enough acid will kill it. When foods, especially vegetables, were preserved by pickling, the vinegar destroyed the botulism. But with the Industrial Revolution and the advent of vacuum-packed canning, botulism ran rampant. It is a disease that strikes the nervous system, paralyzing the muscles. Death usually comes—very painfully—from the inability to breathe because of paralysis of the diaphragm. Not dying is no guarantee of recovery; blindness and paralysis can remain. To make things worse, unlike other FBIs, botulism can be in food and present no signs: no bulging can, no nose-holding stench, no slime.

Eating Disorders: Anorexia and Bulimia

In Victorian England and America, an appetite for food was equated with an appetite for sex, which was taboo. The foods that were thought to arouse unhealthy appetites in girls and women were coffee, tea, chocolate, mustard, vinegar and pickles, spices, nuts, raisins, warm bread, pastry, candy, and alcohol. Meat was the worst—it would surely lead to insanity or nymphomania or both.[41] A woman seen eating meat and potatoes put herself on a level with a barnyard animal. Many women took to eating in secret, reversing the trend for women to eat in public that was begun by Caterina de' Medici almost 400 years earlier.

Men's animalistic sexual impulses needed to be controlled, too. Piano legs were covered so men's wicked thoughts would not be stimulated by the sight of a leg—any leg. A glimpse of a lady's leg was nearly impossible because her ankle-length skirt and petticoats would have to ride above her knee-length high-button shoes—and even then she was wearing stockings you couldn't see through. These sexual avoidances carried over into the language of food. Polite people offered their guests "white meat" or "dark meat" because one simply did not utter the words "breast" or "leg."

In this world of rigid control of women and sexuality, manners and food, a strange malady began to appear, mostly in middle- and upper-class teenage girls. In a time of an abundance of food and wealth, these girls wasted away and sometimes died because they would not eat. The disease was first named anorexia nervosa in 1868 by an English physician.[42] It experienced an upsurge in the 1960s.

There are two main forms of the disease. Anorexia involves starving. Bulimia is binge eating, then purging the food out of the body by extreme exercise, laxatives, enemas, vomiting—at first, forced by putting the fingers down the throat; later, at will. Both are characterized by being more than 15 percent below *minimal* normal body weight, missing three consecutive menstrual periods, and abnormal preoccupation with appearance. The numbers on the scale tell these young women that they are seriously underweight but when they look in the mirror all they see is fat. Now, about 11 percent die.[43]

Good Help Is Hard to Find

In the late-nineteenth-century United States, keeping homes clean and preparing meals required a great deal of work. In the country, someone had to go outside, pump water out of the well, and bring it back into the house, one bucket at a time. In cities, barrels of water had to be lugged upstairs. Getting human and household waste out of houses and apartments in cities was easier—open a window and let gravity take over. Animal garbage collectors—pigs—roamed the streets. By the 1880s, cities began building sewage systems, but they were storm sewers, not sanitary.[44] Houses were lit by kerosene after oil was discovered in Titusville, Pennsylvania, in 1859. It was a dirty fuel, leaving black soot on lamp, walls, fabrics (and lungs), and it required cleaning, too. Who would do all this work?

Middle-class women were unhappy with their servants. The "servant problem" as it was called, was really this: women who had a choice went to work in factories. They wanted to earn and keep their own money. They didn't want to work six-and-a-half days a week in somebody else's house, have their mail opened and their lives monitored. In America, there was not a class of people raised to be servants as there was in Europe. Immigration, disrupted by the Civil War, resumed with a flood of immigrants at the end of the nineteenth century. But people don't come to America so they can be servants.

In contrast to the wealthy young women who starved themselves, working-class young women who smoked, drank, and kept "bad company" with people their parents didn't like were sent to prison, sometimes for years. Often these young women felt that because they were earning their own money, no one could tell them what to do. Their offense was that they were behaving like men. In New York, they were sent to the women's reformatory north of New York City at Bedford Hills. From there, they were paroled as household and kitchen help to middle-class women who were having trouble finding servants. It was an ideal situation for the housewives: if their "girl" didn't do what they wanted, they had the entire prison system and the police force to discipline her.[45]

Vassar: The First College for Women

Also up the Hudson River, 72 miles north of New York City, in Poughkeepsie, was a different kind of institution for women. In the 1860s, a British immigrant, brewer Matthew Vassar, wanted to do something to make himself famous. So he funded a college that he declared would be for women what Harvard and Yale were for men. He did this in the face of the best (male) medical advice at the time, that if women used their brains they would damage their reproductive organs. Menus from shortly after the college's founding reveal typical nineteenth-century American institutional food, heavy on protein and starch. The menus fit into the nineteenth-century trend to have a substantial breakfast—one weekday it was Boston brown bread, fish hash, beefsteak, and fish eggs. The main meal was midday—roast beef, corned beef, hominy, bread pudding, and mackerel (in that order on the menu). Supper was light—sometimes only prunes or biscuits and applesauce.

For about a century, these meals were cooked in individual dormitory kitchens and served in wood-paneled dining rooms on tables covered with white cloths, under chandeliers. The young women had to dress up for dinner, which until the late 1960s meant wearing skirts. But breakfast and the midday meal were more informal. This atmosphere created a sense of family among the students, who often referred to each other as "sister."

However, in the last decades of the twentieth century, it became too expensive to have a dining room in every dormitory, so one central dining hall was created. By then, the college had also become coeducational. Women attending Vassar and the other colleges that opened to them in the late nineteenth and early twentieth centuries would have a profound impact on America and the world in the coming generations.

They also had a profound influence on chocolate. The first written reference to fudge making comes from Vassar in 1887.[46] The craze spread to other women's colleges, especially Smith and Wellesley in Massachusetts. The Vassar recipe is a simple, basic one of cream, sugar, butter, and chocolate. Smith added brown sugar; Wellesley contributed marshmallow creme. Ninety percent of the recipes for fudge in the United States today are based on these three recipes.[47] As chocolate became more popular, it became associated with one very romantic holiday that began to be celebrated in the nineteenth century, Valentine's Day.

World's Fairs and Amusement Parks—The "All-Electric Home"

On September 4, 1882, at 3:00 P.M., an event occurred that changed the world: a switch was thrown, and New York City lit up with Thomas Edison's new invention—electric lights.[48] It transformed night into day. Broadway became "The Great White Way," and New York became famous for its night life. Electricity and machines were used for play, too, in New York's playground, Coney Island. After 1884, people out to enjoy themselves could get on the gravity-powered ride that became the roller coaster. They could eat a Coney Island Red Hot before it was called a hot dog. At Nathan's Famous, they could feast on huge clams on the half-shell. They could stroll while eating cotton candy, a spun sugar confection invented by German immigrants.

Valentine's Day, February 14

Valentine's Day is the second most popular day for dining out (after Mother's Day) and for sending greeting cards (after Christmas). It has its own cuisine and rituals based on a combination of Greek, Roman, and Christian cultures. In the Roman Empire, February 14 was a fertility festival, but around the year 498, Pope Gelasius declared it St. Valentine's Day. There are multiple candidates for St. Valentine, all Christian martyrs: Valentine performed secret marriages for young lovers. Or he helped Christians escape from prison. Or he was in prison and sent a love letter signed, "From your Valentine."[49]

Cupid, the chubby little winged cherub who shoots arrows into the hearts of unsuspecting humans, was originally the ancient Greek god of love, a physically perfect, gorgeous athlete. (In Rome his name was Eros, which gives us *erotic*.) His mother—Aphrodite in Greece, Venus in Rome—was jealous of a beautiful young woman named Psyche (Soul), so she sent Cupid to make Psyche fall in love with an ugly guy. But Cupid took one look at Psyche and fell in love with her himself. He made her promise never to look at him or they would be separated forever. Psyche loved him blindly, but her sisters kept pushing her to sneak a peek. One night, Psyche got a lamp and looked at Cupid while he was asleep. Her hand trembled with happiness, spilling hot oil on Cupid's shoulder. Burned physically and emotionally, he left, because "Love can't live without trust."

Broken-hearted, Psyche went to Aphrodite and begged to see him (he was there recuperating). Aphrodite tried to get rid of Psyche by giving her impossible tasks. But Psyche completed all of them, even going through hell—literally—because she loved Cupid so much. Cupid recovered and he wanted her, too. Zeus, king of the gods, gave Psyche some ambrosia—the food of the gods—which made her one of them. He declared that Cupid and Psyche were married forever, because Love and the Soul can't live without each other.[50]

During the Middle Ages, St. Valentine and Cupid mingled and Valentine became the patron saint of lovers. Cards were exchanged. The oldest valentine in existence was written in 1415. In the 1840s, an American woman, Esther A. Howland, is credited with the first mass-produced valentines. Now, in addition to cards, lovers send flowers, especially roses, and especially red roses to symbolize passion.

Valentine's Day cuisine is aphrodisiacs: champagne, caviar, oysters, foie gras, passion fruit, and truffles (fungus and chocolate). Restaurant decor goes pink and red: menus, linens, flowers, aprons. So does the food: raspberries in vinaigrette, coulis, gelée, soufflé. Food is also heart-shaped: pâté, ravioli, cakes, tarts, muffins, pancakes, cookies, candies. But these offerings aren't guarantees—Cupid is still very mischievous.

Eleven years after New York was illuminated, electricity lit up a building in Chicago. The 1893 World's Fair in Chicago was called the Columbian Exposition, in honor of the four hundredth anniversary of Columbus's discovery of the New World. (They were a year late because it took longer than expected to arrange it.) Its intention was to do for America what the Crystal Palace Exhibition in London had done for England in 1851—show off the wealth and power of the country. Pavilions and exhibits at the Columbian Exposition had to adhere to strict architectural guidelines to create a giant "White City"—so white that black Americans, even famous ex-slaves like Frederick Douglass, were not allowed in as either workers or spectators. They were, however, exhibits. One was a cook, an ex-slave named Nancy Green, dressed up as a slave, smiling and serving pancakes—Aunt Jemima.

Almost 50 years after the all-electric home was introduced, electricity was still being perfected. The Soda Fountain, *April 1917.*

Another exhibit was about electricity. It showcased the "All-Electric Home" of the future, a paradise of "electric stoves, hot plates, washing and ironing machines, dishwashers, carpet sweepers, electric doorbells, phonographs, fire alarms, and innumerable lighting devices"[51]—all of which eventually did come into widespread use, but more than 50 years later.

HOLIDAY HISTORY:

Columbus Day, October 12

The Columbian Exposition in 1893 began the celebration of Columbus Day in the United States, still celebrated in cities with large Italian populations. The Pledge of Allegiance was written for this fair, although it didn't have the words "under God" in it until the 1950s, as a reaction to communism. Like Thanksgiving, what is a holiday in the rest of the United States is a day of mourning for Native Americans.

Nineteenth-Century Health Food Movements

In 1857, German physicist Rudolf J. E. Clausius discovered a unit of heat that he called a calorie. It was the amount of energy required to raise the temperature of one gram of water one degree Celsius. One pound of body fat equals 3,500 calories. With the discovery of the calorie, could health food and dieting be far behind?

Vegetarianism

There were two phases to nineteenth-century vegetarianism. The first was pre–Civil War and began in the 1830s. The second was in the Gilded Age. One idea behind health food in the nineteenth century was that if men stopped eating like animals—meat—they would stop behaving like animals. This objectionable animal behavior included selfishness, sex, and war.

In the 1830s, Dr. Sylvester Graham claimed that the refined white flour that was prized as upper-class food was really a sign of man's fall from his wholesome natural state to an artificial, civilized one. Graham advocated flour made from coarse ground whole wheat, the rough kind fed to the peasants in the Middle Ages. And no commercial baker could make real bread. That could be done by only one person: "It is the wife, the mother only—she who loves her husband and her children as woman ought to love."[52] The flour was named after him first, then the crackers made from it. Today, it is almost impossible to find just plain Graham Crackers. They are marketed as "Low-Fat Grahams" to differentiate them from Honey Grahams, Cinnamon Grahams, Teddy Grahams, Cheddy

Grahams, and the other grahams that mock their inventor's intentions. Often, graham flour is the third or fourth ingredient, after fats and sweeteners. Serving suggestions on the boxes: dip graham crackers into frosting or Cool Whip.

One person who carried health and self-sufficiency to an extreme was philosopher Henry David Thoreau. From July 4, 1845, to September 6, 1847, he engaged in an experiment to prove that man didn't need meat or civilization. Thoreau lived simply in the woods at Walden Pond in Massachusetts, and recorded his observations about the meaning of life, the Industrial Revolution, and detailed what he ate, how he prepared it, and how much it cost. Thoreau believed in vegetarianism, which most Americans did not:

> One farmer says to me, "You cannot live on vegetable food solely, for it furnishes nothing to make bones with"; . . . walking all the while he talks behind his oxen, which, with vegetable-made bones, jerk him and his lumbering plough along.[53]

Thoreau lived on food he purchased, picked, or planted. He bought rice, molasses, rye and cornmeal, flour, a bit of salt pork or lard, and sugar. He supplemented these foods seasonally with wild fruits and nuts like grapes, wild apples, chestnuts, and ground-nuts *(Apios tuberosa)*. He also cultivated enough beans, potatoes, and peas that he was able to sell his surplus for a profit. Thoreau's total food cost per week: 27 cents.[54] He proved that it could be done, but being alone almost all the time is not for everyone.

Kellogg vs. Post: The Battle for Breakfast

There was a battle going on in Battle Creek, Michigan, between the Kellogg brothers. John Harvey wanted to keep the cereal they made sugar-free. W. K. wanted to add sugar. They were both blindsided by C. W. Post, who didn't have a brother to argue with. Post wanted to add sugar to the cereal he made, so he did. W. K. finally added malt sweetener to Corn Flakes. John Harvey went his own way, establishing the Battle Creek Sanitarium—the "San"—which became the center of the late-nineteenth-century health food movement and the forerunner of modern spas. By 1888, its staff of doctors, nurses, physical therapists, and dietitians was handling 600 to 700 patients at a time. Vegetarian, it catered to upper-class patrons like Eleanor Roosevelt (later first lady) and Henry Ford. Dr. Kellogg emphasized the importance of chewing food. Another nineteenth-century health food doctor, Salisbury, was obsessed with chewing, too. He invented a patty of prechopped meat formed into the shape of an oval for those who couldn't or wouldn't chew properly. It was named after him: Salisbury steak. Dr. Kellogg wrote a song about chewing. (Although the original song is gone, it was re-created for the 1994 movie about the San, *The Road to Wellville*.) He was terrified of constipation because he believed it caused "autointoxication"—self-poisoning. Absolutely convinced that masturbation was one of the greatest sins, he advised parents to raid their children's bedrooms at night to catch them in the act. He also advocated what is now called "female circumcision"—cutting the female genitals to prevent sexual enjoyment. He said this should be done without anesthetic.

Kellogg wrote many treatises on diet and food. Aided and abetted by his wife Ella, he came up with the idea that pasta should be boiled for an hour. He ignored humans' flesh-tearing teeth and claimed that all animals were originally nut eaters. Many of his recipes were based on nut butters, especially peanut butter, which Kellogg learned about from George Washington Carver, an agricultural genius.

Carver was born a slave. Booker T. Washington, head of the famous Tuskegee Institute in Alabama and also born a slave, asked Carver to be head of the Agriculture Department. Carver accepted, and stayed for 46 years.[55] Carver saved the economy of Alabama, which had been destroyed by boll weevils, insects that kill cotton. Carver suggested that the farmers grow peanuts instead. The peanuts stored well and could be used for food, even in winter. They could be pressed for oil, and they could be fed—peanuts and leaves—to livestock.[56]

Kellogg promoted peanut butter at the San. This food, originally associated with slaves and African-Americans, was looked down on by middle-class Americans. But the upper-class people who went to the San didn't have to worry about status. They accepted Kellogg's claim that peanut butter was healthy, and spread the word. Anti-vegetarians argued with Kellogg that eating meat must have been the right thing because the human race survived, and along the way invented cooking to make meat digestible. But Kellogg's goal was "to rescue civilization from the 'race-destroying effects of universal constipation and worldwide autointoxication [self-poisoning].'"[57]

"Atlanta holy water": Coca-Cola

Just as apothecaries in the Middle Ages sold sugar and drugs, pharmacists in the Gilded Age sold sugar-water beverages in their drug stores. The drugstore soda fountain, a long counter like a bar where patrons are served nonalcoholic beverages, is an American invention. So is the soda jerk, so called because he jerks down on the handle of a machine that mixes soda—artificially carbonated water (invented in 1767)—and flavorings into hundreds of combinations. By the 1880s, several of these beverages were patented. Their inventors became millionaires by selling for a nickel what cost less than half a cent per portion.[58] They were root and herb concoctions and claimed health benefits.

EARLY SOFT DRINKS[59]

YEAR	BEVERAGE	WHERE	HEALTH CLAIM
1876	Hires Root Beer	Philadelphia, PA	Purifies the blood
1885	Moxie Nerve Food	Lowell, MA	Cures nervousness and paralysis
1885	Dr Pepper	Texas	Aids digestion

Atlanta physician and pharmacist John Stith Pemberton's goal was to invent a potion to free himself from his addiction to morphine, a depressant or "downer" drug. In 1885, he invented Pemberton's French Wine Coca, patterned after other fortified wines, like Vin Mariani. It contained two new wonder drugs, coca from Peru's coca leaf and caffeine from the African kola nut. Both were stimulants and also supposedly aphrodisiacs. He claimed it was good for what ailed Americans: exhaustion, constipation, melancholy, impotence, headaches, hysteria, and addiction to opium and morphine, both legal then. (These claims were false.) When Atlanta banned the sale of anything with alcohol in it, Pemberton took the wine out of his Wine Coca, added seven secret ingredients, known only as 7X, and Coca-Cola was born.

The first ad for Coca-Cola appeared on May 29, 1886. The year after that, Pemberton took out a patent on Coca-Cola; the year after that he died. The Coca-Cola Company became a corporation in 1892. The formula for Coca-Cola was supersecret for more than 100 years, until 1993, when journalist Mark Pendergrast, researching a history of Coca-Cola, went through their archives. By mistake, they gave him a file that contained Pemberton's original formula for Coke. With two exceptions—vanilla from South America and the kola nut from Africa—all of the ingredients in Coca-Cola, including all seven of the supersecret flavorings and the sugar, are Asian. Using orange blossoms is distinctively Middle Eastern. It could almost be out of al-Baghdadi's medieval cookery book.

Coca-Cola was marketed as a medicine until 1898, when Congress taxed medicines. Then Coca-Cola decided it was a beverage. Until 1899, it could only be enjoyed at soda fountains, because the one ounce of Coca-Cola syrup mixed with carbonated water went flat quickly. Then two lawyers from Chattanooga, Tennessee, had what Coca-Cola's board of directors thought was such a waste-of-time idea that they signed a contract giving the lawyers—for nothing—the right to sell Coke *in bottles*. (As stupid business deals go, this one is right up there with IBM's declaration that computer software would never be worth anything, so Bill Gates could keep all the rights to his operating system programs.)

Coca-Cola's board evidently had not kept up with what was going on in the world of bottle technology. Carbonated beverages in bottles were a problem. The methods for closing the top involved some kind of a stopper—glass, cork, or metal—held on with some kind of a clamp or twisted wire. They all leaked. Unless they blew up. Until 1892, when the crown was invented. This is the crimped metal top applied with pressure that still seals soft drink bottles today. Coca-Cola fortunes weren't made from just the soda; manufacturers of bottles, bottle tops, and the factories that sealed them made fortunes, too.[60]

In April 1898, the United States went to war and Coca-Cola went, too. The name of a new drink made with rum, Coca-Cola, and lime juice represented what Americans intended to do. It was the *Cuba Libre*—Free Cuba. Four months later, Spain had been driven out of its last colonies and the war was over. In the

Ad for Hoff's Malt Extract. Like Coca-Cola and other beverages at the time, it claimed to cure a multitude of ills. *Munsey's Magazine, 1897.*

Caribbean, the United States acquired Puerto Rico and Guantánamo Naval Base in Cuba. In the Pacific, it gained Guam and the Philippines.

The United States was on its way to becoming a world power. But Europeans had a head start.

Europe: Nutrition, Sanitation, Evolution

In the nineteenth century, scientists and engineers, mostly in northern Europe, took the theories and instruments discovered during the Scientific Revolution and continued to create practical applications for them. They created machines that caused revolutions in industry, medicine, and science. Millions of people who had lived on small farms streamed from the country into the cities, where they lived in crowded unsanitary conditions and worked in factories with little ventilation 12 or more hours a day. Even children as young as six operated dangerous machinery. Thousands of people died. Scientists no longer attributed these deaths to angry gods; instead, they looked at nutrition and sanitation. In southern and eastern Europe, peasant farmers left their countries and streamed into the cities in the United States. In northern Europe, scientists studied plants and animals and arrived at new theories about life.

France: Yeast

Something was destroying the wine, beer, and milk of France; they were going sour and had to be thrown away. It was a disaster and a mystery. There was nothing wrong with the grapes as they grew on the vines, or the milk as it came from the cow, or the beer at first. Although fermentation had been known for 5,000 years, since the Egyptians discovered that it turned grain into beer, exactly how it occurred remained a mystery. Perhaps the scientists could help.

Louis Pasteur spent the middle of the 1850s to the 1860s examining liquids. Through his microscope, he became the first person in the world to see yeast, the organisms that cause fermentation. He also discovered that if you heated liquid to a certain point, the organisms that caused it to sour were killed, while the ones that made it ferment and turn into wine lived. The scientific community believed that these organisms were the product of fermentation; Pasteur said they were the cause. He was ridiculed, but he was right. The process of heating foods to destroy organisms that cause spoilage still bears his name: pasteurization. In the United States in the twenty-first century, cheese makers want to use raw, unpasteurized milk because heating milk changes it. So far, the U.S. Food and Drug Administration has said no.

France: *Phylloxera*

As part of scientific research, plants and animals were exchanged worldwide, continuing the Columbian Exchange. Sometimes the results were disastrous. *Vinifera* vines from North America caused an epidemic of *phylloxera* in Europe. *Phylloxera* is a tiny yellow aphid that sucks the sap out of the roots of *vinifera* grapes, while aboveground the plant shows no sign of illness. Then, suddenly, the whole plant dies. *Phylloxera* spreads easily on wind, water, and soil stuck to shoes and equipment. Between the 1860s and 1900, it killed about one-third of the *vinifera* grapes in Europe. The cure: import American rootstock and graft French grapes onto it. By 1900, less than one-third of the *vinifera* grapes growing in France were on original French rootstock; the rest were growing on American vines.[61]

Ireland: Swift's "Modest Proposal" for Ending Famine

Another import from the Americas was the major source of food for the Irish. In the nineteenth century, the British presence in Ireland continued to be a source of friction as British landlords grew richer while Irish peasants were on the brink of starvation. A century earlier, in 1729, Jonathan Swift, the British author who is most famous for writing *Gulliver's Travels*, had written a short piece called "A Modest Proposal," subtitled "For Preventing the Children of Poor People in Ireland From Being a Burden to Their Parents or Country, and for Making Them Beneficial to the Public." It was a bitter, dark satire about the extreme poverty among the Irish and how to cure it:

> [A] young healthy child well nursed is at a year old a most delicious, nourishing and wholesome food, whether stewed, roasted, baked, or boiled, and I make no doubt that it will equally serve in a fricassee, or a ragout. . . . A child will make two dishes at an entertainment for friends, and when the family dines alone, the fore or hind quarter will make a reasonable dish, and seasoned with a little pepper or salt will be very good boiled on the fourth day, especially in winter.[62]

The starving Irish missed the humor, because they felt the British would have done it if they could have gotten away with it. A century later, there was still inequality in food distribution. The Irish, like the serfs in the Middle Ages and the slaves in the American South, raised the food but were not allowed to eat it, because it was exported for profit. The mainstay of the Irish diet was a New World root vegetable, the potato.

Ireland: The Potato Famine

The potato, which would grow in poor soil where nothing else as nutritious would, allowed the population of Ireland to increase more than it would have on any other food. Potatoes are extremely nutritious. They contain iron, protein, carbohydrates, and vitamin C. The Irish usually ate potatoes boiled in their skins. The pot was placed on the floor, and everyone gathered around it. Mashed potatoes were invented here: take the potatoes, some of the potato water, add salt, mustard, and sometimes buttermilk. An adult male ate 13 or 14 potatoes per day and very little else. Occasionally there were eggs or oats.[63]

Then, in the 1840s, a disease turned the leaves and stems of the potato plants black and rotted the roots. The potatoes died, and so did the Irish. As a solution, corn—maize—was imported from America. But Irish mills, made for processing soft grains like oats and wheat, couldn't make a dent in corn. The corn rotted; the people starved. They picked nettles that grew on graves. Like Mongol horsemen, they slit the necks of their farm animals and drank the blood. Sometimes the animals died, too.

Approximately one million Irish died during the famine. Another million decided they would go to a new place, a place where there was food, where they would not be persecuted because of their religion. They would start over in America. And they would bring their strong Irish identity with them.

HOLIDAY HISTORY:

St. Patrick's Day, March 17

St. Patrick's Day is the most widely celebrated festival in the world.[64] It honors the patron saint who arrived in Ireland—called the "Emerald Isle" because of its lush green landscape—in A.D. 432, converted the people to Christianity, and banished all the snakes (although evidence indicates there never were snakes in Ireland). The 75 St. Patrick's Day festivals in the United States involve much wearing of the green; dancing to Irish drums, strings, and bagpipe music; and eating traditional corned beef and cabbage and drinking green-colored beer. The first St. Patrick's Day celebration was in 1762. It was in New York City because the Irish in Ireland, under British rule, couldn't celebrate being Irish. Chicago was the first city to dye its river green on St. Patrick's Day.

The United States: Luther Burbank

The Irish were so poor that many of them could only afford to go to the closest port in North American—Boston, Massachusetts. There, a scientist named Luther Burbank (1849–1926) who had been influenced by evolution and the advances in agricultural science in Europe, heard about the potato famine. Burbank was determined to invent—"build" was his word—a better potato, one that would be more resistant to disease, by cross-breeding potatoes to create a hybrid. The Burbank potato was further modified and became the Idaho potato. Burbank was a genius, self-taught, or as he used to say, his school was "the University of Nature."[65] He moved to Napa, California, where he experimented with more than 4,500 species of plants, including seeds and seedlings from India, France, Chile, Persia, Mexico, and Japan, and "built" many other new plants, including the Santa Rosa plum; the plumcot, a plum-apricot cross; and the Shasta daisy. He also created a white blackberry, called Iceberg, but no one was interested.

Bavaria: Ludwig, the Mad King, and the Fairy-Tale Kitchen

At the opposite end of the social scale from the starving Irish was the king of Bavaria. In 1864, 19-year-old Ludwig II became the king of beautiful Bavaria, in the Alps in southern Germany. Most Americans know Bavaria because of the cars made by Bavarian Motor Works (BMW) and because in German, Bavaria is "Bayer"—as in aspirin. Ludwig loved palaces and swans, which were on the Bavarian coat of arms. To provide work for his subjects in a slow economy, he began building castles. They were nineteenth-century Gothic, patterned after the medieval castles he grew up in. The paintings, frescoes, tapestries, and sculptures celebrated heroes from German mythology like Siegfried slaying the dragon. The ceilings were decorated with scenes from the operas of famous German composers like Wagner. Mechanical swans swam in man-made streams. But the castles were bankrupting the kingdom. In 1886, when Ludwig announced he was going to build a fourth castle, he drowned under mysterious circumstances. Some say that nobles lured him onto a boat, went to the middle of the lake, and pushed him overboard.

At one castle, Neuschwanstein—"New Swan Castle"—built from 1869 to 1886, Ludwig spared no expense in creating an ultramodern kitchen. Huge round polished granite columns supported an arched and vaulted ceiling. The kitchen also boasted a granite fish tank, hot and cold running water, a grill, an enormous cooktop that vented under the wood floor, and a wall oven. Rising heat was put to work in two ways. As it passed from the stove to the chimney, it was directed through a plate warmer. Then, hot air in the chimney turned the blades of a turbine connected to a gear that automatically turned the spit roasters. Before elevators, dumb waiters hauled firewood for the stoves and sent the cooked food up three floors to the elaborate dining room.[66] Most Americans have never seen Neuschwanstein but they would recognize it instantly—it is the model for Sleeping Beauty's Castle at Disneyland, but infinitely more beautiful.

Ludwig II's grandfather began a festival that is still going strong today. For two weeks every year, the Bavarian city of Munich hosts the world's largest beer festival, the Oktoberfest.

The Franco-Prussian War of 1870: Escoffier Cooks for the Army

In 1870, France and Germany went to war. French army officers scrambled to corner the best cooks. It just wouldn't be civilized to go to war without a chef. One of the rising chefs in Paris was August Escoffier, a 22-year-old from the French Riviera. He was gifted and he was motivated, and he became the chef to the General Staff.

At the beginning of the war, Escoffier was preparing haute cuisine close to the battlefield: *blanquette de veau*, roast sirloin, and rabbit in pork fat, cognac, and white wine. He knew food would become scarce, so he planned ahead. He became his own farmer, purveyor, and forager. He set up a secret little farmyard so he could have fresh eggs, milk, chickens, geese, rabbits, pigs, sheep, and turkeys. Supplemented with the officers' own stashes of wine and brandies, it paid off. During a siege, the General Staff continued to eat well long after the other cavalry officers had eaten their last good meal—and their last horse (in French, *cheval*). Eventually, however, Escoffier, too, was reduced to using the cavalry officers' horses in *pot-au-feu de cheval* and *cheval aux lentilles*. He and another chef were taken prisoners of war and escaped, but they were captured again when they tried to get jobs in a German *pâtisserie*.[68]

Alsace: Franco-German Cuisine

One disputed area was the province of Alsace, east of Champagne, on France's border with Germany along the Rhine River. Not surprisingly, the cuisine shows a hearty Franco-German fusion. The food from this area that is probably most familiar to Americans is quiche, the savory custard tart with bits of bacon or ham (traditionally, no cheese) which became popular in the United States in the last decades of the twentieth century.[69] Quiche goes well with the white wines the region produces, like Riesling. But Alsatians consume twice as much beer as people in other parts of France; like nearby Belgium, they use it in cooking, too, especially in soup. Alsatians love *choucroûte* [shoo-KROOT]—sauerkraut with pork and sausages. Strasbourg is famous for its Gothic cathedral and *pâté de foie gras* baked in a pastry crust; Munster is famous for its soft cheese. The bread, unlike the white bread so prized elsewhere in France, can be dark like German bread, made with rye or whole wheat. Typically German seasonings found in Alsatian cuisine are juniper, caraway, and horseradish.[70]

Along with French *tartes* and *petits fours*, pastry shops in Alsace make German Black Forest cake (*Schwarzwälder Kirschtorte*), layers of chocolate *genoise*, whipped cream, and morello cherries drenched in kirsch—cherry brandy—and named after the nearby forest. No Alsatian bride sets up housekeeping without the distinctive deep, swirled mold for *Kugelhopf* (a German word), a sweet bread studded with nuts and raisins that used to be for special occasions but now is a breakfast standard. The mold gets its name from *Kugel*, meaning ball, and *Hopf*, from hops, because formerly beer made the batter rise. Terra cotta molds were preferred over copper because they absorb butter, making the crust on each bread better than the last. In addition to the molds for wafers—*gaufres*—Alsatians have numerous molds for shaped spiced cakes or gingerbreads: a star for Christmas, fish or eel (once abundant in the Rhine River) for New Year, a fleur-de-lys for Epiphany, a lamb for Easter, a baby for a baptism, and the famous French rooster for patriotic events.[71]

Before the Franco-Prussian War ended in 1871, Prussia had put Paris under siege. The starving French ate their pet dogs and cats and then the zoo animals. The victorious Germans, from the Palace of Versailles, announced to the world that the German Empire had been created. They took Alsace-Lorraine and forced France to pay a large sum of money before the German army would march out of Paris.

The Austro-Hungarian Empire

Austria's most well-known foods are Wiener schnitzel (Vienna veal cutlets) and apple strudel, a flaky filled pastry. The cutlets are breaded and fried (sometimes stuffed first). Paprika schnitzel is cutlets seasoned with paprika, sauced with sour cream and a touch of tomato. Apple strudel is sweetened with sugar and raisins, made tart with cinnamon. Americans know strudel only as sweet pastry, but in Austria it can also be savory, filled with fried brains or mushrooms. Cream puffs (profiteroles), too, can have savory fillings like ham, liver, or chicken, with a béchamel-based sauce. The Eastern European staples—cabbage, caraway, mushrooms, and sour cream—are often combined with pork and potatoes. A common accompaniment for meat is parsley potatoes. Recipes for sauerkraut abound. *Liptauer* is cream cheese seasoned with capers, herbs, and anchovies. It can be an appetizer or a light meal, spread on bread or toast like an open-faced sandwich. *Nockerl* are dumplings either dropped into soup from a spoon or pushed through a sieve with large holes. Beets, kohlrabi, and other root vegetables are used in soup and salad. Another famous dessert is *Sachertorte* (supposedly named after

Mr. Sacher, a hotel owner), a chocolate cake spread with apricot jam and a chocolate glaze.

The Hungarian part of the Austro-Hungarian Empire had its own sophisticated cuisine, especially in the capital city of Budapest. The signature spice is paprika, like all the vegetable peppers, a New World native, but genetically modified into something uniquely Hungarian. Bell peppers are also stuffed, as is cabbage. But the most famous Hungarian dish is the stew called *guylas* [GOO-lash]. If you are eating anything *à la Eszterhazy*, it is named after an old noble family and is definitely *de luxe*.

FOOD FABLE:

Rigó Jancsi (Gypsy Johnny)

(EXCEPT THIS ONE IS TRUE)

On Christmas Day, 1896, the princess and the gypsy ran away together. Later they were married. A new dish was added to Hungarian cuisine to celebrate this. Like the princess and the gypsy, it was a beautiful, exciting, and rich combination that became an instant worldwide classic. And why not? It's a chocolate sponge layer cake spread with apricot jam, chocolate cream filling, and a chocolate glaze.

But many people in Hungary were too poor to afford the new confection. They would go to a new place, where the land was rich and the streets were paved with gold. They would start over in America.

Italy: Unified Country, Regional Cuisine

"Una tavola senza vino é com'una giornata senza sole." (*"A table without wine is like a day without sunshine."*)

—Italian saying

In the beginning of the nineteenth century, Italy was eight separate states. One was ruled by Italians, one by the pope; the others belonged to foreign countries. Since the fall of the Roman Empire in A.D. 476, Italy's city-states had been conquered and reconquered, ruled by French, German, Spanish, Arabs, Byzantine Greeks, and Normans who enriched themselves at the expense of the people, then left. In 1871, Italy ceased being a series of loosely connected city-states and became one country. It was unified politically, but still fragmented culturally. Each former city-state had its own cuisine, culture, and dialect. These differences in Italian were not like the differences in American English, with merely slightly different accents. They used different words. To overcome this, Italy made education mandatory in 1879.

Northern Italian Cuisine

Twelve years later, in 1891, the most influential cookbook in Italy was published, *La scienza in cucina e l'arte di mangiar bene—The Science of Cooking and the Art of Eating Well*. It was subtitled *Manuale practico per le famiglie—Practical Manual for Families*. It reflected the styles and eating habits of the new middle-class city dwellers, especially in the north. This type of Italian cuisine didn't become popular in the United States until the end of the twentieth century, because only 20 percent of the immigrants who came to America at the end of the nineteenth and beginning of the twentieth century were from the north.

Emilia-Romagna has been called the "richest gastronomic region in Italy."[72] This area is rich in dairy farms that produce butter and Parmigiano-Reggiano cheese. Grains in the north also include rice and corn for risotto and polenta, often to accompany *osso buco*—bone with a hole—stewed veal shank. From the seaport city of Genoa comes *pesto genovese*, an uncooked sauce of basil, olive oil, pine nuts, and Parmigiano-Reggiano cheese. Prosciutto di Parma is a northern Italian ham. Dried sausages like salami are also from the north. Mortadella, an uncured sausage, is known in the United States by the mangled pronunciation of the name of the city where it is made—Bologna—which Americans call "baloney."

The meal begins with *antipasti*—appetizers—but there is no one main course, as meat often is in an American meal. As cookbook author Marcella Hazan explains: "There are, at a minimum, two principal courses, which are never, never brought to the table at the same time."[73] But this was very different from how the vast majority of the population of southern Italy ate.

Southern Italian Cuisine: The Mezzogiorno

The southern half of the Italian boot, the part below Rome, is known as the Mezzogiorno—literally, midday or noon—because it is where the sun shines brightly. In 1806, feudalism ended in Italy but not the extreme class divisions between the minority of upper-class wealthy and the majority who were barely surviving as farmers. Most people in southern Italy lived in one-room, two-level huts. On the dirt floor on the bottom level lived the animals—a few chickens, maybe a pig for sausage. Up a ladder in a loft was where the family slept. The food was not very different from what Don Quixote and Sancho Panza had in Spain 200 years earlier, or medieval peasants 1,000 years earlier—lentils, bread, onions, maybe some cheese and fruit. Meat was on the peasant table only twice a year, at the major Catholic holidays—a chicken or capon for Christmas, roast kid at Easter. Pasta, too, was a luxury. Like the Irish peasants or the slaves who did all the work in the American South, southern Italian peasants raised the animals, sowed the seeds, and harvested the crops, but they didn't get to eat them. The food went to the upper classes.

In the cities it was different. Upper-class cuisine made full use of the bounty for which the Mezzogiorno had been famous and had been fought over since it was settled by the Greeks in the fourth century B.C.—wine, figs, raisins, citrus fruit, sheep and goat, cheese, olive oil, grain. The sea was rich with *frutti di mare* or seafood (literally, "fruit of the sea") *calamari* and *polpi*—squid and octopus.

Pasta and Pizza

By the eighteenth century, the city of Naples (Napoli) had become the pasta capital of the world, with almost 300 pasta businesses. Some of it was sold by street vendors and eaten, in those long strands, by hand.[74] Sauce made with plum tomatoes, especially from the area of San Marzano, has also come to be identified with southern Italian cooking, although the tomato does not appear in Italian cookbooks until almost 1700, and then the recipe is for "Spanish style" tomato sauce.[75] Pasta was layered with tomato sauce and ricotta cheese and topped with mozzarella to make lasagne, or stuffed with ground meat or ricotta cheese and herbs to make square ravioli or round *agnolotti* and then covered with sauce. Parmigiano-Reggiano or pecorino (sheep) cheese is traditionally grated over the top. Meats cooked in the sauce were reserved for special occasions and were a separate course, served after the pasta. Pasta was eaten with peas—*pasta e piselli*; or with beans—*pasta e fagioli*, which became *pasta fazool* in Neapolitan dialect.

Pasta drying in the streets of Naples. *Courtesy Library of Congress, Prints & Photographs Division, LC-USZ62-93348.*

Pizza, a round, flat bread with various toppings, is another typically Neapolitan food. The word *pizza* is related to *pita* and has been used since the tenth century. Neapolitan pizza has a crisp thin crust, while Sicilian pizza has a thicker, more breadlike crust. Simple pizza is dough topped with tomatoes, olive oil, garlic, and oregano. A more elaborate version is Pizza Margherita, created for Italy's Queen Margherita. It is *tricolore*—three-colored—to represent the Italian flag. The tomato sauce is red, the mozzarella is white, and the fresh basil leaves are green. A flat wooden paddle called a peel is used to slide the pizza into a very hot—750°F—brick oven.

Baking and Religion

Baking in Italy was very connected to religion. Each one of the numerous festivals and saint's days required its own special breads or desserts. Some holidays were celebrated throughout Italy, like Madonna Assunta, the assumption of the Virgin Mary into heaven, August 13 to 15; and St. Lucy's Day, the Feast of Lights, on December 13. (Sweden's St. Lucia's Day is based on this. See page 190.) Breads in the shape of *ossa di morti*—bones of the dead—were baked in honor of the Day of the Dead, November 2. For Easter, a special, rich, yeast-risen egg bread was baked, as well as pies filled with ricotta and rice, barley, or kernels of wheat. Another Easter pie is savory, baked in a crust spiced with black pepper and filled with diced prosciutto, other meats, cheeses, and an egg binder. But many feast days were for local patron saints. For example, the feast day of San Maura, the patron saint of people with arthritis and rheumatism, January 15, is celebrated with small breads in the shape of canes.

The pastry and confectionery arts were highly developed in southern Italy because the Arabs had cultivated sugar in Sicily since the Middle Ages. Italian sponge cake might originally have been called *pan di spugna* (sponge bread), or it might be Spanish in origin—*pan di Spagna* (Spanish bread). It is deliberately a bit dry and lightly sweetened, so it can be sliced into layers and moistened with liqueurs like rose-scented *rosolio*, or *strega*, made from herbs and elderberries, and topped with fresh fruit or jam. A more elaborate version calls for the cake to be sliced, drenched in rum, spread with vanilla and chocolate *crema pasticciera* (pastry cream) or ricotta cream, and topped with whipped cream. This is similar to an English trifle, and is called *zuppa inglese*—English soup—because of the rum; it needs to be eaten with a spoon. *Zeppole*, fried and filled with pastry cream, are made for St. Joseph's Day on March 19. The technique for making *zabaglione* (now *zabaione*) *marsala* is the same as the beginning of a *semi-freddo*: whisk egg yolks and sugar for several minutes to aerate and thicken. Various areas of Italy (and Europe) make a simple pastry of dough, twisted or knotted, fried, and sprinkled with confectioners' sugar. *Struffoli* are small fried dough balls coated in warm honey and topped with colored sprinkles. Ricotta was also given special treatment in desserts in southern Italy and Sicily.

Sicilian Cuisine

Ricotta means "recooked," just as *biscotti* means "twice cooked." Originally made from goat or sheep milk, ricotta was a by-product from making a sharp, hard, aged Italian cheese, provolone (nothing like the tasteless round rubber log that is sold as domestic provolone in the United States). Now, ricotta is made on its own. Dried, it becomes ricotta *salata*, tangy and crumbly.

It is used in Sicily's most famous dessert. Cannoli is a study in contrast: a crunchy unsweetened fried pastry tube filled with smooth, sweetened ricotta. Now the dough is wrapped around hollow metal cannoli forms (*cannolini* are the small version) but in the nineteenth century, pastry chefs used *canna*—cane stalks or reeds. Cassata is another Sicilian dessert made with ricotta, a combination of sponge cake, ricotta, wrapped in green-tinted almond paste now, but in earlier times, pistachio paste—a Middle Eastern influence. Cassata can be traced back to the Arab *qas'ah*, the mold that shaped it.[76] Cassata *gelata* is its frozen cousin, which adds layers of three different flavors of *gelato*.

CULINARY CONFUSION:

Ice Cream and Gelato

Traditional Italian gelato—it means "frozen," like *helado* in Spanish—is different from French and American ice creams. French ice cream is thickened and enriched with eggs. American ice cream—Philadelphia-style ice cream—has more cream than French ice cream, but no eggs. It also has what ice cream manufacturers call "overrun"—air whipped into it. Gelato has very little air, so it is denser than American ice creams. Gelato was originally made with goat's milk, which has less fat than cream. There are also refreshing ices—*granita*—made with water, sugar, and lemon juice, mulberries, cinnamon, or jasmine flowers.[77]

Sugar is also used in Sicilian main dishes, which can be *agrodolce*—sour and sweet. *Caponata* is an eggplant relish made with vinegar and sugar. Sometimes foods are sweetened with orange or tangerine juice, raisins, or currants. Caper berries are common, too. The north African and Arab influence shows in *cuscus*, the use of rice, spinach, and the many dishes with chickpeas. From the sea come swordfish, sardines for stuffing, and tuna and anchovies for pasta sauce. Again, these were upper-class foods. The American ex-slave Booker T. Washington visited Sicily and was shocked at the lives of the peasants:

> The Negro is not the man farthest down. The condition of the coloured farmer in the most backward parts of the Southern States in America, even where he has the least education and the least encouragement, is incomparably better than the condition and opportunities of the agricultural population in Sicily.[78]

In the early 1890s, successive years of drought damaged the grain, grape, and citrus crops in Sicily, and *phylloxera* wiped out vines throughout the Mezzogiorno. But hunger was not the only thing that drove 40 percent of Sicily's population away. Lack of industrialization and sanitation also played a part. A government that demanded seven years of service in the armed forces, that turned troops loose on its citizens with orders to arrest anyone with "the face of an assassin," 20,000 deaths from malaria every year, and American industrialization that undercut the price of sulfur, Sicily's chief export, all churned up the idea of leaving. Finally, three years of cholera epidemics in the mid-1880s that killed 55,000 people, and volcanic eruptions and a tidal wave that killed 100,000 more in 1908 seemed like signs from God to the 1.5 million people who decided, weeping and cursing, that leaving Sicily was the only way they could survive.[79]

They would start over in America.

England: Darwin and Evolution

In 1859, Charles Darwin published *On the Origin of Species* and proposed a revolutionary theory of how plants and animals survived. From his observations in the Galapagos Islands, west of Ecuador in the Pacific Ocean, Darwin deduced that living things evolved or changed to survive. Darwin believed that nature weeded out the weak and constantly adapted to new situations to live.

Evolution was and still is a controversial theory. The complex ideas were reduced to a phrase—"survival of the fittest"—that was used to justify the enormous wealth the robber barons accumulated and kept. The people who were doing all the work in the factories weren't "fit" so they didn't deserve a decent wage.

Czech Republic: Mendel and Genetics, Bees and Peas

In an abbey in Brno, a community of farmers in what was then Moravia and what is now the Czech Republic, a monk named Gregor Mendel (1822–1884), the son of farmers, read Darwin's *On the Origin of Species*. Mendel had become fascinated with a new science—agriculture. The abbot in charge of the abbey was very interested in science, too, so the abbey had a garden of rare plants, an herbarium, and a greenhouse. It was in this greenhouse, in 1856, that Mendel began doing experiments with peas *(pisum sativum)*, using new methods of scientific experimentation. Ten years later, in 1866, he published the results of his findings in a local agricultural paper. Nobody noticed. But 35 years later, his report was rediscovered and became the basis for the science of genetics. His theories became widely known as "Mendel's laws of heredity." Now, "Mendelian traits" are called "genes," and Mendel is hailed as "the father of genetics."[80] Mendel's experiments laid the groundwork for genetically modified foods and the human genome project, completed in 2003, which identified all the genes in the human body. As one scientist said, "the road to the [discovery of DNA] started in the Abbey in Brno."[81]

England: Dr. Snow and the Water Supply

In 1854, a cholera epidemic struck London. This disease causes death by depleting the body of all fluids, violently and rapidly. But this epidemic was strange: people in one neighborhood got cholera while a block away they didn't. A physician, Dr. John Snow, finally figured out why: people were getting their water from different wells. Those who got cholera used a well that was contaminated by people dumping the contents of their sick babies' diapers down it. (Perhaps number one on the "Things You Never Thought You'd Have to Tell People Not to Do" list.) According to legend, Dr. Snow had the handle from that pump removed, and ended the cholera epidemic. From this and other scientific observations came germ theory and an understanding of how diseases spread. The transmission of cholera, typhoid, salmonella, and other sanitation diseases is fecal-oral—you get them from poor personal hygiene, sometimes as simple as not washing your hands after you go to the bathroom. In the mid–nineteenth century, London and Paris established public health departments to deal with sanitation.

These efforts by middle- and upper-class reformers to clean up the cities wasn't all from the goodness of their hearts. Having so many sick people and so much filth in the cities was a threat to the health of everyone. Doctors reported city dwellers in Europe living in conditions like those of the slave cabins in the American South, but with much less ventilation: one room that was six feet high, and "ten to fourteen or fifteen feet wide. . . . The walls are plastered with garbage. . . . Everywhere are piles of garbage, of ashes, of debris from vegetables picked up from the streets . . ."[82]

Isabella Beeton: *The Book of Household Management*

In England, the people who owned the factories, supplied the raw materials, and sold the finished product became a prosperous new middle class with new eating habits. A book that describes this new middle class life is Isabella Beeton's 1,112-page *Book of Household Management*, published in London in 1861. It contains:

> Information for the Mistress, Housekeeper, Cook, Kitchen-Maid, Butler, Footman, Coachman, Valet, Upper and Under House-Maids, Lady's Maid, Maid-of-All-Work, Laundry-Maid, Nurse and Nurse-Maid, Monthly, Wet, and Sick Nurses, Etc. Etc.; Also, Sanitary, Medical, & Legal Memoranda.[83]

Clearly, the new British middle-class housewife was a household manager, in charge of a many-roomed house, nutrition and sanitation for her family and a large staff, including child-rearing, invalids, what invalidates a will, and how to keep hair from falling out.

It is not surprising that a cookbook published so soon after Dr. Snow's discovery of the cause of cholera and its cure—boiling—would contain many boiled foods. These new middle-class people were meat-eaters. Out of 845 pages of recipes, 255 are for meat, most cooked by boiling. She cites laboratory studies supporting the health benefits of boiling, because "the juice of flesh is water, holding in solution many substances . . . which are of the highest value as articles of food."[84] A 53-page chapter about vegetables—mostly boiled—even has a recipe for boiled salad: boil two heads of celery and one pint of French beans separately until tender, cut celery into two-inch pieces. Garnishes are chopped lettuce, blanched endive, or boiled cauliflower.[85] Suggested sauces are made of (1) milk, oil, vinegar, mustard, sugar, salt, and cayenne; (2) eggs, cream, vinegar, mustard, salt, white and cayenne pepper; or (3) egg, oil, cream, vinegar, mustard, sugar, salt.[86] There are also four chapters that reflect the British love of dessert and tea time—one chapter on puddings and pastry; one on creams, jellies, soufflés, omelets, and sweet dishes; another on preserves, confectionery, ices and dessert dishes; and one on bread, biscuits, and cakes.

The book is a masterpiece of organization. Each recipe provides information on ingredients, method, time, average cost, how many portions it makes, and when the ingredients are in season. Most measurements are by weight; exceptions are "a heaping tablespoonful" or "2 dessert-spoonfuls." Each recipe is numbered, so cooks can find them and cross-reference them easily.

It is ironic that the woman who was an authority on sanitation died from a sanitation disease. In earlier times, a female midwife stayed with a woman during her "lying-in" as birth was called, and did only that. When men took over the medical profession, they came to women giving birth after setting broken legs, treating infections, doing autopsies. Maybe they washed their hands. Women began to die of an infection called childbed (puerperal) fever, and so did Isabella Beeton, after giving birth to her third child. She was 28 years old.

The new middle-class European life that Isabella Beeton was part of depended on factories. Factories needed raw materials. The European powers turned to other continents to provide the raw materials they needed and markets to sell the goods they manufactured.

At the end of the nineteenth century, desperate peasant farmers from Ireland and southern and eastern Europe went to the United States in search of a better life. Northern European states—with businesses and the armies to protect them—went to Africa and Asia to colonize.

Africa and Asia

Food Patterns

Africa and Asia have distinctive food patterns that include the many cuisines and cultures that cross these two vast continents. In the introduction, we raised the question, What makes a meal? Anthropologist Sidney Mintz answered it in 2001. He calls it the core-fringe-legume pattern—CFLP for short. "The core is usually a complex carbohydrate such as rice, wheat, or maize, which provides 70 to 80 percent of the calories. The fringe is usually a spiced mixed vegetable, meat, or fish, often complemented by a third element—the legume," sometimes soy or other beans.[1] This is an ancient food pattern and is still how most of the world's population eats. Cattle-centered English-speaking countries are an exception. CFLP certainly applies to Africa and Asia, as we shall see.

Africa: Shea Butter, Kola Nuts, Monkey Bread

Africa is an enormous continent. It has the longest river in the world, the Nile; the largest desert, the Sahara; and the fourth tallest mountain, Kilimanjaro—at

19,340 feet, almost a mile higher than the highest peak in the continental United States, California's Mt. Whitney. Its other climate zones range from Mediterranean in the north and south to rainforest at the equator. It also has vast savannas—grassy plains—where herds of lions, leopards, and zebras roam. Among Africa's native food plants are okra, watermelon, sorghum, some varieties of rice, various beans and peas, and yams.

CULINARY CONFUSION:

Yam and Sweet Potato

What Americans call yams are not yams. They are a darker kind of sweet potato, native to the Americas, a member of the morning glory family. The true yam, found in Africa and Asia, is a large, starchy root that can grow six feet underground, which makes it difficult to dig up. According to Alan Davidson, "It was probably slave traders who introduced the sweet potato to Africa, where it was called *igname* or *nyam*, which simply means 'yam.' Since that time the sweet potato has been steadily displacing the true yam as a major carbohydrate food in tropical Africa."[2]

Yam—true wild yam—must be harvested and prepared carefully because some varieties are so poisonous that the Mandingo people used them on arrows. Only famine could drive the Mandingo to eat these yams, and only after repeated washing and very careful cooking.[3]

HOLIDAY HISTORY:

Yam Festival

For tribes like the Ashanti and the Ibo, yams were important in fertility rituals. At harvest time, a male criminal was beheaded so that his blood flowed into the hole in the ground where the first yam had been pulled out. Then water was sprinkled on the field. Then the king ate yams, and after him, his subjects.[4]

The Middle Ages: African-Arab Cuisine

In antiquity, Near Eastern, Greek, and Roman peoples came to trade in Alexandria, Egypt. They introduced wheat, barley, sheep, and goats. However, wheat and barley did not spread throughout Africa because the climate was not hospitable to them. Then from the seventh century through the fifteenth century, the Arabs dominated. Caravans of camels brought spices like cumin, coriander, cinnamon, ginger, and black pepper to the Mediterranean coast on the north, and the Red Sea and Indian Ocean coasts on the east of Africa. Accounts of these Arab merchants are our main source of information about food in West Africa until Portuguese explorers arrived in 1448.

Tribes in West Africa in the Middle Ages fell into three groups: (1) hunter-gatherers whose important sources of protein were wild meats and fish; (2) those who grew food—grains, legumes, fruits, and vegetables; and (3) those who kept animals like cattle, sheep, goats, and camels.

Hunter-Gatherers

Tribes that relied on wild animals hunted antelope, giraffe, ostrich, hippopotamus, crocodile, elephant, snake, gazelle, hare, lizard, and sea and river turtle. They used bows and arrows, sometimes with poisoned tips, spears, javelins, and hunting dogs.[5] Meat was sliced into strips and dried in the sun. Fish was salted. Today, fish is also dried or smoked.

One of the foods they gathered was a caffeine stimulant: the kola "nut," the fruit of the kola tree. The tree is in the cocoa family *(Sterculiaceae)* and grows to 60 feet. The fruit looks like a chestnut, tastes slightly bitter, and was a favorite of royalty. It became a favorite of the world as the cola in Coca-Cola.[6]

Cultivated Grains and Grasses

For the tribes that grew most of their food, the three most important cultivated grains and grasses were millet, sorghum, and rice. Millet was cooked as porridge, ground into flour, or used as a beverage with sour milk or fruit juice added. In some areas, a pancakelike baked bread made of millet flour was a luxury reserved for kings. If millet fermented long enough, it became millet beer. Two other common alcoholic beverages were mead, made from fermented honey, and palm wine from fermented sap. They were sometimes offered to the dead.[7]

The second grain, sorghum, is a "round white grain like chick-pea." It was cooked and eaten as porridge or pounded and combined with honey and sour milk as a drink for humans; it also provided food for animals.[8] Grains and grasses were pounded into flour with stones. In areas where there were no stones, wooden mortars were used.

The third cultivated grain was rice: *Oryza glaberrima,* native to West Africa; and *Oryza sativa,* brought later from Asia. Rice could be boiled: plain in water, with butter, with butter and honey, with meat, served with a vegetable sauce, or made into thin cakes that were roasted in shea butter.[9]

Shea Butter

Shea butter was one of three fats commonly used by the native peoples, along with palm oil and sesame oil. A fourteenth-century Arab described how shea butter was made from

> . . . a fruit resembling a lemon, which tastes like a pear. Inside there is a fleshy stone. They take this stone, . . . crush it and out of it comes something like butter which is used to whitewash houses, to put into lamps and to make soap. When they wish to make this butter edible, . . . it is put on a gentle fire, covered and left until it is boiling fast. . . . Then it is cooled and used in food like butter.[10]

A fourth vegetable fat, argan oil, was used in Morocco and is beginning to be available in the United States in the twenty-first century.

Legumes and Fruit

Among legumes, kidney beans, cowpeas, and broad beans were prominent; slaves brought these with them to the American South. Vegetables included onions, garlic, cucumbers, and gourds. Hollowed-out gourds were used to store shea butter, and also as bowls for common people. The royal West African table was set with gold dishes and cups.

Fruits included watermelon and other melons, the sweet-sour tamarind, and the fruit of the baobab tree, which is high in vitamin C. The white, pulpy fruit is called "monkey bread."[11] The jujube, the small fruit of a wild tree, was used to make a breadlike dough after the pits were removed. It reportedly tasted like gingerbread.[12] Dates grew wild in Western Africa, but date palms were not cultivated until after the Arabs conquered North and West Africa.

There was one food that the people who lived in the Sahara prized as being the best food on Earth, delicious as well as healthy—truffles, sometimes as large as three pounds. The native people cooked them with camel meat; the Arabs cooked them in milk or water, or broth with fat, or just peeled them and roasted them on coals.[13]

Meat

Meat was rare in the cuisine of most indigenous people in West Africa, usually reserved for rituals or feasts. Like the Arabs, they preferred mutton, goat, and camel meat.[14] The Arab influence also showed in the breed of sheep the Africans raised. It was the Arab fat-tail, prized not for wool, but for tail fat and milk, which was made into butter and cheese. Tribes in southern Mauritania consumed camel milk, butter, and meat, sometimes preserved by drying. They probably slaughtered the camels that were at the end of their usefulness for caravans. In a survival situation, camels were killed so that humans could drink the water in the camel's stomach.[15]

The Nineteenth Century: Working for Peanuts

In the 1400s, Portuguese and other Europeans began to explore the African coast. In the 1500s, slave traders arrived. They brought New World peanuts to grow to feed slaves during the Middle Passage from western Africa to North and South America. Chile peppers migrated south from the Iberian peninsula. However, Europeans were restricted to the coasts until the nineteenth century, when technology enabled them to penetrate the interior of Africa.

In the nineteenth century, Europeans invaded Africa, bringing their cuisines and their cultures with them. Between 1878 and 1913, every country on the African continent with the exceptions of Liberia on the west coast and Ethiopia on the east fell to a European power; in 1935, Italy took Ethiopia. First came missionaries. Farmers followed missionaries, and the military came to protect the farmers and the businesses that grew as the European population grew.

Three things enabled Europeans to colonize Africa: (1) quinine, a New World herb that warded off malaria; (2) the steamship, which made sailing upstream into the interior of Africa possible; and (3) machine guns, which allowed a handful of men to control millions.

France had the greatest amount of territory, almost 36 percent of the continent, which it controlled with the French Foreign Legion. Most of it was in the northwest. England followed with more than 32 percent, mostly in the east and south, including modern Egypt and South Africa. Germany, Belgium, Portugal, Italy, and Spain split what was left. This is why there are French croissants and baguettes in Nigeria and the Ivory Coast in West Africa, Italian spaghetti in Ethiopia and Eritrea on the east, and Indian curry and chutney in British East and West Africa.

The British attitude toward people of other cultures was profoundly racist. Cecil Rhodes stated: "I contend that we [Britons] are the first race in the world, and the more of the world we inhabit, the better it is for the human race."[16] These colonial powers caused complete disruption of the life and the land, the cuisine and the culture. They forced the native people to grow nonnative staple crops like peanuts and cacao, which displaced native African foods.

By the end of the nineteenth century, Africa was the world's leading producer of cacao. This caused the economy to shift from a self-sufficient barter system to cash, because the native people now had to buy food with money, so they had to work for wages. Some went to work on rubber plantations in the Belgian Congo, under the extremely harsh rule of King Leopold. Workers who didn't do their work well enough or quickly enough had their hands or feet cut off. The Congo was also rich in copper and tin. But South Africa was a gold mine—literally. And a diamond mine.

Much of modern African cuisine is the colonial cuisine that Arabs brought to Africa in the Middle Ages and Europeans brought in the nineteenth century. Because of Africa's geographical and cultural diversity, it has developed distinct regional cuisines.

African Spices

Throughout Africa, the main spice is chile peppers, brought from South America by the Portuguese and the Spanish. There are words for chiles in many languages in Africa: in French, it is *piment*; in Swahili, *pili-pili*, *peri-peri*, and *piri-piri*, which is also the name of the chile-spiced stew that is the national dish of Mozambique, Portugal's former colony. Chiles are also used in *harissa*, Tunisia's main condiment; in *ras el hanout*, literally, "best in the shop," the signature spice blend in Morocco; and in *berbere* [bare-BARE-ee] in Ethiopia. In Africa, chiles are spice, medicine, aphrodisiac, and the food that is supposed to make them immortal.

AFRICAN SPICES
(THESE CAN VARY GREATLY ACCORDING TO THE CHEF)

	RAS EL HANOUT MOROCCO[17]	HARISSA TUNISIA[18]	BERBERE ETHIOPIA[19]
allspice			✦
anise	✦		
basil	✦		
bay leaf	✦		
caraway seed	✦	✦	
cardamom	✦		✦
chile peppers	✦	✦	✦
cinnamon	✦		✦
cloves			✦
coriander	✦	✦	✦
cumin	✦	✦	
fennel seed	✦		
fenugreek	✦		✦
garlic		✦	✦
ginger	✦	✦	✦
nutmeg	✦		✦
onion			✦
oregano	✦		
paprika			✦
pepper—black	✦		✦
pepper—cayenne	✦		✦
rose hips	✦		

Northern African Cuisines—The Maghreb

The cuisine of North Africa—called the Maghreb—was influenced by the Arabs, the Italians and Sicilians, the French, Spanish, and Portuguese. One Arab influence is a stew of meat and fruit or meat and vegetables—in Arabic, the *tajin* or *tagine* [TAH-zhin] of al-Baghdadi (*touajen* is the plural). It is prepared in the cooking vessel of the same name. Its cone-shaped top allows steam to escape. Or the *tajin* can be cooked in the bottom of a pot with a steamer insert. The steam from the *tajin* wafts up to cook the couscous in the top section. Couscous, the staple food in northern Africa, probably originated with the native Berber tribe. It is tiny balls (one-eighth to less than one-sixteenth of an inch) of semolina wheat (the kind used for pasta), barley, millet, or later, maize flour mixed with salted water.[20] It can also be steamed by itself in a *couscousière* [coose-coose-ee-AIR], a French word, or cooked in the stew.

The Arab influence also shows in spiced meat that is cubed into kebabs or ground and shaped into *kefta*, round like meatballs, flat like a hamburger, or oval. Kebabs and *kefta* are cooked on skewers over a charcoal fire. *Kefta* can also be fried. Olives and lemons cured in salt are common, too. Spiciness is provided by a Moroccan spice mix, *ras el hanout*. In her beautiful cookbook, *Arabesque*, Claudia Roden says that *ras el hanout* "is a legendary mixture of 27 spices including the golden beetle that is the aphrodisiac Spanish fly."[21] Now, chefs make their own mixtures and keep them secret. Spices are sold in bulk at the *souk*—the marketplace.

The Moroccan masterpiece is *bastilla* (one of various spellings) [buh-STEE-yah], layers of contrasting tastes and textures wrapped in flaky dough. The Moroccan pastry, even thinner than phyllo (or filo), is called *warqa* ("leaf"). The layers inside are chicken (originally pigeon or squab) stewed in spices until it falls off the bone. The reduced stewing liquid, along with lemon juice, is mixed with eggs and scrambled until silky. Crunchy chopped almonds are sautéed in butter, dusted with cinnamon and sugar, and sprinkled on top before it is all enveloped in buttered *warqa* and baked.

Clarified butter, called *samna, sman,* or *smen,* is one of the fats used in cooking. Like ghee in India, clarifying the butter by heating it and skimming off the milk solids helps to keep it from going rancid. To eat *bastilla,* you break off a piece and eat it with your hands—only the right hand, because Arabs reserve the left hand for personal hygiene. It is customary to use only the thumb and the first two fingers, to show restraint, instead of greedily using all four.[22] As rich as it is, *bastilla* is not the main course—just the first or second.

The desserts in northern Africa are also Arab-influenced and very sweet with sugar syrup or honey. One is a serious aphrodisiac—it contains both Spanish fly and hashish. Everything is washed down with spearmint tea, poured dramatically from high above the table.

West African Cuisines

West Africa has tropical beaches and tropical fruit from all over the world: pineapple, mango, papaya, coconut. An abundance of fish is preserved by drying, smoking, or salting. Although West Africa is a large grower of cacao, it is not processed there. The beans are shipped to Europe or the United States for processing, then shipped back to Africa as candy, so it is expensive and usually found only in cities and eaten by foreigners.[23] West African meals are one course, one-pot stews, often thickened with peanuts. Palm oil is the standard fat. The staple starch is *fufu* (also *foofoo* and numerous other spellings), made of cassava, maize, yams, plaintains, or rice pounded and mashed, then boiled, steamed, baked, or fried.[24] Chicken is the most valued meat, but snails are eaten more often. Game meat is also eaten: aardvark, eland (a large antelope), venison, ostrich, gazelle, hippopotamus, giraffe, crocodile, a seven-pound frog, rat, and bat.

In the absence of a Muslim influence, there are also palm wine, roast pork, and homemade beer, brewed from "corn, sorghum, or millet; in the rain forests, mashed bananas are the base." In southern Africa, beer is brewed from the fruit of the Maroela tree, which falls to the ground and ferments. What the humans don't harvest, the elephants eat. It makes them drunk and dangerous.[25]

Snack foods include locusts steamed, sautéed, and seasoned with chile; and termites. African termites build enormous mounds aboveground; anteaters (aard-varks) use their sharp claws to tear down the claylike walls, and long snouts and sticky tongues to penetrate the narrow tunnels inside the mounds. When the ter-mites fly and swarm, looking for a new place to build, humans catch and eat them. They are very high in protein and supposedly taste like peanut butter. One popular Nigerian street food sounds perfect for Super Bowl Sunday: beef marinated in beer, rolled in ground peanuts and chile, then grilled over charcoal.[26]

Southern African Cuisines

Many of the ports of Africa were originally settled by European countries as stations where their ships could stop for repairs and supplies, including food. South Africa, almost halfway between Indonesia and the Netherlands, served this purpose for the Dutch East India Company, which first established a colony there in 1652. They immediately planted fruits and vegetables that would keep the ships' crews healthy and free from scurvy and other vitamin-deficiency dis-eases: "sweet potatoes, pineapples, watermelons, pumpkins, cucumbers, radishes, and citrus trees such as lemons and oranges."[27] They also made a dried meat, like jerky, called *bildong*. By the eighteenth century, the Dutch brought slaves from Malaysia and their spicy cuisine, including one dish called *kerrie-kerrie*, later shortened to "curry." Another Malaysian spice mixture composed of onions, gin-ger, dried shrimp or prawns, and chile powder, is called a *sambal*.[28]

Eastern African Cuisines

In eastern Africa, in Ethiopia and Eritrea, the staple food is a bread called *injera*. Like a thick, elastic sourdough crêpe, *injera* is "the daily bread, tablecloth, and silverware."[29] It is made from teff, a tiny, low-gluten grain, and cooked on top of the stove in a sauté pan. The bottom of a round tray the diameter of a small table is lined with *injera*. Then a stew or sauce, called *wot*, is put on top of the *injera* and soaks into it. You break off pieces of *injera* the size of the palm of your hand, and scoop up the food. The table is low; diners sit on backless stools.

A spicy chicken stew called *doro wot* is sometimes called the national dish of Ethiopia. *Sega wot* is beef based; *kik wot* is made with red lentils. The *wot* can be Arab influenced, like lamb stew seasoned with ginger and cinnamon, or show an Italian influence with tomato paste. Coffee originated in this part of Africa, so it is an important beverage.

The signature Ethiopian spice mix is called *berbere. Berbere awaze* is the spices in paste form. A hotter spice mix is *mitmita;* it is also available as *awaze.* Another standard Ethiopian ingredient is *niter kibe,* butter that is clarified and spiced.

INGREDIENTS:

Niter Kibe—Ethiopian Spiced Butter

1 tablespoon fresh ginger, finely grated	2 pounds salted butter
1 cinnamon stick, 1 inch long	½ cup yellow onion, peeled and coarsely chopped
3 whole cloves	
1½ teaspoons turmeric	3 tablespoons garlic, peeled and finely chopped
¼ teaspoon cardamom seeds	
⅛ teaspoon nutmeg	

Eastern Africa also has strong Indian influences because the British brought experienced workers from India to work on the railroad in Africa, including one young man named Gandhi, who later led the successful fight for India's independence.

India: Not Just Curry and Chutney

India is a bit more than one-third the size of the United States, but it has three times as many people. Geographically, its northern border is the Himalayas, the highest mountain range in the world, reaching almost 30,000 feet—twice as high as California's Mt. Whitney, the highest peak in the continental United States. India's southern tip is in the tropics. It is desert in the northwest; the enormous delta of the Ganges, India's holy river, is in the northeast. Since ancient times, winds have propelled ships west from India to the Arabian peninsula and the east coast of Africa. To the east of India across the Bay of Bengal lie Thailand, the Spice Islands, and Indonesia; farther east is China.

In addition to trade contact, India was invaded from the west by the Arabs. Later the Portuguese established a colony in Goa on the southwest coast; on the southeast coast, Pondicherry became the headquarters of the French East India Company in 1664. By the nineteenth century the British had driven them all out and had complete control of India.

The British brought tea cultivation to India. The Indian people made tea their own by adding spices: ginger, black pepper, cinnamon, cardamom, cloves, sugar. Then it became *chai*—the Indian word for tea.

The "Jewel in the Crown"

India was called the jewel in the crown because it was England's most valuable colony. During the Industrial Revolution, it provided natural resources for England's factories, and its population at that time of 300 million people was a huge market for England's manufactured goods. In the 1860s, India's cotton for England's textile factories became extremely important when cotton from the United States was cut off by the American Civil War.

India's geographical diversity, fertile land, multitude of ethnic groups, and location in the center of Asia on strategic trade routes created distinctive regional cuisines. Until recently, however, much of the cuisine that the rest of the world knew as Indian was the cuisine of the Mughals. This was spread by the British, because the Mughals were in power from 1526 to 1857; they were the ones the British conquered to gain control of India.

Dal, Rice, *Roti*

Throughout India, *dal* [doll] is a staple dish. *Dal* refers to raw and cooked legumes: lentils, chickpeas, beans, and peas. According to food historian Colleen Taylor Sen, there are "More than fifty kinds of *dals* on the market, and they are sold skinned and unskinned, split and whole."[30] The lentils Americans know are brown. In India, they also come in red, black, yellow, pink, and green, and in various sizes. They require hours of soaking and cooking. Rice is also a staple, as is wheat bread called *roti*, which is held in tongs and cooked over an open flame.

In *Food Culture in India*, food historian Colleen Taylor Sen has a four-page chart with more than three dozen different kinds of bread made in India. They include flat lentil-flour *pappadums*; *puri* or poori, deep-fried in ghee (clarified butter); and yeast-risen wheat *naan*. A special baking technique is applied to *naan:* it is slapped onto the side of a tandoor, an upright, free-standing clay oven. From northwestern India, on what is now the Pakistani border, comes tandoori-style meat. This is marinated in yogurt and spices, then cooked in the tandoor over hot coals.

CULINARY CONFUSION:

Curry

Curry is an inaccurate catch-all term that was spread by the British, who did not differentiate among India's diverse regional cuisines. It can also refer to an even greater sin, commercial curry powder. Indian cooks grind their own spice mixes as they need them based on religion, region, whether they are cooking meat or vegetables, and their own preferences. The word *curry* is in front of the various dishes in this section because that is how many English-speaking people know them. The dishes should be referred to by their Indian names.

INGREDIENTS:

Pork Vindaloo[34]

Marinade

cider vinegar	fresh ginger
garlic	salt
red pepper flakes	turmeric

Sauce

mustard oil	fenugreek seeds
onions	bay leaves
cinnamon	tomato paste
cloves	paprika
cardamom pods	chile powder
nutmeg	green chiles
cumin seeds	cilantro
coriander seeds	

....

Portuguese Curry—Vindaloo

In 1510, the Portuguese arrived in Goa on India's southwest coast. It was the center of the spice trade and was controlled by Muslims. By the end of the century, the Portuguese had driven out the Arabs, taken over the spice trade, and brought their cuisine and culture to India. The Portuguese remained in Goa for 450 years. The chile peppers they brought to India were adapted quickly and spread throughout the country, across cuisines. This means that any food that is considered traditional Indian but has chile peppers dates back less than 500 years. The Portuguese took black pepper, ginger, cinnamon, and cardamom to Europe with them. Curries from Goa still show up in Portuguese cookbooks.

According to food historian Cherie Hamilton in *Cuisines of Portuguese Encounters*, Goan cuisine is Portuguese cuisine with Indian ingredients and spices. The Portuguese introduced pork, as cuts of meat and in sausage. From their colony in South America, Brazil, they brought cashews and pineapples. From elsewhere in the New World, they introduced peanuts, papayas, potatoes, tomatoes, and sweet potatoes.[31]

They also introduced the concept of soup, like a fish head soup with the two most prominent spices in Goan cuisine, saffron and ginger.[32] A clear example of Portuguese-Indian fusion cuisine is Goan rice, which is called *arroz pilau. Arroz* means rice in Portuguese; *pilau* means rice in Hindi. The Portuguese components are sausage, beef broth, garlic, and chiles; the seasonings are Indian: ginger, cinnamon, cloves, cardamom, and turmeric.

Perhaps the most famous Goan dish is a curry, pork *vindaloo*. The name comes from Portuguese, *vinho e alhos*—vinegar and garlic. As Christians, the Portuguese ate pork; the Muslims and Hindus in Goa did not. In 1560, the Inquisition of the Catholic Church began in Goa. It ordered the Hindu temples destroyed and decreed that only Christians could hold public office. With Hindus gone or converted, eating pork became common in Goa, as did drinking alcohol. As Lizzie Collingham points out in *Curry*, "Nowhere else in India did European settlement have this impact."[33]

Portuguese desserts, with their egg custard bases, marzipan, and tarts created another new category of Goan cuisine. They were combined with local ingredients like coconut milk and bananas to produce European-style cakes and fritters, often made by nuns in convents.

Bengal—Northeastern India

Bengal contains the delta of the Ganges, India's holy river, which flows through the city of Calcutta—now spelled Kolkata—before it empties into the Bay of Bengal. Rice and fish are the staples, along with potatoes, eggplant, pumpkin, okra, leafy greens, and *dal*. The spices are "turmeric, dried red chile, cumin seed, fresh green chile, coriander powder or seed, ginger, small and large onion, garlic, lime, mustard seed, black pepper."[35] The common cooking oil is mustard oil. "A Bengali meal follows a definite progression of flavors from bitter through salty and sour and ending with sweet."[36] The bitter is provided by bitter melon. The love of sweets involves the Portuguese, who had multiple posts in the Bay of Bengal beginning in the early sixteenth century, shortly after they colonized in Goa. They brought their knowledge and love of confections with them.[37]

Southern India

In southern India, many vegetarian dishes are made from rice and lentils ground into flour. *Idli* is a white, steamed, spongy small ball. It can be made in a mold like *abelskivers*, the Danish round pancake. *Dosas* are thin, like crepes. Stuffed with vegetables, they become *masala dosa*. Both *idli* and *dosas* are served with spicy chutney, now often tomato, like a sauce. The leaf of the curry plant, which tastes like a combination of curry spices, is used in the cooking of southern India. The long coastline provides hundreds of varieties of fish, so the area along the coast is not vegetarian.

Mughal Curry—Rogan Josh

The Mughals were nomads from northern Asia, but they had already adopted much of Persian cuisine and culture before they conquered northern India. During the Mughal Dynasty (1526–1857), chickens destined for the emperor's table "were hand-fed with pellets flavored with saffron and rosewater and massaged daily with musk and sandalwood." To lessen their homesickness, the Persian Mughals planted orchards of stone fruits—peaches, apricots, plums, and cherries; nuts—walnuts, pistachios, almonds, and chestnuts; and apples, pears, and pomegranates. Other Persian favorites—melons and grapes—grew in the royal gardens.[38] They also loved the homegrown Indian mango.

A British visitor to the Mughal court from 1615 to 1619 described a three-person banquet where the number of dishes each person received was based on his importance. The host got 60 dishes, the guest of honor 70, the least important person 50. The food, including rice boiled with ginger, pepper, and butter, and a meat curry with onions, herbs, and spices was "exceedingly pleasing to all Palates." But sitting cross-legged on the floor the entire time was exceedingly difficult.[39]

Mughal cuisines include the cuisine of Kashmir, in the foothills of the Himalayan mountains. This is where the nobles went in the summer to escape the heat in the lowlands, and where one curry, *rogan josh,* originated. As Lizzie Collingham points out in *Curry,* "rogan means clarified butter in Persian, . . . josh means hot" (as in heat, not spicy; see Crossing Cultures: "Curry" chart).[40] Another Mughal specialty is *biryani,* a meat and rice dish that is like a Persian *pilau.*

HOLIDAY HISTORY:

Mishani

"Every important occasion in Kashmir is celebrated with a *mishani,* a meal that traditionally consists of seven dishes—all of them made from lamb. It includes roast leg of lamb; cubes of lamb spiced with cardamom, cumin seeds, and cinnamon; grilled lamb kababs; spiced lamb liver; lamb kidneys; shoulder of lamb; and delicate lamb meatballs pounded with yogurt and spices."[41]

It was during the Mughal Dynasty that Shah Jahan built one of the most beautiful buildings in the world, the Taj Mahal. It is a white marble tomb encrusted with gold that he built for his wife in Agra, north of New Delhi. It took 22 years to build, from 1631 to 1653.

Delhi Curry—Garam Masala

Another mix of curry spices of Persian origin is found south of Kashmir, in north-central India around the area of New Delhi, the capital. *Garam* means hot; *masala* means "ingredients or materials."[42] *Garam masala* is milder than *rogan josh* because it contains no fresh chiles. This is the cuisine that Americans were introduced to by Indian chef Madhur Jaffrey in her groundbreaking 1973 book, *An Invitation to Indian Cooking.* As an upper-class Indian, she did not cook until she went to school in England, got homesick, and taught herself to cook her native cuisine from letters her mother sent her.

"CURRY"

TYPE REGION COUNTRY	GARAM MASALA CENTRAL INDIA[43]	ROGAN JOSH NORTH INDIA[44]	VINDALOO SOUTHWEST INDIA[45]	PONCH PHORON NORTHEAST INDIA	BALTI PAKISTAN[46]
ajwain*					
anise, star					✦
asafetida		✦†			
bay leaf					✦
cardamom	✦	✦	✦		✦
chile			✦		✦
cinnamon	✦	✦	✦		✦
cloves	✦	✦	✦		✦
coriander	✦	✦	✦		✦
cumin	✦	✦	✦	✦	✦
fennel		✦		✦	✦
fenugreek		✦†		✦	✦
garlic		✦†	✦		✦
ginger	✦	✦	✦		✦
kalonji (black onion seed)	✦			✦	✦
mustard seed			✦	✦	✦
paprika		✦			
pepper—black	✦	✦	✦		
pepper—cayenne		✦	✦		
saffron		✦			
turmeric			✦		

* Ajwain is a spice that tastes like thyme or caraway, but more pungent.

† Muslims use garlic and onion; Hindus use asafetida and fenugreek in *rogan josh*.

The Taj Mahal, India. *Courtesy Corbis Digital Stock.*

East of Delhi is Lucknow, where the specialty is *korma*. This is a sauce variation using *garam masala* spices, but with a cream enrichment at the end.

Anglo-Indian Cuisine

In the eighteenth century, the household of a British official in India had its own deer, cows, calves, sheep, kids, ducks, geese, and rabbits, so an important dinner could include 15 or 16 meat courses. One woman described an average daily main meal in 1780: "We dine at 2 O'clock in the very heat of the day. . . . A soup, a roast fowl, curry and rice, a mutton pie, forequarter of lamb, a rice pudding, tarts, very good cheese, fresh churned butter, excellent Madeira."[47] Nap time followed, then socializing and visiting. Supper was a light evening meal. In the nineteenth century, the meals were reversed—the midday meal was light, called *tiffin*, from the British word that is the equivalent of "snack." The heavy main meal, at 7 or 8 P.M., was a social event. This shift in cuisine reflected a shift in power in India.

The event that caused the shift involved food. In 1857, a rumor, untrue, spread among the *sepoys*—Indian soldiers in the British East India Company army—that the rifle cartridges were smeared with beef and pork fat, which went against their religions. The *sepoys* were incensed because they had to break the cartridges open with their teeth. They mutinied. It took a year for the British to regain control of India, and when they did, all opposition was crushed. The time of the British rule until India became independent in 1947 is called the Raj [rah-zh].

During the Raj, a British army officer could live and eat like a *raja*—king. The arrival of wives from England shifted food away from native Indian to Anglo-Indian or purely British: roast meats, puddings, and sandwiches. Breakfasts were substantial: boiled or fried fish or prawns, a curry or casserole, cold mutton, bread and butter or rice, plaintains or oranges. Kedgeree was a popular British breakfast.

RECIPE:
Kedgeree

"Any cold fish, 1 teacupful of boiled rice, 1 oz. of butter, 1 teaspoonful of mustard, 2 soft-boiled eggs, salt and cayenne to taste," all mixed together and served hot.[48]

Curry was popular with Anglo-Indians, but not in its original meaning as a spiced relish from south India. Instead, it became a catch-all word that could mean broth, a wet stew, or a dry dish. They were served with chutney. Indian servants prepared and served the food.

Drinking increased. The beverage of choice was claret. An acceptable ration for a man was three bottles after dinner; for a woman, one a day. They also drank champagne, brandy, and beer.[49]

CULINARY CONFUSION:
Chutney

Indian chutney is not what Americans know as chutney, which is probably some variation of Major Grey's. This bottled chutney is heavy and thick, with chunks of fruit—mostly mango—cooked in sugar and vinegar. Indian chutneys are simple combinations like jalapeños, mint, yogurt, and cilantro; or tomato, vinegar, a bit of sugar and spices; or freshly grated coconut, chiles, ginger, and lemon juice. Tamarind is used, too, to add a bit of sourness. Indian chutneys are much thinner than Major Grey's, more like sauces than jams or preserves.

India also produced a crop that proved crucial in expanding the British Empire. It was grown cheaply in India, then transported to China on British ships and sold to the Chinese. The plant's name in Latin is *papavera somnifera*—"poppy-put-you-to-sleep"; the product processed from its sticky juice is opium.

China: Tea and Opium

Tang and Song, 618–1279

More than a thousand years before the British arrived, a great new dynasty arose in China. The Tang (618–907) reconquered lands that had not been in the possession of China since the end of the Han Dynasty in A.D. 220 and redistributed them to the peasants. Much of the expansion of China occurred during the reign of China's only female emperor, Wu Zhao. She was the power behind the throne for 30 years before she finally proclaimed herself emperor in 690. During the Tang period, bananas, dates, citrus, and taro palm were grown in the south. So was litchi, the sweet fruit that was a favorite of the emperor's court. Foods traveled to China via Muslim traders on the Silk Road from Persia and Central Asia: sugar cane, spinach, lettuce, almonds, figs, and grapes in various forms—syrup, raisins, wine.[50] However, another beverage had their attention: "The age was marked by an obsessive concern with ale. Rarely in the history of the world has alcoholism been so idealized." The use of hallucinogenic drugs was also widespread. Both seemed to be part of a desire for escapist release in a time of many famines.[51] Costly wars and high taxes to pay for them further weakened the dynasty. One of the items taxed was salt, which provided half of the state's income.[52] Salt smugglers took what they could. Finally, in 907, in a series of events reminiscent of the fall of Rome, rebels from border areas ransacked the capital, Chang'an, and killed the last emperor, a child. After several years of war, the Song Dynasty took power over a China that was smaller but more stable.

During these two dynasties, China's population grew, and grew increasingly urban and sophisticated. The entire country contained 100 million people, the most in the world and the most advanced. At least 10 cities had as many people as Rome and Baghdad at their height: one million. There was also a million-man standing army for which the government bought massive amounts of food. It was the only place in the world that knew the secret of how to make silk. Some things in widespread use in China: the fine porcelain that the West still calls "china," gunpowder, the printing press, tea.

The Tao of Tea

Just as Christianity spread on the roads in the Roman Empire, tea spread throughout China on the Silk Road, often with Buddhism. Buddhist rituals were performed in Chang'an, the end of the Silk Road, which was an international trading city.

FOOD FABLE:

Where the Tea Leaf Comes From

In the fifth century A.D., Boddhidarma, the monk who brought Buddhism to China, was having trouble meditating—he kept falling asleep. He just couldn't keep his eyelids open, so he tore them off and threw them on the ground. They took root and grew into tea plants.

Like all legends, this one has some truth in it. It is possible to see the shape of an eyelid in the oval of a tea leaf, and tea has caffeine, which will keep even sleepy monks awake. Tea is a member of the camellia family, a glossy-leaved bush that also produces large-bloomed flowers. Its scientific name is *Camellia sinensis* or *Camellia assamica*—camellia from China or Assam, a region in northeast India, although it probably originated in Southeast Asia in what is now Vietnam.

Tea began as an exotic medicinal drink, the cure for everything from epilepsy to lung disease to dysentery. It got a popularity boost in the eighth century when Lu Yü wrote *The Book of Tea*. While Arabs and Europeans looked to gold to provide the secret of eternal life, the Chinese thought tea was the key. At the end of the twentieth century, scientists discovered that green tea is a powerful anti-oxidant, a cancer-fighting agent.

Yin and Yang

The Chinese also thought that correct balancing of Tao, the energy force behind the universe, would lead to immortality. Like the Greek gods who had both positive and negative sides, and like the European system of humors on which it is probably based, Tao has opposing components, yin and yang. Yin is female, passive, cool. Yang is male, aggressive, hot. (Feng shui is this principle applied to buildings and landscape.) The Chinese believed that if humans harnessed yin and yang properly, if they could find the right combination of foods, they could become immortal. To try to attain immortality, five Tang emperors in a row took "immortality drugs"—probably heavy metals—and died.[53]

China's Tang Dynasty was a time of great advances in the arts, such as poetry, but it was during the Song Dynasty, specifically between 960 and 1279, that distinctive cuisines emerged in three regions: north; south, around the Yangtze River delta; and Szechwan. Cantonese came later. Northern Chinese cuisine was dominated by the city of Peking. Millet, meat, and dairy products were a large part of the total food consumed. Wheat was also grown and the flour used for dumplings, fried dough strips, and noodles. It was blander than southern cuisine, which was based on rice, fish, pork, vegetables, and fruits. Szechwan cuisine was also based on rice. Tea was popular, too. It was missing two foods that characterize it now, hot peppers and peanuts, because they were from the New World and had not been introduced to China yet. But even then the food was hot, seasoned with a "vegetable that resembles the pea; . . . it will cause gasping and gaping."[54]

TEA CHRONOLOGY

3,000 B.C.	Tea consumed in China
A.D. 3rd century	Tea first appears in written Chinese
5th century	Boddhidarma legend about sleepy monk and origins of tea
618–907	Chinese consider tea a powerful medicine and secret to long life[55]
8th century	*The Book of Tea (Cha Ching)*, written by Lu Yü in China
804	Japanese monk brings tea to Japan
1215	Esai, monk who brought Buddhism to Japan, writes tea treatise, *Kissa Yojoki*
16th century	Sen Rikyu transforms tea ceremony into Japanese cultural event
16th century	Portuguese priest writes about tea
1610	Dutch bring teapots to Europe
mid-18th century	Tea is huge fashion in Russia; they invent samovar
December 16, 1773	Boston Tea Party in Massachusetts
1839–1842	Opium Wars—England forces opium on China to pay for tea
20th century	Tea bags come into use
late 20th century	Americans invent Mrs. Tea to make instant iced tea; no longer produced
late 20th century	Americans consider tea a powerful medicine and secret to long life

The Song period, which followed the Tang, was a time of plenty in China. As trade increased, so did the merchant class and so did their desire for new, exciting foods. In 1027, to avoid famine, the emperor ordered green lentils from India and a new strain of rice from Champa (present-day Vietnam) to be grown in southeastern China. The Champa rice matured faster so two crops could be grown in one season, and it was drought tolerant so it could grow where rice had never been grown before. Other kinds of rice were "official" (the only kind that could be used to pay taxes); glutinous rice for wine; "red rice, red lotus-seed rice, yellow keng-mi, fragrant rice, and 'old rice,' rice sold off at a discount by the official granaries."[56] However, among the upper classes, polished white rice was the standard, just as refined white bread was the standard in Europe.[57]

RICE CHRONOLOGY (ORYZA SATIVA)

6500 B.C.	Rice cultivated in Yangtze Valley, China
2000 B.C.	Rice in northern India and southeast Asia
300 B.C.–A.D. 200	Rice reaches Japan and the Middle East
A.D. 1st century	Rice in Indonesia and probably the Philippines
A.D. 500–600	Rice grown in Egypt
after 700	Muslims spread rice throughout Mediterranean and to West Africa
1027	Champa rice grown in China
13th century	Rice in northern Europe
15th century	Rice in northern Italy
1700	Rice grown in Carolinas in North America with African slave labor
c. 1900	Varieties capable of growing in colder climates are grown in Japan
1980s	Genetically engineered IR36 planted in more than 10% of world's rice fields

There were "Seven Necessities" that people had to have every day: "firewood, rice, oil, salt, soybean sauce, vinegar, and tea."[58] At various times, the government had monopolies on salt and tea, and also on wine. The wealthy went far beyond these mere seven necessities. The food explosion was evident in huge cities like Kaifeng and Hangchow, which had separate markets for different foodstuffs in different parts of the city: markets for grain; two for pork; meats besides pork, like beef, venison, horse, fowl, rabbit; vegetables; fresh fish; preserved fish; fruit; oranges; and more. In butcher shops, five butchers at a time lined up at tables, cutting, slicing, and pounding cuts of meat to order.[59] The food for the imperial household was bought at its own special markets.

During the Song Dynasty, upper-class diners moved from sitting on the floor to chairs. Multicourse dinners were brought to lacquered tables set with porcelain dishes and sometimes silver chopsticks and spoons. Meals were prepared by household staffs that could number in the hundreds. The emperor's kitchens had a staff of more than a thousand working under guard. For a change of pace, there were wine and tea houses, and restaurants and caterers that cooked food to order that was as good as or better than that available in the wealthiest homes. For the lower classes, there were street vendors, noodle shops, and smaller restaurants like the *taberna* and *popina* of ancient Rome that provided prepared food. Some snack shops specialized in one kind of food, like *ping*—little "cakes" that were sweet or savory, stuffed or plain, steamed or fried. All of the chefs who prepared these foods were male, with perhaps only a few female exceptions. If they were literate, these chefs could find recipes printed in Chinese encyclopedias and in *The Illustrated Basic Herbal*, which appeared in 1061 and contained descriptions and drawings of hundreds of foods.

State banquets were the most lavish ceremonies, with over 200 different dishes and table service of jade, pearl, and silver.[60] A person's importance at a function like this was measured not just by where he sat, but also by how many courses he got. Other festivals celebrated Buddhist holidays. Ancestors were always honored at these events.

The Song Dynasty was a time of peace and prosperity in China, but the peace came at a price. China kept the barbarians at bay by paying them off with "gifts" of silver and silk. The Song split into northern and southern factions; a war between them followed. This made China vulnerable to invaders.

The Mongols: Living High on the Horse

In the thirteenth century, across the vast, dry, flat grasslands of Asia—the steppes—galloped the Mongols, led by Genghis Khan. What the Vandals and the Goths were to Ancient Rome, the Mongols were to China—barbarian invaders from the north. The Mongols' merciless tactics terrified their enemies. They would surround a city and demand its surrender. If the city didn't surrender, they killed everyone. If the city did surrender, they killed everyone. The Mongols could ride for days, switching horses without getting off. They invented stirrups to make themselves bipedal while riding a horse, for the same survival reason that early man became bipedal: it left their hands free to use weapons. They could stand up in the stirrups without falling off the horse and still be able to guide it with their knees and feet. They could also twist and shoot to the side or behind them. Standing, they were higher than the horse's head so they could shoot arrows over it.

In the process of conquering China, the Mongols changed from nomads to not just settled, but urban—quite a leap. And their food shifted from cooking to cuisine. The nomadic Mongols were pastoral people, driving their flocks before them. They lived on dairy from their sheep and goats—milk, butter, cheese—but they were also fueled by horse-power. Their favorite food was fermented mare's milk, called *kumiss*. Unlike cow's milk, mare's milk is high in vitamin C. When there was nothing else to drink or when they were riding and couldn't stop to rest, they drank their horse's blood. They made a slit in the horse's neck and knew just how much blood to suck without hurting the horse. Sometimes they ate horse meat. They also hunted—Siberian tigers, wolves, bears, wild boar—and usually boiled their catch, on the bone, with "seeds, grains, tubers, roots, fruits and berries, etc., even green vegetables, whatever was available." The resulting thick soup was synonymous with the Mongol word for food: *shülen*.[61]

CROSSING CULTURES:

FILLED DUMPLINGS

COUNTRY	NAME	DOUGH	FILLING
Argentina	empanada	pastry	meat, cheese
Armenia	boereg	phyllo	cheese
China, south	won ton	noodle	seafood, pork
China, north	bao	bread	seasoned pork
England	pasty	thick pastry	meat
Ethiopia	sanbussa	thin pastry	beef or lentils
Greece	spanakopita, tiropita	phyllo	spinach, cheese
India	samosa	pastry	vegetables, potato
Indonesia	sambusa	pastry	meat, vegetables
Iran	manti	yogurt pastry	meat
Iraq	sambusak	bread	meat, pulses
Italy	ravioli/calzone	noodle/bread	meat, cheese
Jewish	kreplach	noodle	meat
Korea	man-du	noodle	meat, vegetables
Lebanon	barak/sambousek	phyllo/puff pastry	meat/cheese
Mexico	enchilada	corn tortilla	meat, cheese
Morocco	briwat	phyllo (warqa)	savory or sweet
Poland	kolodny	noodle	meat
Portugal	empada/boureka	pastry	pork, shrimp
Russia	pierog	sour cream pastry	ground beef
Tibet	momo	noodle	yak meat, vegetables
Tunisia	brik	warqa	egg
Turkey	manti/börek	noodle/pastry	savory or sweet
U.S.	dumpling	sweet pastry	sweetened fruit
Uzbekistan	manti	noodle	lamb

In the thirteenth and fourteenth centuries, this changed. The Mongols shifted from cooking to cuisine. This new Mongol cuisine was like the culture: open to new ideas and techniques. The soup now had foreign spices and vegetables. As food historian Paul Buell points out, the Turks played a large part in the change to the new cuisine. The Mongols appointed Turks to important positions as government officials because the Turks were literate and among the upper classes in other cultures. The Turks had been in contact with Muslim Arabs and their cuisine and also with Persian cuisine. They were familiar with grains, which the Mongols were not; they had many different kinds of dough—for bread, noodles, pastry—and they used the *tannur*, a freestanding clay oven. (In India, *tandoor*.) Through the Turks, many Middle Eastern foods were introduced to China. It is rare that food historians have such a clear-cut indication of where foods came from, but chickpeas, ghee, and parsley were known to the Mongols respectively as "Muslim beans," "Muslim oil," and "Muslim celery." Recipes for sheep's head and *halwa* are labeled "Muslim recipes."[62]

These new foods were enjoyed not only in Peking, but spread throughout the empire. Other foods crossed cultures, too, like *manty*, a filled dumpling which food historian Paul Buell says is "probably originally a Central Asian food" that spread west to Turkey and through the Turks, beyond.

Genghis Khan's grandson, Kublai Khan, ruled from 1260 to 1294 from the new capital he created in Peking (now Beijing). He called his dynasty Yuan, which means "beginning." Kublai Khan ruled the largest land-based empire the world has ever seen—west into India and Poland, east to Korea. He decided to extend it farther. Kublai Khan sent messengers to Japan, demanding that they pay tribute to him—in effect, admit they were inferior, submit to his rule, and give him money. He expected Japan to submit, as all the other countries had. But Japan, under the rule of samurai warriors, did not submit.

By the time the Portuguese arrived in China, the ancient empire of China had made several forays to the west in huge sailing ships with red silk sails. However, China's rulers were not impressed with what the West had to offer in either cuisine or culture. As Europe became increasingly secular and interested in business, China's rulers decided that they would remain agrarian; that farming, not business, was the way to prosperity and a life of harmony. They closed themselves off from the rest of the world. The emperor decreed that only one city would remain open to foreign trade. It was in southern China: Canton to the British, Guangzhou to the Chinese.

Cantonese Cuisine

"Cantonese food, at its best, is probably unequalled in China and possibly in the world."[63]

The freshest ingredients, drawn from all regions of China, split-second timing, a wide variety of techniques, hundreds of superb dishes, and the ability to quickly absorb new foods and techniques—like baking—from other cuisines make for an ever-expanding, innovative cuisine. Unfortunately, what most Americans know as Cantonese cuisine—isn't. The sweet and sour pork, chop suey, chow mein, greasy egg rolls, and fried rice that became popular in the United States in the 1950s and 1960s are not at all representative of Cantonese cuisine. It was dumbed down and sweetened up for American taste buds. The Cantonese have even fewer desserts than other areas of China, so they do not use sugar with a heavy hand in their main dishes. Cantonese cuisine uses—sparingly—chile sauce, hot mustard, vinegars, sesame oil, and soy and oyster sauces. Fish and seafood—oysters, sea cucumbers, squid, jellyfish, and croaker—are Cantonese specialties. They are often steamed, stir fried, or deep fried. They are not slathered in cornstarch, canned pineapple juice, and questionable flavor enhancers like MSG—monosodium glutamate. The Cantonese regard this kind of cooking and the people who eat it the same way the Romans regarded people who had never had bread and put meat under their saddle to warm it up—as barbarians.

FOOD FABLE:

The Origin of Chop Suey

It is a myth that chop suey is of American origin. As the story goes, someone went to a restaurant in San Francisco's Chinatown just before closing time, so the chef threw together all the leftover odds and ends. Chop suey is leftovers, but from Canton, where *tsap seui* means "miscellaneous scraps."[64]

The delicacy of Cantonese cuisine comes out in *tim sam (dim sum)*, which means "small eating." These are bite-size dumplings, pieces of dough wrapped around a spiced meat or seafood filling, then steamed. Sometimes they are wrapped in lotus or bamboo leaves and steamed, the way Mexican cuisine uses corn husks to wrap tamales, or other cultures use banana leaves. Cantonese cuisine is also the cuisine of the islands of Macau and Hong Kong. By treaty, England gave Hong Kong back to the Chinese on July 1, 1997. Many people left Hong Kong and brought their cuisine with them; there are now many fine Cantonese restaurants in the United States.

The Opium Wars

In the nineteenth century, the British treasury had an unfavorable balance of trade with China. The British wanted tea; the Chinese wanted nothing except payment in silver. The British had to find something to sell to China. They decided on opium—a depressant drug, a "downer." It was highly addictive so there would be return customers. The Chinese emperor objected to Queen Victoria; she ignored him. There was a war, but the Chinese navy was no match for British steamships and guns. By 1842, the Opium Wars were over and China was forced to give the island of Hong Kong to the British. It was also forced to open other major cities for trading in addition to Canton. Foreign money, businesses, governments, and guns were calling the shots in China. This destabilized the government, which caused civil wars in China for almost a century. In 1911, thousands of years of empire, and the emperor, came to an end. More civil unrest followed. This made China vulnerable to invasion by Japan in 1937.

"Coolies," the New Slaves

The conquering of China and India in the nineteenth century also resulted in the enslavement of the populations. Chinese and Indians became a new source of slave labor throughout the world. They were known as "coolies." The African slave ships were the model for the coolie ships, and as on the African ships, the coolies mutinied and died. Sometimes Chinese lured other Chinese into servitude with offers of jobs as cooks for the French in Canton, or with the Chinese army. Chinese and Indian workers were shipped as far away as the Caribbean, where they worked 21 hours a day making sugar. Others ended up in California in the gold fields or working on the railroad. And, of course, they brought their cuisines and their cultures with them.

Korea: Kimchee and *Pulgogi*

Rice is the staple of Korean cuisine. Glutinous lowland rice, *tapkok*, is eaten. An upland variety is used for flour and beer. Flour is also made from ground mung beans. The staple condiment and national dish, which comes in more than 200 varieties, is kimchee. It is traditionally made every fall—cabbage season—in Korean homes. Cabbage (and sometimes radishes), chile pepper, and garlic are packed into stone crocks and fermented. What Americans know as Korean barbecue is *pulgogi*—meat or seafood marinated in soy sauce, sesame oil, garlic, ginger, pepper, and green onions, then broiled. Wheat or buckwheat noodles or dumplings like won tons but larger are served in soup. Soup provides the liquid during a meal; beverages like rice water or barley water are consumed after. What Americans would consider dessert—rice cakes or fruit—is eaten between meals as a snack.

The Koreans, like the Japanese, are formal people. There are many rules controlling relations between people and regarding food. Koreans consider it rude to look people in the face while speaking to them or to compliment anyone, like the cook, directly. It is more polite just to say that the food is good. Elders are deeply respected. They are spoken to first, served food and drink first, and eat first. No one can begin eating until the oldest person does. Dining tables are low; diners sit on cushions on the floor. The service is *à la française*, with all courses presented at once. Chopsticks and spoons are the utensils. Fingers are never used. The meal is over when the oldest person is finished. When dining out, Koreans never split the bill or ask for separate checks. The entire bill is paid by the person who had the idea to go out.[65]

Vietnam: Spring Rolls and Pâté

Geographically, Vietnam is divided into three parts, which influence its cuisine: the Red River in the north, the Mekong River in the south, mountains in between. It is the middle section, known as Champa, which sent a fast-maturing strain of rice to China. The south is a tropical rice-growing area. Vietnam also has three major influences on its cuisine: to the northeast, its ancient colonial master, China, which controlled Vietnam until 939; India to the west; and France, its more recent colonial master. By 1883, France had expanded its empire to include French Indochina—the modern countries of Laos, Cambodia, and Vietnam. Then there are the Portuguese, who arrived in Vietnam in 1516, bearing chile peppers. Between 1623 and 1698, people from the north and central sections migrated south and founded Saigon, now Ho Chi Minh City.

One of the hallmarks of native Vietnamese cuisine is using lettuce leaves to wrap vegetables and herbs. The Chinese influence in the north shows in stir-frying and chopsticks, and the use of black pepper as the hot spice. Vietnamese fermented fish sauce, *nam plah*, replaces soy sauce. Vietnamese spring rolls are more delicate than Chinese because the wrappers are made of rice flour instead of wheat flour. The Indian—and Portuguese—influence shows in curries in the south, where the hot spice is chile peppers. Herbs include lemon grass, cilantro, Thai basil, and mint. From the French, also in the south, centered in Saigon, the Vietnamese learned pâtés. Noodle soups, called *phô* [fuh], are important national dishes.

Indonesia: The Spice Islands

Southeast of India is Indonesia, the fourth most populous country in the world. Indonesia is a chain of large islands in the South Pacific. The area is subject to nature at its most violent: volcanoes whose ash provides fertilizer, earthquakes, and tidal waves. The world became acutely aware of Indonesia on December 26,

2004, when massive undersea earthquakes triggered tsunamis that killed hundreds of thousands and left millions homeless throughout the Indian Ocean. Hardest hit was Indonesia's northernmost province, Banda Aceh.

As in other Asian countries, rice is the main ingredient in Indonesian cuisine: "The standard everyday meal for millions of country people in Indonesia consists of boiled white rice, a little dried fish, and some chilli peppers. It must be white, fully milled, rice; brown rice, with the bran still on, may be more nutritious but is reserved for very young children and invalids."[66] This is in sharp contrast to the feast called *Rijsttafel*—Rice Table. This is a purely Dutch invention, patterned after the Indonesian custom of putting all the food on the table at once, like *service à la française*. Except that the Dutch took all different kinds of Indonesian food out of context and served it all at once. It would be as if people from another country came to the United States and claimed that a typical American holiday dinner was New Year's Eve champagne and caviar, Super Bowl guacamole, Valentine chocolate hearts, Fourth of July hot dogs, Thanksgiving turkey, and Christmas ham.

HOLIDAY HISTORY:

Selametan[67]

A *selametan* is an ancient native feast that existed before Muslims came to the Spice Islands. *Selametans* mark major rites of passage—birth, marriage, pregnancy, death—but they can also be to give thanks for a good harvest, to bless a new house, or before a trip. Whatever the occasion, it is a celebration of sharing and of community. It is also a time to make offerings to the spirits that control good fortune.

The centerpiece of a *selametan* is rice, either white cooked in coconut milk—*nasi gurih* or *nasi uduk*—or yellow from turmeric—*nasi kuning*. But how many dishes are served with it, which dishes, and how spicy they are, varies with the event. The cooking and cleaning up are communal, too.

The example Indonesian chef Sri Owen gives is a *selametan* for a woman in the seventh month of pregnancy, so there are seven hard-boiled eggs. The traditional vegetables are "*kacang panjang* (yard-long beans), *kangkung* (water spinach), *taoge* (beansprouts), and . . . *kol* (cabbage). The *bumbu* or coconut dressing should not be . . . chilli-hot because a pregnant woman must not eat hot food. There should also be a steamed coconut relish . . . mixed with some minced beef and wrapped in seven banana-leaf packets."

Like other countries in Asia, Indonesia was influenced by other Asian countries and by European explorers and colonizers. In the area around modern Singapore, there still exists a Chinese-Malaysian cuisine with a Portuguese name. *Nonya* is Portuguese for "grandmother," because it is rustic home cooking, like a noodle soup with tofu and coconut milk called *laksa*.

The Philippines: Chinese-Spanish Fusion

The Portuguese explorer Magellan "discovered" the Philippines in 1521 and was served a banquet of rice and stewed pork followed by roasted fish, ginger, and wine.[68] Rice and pork still figure prominently in Philippine cuisine, as they do in Chinese cuisine, while fish and vegetables are the mainstay of the island table. Because they were Spain's colony for hundreds of years, the main influence on Philippine cuisine is Spanish, along with Chinese, Malaysian, and Indonesian. The Spanish brought the olive oil, vinegar, onions, and garlic native to their own cuisine. From their colonies in Central and South America they brought foods native to the Americas: peanuts, chile peppers, tomatoes, potatoes, sweet potatoes, and corn. Like the Hawaiians and other Pacific island peoples, the Filipinos roast whole suckling pigs. Like the Malaysians, Indonesians, and southern Indians, Filipinos stew many foods in coconut milk. From American cooking, Filipinos learned about pies, but they made them their own by using local fruit like mango. Among the national dishes of the Philippines are *adobo*, meat stew with a vinegar-garlic sauce base, like *vindaloo*; *ginataan*, coconut milk stew; and *lumpia*, the Philippine version of spring rolls—vegetables wrapped in rice paper, like a burrito—that are found throughout Asia. Like other Asians, the people in the Philippines did not want foreign rule, Spanish or American, and fought against American rule for many years.

However, two countries in Asia—Thailand and Japan—managed to remain independent of European rule.

Thailand (Siam): Lemongrass and Jasmine Rice

Thailand owed its independence to its extraordinary ruler, King Rama IV (ruled 1851 to 1868). He was a Buddhist monk for 27 years before he became king. His training in patience and humility, along with his own intelligence and shrewdness, served him well as he negotiated with American and European diplomats during his reign. With two-thirds of the land in Thailand unsuitable for farming, it began to trade with Western countries, which valued Thai rubber, tin, and teak.

Thailand accepted some beneficial things from Western Christian missionaries, like the printing press and smallpox vaccinations, but kept its culture. This included slavery. Most Westerners know about nineteenth century Thailand from the 1870 autobiography written by Anna Leonowens, the British woman who tutored the king's family. *Anna and the King of Siam* became the Broadway play and movie *The King and I*, remade in 1999 as *Anna and the King*, starring Jodie Foster. Thais object to these accounts and they are banned in Thailand.

The staple food in Thailand, as in other Asian countries, is rice. Every year, a sacred ceremony signals the beginning of the rice planting season.

Thai Royal Plowing Ceremony

"Traditionally, the rice growing season in Thailand commences in May with the Royal Plowing Ceremony. It takes place near Bangkok's Grand Palace, in a spacious, grassy expanse called *Sanahm Luahng* ('the field of the King'). During the ritual, an official . . . appointed by the king uses a ceremonial plow drawn by white bulls to plow a long furrow into the field. He is followed by chanting Brahman priests and by four women carrying baskets of rice seed. The women scatter the seed in the plowed furrow. Once it has been sown and the ceremony is concluded, the onlookers scramble for the rice seed in the furrow, as it is believed that if these seeds are mixed with one's own, a good crop will be ensured."[69]

The rice they were planting in the ancient Royal Plowing Ceremony was not Thailand's most famous rice—jasmine—because that didn't exist until 1945. This long-grain rice was the result of a genetic modification experiment and grows best in northeastern Thailand.

Thailand, between China to the east and India to the west, has much in common with the cuisines of both countries. With southern Chinese Szechuan and Yunan cuisine, Thailand shares the use of two New World foods, peanuts and chiles. Noodles like crisp-fried *mee krob* also show the Chinese influence. It has curries *(gaang)* in common with India. The name of one curry is a clue to who introduced it: *massuman* is Thai for *musselman*, an early English corruption of "Muslim." The signature seasoning is a pungent fermented fish sauce called *nam plah*, literally "fish water." Fresh herbs like small-leaved Thai basil, mint, and cilantro are a bright contrast to *nam plah*. Cilantro roots, which are cut off in western markets, add a more intense cilantro flavor to Thai cooking. Citrus sharpness and sourness come from lime—juice, zest, and leaves. Lemongrass *(Cymbopogon citratus)* also provides a fresh intense citrus taste. Lemongrass has a solid green stalk about the diameter of a pencil or marker. In American markets, it is usually sold in bunches of three to four stalks, each about a foot long. Many of these ingredients are present in one of Thailand's most famous dishes, hot and sour shrimp soup—*tom yung kung,* sometimes called *tom yum goong*.

By contrast, Thai drinks and desserts are very sweet, like Arab desserts. Thai iced tea is made with sweetened, condensed milk, which was available in cans—clearly a recent, industrial item—so spoilage was not a problem. The dessert mango with sticky rice is made with palm sugar. Desserts perfumed with jasmine essence were probably introduced by Arabs.

INGREDIENTS:

Tom Yung Kung (Dom Yam Gung)

THAI HOT AND SOUR SHRIMP SOUP[70]

1 tablespoon vegetable oil	2 green Serrano chiles
Shrimp shells	1 red Serrano chile
8 cups chicken stock	2 pounds fresh (green) shrimp (20 ct)
3 stalks lemongrass	1 tablespoon nam pla
4 citrus leaves	2 tablespoons cilantro, chopped
1 teaspoon lime zest	3 green onions, chopped
Juice of 2 limes	1½ teaspoons salt

INGREDIENTS:

Mamuang Kao Nieo

MANGO WITH STICKY RICE[71]

1½ cups glutinous rice	½ teaspoon salt
1 cup thick coconut milk	5 ripe mangoes
½ cup palm sugar	4 tablespoons coconut "cream"

Japan: Tempura and Umami

China and Japan are linked by location. Huge China, wealthy in natural resources and food, lies west of the much smaller Japan, an island country with no natural resources except water and people. Like Greece, most of Japan's land is mountains that contain no mineral wealth. Like California and the rest of the Pacific Rim, it lies on an earthquake fault and has volcanoes. So Japan had to either trade with or conquer other countries to meet the basic needs of its population. Many of Japan's foods—but not its cuisine—and much of its culture, such as art, religion, and pictographic writing, originated in China. The diets of both countries rely on rice. Rice was cultivated in China about 8,500 years ago, but did not reach Japan until between 300 B.C. and A.D. 200. Japanese rice—*japonica*—is short grained and "glutinous," which really means sticky, because there is no gluten in rice.

Great Buddha of Kamakura, Japan, 1252. The temple that originally housed the 93-ton metal statue was washed away by a tsunami in 1495. *Courtesy Corbis Digital Stock.*

Japan refers to itself as the Land of the Rising Sun, which is depicted as a huge red ball on its flag. The Japanese believe that they are descended from the sun goddess, Amaterasu, who gave humans three gifts. One was the sacred iron sword, which figured prominently in Japanese culture.

It is a culture of intense extremes. On one hand, there is great attention to detail and the creation of beauty. An example is a simple activity elevated to art, like drinking tea. On the other hand, there is a violent warrior mentality. Cultural anthropologist Ruth Benedict describes this split in her book *The Chrysanthemum and the Sword*.

The Way of Tea

In A.D. 804, a Japanese monk brought tea back from China. In 815, he introduced it to the emperor, and that began the tea tradition in Japan. The first treatise on tea, *Kissa Yojoki*, was published in Japan in 1215, the year the Magna Carta was signed in England and the pope declared that communion wafers were the literal body of Christ. The treatise was written by Esai, the monk who also introduced Zen Buddhism to Japan. The Way of Tea stated that there were four values connected to tea practice: reverence, respect, purity, and tranquillity. However, the rituals associated with tea at this time in Japan had little to do with religion. As a new fashion from China, it caught on among the upper classes. Bored nobles dressed up in their finest clothes and went to tea houses to play games: who could taste a tea and guess its exact place of origin? Then they bet on the outcome and handed out prizes like bags of gold to the winners. Tea purists objected to this deviation from the Way of Tea. They got the tea games banned. But the games were too popular; finally, the ban went and the games stayed.

It would be centuries before the Japanese tea ceremony returned to its roots and found its form. During that time, the Japanese would repel foreign invaders and develop a unique sense of identity, with a cuisine and culture to match.

Mongol vs. Samurai

In the Middle Ages, knights in Japan were called samurai [SAM-ur-eye]. These warriors followed the code of Bushido, similar to the code of European knights: they were brave and loyal and willing to die for their earthly lord. A samurai would never surrender. He would kill himself instead or his entire family would be dishonored; it was more honorable to die in battle. Samurai swords were large and deadly; the same skills make Japanese kitchen knives some of the best in the world today.

Into this samurai warrior culture, the Mongol ruler Kublai Khan sent his messengers, demanding that Japan submit to Mongol rule. The Japanese ignored him for 10 years. In 1274, the Mongols tried to invade Japan, but a storm drove them back. Kublai Khan sent more messengers. The samurai chopped off their heads. In 1281, the Mongols tried to invade Japan again. A storm scattered the fleet; great waves sank the ships. The Japanese believed that their gods had saved them by sending a divine wind, called kamikaze [kah-mi-KAH-zee]. They used the same word at the end of World War II to describe their suicide pilots who dive-bombed American ships. The Mongols did not try to invade Japan again. Japan remained unconquered until 1945, the end of World War II, when Americans occupied the country.

The Samurai in the Tea House

By the sixteenth century, there was a new nationalism in Japan, a sense of their special identity. This can be seen in the tea ceremony, which shifted from a borrowed cultural practice to a uniquely Japanese one. The greatest tea master of all, Sen Rikyu (1522–1592), revived the Way of Tea and its four principles: reverence, respect, purity, tranquillity.

Sen Rikyu replaced the elaborate imported Chinese tea cups and Chinese vases made of semiprecious stone with modest Korean-made tea cups and simple bamboo baskets.[72] He also made the tea room smaller and more intimate, nine feet square. Then he put a rack by the door where the samurai had to hang their swords. But the sword had served a purpose at the table, as a divider to stake out personal space. A fan was substituted for the sword, which is why it is considered extremely aggressive to open a fan in a teahouse—it is the equivalent of brandishing a sword.

The ritual of taking a walk around the gardens in the back of the tea room before the ceremony serves a purpose, too. It appears to be an appreciation of nature and part of the ritual, but it is also a look-see to make sure no one is lurking in the garden waiting to assassinate the unarmed samurai.[73] In the sixteenth century, the tea house was a masculine world: the tea master was a man; flower arranging—then, *tatebana*, now *ikebana*—was a masculine art.

HOLIDAY HISTORY:
Japanese Tea Ceremony

The tea ceremony is interactive art that involves and heightens all the senses. The first is smell. Incense is burning as you walk in. Then you hear a whisper like a gentle breeze in the trees—the flame under the teakettle. A flower arrangement (a new art in the sixteenth century) soothes your eyes. As you sit on the straw tatami mat on the floor, you are aware of the feel of your silk kimono against your skin. You watch the movements of the tea master as he offers tea to Buddha. Then you drink a bowl of thick, bracing, bitter green tea.

The food is a series of small courses called *kaiseki*, from the words that mean "sitting together." It "is the flower of the Japanese cuisine," as Jennifer Anderson states in her book *An Introduction to Japanese Tea Ritual.*[74] The food is simple and simply prepared, with a concentration on the quality of the ingredients, on presentation, and on the spirit in which the food is offered and consumed. It can begin with a drink of ice water, hot water, chrysanthemum tea, plum wine, or sake—Japanese rice wine. These might be followed by two bowls, one rice and one *miso* soup. Then raw fish garnished with horseradish, edible chrysanthemum petals, and chrysanthemum greens. After more sake, the centerpiece is brought out on a separate tray, perhaps "a shrimp ball, a little piece of green *yuzu* citron, a leaf of spinach, and a shiitake mushroom in a clear stock of the best quality *dashi*."[75] A grilled course follows, either meat or fish. The meal ends with a broth made of brown rice and salt water accompanied by pickles. These foods are served with much politeness and bowing. They are eaten with new chopsticks.

The tea room is a utopia. Nothing from the outside intrudes. The conversation in the tea house is about the tea house, the tea, the flower arrangement. This forces you to focus on what is in front of you, on the beauty in the simplest everyday things, on how the Zen of the tea ceremony is the harmony of the universe. When you come out, you are altered.[76] The tea ceremony is a flawless execution of the combination of art, food, and religion that began in cave paintings 35,000 years ago in Europe.

But when the samurai comes out of the tea house, he puts his sword on again.

Samurai Culture, Portuguese Cuisine

Into this atmosphere of Japanese nationalism the Portuguese arrived in the 1540s to trade and preach Catholicism. This encounter was a shock to the Japanese, who had no idea that people existed who were not Asian. At first the Japanese were very interested in the new technology the Portuguese brought with them—guns—and in the new religion. Approximately 300,000 converted to Catholicism.

But there was a culture clash. Samurai culture was centered around the sword and swordcraft—skill in making and using swords. There was no place in Japanese identity for killing from a distance with guns. It was not heroic for people raised on the elaborate rituals and codes of honor based on man-to-man and hand-to-hand combat. The foreign technology and the foreign religion were banished from Japan. In 1587, Emperor Hideyoshi gave foreign priests 20 days to leave the country. He claimed that Catholics were persecuting followers of Buddhism and Shinto, and that Portuguese merchants were selling Japanese people into slavery. In the following decades, the choice for Catholics—foreign and native Japanese alike—was to renounce their faith or be tortured to death. Thousands renounced, thousands died.

By 1639, about 100 years after the Portuguese arrived, Japan had followed China's example: it became a closed country. It was illegal for Japanese to leave the country and for Catholics to enter it. Contacts with foreigners were restricted to one city, Nagasaki. But the Portuguese had left their mark on Japanese cuisine. They contributed the battered and fried foods called tempura and the word for bread—*pan*, as in *panko*—Japanese bread crumbs.[77] The Japanese left the gun but took the tempura.

Japan Westernizes

Japan stayed closed for more than 200 years, until people from a country that didn't exist in 1639—the United States—sailed into Tokyo Bay with four steam-powered warships in 1853. A letter from the president of the United States said that it would be "extremely beneficial to both" Japan and the United States to allow "free trade between the two countries." The United States wanted its ships to be able to put into ports in Japan to refuel, and would pay, "in money, or anything else your Imperial Majesty's subjects may prefer."[78] Commodore Perry, the commander of the American fleet, said that while the Japanese were thinking the offer over, he would go get a larger fleet of warships and return for their answer.

The Japanese saw the cannons on the ships and the writing on the wall. In 1867, a civil upheaval ended the feudal government that had ruled for 600 years. The new government Westernized. This period is known as the Meiji [MAY-jee] Restoration, which means "enlightened rule." Japan turned its samurai will and discipline to modernization and cooperation with the West. One of its models was Germany, newly united and heavily militarized.

By 1894, Japan had dozens of warships and an army of half a million men. It invaded mainland Asia by winning a war against China in Korea. It also won the island of Taiwan. Japan then advanced into the Chinese province of Manchuria, on the Russian border. This led to a war with Russia. In 1904, after Russia refused to settle the war on Japan's terms, Japan launched a surprise attack and destroyed most of the Russian navy. These stunning victories allowed Japan to occupy Korea; in 1910, Japan annexed Korea.

A New Taste: Umami

In 1908, a scientist in Japan made a discovery that was important in the food world: Dr. Ikeda identified a fifth taste, umami, or savory. Up until then, the world still believed in the four tastes that the Greek philosopher Aristotle had described in the fourth century B.C.: sweet, sour, bitter, and salty. Dr. Ikeda found umami in *dashi*, the Japanese stock. This is not like European stock, which was made from veal, beef, or chicken. *Dashi* is made from kelp and dried, flaked tuna. Kelp is seaweed, known as *kombu* in Japanese. Both *kombu* and dried tuna are intense flavors. But they are not sweet, sour, bitter, or salty.

The taste of umami is created by an amino acid called glutamate. Umami is found in many meat, fish, and dairy foods, especially sharp aged cheeses like Parmigiano-Reggiano. Umami has also been identified in tomatoes, potatoes and sweet potatoes, asparagus, shiitake mushrooms, fermented beans, truffles, and green tea.

Dr. Ikeda was ahead of his time. He published his results, but his idea of a fifth taste fell on deaf ears in the West. It was not until the 1980s that European and American scientists and chefs "discovered" umami.

A New Empire

At the beginning of the twentieth century, almost every country on the continents of Africa and Asia was the colony of a Western power. In Africa, cuisines and cultures throughout the continent were under severe stress. A cash economy forced people away from traditional bartering. Having to work for wages to grow foods they did not eat drove them off their land and away from the kin and tribal relationships that were reinforced by communal eating.

JAPANESE BASIC FOODS

Daikon	Large white radish, originated on Aisan mainland
Dashi	Stock of kelp and dried, flaked tuna; source of umami
Donburi	Rice bowl—the food and the vessel
Manju	Rice cakes filled with sweet bean paste
Mirin	Rice wine, lower in alcohol (can be <1%) than sake
Miso	Fermented rice, barley, or soy; miso soup, with rice = fundamental foods
Mochi	Sweet rice cakes made of steamed rice finely ground and shaped; made from mochigome rice (literally, "rice sticky"). Origins are religious; offered to the gods. During Heian 794–1192 became part of New Year.[79] Mochi bits—small cubes—now used as topping on frozen yogurt; Mikawaya in Los Angeles, CA, introduced mochi-covered ice cream in 1994.
Nori	Dried seaweed (kelp)
Ponzu sauce	Tart citrus (yuzu, lemon, etc.) and mirin-based sauce; from Portuguese *pomar*, orchard (probably from "apple"); Dutch *pons* = citrus orchard. Japanese *zu* = vinegar. Used for sashimi, grilled meat and fish.
Ramen	Thin wheat noodles
Sake	High-alcohol rice wine, approx. 20%
Shabu-shabu	Means "swish-swish." Hot pot; not as sweet as sukiyaki; twentieth-century invention; from Chinese; diner cooks the protein or vegetables in hot broth or dashi by swishing them around.
Shoyu	Soy sauce
Soba	Thin noodles, especially buckwheat; opposite of udon. Preferred in Tokyo; high in B vitamin thiamine, so avoids beriberi from only rice; traditional on New Year's Eve; served chilled in summer.
Sukiyaki	Hot pot usually with beef; contains sugar, unlike shabu-shabu
Surimi	Fish cake of white fish (fish stick, gefilte fish); imitation crabmeat—Krab
Tempura	Food battered and deep fried; from the Portuguese
Tonkatsu	Pork cutlets
Udon	Thick wheat noodles
Wasabi	Japanese horseradish; *Brassicaceae* family
Yaki	Broil
Yakiniku	Meat grilled at the table

Asians, too, were in despair. Giant China was helpless, forcibly opened in the Opium Wars. Southeast Asia was under the control of France. Indonesia had been in Portuguese, then Dutch hands for centuries. The British had a lock on India. The United States had a foothold in the Philippines. Thailand walked a tightrope to remain independent.

Japan alone was poising itself to become an empire in Asia and a power in the world. Even so, Japan was crowded and economic opportunities were limited. Many Japanese decided to start over in the Americas. They went to work on coffee plantations in Peru; on pineapple plantations in Hawaii, which became a U.S. territory in 1900; and on farms in the United States itself. In California, they lived in communities known as Little Tokyo in Los Angeles and San Francisco. However, racial laws prohibited them from becoming citizens or owning land, regardless of their patriotism or their considerable skill at farming. People in California did not want their children going to school with Japanese children. They demanded that Japanese stop migrating to California.

In the beginning of the twentieth century, this created an international incident. It increased the tension between Japan and the United States as both countries, new powers on the world stage, struggled for supremacy.

The Purity Crusade, Cuisine *Classique,* and Prohibition

1900–1929 IN EUROPE AND THE UNITED STATES

By 1900, a little more than a century since breaking away from England, the United States had become a world power. After winning the four-month Spanish-American War in 1898, the United States had acquired Puerto Rico and Guantanamo Naval Base in Cuba in the Caribbean, and Guam and the Philippines in the Pacific. It also had a new drink, the Cuba Libre (Free Cuba)—rum, Coca-Cola, and lime juice. From a late start in the Industrial Revolution, American factories were now outproducing England, Germany, and Belgium *combined.* American beef and wheat were feeding the world. It had many millionaires, and in 1901, the world's first billion-dollar corporation, United States Steel. The new industrial giant was built in great part by immigrant labor.

The New Immigrants and the Melting Pot

They came to America by the millions—26 million between 1870 and 1920.[1] They were Italians, Norwegians, Irish, Jews, Greeks, Poles, Hungarians, Lithuanians, Czechs, Bohemians, Moravians, Romanians, Bulgarians, Swedes, Finns, Latvians, Estonians, Russians, and others. They arrived at Ellis Island in New York Harbor with few possessions and almost no money—the average male had

$17.^2$ So they stayed where they landed, swelling the cities on the East Coast—New York, Boston, Philadelphia—to bursting. In addition to these millions of immigrants with strange food, languages, clothes, and customs, Americans were leaving their farms and moving to cities to work in factories. New York City became the most densely populated place on Earth. From 1910 to 1940, Japanese, Australians, and others arriving on the West Coast were processed at Angel Island in San Francisco Bay.

Italian-American Cuisine

"Not yet Americanized. Still eating Italian food." The legendary late-nineteenth-century female social worker who wrote this might have been referring to macaroni, which horrified meat-and-potatoes-eating Americans. If the pasta wasn't bad enough, that sauce of olive oil and garlic and tomatoes would surely kill you. And pizza—that same tomato sauce, but on bread. Only one thing could make it worse—fry the bread dough, then ladle tomato sauce on top and sprinkle it with cheese. The name said it all: *pizza fritta*—fried pie. And when their babies teethed or had colic, these people rubbed wine on their gums or even gave them a sip. Italians would never become real Americans or understand American food.

Usually, the Italian men came to America first. They learned to cook or found rooming houses run by other Italians where they got meals. For about 50 percent of the Italians, the trip to America was temporary, a way to make the money they needed to return to Italy and buy land or open a small business. Others sent for their wives and families later.

As Italians became more prosperous in America, these women who could make a meal out of very little in the old country found they had a great deal to work with in the new one, especially meat. On Sundays and holidays, after the pasta course, there might be a special tomato sauce with meatballs, sausage, pork spareribs, and *braciole* [brah-CHO-lay]—flank steak sprinkled with salt, pepper, Parmigiano or pecorino cheese, chopped garlic, parsley (and fresh basil in season), rolled and tied with string, browned in olive oil and garlic, then simmered in the sauce.

FOOD FABLE:

Spaghetti and Meatballs

Spaghetti and meatballs—pure and simple, authentic Italian food, unchanged from Italy, right? Wrong. Spaghetti and meatballs is an American invention. Italians do not eat the pasta course and the meat course together. It's pasta first, then meat. This is demonstrated in the movie *Big Night*, about two Italian brothers, Primo and Secondo (First and Second, the order of their birth and also the names of the food courses), who open a restaurant in America. One woman customer gets a plate of spaghetti and keeps asking where the meatballs are. One of the brothers tries to explain that it is the pasta course. Finally, exasperated, he bursts out, "Sometimes the spaghetti just likes to be by itself!"

Mothers taught daughters to cook without recipes, just by feel. They avoided cooking classes. The second generation, the children of the immigrants, who went to American schools and learned to read and write English, began to figure out the measurements and write recipes down. The Christmas and Easter traditions of making mountains of pastry, sweetened egg bread, sweet ricotta pies, or savory prosciutto pies to offer to relatives and friends continued. Until the end of the twentieth century, many of the best Italian foods were not commercially available; they were made in the home.

Italian immigrants, with one foot in Italy and one in America, celebrated holidays with the cuisines of both countries. On Thanksgiving, Italians ate an Italian holiday meal: soup, lasagne, meatballs and sausage, and Italian bread. Then they ate the full American holiday meal: turkey; cranberry sauce; stuffing made with Italian bread, Italian sausage, and giblets; mashed potatoes; and sweet potatoes. There would also usually be an Italian vegetable like broccoli with olive oil, lemon juice, and garlic. The salad of fresh greens came last, as it had in Italy, followed by fresh seasonal fruit like pomegranates, pears, and tangerines. Then came American pumpkin pie and apple pie, and finally, in the Italian tradition, a bowl filled with walnuts, almonds, dried figs, and maybe pomegranates to munch on. For Italians and Italian-Americans, Thanksgiving was a traditional Italian holiday meal with a traditional American holiday meal sandwiched in the middle.

For Italians, as for other immigrant groups, festivals reinforced the immigrants' sense of community in their new country, like the Feast of San Gennaro.

HOLIDAY HISTORY:

San Gennaro in New York's Little Italy, September 12–22

The *festa* of San Gennaro is the largest Italian-American celebration in the United States. San Gennaro, the patron saint of Naples, was decapitated on September 19, A.D. 305, for believing in Christ. The street fair began in New York's Little Italy in 1926. Now it takes place from September 12 to 22 every year (except 2001, when it was canceled because of September 11). More than a million people turn out to watch the religious processions as the statue of San Gennaro is paraded down Mulberry Street, and to buy Italian food—especially sausage and pepper submarine sandwiches—from more than 300 street vendors. In 2002, a cannoli-eating contest was added.

Jewish-American Cuisine

Many foods that Americans think of now as typically American, or typically New York, originated with the two-and-a-half million Jews who migrated from eastern Europe. Jews settled on New York's Lower East Side, the alphabet avenues—A, B, C, D—around First Avenue. The Jews, too, took advantage of the abundance of food in America to develop their own cuisine and cook every day the food that had been reserved for holidays or for the upper classes in Europe. Noodles and dumplings like kreplach and knishes could be filled with meat in addition to the traditional potatoes. Chicken soup, bagels, bialys, lox and cream cheese, sour cream, cheesecake, borscht, and gefilte fish could be eaten often. German Jewish delicatessen food, heavy on meat—kosher sausage, salami, pastrami—became the new tradition for all Jewish immigrants. Delicatessens called "appetizing" stores sprang up in the New York Jewish community. Many of these foods became mainstream American, like "New York" cheesecake, lox and bagels, and chicken soup.

Jewish women, responsible for food preparation, demanded high-quality food and boycotted and demonstrated when they didn't get it. American food companies advertised in the Yiddish press; some, like Heinz, even started producing kosher foods. These people who had known starvation in the old country could afford meat. Rabbis and the Yiddish press reminded Jews to observe the dietary laws, because temptations to eat outside the culture were everywhere. Some Jews were curious, especially those who worked closely with Italians. Jewish children were exposed to the foods of Americans and of other immigrants at school.[3]

Cookbooks written by Jewish women or by settlement houses—places the immigrants could go to learn how to settle into the United States—helped the Jewish community learn how to use the resources available to them. The first one was published in 1901 by Lizzie Black Kander. *The Settlement Cookbook: The Way to a Man's Heart* had Jewish and non-Jewish recipes. Unlike Italian women, Jewish women eager to improve their skills signed up for free cooking classes provided by local governments and charities.

Greek-American Cuisine

The Greeks, too, came from a life of extreme poverty in Greece, where they slept on sheepskins on the floor, subsisted on beans and a little olive oil, and had few possessions. They came looking for work on the railroad, the factories, the mines. Like the Italians, bread was sacred to the Greeks. If you dropped it on the floor, you picked it up and made the sign of the cross and ate it. You never threw it away. Women were the cooks, but men roasted lamb on a spit, taking turns squatting on the ground to turn it constantly.[4] Families observed the religious holidays, especially Easter:

> Fasting began in earnest for us two weeks before Easter. Neither fish, poultry, nor meat could be eaten because of the blood in them, in memory of Christ's shedding His blood. Nor was anything that came or was made from blooded animals allowed: milk, eggs, cheese, yogurt. Many households lived on beans, lentils, and greens, and some mothers would not use olive oil for taste because it was holy. Our food was bread, pickled peppers, squid with rice, spinach with rice, beans with rice, and, for something sweet, halvah. Between meals we munched on salted, dried chick-peas.[5]

The Easter fast was broken with roast lamb and Greek Easter bread, which, like the other European Easter breads, is sweet and rich with eggs and butter, and has colored hard-boiled eggs baked into the top. Other sweet breads can be braided, like Jewish challah.

Other traditional Greek dishes are *avgolemono*—chicken soup with rice and lemon, thickened with egg; *skordalia*—garlic, mashed potato, and almond sauce; *dolma*—stuffed grape leaves; moussaka—like lasagne, but with layers of eggplant instead of pasta in tomato sauce and béchamel; and Greek salad, which has tomatoes, cucumbers, onions, green bell peppers, black olives, and feta cheese, but not lettuce. Common vegetables are eggplant, spinach, artichokes, and potatoes. After lamb, fish and seafood are main courses, either sprinkled with olive oil, lemon, and oregano and baked, or fried in olive oil. Rice pilaf and noodles are the starches, along with potatoes. The signature herb is dried oregano.[6]

The Greek immigrant women, like the Italian women, had very long hair that they wore in a knot at the nape of the neck. After they arrived in America, many cut their hair short, even against the wishes of the men, in the American fashion—a symbol of assimilation and freedom.

The Greek men spent their evenings as they had in Greece—in coffeehouses, dressed in their good clothes, smoking, talking politics, playing cards, and reading the Greek-language newspaper or, if they were illiterate, listening as it was read. The coffeehouse was also bank and post office: "The men left their savings with the *kafejis* (coffeehouse owner) when they went away in search of work, and they had their mail sent in his care." But they did new things, too, in the coffeehouses in America—study Greek-American dictionaries, learn how American laws worked, and how to pass the test to become an American citizen. "Of the three early institutions—coffeehouses, Greek-language newspapers, and churches—the coffeehouses came first."[7]

Some of the best Greek-American food is still prepared in enormous quantities by women for church functions, like the Greek Orthodox Church of the Annunciation in Modesto, California, where the women make world-class pastries like baklava, *diples*—honey rolls; *kourambiedes*—powdered butter cookies; and *paximathia*—ancient Greek biscotti.

Polish-American Cuisine

Another group with a strong culinary tradition, Poles, settled in the Midwest, especially Chicago, Illinois, and Milwaukee, Wisconsin. Like the Italians, Jews, and Greeks, the Poles who came to the United States from 1880 to 1920 were poor people who brought a rich cuisine that they were finally able to afford and enjoy. Poland, located between Germany and Russia and at various times part of both, shows those influences in its cuisine. The most famous Polish dish is a stew called *bigos*, or hunter's stew.

Bigos—Polish Hunter's Stew

Heavy with freshly killed meat, *bigos* was traditionally served to royalty after the hunt. Today, it is made with all of the following meats in one stew: beef, lamb, pork, venison or hare, chicken or duck, ham, sausage, and veal. Onions, mushrooms, and sauerkraut provide tang, Madeira makes it mellow, roux is the thickener. It is made in large quantities, and is very time consuming, since each meat is first cooked separately.

Less complicated and more common Polish dishes are made from cabbage, cauliflower, Brussels sprouts, and root vegetables like celery root, parsley root, and carrots. Caraway and dill are the signature spice and herb. Dill pickles are used as seasoning. Mushrooms are often combined with sour cream in fillings or patties; fruit soups are made of berries or stone fruits like apricots and plums. There is even a beer soup, spiced with cinnamon, thickened with egg yolks, and boosted with rum. The French influence shows in pastry and quenelles, even in the dough for Russian-style *pierogi*, filled with meat or cabbage. The Polish version of *kulebiak* is less complicated, with fewer layers. Organ meats and brains appear in soup, pâté, and as filling for crêpes. The Ukrainian beet soup, borscht, becomes Polish *barszcz*. Polish-Americans still celebrate their cuisine and culture today.

Polish Fest

America's largest Polish festival is the Milwaukee, Wisconsin, Polish Fest. For three days in June, thousands of people feast on Polish, German, and other European specialties. *Feinschmeckers* (gourmets) will be glad that *wurstmachers* (sausage makers) have been busy turning out more than 70 varieties of sausage—bratwurst, beerwurst, knackwurst, yachtwurst, wieners, liver sausage, braunschweiger, salami, bologna, German-style mortadella with pistachios, and summer sausage—along with pastrami, ham, smoked pork butt and shoulder, and bacon. Beer is the beverage of choice, to quench the thirst from sausage and nonstop polka dancing. See www.polishfest.org for more details.

Progressives and the Purity Crusade

The Progressive era, approximately 1901 to 1920, like Reconstruction, was a time of intense, profound political and social change in America. It crossed party lines, from Republican presidents Theodore (Teddy) Roosevelt and William

Howard Taft to Democrat Woodrow Wilson. Three events occurred in the United States in 1903 that took industrialization to new heights and changed the world forever: (1) in Detroit, Henry Ford produced the first car with a gasoline combustion engine; (2) in Kitty Hawk, North Carolina, the Wright Brothers flew the first airplane; and (3) in Hollywood, *The Great Train Robbery*, at 18 minutes long, the first movie that told a full story, was released.

In cities, food distribution became mechanized. Horn & Hardart had a chain of automats. Putting coins in a slot opened the latch on a little door so customers could pick the food they wanted, visible behind glass in vertical cases.

Reacting to the changes brought about by industrialization, urbanization, and immigration, the Progressive reformers, middle-class men and women from all parts of the country, wanted to clean up democracy, the food supply, and human behavior. This is reflected in four Constitutional amendments: in 1913, the Sixteenth Amendment created an income tax, and the Seventeenth took election of senators away from state legislatures and put it in the hands of citizens directly. In 1919, the Eighteenth Amendment made alcohol illegal, and the Nineteenth gave the vote to the last group of Americans that still had no voice—women.

The Progressive buzzword was "pure"—pure food, pure living, pure morals. Progressives felt that American morals were eroded by unscrupulous businessmen cutting corners and polluting the food supply.

The Basement Bakers: Labor Unions and the *Lochner* Case

Contamination of the bread supply was of great concern to Progressives. In 1894, the *New York Press* printed an editorial about the horrendous working conditions of bakers. American food professions still operated like medieval guilds: journeymen bakers worked more than 100 hours a week, usually in extremely unhealthy conditions in primitive cellars. They worked at night, breathed in flour dust, and had a lower life expectancy than other workers: "most of them dying between the ages of forty and fifty."[8] In 1897, the state legislature unanimously passed the New York Bakeshop Law, which limited the number of hours a baker could work to 10 per day or 60 per week. It required "all buildings or rooms occupied as biscuit, bread, pie, or cake bakeries" to have ceilings at least eight feet high; floors of cement, tile, or wood (meaning not dirt); walls of plaster or wood (meaning not dirt); "air shafts, windows, or ventilating pipes"; drainage and plumbing; and a bathroom separate from the food prep and storage areas. It also stated, "No person shall sleep in a room occupied as a bake room," and barred all domestic animals except cats from bakeries, indicating a rodent problem.[9]

In 1905, the U.S. Supreme Court overturned the section of the Bakeshop law that limited working hours. The ruling in *Lochner v. New York* stated that the government had no right to interfere with business. For the next 32 years, until it was overturned in *West Coast Hotel Co. v. Parrish* in 1937, the *Lochner* decision blocked attempts to improve working conditions in any profession.

FOOD ADULTERATION, END OF NINETEENTH CENTURY[10]

FOOD	ADULTERATED WITH
Beer	glycerin, grape sugar, tannin, salicylic acid, bicarbonate of soda, valerian to "'stupefy' the drinker and prevent vomiting"
Brandy	sour wine
Bread	adulterated flour, ashes, copper sulfate
Butter	lard, vegetable fat, starch
Canned foods	copper, tin, chemical preservatives
Cayenne Pepper	red lead, iron oxide, rice flour, salt
Cheese	mercury salts
Cocoa/Chocolate	iron oxide, animal fats, dye
Coffee	chicory, acorns, shells, burnt sugar, beans, peas
Flour	sand, plaster of Paris, ground rice
Fruit Juices	salicylic acid, artificial flavoring
Ginger	cayenne pepper, mustard, turmeric
Lard	caustic lime, alum, starch, cottonseed oil, water
Milk	water, burnt sugar, yellow annatto and aniline dye, formaldehyde, borax, nitrates, dirt, manure, urine, bacteria
Mustard	lead chromate, lime sulfate, turmeric, flour
Pepper	mustard, flour, nut shells
Pickles	alum, apples, flour
Vinegar	sulfuric acid, hydrochloric acid, burnt sugar

Cigarettes were adulterated, too, with tree bark, opium, and "tobacco and cigar butts picked up from the streets."

But what the bakers couldn't get by law, they got by bargaining. In 1912, union bakers in New York City negotiated their work day down to 10 hours. The men in the food trades might not have been successful in their bid for better working conditions if it hadn't been for the almost 200 teenage girls who burned alive or jumped to their deaths in 1911 when a fire swept through the Triangle Company clothing factory where they worked. The girls had been locked in to keep union organizers out. As a result, New York State launched a four-year investigation that aimed to improve working conditions in all industries.

Bread was only one item that concerned Progressives. So-called medicines weren't any better. Over-the-counter syrups—called "soothing" or "quieting"—soothed and quieted because they contained cocaine and/or opium, and sometimes as much as 23 percent alcohol. Take four times a day.[11] The public outcry for change was deafening. Some states passed laws, but the problem was countrywide. Progressives wanted the federal government to step in. They found a champion in Harvey Washington Wiley, the chief of the Bureau of Chemistry in the U.S. Department of Agriculture (USDA), and his very public approach to the problem.

The Poison Squad

Dr. Harvey Washington Wiley was a one-man crusade against adulterated food. As the USDA was structured then, Wiley was prosecutor, judge, and jury in cases where food was suspected of being contaminated. This made him the darling of women's groups across the United States and the fly in the soup for food producers. In 1903, Wiley began experiments to prove that adulterated food and preservatives damaged health:

> The experiments involved setting up a kitchen and dining room in the basement of the chemistry building of the Department of Agriculture, recruiting 12 healthy young male employees to undergo a series of tests, and undertaking extensive laboratory measurements.[12]

Newspapers christened the young men "The Poison Squad." Wiley patterned his experiments on those done by U.S. Army Surgeon Walter Reed, who had just proved that a mosquito transmits yellow fever. Previously, it was thought that yellow fever could be caught by contact with contaminated utensils, soiled bedding, clothing, and other items that had been in contact with yellow fever patients. But Reed had put young men (army "volunteers") in rooms to live with these items, and they hadn't gotten sick. Wiley was going to do the same, to prove that preservatives were bad for health. He fed the young men food with formaldehyde, alum, borax, and sulphurous acid, among other things.

But these experiments were not very scientific. He had no norm, no control group—men who *weren't* eating preservatives—to compare them with. What Wiley really wanted was a ban on Coca-Cola. But Americans were more concerned about contaminated meat.

The Meatpacking Industry and *The Jungle*

In 1905, the same year as the *Lochner* case, a stomach-turning story about the meat processing industry appeared in a series of magazine articles. Upton Sinclair's book *The Jungle* was the caboose on the train of events that led to the passage of the Meat Inspection Act in 1905 and the Pure Food and Drug Act in

1906. Women's groups had been lobbying for years for laws to clean up the food supply. During the Spanish-American War in 1898, young men in the prime of life had died from eating bad food, canned meat they called "embalmed beef." The process that began with Napoleon and Appert to guarantee safe food for the army was used to pawn off rotten food that the corporate giants couldn't sell anywhere else. Americans were outraged. They were further outraged when Sinclair described meatpacking plants where animal blood flowed in rivers; food and humans were covered with flies; workers fell into vats and were processed as lard; rat feces, rat poison, and dead rats ended up in sausage along with rusty, filthy water from garbage cans; and chemicals made rotten, contaminated meat odorless and healthy looking. Sinclair wrote the book to show the terrible working conditions of the immigrants—his main characters are a Lithuanian family in Chicago—but readers panicked over what was being done to their meat. Sinclair said, "I aimed at the public's heart, but I hit its stomach." In an unprecedented display of power, the federal government stepped in and began to regulate the country's meat- and food-processing plants. The public called it "Dr. Wiley's Law."

United States vs. Coca-Cola—Caffeine on Trial

In 1911, Wiley finally succeeded in bringing Coca-Cola to trial on two grounds: misbranding, because it *didn't* contain cocaine, which the label implied (it had been removed by 1902), and fraud, because it *did* contain caffeine, which the label omitted. If it had contained cocaine, it would have been illegal. No problem—consumers sprinkled cocaine powder into their Coke. But Wiley's pet peeve was that Coca-Cola consumption was so widespread in the South that even children had the "Coca-Cola habit"—as in drug habit. He believed their parents had a right to know it contained caffeine; Southerners generally were portrayed as addicts. Wiley's moral crusade against Coca-Cola was so successful that the U.S. Army banned it in June 1907—but reinstated it in November. Soldiers had used Coca-Cola in two ways: mixed with whiskey in a highball, and as a hangover cure.

The trial, which began 50 years almost to the day after the Civil War started, reflected the North-South split that was still an open wound. Coke was a Southern company, Atlanta-based, on trial in a Southern city, Chattanooga, Tennessee. During the Civil War, Chattanooga was the rail center for the South—until Sherman cut it. Wiley had served with Sherman, and Wiley's boyhood home had been a stop on the Underground Railroad. The jurors stayed in a hotel owned by a Coca-Cola executive. The judge ruled that Coke was not misbranded, but Coke eventually reduced the caffeine content. It also changed its marketing to make sure that no child under 12 was shown drinking it. (That policy went out the window in 1986.) Wiley retired from the USDA a year after the trial began.[13]

Efficiency Experts and Domestic Science: Ellen Richards

In the beginning of the twentieth century, efficiency in business became almost a new religion. Scientists, engineers, and efficiency experts like Frederick Taylor, and Frank and Lillian Gilbreth, were the saviors of time—and therefore of money. They believed everything could be measured, and the measurements could be used to improve society. They used standardized tests, like the IQ (Intelligence Quotient) test, to measure human potential. Recently, scientists taught sign language to Koko, a gorilla. Then they gave Koko a standard IQ test. Normal human IQ is between 85 and 115. Koko scored 95 points, and would have scored higher but the test was culturally biased against gorillas. It was a food question that tripped Koko up: "Of the following five things, which two are good to eat? 1. a flower; 2. a block; 3. an apple; 4. a shoe; 5. ice cream." Koko picked flower and apple, but the correct answers were apple and ice cream. However, a case could be made for Koko's choices, especially now when edible flowers are not unusual in salads and soups.[14]

Ellen Richards, a graduate of Vassar, was the first woman to enroll at MIT, the Massachusetts Institute of Technology. In 1870, she had to enroll as a special student because no woman had been there before. She proceeded to use her knowledge about chemistry to improve the lives of the women who managed households, and to teach them to identify adulterated foods. She published many books about sanitation and nutrition, in addition to cooking. Her first book was *The Chemistry of Cooking and Cleaning*. She spearheaded a movement to teach women the cutting scientific edge of food preparation and housekeeping, because with good household help hard to find, many more women were having to do these

Science and efficiency were used to advertise this 1907 hand-cranked bread machine. Woman's Home Companion, *June 1907.*

things themselves with the help of the new electric appliances. Women formed organizations to spread this information, like the Cooking Teachers' League and the National Household Economic Association. Ellen Richards was president of the American Home Economics Association until 1910. By then, the new profession of domestic science was firmly established.[15]

Ellen Richards was just one of the many women who crusaded for change. Anna Jarvis, a West Virginia woman, was responsible for creating a new holiday to honor mothers in the United States.

1905 ad for McDougall Kitchen Cabinets. *From Munsey's Magazine.*

HOLIDAY HISTORY:

Mother's Day, the Second Sunday in May

Mother's Day is the most popular day to eat out in America.[16] It came about because Anna Jarvis vowed to fulfill her mother's wish to have one special day set aside to honor every mother "for the matchless service she renders to humanity in every field of life." Anna's mother, also named Anna Jarvis, spent her life in service to others. Before the Civil War, she initiated Mothers Day Work Clubs to try to remedy the high infant mortality rate caused not just by disease but also by poor nutrition and sanitation—seven of her 11 children died in childhood. During the Civil War, the Mothers clubs shifted to nursing injured soldiers, regardless of which side they were fighting for.

After Anna Jarvis died in the second week in May 1905, her daughter began a letter-writing campaign to state and federal legislators and other prominent people to make Mother's Day a national holiday. She handed out white carnations, her mother's favorite flower, now the traditional Mother's Day flower. In 1914, Congress passed a resolution making it a national holiday, and President Woodrow Wilson issued a proclamation. The Mother's Cookies Company began the same year and continues today. Songs celebrating mothers soon followed, as did advertising from florists and greeting card companies. Anna was horrified at the commercialization. The church where Anna Jarvis worshipped, Andrews Methodist Episcopal Church in Grafton, West Virginia, built in 1873, is now the International Mother's Day Shrine.

Brunch

Brunch, a traditional way to celebrate Mother's Day, is purely an American invention. The word *brunch*—a combination of breakfast and lunch—was not even in the Oxford English Dictionary until recently, although it was in American dictionaries. It originated during the Gilded Age in nineteenth-century America, when women began having "breakfast parties."

RECIPE:

Claire Criscuolo's Squash Blossom Pancakes

SERVES 6 (MAKES ABOUT 32 PANCAKES)

8 to 10 squash blossoms or 3 dozen whole flowers

2 cups unbleached all-purpose flour

2 teaspoons baking powder

3 eggs

1 cup water

¼ cup finely chopped fresh flat-leaf parsley or a mixture of parsley and fresh basil

Salt and pepper to taste

½ cup olive oil

1 Remove the stems from the squash blossoms. Rinse and coarsely chop if using 8 to 10.

2 Measure the flour and baking powder into a large bowl. Stir to combine.

3 In a separate bowl, whisk together the eggs and water.

4 Add the egg mixture to the flour mixture all at once, using a rubber spatula to scrape out the bowl. Stir to combine.

5 Add the chopped squash blossoms, parsley, basil, salt, and pepper to the batter. Stir well to combine. If using whole blossoms, dip them in the batter to coat thoroughly.

6 Line a cookie sheet with a double layer of paper towels and set it by the stove.

7 Heat 3 tablespoons of the olive oil in a large nonstick skillet over medium heat. Drop heaping teaspoons of the batter into the hot oil, fitting as many as you can without crowding. Cook for 2 to 3 minutes, or until the undersides are medium golden brown. Turn and cook the other sides for about 2 minutes, or until medium golden brown. Transfer to the towel-lined cookie sheet.

8 Continue frying the remaining batter, heating additional oil as needed. Serve hot, at room temperature, or chilled.

Adapted from Claire's Italian Feast *by Claire Criscuolo, chef-owner of Claire's Corner Copia, New Haven, CT (www.clairescornercopia.com).*

Brunch is an opportunity for chefs to go past the customary breakfast and lunch foods to quiche, seafood Newburg, frittatas, and even more elaborate creations. In Kennebunkport, Maine, chef Christian Gordon at Federal Jack's has revamped a Delmonico's invention from the 1920s, eggs Benedict—an English muffin topped with ham, poached eggs, and hollandaise sauce—into a croissant topped with poached eggs, lobster, and hollandaise. Mother's Day brunch at the elegant Raffles Hotel in Singapore has featured a salmon station, a carving station, and a "live station" with pan-fried foie gras with rhubarb grenadine compote and Old Port Wine jus.

Brunch is also an excuse to start drinking early in the day. A traditional brunch drink is the mimosa, made with champagne and orange juice. The Mimosa Royale adds Chambord. At the Kapalua Bay Hotel in Hawaii, mimosas came in Tropical—champagne, peach schnapps, and orange juice; Strawberry—champagne and strawberry juice; and Plumeria Terrace—apricot brandy and orange juice. Other traditional brunch drinks are the Bloody Mary—vodka and tomato juice; and its nonalcoholic cousin, the Virgin Mary.

Fathers demanded equal time, and Father's Day began to be celebrated unofficially. In 1966, President Lyndon B. Johnson made it official when he declared Father's Day, the third Sunday in June, a national holiday.

Guess Who's Not Coming to Dinner?

President Theodore Roosevelt didn't understand the public's reaction. He had simply invited a great American leader to dinner. Except that the leader was black—Booker T. Washington, the former slave and founder of the Tuskegee Institute in his native Alabama. Senator Benjamin Tillman of South Carolina said, "The action of President Roosevelt in entertaining that ni___r will necessitate our killing a thousand ni___rs in the South before they will learn their place again."[17] When Ida B. Wells, a black Southern journalist, wrote articles against lynching, she got out of the South one step ahead of the lynch mob herself. W. E. B. Du Bois [doo-BOYCE] became the first African-American to earn a Ph.D. from Harvard and was one of the founders of the NAACP (National Association for the Advancement of Colored People) in 1910.

Then Woodrow Wilson, the son of a minister, former president of Princeton University, and the Progressive governor of New Jersey, was elected president in 1912. His high moral ground appealed to many voters, but Wilson was from Virginia. He segregated the White House, installing separate drinking fountains, bathrooms, and cafeterias. The rest of the government followed suit. For the next 20 years, until President Franklin Delano Roosevelt and his wife Eleanor moved there in 1933, the only blacks in the White House were the kitchen help.

Escoffier and Ritz: Cuisine *Classique* and the Grand Hotels

Auguste Escoffier, like Carême, never wanted to be a cook. Like Carême, he wanted to be an artist, a sculptor. He was born on October 28, 1846, in the south of France. At the age of 13, he became an apprentice cook in a restaurant owned by his uncle in Nice, the Restaurant Français. His brilliance was noticed and when his apprenticeship was over, he was presented with the dream of every cook in the provinces: a job in Paris. He went but left in 1870 to be a chef in the Franco-Prussian War. Then he returned to Paris.

At a time when deluxe grand hotels were being built all over the world to cater to wealthy travelers, the meeting of Escoffier and Cesar Ritz changed the food and hotel industries forever. The Savoy Hotel in London was built with American hotels as a model and to rival them in attracting wealthy patrons. Americans invented the electric light and the telephone and expected these things when they traveled. Always looking for a short-cut, Americans also invented the shower, known then as the "shower-bath," and really liked indoor plumbing. Ritz understood this; his hotel reflected it.

Escoffier invented new dishes, many named after famous people, usually women. For example, *Pêches Melba* (Peach Melba) was named after the famous Australian opera singer Nelli Melba. Originally, the dish was too complicated and might not have caught on, but Escoffier replaced an elaborate ice swan and spun sugar sculpture with a raspberry sauce, and it became a hit. Other dishes were named after princesses and the actress Sarah Bernhardt, who became a personal friend of Escoffier; she sent him a heartfelt note of sympathy when his son was killed in World War I.

Escoffier Organizes the Kitchen: The Kitchen Brigade

Escoffier made the second great step to standardizing French cuisine. Just as Carême organized the sauces, Escoffier organized the kitchen. The man who was born in the nineteenth century and trained in a medieval system of apprenticeship brought twentieth-century methods of organization to the kitchen. The Kitchen Brigade was a military-style chain of command from the top to the bottom. The chef is in charge of food production. He or she plans menus, decides what food and supplies need to be ordered, determines costs of menu items, and plans work schedules. In some large establishments, the chef's duties are more administrative and creative, so the sous [soo] chef, which means "under" in French, supervises the kitchen and the staff. Each area of food production has a station chef or *chef de partie*. The *chefs de partie* sometimes have assistants, called *commis*. The *tournant*—swing cook—fills in as needed. The *aboyer* (literally, "barker") calls out the orders. Depending on the size of the establishment, the kitchen brigade can be expanded or condensed. This is the classical Kitchen Brigade.

CHEF				
SOUS CHEF (UNDER-CHEF)			**PÂTISSIER (PASTRY)**	
Chefs de Partie (Station Chefs)			Confiseur (candy)	Boulanger (baker)
Saucier (sauces)	Poissonier (fish)	Rôtisseur (roasting)	Glacier (cold desserts)	Decorateur (specialties)
Grillardin (grilling)	Friturier (frying)	Entremetier (hot appetizers)		
Potager (soup)	Legumier (vegetables)	Garde Manger (pantry—cold food)		
		Boucher (butcher)		

The organizational model of the Kitchen Brigade has been used for a brigade for the front of the house, supervised by the maître d'hôtel or the host who greets the customers. The wine steward controls the house wine stock, list, and table service. The head waiter supervises the waitstaff.[19]

Escoffier Organizes the Cooking: *Le guide culinaire*

"I wanted to create a useful tool rather than just a recipe book."[20]

In 1903, Escoffier published his massive book *Le guide culinaire—The Culinary Guide*. It does more than tell *how* to cook foods, it tells *why*, and in detail. With 5,000 recipes, it has stocks, roux, and sauces, the bases of French cuisine, first. Then garnishes, soups, hors d'oeuvres, eggs (202 recipes), fish, meat, poultry, and game. One separate chapter is about roasting; Escoffier had held the difficult position of *rôtisseur*, or roasting chef. This was a real juggling act. The chef had to constantly turn a giant spit over an open fire with different kinds and cuts of meat and poultry on it and make sure that they all cooked to exactly the right degree of tenderness at exactly the right time. He recommends which cuts of meat are best for formal presentation, like beef ribs (which need a trained carver); and which ones are suitable only for the family table, like pork shoulder. Like Hannah Glasse 150 years earlier, he advises tearing the ears of a hare to determine its age (the younger, the easier to tear) and warns about English puddings and meat pies because once they are assembled, nothing can be done to correct the seasoning or any mistakes. He instructs that poultry and game should be barded—partly covered with thin slices of salt pork or pork fat—to retain moistness while roasting. He puts the nail in the coffin of some older ways of presentation: "The Medieval way of decorating roast game birds with their feathers has fallen into disuse."[21]

Escoffier is also very concerned with safety. His section on deep frying recommends using beef kidney fat but not mutton fat, because it froths up and might overflow. (He also doesn't like the taste, unlike Middle Eastern cooks, who prize it.) It is also crucial to have equipment that is easy to use and not defective. Although he does not come out and say so, it is clear that Escoffier has witnessed some terrible kitchen accidents and is very protective of his kitchen staff.

"Where Ritz goes, we go!"—the Prince of Wales[22]

The Prince of Wales, the future King Edward VII of England, was an admirer of Escoffier and made the Savoy *the* place to go. He was also the undoing of Ritz. The coronation was going to be the most important event ever held at the Savoy. The driven, perfectionist Ritz planned

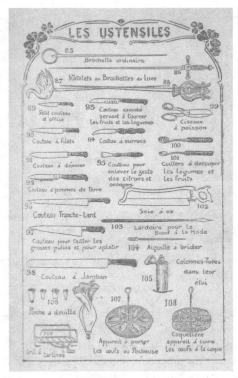

Cooking utensils at the time of Escoffier include elegant skewers, knives, larding needles, pastry bag and tips, and egg poachers. Cuisine de la Madelon, *ca. 1905.*

for months so that every detail would be flawless. Two days before the coronation, Edward developed appendicitis and the coronation was postponed. The effect on Ritz was nearly fatal. He didn't fall on his sword like Vatel, but he went into shock and had a complete emotional breakdown. He never worked in a hotel again. The man who brought electricity and private indoor plumbing to hotels, who elevated a chef to management for the first time, who always made sure that everything ran smoothly, who could fix anything, couldn't be fixed. He died 16 years later, alone in a sanitarium in Lausanne, Switzerland, not far from where he was born and where he had made his brilliant beginning.

"The Paris of the West" and the Escoffier of the West

San Francisco, California, wanted to become "the Paris of the West," and they had a chef who fancied himself the Escoffier of America—chef Victor Hirtzler

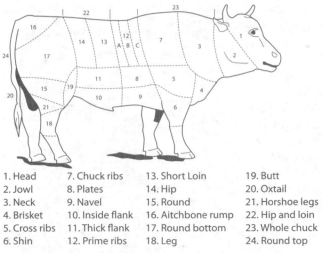

1. Head	7. Chuck ribs	13. Short Loin	19. Butt
2. Jowl	8. Plates	14. Hip	20. Oxtail
3. Neck	9. Navel	15. Round	21. Horshoe legs
4. Brisket	10. Inside flank	16. Aitchbone rump	22. Hip and loin
5. Cross ribs	11. Thick flank	17. Round bottom	23. Whole chuck
6. Shin	12. Prime ribs	18. Leg	24. Round top

Beef, American cuts, 1920. *From* The Epicurean *by Charles Ranhofer. Chicago: The Hotel Monthly Press, 1920.*

of the Hotel St. Francis. He was born in Strasbourg, apprenticed at 13, trained at the Grand Hotel in Paris, and served as food taster to Czar Nicholas II of Russia. On April 18, 1906 at 5:13 A.M., the St. Francis and the Fairmont hotels rode out the great San Francisco earthquake, 8.3 on the Richter scale, with some cracking and buckling. The kitchens were open, serving thousands of hotel guests and displaced San Franciscans and visitors, including opera singer Enrico Caruso and actor John Barrymore. But they couldn't withstand the fires that erupted all over the city when the gas lines ruptured and the water ran out. The two-year-old St. Francis Hotel was completely destroyed. So were warehouses full of wine; it was a severe blow to the Napa wine industry.[23]

Two years later, the new St. Francis opened on the same spot with Hirtzler still the chef. In 1910, he published his own book of recipes, *L'art culinaire*. In 1919, it was expanded and set in a day-by-day format: breakfast, lunch, and dinner 365 days of the year. Hirtzler was clearly competing with Escoffier. Like *Le guide culinaire*, *L'art culinaire* contained 202 recipes for eggs. It, too, had recipes for calf's brains, sweetbreads, foie gras, truffles, tongue, lobster, lamb kidneys, rooster combs, and oxtails. But Hirtzler also specified American foods: California oysters, California raisins, California artichokes, avocados (called "alligator pears"), Alaska black cod, reindeer. Most of Hirtzler's dishes reflect his classical French training, like puff pastry, sauce Périgord, hollandaise, and bearnaise. But Hirtzler was also feeding Americans, so "hamburger steak" and "homemade beef stew" are on the menu, along with gingerbread; cobbler; Southern corn pone; cactus fruit; cream of celery, Kalamazoo; hare soup, Uncle Sam; Maryland beaten biscuits; Philadelphia pepper pot; Kentucky sauce; Petaluma cream cheese; Boston baked beans; Boston brown bread pudding; and Boston and Manhattan

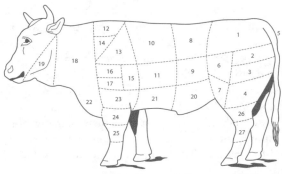

1. Culotte
2. Tranches petit os
3. Milleu du gite à la noix
4. Derrière
5. Tendre de tranches
6. Tranche grasse
7. Pièce ronde partie
8. Aloyau ave filet
9. Bavette d'Aloyau
10. Côtes couvertes
11. Plat de côtes
12. Surlonge partie
13. Derrière de paleron
14. Talon de Collier
15. Bande de Macreuse
16. Milleu de Macreuse
17. Boite a molele
18. Collier
19. Plat de joue
20. Flanchet
21. Milieu de poitrine
22. Cros bout
23. Queue de gîte
24. Gîte de devant
25. Cros du gîte
26. Gîte de derrière
27. Cros du gîte de derrière

Beef, French cuts (Boeuf coupe à la française) [original spellings]. *From* The Epicurean *by Charles Ranhofer. Chicago: The Hotel Monthly Press, 1920.*

clam chowders. Escoffier lists only one recipe using chocolate; Hirtzler, in the hometown of Ghirardelli, has many, including chocolate cream pie. Hirtzler also did something that Escoffier never did—he named dishes after himself. There are Celery Victor, Chicken Salad Victor, Crab Cocktail Victor, Victor Dressing, and Coupe Victor. Chef Victor Hirtzler lives on today in the Victor Restaurant at the top of the St. Francis Hotel.

However, a classically trained chef from Europe had to make accommodations to cooking in the United States. Even if dishes had the same name, *charcuterie* was very different. For example, there is no French equivalent of ribs, prime or otherwise, while America's bottom round is several different cuts in France.

Dining on the Railroad: The Harvey Girls Civilize the West

Anywhere that considered itself civilized served French food in the style of Escoffier, even remote regions of the American West. Disgusted with the poor food at railroad stops, British-born Fred Harvey established a string of first-quality restaurants that stretched from Chicago south and west to San Francisco, along the Atchison, Topeka, and Santa Fe Railroad. In the 30 minutes patrons had while their train was stopped, the Harvey houses served food that was per-haps French, or at least French sounding. For example, "Cream of Chicken Reine Margot, Consomme Careme, Jumbo Bull Frog Almandienne, and Medai-llon of Salmon Poche, Sauce Mousseline" [their spellings]. American foods included mashed potatoes, raspberry sundae, Manhattan clam chowder, roast homemade veal loaf, broiled live baby lobster (whole), and Saratoga chips (aka potato chips).[24] These dishes were served in Wichita, Kansas; Guthrie, Oklahoma; Amarillo, Texas; Trinidad, Colorado; Clovis, Deming, and Raton, New Mexico; and Needles, Mojave, and Merced, California.

At first, waiters served the food, but they got into fights—with their fists, with knives, with guns. They destroyed kitchen equipment and missed work. Harvey's solution: fire the men and hire women. The Harvey Girls were single white women "of good character" from 18 to 30 years old who answered ads in newspapers in the East and Midwest. Some came because there were many more men than women in the West, but the six-, nine-, or 12-month contract each woman signed said she could not get married during that time without losing her job, her pay, and her railroad pass.

A large staff was necessary to get food on the tables so quickly in the à la carte lunchroom and a dining room, and the waitresses were the majority: "in order of importance, a manager, a chef, a head waitress, between 15 and 30 Harvey Girls, a baker, a butcher, several assistant cooks and pantry girls, a housemaid, and busboys."[25] Harvey chefs were mostly European. The front of the house—the Harvey Girl waitresses—were all white. Their professional waitress uniform was long and black—dress to the floor, sleeves to the wrist, high collar. Over this was an immaculate white apron. They worked 10 hours a day, six or seven days a week. The kitchen workers reflected the population of the Southwest—black, Hispanic, and Indian.

The railroad subsidized the restaurants, which they allowed to operate at a loss, because "Fred Harvey Meals All the Way" was a guarantee of good food that sold train tickets. Harvey was a perfectionist who showed up in his restaurant kitchens unannounced and "looked the place over as if he suspected a murder had been committed and the search was for clues."[26] He fired people if he didn't like their attitude or if they tried to cut corners by squeezing orange juice ahead of time instead of when it was ordered. Other railroads also relied on the dining car to bring in customers. They even ran their own bakeries and used local produce.

Mobile Dining de Luxe—the Titanic

The stringent fine dining standards of the railroads were also applied to ships. Crossing the Atlantic Ocean by luxury liner was done by a small elite; only 205,000 passengers crossed in 1902.[27] An acronym to describe the way the wealthy made the crossing became a synonym for luxury: "posh." It stood for "Port Out, Starboard Home," which ensured that the cabin would always be facing the south and the sun.

The 883-foot-long *Titanic*, 46,328 supposedly unsinkable tons with 11 decks, struck an iceberg in the North Atlantic on April 14, 1912, at 11:40 PM and sank less than three hours later, at 2:20 AM on April 15, 1912. Its lounge was patterned after the Palace of Versailles; it had a marble drinking fountain, Turkish baths, a gymnasium, and was the first ocean liner to have a swimming pool and squash courts. Among its passengers were 10 millionaires, people with names like Astor, Guggenheim, Widener, and Rothschild. For the dinners that were served to the 322 first-class passengers in their own dining room, the Goldsmiths and Silversmiths Company of Regent Street in London had provided 10,000 pieces of plate.[28]

It was a British ship, so dinner was announced by buglers playing "The Roast Beef of Old England."[29] The last meal served was on Sunday night, April 14, 1912, and it was supposedly the most lavish served on the ship: oysters, salmon, filet mignon, roast duckling, foie gras, squab, asparagus, chocolate and vanilla éclairs, and French ice cream for the finale.[30] It took a staff of about 60 chefs and 40 assistants (mostly French), and 50 waiters (mostly Italian) to get the 2,000 breakfasts and dinners prepared and served.[31]

That last night, Sunday dinner had been served and the kitchens were closing down. The shipbuilder popped in to thank the baker for a special bread. Almost everyone on the ship retired for the night, looking forward to being in New York in 48 hours. But the ship sideswiped an iceberg that slit a 300-foot gash in its side. For the first time, radio operators used the new code—SOS for "Save Our Ship"—at sea. The ship *Carpathia* picked up the last of the 711 survivors by 8:00 A.M. This was fortunate, because no one had bothered to put food or water or compasses on the lifeboats of the unsinkable ship. One thousand, four hundred and ninety people drowned on the *Titanic*. The highest proportion of passengers saved was from first class, the lowest, from third class. The staff couldn't even think about getting on a lifeboat until all the passengers were on. As far as historians can determine, all of the kitchen staff died except one. A 17-year-old cook was saved by accident. He was helping a woman carry a child and was swept overboard when the ship went under. He was picked up by a lifeboat.[32] Almost twice as many kitchen staff died on the *Titanic* as at Windows on the World on September 11, 2001. The press busied themselves with obituaries of the rich and famous on the *Titanic*, but only one person tracked down the names of as many of the kitchen staff as possible and printed obituaries of them—Escoffier.

Escoffier at Sea: Bigger than the Titanic

Germany had been competing with England ever since the Industrial Revolution began in the 1750s in England. As the British expanded into Africa and Asia, so did the Germans. Now, the Kaiser was increasing the German navy in a direct threat to British supremacy on the seas. Nationalism was rising in Germany, but in the kitchen the Kaiser wanted only French food and French cooks. On May 25, 1912, the Hamburg-American liner *Imperator*, 52,000 tons, 900 feet long, was launched. It was Germany's answer to the *Titanic*, bigger than the *Titanic*, and had learned a lesson from the *Titanic*, which had sunk a month earlier: the *Imperator* carried extra lifeboats. The *Imperator* had a swimming pool, marble bathtubs, and other fittings that made her top heavy so that she rolled badly.[33] It was Escoffier's first trip across the Atlantic, on his way to open the kitchen at the Hotel Pierre in New York City. Tensions were high in Europe; the smell of war was in the air. After an imperial banquet for more than 100 people, Escoffier talked to the Kaiser, hoping to influence him about keeping peace in Europe. Escoffier had been through one war with Germany and did not want another one.

World War I and the Russian Revolution

Two years after Escoffier and the Kaiser spoke, World War I began. On June 28, 1914, in Sarajevo, the capital of Bosnia, Archduke Ferdinand, heir to the Austro-Hungarian Empire, and his wife were shot and killed.

The Balkans: Powder Keg of Europe

Bosnia was one of several independent new nations on the Balkan Peninsula in southeastern Europe that had broken away from the weakening Ottoman Empire. Others were Greece, Romania, Bulgaria, and Serbia. The area was a powder keg because of longstanding religious and ethnic hatreds. It was where Roman Catholic Europe met Orthodox Greeks and Asian Muslims. Caucasians, Slavs, and Turks bumped borders as each nation sought to expand. (This area exploded again in 1991 with "ethnic cleansing." United Nations troops restored a tense order.) The Russian and the Austro-Hungarian Empire giants also thought the weak new Balkan countries would be easy pickings to increase their own territories.

As a result of the archduke's assassination, Germany, the Austro-Hungarian Empire, and Italy went to war against France, England, and Russia. Later, Italy changed sides, Russia left the war, and the United States joined France and England. The ability of technology to inflict wounds was much more advanced than medicine's ability to heal them at that time. The new technologies were airplanes, chemical gases, motorized tanks, and machine guns. The defense against these was primitive: dig a trench in the mud and hide. The casualties were astronomical: approximately one million men per battle at Verdun and the River Somme in northeastern France.

Armenian Cuisine

The fighting in World War I extended east to the Muslim Ottoman Empire, which had a large population of Armenian Christians who wanted their own country. Armenian cuisine is a mixture of Turkish, Greek, Syrian, Persian, and Arabic cuisine. Like the cultures to the east of it, Armenian cuisine has flat bread, rice pilaf, and barley; like the cultures to the west, it has noodles. Like the cuisine of its neighbor to the west, Bulgaria, yogurt is a staple food, used in everything from hot and cold soups to dips, cheeses, stews, pastries, beverages, salads, and cakes. Chickpeas and lentils are widely used. Eggplant appears fried, stuffed, baked, mashed, in hot and cold casseroles, in salad, and with and without meat, usually lamb, like the layered Greek casserole, moussaka; and the Persian *imam bayaldi*, which the Armenians call *iman bayeldi*. Okra finds many uses here, along with zucchini, cauliflower, spinach, cabbage, and *dolma*—stuffed vegetables, especially grape leaves. An Armenian specialty is bulghur—cracked wheat—used in tabbouleh salad and pilaf. Desserts are made of *kadayif* (the Persian *kataif*), a shredded wheat dough, and phyllo, and are drenched in sugar syrup, like *paklava* (Greek baklava). They use the fruits and nuts of the eastern Mediterranean—raisins, dates, apricots, walnuts, almonds. Sesame is used in oil and paste form—*taheen*, or *tahini* in Lebanon and Syria, to the south.

In 1915, during World War I, the Armenians fought for their independence against the Turks. More than 600,000 Armenians died. Many of the survivors migrated to the United States, to the Central Valley of California and the city of Fresno, where they grew grapes and went into the dried fruit business, especially raisins. Some famous Armenian-Americans are the writer William Saroyan and actress-singer Cher (Cherilyn Sarkisian).

The United States: From Hot Dog to "Liberty Dog"

The United States joined World War I in 1917, after Germany resumed unrestricted submarine warfare and sank American merchant ships in the Atlantic. The war was not popular; many felt that the United States had no business in a European war. The draft was difficult to enforce: approximately a quarter of a million men simply didn't show up, and before Social Security numbers came into use in 1935 there was no way to track them. World War I was also a problem for many American immigrant groups. The Irish hated the British, America's ally; the Jews objected to another ally, Russia, from which they had

Just before the United States entered WWI, advertisers used patriotism and defense as marketing tools. *1916 poster.*

fled. America also had a large population of German-speaking immigrants and citizens of German descent, but Germany was the enemy. Americans turned against everything German—in principle. They wouldn't eat hot dogs and sauerkraut, which were German, but they would eat "liberty dogs" and "liberty cabbage," which were 100 percent American. Americans of German descent stopped speaking German at home, so they wouldn't slip up and speak it on the street, where it was dangerous. German language newspapers went out of business, towns named Germantown or Berlin changed their names. German-American festivals ceased. Italy and Italian immigrants, too, were the enemy until Italy switched sides midway through the war. Then Italian food became "spaghetti, food of the ally."[34]

Men and women volunteered for the war effort. Some, like the writer Ernest Hemingway, went to Europe and drove ambulances. On the home front, Americans grew victory gardens to feed themselves and to add to the national food supply. They substituted peanut flour for wheat flour. Daylight saving time was instituted to help the farmers.

The Russian Revolution—"Bread and Peace"

In 1917, the year the United States entered the war, Russia left. It had already lost more than seven million men and was facing a revolution. Food played a huge part in the Russian Revolution in 1917. Peasant farmers made up the majority of the army, so when they got drafted, crops didn't get planted or harvested. There were food shortages in the country and food riots in the city. The cry of the communist revolutionaries was "Bread and Peace." Finally, even the czar's close advisers begged, pleaded, then demanded that he give up the throne. He did, assuming that one of the other countries in the world would welcome the royal family. But he was an absolute monarch, cruel and oppressive. That form of government had not existed in England and France since the seventeenth and eighteenth centuries, respectively, and they wanted nothing to do with it. The United States had multiple reasons for not sheltering the czar. As the first democracy, it was opposed to him philosophically. As the home of millions of immigrants, many of them Jews who had just fled the czar's oppressive rule and were living in densely packed cities, the United States couldn't risk the civil disturbances the czar's presence would certainly cause. The czar, czarina, their four daughters, and their one son were executed by the communists.

Russian Cuisine

Russia is an enormous country that spans two continents. Its west, with large cities like Moscow and St. Petersburg, is in Europe. Eastern Russia is in Asia and borders Mongolia and China. In southern Russia, the province of Georgia borders Turkey. So Russian cuisine is many cuisines with many influences. On the eve of World War I, Russian cuisine and culture were at the top of European life—for the upper classes. The lower classes were poor and starving.

In the 200 years since Peter the Great had decided to Westernize his country, Russia had become a power in European politics and cuisine. The potato had become a staple. So was black bread made from dark rye and coffee. In the cold Russian climate, root vegetables like turnips and beets were staples, too, in borscht—beet soup with a sour cream enrichment. Dill and caraway were the common herb and spice. From its Asian side, Russia gets *pel'meni*—dumplings like ravioli or wontons made of flour-and-egg noodle dough filled with fish, mushrooms, or meat (originally, horsemeat). Preserving foods was not a problem in Siberia, where even the ground was frozen a great deal of the year. A wide variety of foods in Russia were also preserved by pickling—cucumbers, mushrooms, apples, lemons, and cabbage, in sauerkraut. Rustic Russian standards are *shchi*—cabbage soup; *kasha*—buckwheat groats; and *kvass*—a fermented drink that can be made from leftover black bread, fruits, or vegetables.

Pierogi (*pirozhki* for the smaller version) are turnovers in a flaky pastry, with sour cream added, filled with ground meat, rice, eggs, mushrooms, or cheese. These versatile pies can be either street food or served at a banquet. A more elaborate upper-class filled pastry is *koulibiac*, the fish *en croûte* that Carême brought back to Paris with him in the early nineteenth century. Other pre-Revolution Russian classics are Beef Stroganoff, beef in a sour cream sauce; sturgeon soup with champagne; and Salad Olivier, originally chicken and potatoes with mayonnaise. Another luxurious Russian dish is named after the capital of Ukraine. According to Russian food historian Darra Goldstein, Chicken Kiev is "a symbol of Russian *haute cuisine*."[35] Kiev-born Russian cookbook author Anne Volokh dates it to "the early 1900s."[36]

....

INGREDIENTS:

Chicken Kiev

Chicken Kiev has only a few main ingredients: chicken breast filets pounded and stuffed with herbed butter, lemon juice, and French mustard, then rolled, dipped in flour, beaten egg, and bread crumbs, and deep fried in oil. When the diner cuts into the chicken, the butter bursts out. In some restaurants, the server makes the first cut because it can be messy.

....

Appetizers are called *zakuski*, and can include pickled spiced cherries, cucumbers or mushrooms in sour cream, beet salad, and stuffed cabbage. The most famous *zakuski* are the trio of small buckwheat crêpes called *blini*, the caviar placed on them with a small silver spoon, and vodka to wash it all down. *Blini* were also traditional during Butterweek, the Russian equivalent of Mardi Gras, when they were buttered and topped with sour cream. Caviar is the roe, or eggs, of the sturgeon fish, found in the Caspian Sea. It comes in several grades—osetra, sevruga, and beluga, the largest. The czars ate special golden caviar from the sterlet fish.[37] Vodka was "infused with anywhere from 3 to 40 flavors—sage, heather honey, angelica root, ginger root, anise, juniper berries, Crimean apple and pear leaves, mint, young shoots of mountain ash, nutmeg and nutmeg blooms, vanilla, cinnamon, cardamom, cloves."[38]

Pre-Revolutionary Russians of all classes were great tea drinkers at any time of day. The lower classes sucked their tea through a sugar cube held between the teeth. The upper classes had evening teas that were elaborate and competitive: six kinds of cake, each from a different bakery.[39] The hostess poured tea "into porcelain cups for the ladies and glasses for the men. The glasses were inserted into *podstakanniki*, metal or filigreed silver holders."[40] The centerpiece was the samovar.

The Fabergé Russian Royal Easter Eggs

The Russian royal family had an Easter tradition based on the peasant tradition of painting eggs. Some of the more elaborately decorated eggs come from the Russian Christian Church in eastern Europe, especially Ukraine. *Krashanky* are hard-boiled eggs dyed one solid color, meant to be eaten. *Pysanky*, purely decorative, are made from raw eggs dyed many times in multicolored elaborate patterns. Each color has a symbolic meaning: yellow means a successful harvest; green represents the rebirth of spring; black is the dark before the dawn, when the souls of the dead travel, especially between the first and third crow of the rooster. The dyes were made from plants: red from beets; orange from onion skins; blue from red cabbage leaves; brown from nutshells. Now, everything from tiny quail eggs to enormous ostrich eggs is decorated.

Every year the Russian royal family exchanged Easter eggs, but they weren't folk art. They were made by Fabergé, the royal jeweler, out of gold, silver, platinum, and crystal studded with diamonds, rubies, pearls, emeralds, and sapphires. Each egg had a surprise inside, often mechanical. For example, a platinum egg 10 ¼ inches high opened up to reveal miniature gold railroad cars that hooked together and ran when wound up with a key. A tiny golden replica of the royal yacht floats in a crystal sea; the whole thing is 6 inches high. A miniature version of the coach in which the czar and czarina rode to their coronation in 1896 comes out of a golden and jeweled egg, 3¹¹⁄₁₆ inches long. The last egg was "modest," a red cross on a white background, because it was just beginning to dawn on the royal family that it might be in poor taste to flaunt their wealth in the face of famine and war. Too late.

The Easter egg for 1911 was a miniature orange tree, 11¾ inches high, with a gold trunk, studded with "oranges" and "orange blossoms" made of precious stones. A secret "orange" made a little bird pop up out of the tree and sing. In 2000, when an exhibit of Fabergé eggs was on display at the Riverfront Arts Center in Wilmington, Delaware, Executive Pastry Chef of the Hotel du Pont, Michele B. Mitchell (a 1988 graduate of the Johnson & Wales Pastry Arts Program) and her staff re-created the Orange Tree Egg out of sugar work, chocolate, fondant, gold leaf, and silver dust. It was three and one-half feet tall and took about 100 hours to create. They also made 45 miniature Orange Trees as room favors. The top half of the small tree dome came off to reveal truffles inside, as a turn-down service for the VIPs at the gala opening of the exhibit, which was held at the hotel.

The Cities: People Eat Communally

The Russian Revolution com-pletely changed the relation-ship of the citizen to the state and to the food production and distribution system. Lenin, the leader of the new communist Bolshevik government, pulled

Chocolate Fabergé egg sculpture. *Created by Michele Mitchell, Executive Pastry Chef of the Hotel du Pont, Wilmington, Delaware.*

Russia—called the Union of Soviet Socialist Republics, or USSR—out of World War I. After a further four years of civil war, from 1917 to 1921, there was no more private ownership of property; it all belonged to the state, communally. Gone, too, were the titles. No more princes or princesses, dukes or duchesses. As in the French Revolution, they were all either dead or fled. Everyone was equal in the new classless society where people addressed each other as "comrade." This meant drastic changes in all levels of society and in the food people ate, where and when they ate it, and how they grew it.

In the cities, the government took over the restaurants, hotels, and mansions that had been used by the upper classes and turned them into communal dining places where all workers had to eat. [41] Then they organized food preparation and distribution throughout the entire country as if it were one enormous kitchen. Communal dining was also intended to free women from their traditional kitchen duties so they could work in factories or on farms. Shortages of skilled kitchen staff resulted in small portions of food that tasted terrible, prepared in unsanitary conditions, and led to epidemics and strikes. Meals were "tiny plates of barley gruel" or "soup with herring head or rotten sour cabbage." Moldy grains, bread the consistency of clay, and "coffee" made from acorns rounded out the meal.[42]

People still wanted the food they were used to, and some of them had the money to pay for it. Secret restaurants sprang up. With the right connections and the right password, you might be lucky enough to find yourself in a place with tablecloths and napkins, eating roast meat and vegetables and something made with flour and sugar.[43] The country desperately needed to produce more food; the daily bread ration had dropped from one pound per person in 1917 to 2 ounces in 1919.

The Country: People Farm Communally

After Lenin died in 1924, St. Petersburg, the city founded by Peter the Great in 1703, was renamed in Lenin's honor: Leningrad. Stalin took over the USSR, with a five-year plan for agriculture and industry. His goal was to make the country an industrial giant equal to the United States. To do this, he needed equipment and engineers. International Harvester, the American company that made threshing machines, opened a factory in the USSR. To buy the heavy industrial equipment the USSR needed, they sold the only thing they had: grain. They sold millions of tons of grain; millions of Russian people starved. Large farms were split up and people were forced to farm together. Without the incentive of keeping food for themselves or selling it at a price they wanted, food production dropped. Many of the successes that Stalin claimed in food and industrial production were only numbers on paper that bore no resemblance to reality.

The Punitive Treaty of Versailles and the Seeds of World War II

World War I ended in 1918, at the eleventh hour on the eleventh day of the eleventh month: 11:00 A.M., November 11. The day and time were chosen purposely so that no one would ever forget the horror of the War to End All Wars. There certainly would never be another war. Who would be insane enough to go through anything like that again?

In 1919, the victors—England, France, the United States, Italy, and Japan—got together at the Palace of Versailles to draw up a peace treaty and decide what to do with Germany. The result was the Treaty of Versailles. The adjective that has always been used to describe the treaty is "punitive"—punishing. Germany had to publicly admit that it started the war; it had to repay England and France for the war; its colonies in Asia were given to Japan; its colonies in Africa were divided between England and France; its western border, the province of Alsace-Lorraine, taken in the Franco-Prussian War in 1870, was returned to France; its eastern border, a strip of land known as the Danzig Corridor, became part of the newly created country of Poland. These conditions made economic recovery nearly impossible for the Germans. Money became worthless. One American dollar was worth more than 800 million German marks. Food prices skyrocketed—a loaf of bread cost a shopping cart full of money. The United States objected to the treaty, sure that these harsh surrender terms would only enrage the German people and make them want revenge.

The map of Europe was literally redrawn because of World War I. The Austro-Hungarian Empire was broken into the separate countries of Austria, Hungary, and Czechoslovakia. It also ceded territory to Italy, Romania, and Bulgaria. Bosnia, Serbia, and Albania were combined to create Yugoslavia. Western Russia became the new Finland, part of Poland, and the smaller countries of Estonia, Latvia, and Lithuania.

The map of Asia was changed, too. The Ottoman Empire had fallen. Earlier, it had lost its territory in the Balkans in southeastern Europe. Now, it had also lost territory in southwestern Asia. New countries were created: Syria, Iraq, Jordan, and Saudi Arabia, named after the powerful Saud family. Saudi Arabia was an Islamic state, very conservative, where alcohol was and still is illegal. The core of the Ottoman Empire, the city of Istanbul in Europe and the Anatolian plain in Asia, became Turkey, an independent country in 1923, still part European and part Asian: its legal system was separate from its religion.

In eastern Asia, Japan was making its bid to become an empire after the fall of the Chinese empire in 1911. Working as a dishwasher in the kitchen at Ritz's Savoy Hotel in London was a young man from French Indochina who wanted freedom for his country. He tried to see America's President Wilson to show him the document he had drafted for his country patterned after the American Declaration of Independence, but Wilson wouldn't see him. More than 40 years later, the United States was forced to deal with Ho Chi Minh in his own country—Vietnam.

After four years of horror, the world was glad the war was finally over. It was tired of death and economizing. It was time to party.

The Roaring Twenties in the United States

A major change occurred in the global economy as a result of World War I. The United States emerged from the war a creditor nation. This meant that for the first time, other countries owed the United States money. The war was expensive; European countries had borrowed money from the United States to pay for it. As a result, the center of world banking shifted to New York City, where it remains today, even though the United States is now a debtor nation—it owes money to other countries.

American soldiers returning home brought the more easygoing morality they had been exposed to in Europe with them. Young people who had seen too much death developed a hedonistic, carpe diem [CAR-pay DEE-um] attitude— "seize the day" or "eat, drink, and be merry"—because tomorrow you might die. But some found their jobs gone and their neighborhoods changed because of African-Americans who had migrated north to work in factories during the war. Angry whites rampaged through black neighborhoods, lynching in Chicago and

East St. Louis; they burned the entire African-American section of Tulsa, Oklahoma, to the ground.

1920 was a watershed year in American history. For the first time, more Americans lived in cities (figured at 8,000 people) than in the country. It was the year of the first transcontinental airplane flight—no passengers, just mail; and of the first international black congress, at which African-Americans issued their own declaration of rights. Americans heard the first radio broadcast. Six years later, they heard the first radio advertising jingle; it was for a new breakfast cereal, Wheaties.[44] Two Constitutional amendments went into effect. The eighteenth outlawed alcohol. The nineteenth granted women the right to vote.

"[T]he manufacture, sale, or transportation of intoxicating liquors . . . is hereby prohibited."

On January 17, 1920, the Eighteenth Amendment to the U.S. Constitution shut down the seventh largest industry in the country. It didn't happen overnight. The Temperance Movement began in the early nineteenth century as religious opposition to rum drinking. That is why coffee replaced rum as the standard beverage of the United States Army in 1832. The Temperance Movement gained momentum in the middle of the nineteenth century when beer-drinking German and whiskey-drinking Irish immigrants began arriving in large numbers. At the end of the nineteenth century came wine-drinking Italians and Hungarians, vodka-drinking Poles and Russians, beer-drinking Czechs and Lithuanians.

American women countered with the Women's Christian Temperance Union (WCTU), and took to picketing in front of bars and sometimes smashing them with hatchets. Progressive reformers thought that alcohol caused a wide

"Liquid profits." During Prohibition, soft drink consumption rose with the aid of refrigeration.

variety of social ills. Workers who spent the weekend binge drinking missed work on Monday, or showed up hungover and had accidents—"Blue Monday." Factory workers who got paid in cash on Friday went to the bars across the street and drank and gambled their pay away so their families had no money for food. Young sons who went into bars looking for their fathers would become juvenile delinquents. Daughters would turn to prostitution to put food on the table. And a drunk voter could be bought. Progressives thought that prohibiting alcohol would cure all these problems.

The alcohol industry didn't mount a serious campaign against the prohibition movement because beer and wine producers couldn't believe it would affect them. To European immigrants, unfamiliar with the tradition of Puritanism in the United States, beer and wine were like water, or were consumed instead of it. They thought that at the worst, only hard liquor—distilled spirits—would be prohibited, which would mean more business for them. But *all* alcohol over one-half of 1 percent was prohibited.

There was a loophole: suddenly, people were getting prescriptions for alcohol "for medicinal purposes." Hard-core alcoholics sneaked into churches and synagogues to steal the sacramental wine, or drank the alcohol that fueled small appliances like curling irons.

Wine production plummeted from 55 million gallons in 1919 to four million gallons in 1925. However, grape production, which dropped right after the Eighteenth Amendment was passed, rose again. Clever vintners marketed grape juice and "bricks" of dried grapes with labels warning consumers UNDER NO CIRCUMSTANCES to add water and yeast or the grapes would ferment and turn into wine. Some estimates are that wine consumption doubled by the end of the decade.[45]

Prohibition destroyed the California wine industry, which had come a very long way since 1880, when British author Robert Louis Stevenson *(Treasure Island, Kidnapped, Dr. Jekyll and Mr. Hyde)* spent his honeymoon near Mount St. Helena and wrote with great foresight:

> Wine in California is still in the experimental stage. . . . The beginning of vine-planting is like the beginning of mining for precious metals: the winegrower also "prospects." One corner of land after another is tried with one kind of grape after another. This is a failure; that is better, a third best. . . . The smack of Californian earth shall linger on the palate of your grandson.[46]

Prohibition was also a one-two knock-out punch for French restaurants. It wasn't just the wine consumed with the meal—it was the alcohol-based marinades and sauces. You can't have coq au vin without the *vin* or *boeuf bourguignon* without the burgundy. No more Cherries Jubilee or Crêpes Suzette if there's no alcohol to flambé. White-gloved waiters who were skilled in these spectacular tableside presentations were also out of work.

Crime: The Beer Wars and Al Capone

Prohibition, which had begun with the intention of decreasing crime, increased it. Law-abiding Americans who saw nothing wrong with having a drink became casual lawbreakers. When drinking was legal, bars had to close at night. When it became illegal, bars could stay open around the clock. People went to the new underground drinking places, called "speakeasies" because they knocked on the door and whispered the password. In the countryside in cold parts of the country, water tanks were filled with apple cider. The juice fermented during the day and the water froze at night. Skimming the ice off every morning reduced it to apple jack—homemade apple brandy. Violent crime increased, too, as the gangs that smuggled liquor in trucks from Canada or by ship along the coasts fought each other using World War I surplus Thompson submachine guns—Tommy guns. And since they were taking a risk, it was much more profitable to sell distilled spirits with a higher alcohol content than bulky beer.

Crime was especially violent in Chicago, where gangsters killed each other for control of breweries, which continued to operate by bribing officials. Dozens of innocent bystanders got caught in the crossfire of drive-by shootings. On Valentine's Day, February 14, 1929, Al Capone's gang machine-gunned seven rival gang members in a garage on Clark Street. This was too much. The government sent in federal agents, who became known as "The Untouchables," to get Capone. They realized that it would be impossible to get him on criminal charges because he would just kill anyone who testified against him, so they convicted him of not paying $215,000 in income taxes. He was sent to the federal prison in Atlanta, Georgia, until 1934, when he was shipped to the new super prison on an island in San Francisco Bay—Alcatraz.

The architects of Alcatraz thought of everything, including the food. They decided that because so many prison riots started because of poor food, the food in Alcatraz would be superior to that of any other prison in the United States. This advice was forgotten later at the maximum security prison in upstate New York at Attica, where one of the causes of the worst prison riot up until that time on September 5, 1971, was food. The prison administration bought pork, an inexpensive meat. However, a large percentage of the prison population was African-American Muslims, who couldn't eat it.[47]

Ice Cream, You Scream—the Good Humor Man Meets the Mob

With alcohol technically off limits during Prohibition, Americans went crazy for candy and ice cream. Hotels and restaurants turned bars that had sold cocktails into soda fountains. The 1920s saw the birth of Milky Way, Butterfinger, Oh Henry, and Mounds bars. These followed the Hershey bar, which had been created by Milton Snavely Hershey, the son of German immigrants, in Pennsylvania. In Youngstown, Ohio, Harry Burt invented a hard candy on a stick, which he called the Jolly Boy Sucker. What he really wanted to do was put a chocolate coating on an ice cream bar. Problem: the ice cream melted or the coating clotted. He finally got it to work, but holding it was messy. The solution: put a stick in it, like his other candy.

Burt called his confection "Good Humor" because he said that it put him in a good humor to eat it. He got a patent, then he got an old truck, painted it white, put on a white uniform, attached bells from an old sleigh, and rang them as he drove slowly down the street, attracting children. As he became successful, gangsters wanted a percentage of the profits. When he refused, they blew up his trucks. The Good Humor Man and

Commercial hand-cranked ice cream freezers. *The Western Druggist, April 1894.*

his white Ford truck were a standard fixture in the 1950s and 1960s as Americans moved to the suburbs, one of the last foods still delivered to homes. In 1977, Good Humor shifted to selling in supermarkets but gave its drivers the option to become independent contractors. Few did. In the twenty-first century, in some places, restored Good Humor trucks still travel down city streets. But ice cream routes are lucrative, so there is still fierce competition among ice cream vendors.[48]

Americans liked ice cream but production was limited until 1902 because it was all laboriously hand-cranked. Then the brine freezer came into use and production more than doubled between 1904 at 12 million gallons and 1909 at 29 million gallons.[49]

ICE CREAM AND YOGURT CHRONOLOGY—UNITED STATES

1780s	Thomas Jefferson handwrites recipe for vanilla ice cream
1846	Nancy Johnson, Pennsylvania dairy maid, invents hand-cranked ice cream freezer
1851	Baltimore, MD—Jacob Fussell opens first ice cream manufacturing plant in U.S.
1856	Fussell—"father of the wholesale ice cream industry"—opens ice cream factories in Boston and Washington, D.C.; packs ice cream in ice, ships by train to major cities
1859	U.S. ice cream production is 4,000 gallons[50]
1878	Mechanical ice cream scoop invented by William Clewell[51]
1899	U.S. ice cream production is five million gallons, still hand-cranked[52]
1900	International Ice Cream Association (IICA) founded[53]
1902	Brine freezer introduced; beginning of mass production of ice cream
1904	Ice cream cone is popular at St. Louis World's Fair; production is 12 million gallons
1909	Ice cream production reaches 29 million gallons[54]
1919	Ice cream sandwich I-Scream Bar, renamed Eskimo Pie, invented in Iowa
1919	Dannon Yogurt founded by Isaac Carasso
1920	Ohio candy maker Harry Burt invents Good Humor—ice cream on a stick
1920s	Mechanized packaging, 10 times faster, begins to replace hand-packed ice cream
1933	Prohibition repealed; ice cream consumption drops drastically
1936	Greek immigrant Athanassios Karvelas, aka Tom Carvel, begins Carvel Corporation
WWII	U.S. Army manufactures 80 million gallons of ice cream
1947	Dannon introduces yogurt with fruit on the bottom
1953	Brothers-in-law Burt Baskin and Irv Robbins combine their Pasadena and Glendale, CA, ice cream stores into Baskin-Robbins; free samples on pink plastic spoons
1960	Häagen-Dazs formed in New York City by Polish immigrant Reuben Mattus
1961	Good Humor sold to Lipton, subsidiary of multinational Unilever[55]
1977	Good Humor shifts from selling on the street to supermarkets
1978	Ben & Jerry's opens in a rundown former gas station in Burlington, Vermont
1983	Pillsbury buys Häagen-Dazs
1984	July becomes National Ice Cream Month; third Sunday is National Ice Cream Day
1998	Häagen-Dazs creates Dulce de Leche, first mainstream Mexican-inspired flavor
2009	Ice cream accounts for more than $21 billion in annual sales in the U.S.[56]
2010	Dannon plant in Minster, Ohio, is world's largest; 230,000 cups of yogurt per hour[57]
2010	Baskin-Robbins is world's largest ice cream store chain; 2,800 in U.S.; 5,800 world

The Immigration Door Slams Shut

In 1924, the Immigration Act cut immigration for two groups—southern Europeans and eastern Europeans, mostly Italians and Jews—to a minimum. By this time, many Americans regarded Italians as a "criminal class." and Jews as radicals who wanted to overthrow the American government. Italy's fascist dictator, Mussolini, also stopped the hemorrhage that had reduced the population of Italy by one-third by refusing to issue exit visas.

Exceptions: Mexicans were not restricted from coming into the United States because farmers needed cheap labor. But once in, they were severely restricted as to where they could go and what they could do. Mexicans who attempted to leave the fields and move to the cities were stopped—by the police, if necessary.

Mexicans were considered "colored" and were subjected to the same Jim Crow laws as African-Americans in the South: forced to ride in the back of the bus; to use separate public facilities, waiting rooms, and water fountains; and to go around to the back door of restaurants to get food. In 1927, Asians were added to the list when the Supreme Court ruled, in the case *Lum v. Rice*, that a Chinese girl could not enroll in a Mississippi school because she was "colored."

Women in a tortilla factory. *Courtesy Security Pacific Collection/Los Angeles Public Library.*

The Harlem Renaissance

There was another unintended loophole in the immigration laws. People with British passports were always allowed into the United States. Britain owned many islands in the Caribbean, so all the inhabitants were British citizens with British passports. And they were black. Many people from the Caribbean used this opportunity to migrate to New York City, where they became one-quarter of the population in Harlem and the heart of a cultural flowering of poetry, novels, art, and music called the Harlem Renaissance.

At Harlem nightclubs like the Apollo, performers and staff were all black, but only white customers were allowed in. Jazz and blues, uniquely American music with roots in Africa, came up from New Orleans to St. Louis, Kansas City, and Chicago after World War I when the U.S. government forced New Orleans to close down the red light district, Storyville, because too many sailors were getting into trouble (or ending up dead) there. Jazz greats like Louis Armstrong said good-bye to their families and got on the trains headed north.

A black leader emerged from this movement, Jamaican Marcus Garvey. He said that his people were not "colored," they were Negro, and make sure you spell that with a capital *N*. He preached pride, and urged blacks to go to black stores, black banks, and black businesses. The U.S. government deported him back to Jamaica.

The Ideal American Woman

In the 1920s, Americans became obsessed with appearances. People stopped asking what good deeds a person had done and said instead, "What does he/she look like?" Americans discovered beauty contests, diets, salad, and sliced bread. When women got the vote, they felt that they were finally recognized as the equals of men. They cut their hair short like men, raised their hemlines to the knees, and declared that they were liberated. 1921 saw the birth of two mythical American women. One sprang from the glitz of Atlantic City, New Jersey; the other was conceived in a boardroom in the grain-growing heartland in Minneapolis, Minnesota. One was all about appearance; the other was pure function. One had physical reality but no substance; the other was all substance but a physical fiction. Miss America and Betty Crocker were flip sides of the same coin, two opposite images of the ideal American woman. They have both changed over time to reflect how women's appearances and roles have changed, as the official Betty Crocker portraits show.

The evolution of Betty Crocker. Top: 1936, 1955, 1965, 1969. Bottom: 1972, 1980, 1986, 1996. *Courtesy of General Mills Archives.*

Betty Crocker began as a serious-looking, unsmiling housewife. By the 1950s, she still looked like somebody's grandmother or aunt, but she was smiling. The women's movement that crystallized around the publication of Betty Friedan's book *The Feminine Mystique* in 1963 showed in the Betty Crocker pictures of 1968 and 1972, which looked like professional women who worked outside the home. The 1986 Betty Crocker looked a little more shrewd and tough than the others, as if she had a Masters in Business Administration and wouldn't cook food as much as order others to do it. The Betty Crocker of 1996 was softer, more casual and approachable, and had the biggest smile yet. There was also a search for handwriting that would look like Betty Crocker's, because she answered thousands of letters about cooking from American women. Betty Crocker became a merchandising empire. She had her own radio show and cookbook.

The emphasis on appearances extended to food. The invention of color printing made advertising in magazines, newspapers, and posters easy and affordable. Consumers wanted food that looked just like the perfect pictures. This explains why the tasteless Red Delicious is the best-selling apple in America: it looks like the apple in children's alphabet books (*A* is for *apple*).

Movie Star Cuisine

By the 1920s, Hollywood and its movie stars had become big business, even though the movies didn't have sound until 1927. Movie stars lived in enormous homes that looked like French châteaus, Italian villas, Spanish haciendas, or European palaces. Their estates had swimming pools, tennis courts, marble floors, gatehouses, vast lawns. Wild parties took place.

They ate at restaurants that were just as spectacular and visual as their homes and the movies they appeared in. The 1,000-seat Cocoanut Grove nightclub (1921–1989) used artificial palm trees salvaged from heartthrob Rudolph Valentino's movie *The Sheik*. Fake monkeys and fake coconuts lived in the trees. Later, in the 1930s and 1940s, The Grove, located in the Ambassador Hotel, broadcast the live Big Band music of Guy Lombardo, Rudy Vallee, and Ozzie Nelson nationwide.[58]

Sexy Clara Bow, who had "It" owned the It Café on Vine Street in Hollywood. In Tijuana, just over the border in Mexico, where movie stars went to play, Chef Caesar Cardini supposedly invented the Caesar salad of romaine lettuce, Parmigiano-Reggiano cheese, and anchovies, which became popular.

Actors had to eat sparingly, mindful that the standard contract with the movie studios had what the actors called a "potato clause." It said that any change in appearance could be grounds for terminating the contract—for example, if they gained weight. Chef Bob Cobb of the Brown Derby helped them stay slim. You couldn't miss the Brown Derby (1926–1985), first on Wilshire Boulevard, then another on Hollywood and Vine—it was shaped like a giant derby hat. In the Derby kitchen, Bob invented the chopped salad of lettuces with bits of chicken, bacon, and avocado named after him.

After 1930, those who didn't care about their weight could go to Mama Weiss's Hungarian Restaurant in Beverly Hills. According to legend, movie star Lana Turner was discovered at another Hollywood institution, Schwab's Drugstore on Sunset Boulevard, near what is now the Kodak Center where the Academy Awards are held. She wasn't, and Schwab's closed in 1988.

The Discovery of Vitamins and Penicillin

In the 1920s, scientists began to discover exactly what was in food. They called these properties "vitamines," a combination of *vita*, meaning "life," and *amine*, for amino acid, and named them with letters of the alphabet. Vitamin A, in liver and carrots, affects eyesight. Deficiency causes night blindness; excess results in nausea, joint pain, and death. B vitamins, in brown rice, pork, and liver, make the nervous system function. Vitamin C counteracts scurvy. Vitamin D, the "sunshine vitamin," is in milk and helps to build bones. Without it, bone-deforming rickets occurs. Vitamin K causes blood to clot. There are other vitamins, and scientists are still discovering the properties of foods.

In 1929, Alexander Fleming, a British physician, noticed that something was destroying his experiment. Some mold from bread had gotten into it and killed it. He had discovered *Penicillium notatum*, the first antibiotic (Greek: *anti* [against] and *bios* [life]). Soon after, other antibiotics like the sulfas, the mycins, and tetracycline were discovered. Penicillin came into widespread use in the United States after World War II, when it was mass-produced for use in the war. Fleming was knighted and was one of the winners of the Nobel Prize in 1945 for his discovery.

The Rise of the Supermarket

As 1929 began, life was looking good. The Industrial Revolution had arrived in the American home. Electricity and new appliances replaced household servants: electric stoves and refrigerators, vacuum cleaners, washing machines, toasters, sewing machines, teakettles. People could save time by purchasing their bread already sliced and their vegetables frozen in a process invented by Clarence Birdseye after he saw Eskimos quick-freezing food. (Then Marjorie Merriweather Post, of the Post food family, bought Birdseye's operation and changed the name to General Foods.) Americans ate canned food and fed their infants the convenient new baby foods made by Gerber.

They bought all these foods in the new one-stop supermarkets. The Alpha Beta supermarket had everything in alphabetical order; customers could walk up and take what and how much they wanted instead of waiting for a clerk to help them, like in the old general stores. Another food giant, the A & P—the Great Atlantic and Pacific Tea Company—was selling one-tenth of all retail food in the United States and doing one billion dollars a year in business.[59] The USDA was inspecting meat, and Coca-Cola was free of coca. The Public Health Service monitored 29 diseases, including food-borne illnesses, in every state, the District of Columbia, Hawaii, and Puerto Rico. There was one car for every five people in the United States, compared with one for 43 in England, and one for 7,000 in Russia.[60] There were many fun things to do, like driving around in the car with friends, going to movies and dances and parties. Anyone who really wanted a drink could get one. America was in a party mood. Party, party, party.

The Fall of the Stock Market

In October 1929, the stock market crashed. It was the greatest financial flop in American history up to that time. Stock prices bottomed out; millions of people lost their jobs. People who had been worth millions were suddenly wiped out. They committed suicide by jumping out of their office windows. During the presidential campaign in 1928, Herbert Hoover had promised Americans that if he was elected, he would put "a chicken in every pot." After the stock market crash, many Americans not only didn't have a chicken, they didn't have a pot.

The party was over.

Soup Kitchens, Spam, and TV Dinners

The Depression and the New Deal

The United States was more industrialized than any other nation, so it was hit hardest by the Depression. Unemployment across the United States reached deep into the middle class. Many people lost their homes. They lived in empty lots or down by the railroad yards, in shacks made of old pieces of tin or cardboard boxes. They heated themselves by making fires in barrels; they ate garbage and food scraps they scrounged or begged. These new "towns," called "Hoovervilles" in bitter honor of president Herbert Hoover, sprang up all over the United States. Hoover, a Republican, told Americans who saw their lives getting worse that "Prosperity is just around the corner."

Soup Kitchens and Bread Lines

With millions of people out of work, public funds and private charities were quickly overwhelmed. Gangster Al Capone saw the Depression as a public relations opportunity to present himself as the patron saint of Chicago; he set up its first soup kitchen and fed 3,000 people a day. It didn't keep him from being sent to prison.[1] Some organizations handed out free bread, but accepting charity at that time was regarded as shameful, and people standing in line to receive free food often tried to hide their faces. The Los Angeles County sheriff's department did better than soup and bread lines—it hosted an annual barbecue. The meat was pit-cooked for 14 to 15 hours, the West Coast equivalent of the New England clambake, but with beef. First, they cut the number of people who needed food by deporting thousands of Mexicans back to Mexico.

RECIPE:

Los Angeles County Annual Barbecue[2]

MAKES 75,000 8-OUNCE SERVINGS

Amount	Ingredient
40,000 pounds	prime steer beef, forequarter only, cut in 25-pound chunks
300 crates	tomatoes, chopped
4,000 pounds	onion, chopped
50 pounds	garlic
700 pounds	salt
125 pounds	black pepper
25 pounds	green chile peppers, seeded and chopped
50 pounds	ground celery seeds
50 pounds	ground oregano
10 pounds	ground cumin seed
100 pounds	vinegar

Hoover lost resoundingly in his bid for reelection in 1932 to Democrat Franklin Delano Roosevelt (FDR). Polio had almost killed FDR; it left him in a wheelchair, although he was usually photographed without it. It also left him knowing what human beings can accomplish if they have enough will power.

"I see one-third of a nation ill-housed, ill-clad, and ill-nourished."

—President Franklin Delano Roosevelt[3]

Roosevelt, inaugurated on March 4, 1933, told the American people the truth—the Depression, entering its fourth year, was getting worse, not better. This, along with an unprecedented, steep rise in violent crime, much of it connected to gangsters and Prohibition, had Americans hungry (and thirsty), angry, scared, and losing confidence in their government. People literally ran to the bank and took their money out—first come, first served. If you got there late, your money was gone. Many Americans wondered if capitalism and democracy were going to survive or should be replaced with something else. In Russia, Stalin's communist five-year plan was succeeding, at least according to Stalin; in Germany, Hitler's National Socialist party, the Nazis, was feeding people and turning the economy around. FDR reassured the American people: "We have nothing to fear but fear itself."

Roosevelt's administration, called the New Deal, had a three-pronged approach to the economy. The New Deal's three "R's" were relief, recovery, and reform. The federal government would provide financial relief to people in the form of jobs and money, begin programs to help economic recovery, and reform the laws controlling banks and the stock market. In the first hundred days after his inauguration, Congress was happy to pass any programs the president proposed.

CCC—Civilian Conservation Corps: Paying People to Work

One of FDR's first priorities was to stabilize the economy. He immediately declared a "bank holiday" and closed every bank in the country until federal auditors could decide which ones were healthy. Deposits in the banks that reopened were insured up to $5,000 by a new agency, the Federal Deposit Insurance Corporation—FDIC. There were so many agencies that they were referred to only by their initials. These "alphabet agencies" had names like CCC and AAA.

On March 31, 1933, FDR signed the bill creating the Civilian Conservation Corps—the CCC. Its goal was to prevent the many angry, unemployed young men living in Hoovervilles and hanging around street corners from turning into gangs and revolting against the United States. Just as almost 2,000 years earlier, the Romans gave free bread and entertainment to the urban poor to avoid civil disorder, the Roosevelt administration got 19- to 22-year-old men off the city streets and into the countryside. Soon, there were men in 1,450 CCC camps throughout all 48 states building roads, clearing trails, and planting trees. They were supposed to receive the standard army ration of 12 ounces of flour, 10 ounces of fresh beef, 10 ounces of potatoes, and 5 ounces of sugar per man per day, but army physicians increased it by 5 percent when they discovered that all the men were undernourished. The menu included a variety of foods, but the constants at all three meals were the basis of the typical American diet: meat, potatoes, bread, butter, coffee. Dairy products were also abundant in fresh milk, butter, creamed vegetables, and puddings.

MENU:

CIVILIAN CONSERVATION CORPS[4]

BREAKFAST	DINNER (LUNCHEON)	SUPPER
Oatmeal	Roast Pork and Gravy	Braised Ribs of Beef
Fresh Milk	Baked Potatoes	Mashed Potatoes and Gravy
Fried Eggs and Bacon	Creamed Peas	Creamed String Beans
Hashed Brown Potatoes	Cabbage Slaw	Fresh Fruit Salad
Bread and Butter	Bread and Butter	Bread and Butter
Coffee	Rice Pudding	Apple Pie
	Coffee	Hot Cocoa and Coffee

The men had to send their pay home so their families could buy food and pay mortgages. Now these men and their families felt good about their country. So did the farmers who sold their food to the government.

AAA—Agricultural Adjustment Act: Paying People Not to Work

The problem with American farms was the same as with American industry—overproduction. Food cost very little. Shipping it, however, was expensive. It cost farmers in the Midwest more to ship their food to the cities than they could charge for it. They would lose money. So they destroyed the food. Newsreels showed farmers dumping gallons of milk, rivers of milk, into the gutter while hungry babies in cities cried and got rickets. Something had to be done. Roosevelt's solution was the Agricultural Adjustment Act—AAA. This revolutionary law paid farmers *not* to farm. They had to plow their fields under. The AAA was eventually declared unconstitutional and replaced with other farm subsidies.

The New Deal changed the relationship between the American people and their government profoundly. The government giving charity was contrary to the American idea of rugged individualism, that people would take care of themselves without help from anyone, especially the government. On the other hand, European countries where social welfare programs had existed for decades considered America backward and barbaric because it didn't have these programs.

The New Deal also changed the relationship between the government and black Americans. FDR immediately ended segregation in the White House, and his programs gave professional jobs to black people. The first lady, Eleanor Roosevelt, had many black friends and worked actively to help them achieve equality. She was also the president's "legs," going places he couldn't. There were jokes about Eleanor sightings, just as there are jokes now about Elvis sightings—Eleanor was spotted down a coal mine, up on a bridge being built, at a farm, in a school. But the Eleanor sightings were real; she *was* everywhere, making the federal government a living presence for ordinary Americans. She was more of a force in the life of America than any other first lady.

Alcohol in the New Deal

One of the first things FDR did after his inauguration was ask Congress to make beer and wine legal again. On March 22, 1933, Congress passed the Beer and Wine Revenue Act on the grounds that the country needed the tax money. (Roosevelt thought they needed a drink.) One newspaper cartoon showed FDR as a waiter, towel over his arm, a tray loaded with foaming beer, running to a table. The caption read, "I Call That Service."

By the end of FDR's first year in office, all alcohol was legal again. On December 5, 1933, the Twenty-first Amendment to the U.S. Constitution repealed the Eighteenth Amendment. Prohibition was over. However, the decision of whether to be wet or dry was left to the individual states. Some, like Utah, remained dry for decades. 1933 was also the year that a California man invented a handy gadget that solved a problem that had been a bane to mankind: it took the pits out of green olives, making them suitable for dropping into martini glasses.[5]

Although people could begin drinking again, the industries that produced alcohol had gone out of business or been closed for 13 years. In 1933, there were approximately 130 wineries left in California, and approximately 150 total in the United States, down from more than 1,000 before Prohibition. Equipment was rusted, casks rotted. The 1934 vintage "may well have been the worst commercial

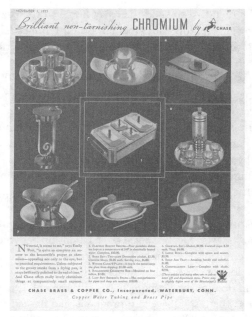

Advertisement for barware one month before Prohibition ended. Vogue, *November 1, 1933.*

American wines ever produced. Some, still fermenting when first shipped, literally blew up on store shelves."[6] The reputation of wine fell, further depressing the wine industry. It took decades to recover.

Bill W. and Dr. Bob: Alcoholics Anonymous—AA and the 12 Steps

Once drinking was legal again, some people began to admit, after years of trying to deal with it themselves, that they were alcoholics. Two, Bill W. and Dr. Bob, both Vermont natives, had experienced severe blackouts (24 hours at a time) and multiple hospitalizations and were considered hopeless. Bill W. was on the verge of being committed to an institution when a friend told him about the Oxford Group, a worldwide religious organization founded by a Lutheran minister and dedicated to changing the world "One Person at a Time." One of the men Bill W. met at a meeting had gone to Europe in desperation to see the famous psychoanalyst Carl Jung, who told him that medicine and science could do nothing to help him; it would take a spiritual conversion. Bill W. had such a conversion, and then "there came a vision of a society of alcoholics, each identifying with and transmitting his experience to the next—chain style."[7] He proceeded to bring this philosophy to others, including Dr. Bob. The official date of the beginning of Alcoholics Anonymous (AA) is June 10, 1935, the day that Dr. Bob took his last drink. In 1938, the 12 Steps—the guidelines to recovery—were developed. AA has spawned Overeaters Anonymous, Narc-Anon for drug addicts, and many other 12-step programs. In Germany, Hitler dealt with alcoholism by sterilizing 20,000 to 30,000 alcoholics.[8]

The Dust Bowl—Black Blizzards in the Dirty Thirties

Not only the economy, but also nature was in precarious shape. The Dust Bowl was the name given to the ecological disaster that swept across the American southern Great Plains in the 1930s. Land in western Kansas and eastern Colorado, south to the Oklahoma Panhandle and Northern Texas, and northeastern New Mexico, had been used for grazing cattle on native grasses that clung to the soil. During World War I, when the world needed wheat, this area shifted to wheat production, which meant that it was plowed. After the wheat was harvested there was nothing to hold the soil down. When drought came, the soil went airborne, creating black blizzards across the plains and the eastern United States. Farmhouses, outhouses, barns, cars, and farm equipment were buried under dirt drifts sometimes 20 feet deep. It was worse than snow; snow eventually melts. Humans who breathed it in got "dirt pneumonia"; animals died.

Twenty-five percent of the population in the states affected by the Dust Bowl went west, mostly to California, looking for work and land. They were memorialized in John Steinbeck's 1939 novel *The Grapes of Wrath*, and in the 1940 movie version. The 75 percent who stayed had to change what they grew and how they grew it. According to food historian Anne Mendelson, "in the shift to intensive, mechanized farm production, growers were obliged to concentrate on factors like hardiness, high yield, disease resistance, and transportability. Thus, the genetic diversity of American crops generally shrank between the wars."[9]

Vitamin Deficiency: Pellagra

In the American South, African-American sharecroppers, descendants of slaves, lived in poverty, tied to the land they lived on and farmed, which was owned by whites. During the Depression, they became even poorer. Many suffered from sore muscles and joints, dizziness, insanity, and death. Italy and Africa also had epidemics of this disease, which was given an Italian name based on one of its outstanding features, rough skin: pellagra. Scientists came up with various theories about its origins: it was caused by corn infected with ergot, or it crossed over from animals. Finally, in 1915, a scientist from the U.S. National Institute of Health proved that pellagra occurs in areas where corn, deficient in niacin, one of the B vitamins, is the staple food. During the Depression, the American Red Cross cut the number of deaths from pellagra by one-third by distributing yeast to sharecroppers.[10] Other foods high in niacin are liver, legumes, and fish, especially tuna and salmon.

Depression Innovation—New Foods and Marketing

During the Depression, American ingenuity went into overdrive to come up with new ways to sell food. Apple sellers appeared on street corners in cities.

Little pieces of paper that told fortunes were baked into cookies in Chinese restaurants. Movie theaters started selling popcorn and soon discovered that popcorn was more profitable than movie tickets.[11] Before that, going to a movie was like going to a play. The theater was an elegant "palace" with heavy velvet draperies and chair coverings, gold on the walls, elaborate paintings on the walls and ceiling. You did not eat. Movie theaters also had nights where they gave away dishes and other prizes. Oregon fruit growers Harry & David used the U.S. mail to save their pear orchards and their business and became the largest mail-order shippers in the United States.

Refrigeration advanced enough that walk-in refrigerators and freezers were invented, which revolutionized commercial food preparation and, later, home food preparation.

The Joy of Cooking and Depression Cooks

After the stock market crash, many upper-middle-class women found themselves merely middle class or worse. They suddenly had to live without household help, the maids and cooks on whom they had always relied. One woman who found herself in what was referred to then as "reduced circumstances" was a 53-year-old widow of old German stock in St. Louis, Missouri. When Irma Rombauer began collecting recipes from women friends and restaurateurs, some in her family called what she was doing a "hobby" or a descent into insanity, because they knew "Irma's a TERRIBLE cook."[12] Others, like her son Edgar, knew that Irma had taken cooking classes and was respected as a hostess.[13]

Irma was motivated: she was looking financial ruin and poverty in the face if she failed. She persisted, carefully tested the recipes, and in 1931, using half of all the money she had, she self-published 3,000 copies of *The Joy of Cooking*. Her daughter Marion Rombauer Becker, educated at Vassar and an artist, provided the cover art and illustrations. The book was subtitled *A Compilation of Reliable Recipes with a Casual Culinary Chat*.

As Anne Mendelson, the Rombauer/Becker biographer, points out, in the second edition, the one that became a national cookbook in 1936, Irma "hit on . . . a new way of writing recipes." Instead of listing the ingredients, then giving the instructions, she swirled them together like a marble cake:

"Sift ------------------------ ¹/₂ cup sugar

Beat until soft ------------ ¹/₄ cup butter"[14]

The format was continued in following editions by her daughter and then her grandson Ethan Becker, a Cordon Bleu Cooking School graduate.

Another woman who turned her kitchen into a gold mine during the Depression was Margaret Rudkin. The Connecticut woman invented a special whole-grain bread for her son, who was suffering from allergies. Her bread developed a local reputation, so she placed it in stores. When bread was selling for a dime a

DEPRESSION INNOVATION

YEAR	GENDER	PLACE	PRODUCT
	Corp.	US	Popcorn in movie theaters
1929	M	MA	Howard Johnson's—first restaurant franchise
1930	Corp.	MA	Ocean Spray Jellied and Whole Berry Cranberry Sauce
1930	M	IN	Twinkies
1931	F	MO	*Joy of Cooking* published
1931	Corp.	MN	General Mills markets Bisquick
1932	M	TX	Frito's Corn Chips
1933	–	US	Prohibition ends; soft drink manufacturers urge soda as mixers
1933	Corp.	US	Miracle Whip dressing introduced at Chicago World's Fair
1934	Corp.	US	Ritz Crackers (Nabisco)
1934	M	OR	Harry & David begin mail-order business for their pears
1934	F	US	Girl Scouts begin cookie sales
1934	Corp.	CA	Los Angeles Farmers Market opens at 3rd and Fairfax
1935	M	OH	Alcoholics Anonymous founded
1936	Corp.		Oscar Mayer Wienermobile rolled out
1936	M	AR	John Tyson, truck driver, buys a chicken hatchery
1936	M	NY	Carvel ice cream introduces "Buy one, get one free"[17]
1937	F	CT	Pepperidge Farm begins; sells bread above market price
1937	F	OK	Bama Pie Company incorporated; sells personal-size pies
1937	F	MA	Toll House Cookies accidentally invented by Ruth Wakefield
1937	Corp.	US	Kraft Macaroni & Cheese introduced to national market[18]
1937	Corp.	US	Parkay Margarine introduced
1937	Corp.	US	Spam
1938	M	PA	Chef Boyardee incorporates; originally in Cleveland[19]
1938	M	TN	Lay's Potato Chips
1939	Corp.	US	Nestlé makes Toll House Real Semi-Sweet Chocolate Morsels

loaf, Margaret insisted on charging a quarter and got it. That was the beginning of Pepperidge Farm.[15]

In Los Angeles, pies baked in her kitchen provided income for Marie Callender. In Texas, Cornelia Alabama Marshall realized that not everyone could afford her full-size pecan and fruit pies, so she loaded up her husband's truck with individual three-inch pies and sent him out to construction sites. The pies became known by her middle name, "Bama Pies"; she was "Grandma Bama."[16]

In 1935, a young man from Oregon with some college and a bit of experience as an actor needed to make money, so he began a catering business. Two years later he opened a small shop called Hors d'Oeuvre Inc., and began the career that led to his becoming known as the "Father of American Cooking." James Beard published his first book, *Hors d'Oeuvre and Canapés*, in 1940. He wrote many books, including *Cooking It Outdoors*, the first cookbook that went beyond scouting or survival food and treated outdoor cooking seriously. He was also the first person to have a television show on cooking. When Beard died in 1985, Julia Child decided to preserve his brownstone home in New York's Greenwich Village as a foundation to promote fine food and drink, and as a memorial to the Father of American Cooking.

Poisoned Food: Japan's Biological War against China

Japan invaded China in 1931, then escalated its attacks in 1937. Japan intended to take China's massive natural resources, including food. The Japanese committed many atrocities, including the Rape of Nanking. In less than two months, the Japanese raped, dismembered, looted, tortured, and burned at least 100,000 people, most of them civilians. Japan denies this ever took place, even though they filmed it. In 2002, Japan opened a museum about World War II; it included nothing about Nanking.

The Japanese used food as a weapon against Chinese civilians, including children. Japanese scientists put anthrax in chocolates and plague in cookies. They dumped typhoid down wells, sprayed fields with contaminated grains of wheat and millet, and released rats carrying plague fleas into cities. Chinese food customs—like fish peddlers who went from village to village—unknowingly helped to spread the diseases. Japanese doctors came to vaccinate people in the affected areas—but the "vaccines" were injections of cholera. They burned down villages and said they were cleansing them. They developed a concentrated version of toxin from the liver of the Japanese blowfish—*fugu*—to kill people, but a U.S. bombing raid destroyed the research facility. These tactics were extremely effective: six million Chinese civilians died.

1939: World's Fair and World War

The last year of the decade ended with the best of events and the worst of events. The best: the New York World's Fair opened. Pavilion after pavilion displayed technological progress and the hope for a better life in the future. The French pavilion had a restaurant, called simply Le Pavillon, which was the latest in French food. After the fair closed, the restaurant went directly into New York City where it became a landmark for years and the training ground for many chefs, including the White House chef during the Kennedy administration in the 1960s.

The worst: in August 1939, Hitler and Stalin entered into a nonaggression pact: neither Germany nor Russia would attack the other. The two countries, very wary of each other, were separated only by Poland, which they both claimed. In effect, Stalin was giving Hitler the go-ahead to invade Poland. Britain and France, which had been counting on the threat of Russia to deter Hitler, were furious. They informed Hitler that if he invaded Poland, Germany would be at war with them.

World War II

Germany invaded Poland on Friday, September 1, 1939, plunging the world into war again for the second time in a little more than two decades. England and France, true to their word, then declared war on Germany. The match was uneven. In defiance of the Treaty of Versailles, Germany had been preparing for war for the better part of a decade while England and France had not. The heart of Germany's industrial production, the Ruhr Valley, was dominated by the Krupp family. They began in the sixteenth century as manufacturers of cutlery who traveled from town to town peddling knives.

Germany easily took Poland, then overran Denmark and Norway. In Denmark, when they ordered every Jew to wear a yellow star, everyone, including the king and queen, wore a yellow star. The Nazis continued west toward the Netherlands. As the Dutch army rushed to defend its borders, the Nazis attacked the interior of the country with a new kind of warfare, soldiers dropped from airplanes behind enemy lines—paratroopers. Overwhelmed, the Netherlands surrendered. Then Luxembourg. Then Belgium. In May 1940, France fell. For more than a year, England, the last country in Europe not under Nazi control, fought the entire Nazi empire alone in Europe and in Africa, where the Nazis were trying to capture the Suez Canal and get to the oil in the Middle East. The

United States helped England by providing ships, ammunition, oil, and food through the Lend-Lease program. Hitler was going to invade England and then the United States—right after he finished off Russia.

The Nazi Siege of Leningrad: "Starve them"

The Nazis looked at the Slavic people of Russia the same way they looked at the Jews, as *untermensch*—subhuman. On June 22, 1941, the Russian people found out that Hitler had broken the Non-Aggression Pact when the German air force, the Luftwaffe, launched a blitzkrieg—a lightning strike—against the USSR and destroyed almost their entire air force before it could get into the air. Then Germany invaded on the ground. By September 8, 1941, the city of Leningrad was surrounded and under siege. The Nazis used incendiary bombs to deliberately set the warehouses on fire and burn the food supply. Two thousand five hundred tons of burning sugar caramelized, flowed through the streets, then hardened. The government broke pieces off and sold the sugar in chunks.[20] The Nazi strategy: wait until winter, and let the people of Leningrad starve. Then they would surely surrender.

Hitler had a special interest in Leningrad: it contained the largest food plant seed bank in the world—more than 250,000 specimens. The seed bank at the Institute for Plant Industry was the life's work of Nikolai Vavilov, whose passion was increasing the world food supply. Vavilov had gone backwards in the Columbian Exchange to pinpoint the origins of food. There, he reasoned, he would find other varieties of foods, ones that existed before humans engineered them into their current forms. He made more than 200 trips to remote areas on every continent except Antarctica to collect the seeds. With these, Hitler could control the world's food supply and provide superfood for his Nazi supermen.[21]

December 7, 1941: Pearl Harbor

President Roosevelt told Japan to get out of China. When Japan didn't, the United States cut off Japan's oil supply. Japan's response was to bomb U.S. military bases in Pearl Harbor, Hawaii, on Sunday, December 7, 1941, shortly before 8 o'clock in the morning. Pearl Harbor was only one prong in a multitarget attack. At the same time they bombed Pearl Harbor, the Japanese also bombed the Philippines, Guam, Wake Island, Hong Kong, and other places in the Pacific.

A kitchen worker was one of the heroes of Pearl Harbor and the first African-American hero of World War II. Mess Attendant First Class "Dorie" Miller, a Texas high school fullback and heavyweight boxing champion on the USS *West Virginia*, manned a .50-caliber machine gun on the deck of the *West Virginia* and started firing even though he had not been trained to—the segregated armed forces taught only white sailors to use guns. Rumors spread that he shot down several Japanese planes, but Miller said he thought maybe he got one. He was awarded the Navy Cross for bravery. The African-American community wrote to President Roosevelt to have Miller admitted to the United States Naval Academy. It never happened. Miller was serving as Ship's Cook Third Class when his ship, the *Liscome Bay*, was torpedoed by a Japanese submarine and sank on November 24, 1943. Miller was awarded the Purple Heart after his death, and a ship named after him, the USS *Miller*, was commissioned in June 1973.[22] In 2001, the actor Cuba Gooding Jr. played Miller in the movie *Pearl Harbor*.

Congress declared war on Japan on Monday, December 8, 1941. While they were debating whether to also declare war on Japan's allies, Germany and Italy, Germany and Italy declared war on the United States. Then the factories in the greatest industrial cities in the greatest industrial nation the world had ever seen—Detroit, Pittsburgh, New York, Chicago, Los Angeles—shut down. When they reopened, jeeps and trucks, not cars, drove off the assembly lines at General Motors, Chrysler, and Chevrolet in Detroit. Steel for battleships and bombers rolled out of the mills in Pittsburgh 24 hours a day, seven days a week.

When Pearl Harbor was bombed, Leningrad was deep in winter and its fourth month of siege. In January 1942, the bread ration dropped to four ounces per person per day. Two hundred thousand Russians starved to death. But they did not surrender.

Japanese in America: Executive Order 9066

The sneak attack on Pearl Harbor enraged and terrified Americans, especially on the West Coast, where they were afraid the Japanese living in the United States would engage in sabotage to help Japan invade the country. The Japanese were in a bind: they couldn't prove their loyalty because it was against the law in America at that time for anyone born in Japan to become a citizen. President Roosevelt issued Executive Order 9066: arrest every person of Japanese ancestry, even people who were citizens because they were born in the United States. Japanese-Americans fought Executive Order 9066 all the way to the Supreme Court, which ruled against them in *Korematsu v. United States*.

The Japanese were sent away from the Pacific coast to detention centers in remote inland areas. So were Japanese in Canada and Peru. In the camps, they continued to do what they had always done: grow fruits and vegetables, which they ate and sold to the soldiers at the camp. One of the camps was Manzanar, in the Mojave Desert between the Sierra Nevada Mountains and Death Valley in California; escape was impossible. But many young Japanese-American men did get out: they joined the armed forces. The Japanese 442nd regiment fought in Europe and became the most highly decorated unit in the American military in World War II.

K-Rations

When the United States went to war, so did its food manufacturers. Millions of service men and women needed to be fed in training camps, on ships, in the Pacific, in Africa, and in Europe. The food needed to be nutritious, ready to eat or easy to prepare, and portable. Much of the food for the military was made by Hormel and Kraft. Soldiers on the front lines drank instant coffee made by 12 different companies in the United States, including Maxwell House and Nescafé.[23]

The letter "K" was chosen randomly as a name for for WWII rations to differentiate it from earlier "C" and "D" rations. K-rations were small individual boxes containing one meal labeled "Breakfast," "Dinner," or "Supper." Nothing was called "Lunch." The boxes were dipped in wax to waterproof them. At the beginning of the war, all the boxes were plain brown cardboard. Later they were color-coded in brown, green, and blue for breakfast, dinner, and supper, respectively. The colors also supposedly boosted morale.

K-RATIONS[24]

BREAKFAST	DINNER	SUPPER
Canned meat product	Canned cheese product	Canned meat product
Biscuits	Biscuits	Biscuits
Powdered coffee	Powdered beverage	Powdered coffee
Fruit bar	Candy	Candy
Chewing gum	Chewing gum	Chewing gum
Sugar tablets	Granulated sugar	Granulated sugar
Cigarettes	Cigarettes	Cigarettes
Can opener	Can opener	Can opener
Wooden spoon	Wooden spoon	Wooden spoon
Compressed cereal bar	Matches	Bouillon powder
Water-purification tablets	Salt tablets	Toilet paper

The K-rations reflected American habits: cattle- and wheat-based main courses; stimulants in sugar, chewing gum, caffeine, and tobacco. The meals were almost identical, with the exception of a compressed cereal bar at breakfast, dairy at dinner, and bouillon powder at supper. Water purification tablets were provided at the beginning of the day, salt tablets in the middle to avoid dehydration from lost minerals, toilet paper at the end.

Spam

The "canned meat product" in the army rations came from Hormel. During World War II, the U.S. government bought 90 percent of everything the Hormel Company put in a can. Some of Hormel's products included Hormel Chili Con Carne, Dinty Moore Beef Stew, and canned hams. But the product most identified with Hormel was Spam—spiced ham—"Hormel's New Miracle Meat in a Can."[25] GIs and allied troops ate Spam fritters, Spam soup, Spam sandwiches, Spam salad, Spam stew, Spam and macaroni, Spam and dehydrated eggs, Spam and dehydrated potatoes, Spam meatballs, Spam chop suey, Spam and Spam and more Spam—more than 100 million pounds of it.[26] Every bit of Spam was used, including the packaging. The valuable metal in Spam cans was recycled as pots and pans and stills to make alcohol. Spam grease lubricated guns, conditioned skin, and became candles. There was so much Spam that soldiers called Uncle Sam, "Uncle Spam."[27]

Spam was also shipped overseas to America's allies as part of the Lend-Lease program. In England, it was eaten by civilians in air-raid shelters and cleverly disguised under French sauces in fine restaurants. They thought Spam was an acronym for "Specially Prepared American Meat."[28] In Russia, Spam fed the army. After the war, the Red Cross fed Spam to grateful, starving European refugees, who thought it was a luxury.

Food Rationing

To help the war effort, the American government asked consumers to voluntarily cut back on their consumption of vital foods like meat. It had worked in England. But Americans are not British. They didn't cut back until laws set quotas and forced them to. In response to rationing, Americans did the same thing they did when Prohibition went into effect: they took their babies out of carriages, grabbed their children's toy wagons, went to the stores, picked the shelves clean, and hoarded. Then the slogan was: "Use it up, wear it out, make it do or do without." Some of the things Americans on the home front did without (or with very little of) were rubber, gasoline, sugar, butter, meat, milk, and eggs. Without rubber for their car tires, Americans didn't go on vacation. They did, however, go to the movies in record numbers, so popcorn consumption tripled. A chemist named Orville Redenbacher went into the popcorn business to feed the new movie theaters, including drive-ins, which had opened in 1933.

Nutrition for National Defense

Nutrition became a matter of national defense. Men were "rejected for service with the armed forces because of faulty nutrition and thousands of man-hours are lost on the production lines for lack of proper food."[29] It was up to the housewives of America to change this and save the country—even though they might be working full-time in defense plants themselves. Newspaper and magazine cooking columns invented recipes based on shortages. Meat was extended with eggs, bread stuffing, rice, and cereal. Recipes for pseudo-ethnic foods were supposed to tempt the palate: Italian Liver (tomato, green pepper, and mushroom sauce on spaghetti); Tamale Pie; Spanish Rice; Swiss Steak. For the truly desperate, there was "Gypsy's Joy," made of rice, water, bacon fat, condensed tomato soup, cooked ham, and "crumbled, nippy cheese."[30] Extensive use was made of macaroni: au gratin, loaf, ring, with spinach, in a casserole with fish and corn; fish was not rationed. Welsh "rabbit" made a come-back. Bacon fat was everywhere. Food writer Mary Frances Kennedy (M. F. K.) Fisher wrote a book called *How to Cook a Wolf*, about how to make nutritious meals with limited items. Americans continued to discover that Italian food was cheap, nutritious, and delicious.

Not just what was prepared for lunch, but how it was packed was connected to national security: "Some defense plants insist on paper bags which can be inspected as they enter the plant. . . ."[31] Housewives were urged to collect and recycle cosmetics jars, peanut butter jars, salad dressing bottles, cottage cheese and ice cream cartons to pack food along with the standard thermos bottle.

Candy and the War Cake

Even with rationing, the United States was wealthy in food. It sent its men into battle with what only a few years before had been a luxury item: chocolate candy. Sugar was rationed for home use but was available for the commercial produc-tion of chocolate and soft drinks. Hershey, Mars, Coke, and Pepsi got sugar. When Congress was on the verge of declaring the manufacture of candy illegal because it wasn't important to the war effort, Hershey convinced them that chocolate was crucial as a morale booster—it would remind the boys of home and what they were fighting for. So America's soldiers went to war and ate Her-shey Bars, and M&Ms from Hershey's competitor, Mars.

Chances were good that the sugar came from sugar beets that were grown, cultivated, and harvested by Mexicans. With more than 16 million Americans in the armed forces, farms needed laborers. The United States began the *bracero* (laborer) program (from *brazo*, the Spanish word for "arm") to bring back the Mexicans they had just deported. Under the *bracero* program, approximately four million Mexican agricultural workers came into the United States until the pro-gram was discontinued in 1964.

With sugar rationed, desserts were in short supply. In America's down-under allies, Australia and New Zealand, women baked ANZAC biscuits—an acro-nym for Australia and New Zealand Army Corps. They were made of oats and flour, sweetened shredded coconut, and honey.[32] In the United States, some cooks used Coke and Pepsi as sweeteners: bake a cake, poke it full of holes, pour the cola in. "The War Cake" was made without butter, eggs, milk, or white sugar. It used brown sugar and water sweetened by soaking raisins in it, a technique used in the Middle East since ancient times. It tasted good and kept long enough to be shipped overseas to men and women in the armed forces.

RECIPE:

The War Cake[33]

2 cups brown sugar	1 teaspoon cloves
2 cups hot water	3 cups flour
2 tablespoons shortening	1 teaspoon soda
1 teaspoon salt	1 package seedless raisins
1 teaspoon cinnamon	[no weight or measurements given]

Boil together the sugar, water, shortening, salt, raisins and spices for five minutes. When cold, add flour and soda dissolved in a teaspoonful of hot water. This makes two loaves. Bake about 45 minutes in a 325° F. oven. This cake is of good texture and will keep moist for some time.

.....

Americans were comparatively lucky in World War II. American civilians struggled to come up with creative ways to make cakes without key ingredients, and American soldiers complained about having to eat Spam, but none of World War II was fought in the United States, and nobody starved to death because of food shortages in America.

Prison Camp Food

The 140,000 men held prisoner by the Japanese would have laughed at rationing in the United States. The men were all severely malnourished and suffered from vitamin-deficiency diseases like beriberi, pellagra, scurvy; thousands died. In their weakened state they also got malaria, dysentery, cholera, and typhus. Some swelled up grotesquely; others went blind. Any small cut or mosquito bite could mean gangrene and death within days. The Japanese guards told the men their problem was that they needed to exercise more.[34] Scattered in camps throughout Asia, the prisoners—British, Dutch, Australian, American—worked at hard labor in salt mines or building a railroad in Burma (like in the movie *The Bridge on the River Kwai*). The U.S. Army ration for each enlisted man in peacetime was approximately four-and-one-half pounds of food per day. In combat, it was much higher. The official Japanese ration for prisoners of war doing strenuous physical labor was one pound, 11 ounces of food per day.[35] One bright spot in the months—for some, years—of imprisonment was when Red Cross packages arrived filled with food, cigarettes, and antibiotics. The men quickly traded items. Chocolate, tobacco, canned meat all changed hands. One food was almost never traded: cheese. The men had not had dairy in any form in so long that they craved it and held onto it. An exception: men who couldn't stop smoking starved to death because they traded their food for cigarettes.

In the United States, approximately 400,000 German prisoners of war were treated precisely according to the Geneva Convention of 1929, which stated that captured soldiers were to receive the exact same food that the capturing army fed its own troops. Troops were not subject to rationing; civilians were. So, during

World War II, German prisoners of war in America ate better than American citizens.

The Hollywood Canteen

Hollywood actors and actresses volunteered their time and services to help the war effort. Male mega-stars like Clark Gable, Jimmy Stewart, and Tyrone Power joined the armed forces. Actresses flew across the country selling bonds. In Hollywood, some of the biggest stars could be found at night at the Hollywood Canteen handing out coffee and doughnuts and chatting and dancing with men in the armed forces. Black and white movie studio musicians played live music. These humane gestures escalated into political acts when word got out that there were "mixed" couples—blacks and whites—dancing together. There was talk of segregating the Canteen. That ended when two-time Academy Award–winner Bette Davis and John Garfield—major Warner Bros. stars and founders of the Canteen—said if that happened, the actors wouldn't come. Without actors, there would be no Canteen. So, unlike the armed forces in WWII, or nightclubs in the United States, the Hollywood Canteen was integrated.[36]

The "Final Solution"

In early 1943, Hitler put into effect his "Final Solution," the plan to kill all the Jews in Europe. When Hitler was asked how he thought he could get away with killing millions of Jews, he said, "Who remembers the Armenians?" This was a reference to the Armenians living in Turkey, who supported Turkey's enemies during WWI, and who were killed by the Turks. Jews, Gypsies, homosexuals, political prisoners, disabled people, and even Christian ministers were rounded up and shipped in boxcars without food, heat, or sanitary facilities to concentration camps throughout Europe. Twelve million people, including six million Jews, starved to death, died of disease, or were sent to the gas chambers in camps like Auschwitz in Poland. People who were ordinarily civilized and kind became concerned only with their own survival. The motto in the camps was: "Eat your own bread, and if you can, that of your neighbor." A sign that humanity was returning at the end of the war was when people started to share food again.[37]

In his zeal to kill Jews, Hitler had not forgotten to keep killing Slavs. Leningrad was still under siege. No animals were left in the city. The people had eaten all the stray cats, dogs, and birds. And their own pets.

The Greatest Tank Battle in History; Mass Starvation

In July 1943, on the flat fields of the Ukraine, near the town of Kursk, the greatest tank battle in history took place. For two weeks, the Germans and Russians fought each other with everything on wheels. The Russians finally emerged as the victors in what some historians consider the turning point of World War II, but it demolished the land that was the breadbasket not just of the Soviet Union, but of Europe.

In Leningrad, still under siege, starving people ate anything that offered any semblance of nourishment—leather shoes, briefcases, lipstick. They stripped wallpaper off plaster walls and ate the wallpaper paste. Then they ate the wallpaper. Then they ate the walls. Women who had given birth but were so malnourished that they had no milk opened a vein so that their babies could suckle. At the Institute for Plant Industry, they starved rather than eat the seeds.

As 1944 approached, millions of people were dying all over the world, many of starvation. In India, there was a "man-made" famine: British administrators miscalculated the severity of crop shortages, and almost six million Indians starved to death or died from diseases brought on by malnutrition. In Japan, strict food rationing was in effect. They were also short on medical supplies, oil, and many other crucial items. In the Netherlands, Anne Frank, a 14-year-old Jewish girl in hiding with her family, wrote in her diary about the terrible monotony of their diet, which included slimy, very old preserved cabbage. Other people in the Netherlands ate tulip bulbs boiled to mush or sliced and fried like chips. In England, children got their vitamin C from a syrup made out of rose hips.[38]

In Leningrad, people resorted to cannibalism. Children didn't dare go outside.[39] The siege finally ended in January 1944. The death toll from starvation was approximately one million people, one-third of the city's total population; more were killed by the bombs.[40] During all that time, the only ones who expected the people of Leningrad to surrender, the only ones who ever uttered the word "surrender," were the Nazis.

The Atom Bomb

In the United States, President Franklin D. Roosevelt died on April 12, 1945, and left his successor, President Harry S Truman, with a difficult decision. A plainspoken man from Missouri, Truman's motto was, "If you can't stand the heat, stay out of the kitchen." The decision was whether or not to drop the new $2-billion weapon the United States had developed, the atomic bomb. Truman knew he was in the kitchen, and the heat was turned up full blast. On August 6, 1945, the United States dropped the first atom bomb on the city of Hiroshima, Japan. The center of the city was pulverized. Approximately 100,000 people were killed outright; thousands died later from the aftereffects of radiation. When Japan's military leaders, with their samurai never-surrender philosophy, still didn't surrender, the United States dropped another atom bomb on Nagasaki on August 9. Several days later, Japan surrendered, ending World War II.

The airplanes that had dropped bombs began dropping crates of food. Some prisoners of war, so hungry, ate too much and died. Sometimes the parachutes on the 250-pound packages didn't open, and buildings and people were destroyed. One of the last American casualties of World War II was a Marine killed by flying Spam.[41]

The Cold War

World War II caused a major shift in global politics and economics. The United States, England, and Russia had used American oil in eastern and western Europe, Asia, Africa, and the Pacific and Atlantic oceans to fly airplanes; run tanks, trucks, and jeeps; and sail ships. After World War II, the United States was still producing oil, but not enough to meet its needs. The world's attention shifted to the area that was rich in oil—the Middle East—especially the countries of Iran and Saudi Arabia.

The Russians took heavier casualties in World War II, both military and civilian, than any other country. About 20 million people had died, either killed in the war or by starvation. (In comparison, about 290,000 Americans died in the war.) In the Russian countryside, more than half the horses were gone; only three million pigs were left out of 23 million. Almost five million houses were destroyed, as well as hundreds of thousands of tractors and wagons and thousands of farm buildings.[42]

The USSR and the United States, countries that had been uneasy allies in World War II, became bitter enemies, especially after the USSR exploded its own atom bomb in September 1949. In October 1949, Mao Zedong triumphed over Jiang Jieshi in China's civil war and announced that the most populous country on earth—500 million people then, one-fourth of all the people on the planet—was the communist People's Republic of China. Thousands of Chinese fled communist China and went to the island of Formosa, now called Taiwan.

This was the Cold War between two different political and economic systems, capitalism and democracy versus communism. It consisted of a massive military build-up including nuclear weapons and espionage. Americans dug bomb shelters in their yards and stocked them with canned goods just in case the Cold War heated up.

The United States poured millions of dollars into European countries, especially Italy, France, and Greece, to help them recover and to keep them from becoming communist. The American Army brought a new word into the Italian language: *ciao*. It is pronounced "chow" and means "hello" or "good-bye." It came into use after World War II, when starving Italians begged for food from American soldiers and knew only the one word of English they heard soldiers say when they went to eat—"chow."

Food had become a political issue in Italy in the 1930s when the fascist dictator Mussolini declared pasta passé because it was making Italians soft and sluggish. Mussolini's New Roman Empire needed new foods to make its people strong and hard. A huge debate arose all over Italy. The keep-the-pasta movement was supported with protests and petitions. Others wanted the new cuisine, dishes with names like "Raw Meat Torn by Trumpet Blasts" and "The Ox in the Cockpit." Finally, a conference of chefs was held to decide the issue for the culinary community; what the chefs decided was to beat each other up.[43] At the end of the war, an Italian mob killed Mussolini and hung him from a lamppost on a butcher's meat hook.

The period immediately following World War II saw a move for independence in colonial countries. In India, devastated by famine and disease, the Indian army followed Indian officers who wanted independence from Britain. A religious leader who preached nonviolence, Gandhi, used the same strategy to gain independence from England that Americans had used almost 200 years earlier: boycott British goods. One of these was salt, because England had a monopoly on salt production in India. From 1930 to 1932, Gandhi led hundreds of thousands of Indians to the sea on Salt Marches. Getting salt by evaporation from the sea broke the law—and the monopoly—and encouraged the Indian people to engage in other acts of civil disobedience until they were granted their independence in 1947. Fighting immediately broke out between Hindus and Muslims until the new country of Pakistan was created as a Muslim state out of western India. Gandhi tried to make peace, but was assassinated by a Hindu who thought he was too pro-Muslim. In the Pacific, the Dutch granted Indonesia independence in 1949.

For the 16 million Americans in the armed forces returning home, many wanted to change jobs. Some had discovered during the war that they had a talent for cooking. In 1946, the cooking school that became The Culinary Institute of America was founded in New Haven, Connecticut.

FOOD FABLE:

American Soldiers and World War II Food

The myth was that American soldiers, impressed by the food they were exposed to in European countries, especially Italy and France, came back to the United States eager to eat more of it. This would be inaccurate. During and after the war, there were tremendous food shortages in Europe. The food exchange went from Americans to Europeans, not the other way. The Italian food that GIs had been exposed to, many for the first time, was given to them by the army—canned Chef Boyardee spaghetti.

Also in 1946, an American woman from Pasadena, California, a graduate of Smith College, class of 1934, went with her husband to Paris, where he was stationed at the American Embassy. She went to the Cordon Bleu cooking school there and became fascinated with French cooking. She wanted to spread the word on how good French food was and show Americans how to make it. And that is exactly what Julia Child did when she returned to the United States.

The Cold War heated up and became a shooting war, called a United Nations "police action," in Korea from 1950 to 1953. It later became the subject of the movie and TV series *M*A*S*H*. This caused a huge build-up of the military in the United States that continues to the present.

The Fast-Food Fifties

"Better Living through Chemistry" was the slogan in the 1950s, along with "I Like Ike," which referred to five-star general Dwight D. Eisenhower, who led the Allies to victory in World War II and the Republicans to victory at the polls, serving as a two-term president from 1953 to 1961. After World War II ended in 1945, men returned from overseas, women gave up their factory jobs, and they proceeded to do things in record numbers: get married; move to the suburbs into houses built on what had often been farmland and financed by new government programs for veterans like the GI Bill; buy cars; and buy new appliances like stoves, refrigerators (20 million in one five-year period), dishwashers, washing machines, dryers, backyard barbecues (really grills), and the new home freezers invented by Amana.

They also bought televisions in record numbers and watched shows that reflected an idealized version of their prosperous new life. In *Father Knows Best*, *Ozzie and Harriet*, and *Leave It to Beaver*, Mom, freed from household drudgery by her new appliances, was serene and perfectly dressed and put meals on the table with no trouble.

In 1959, an entire episode of the popular TV show *Lassie*, about a collie dog and the rural family she lived with, dealt with "The New Refrigerator." Mother is dying to get rid of the old ice box, with its "dripping pan" and "no room." There is a linguistic shift as they remind each other to call the new appliance by a new word—"refrigerator." After Father brings the refrigerator in and plugs it in, the whole family stands around looking at it, beaming and listening to the motor. Almost moved to tears, mother caresses it and says, "Let others have their mink coats." The refrigerator also changes their relationship with the man who delivers ice to the house. Now they will see him only when he brings coal and oil in the winter.

Post-WWII Americans also had children in record numbers—50 million from 1945 to the end of the 1950s. This Baby Boom resulted in food marketing aimed specifically at children. In 1951, Tony the Tiger appeared to sell breakfast cereal. Flaked fish sticks transformed fish into finger food, appealing to children. Adults continued eating the foods they had been served in the armed forces: instant coffee and Spam.

TV Dinners and Jiffy Pop

Fast food and frozen food combined in 1954: Swanson introduced TV dinners. These frozen, precooked meals only needed to be popped in the oven and reheated. For 99 cents, the consumer got an aluminum tray divided into compartments with an entree, vegetables, and dessert. As more people stayed home to watch television, movie attendance dropped and so did popcorn consumption. Popcorn producers retaliated with Jiffy Pop—prepackaged and oiled popcorn in an old-fashioned style popper with a handle for the home audience.

In 1955, the principle of the assembly line finally came to food when milk-shake salesman Ray Kroc bought the McDonald brothers' hamburger stand in San Bernardino, California. Down the street was the restaurant that became Taco Bell.[44] Disneyland also opened in July 1955, and was so successful that they ran out of food on the first day.

At about the same time, another legend was born. This one was totally fake, but caught on and is celebrated around the world now.

HOLIDAY HISTORY:

St. Urho's Day, March 16

In 1956, Richard Mattson, a Finnish-American in Minnesota, got tired of listening to his Irish-American friends sing the praises of their patron, St. Patrick, and how he drove the snakes out of Ireland. So Mattson made up a Finnish saint, St. Urho (Hero), who drove the frogs out of Finland and saved the grape harvest (a real feat—Finland is as far north as Alaska). Nevertheless, the story caught on, with the frogs changed to grasshoppers (perhaps because of the grasshopper plagues in nineteenth-century Minnesota). St. Urho's colors are green for the grasshoppers and purple for the grapes. His day is March 16, purposely beating St. Patrick by one day.

Special foods connected with St. Urho's celebration include real grasshoppers in cookies, caramel corn, fritters, and enchiladas (perhaps for those from southern Finland). There is also *kalamojakka*, a Finnish fish and potato stew, which the saint ate every hour to keep up his strength while fighting the grasshoppers. The St. Urho's Grasshopper drink is made with green crème de menthe, white crème de cacao, and Finlandia vodka. The festivities include parades, songs, poems, polkas, statues, and chants of St. Urho's curse: *"Heinäsirkka, heinäsirkka, mene täältä hiiteen!"* ("Grasshopper, grasshopper, go to hell!").[45]

Civil Rights: African-Americans and the *Brown* Decision

Civil rights advocates had been using lawsuits to chip away at segregation in the United States. They were aided by black athletes whose talents were so spectacular they could not be ignored. Jesse Owens ran like the wind at the Nazi Olympics in Berlin in 1936 and won four gold medals. In 1938, the phenomenal fists of Joe Louis, the Brown Bomber, beat Germany's Max Schmeling for the world heavyweight boxing championship. In 1947, UCLA graduate Jackie Robinson integrated baseball when manager Branch Rickey put him in the line-up for the Brooklyn Dodgers (they moved to Los Angeles in 1958). The Tuskegee Airmen, black pilots, also served with distinction in World War II.

In the South, discrimination continued after World War II. In restaurants, the front of the house was segregated—reserved for whites only—but blacks still did the cooking and serving. Blacks felt that they had served their country honorably and risked their lives and should be treated equally. In 1948, one veteran, wearing his uniform and war medals, refused to move to the back of the bus. White men pulled him off the bus, beat him, and blinded him. An angry President Truman picked up a pen, issued an executive order, and integrated the army.

In 1954, the NAACP—National Association for the Advancement of Colored People—and others in the civil rights movement brought a case before the Supreme Court. In a rare unanimous decision in *Brown v. the Board of Education of Topeka, Kansas*, the Supreme Court justices stated that segregation was wrong. Period. Then they ordered that schools be integrated. The South resisted. The governor of Alabama said, "Segregation today, segregation tomorrow, segregation forever." It was going to be a long fight.

Civil Rights: Hispanics and César Chávez

Another group was fighting for survival, too. The plight of migrant workers was shown to Americans in "Harvest of Shame," a CBS-TV documentary that aired, deliberately, the day after Thanksgiving in 1960. Narrated by respected newsman Edward R. Murrow (who was the subject of the 2005 movie *Good Night and Good Luck*), it showed the deplorable conditions under which migrants worked for $900 per year. One thing that made their lives so difficult was the short-handled hoe. The 12- or 14-inch handle forced workers to literally bend in half for up to 12 hours a day out in the fields. At the end of the day it was nearly impossible to stand up. There was also no place for workers to go to the bathroom. A leader emerged. César Chávez forged a political movement of migrants and appealed to the American public to boycott table grapes (not wine grapes) and lettuce until those producers provided more humane working conditions. Chávez had a slogan: *Si se puede* (Yes, we can). And they did. César Chávez Day is celebrated on March 31.

The Cuban Revolution: Castro and Rum, 1959

On New Year's Eve, December 31, 1958, revolutionary Fidel Castro finally succeeded in taking Cuba's capital city, Havana, and overthrowing the government. Dictator Batista had been friendly to American businesses, including organized crime and the casinos and other operations they ran. This is illustrated in the movie *The Godfather II*, when the representatives of organized crime and American businesses literally cut up a cake in the shape of Cuba and take pieces. Most Cuban people were extremely poor, suffering from malnutrition and starvation. They ate *sopa de gallo*—rooster soup—an ironic name because there was nothing in it except water and brown sugar. To try to equalize food distribution, Castro instituted food rationing.[46] He also nationalized the rum industry, which means that the country took it by force. The Bacardi family fled to Puerto Rico. Castro also promised free elections. The Cuban people are still waiting.

Many Cubans, especially the educated upper class, moved to America after the revolution and brought their cuisine and culture with them to Little Havanas, like the one in Miami, Florida. Like other countries in the Caribbean,

Cuban food shows the influence of Spanish, African, and native cuisines. The staples are Spanish black beans and rice, and native plaintains, a type of banana. The Spanish influence also shows in pork marinated in Seville orange juice and stewed with onions, chicken roasted with garlic, and meatballs—*albondigas* [ahl-BON-dee-gahz]. Desserts feature tropical fruits—banana, coconut, pineapple, guava—in puddings, pies, and flan, a Spanish-style custard. The rum drinks that Americans are most familiar with, in addition to the rum-and-Coke Cuba Libre, are the daiquiri [DACK-ree], made with white rum and fruit; and the piña colada [PEE-nya ko-LAH-dah], which adds pineapple. At the end of the twentieth century, the *mojito* [moe-HEE-toe], made with rum, mint, lime juice, sugar, and carbonated water, became popular.

Hawaii Becomes a State, 1959

Also in 1959, Hawaii became a state. Alaska joined the United States in 1960, making a total of 50 stars on the American flag. Mainland Americans suddenly "discovered" the tropical Hawaiian islands, 2,500 miles away. James Michener's best-selling novel *Hawaii* became a blockbuster movie in 1966. A 1970 sequel, *The Hawaiians*, in a moment of deep fiction, showed Academy Award–winner Charlton Heston changing the economy of Hawaii forever by stealing the pineapple from South America in the nineteenth century and bringing it to Hawaii. In reality, pineapples came to the Pacific with Captain Cook in the 1770s. Hawaiians began canning them in 1892. (They were grown in Europe shortly after Columbus found them on Guadeloupe in 1493.) Elvis Presley visited *Blue Hawaii* in 1961 and returned to enjoy *Paradise Hawaiian Style* five years later. On television, the islands provided exotic scenery for three series: *Hawaiian Eye* from 1959 to 1963, *Hawaii Five-O* from 1968 to 1980 (and 2010), and *Magnum, P.I.* from 1980 to 1988. The main characters were *haoles* [HOW-lees]— white people—with Asian locals taking a distant second place or absent.

Religious and Food Missionaries

Haole Mark Twain visited Hawaii—then called the Sandwich Islands—in the 1860s, when there were still people alive who remembered native life and customs before missionaries arrived in the 1820s and converted them to Christianity. Dogs were raised for food and prized; 300 were sacrificed when King Kamehameha died in 1819. The dying king had to be carried from the house he slept in to the house where he ate because eating and sleeping in the same building was taboo. His wives had to eat in a separate house.[47] It was also taboo for women to eat bananas, pineapples, or oranges; the missionaries changed that.[48] Twain tried a cherimoya—"deliciousness itself"; a tamarind—"sour"; and saw natives eating raw fish—"Let us change the subject!"[49] In the marketplace he saw poi, a staple Hawaiian starch that "looks like common flour paste," and was kept in four-gallon bowls made of gourds. The natives "bake it [taro root] underground, then mash it up well with a heavy lava pestle, mix water with it until it becomes a paste, set it aside and let it ferment, and then it is poi."[50] It was eaten by sticking a forefinger into the bowl.

In the 1920s, 100 years after the religious missionaries came to Hawaii, food missionaries—home economists from Columbia Teachers College in New York City—introduced standard American food to Hawaiian schools: ground beef in the form of hamburger, meatloaf, and Salisbury steak.[51] Hawaiians refer to themselves as "locals" to distinguish themselves from *haole* missionaries and tourists. "Local Food" is their fusion of native, Japanese, Chinese, Filipino, Pacific Islander, and American cuisines. Rice is a staple starch. A whole pig marinated and roasted underground is the centerpiece of the luau. Spam appears in its Japanese form as Spam sushi and Spam tempura; in its Chinese form as Spam wonton; and in its Filipino form as Spam lumpia. As food historian Rachel Laudan notes, "in Hawaii Spam continues to be something to be reckoned with."[52] In 1959, the year that Hawaii became a state, Hormel sold its one billionth can of Spam.[53]

The Puu Puu Platter

Hawaii is part of Polynesia, now called the Pacific Islands: the Marianas, the Solomons, Guam, Fiji, Samoa, New Caledonia, the New Hebrides, and others. In the 1950s and 1960s, something that claimed to be Polynesian food appeared in American restaurants. Sweet, fruity drinks were garnished with small pastel paper umbrellas. The puu puu platter was an excuse to deep-fry food and smother it in canned pineapple chunks, maraschino cherries, and corn syrup. Real Polynesians eat food steamed or baked in banana leaves; taro, poi, yams, plantains, coconut, and fresh tropical fruit. They also eat fried forest rat and insects. The stewed flesh of fruit-eating bats *(civet de roussette)* is regarded as such a delicacy that some species are near extinction.[54]

Fine Dining: Life as a Work of Art

In the 1950s, Americans began a love affair with things Italian and French. On one of America's most popular television shows, *I Love Lucy*, Lucy and her real-life and television husband Ricky went to Europe. Lucy got more "local color" than she bargained for when she climbed into a wine vat to stomp grapes with her bare feet and ended up in a wrestling match with a strong, angry Italian woman. *Roman Holiday* (1953) was about a runaway princess; even ancient Rome was featured in a series of movies about the Roman Empire, including Shakespeare's *Julius Caesar*. Italian movie stars Sophia Loren and Anna Magnani were so well liked by American audiences that they won Academy Awards for Best Actress.

France was equally photogenic. *An American in Paris*, about an American GI who stays in Paris to paint after the war, won the Academy Award for Best Picture of 1951; in *Sabrina* (1954), the plain-Jane title character went to a cooking school with a view of the Eiffel Tower and came back looking like a *Vogue* model—and she could crack an egg one-handed. *To Catch a Thief*, directed by suspense master Alfred Hitchcock in 1955, showed the glories of the French Riviera. It also had dialogue that was very suggestive for the time: gorgeous Grace Kelly asks Cary Grant if he wants a breast or a leg—but all she's offering him is chicken. Brigitte Bardot, the French "sex kitten," popularized the new bikini bathing suit. Americans went on whirlwind tours through Europe, where the dollar was strong, and tasted the food for the first time.

In France, a new style of cooking began in the 1950s. Its leading chefs were Ferdinand Point, Paul Bocuse, Michel Guérard, Jean and Pierre Troigros, and Alain Chapel. This new style altered the *grande cuisine* of Escoffier in several ways. It broke the three-century-old tradition of relying on roux as a thickening agent and used lower-fat stock reductions instead. Escoffier's parsley garnish was gone. Presentation was Asian-influenced and asymmetrical, with the focus on color, texture, size, shape. Food was "art on a plate."

The great American architect Frank Lloyd Wright believed in life lived as art, too. At Taliesen, the school he founded in Spring Green, Wisconsin, it is the job of one student to get up early every morning and create a work of art for the others. This work of art is composed of furniture, napkins, cups, and saucers. The tables in the dining room are a variety of shapes, like tinker toys: round, square, rectangular. The student arranges them in a new design, chooses napkins and place mats, picks wildflowers in season. This way, first thing every day, everyone is stimulated and challenged by new shapes, forms, colors, textures. And that's *before* the food. It is an old concept that is still new and meaningful.

In 1973, two food critics, Gault and Millau, gave this new cooking a name—Nouvelle Cuisine. Again; cuisine had become *nouvelle* in eighteenth-century France, too.

The Sixties: Revolutions in Color

The 1960s was a decade of political and social upheaval throughout the world. Students rioted in Paris, New York, and California for various reasons. Civil rights and social injustice were foremost. Millions of Americans protested the war in Vietnam, a former French colony. It was a social revolution that changed the way history was written and changed food writing, too. Before the 1960s, most history was "from the top down" or "great man"—about what important people, usually white men, had done. In the 1960s, people of all races, classes, and genders began writing their own history "from the bottom up"—about how the masses of ordinary people had changed history, too.

"Black is beautiful"

African countries revolted, shaking off their colonial masters. And African-Americans pointed out that 100 years after President Lincoln freed the slaves in the Civil War, they still couldn't vote, serve on juries, attend schools with white people, or sit at public lunch counters. In 1963, hundreds of thousands of Americans of all races, ages, and genders marched at the Washington Monument and heard the Reverend Dr. Martin Luther King tell the world, "I have a dream" that people will be judged by what's inside them, not by the color of their skin, while millions more saw him on television. Black men shook off a hundred years of being insulted by being called "boy" and started addressing each other as "man." The new slogan for black pride was "Black is beautiful." Because of the Civil Rights movement, advertising icons like Aunt Jemima and Uncle Ben got face lifts to look more like professional people and less like happy slaves.

Americans continued their love affair with speed in cars, airplanes, and food. At first, if you wanted food you had to go to a restaurant. Then you could call ahead and the food was ready when you got there. At some restaurants, you didn't even have to go inside—there was a drive-through window. In the 1960s, food got even faster—the restaurant came to you. Domino's Pizza was the first fast food delivered to your door. And Julia Child came to your television.

Cordon Bleu and White House—Julia Child and Jackie Kennedy

In 1961, *Mastering the Art of French Cooking*, written by Julia Child, Simone Beck, and Louisette Bertholle, was published. It revolutionized Americans' relationship to food, especially French food. Julia Child's purpose was to take the mystery out of French cooking, to make it accessible to anyone in America, and she did. The kitchen on Julia Child's television program looked like an average American kitchen because it was hers, designed by her husband Paul. She cooked on an electric stove top, used average kitchen knives and ingredients that could be found in any American supermarket. Quiche and other French foods became extremely popular.

In 1963, Julia Child revolutionized the teaching of cooking when she appeared on Boston's public broadcasting station WGBH as *The French Chef*. In 1966, her picture was on the cover of *Time* magazine, which called her "Our Lady of the Ladle." The television programs *Julia Child and Company, Julia Child and More Company,* and *Dinner with Julia* followed. In 1981, she was one of the founders of the American Institute of Wine and Food (AIWF). In 1989, she wrote *The Way to Cook*, the first cookbook offered as a main selection by the Book-of-the-Month Club. She was one of the founders of the James Beard Foundation and, with Jacques Pepin, of the new culinary history program at Boston University. Her name is on an award for Best Cookbook given by the International Association of Culinary Professionals (IACP), which she also helped to found. Her numerous books are on the shelf of every professional and amateur cook in America. Her kitchen is at the Smithsonian National Museum of American History. Her generosity and commitment to food were everywhere. In 2009, Meryl Streep played Julia Child in the movie *Julie and Julia*. Amy Adams was Julie Powell, a young woman who cooked her way through *Mastering the Art of French Cooking* in 365 days and blogged about it.

Although Julia Child made it possible to cook French food without special equipment, a hardware store owner in Sonoma, California, north of San Francisco, liked special equipment. Chuck Williams went to France and brought equipment back to his store. It was immediately popular, so he opened another one, in Beverly Hills, then more. As a character on a television show remarked, "Once you've discovered fire, it's just a short hop to Williams-Sonoma."[55]

President or Pastry?

French food reached Washington, D.C., too, in 1961, when John Fitzgerald Kennedy (JFK), the young, good-looking, Harvard-educated, Irish Catholic senator from Massachusetts, and his wife, Jacqueline Bouvier Kennedy, became president and first lady. The White House became a social focal point of the United States. The Kennedys hired a chef who was trained in classical French cooking, René Verdon. Jackie, as she became known, was of French descent, and had spent her junior year at Vassar in France. When the couple attended state dinners in France, she spoke to the guests in French; when they went to South America, she gave speeches in Spanish. Unfortunately, the first lady was not fluent in German, so when Kennedy went to Berlin and gave a speech to show solidarity with the people of Berlin, which had been split into two cities by a wall the communists built, he said, "*Ich bin ein Berliner.*" There was controversy for a while over whether what he had said translated as, "I am from Berlin" or "I am a Berliner"—which is a jelly doughnut. German grammarians finally ruled that Kennedy had affirmed his humanness and his humanity, and said that he was from Berlin.

The Green Revolution—Farming

In the 1960s, overabundance caught up with Americans—obesity became a problem. Weight Watchers held its first meeting in 1963. Other diet organizations followed: Overeaters Anonymous, patterned after the Alcoholics Anonymous program; Australian Jenny Craig; a Christian Weigh Down Diet, which urged its members to get "slim for Him."[56] Millions of Americans were going to health clubs and drinking diet soda—Diet-Rite, Tab, Diet Pepsi, Fresca. In 1975, dieting even reached beer when Miller introduced Lite Beer. The slogans were "Thin is in" and "You can't be too rich or too thin," except that there was an increase in the eating disorders first named in the nineteenth century, like anorexia nervosa.

However, millions of people in the world were starving. The industrialized nations saw food as an issue of national security: underfed populations in other countries could revolt and change the global balance of power. Science had nearly wiped out malaria by spraying with DDT, invented a liquid vaccine that prevented polio, and cured infections with antibiotics like penicillin and sulfa.

After these medical miracles, what was left? Miracle food—genetically engineered soy, and dwarf rice that had a short growing time, a phenomenal yield, and would grow anywhere in Asia would stamp out famines like the one that killed approximately 20 million people in China between 1958 and 1961.[57] The United States, the largest grower of rice in the world, built the International Rice Research Institute in the Philippines. In 1965, Ferdinand Marcos was elected president of the Philippines on the slogan, "Progress is a grain of rice." The technical name of the rice was IR8, but it was called *Than nong*, after the Vietnamese god of agriculture. It not only grew much faster, so it could produce two crops each year, it also yielded more rice per plant. This was the beginning of the Green Revolution, the plan to feed the world by applying science and genetic breakthroughs to farming.

The Blue Revolution—Aquaculture

The same intensive farming was taking place in the water, with salmon, shrimp, mussels, tilapia, and trout. Aquaculture had its proponents and opponents. Supporters claimed that fish farming would increase yield and help feed the world. Opponents pointed out that farming some fish—like salmon, which eat other fish—disrupts ecosystems as smaller fish do not provide food in their own ecosystem because they are captured to feed larger fish somewhere else. Opponents also question the quality of the farmed fish, which become fatty swimming in pens instead of the ocean, and have to be dyed to look the way they do in the wild. Nevertheless, fish farming "is probably the world's fastest growing form of food production. . . . Some people believe that, by 2030, aquaculture will supply most of the fish people eat."[58]

The Anti-White Revolution—Counterculture Cuisine

The social revolutions of the 1960s included food revolutions. For the first time in history, some people were eating with a consciousness about the global environmental consequences of where their food came from and how it was produced. The new buzz word was "ecology"—recognizing that all living things, including humans, were connected. In a "back to nature" movement, some Baby Boomers revolted against industrialization by living on communes patterned after Israeli kibbutzim and doing manual labor. They grew fruits, vegetables, and herbs, milked farm animals, and in a gesture of political solidarity with nature and the civil rights movements, revolted against white things, especially white foods: "Minute Rice, Cool Whip, instant mashed potatoes, white sugar, peeled apples . . . and, of course, Wonder Bread." Instead, they baked bread with whole grains, ate brown rice and brown eggs.[59] Corporate responsibility and accountability were born here, too, as the Baby Boomers demanded to know which corporations had ties to the military-industrial complex and the Vietnam War.[60] When this counterculture cuisine crossed over to the cities, it took the form of salad bars, herb tea, and whole-grain bread. In the language of the 1960s, this "raised the consciousness" about environmental issues—so much that Earth Day was celebrated for the first time on April 22, 1970. By the 1970s, corporate food producers, restaurants, and supermarkets realized that there was money in counterculture cuisine and were manufacturing and corporatizing this counterculture cuisine.

Space Age Technology

At the same time that the "back to nature" movement was growing, technology was changing American kitchens. WWII radar led to the microwave oven. The Raytheon Company produced the first commercial one in 1947, the Radarange. Like the first computers, which filled an entire room, these early microwaves were enormous. Tappan's first domestic model, in 1952, "stood five and a half feet high . . . [and weighed] 750 pounds." And cost thousands of dollars. It was not until 1967 that Amana sold a viable microwave for home use at $495. By 1975, microwaves "outsold gas ranges."[61]

Space Age technology contributed Tang—powdered orange juice—which went into space with astronauts and into American kitchens. A revolutionary new line of cookware was advertised as being made of the same material as rocket nosecones. CorningWare, introduced in 1958 by the Corning Glass Works Company in New York, could go from freezer to oven to direct stovetop flame without cracking or burning. It was easy to clean, and the white square or rectangular pans with the little blue cornflower design looked good enough to put right on the table as serving dishes. They cleaned up in the dishwasher.

In the coming decades, prosperity would increase and credit cards would become available to everyone. Americans' new interest in food and love of convenience would take American cuisine in two different directions. One would go toward ethnic and exotic, sparing no expense; the other wanted faster food and more of it for less money. Technology would serve them both.

Agribusiness vs. Organic

From the 1970s into the second decade of the twenty-first century, food continued to go in two different directions. On the one hand, there was agribusiness, huge multinational corporations that practiced intensive farming of food and animals. Massive pollution of the food supply and epidemics among animals caused by poor sanitation led to more people insisting on the opposite. Organic food was free of pesticides and additives, preferably locally grown to leave as small a footprint on the planet as possible. Agribusiness used artificial flavorings and trans fats; organic used natural flavors and pushed successfully for laws making trans fats illegal. Agribusiness provided high fat, high sugar, high salt school lunches; organic got Congress to pass the Wellness Policy for schools and got salad bars put in schools.

The Seventies: Food Revolutions
California Cuisine: Alice Waters
In 1971, a landmark in the history of food took place in Berkeley, California—Alice Waters opened Chez Panisse restaurant. She named it after a character in the French film *Fanny* (1961). Panisse's modest restaurant is the heart of the

town because of his unconditional love. The movie takes place in Provence in southeastern France, the home of the cuisine that inspired Waters.

Like many other famous food people, she didn't start out intending to have a career in food. She was a kindergarten teacher who went to France and fell in love with the country and the food. When she found mesclun salad greens, she brought the seeds back and grew them herself. She was also inspired by British writer Elizabeth David's passion for Mediterranean cooking, her desire to bring the "flavour of those blessed lands of sun and sea and olive trees into . . . English kitchens."[1] In turn, Waters and Jeremiah Tower, one of the most influential chefs at the restaurant, influenced another generation of chefs and food producers like Mark Miller, Lindsey Shere, Wolfgang Puck, and Francis Ford Coppola.

Another food landmark occurred in 1971, also on the West Coast. Three friends got together and opened a coffeehouse in Seattle, Washington. They named it Starbucks, after a character in *Moby Dick*, Herman Melville's nineteenth-century novel about an obsessed sea captain's hunt for a great white whale.

California Cuisine: Wine

In the 1970s, California wineries finally began to recover from Prohibition. In the 1920s, the grapevines had been ripped out and the land planted with peaches, plums, and nuts. Solidly built stone wineries that had been producing prize-winning wines since the nineteenth century were abandoned. When Prohibition ended in 1933, the fruit and nut orchards were ripped out and the land replanted with vines. But it was the Depression and then World War II, so many of the wineries did not function until after 1945.

In 1976, the bicentennial of the United States, two Napa Valley vineyards shocked the world of wine. In a blind tasting, Stag's Leap took first place in red wines; Chateau Montelena took first place in whites. The wineries they beat—French—had been leaders in the world of wine. The Napa wineries won fair and square: in France with French judges.[2] This is the basis of the 2008 movie *Bottle Shock*. The reclamation of what *Smithsonian* magazine calls these "Ghost Wineries" continues into the twenty-first century.

Minceur, Spa, and Vegetarian Cuisine

Nouvelle Cuisine, pared down even more and stripped of fat, resulted in super-lean cuisines like spa cuisine and cuisine *minceur* (French for "lean cuisine"). Many people thought that cutting out fats was the way to immortality. Nathan Pritikin, who ran the Pritikin Longevity Center near the beach in Santa Monica, California, touted the physical benefits of eating no fat and jogging. In 1983, *The Pritikin Promise: 28 Days to a Longer Life* became a *New York Times* best seller. The Pritikin diet allowed no fat, sugar, or oil. Around the same time, a young medical doctor, Dr. Dean Ornish, had an idea that patients recovering from heart attacks and surgery would do better with less medicine if they changed their diets drastically. He contacted a food writer, Martha Rose Shulman, who came up with "heart healthy" recipes. The pilot program was a great success. The American Heart Association adopted the concept, and soon restaurants were sporting menus with a ♥ next to the healthy approved dishes. Shulman went on to write many other cookbooks, like *Mediterranean Light* (Martha-Rose-Shulman .com).

Spas like the Golden Door north of San Diego, California, founded in 1958 (the same year as the Barbie doll), provided very low-calorie cuisine based on organic fruits and vegetables from their own gardens and prepared by classically trained chefs. In 2010, the Golden Door's weekly rate was $7,750.[3] Spas designed around feng shui used herbs and vegetables like carrots, lemongrass, ginger, and mandarin oil (sometimes organic) for facial masques, body wraps, and massages. Farmers' markets and food festivals sprang up all over the United States in response to the demand for the freshest ingredients.

In 1973, the Moosewood Restaurant, a collectively owned vegetarian restaurant, opened in Ithaca, New York. The food and the seasonings made vegetarian cooking exciting, spicy, and ethnic. Cookbooks like *The Moosewood Cookbook*, *The Enchanted Broccoli Forest*, and others followed. They gave vegetarianism a new taste and reinvigorated a movement that had been out of fashion since the end of the nineteenth century.

At the other end of the food spectrum were desserts. In 1977, a woman opened a store in Palo Alto, California, in spite of having been told by everyone that she could never make a living selling nothing but cookies. Mrs. Fields proved them wrong. The following year, two friends learned how to make ice cream through a correspondence course from Pennsylvania State University and converted a run-down gas station into an ice cream parlor in Burlington, Vermont. Ben & Jerry became an ice cream empire.

Urban Renewal and Gentrification: Boston Market and B&Bs

Faneuil Hall Market, Boston, which spawned the Boston Market restaurant chain, was one of the first urban redevelopment projects. It took a downtown area that had been warehouses and renovated it into small retail and food shops. Other cities followed this successful example. New Yorkers discovered old factories and warehouses with solid wood floors that could hold thousands of pounds and turned them into lofts. In more remote areas, old farmhouses and even lighthouses were turned into the newest getaway craze, the bed and breakfast—B&B.

Unlike an impersonal hotel, the B&B provided chatty owners who lived on the premises, comforting fireplaces in the bedrooms (and sometimes the bathrooms), goose down quilts, liqueur nightcaps, and freshly baked breads and muffins for breakfast. The California coast abounds in B&Bs. One town that made a fortune turning California redwoods into lumber and then went into a decline revived by recycling its past and restoring its architecture. Eureka, California, has more buildings on the National Register of Historic Places than any other town in the United States. Eureka and the surrounding area north of San Francisco boast many B&Bs, hotels, restaurants, and private homes that began as Victorian mansions with the elaborate trim and detail known as "gingerbread." The picture of a B&B in Ferndale, California, is a real "gingerbread" house—the Gingerbread Mansion Inn.

The Gingerbread Mansion Inn. *Courtesy Bob Von Norman.*

The Eighties: Political and Restaurant Revolutions

Profound changes took place in world politics in the 1980s. In 1989, during the administration of Republican President Ronald Reagan, the communist government of the USSR fell. So did the Berlin Wall—Germany was unified again. Free for the first time in the greater part of a century from the military-enforced dictatorship of communism, many areas fragmented along the religious and ethnic lines that had existed for hundreds of years. Czechoslovakia split into the Czech Republic and Slovakia. In the former Yugoslavia, war broke out between Serbs and Slavs again.

In the 1980s, American Baby Boomers, the generation that screamed its way through the 1960s with "Never trust anybody over 30," hit 30 and panicked. Looking for immortality, they drank designer waters, joined health clubs, and exercised until their joints wore out. They sought "natural" herbal and vitamin solutions for their problems. St. John's Wort eased their depression, glucosamine and chondroitin soothed their joints, echinacea was supposed to cure their colds. They took ginkgo biloba to help them remember when to take everything else.

The Zagat Guide

The 1980s felt the effects of two events that took place at the end of the 1970s. In 1979, two New York City attorneys, both Yale Law School graduates (he went to Harvard, she went to Vassar), turned a hobby into a business. Their informal system of rating restaurants for friends evolved into best-selling guides for Tim and Nina Zagat and revolutionized the business of restaurant criticism. Unlike newspaper and magazine reviews, Zagat reviews don't depend on just one person. Over 100,000 people review restaurants in 45 cities by filling out a detailed questionnaire.

The Iranian Revolution Comes to Beverly Hills Restaurants

There was another important shift in world politics in the 1970s. In 1971, England withdrew from the Middle East, leaving a power vacuum. In 1979, an Islamic fundamentalist revolution led by a religious leader, the Ayatollah Khomeini, overthrew the Shah of Iran (*shah* means "king") and took the American embassy in the capital, Teheran, and all of its employees hostage. The shah and the royal family had to flee, as well as thousands of Iranians who were used to doing business with Western countries, especially the United States. The women didn't wear long dresses and veils; they went to college, had jobs, and drove cars. By the early 1980s, there was an influx of Westernized Iranians in the United States, especially in Beverly Hills, California.

These Iranians/Persians brought their cuisine and their culture with them. Iranian restaurants, groceries, and bakeries sprang up in Beverly Hills and West Los Angeles, including one restaurant with a *tannur*, the freestanding clay oven like an Indian tandoor. Signs in the Farsi language lined Westwood Boulevard just south of the University of California. Menus offered items like hummus; *polos*, rice-based meat dishes; and *fesenjan*, meat stew in a smooth pomegranate and walnut sauce. Fine pastry shops that sold baklava side-by-side with éclairs and *petits fours* showed the French influence on Middle Eastern food.

Iran stopped selling oil to the United States. Prices rose. Americans experienced something they had not experienced since World War II—shortages. They got up before dawn to drive to gas stations and wait in long lines for a limited number of gallons of expensive gas. One long-term result of the oil crisis of the 1970s was that Japan, always short of energy, made a conscious decision to focus on electronics, including energy-efficient ones. Now, this technology runs many appliances. Electronic sensors stop cooking food when it's done, switch lights off when people leave a room, sense what's in the dishwasher.

The New Immigration and Ethnic Restaurants

U.S. immigration laws passed in 1965 began to have an effect in the 1980s with an explosion of new immigrants—about one million a year in the last two decades of the twentieth century. The immigration wave that had occurred in New York and other Eastern cities at the end of the nineteenth century occurred on the West Coast at the end of the twentieth, with one crucial difference. The Eastern cities got immigrants from southern and eastern Europe; immigrants to the West were from Asia, the Middle East, Africa, and Central and South

America. Just as New York had Little Italy, German Yorkville, and the Jewish Lower East Side, southern California has Little Saigon, Little India, Little Ethiopia, Koreatown, Cambodia Town, Thai Town, and a sprawling new Chinatown in the San Gabriel Valley northeast of Los Angeles. These are in addition to Little Tokyo downtown and a Japanese community on the west side.

The census of 2000 showed that for the first time, whites were not a majority in California. The Hispanic migration was so massive—almost 50 percent of the population of New Mexico, for example—that many of the immigrants do not assimilate; they live in parallel cultures. This immigration caused an explosion of ethnic restaurants. On the same street with Jamba Juice and Jack in the Box are Islamic *halal* butchers, Mexican *panaderias* selling *tres leches* cakes, sushi bars, Brazilian sports bars for watching soccer, Hong Kong–style seafood restaurants, Franco-Caribbean restaurants, Lebanese hookah bars, Filipino and Indonesian grocery stores, bagel bakeries, Argentine *empanadas*, Thai BBQ, and Iranian restaurants. Now, "Southwestern" can mean Tex-Mex or a region of India. And antipasto, *antojitos*, and amuse-bouches were joined by Spanish *tapas*, Middle Eastern *mezze*, Indian *chaat*, and the Japanese *bento* box.

McDonald's in China: Burger or *Bao*?

At the end of the twentieth century, industrialization arrived in Asia and brought about the same changes in cuisine and culture that it had caused in England in the eighteenth century and in the United States in the nineteenth: people moved from the country to the cities for more opportunities; cities became crowded and polluted; class differences increased based on who owned businesses and who did the labor; traditional gender roles shifted. People who had lived on the land were no longer near the source of food or their families, so rituals were disrupted. You don't have a *selametan* with strangers.

McDonald's, the most global of restaurants, opened in Asia. It made accommodations to local cuisines and cultures and also influenced them: vegetable McNuggets and "a mutton-based Maharajah Mac" in India; *halal* food in Muslim areas.[4] In Turkey you could get a McBurek; in Greece, a Greek Mac—a spiced burger in a pita. For a while, Australians down under got their local favorite, the McOz, a quarter pounder with beets on top. New Zealand customers got the KiwiBurger, which added a fried egg to the beet topping.

McDonald's opened in Beijing, China, in 1992. At 700 seats, it was McDonald's largest restaurant to that time.[5] Now, "seven of the world's ten busiest McDonald's restaurants are located in Hong Kong."[6] McDonald's was a model of American efficiency and created newer, higher standards of hygiene in food and restaurants. It started by moving the toilet out of the kitchen, where it had traditionally been to cut plumbing costs.[7]

But a hamburger on a bun and French fries—a full meal to Americans—doesn't fit the Chinese definition of a full meal, which has rice and vegetables. So McDonald's is considered snack food.[8] In Hong Kong, it doesn't fit the definition of meat, either. It's *bao*—a dumpling stuffed with meat.[9] In Hong Kong, Coca-Cola, exotic and imported, like sugar in medieval Europe, was treated as a medicine—served hot, with ginger and herbs.[10]

Although the service is fast by American standards, for Chinese, fast food is something bought from a street vendor. Going into a restaurant with tables means sitting—and lingering.[11] Chinese stay twice as long in McDonald's as Americans, 20 to 25 minutes compared to 11.[12]

In China, the most populous country on Earth, it has been government policy since 1980 not to have more than one child. So the second generation of only children has no brothers or sisters, and because their parents are only children, they also have no aunts, uncles, or cousins. Enter Ronald McDonald, who is called "Uncle McDonald," and his female counterpart, "Aunt McDonald." They are the extended family that is gone in China. They do what a good aunt and uncle do: take an interest in the children, talk to them, and play games. Sometimes they do this while celebrating a child's birthday, an American custom previously unknown in China, but which has caught on as single-child families and prosperity combine to create child consumers. Aunt and Uncle McDonald also visit the children at school and at home.[13]

Another American custom new to Asia is "friendliness." Americans are used to "service with a smile"; Asians see strangers smiling as faking to butter them up and cheat them. Asian seriousness about the job, including food service, comes across to Americans as "a deliberate attempt to be rude or indifferent."[14]

A poultry market in Vietnam. *Photo courtesy of Ron and Sylvia Mracky.*

Southeast Asian Cuisines

Since much of what Americans knew about Southeast Asian cuisines in the 1980s was connected to the Vietnam War, they didn't like them. Soldiers complained about fermented fish sauce, *nuoc mam* in Vietnam, *nam pla* in Thailand. Eventually, Americans acquired the palate necessary to appreciate these sophisticated combinations of Asian fusion food. Nouvelle Vietnamese restaurants like Michelia in Los Angeles, under the direction of chef-owner Kimmy Tang, served Vietnamese food influenced by France, China, Italy, Thailand, and California.

INGREDIENTS:

Chef Kimmy Tang's Saigon Roll

Traditional Spring Roll	Nouvelle Vietnamese—Chef Tang
8 cooked shrimp	8 peeled shrimp
8 cooked slices bacon	1 teaspoon canola oil
½ pound cooked rice noodles	---
8 mint leaves	8 mint leaves
8 basil leaves	---
8 lettuce leaves	¼ pound mixed baby greens
1 handful bean sprouts	---
1 small cucumber, julienned	1 small cucumber, finely julienned
---	½ pound jicama, finely julienned
---	⅛ pound pickled carrot, finely julienned
---	1 stalk green onion, thinly sliced
---	4 thin slices ginger, finely diced
4 sheets of rice paper, for wrapping	4 sheets of rice paper, for wrapping

---

Hong Kong was a special case in world history. When England's 99-year lease on the tiny island expired in 1997 and ownership reverted to communist China, thousands of people left. Many were middle-class professional people used to a capitalist society who did not want to be under the rule of communist China. They took their Cantonese-influenced cuisine when they went to Thailand, Vietnam, and the United States. Called Chiu Chow [zhoo chow], it is seafood-intensive, based on cooking in seasoned broth.

Changes in Cookbooks and Kitchens

In America, these immigrant groups followed the same pattern as earlier groups. At first, cooking was done at home, then in restaurants that catered to the immigrants, then in crossover restaurants for the general public. The first Thai cookbook, *The Original Thai Cookbook* by Jennifer Brennan, wasn't published in the United States until 1981. By the end of the 1990s and the beginning of the twenty-first century, mainstream American publishing was producing many cookbooks devoted to the foods of Southeast Asia. These are in the new style of cookbook writing, which includes not just cuisine, but culture, history, and memoir. More and more, in the global world and the global economy, people want to know not just what they are eating, but why and where it came from. Like the cuisine, the authors of many of these books have lived on more than one continent and are multicultural.

There were changes in more than just the food in restaurants. Hispanics went into kitchens in record numbers. By 2002, they were 25 percent of all commercial cooks, including in high-profile restaurants.[15] Women, too, caused changes in the front and back of the house. When a Los Angeles businesswoman took her male partner to dinner at an elegant French restaurant in 1980, her menu had food items but no prices on it. The man's had food *and* prices. It was common practice at some upscale restaurants to give menus with prices only to men because it was assumed that they would be paying the bill; women were not supposed to concern themselves with numbers and money. A lawsuit later, all

This menu offers items from all parts of the pig. *Photo courtesy John Bandman, Certified Chef of Cuisine and Educator, New York Restaurant School at Art Institute New York City.*

patrons at restaurants get the same menu.[16] Although women had been able to get credit in their own names since 1973, it was still unusual for a woman—even a professional woman—to buy dinner for a man. In the twenty-first century, it is commonplace.

Northern Italian

In the 1980s, Americans discovered Italian food all over again. This time it was the (mostly) tomato-less northern Italian food from Tuscany, Emilia-Romagna, and Genoa. Pesto Genovese ("from Genoa")—basil, pine nuts, olive oil, and Parmigiano-Reggiano cheese—became popular and soon had innumerable imitators. Parsley, sage, and cilantro were mixed with pecans, almonds, walnuts, or pumpkin seeds. Rice and corn, in risotto and polenta, replaced pasta as the starch. Tiramisu—literally, "pick me up"—became a popular dessert. It was assembled, not cooked, made from food that would be on hand in an average Italian household: coffee, lady fingers or leftover sponge cake, mascarpone cheese, cocoa. In 1975, nouvelle spread to Italian when Pasta Primavera ("springtime")—pasta with vegetables—was invented at New York's Le Cirque restaurant. Spaghetti and meatballs in tomato sauce were *finito* in upper-class restaurants. For a while.

Fetal Alcohol Syndrome

In 1989, Michael Dorris, a Native American professor of anthropology at Dartmouth College in Hanover, New Hampshire, published a book called *The Broken Cord*. It was the agonizing story of his discovery of the disease from which his adopted Native American son was suffering, fetal alcohol syndrome or FAS. Drinking during pregnancy could cause severe central nervous system damage, seizures, and shorten life. He exposed the history of United States–Native American relations that had led to such despair that on the reservations young men carry can openers in their pockets to puncture spray cans of Lysol, smear the gel on bread, eat it to get high—and suffer severe nervous system damage. Soon after *The Broken Cord* was published, Congress passed a law stating that labels warning women of the dangers of consuming alcohol during pregnancy had to be placed on all bottles of alcoholic beverages.

The Nineties: The Celebrity Chef

In 1991, the communist government of the USSR came to an end and the Cold War was over. But a war for control of the television food audience was heating up. The Food Network, a new cable channel based in New York City, began in 1993. By then, the chefs who had been changing cuisine and opening restaurants were well known in the culinary world. With the Food Network, they became household names. With the advent of reality shows in the twenty-first century, anyone who was a complete unknown had the chance to become a star on a 30-minute show on the Food Network.

Food Network and Food Empires: Puck, Stewart, Lagasse

In the 1970s, a shy young Austrian named Wolfgang Puck was the chef at Ma Maison, a trendy Hollywood restaurant with an unlisted telephone number. In 1982, he broke out on his own and opened Spago on Sunset Boulevard in West Hollywood, California. Puck reinvented pizza. He used the dough as a base for fusion food from worldwide cuisines: Black Forest ham and goat cheese; smoked salmon and golden caviar; duck sausage, chile oil, and mozzarella; and chicken, jalapeño peppers, and fontina cheese. His pasta could be spicy, spinach, or black with squid ink; and sport sauces or fillings of pumpkin, foie gras and truffles, smoked scallops, or sweetbreads. Bland white hothouse mushrooms disappeared, replaced with shiitake, oyster, chanterelle, enoki, cremini, and porcini. Puck's food became wildly popular, especially with celebrities, who gathered at the restaurant informally at first for what became Puck's famous—and very exclusive—Academy Award parties. He owns multiple restaurants, frozen Puck pizzas and soups are sold now in supermarkets, and he also provides food for Century City Hospital west of Beverly Hills. In January, 2001, Puck began his own television show on the Food Network.

Martha Stewart went from middle-class Polish-American girl to model to Barnard graduate to Wall Street stockbroker to Connecticut caterer to Martha Stewart OmniMedia to prison for insider trading, and back again. The Polish-American seemed to discover what alchemists in the Middle Ages couldn't: how to turned everything she touched into gold. She transformed "housekeeping" into "homekeeping," and her line of paints, linens, and housewares brought affordable beauty and sophistication to mainstream K-Mart. According to professional bakers, she also changed what people expected from their wedding cakes, expanding far beyond yellow and white, and with creative decorations. By the beginning of the third millennium, many brides and grooms were bypassing traditional wedding cakes in favor of individual strawberry shortcakes (especially June brides, when strawberries are in season), devil's food cake, fruitcake, pies, cupcakes stacked up in a pyramid like a French *croquembouche*, and even cakes made from rounds of cheese.

Emeril Lagasse, a Portuguese-American from Massachusetts and 1978 graduate of Johnson & Wales in Providence, Rhode Island, developed a tremendous following. Audiences responded to his outgoing everyman personality and signature phrases "Kick it up a notch" and "BAM!" as he zapped his food with spices. He owned several restaurants and had a one-hour daily television show, and a line of sauces, cookware, and cookbooks. Lagasse became so popular that the Food Network sometimes seemed like "all Emeril, all the time."

Some other popular shows that have been on the Food Network: Rachael Ray's *30 Minute Meals*, Giada De Laurentiis's *Everyday Italian*, Sara Moulton's

Cooking Live, Gale Gand's *Sweet Dreams*, and the *Too Hot Tamales*, Susan Feniger and Mary Sue Milliken. Bobby Flay traveled across America, unearthing clambakes in Massachusetts and the stew called "burgoo" in Kentucky. Mario Batali and his sidekick Rooney ate their way across Italy from antipasto to gelato. A knock on the door could be Gordon Elliott, bringing along a chef to surprise Mr. and Mrs. Average American and family with an amazing dinner cooked from odds and ends they found in the refrigerator, freezer, and kitchen cabinets. Alton Brown explained food chemistry with the aid of pop-up experts and graphics. *Food 911*'s Tyler Florence could cure a sick bouillabaisse or whatever else ailed your food.

One of the most popular shows on the Food Network was *Iron Chef*. The show began in 1993 on Fuji TV in Japan and premiered in the United States in 1999. Dubbed from Japanese, this one-hour show pitted male chefs cooking in Japan against each other. Each show centered around a theme food; it could be giant clam, eggplant, pumpkin, or anything else. It is cooking as spectacle, cooking as contest, cooking as gladiatorial combat. It is the "straight" version of a comedy routine that John Belushi invented in 1976 on the television show *Saturday Night Live*. In "Samurai Delicatessen," Belushi's Samurai Chef character screamed at customers as he hacked deli meats and vegetables to ribbons with a huge samurai sword.

Iron Chef spawned an equally popular spin-off: *Iron Chef America*. The first American iron chefs were Bobby Flay, Mario Batali, and Wolfgang Puck. In 2005, the first female iron chef joined the line-up: Cat Cora, a Greek-American raised in the American South.

Comfort Food

The term *comfort food*, meaning a food that relieves stress, often because of associations with good childhood memories, was used as far back as the 1950s. It was added to the Oxford English Dictionary in 1997, with the meaning expanded to foods high in sugar or carbohydrates, which might increase the levels of mood elevators tryptophan and serotonin in the brain. Comfort foods vary by culture, region, and gender, but some major ones in the United States are potato chips, ice cream, and sweets.[17] Macaroni and cheese is one of the dishes fueling the global cheese market, which is expected to grow by "more than 20% between 2008–2015."[18]

As the Baby Boomers aged, they lapsed from their low-fat diets and intense workouts and went back to the comfort foods of their 1950s childhoods: meatloaf with gravy and mashed potatoes, and Rice Krispie Treats. They also comforted themselves with $6 billion worth of cookies a year and food they had eaten sitting around fires at summer camp.[19] Two of the old favorites were Banana Boats—scooped-out bananas stuffed with chocolate and marshmallows and heated slowly at the edge of the campfire—and s'mores.

RECIPE:

S'mores[20]

First, make a campfire. Then, take a Graham cracker and cover it with a chocolate bar. Then, put some marshmallows on a stick and roast them over the campfire. Slide the hot, toasted marshmallows off the stick (making sure to get some on your fingers, so you have to lick them) and onto the chocolate bar on the Graham cracker. Cover with more chocolate bar, and top with another Graham cracker. The hot marshmallow melts the chocolate and welds the entire sandwich together. It is a symphony of taste and texture, and everybody wants "s'more."

Soon, s'mores went upscale, served with a knife and fork in restaurants with tablecloths, napped in pools of raspberry coulis. There was even a s'mores martini made with Absolut Vanilla liqueur and Godiva White Chocolate liqueur.

Golden Rice: GM vs. Organic

Technology changed food preservation and food. Agribusiness introduced irradiated food to extend the shelf life of food. "Nuked" food like soups appeared in pop-top or pour-spout boxes even in health food stores. Around the world, there was an increase in genetically modified food—GM. The purpose, as it had been since prehistory, was to produce greater yields of foods that resisted disease. France resisted the foods. Other European countries were not keen on GM either; they especially didn't want it applied to wines. In France and Italy, where wine is a traditional and sometimes family business going back generations and hundreds of years, wine and wine-making methods are sacred. But Italians have accepted GM wheat used for pasta. In 1990, California passed the toughest organic food law in the United States to that time.

GM Golden Rice, which scientists called "Miracle Rice," not only has an improved yield, but also packs a nutritional boost of vitamin A from beta carotene, which gives corn and carrots their color. Lack of vitamin A causes about one million children a year to die, while as many as 230 million more are in danger of going blind. The problem is especially acute in countries where rice is all they have to eat, because rice has no vitamin A. With millions in funding provided by the Rockefeller Foundation, a nonprofit organization, scientists in Europe, the United States, and Asia spent more than a decade developing Golden Rice. The seed was given away free to farmers in Asia, so the only profit would be to the people who needed the rice.

A hot topic is who holds the patent on these invented foods. As the laws stand now, farmers anywhere who have developed their own seeds—for example, an heirloom tomato—are not protected by the law unless they patent the seed. This makes farmers in developing countries vulnerable to multinational companies sending out biopirates, taking the seed, and patenting it themselves.

CHRONOLOGY: GENETIC MUTATIONS/ENGINEERING[21]

1500s	Europe	Cauliflower produced
1750	Belgium	Brussels sprouts appear, genetic mutation
early 1800s	Brazil	Seedless navel orange appears, genetic mutation
1840	Germany	Von Liebig writes *Organic Chemistry and Its Applications in Agriculture and Physiology,* explains soil fertility, changes farming
1859	England	Darwin writes *The Origin of Species*, theory of evolution
1860	Germany	Crops grown hydroponically—in water only, no soil
1866	Czechoslovakia	Mendel discovers laws of "heredity factors" (later called genes)
1873	California	2 seedless navel orange trees begin California citrus industry
1873	U.S.	Burbank "builds" what becomes the Idaho potato, sells it for $150
1873	Japan	Dwarf wheat with large head that doesn't fall down produced
1907	Florida	Pink grapefruit appears on one tree, genetic mutation
1930	U.S.	Plant Protection Act allows new breeds to be patented
1945	Thailand	Jasmine rice invented
1950s	Iowa	Triticale invented, GM cross between wheat and rye
1953	England	Watson and Crick discover structure of DNA—double helix
1954	U.S.	**GREEN REVOLUTION BEGINS:** American scientists cross Japanese dwarf wheat with Mexican wheat, increase yield phenomenally
late 1950s	France	Tissue culture cloning developed
1965	U.S.	Orville Redenbacher introduces huge new popcorn
1966	Asia	IR8 rice, GM: "the most widely planted variety of rice, or of any other food crop, the world has ever known"[22]
1968	New York	Rio Red Grapefruit created using thermal neutron radiation
1974	Canada	GM rapeseed becomes canola, for "Canadian oil"
1978	U.S.	GM bacteria that clean oil spills are first patented living organisms
1982	U.S.	GM human insulin available, better than previous insulin (pig)
since 1985	Worldwide	More than 1,000 crops created by chemical or radiation mutation

(continues)

1990s	Italy	One-third of durum wheat grown for pasta is GM Creso, created with neutrons and X-rays
1998	U.S.	Almost 50% of soybeans and 25% of corn modified to protect against insects or herbicides
1999		Golden Rice patented (beta carotene added to prevent blindness)
1999		Chymosin, enzyme made by gene splicing, replaces rennet in 80–90% of cheese in the U.S. and Canada
2001	World	Human genome sequence (all DNA) completed
2002	Europe	Bright purple Graffiti cauliflower, GM, available in U.S.

There are arguments against genetically modified food and against organic food. "Spot checks show the majority of organic produce is contaminated."[23] It can contain pesticide residues, or natural contaminants like bacteria: tuberculosis, salmonella, listeria, campylobacter, and clostridium, which causes botulism; they do not yield as much as modified foods, which is an issue in the face of world hunger; some organic farmers apply "natural" insecticides like *B.t.* toxin to crops while they are growing, but it is the same insecticide that has been engineered into GM seeds.[24] As Canadian scientist Alan McHughen puts it, you can name your poison: "Conventional foods have more pesticide residue contamination; organic foods have more biological contamination."[25]

Food-Borne Illnesses (FBIs) and HACCP

At the end of the twentieth century and into the twenty-first, contamination continued to rise in animal and vegetable foods. Zoonoses [zoo-oh-NO-seez]—diseases that leap from animals to humans—reached frightening proportions in England when bovine spongiform encephalitis, also called BSE or "mad cow" disease, crossed over to humans and caused Jakob-Creutzfeld, a fatal brain disease. The cause was traced to feeding the cows ground-up parts of other animals like sheep. There was widespread panic in Europe briefly, and consumption of vegetables and fish rose.

Avian flu is another animal-related FBI. The virus H5N1 finds ideal conditions among the millions of chickens packed together in huge coops. Salmonella has changed, too. Previously, salmonella was spread by bacteria from the intestinal tracts of animals and birds, especially egg shells contaminated with fecal matter. This decreased radically when the United States mandated stringent procedures for cleaning and inspecting eggs in the 1970s. Now, however, salmonella is in the egg itself even before the shell is formed, transmitted from the ovaries of infected hens that have no symptoms. External disinfecting—washing the eggshells—is useless against this type of salmonella; only thorough cooking of the egg kills the bacteria. Mega-epidemics occur now because of pooling, where eggs or other food products from many farms are brought together. The CDC—U.S. Centers for Disease Control and Prevention—estimates that "if 500 eggs are pooled, one batch in 20 will be contaminated and everyone who eats eggs from that batch is at risk."[26]

On July 25, 1996, the Food Safety and Inspection Service division of the U.S. Department of Agriculture published its final rule on the HACCP system. HACCP [HAY-sip] stands for Hazard Analysis and Critical Control Point. This system identifies seven crucial points in food production that could cause contamination and result in food-borne illness. Food safety became an increasingly serious issue in 2006 when the deadly bacteria E. coli O157:H7 sickened 183 people in 26 states. The source was traced to raw spinach.[27] In 2009, Nestlé recalled its raw, refrigerated, prepackaged chocolate-chip cookie dough after 80 people in 31 states were infected with E. coli O157:H7.[28] The Los Angeles County Health Department made a priority of stopping another FBI, listeriosis [lis-tare-ee-OH-sis], in unpasteurized Mexican-style fresh cheeses.[29] Listeriosis has a "case-fatality rate of 20%, and causes an estimated 28% of all foodborne disease–related deaths," according to the National Institutes of Health.[30] In all of these outbreaks, people were hospitalized, became paralyzed, or died.

Sugar Blues: The Twinkie Defense and Diabesity

In the 1970s, sugar became a villain. It had gone from being a medicine and a cure-all in the Middle Ages, to an upper-class condiment, to a popular sweetener, and finally, to a drug. Sugar intoxication and a sugar "high" were followed by a crash in blood sugar levels that supposedly produced "sugar blues." It even became an excuse for crimes. In San Francisco in 1978, former policeman and city supervisor Dan White shot and killed Mayor George Moscone and openly gay supervisor Harvey Milk in San Francisco City Hall. He claimed that it was not premeditated even though he brought extra bullets and avoided metal detectors by climbing in a window. His defense: "diminished mental capacity," a chemical imbalance in his brain from eating too much sugar-rich junk food just before the murders. This became known as "The Twinkie Defense." The jury found White guilty of only the lesser charge of manslaughter. In 1985, shortly after he was paroled from prison, White shot and killed himself, but there is no record of what he ate immediately beforehand. In 1982, California voters eliminated this diminished capacity defense.[31]

While sugar as a cause of criminal behavior remains open to debate, sugar as a cause of physical illness is well established. Diabetes is a disease in which the pancreas cannot process sugar properly, which can lead to organ damage. Ninety to 95 percent of those with diabetes have what is called type 2. This usually strikes after the age of 40, which is why it is also called "adult onset diabetes."

However, from 1990 to 1998, diabetes increased by one-third in the United States. The vast majority of this increase—76 percent—was among people aged 30 to 39. It is much more prevalent in the Southeastern and Midwestern states and in California. It also has preferences: Native Americans, Alaska Natives, and African-Americans have a much higher incidence of the disease. The two major causes are an increase in obesity and a decrease in exercise. Sixty percent of Americans do not exercise regularly, and 25 percent do not exercise at all.[32] A new word entered the English language: "diabesity."

Fat Blockers and the French Paradox

Americans say they want to lose weight—they just don't want to have to change what they eat or feel deprived while they do it. They want to have their cake and eat it, too. One of the first attempts at fat blocking was an herbal combination unregulated by the FDA. Fen-Phen was removed from the market when its users began experiencing serious side effects, even death. Then came Olestra, which blocked fat absorption in the intestines but had side effects, too, such as diarrhea. There were other fat blockers; low-fat or no-fat desserts that compensated for the lack of fat with an increase in sugar; and baked instead of fried potato chips, for which Lay's mounted one of the most expensive campaigns in advertising history using supermodels and Miss Piggy the Muppet.

CULINARY CONFUSION:

The French Paradox

The French Paradox is that the French eat foods high in fat but have less heart disease than Americans. Many theories have been advanced as to why. Smaller portions? Greater wine consumption? Cigarette smoking? Or maybe it's their *joie de vivre*—joy of living. The entire country stops work in August and goes on vacation. There are also close ties with family. The French workday ends so everyone can go home for dinner, unlike the American 24/7 workday. Whatever the reason, nutritionists predict this will change if the French diet shifts to more fast food.

In 1996, a new physical condition was identified: people who were normal weight and looked thin but had too much body fat. Dr. David Heber at UCLA coined the term "sarcopenic obesity" to describe people who have fat where they should have muscle. Sarcopenia (loss of muscle) usually occurs in elderly people whose muscles wither from lack of use, but sarcopenic obesity can occur in young women who are terrified of gaining weight, so they don't eat enough protein or get enough exercise. According to the height-weight charts, they are the right weight, and they look all right in their clothes, but they are not fit and healthy.[33]

The New Millennium and the Future of Food

"Among the Millennium Development Goals which the United Nations has set for the 21st century, halving the proportion of hungry people in the world is top of the list."

—United Nations World Food Program

"What we eat has changed more in the last forty years than in the previous forty thousand."

—Eric Schlosser, *Fast Food Nation*

On December 31, 1999, much of the world went into a panic over the coming year 2000 (Y2K). Like people in the Middle Ages 1,000 years earlier, some expected the world to end at the beginning of the new millennium; others stock-piled food, water, and ammunition because they feared a worldwide breakdown of the computer systems that control telephones, traffic lights, electricity, and national security systems. None of this came to pass.

What did occur in 2000, however, was that India passed the one billion population mark, making it the second most populous country in the world, after China. Since gaining its independence from Britain in 1947, India's population tripled. Its population is expected to exceed China's by 2030.[34]

Drastic changes had also occurred in American life by the year 2000. Just as by 1920 a majority of Americans lived in cities, by 2000 a majority of Americans lived in suburbs. In the beginning of the nineteenth century, the vast majority of Americans were farmers. In the beginning of the twentieth century, most Americans worked in factories. In the beginning of the twenty-first century, the fastest-growing sector of the economy was service jobs, especially restaurants, which employed 3.5 million people, many at minimum wage. About 50 cents of every dollar Americans spent on food was spent in a restaurant, predominantly fast food, often drive-through—more than $110 billion.[35] The typical American diet of meat and potatoes became hamburgers and French fries, mostly frozen, freeze-dried, high in fat and salt. By 2010, those who couldn't live without a sugar boost were switching the hamburger bun for a glazed donut and using the milkshake as a dip for the fries.[36]

The top five fruits and vegetables that Americans do consume are bland, lack variety, and are not the most nutritious. Two are fresh—bananas and iceberg lettuce, a pale, not dark green leafy vegetable. The other three are tomatoes, potatoes, and oranges, mostly processed as sauce, French fries, and juice, respectively.[37]

Americans concerned about where their food was coming from succeeded in getting governmental guidelines. On December 20, 2000, the United States

Department of Agriculture (USDA) set national standards for organic foods and ordered that labels be applied to foods beginning in 2002, after farms were inspected. To rate a label of "100 percent organic," foods must meet the following criteria: (1) no irradiated food; (2) no genetically altered food; (3) no synthetic insecticides; (4) no chemical fertilizers; (5) no chemical herbicides; (6) no sewage sludge; (7) no growth hormones.[38] In May 2006, the first International Federation of Organic Agriculture Movements (IFOAM) conference on Organic Wild Production was held, in Bosnia and Herzegovina.

The USDA minimum daily nutritional requirements also changed from the four basic food groups to a food pyramid that still relied more heavily on meat than the food pyramids of other groups. It also included canned foods. The U.S. pyramid was also different in what it lacked: other pyramids included exercise and water.

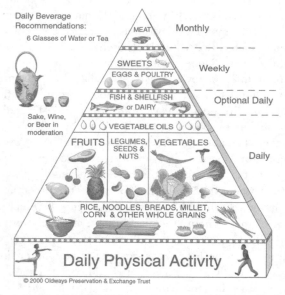

The Asian Diet Pyramid. *©Oldways Preservation & Exchange Trust.*

The Vegetarian Diet Pyramid. *©Oldways Preservation & Exchange Trust.*

The Mediterranean Diet Pyramid. *©Oldways Preservation & Exchange Trust.*

The Latin American Diet Pyramid. *©Oldways Preservation & Exchange Trust.*

The U.S. Food Pyramid, which is interactive. *Courtesy the United States Department of Agriculture, Food and Drug Administration.*

Windows on the World

Tuesday morning, September 11, 2001. At the southern tip of Manhattan stand the Twin Towers of the World Trade Center, the tallest buildings in New York since they were built in 1976. The buildings have their own zip code because every day, 50,000 people file into them to work and to visit. They come from New York, New Jersey, Connecticut, Pennsylvania, and more than 60 countries. And all of them have to eat.

Throughout the building, private chefs are preparing meals. On the 106th and 107th floors—the very top—of One World Trade Center, 79 staff members are in the kitchens of the Windows on the World restaurants. Some are bringing breakfast to the 500 people attending a business seminar. Executive Chef Michael Lomonaco, the gifted man who turned around the 21 restaurant and raised the Windows restaurants to award-winning excellence, will take the 58-second elevator ride up 107 stories in a few minutes, after he gets his new eyeglasses. But Michael Lomonaco will never get into the elevator, because the building will be on fire, filled with exploding jet fuel. Thousands of people died, including the kitchen staffs and hundreds of police and firefighters.

The Zagat Guide says Windows on the World "put diners close to heaven." The view from the top of the world on the 107th floor was indeed spectacular. As you looked down into the harbor, the Statue of Liberty, a gift from France in 1886, raised her torch up toward you. The famous words "Give me your tired, your poor, your huddled masses yearning to breathe free" by Jewish-American poet Emma Lazarus are written on the base of the statue. George Delgado, the mixologist at Windows on the World, invented many drinks, some inspired by the vistas from Windows. His Lady Libertini Martini mimics the colors of the Statue of Liberty.

In January 2006, food workers from the restaurants in the Twin Towers opened a cooperative restaurant called Colors.

The European Union

On January 1, 2002, 11 countries in the European Union began using the same currency, the Euro. The countries, in alphabetical order, are Austria, Belgium, Finland, France, Germany, Ireland, Italy, Luxembourg, the Netherlands, Portugal, and Spain. These countries (with the exception of Finland) had waged almost constant war against each other for 1,500 years, including nine world wars. They had been city-states; had monarchs, civil wars, and revolutions; had been split up, reunified with different boundaries, and finally, turned into democracies or limited monarchies. Now, for the first time since before the Roman Empire fell in A.D. 476, peace reigned among these countries. And menus in every single one had to be rewritten to reflect the new currency.

Drink of the Month—July 2001
George Delgado's Lady Libertini Martini

"The Statue of Liberty . . . may seem diminutive from up here (107 stories up), but what she stands for is far greater than the tallest buildings on earth. . . . As I gaze out over what is now called Liberty Island, I think of this statue's rich history as well as her symbolic significance, and decide that she needs a tributary cocktail of her own. Not just any cocktail would do. It would have to be the truly American classic, the king of cocktails, the Martini.

> 3 oz. Grey Goose Vodka
> ¼ oz. Monin Kiwi Syrup

In an ice-filled mixing glass, add the kiwi syrup and the Grey Goose Vodka (which I consider to be 'the other great gift from France'). Shake it thoroughly and give a quick check on the color. It should match the green, rusted copper color of the Statue of Liberty. If it's too pale, add up to ¼ oz. more of the kiwi syrup. But remember, the syrup is for color only; the end result should be a vodka martini. Now you can strain the cocktail into a chilled martini glass. For aesthetics you may try a red-colored garnish like a speared cherry or an orange twist to represent the 'torch of liberty.'

I wish you could join us here at Windows on the World to make this celebratory tribute, but if you can't, please try this at home and enjoy! Have a happy and safe 4th of July."

© 2001 George Delgado/Promixology, Inc.

Gluttony for Fun and Profit

On February 21, 2002, the Fox Network broadcast a program called "Glutton Bowl." Filmed in a hangar at the Santa Monica, California, airport, the two-hour pseudo-sports event presented chow hounds as athletes, providing Olympic-style commentary about their strategy and training (tip: they chew Tootsie Rolls to build up their jaw muscles). Each five-minute contest began with a 55-gallon drum suspended from the rafters dumping an avalanche of food onto the hangar floor: hard-boiled eggs, quarter-pound sticks of unsalted butter, whole beef tongues, mayonnaise, hot dogs with buns. As displays of decadence go, this is right up there with vomitoriums in the Roman Empire and fountains gushing wine in the Renaissance.

The craving for high-calorie consumption swept the country, in defiance of all health advice to the contrary. It was particularly prevalent at county fairs. If the Krispy Kreme doughnut chicken sandwich wasn't enough of a boost, there were all kinds of foods dipped in batter and deep fried, including Oreos, olives, Twinkies, frog legs, Snickers bars, pickles, cupcakes (frost *after* frying), waffles, burgers, s'mores, avocados, "zucchini weenies" (a hollowed-out zucchini filled with a hot dog, and Coca-Cola. Texans could enjoy chicken-fried bacon slathered with mayonnaise, which food historian and chef Clifford Wright calls "fat-fried fat with fat sauce."[39]

Everything Old Is New Again

Humans continually reinvent and repeat their cuisines and cultures, with new twists. Now, meats like buffalo and ostrich, formerly consumed by Stone Age tribal people, are sold in American supermarkets. Verjus, the juice of unripe grapes and out of vogue since the Middle Ages, is produced commercially in Napa, California, as the wine-friendly alternative to vinegar in salad dressing. In another throwback to the Middle Ages, edible gold reappeared, but this time as a powder to adorn the rims of martini glasses. *Moros y cristianos*, the black beans and rice from Spain, is still a staple in Cuban restaurants, but it is called just *moros*, and in an age of increased health consciousness, sometimes the rice is brown. The Aztec food that the Spaniards couldn't bring themselves to eat in the sixteenth century—*spirulina*—is now sold in health food stores. The sweet-and-sour-sauce combination of the Middle Ages became palatable again as the *gastrique*, a sugar/honey and citrus sauce, even for fish. *Coca-Cola* is the second most recognized word in the world, after *OK*.[40]

In the summer of 2000, locust plagues infested the American West as they had more than 100 years earlier.[41] This time, they were fought with poisons and pesticides instead of hopper dozers. Almost 100 years after the ice cream cone was invented, Chef Thomas Keller of the French Laundry in Napa Valley reinvented it as a savory cone or cornet and scooped salmon tartare into it. Chefs Mark Miller, Stephan Pyles, and John Sedlar took tamales upscale with jerk shrimp, truffle butter, foie gras, roasted pheasant, duck confit, and venison chorizo.

In the late twentieth century, chefs were celebrities again, as Carême was after the French Revolution. Soft drink giants like Coke and Pepsi extended their markets by inventing "health" drinks with herbal additives that, like the patent medicines of 100 years earlier, promised to cure whatever ailed the consumer. The FDA sent them warning letters.[42]

Heirloom tomatoes with names like Black Zebra, Box Car Willie, and Big Rainbow (all genetically engineered in the past) returned to supermarkets, while the food of new ethnic groups joined the food of older ethnic groups in becoming "typically American." Just as Italian and German foods like pizza, hamburgers, and hot dogs had become "typically American," a Mexican food, salsa, replaced ketchup as the leading condiment in the United States.[43]

In the twenty-first century, Americans continue their love affair with pizza, eating 100 acres of pizza per day—three billion pizzas per year.[44] In 2005, Domino's combined the top two American fast foods—pizza and burgers—and produced the Cheeseburger Pizza. Fine wining and dining on the railroad reappeared on the Napa Wine Train. Brunch, an American invention, caught on in France as *le brunch*.[45] The French, declining in influence in the food world in the explosion of global cuisines, tried to redefine their food as *le fooding*, more accepting of spices and ethnic influences. In 2001, the chefs who began nouvelle cuisine—Paul Bocuse, Michel Guérard, Paul Haeberlin, Pierre Troisgros, and Roger Vergé—declared it *fini*.[46] In 2002, California chef Roxanne Klein brought food full circle, from the cooked back to the raw, at her restaurant with no stoves in the kitchen and no food heated higher than 118°F. It closed in 2004. The word *cookies*, which had been used for small sweet treats Dutch in origin and first described in print by Amelia Simmons in 1796, now also means Internet files that keep track of information about users. The Internet also gave America's most popular canned luncheon meat a new meaning and turned it into a verb: spam. And somewhere, deep underground in Georgia, a time capsule is waiting to be dug up in the year 8113, so people of the future can taste Coca-Cola—on the remote chance the company isn't still in business then. But it might have competition—in 2006, a native tribe in Colombia put coca juice in a beverage it markets as Coca-Sek.[47]

At the beginning of the new millennium, American fashion experienced a resurgence of interest in the 1950s, which it called "Midcentury," especially the houses, which were built with wood floors, tile kitchens and bathrooms, fireplaces, and lots of windows. Wealthy Baby Boomers took advantage of low interest rates to remodel their homes or buy new ones, ending up with 10,000 or more square feet. These enormous homes had huge showplace kitchens with tile, wood, faux finishes, and farmhouse sinks to make them look like they came out of French farmhouses or Tuscan villas, but these American kitchens were almost as large as the entire Mediterranean farmhouse. They also boasted commercial-grade, stainless steel appliances; separate wine refrigerators or cellars; over-the-stove, antique-finish, pot-filler faucets; bar sinks; walk-in pantries; and granite kitchen islands. Some expanded the kitchen even more to include plasma TVs, fireplaces, and sofas in what became a new take on the old colonial great room. Elaborate kitchens and living rooms were also built outside. Many of these kitchens were built by people who didn't cook.[48]

These new mansions also had home theaters, so with satellite TV, pay-per-view, and movies that could be bought or rented on the Internet and sent through the mail or directly to your TV, people went out to the movies less. To try to lure customers back, some movie theaters began offering, in addition to popcorn and candy, alcoholic beverages like martinis and beer that patrons could take into the theater. Movie studios promoted their movies and sold DVDs in one place Americans did continue to go—Starbucks.

Native Seeds

The future of food lies in preserving its past. While some plants are cultivated in increasing numbers, hundreds of species become extinct every year. Scientists call this an ecological disaster. Part of the tragedy is that we do not know what new foods or medicines might have been in these plants that are gone forever.

In 1983, Native Seeds/Search (www.nativeseeds.org), a nonprofit organization based in Tucson, Arizona, was founded. It has reclaimed 2,000 varieties of arid plants cultivated by Native American peoples like the Apache, Yaqui, Paiute, Pima, Hopi, and Navajo. Fifty-five percent of the seeds are for the native three sisters—maize, beans, squash. The remaining 45 percent are both Old and New World: black pinto, orange lima, and scarlet runner beans; purple string beans, pink lentils, yellow-fleshed watermelon; wild tomatoes and tomatillos for green salsa. Chile pepper connoisseurs appreciate the locally grown Jemez, Isleta, and Chimayo chiles. Organizations like the Nature Conservancy preserve seeds, too. In addition, governments throughout the world have established more than 100 germ plasma banks to store seeds and cells. In the United States, the NSSL—the National Seed Storage Laboratory—began at Colorado State University in 1958. Today, more than 232,000 types of seeds are stored there, with plans to save more than one million.[49]

Sustainable Seafood

Sustainable agriculture, sustainable livestock, and sustainable fish are all important to the future of food. Seafood, halibut, sole, and all five kinds of salmon from Alaska—pink, chum, coho (also known as silver), sockeye, and king (chinook)—are wild because fish farming has been illegal in Alaska since 1990. Salmon are unique. Born in fresh water, they swim out into the ocean, sometimes thousands of miles, live there for years, then return—only once—to the *exact spot* where they were born to lay and fertilize their eggs, sometimes thousands of feet above sea level. (This is beyond the comprehension of mere humans, even scientists.)

The salmon are caught at spawning time, when they are heaviest and most loaded with nutrients. Wild Alaska salmon eat marine life like shrimp, herring, and squid, which makes them high in antioxidant vitamin E and omega-3 oils. They also change color then, to their distinctive pink. Salmon farmed in pens in places outside Alaska do not load up with nutrients so they do not change color naturally. They are gray. Dye turns them salmon color.

The state of Alaska monitors how many fish are running, water quality, and other factors to ensure no overfishing. Within one hour of being caught (some by hand on a line), wild Alaska salmon are flash frozen in a −40°F blast freezer and glazed with a coat of water that freezes and forms an airtight seal to prevent oxidation.

Alaska Fisherwoman Joy Martin's Salmon Carpaccio

About 2 pounds of salmon, frozen (flash-frozen at sea is best because it removes any chance of parasites, or have the fish market do it)

2 tablespoons salt

Freshly ground pepper

2 tablespoons fresh thyme

2 tablespoons fresh chopped tarragon

2 tablespoons fennel seeds (wild are best), chopped or milled in a grinder

1 cup olive oil

Juice of 2 lemons

2 tablespoons capers

Thaw the salmon. Remove the skin and pin bones. (Most fish markets will do this.) Put the salmon in a nonreactive container. Combine the dry ingredients and sprinkle the salmon on both sides. Add the liquids. Cover the salmon tightly and refrigerate for at least two days and up to five. Turn twice a day. Remove from refrigerator one hour before serving. Hold the fish up to drain all the liquid, strain it, and save. Cut very thin slices of salmon slightly on the diagonal and place them on a serving platter. Whisk the reserved liquid until thick and spoon it over the salmon. Scatter the capers on top.

© *The Fish Lady*

Slow Food and the Ark

In 1989, the Slow Food movement (slowfoodusa.org) was founded in Paris to counter the fast food trend. Now based in Italy, it has more than 80,000 members in chapters called convivia, like ancient Roman banquets, in more than 100 countries.[50] Its symbol is the snail; its main project is The Ark. Like Noah's Ark, its goal is to save the living things of the Earth and to promote biodiversity and high-quality, sustainable food production. Recently, in conjunction with the American Livestock Breeds Conservancy, it reintroduced to the marketplace four excellent-tasting heritage turkeys that have been crowded out by the big-breasted Large White variety.[51] Near extinction are the Naragansett (fewer than 100 alive), Jersey Buff and American Bronze (fewer than 500 breeding birds each), and Bourbon Red (664 breeding hens). The Ark has inspired other private organizations around the world to rescue indigenous food plants and animals and distribute seeds, like Peliti ("oak tree" in dialect) in Greece.

In spite of the efforts of environmentally conscious organizations, some species are dangerously close to extinction. In 2006, five species of fish in the deep waters off eastern Canada were listed as critically endangered—two types of grenadier, blue hake, spiny eel, and spinytail skate.[52] At the same time, the Convention on International Trade in Endangered Species called a halt—supposedly temporary—to all exports of caviar. As wild sturgeon and their eggs have become more rare because of pollution, poaching, and overfishing, the price has gone up. The price of Beluga, the top grade of caviar, more than doubled in one year, to over $200 per ounce, earning its nickname—"black gold."[53] Sturgeon farms are springing up in some countries, including the United States.

The Edible Schoolyard and the Wellness Policy Guide

It has been estimated that at the turn of the 21st century, approximately 15% of U.S. children between the ages of 6 and 19 years (11 million children) were overweight or obese, a prevalence that is unlikely to decline in the near future and that is triple the prevalence among children of the same age in the 1960s.[54]
—New England Journal of Medicine

On Sunday, August 26, 2001 (coincidentally, the eighty-first anniversary of the day the Constitution was amended to give women the right to vote), Chez Panisse turned 30. The $500-per-person celebration was a benefit for the Chez Panisse Foundation. This supports, among other things, the Edible Schoolyard, a project with Martin Luther King Jr. Middle School in Berkeley, California. Alice Waters believed that teaching children about food from gardening to cooking to serving would make them eat better.[55] By 2008, nearly half of the schools in California had a gardening program, with gardening not just outside, but in the curriculum. In core courses like English, students wrote recipes; for math, they measured the garden. These programs also had a backlash: why were the children of Hispanics and African-Americans being taught to dig in the dirt as a way to a better future? Hispanics, the majority of California's farm labor, were trying to get away from farming.[56]

At the end of the twentieth century, school budget cuts got rid of most of the home economics programs started by Ellen Richards and other professional women at the beginning of the twentieth century. It also made cash-needy schools eager for corporate sponsorship. Food giants like Taco Bell and Pizza Hut served students lunches; Coca-Cola machines dispensed soda. In 2002, the Los Angeles Unified School District began to reverse this trend when they voted to take the soda machines out of schools. The children protested. Raised on caffeine, sugar, carbonation, and fats, and used to the taste and mouth feel of artificial flavors and trans fats, they demanded their right to adulterated food and beverages. Harvey Washington Wiley spins in his grave.

In 2004, in an effort to reduce childhood obesity, the U.S. Congress passed the Child Nutrition and WIC Reauthorization Act. This law required every school to have a written Wellness Policy by 2006 stating what kind of physical education it was providing; what kind of nourishing, healthy food it was serving; and how it was educating students and their parents about the connection among diet, exercise, and health. The goal was to involve the entire educational community in helping children become and stay healthy and develop good, lifelong eating habits.[57]

A growing number of projects promote the healing power of nature and of food: the Garden Project at the San Francisco County Jail, run by Catherine

Sneed; the Veterans Administration Hospital garden project in West Los Angeles; Les Dames d'Escoffier school projects throughout the United States; the Vassar Farm; Chef Ann Cooper's school on Long Island; in the Midwest, chefs Charlie Trotter and Rick and Deann Bayless, to name just a few. Before her death at the age of 91 in 2004, Julia Child funded children's educational programs with part of the proceeds from the sale of seeds for Julia Child Heirloom Tomatoes. There are many others, and they all have one goal: ensuring good, healthy food for this generation and for all those to come.

Food terminology changed, too. *Foodie* was joined by *koodie,* a kid who is interested in food. *Waiter* and *waitress* lost passivity and gender when they became generic *runners.* Molecular gastronomy took a closer look at the chemistry and physics of cooking. Taste buds moved front and center in the new discussions of flavor, which finally included umami, first identified in Japan in 1908. Terroir, the taste of place, as Amy Trubek put it in her book of the same name, became the subject of not just sommeliers but scientists.

The Green Movement, not to be confused with the Green Revolution that began in the 1950s, has its roots in the ecology movement of the 1960s and seeks to reverse the "Better Living through Chemistry" trend of the 1950s. It stresses organic food and as few chemicals as possible in the environment. Using tote bags saves paper and plastic at the supermarket; solar panels and gardens on rooftops supply clean energy and food; garbage becomes compost. The Green Movement tries to achieve its goals through not only individual responsibility but also public policy.

In 2006, journalist Michael Pollan wrote *The Omnivore's Dilemma.* It is about what is really in our food supply. Pollan showed that much of our diet is based on corn—not just corn on the cob, but the corn that feeds the beef and pork that then feeds us. The ancient Maya believed that after their creator tried and failed several times to create the world, he finally succeeded with corn. They believed that they lived in a world of maize.[58] Pollan proved it.

Disasters, Natural and Man-Made

On Sunday, December 26, 2004, one of the greatest disasters in history struck Asia as a series of earthquakes under the Indian Ocean west of Australia triggered a series of tsunamis—waves, walls of water up to 30 feet high, traveling more than 500 kilometers per hour. Indonesia was closest and was hit hardest, especially the city of Banda Aceh, where an estimated 80,000 people died in a few minutes. Then the tsunamis swept east to Malaysia, north into Thailand and Myanmar, west across the Indian Ocean to Sri Lanka and southern India, and reached Somalia on the east coast of Africa. The earthquakes ranged in magnitude from 7.5 to 9 on a scale of 10. The aftershocks by themselves were major earthquakes. The tsunamis traveled thousands of miles, affecting 12 countries. They wiped out entire villages and killed hundreds of thousands of people.

One-third of the dead were children. An estimated five million people were left homeless and had their jobs destroyed.

The most immediate problems were getting clean water and food. Sanitation was a serious concern as water supplies were contaminated. People who had spent their lives making a living fishing no longer had boats or nets. Or families or homes. The world responded with massive amounts of aid, but distributing it was difficult with roads and communications destroyed or lacking in the first place. Sometimes local governments were wiped out, too. It will take years to rebuild, generations to forget.

On January 12, 2010, Haiti was hit by a magnitude 7.7 earthquake, which killed 200,000 people and left millions in need of emergency aid, especially clean water, food, and medicine. Then, on February 27, 2010, a magnitude 8.8 earthquake struck Chile. The death toll was less than in Haiti, but here, too, rebuilding will take years.

Haiti's economy had already been devastated by the free trade agreement that went into effect in 1993. Before, Haiti was exporting rice. Now it imports more than 50 percent of its food. Haiti's small-scale farmers were driven out of business because they could not compete with multinational agribusinesses that farm on a huge scale more cheaply. For Haitians, eating locally was much more expensive. For example, rice, a Haitian staple food, cost more—by $1 a pound—when grown in Haiti than imported.[59] To try to help, Odwalla, an American company, created a mango-lime beverage called Haiti's Hope. Odwalla's intention was to use mangoes grown in Haiti and to donate 100 percent of the proceeds to programs that support the mango farmers.[60]

On April 20, 2010, a BP (British Petroleum) oil rig in the Gulf of Mexico near Louisiana blew up. At first, the concern was for the 11 workers killed on the rig. Then Americans realized that tens of thousands of gallons of crude oil were gushing into the water every day. In spite of massive efforts, the spill continued for months. Oil reached the coastal marshes of Louisiana, and the shores of Mississippi, Alabama, and Florida. The spill forced people who had been making their living harvesting food from the Gulf for generations out of business. One was the oldest oyster-shucking company in the United States, P&J Oysters, in business since the U.S. centennial in 1876. Tourism, real estate values, and wildlife were all hit hard in areas affected by the spill. The long-term effects of the chemical dispersants that were used are not known.[61]

Food: Past, Present, and Future

In the second decade of the twenty-first century, world population continues to increase. Providing clean drinking water and producing enough food will continue to be problems. Intensive food production methods create cheaper food, but they also make it easier for diseases to spread.

Americans spend billions stampeding from diet to diet, looking for the quick fix to take the weight off fast. They cut out carbs, cut out beef, eat for their blood type, eat according to the glycemic index. There is even a Stone Age diet. At one point, Delta Airlines offered 14 different types of meals, all with no MSG: Asian; Baby, toddler, and child; Bland; Diabetic; Fruit plate; Gluten-free; Hindu; Kosher; Low-calorie; Low-cholesterol/low fat; Low-sodium; Moslem; Seafood (hot and cold); and Vegetarian (ovo-lacto and pure).[62] Perhaps at birth, future generations will receive printouts of their genotype so they can avoid foods that will damage their cell structure and help them live longer, healthier lives. Or maybe they'll be genetically modified, before or after birth, to remove food or other sensitivities or health problems.[63]

Increasingly in the United States, they'll be leading those lives alone. The 2000 census showed more single people—31.6% of the population—than families—31.3%. These groups have different eating habits. Single-serving foods and small watermelons like the Bambino (Italian for "baby") are just two of the ways food producers target the single market.[64]

Humans continue to search for immortality in food: in fruit juices high in antioxidants; in herbal remedies like extracts of ginger and cucurmin; and in bottled water—in some cases, just tap water with flavoring. Like sugar in the Middle Ages, the farther away it comes from and the more expensive it is, the better it must be for you, like mangosteen and goji berries.

Scientific research has verified the health properties of some of these foods. An 11-year study of more than 40,000 men and women in Japan found that drinking five or more cups of green tea a day reduced the risk of heart disease by 16 percent.[65] Studies at UCLA found that some beverages had positive health benefits. Pomegranate juice helped delay the return of prostate cancer.

UCLA TOP 10 HEALTHY BEVERAGES[66]

1.	Pomegranate juice
2.	Red wine
3.	Concord grape juice
4.	Blueberry juice
5.	Black cherry juice
6.	Açaí juice
7.	Cranberry juice
8.	Orange juice
9.	Tea
10.	Apple juice

Genetic modification of food continues, and continues to be championed by some and reviled by others. The debate over organic and sustainable continues, too, as health food advocates want chemicals that cause cancer in laboratory rats banned. But this isn't as straightforward as it seems:

> Coffee . . . contains more than a thousand chemicals: 28 have been tested, and 19 turned out to be carcinogens in rats and mice. Plants produce many natural pesticides: 71 have been tested, and 37 are carcinogens in rats and mice.[67]

Some scientists question the validity of comparing humans and laboratory animals at all. So, in spite of cracking the code of DNA, discovering vitamins and minerals in food, and conquering sanitation diseases, much remains to be discovered about food and its properties. New foods continue to show up, like the Laotian rat, which became news to people outside Laos in 2005.

In March 2010, the United States Congress passed the Patient Protection and Affordable Care Act. This health care reform bill impacted restaurants in two ways. First, to provide health care for everyone in the country, employers would have to pay more taxes. Second, the bill replaced individual state standards for food labeling with one nationwide standard. Every restaurant chain—defined as 20 or more restaurants—had to comply. The National Restaurant Association (NRA) and the International Franchise Association (IFA) opposed the law because of the new burdens they felt it would impose on restaurants. On the other hand, the law also protected restaurants from frivolous lawsuits over nutrition information.[68]

New Technology

New technology will continue to affect how food is processed and served, and to make food more convenient. Printers using vegetable ink and rice paper crank out edible menus and transfers for name-branding food items and for cake decorating. Licensing recognizable cartoon characters like Mickey Mouse, Barbie, Cinderella, Spider Man, and the Sesame Street Muppets for cake pans and other items is a growing business. Silicone bakeware makes greasing and flouring pans a thing of the past. Computers connecting the front and back of the house have replaced the *aboyer* or barker. Video cameras monitor cash registers and food prep areas.

Scientists are examining taste in new ways. They have discovered that taste is anatomically and genetically determined by how many taste buds you have on your tongue, which is an inherited trait. Scientists categorize people as "nontasters" or "tasters." Nontasters don't taste bitter foods like grapefruit, broccoli, and the other cruciferous vegetables very intensely. They can eat chile peppers and not suffer. Tasters, on the other hand, have many more taste buds and are sensitive to bitter and sweet tastes, and to sensations like carbonation and fat. Among the tasters are "supertasters," people whose tongues are covered with taste buds and who are extremely sensitive.[69]

A revolution in food packaging has also occurred. Cryovac, aka *sous vide*—literally, "under vacuum"—is increasingly used to preserve and package food, replacing tin cans with tear-open packages, even of tuna. Vegetables that can be microwaved in the bag they are sold in eliminate washing vegetables and pans. Microwaves preprogrammed with one-touch cooking for frozen food, pizza, and popcorn replace gas and electric ovens from the 1920s through the 1950s that printed temperatures and cooking times for foods on the inside of the oven door.

Recession Innovation: New Foods and Marketing

Food providers created new marketing methods in response to the economic downturn that began in 2008. In 2009, McDonald's embarked on "the biggest new-packaging initiative in the history of our brand," shifting the emphasis to nutritional values.[70] Other restaurants cut prices or offered special prices at certain times of day. They also enticed customers with all-you-can-eat in all its guises: bottomless, never-ending.[71] Starbucks dropped the price of a cup of coffee to $1.50 and threw in free pastry and copies of *USA Today*. It was still 50 cents more than the dollar meals available at both burger giants, McDonald's and Burger King.

Breakfast began to last all day, sometimes served 24/7. It became the new comfort meal for customers, and a new cash cow for restaurants. According to one study, "restaurants added more than 460 new breakfast products in 2009, more than in the previous two years."[72] Breakfast burritos, hot and cold sandwiches, and wraps joined the standard pancakes and omelets—whole egg or egg white. Quiznos started serving breakfast in March 2010, with its signature toasted sub and its Sammie sandwich. Rival Subway opened its doors for breakfast a month later. At Subway, you could get its foot-long sandwich for breakfast, too; its omelets were made with cage-free eggs. Another study concluded that "breakfast is projected to be a $93 billion business and is absolutely crucial in the 24-hour convenience store environment [C-stores], as more than 35 percent of convenience store food business is in breakfast."[73] Other chains, like Wendy's and Taco Bell, planned to join the breakfast bonanza.

At Applebee's, happy hour, with prices lowered, lasted all day, too, except for dinner rush from 7:00 PM to 10:00 PM.[74] Superbeers, with alcohol content as high as 40 percent, arrived in the United States from Scotland and Germany.[75] In bars, creative mixologists started making drinks differently. Mixology razzle-dazzle includes using atomizers and olive oil sprayers to finish drinks, and spraying house-made tinctures on top instead of incorporating them into the drink by stirring or shaking. Deconstructing the drink this way creates dramatic layers of flavors and aromas, and showcases the house's signature mixtures. Atomizers are quick and also efficient: they cut down on waste by coating the inside of a glass with less of a material, the way that sprays cut down the time bakers spend greasing and flouring pans. Sprays of citrus oils applied to the outside of drink glasses linger on the customer's fingers. Bars also started branding drinks by topping them with egg white or other light-colored foam and spraying colored liquids on stencils with the bar's logo.[76] In April 2009, Le Whif appeared: an inhaler that provides a chocolate experience with less than one calorie.[77]

Food became increasingly mobile. In an updated version of nineteenth-century pushcarts selling popcorn and twentieth-century trucks selling ice cream, food entrepreneurs used trucks and even mobile homes to start their own businesses with a much lower investment than it takes to open a restaurant. In California, food trucks—the "roach coach"—had long been a fixture on movie locations to feed crews. In the Hispanic community, "taco trucks" sold familiar food to workers in upscale neighborhoods. Now twenty-first-century chefs can be found in dessert trucks, grilled cheese trucks, barbecue trucks, even a bustaurant on top of a double-decker bus, all over the United States. Established restaurants are climbing on the bandwagon and sending trucks out, too. Canter's Delicatessen, a Los Angeles institution, put wheels on its matzo ball soup in 2010. In keeping with the new Green movement, the Border Grill truck, also in Los Angeles, runs on biodiesel fuel. Trucks with a restaurant's logo also bring more customers into the restaurant.[78]

On cellphones, Twitter announces truck arrival times and locations. Louisiana-based Smoothie King and Minnesota-based Caribou Coffee were just two of the food chains taking advantage of cellphones to send coupons as text messages.[79] Food promotions also showed up on special channels on cable TV. With mobile coupons and promotions, consumer frustration dropped: no more clipping and filing and then discovering in the check-out line at the supermarket that you left the coupons at home.

Competition for customers was fierce. According to the U.S. Bureau of Labor Statistics, in 2008, American food shoppers could choose from among 25,900 convenience stores and approximately 85,200 grocery stores.[80] Only one of the top 25 grocery stores in 2010 was in existence in 1919—A&P. Two others in the top 25, Kroger and Safeway, appeared on the top retailers list for the first time in 1920 and 1922, respectively.

Good-bye, *Gourmet*; Hello, Food TV

The shift to new digital media, combined with the economic downturn, produced casualties, and most notable was *Gourmet* magazine. It published its first edition in 1941, and its last in 2009. Although it ceased hard-copy publication, it remained on the Internet.

Another casualty was the organic food market. By 2010, the market was growing by only 1.9 percent, compared with its rapid growth of almost 30 percent before the recession in 2007. Conventional crops are heavily subsidized by the federal government, so they are cheaper than organic. Organic certification is expensive and requires that farmers use no pesticides or fertilizers on their land for three years. The new locavore movement—using food produced within 100 miles of where you live, to cut down on the negative environmental impact of

TOP U.S. SUPERMARKETS

1919[81]	1930[82]	2010[83]	NAME
--	--	1	Wal-Mart
--	2	2	Kroger
--	--	3	Costco Wholesale Corp.
--	--	4	Supervalu [sic]
--	4	5	Safeway
--	--	6	Loblaw Cos.
--	--	7	Publix Super Markets
--	--	8	Ahold USA
--	--	9	C&S Wholesale Grocers
--	--	10	Delhaize America
--	--	11	7-Eleven
--	--	12	H. E. Butt Grocery Co.
--	--	13	Meijer Inc.
--	--	14	Sobeys
--	--	15	Dollar General Corp.
--	--	16	Wakefern Food Corp.
--	--	18	BJ's Wholesale Club
1	1	19	A&P
--	--	20	Giant Eagle
--	--	21	Trader Joe's Market
--	--	22	Whole Foods Market
--	--	23	Family Dollar Stores
--	--	24	Winn-Dixie Stores
--	--	25	Associated Wholesale Grocers
2	3	--	The American Stores Co.
--	5	--	First National Stores

transporting food—also ran into difficulties. Organic food is such a small segment of the market that organic food producers can't get enough of what they need locally.[84]

When the organic market was at its height, many agribusinesses acquired or started organic companies, as the North American Food Sales chart shows.

NORTH AMERICAN FOOD SALES

RANK	CORP.	FOUNDED	WHERE	ORGANIC BRANDS	
1	Kraft	1903	Chicago, Illinois	Back to Nature Kraft Organic Planters Organic	DiGiorno Nabisco (1898) South Beach Diet (2005)
2	Tyson	1936	Arkansas	Nature's Farm	
3	Pepsi	1898	North Carolina	Naked Juice Tropicana Organic	Tostito's Organic
4	Nestlé	1860s	Switzerland	Grain Essentials	PowerBar Pria
5	Anheuser-Busch	1852	St. Louis, Missouri	Stone Mill Wild Hop	
6	General Mills	1860s	Minneapolis, Minnesota	Cascadian Farm Muir Glen	Gold Medal Organic Sunrise Organic
7	Dean	1925	Illinois	Alta Dena Organic Cow of Vermont Silk	Horizon White Wave
9	ConAgra	1861 as Van Kamp Pork & Beans	Indianapolis, Indiana; ConAgra formed in 1971 when Nebraska Consolidated Mills changed its name	Alexia Foods Gilroy Foods (roasted vegetables) Healthy Choice Healthy Choice Café Steamers Hunt's Organic	Lightlife Orville Redenbacher's Organic My Fries PAM Organic Ultragrain Flour

(continues)

RANK	CORP.	FOUNDED	WHERE	ORGANIC BRANDS	
10	Cadbury Schweppes	1790	England	Green & Black's Nantucket Nectars Organic	Mott's Organic
12	Kellogg	1906	Battle Creek, Michigan	Bear Naked Keebler Organic Morningstar Farms Wholesome & Hearty— Gardenburger	Kashi Kellogg's Organic Natural Touch
14	Unilever	1890	Anglo-Dutch	Ben & Jerry's Organic Ragu Organic	Breyers Organic
15	Coca-Cola		Atlanta, Georgia	Odwalla	
16	M&M Mars	1911	Tacoma, Washington	Dove Organic Seeds of Change	
17	Dole	1851	Hawaii	Dole Organic	
22	Campbell's Soup	1869	New Jersey Camden	Campbell's Organic Prego Organic V8 Organic	Pace Organic Swansons Organic
23	Hershey	1894	Pennsylvania	Dagoba	
27	Heinz	1869	Pittsburgh, Pennsylvania	Bagel Bites Heinz Organic Weight Watchers	Classico— lowfat sauces Smart Ones
47	Smucker's	1897	Orrville, Ohio	After the Fall Santa Cruz Organic	R.W. Knudsen
74	Danone	1919	Barcelona, Spain	Brown Cow	Stonyfield Farm

While food in print dwindled, food on TV expanded. On the Food Network, Bobby Flay, one of the original Iron Chefs, continued to challenge himself in the kitchen and chefs around the country on *Throwdown*. On *Chopped*, four contestants cooked three courses in one hour, with one left standing. In January 2010, a new show debuted on the Food Network: *Worst Cooks in America.* The contestants were people from all over the country whose children, partners, and colleagues had begged them to learn how to cook. They created their signature dishes: chocolate pancakes that looked like rubber cow patties, peanut-butter-crusted cod, a whole boiled chicken with slices of Swiss cheese slapped over it, asparagus stalks (the tips had been cut off and thrown away), hollowed-out rutabagas with mystery stuffing. Under the guidance of chefs Anne Burrell and Beau MacMillan, some of them learned to cook.

An epidemic of reality food shows spread from the Food Network to other cable stations. British Chef Gordon Ramsay, with 27 restaurants, had five TV shows, among them *Kitchen Nightmares*, on the BBC and other channels. On the Travel Channel, Chef Andrew Zimmern traveled the world and sampled *Bizarre Foods*, while Chef Anthony Bourdain dropped in with *No Reservations*. Fine Living Network showcased a Road Kill Festival and dishes like Tarantula Tempura. The Discovery Channel featured Carol Selva Rajah, chef and author of 11 cookbooks, in a multipart series on Malaysian cuisine. French Chef Alain Ducasse had no TV show, but did have 22 restaurants worldwide, 18 cookbooks, a chain of hotels, two cooking schools, and his own publishing house. Joël Robuchon weighed in with 19 restaurants and 16 cookbooks. Some chefs crossed over into acting: India's Madhur Jaffrey has been appearing on TV and in films since 1964, including *Law and Order* and the movie *Prime* with Meryl Streep in 2005.[85]

In June 2010, the Food Network launched Top Chef University, a completely online cooking school, to teach viewers everything from basics like knife skills and stocks through dessert. There was also a lesson on global cuisines, and one on molecular gastronomy.

Canadian Cuisine

In February, 2010, television gave a big boost to Canadian cuisine and culture when it broadcast the Winter Olympics from Vancouver. The Canadian flag is a big red maple leaf, so it is no surprise that maple in many forms shows up in Canadian cuisine: syrup, sugar, butter, fudge, and maple-glazed chicken breasts. Wild cranberries, blueberries, gooseberries, and cloudberries are transformed into pies, tarts, and puddings, sometimes with the help of maple in one of its forms.

But Beaver Tails, aka Moose Tongues, are flaky buttery pastries sprinkled with cinnamon sugar. In the United States, they're Elephant Ears. Canadians go crazy for Nanaimo Bars, invented for a recipe contest in the town of Nanaimo, British Columbia, in 1986. They are three layers: a base of Graham cracker crumbs, ground nuts, coconut, and melted butter; a filling made with vanilla custard powder (really a cornstarch pudding); and a topping of melted chocolate.[86]

Canada's native or First Nations people make use of native Canadian ingredients. They hunt for wild game—deer, moose, goose, and pheasant—and make salmon jerky.

Ethnic cuisines are found throughout the country: Italian, Ukrainian, Polish, and Scandinavian, among others. The Doukhobors are vegetarians of Russian descent. Ontario has Mennonites, just like Michigan. Chinese restaurants are as popular in Canada as they are in the United States. One specialty is the "Chinese smorgasbord," which supposedly started in Vancouver at the end of the nineteenth century when the Chinese cooked for Scandinavian lumberjacks. Ginger beef is also believed to have originated in western Canada. Newfoundland and Nova Scotia in eastern Canada show the influence of British, Irish, and Scottish cooking, with scones, oat bread, Irish stew, and salt cod.

The French-speaking population centered in Quebec contributes traditional French dishes like onion soup and crème caramel, and newer foods like *poutine,* a French-Canadian word pronounced "poot-tsien" or "poo-teen." The origins of the dish and the word are obscure. It might be related to pudding, like Portuguese *pudim,* or *potée,* French for "a potful." *Poutine* uses French fries the way Americans use spaghetti or corn chips: as a base for toppings. The traditional toppings, added at the last minute to avoid sogginess, are brown gravy and fresh curd cheese. Variations include tomato sauce and mozzarella, guacamole and sour cream, feta cheese, and even foie gras. The possibilities for fusion cuisine are endless.

CROSSING CULTURES:
Sriracha, Global Cuisine in a Bottle

A condiment created in the early 1980s represents the new global fusion of cuisines and cultures. Hot on the heels of salsa and catching on in the United States is Sriracha [SIR-rotch-ah is how its creator pronounces it; most people say sir-AH-cha]. This sauce is made by an ethnic Chinese from Vietnam living in southern California. Its ingredients include chile peppers from the Americas and garlic from Europe. It also has sugar, which originated in Asia, and vinegar, which put it in the Middle Eastern–Italian tradition of *agrodolce*—sweet and sour. The label on the bottle is in Vietnamese, Chinese, English, French, and Spanish. It is named after a province in Thailand, and sold at Wal-Mart.

Sriracha is also an immigrant success story. What began in a household kitchen as a small business with everyone in the family chopping, cooking, and canning now has warehouses and a distribution network to handle the 10 million bottles a year it produces. It is used by individuals to spike slices of pizza, as a dip in chain restaurants, and to provide punch to sauces created by celebrity chefs.[87]

The Food Connection

Regardless of where food is grown, how it is harvested, processed, packaged, or transported, it will still need to be cooked. Every man or woman standing at a stove in a modern kitchen reaches back millennia, from a humanitarian providing food after a natural disaster to Julia Child taking cooking classes at the Cordon Bleu; to the young chef Escoffier foraging for food during the Franco-Prussian War; to the scientists Snow and Pasteur and Koch experimenting to find the causes of sanitation diseases, sour wine, and anthrax; to the homeless 10-year-old Carême walking into a professional kitchen for the first time. We reach back to Appert and his champagne bottles filled with the first bottled food; to the anonymous African-American women cooks sweating in the plantation kitchens of the American South, and the anonymous men cooks freezing in the snow on Napoleon's retreat from Moscow; to American orphans and Chinese slaves; to Russian communal kitchens and American settlement houses; to nuns in convents and women in harems making pastries; to Mongols around a campfire drinking *kumiss*; Romans on a *triclinium* eating roast pig at a banquet; Greeks drinking wine at a symposium; high priests in Egypt and Mesopotamia offering food to their gods. We reach all the way back to that first human who cracked a bone and sucked out the marrow. So whether we are whisking tea in a tea house; cracking a coconut in Southeast Asia; digging a pit for a Native American barbecue, a New England clambake, or a luau; preparing rice for a *selametan*; hanging hams to cure; stomping on grapes in the Mediterranean or potatoes in the Andes; stuffing vegetables or squeezing the juice out of fruit; waiting for a tweet from a truck; sharing soup or breaking bread; we are all connected, and we do it for the same reason: we love the food, and friends are around the fire.

"Let us live and eat in peace and good-fellowship, for when God sends the dawn, he sends it for all."

—Sancho Panza, 1602[88]

FRENCH PRONUNCIATION

1. The Circumflex Accent: ^.

This just means that the letter *s* got dropped on the way from Latin to French; it has nothing to do with pronunciation. For example, *goût* (pronounced *goo*) means taste, which in Latin is *gustus*. *Château*—castle—used to be *castellum*.

2. The Letter S.

The final *s* is not pronounced unless there is an *e* after it, and then it sounds like *z*. For example, the knife cut, *brunois*, is pronounced *broon WAH*. Add an *e*—*brunoise*—and it becomes *broon WAHZ*. The same holds true for *françoise*, *niçoise*, and all the other words that end in *ois*.

3. The Final *E*.

The final *e* in words like *brunoise* is not pronounced. To indicate that the *e* is supposed to be pronounced, an accent mark is added. Then the *e* is pronounced *ay*. For example, *velouté* sauce: without an accent on the final *e*, it would be pronounced *veh loot*, instead of *veh loo TAY*.

4. The Cedilla: ç.

This is used to make a *c* sound like *s*. For example, *niçoise*, as in *salade niçoise*, is pronounced *nee SWAHZ*.

ITALIAN PRONUNCIATION

There are few pronunciation rules in Italian. All the letters are pronounced, and the Italian alphabet has only twenty-four letters, two fewer than English. The letters *j* and *k* are missing; *g* and *c* fill in for them. Some simple things to remember about Italian pronunciation:

1. Plural.

Any word that ends in *i* in Italian is already plural; do not add an *s*. For example, *ravioli* and *cannoli* are plural. *Raviolis* is incorrect. So is *cannolis*.

2. Emphasis.

The emphasis is usually on the second-to-last syllable. For example, *spah GAY tee.*

3. Sometimes the Letter *C* Equals the Letter *K*.

The letter *c* is pronounced hard, as in *cat*. There are two exceptions: *ce* and *ci* are pronounced *chay* and *chee*. Example: the actor Al Pacino's name is pronounced *pah CHEE no*. To keep the hard *c* sound, put an *h* between the *c* and the *e* or the *i*. Example: the Italian pasta dish *checca* is pronounced *KAY kah*.

4. Sometimes the Letter *G* Equals the Letter *J*.

The letter *g* is pronounced hard, as in *got*. There are two exceptions: *ge* and *gi* are pronounced *jay* and *jee*. Example: former New York City mayor Rudy Giuliani, pronounced *joo lee AH nee*. To keep the hard *g* sound, put an *h* between the *g* and the *e* or the *i*. Example: spaghetti. Also, the first syllable of the San Francisco chocolate company Ghirardelli is pronounced *gear*, not *jeer*.

MAJOR WARS AND BATTLES (not ancient)

WHEN	BATTLE / WAR	WHERE	WHO FOUGHT (WINNER IN BOLD)
476	Fall of Western Roman Empire	Rome	**Barbarians** invade Western Roman Empire
732	Battle of Tours#	France	Muslims invade **France**
1066	Battle of Hastings	England	**France** invades England
1096–1212	Crusades#	Jerusalem	Christian Europe invades **Muslim** Levant
1279	Invasion	China	**Mongols** invade China
1337–1453	Hundred Years' War	France	England invades **France**
1453	Fall of Eastern Roman Empire#*	Turkey	Muslim **Turks** vs. Christian Eastern Roman Empire
1492	Reconquista#	Spain	Catholic **Spain** against Muslims and Jews
1571	Battle of Lepanto#*	Eastern Mediterranean	Catholic **Spain, the Pope, Venice** vs. Muslim Turkey
1588	Spanish Armada#*	English Channel	Catholic Spain vs. Protestant **England**
1618–1648	Thirty Years War#	Europe	Catholic vs. Protestant—a draw
1642–1649	Civil War#	England	**Puritans** vs. Cavaliers
1688	Glorious Revolution#	England	**Protestant** vs. Catholic
1688–1697	War of League of Augsburg	**WORLD**	France vs. most of Europe—a draw
1701–1713	War of Spanish Succession	**WORLD**	**England, Austria, Dutch Republic, Portugal, some Germans and Italians** vs. France and Spain
1740–1748	War of Austrian Succession	**WORLD**	Prussia, France vs. **Austria, England**
1756–1763	Seven Years' War (French and Indian War, 1754–1763)	**WORLD**	**England, Americans** vs. French and Mohawk Indians
1778–1783	American Revolution	**WORLD** took part; fought in North America	**American colonies** vs. England

WHEN	BATTLE / WAR	WHERE	WHO FOUGHT (WINNER IN BOLD)
1793–1802	French Revolution	**WORLD** took part; fought primarily in France	**Peasants and bourgeoisie** vs. nobility
1803–1815	Napoleonic Wars	**WORLD**	France vs. **England, Russia, Spain, Belgium, Germany, Austria;** England vs. **U.S.**
1821	Revolution	Mexico	**Mexicans** vs. Spain
1839–1842	Opium Wars*	China	China vs. **England**
1861–1865	Civil War	U.S.	**Free North** vs. slave South
1910–1911	Revolution	Mexico	**Peasants** overthrow dictator
1914–1918	World War I	**WORLD**	Austro-Hungarian Empire, Germany vs. **England, France, U.S., Russia, Italy, Japan**
1918–1924	Revolution/Civil War	Russia	**Communist peasants** against nobility
1939–1945	World War II	**WORLD**	Germany, Italy, Japan vs. **China** (1937–1945), **England** (1939–1945), **Russia**, and **U.S.** (1941–1945)
1947	Independence	India	**Indians** vs. British colonial masters; then Hindus vs. Muslims
1949	Revolution	Indonesia	**Indonesians** vs. Dutch colonial masters
1949	Revolution	China	**Communists** vs. Nationalists
1959	Revolution	Cuba	**Communists** vs. capitalists
1960s	Revolutions	Africa	**Africans** vs. European colonial masters

religious war; * naval battle

SELECTED COOKBOOK AND FOOD BOOKS CHRONOLOGY

DATE	COUNTRY/ LANG	AUTHOR	BOOK TITLE	IMPORTANCE
c. 3500 B.C.	Mesopotamia/ Cuneiform	Anonymous	(fragments)	Earliest written recipes include bird bouillon
c. 330	Sicily/Greek	Archestratus	*The Life of Luxury* (fragmts.)	In verse; mostly about fish
A.D. 1st c.	Rome/Latin	Apicius	*De Re Coquinaria*	First real cookbook; sauces; 1st Eng. translation in 1936
10th c.	Tunisia/Arabic	al-Mālikī	*Riyāḍ al-nufūs*	first mention of dessert *kunāfa*
1061	China/Chinese	Anonymous	*The Illustrated Basic Herbal*	Hundreds of foods described
1215	Japan/Japan.		Kissa Yojoki	First book on tea in Japan
1226	Muslim/Arabic	Al-Baghdadi	*A Baghdad Cookery Book*	Beginning of pastry/confection
13th c.	Muslim/Arabic		Kitāb waf al-at'ima al-mutada	94/155 recipes use rose water
13th c.	Hispano/ Arabic	Anonymous	*Kitāb al-ṭabikh fī al-Maghrib wa'l-Āndalus*	Early reference to couscous
c. 1300	Switzerland/Fr.	Anonymous	*Sion Viander*	Little Arab influence
14th c.	Naples/Latin	Anonymous	*Liber de Coquina*	First lasagne recipe
14th c.	China/Chinese	Hu Szu-hui	*Yin-shan cheng-yao (Good & Essential Things for Emperor)*	Written by Chinese-Turk in Mongol court.
c. 1370	France/French	Taillevent	*Le Viander*	Little Arab influence
1392/3	France/French	Anonymous	*Ménagier de Paris*	Daily household cooking
1474	Rome/Latin	Platina/Martino	*De Honesta Voluptate*	First printed cookbook
c. 1490	France/French	Taillevent	*Le Viander*	First printed French cookbook
1502	England/Eng.	Anonymous	*The Pineson Book*	First printed English cookbk.
1510	Brussels/ Dutch	Vander Noot	*Eeen Notabel Boecxke van Cokerije*	First printed Dutch cookbook
1520	Barcelona, Sp.		*Libre del coch*	Catalan cuisine
1532	Poland/Polish	Anonymous	*Kuchmistrzostwo (The Art of Cooking and Cellaring)*	First cookbook in Polish
1570	Italy/Italian	Scappi	*Opera*	High Renaissance cuisine

DATE	COUNTRY/ LANG	AUTHOR	BOOK TITLE	IMPORTANCE
1604	Brussels/Fr.	Casteau	*Ouverture de Cuisine*	First *pâte à choux*
1651	France/French	La Varenne	*Le Cuisinier françois*	Classical French cooking
1653	France/French	La Varenne	*Le Patissier françois*	Probably by Italian pastry chef
1667	Dutch	Anonymous	*The Sensible Cook*	Dutch Golden Age food
1682	Poland/Latin	Stan. Czerniecki	*Compendium Fercolorum*	First original Polish cookbook
1691	France/French	Massialot	*Cuisinier roïal et bourgeois*	1st recipes w/alpha headings
1742	America/ Eng.	Eliza Smith	*The Compleat Housewife*	1st cookbk printed in colonies
1746	France/French	Menon	*La Cuisinière bourgeoise*	First French cookbk to women
1747	England/Eng.	Hannah Glasse	*The Art of Cookery*	Successful 18th century cookbk
1790	Italy/Italian	F. Leonardi	*L'Apicio moderno*	1st pasta & tomato sauce recipe
1793	France/French	Mme. Méridot	*La cuisine républicaine*	Female author; all potatoes
1796	U.S./English	A. Simmons	*American Cookery*	First American cookbook
1810	France/French	Nicolas Appert	*L'Art de Conserver . . .*	First book on canning
1816	Russia/Russ.	Chef Levshin	*The Russian Kitchen*	First Russian cookbook
1824	U.S./English	Mary Randolph	*The Virginia Housewife*	Influential cookbook
1829	U.S./English	Lydia Child	*The Frugal Housewife*	Reprinted at least 35 times
1839	Naples/Italian	I. Cavalcanti	*La cucina teorico-pratica*	Italian without French influence
1841	U.S./English	C. Beecher	*Treatise on Domestic Econ.*	Democracy, health, and diet
1859	Britain/English	Isabella Beeton	*Book of Household Mgmt.*	British Victorian cooking
1861	Russia/Russ.	E. Molokhovet	*A Gift to Young Housewives*	Best seller; > 4,000 recipes
1864	Australia/Eng.	Edward Abbott	*English & Australian Cookery*	First Australian cookbook
1881	U.S./English	Abby Fisher	*What Mrs. Fisher Knows . . .*	Early African-American cookbook
1881	U.S./English	Ellen Richards	*The Chemistry of Cooking*	First woman at MIT
1891	Italy/Italian	Pellegrino Artusi	*La Scienza in Cucina*	Cornerstone of Italian cooking
1896	U.S./English	Fannie Farmer	*Boston Cooking School Ckbk*	Industrialization and cooking
1898	U.S./Spanish	E. Pinedo	*El cocinero español*	1st Spanish-lang. cookbk in U.S.
1901	U.S.	Lizzie Kander	*The Settlement Cookbook*	Jewish/Jewish-Am. recipes
1903	France/French	Escoffier	*Le Guide Culinaire*	5,000 recipes from the master
1910	Poland/Polish	Ochorowicz-Monatowa	*Uniwersalna Ksiaóka Kucharska (Universal Ckbk)*	Bible of Polish cooking; translated into English 1958

DATE	COUNTRY/LANG	AUTHOR	BOOK TITLE	IMPORTANCE
1931	U.S./English	Irma Rombauer	*The Joy of Cooking*	3,000 copies self-published
1938	France/French	Montagné	*Larousse Gastronomique*	Encyclopedia
1960	Britain/English	Elizabeth David	*French Provincial Cooking*	Influenced generations
1961	U.S./English	Beck, Julia Child, Bertholle	*Mastering the Art of French Cooking*	Makes French cooking accessible to Americans
1968	U.S./English	Claudia Roden	*A Book of Middle Eastern Food*	Includes medieval recipes
1970	U.S./English	Harva Hachten	*Best of Regional African Cooking*	First continent-wide African cookbook
1971	U.S./English	George Lang	*The Cuisine of Hungary*	Recipes and history
1973	U.S./English	Madhur Jaffrey	*Invitation to Indian Cooking*	Written for Americans
1973	U.S./English	Molly Katzen	*Moosewood Cookbook*	Vegetarian, spicy, ethnic
1979	English	Escoffier	*The Culinary Guide*	First English translation
1981	U.S./English	J. Brennan	*Original Thai Cookbook*	First Thai cookbook in U.S.
1982	U.S./English	Alice Waters	*Chez Panisse Cookbook*	Seminal California French
1983	U.S./English	Ornish/Shulman	*Stress, Diet, & Your Heart*	First heart-healthy cookbook
1984	U.S./English	Harold McGee	*On Food and Cooking*	Kitchen chemistry
1991	U.S./English	Ayla Algar	*Classical Turkish Cooking*	History and recipes
1996	Italy/French English	Flandrin and Montanari, eds.; Sonnenfeld	*Histoire de l'alimentation; Food: From Antiquity to the Present*	Invaluable, broad history.
1998	U.S./English	Ntozake Shange	*If I Can Cook/You Know God Can*	African food and history with a poetic soul
1999	England	A. Davidson, ed.	*Oxford Companion to Food*	Encyclopedia
2000	U.S./English	Clifford Wright	*A Mediterranean Feast*	Massive; 500 recipes + history
2001	U.S./English	Eric Schlosser	*Fast Food Nation*	The way Americans eat now
2002	U.S./English	Marion Nestle	*Food Politics*	First hard political/food history
2003	U.S./English	Pinedo; Strehl, ed./ trans.	*Encarnación's Kitchen*	Selections from first cookbook written by a Hispanic in U.S.
2004	U.S./English	Andrew Smith, ed.	*Oxford Companion to Food & Drink in America*	First American food encyclopedia
2004	English /Farsi	N. Batmanglij	*New Food of Life: Ancient Persian and Modern Iranian*	Bold, uncompromising Iranian

Notes

Antipasto/Antojitos/Amuse-Bouches
1 Nabhan, Why Some Like It Hot, 30.

First Course
1 Stephen J. Pyne, *World Fire*, 3.
2 http://www.nytimes.com/2009/04/21/science/21conv.html?pagewanted=print
3 http://hnn.us/roundup/entries/89571.html
4 LA Times, 7/11/2002, 1.
5 Brothwell, *Food in Antiquity*, 32.
6 Tannahill, *Food in History*, 32.
7 Klein and Edgar, *Dawn of Human Culture*, 156.
8 Flandrin and Montanari, *Food*, 17
9 *Ibid.*, 144.
10 Tannahill, *Food*, 15.
11 Achaya, *Indian Food*, 5.
12 Cass, *Dancing Through History*, ix.
13 *Ibid.*, 3–8.
14 *Ibid.*, 7.
15 Frazer, *The Golden Bough*, 21; 24. Janson, *A Basic History of Art*, 32–35.
16 Brothwell, *Food in Antiquity*, 19.
17 Achaya, *Indian Food*, 3.
18 *Ibid.*, 202–203.
19 *Ibid.*, 199.
20 Klein, *Human Culture*, 17.
21 McGee, *On Food and Cooking*, 234.
22 *Ibid.*, 275.
23 Brothwell, *Food in Antiquity*, 194.
24 Woodier, *Apple Cookbook*, 1–2.
25 Courtwright, *Forces of Habit*, 9.
26 Brothwell, *Food in Antiquity*, 165.
27 McGee, *Food and Cooking*, 370.
28 Davidson, *Oxford Companion to Food*, 384.
29 Phillips, *Wine*, 24.
30 Spodek, *World's History*, 48–49.
31 *Ibid.*
32 Brothwell, *Food in Antiquity*, 166.
33 Flandrin and Montanari, *Food*, 40.
34 Bottero, *Oldest Cuisine*, 43.
35 *Ibid.*, 112–113.
36 *Ibid.*, 114.
37 *Ibid.*, 117.
38 *Ibid.*, 26.
39 *Ibid.*, 29–30.
40 *Ibid.*, 35.
41 *Ibid.*, 81.
42 *Ibid.*, 81.
43 Flandrin and Montanari, *Food*, 35.
44 *Ibid.*, 19.
45 *Ibid.*, 118–120.
46 Tannahill, *Food in History*, 47.
47 http://news.nationalgeographic.com/news/2001/05/0518_crescent.html
48 *www.alchemy.com*
49 Woodier, *Apple Cookbook*, 2.
50 Roden, *Middle Eastern Food*, 268.
51 *Ibid.*
52 Spodek, *World's History*, 71.
53 McGee, *On Food and Cooking*, 170–171.
54 History Channel, *Egypt Beyond the Pyramids*.
55 Flandrin and Montanari, *Food*, 13. Brothwell, *Food in Antiquity*, 54.
56 History Channel, *Egypt Beyond the Pyramids*.
57 Tannahill, *Food in History*, 52–53.
58 Flandrin (Edda Bresciani, "Food Culture in Ancient Egypt"), 39.
59 Zborowski and Herzog, *Life Is With People*, 368.
60 *Ibid.*, 368–369.
61 The Holy Bible (Cleveland: The World Publishing Company, 1962), 53. *Exodus*, 5–11.
62 *Exodus*, 12. Zborowski and Herzog, *Life Is With People*, 388–89.
63 Anderson, *Food of China*, 45.
64 Kurlansky, *Salt*, 19–21.
65 Miller, *The Spice Trade*, 43.
66 http://www.math.nus.edu.sg/aslaksen/calendar/chinese.shtml
67 http://www.chinascape.org/china/culture/holidays/hyuan/newyear.html#origin
68 http://www.new–year.co.uk/chinese/history.htm
69 http://memory.loc.gov/ammem/collections/jefferson_papers/mtjtime1.html
70 Kurlansky, *Salt*, 31.
71 Achaya, *Indian Food*, 18–29.
72 *Ibid.*, 11.
73 *Ibid.*, 18.
74 *Ibid.*, 110, 113, 108, 111.
75 *Ibid.*, 38.
76 *Ibid.*, 9.
77 Farb, *Consuming Passions*, 141–146.
78 Anderson, *Food of China*, 6.

Second Course
1 *Food*, Massimo Montanari, "Introduction: Food Systems and Models of Civilization," 69.
2 http://www.theoi.com/Olympios/Demeter.html; Homeric Hymn 2 to Demeter 275 ff.
3 http://seds.lpl.arizona.edu/Maps/Stars_en/Fig/virgo.html
4 In Greek, the final *e* is pronounced like the double *e* in "beet." For example, the Greek goddess of victory, Nike—"Nigh kee."

5 Depending on which translation. *Handbook of Greek Mythology* says pennyroyal; Hamilton's *Mythology* says barley-water and mint.

6 http://www.theoi.com/Olympios/DemeterGoddess.html

7 http://www.theoi.com/Olympios/DemeterGoddess.html, Homeric Hymn 2 to Demeter 205

8 http://www.theoi.com/Olympios/Dionysos.html

9 http://www.theoi.com/Olympios/DionysosGod.html

10 Flandrin and Montanari, *Food*, 94.

11 http://www.theoi.com/Olympios/Dionysos.html, citing Paus. viii. 39. § 4; Theocrit. xxvi. 4; Plut. *Sympos.* iii. 5; Eustath. *ad Hom.* 87; Virg. *Eclog.* v. 30; Hygin. *Poët. Astr.* ii. 23; Philostr. *Imag.* ii. 17; *Vit. Apollon.* iii. 40.

12 http://www.theoi.com/Olympios/DionysosGod.html, quoting Athenaeus, Deipnosophistae 2.36a-b

13 Courtwright, *Forces of Habit*, 10.

14 Flandrin and Montanari, *Food*, 97.

15 Archestratus, *The Life of Luxury*, 21.

16 Flandrin and Montanari, *Food*, 100.

17 http://www.theoi.com/Olympios/DionysosGod.html

18 Isaac Asimov, *Words of Science*, 20; *OED*.

19 Dalby and Grainger, *The Classical Cookbook*, 42.

20 *Ibid.*, 43–44.

21 Taylor, *Olive in California*, 7.

22 Davidson, *Oxford Companion*, 551–553.

23 Taylor, *The Olive in California*, unless otherwise noted.

24 Davidson, *Oxford Companion*, 553.

25 Toussaint-Samat, *History of Food*, 299–301.

26 Farb, *Consuming Passions*, 62.

27 Tannahill, *Food in History*, 61.

28 *Food*, Marie-Claire Amouretti, "Urban and Rural Diets in Greece," 82.

29 Tannahill, *Food in History*, 65.

30 *Food*, Marie-Claire Amouretti, "Diets in Greece," 82.

31 Brothwell, *Food in Antiquity*, 201.

32 Flandrin and Montanari, *Food*, 288.

33 http://penelope.uchicago.edu/Thayer/E/Roman/Texts/Athenaeus/1A*.html

34 Grant, *Founders of the Western World*, 68.

35 Flandrin and Montanari, *Food*, 87, quoting Antiphanes in *Apud Athenaeum*, 370e.

36 Toussaint-Samat, *History of Food*, 622.

37 An identical statue is in Rome, Georgia. Italian dictator Benito Mussolini sent the copy in 1929 as a gift from one Rome to the other to honor the opening of a Georgia silk mill whose parent company was in Italy. During World War II, when Italy was America's enemy, the American statue had to be taken down and hidden after angry citizens threatened to blow it up.

38 Grant, *Founders*, 144–145.

39 http://www.theoi.com/Olympios/DemeterGoddess.html, quoting Ovid, Metamorphoses 5.341

40 Tannahill says the Romans preserved the land and grew grain on it (72–73).

41 Bober, *Art, Culture, & Cuisine*, 190.

42 Miller, J. Innes. *The Spice Trade of the Roman Empire*, 29 B.C. to A.D. 641. Oxford at the Clarendon Press, 1969; 23, 278, 279.

43 Woodier, *Apple Cookbook*, 2.

44 Tannahill, *Food in History*, 64.

45 Davidson, *Oxford Companion*, 672–673.

46 Phillips, *Wine*, 34.

47 *Ibid.*, 34.

48 *Ibid.*, 35.

49 Toussaint-Samat, *Food*, 296–297.

50 The male warrior society of Rome assumed that bee society was just like theirs: headed by a powerful male, like an emperor bee, who brought all the other bees out to wage war. The idea of a queen did not occur to them. Lacey & Danziger, *The Year 1000*, 139.

51 Farrar, *Ancient Roman Gardens*.

52 Shelton, *As the Romans Did*, 75–78.

53 http://penelope.uchicago.edu/Thayer/E/Roman/Texts/Cato/De_Agricultura/C*.html

54 http://penelope.uchicago.edu/Thayer/E/Roman/Texts/Cato/De_Agricultura/G*.html. Cato, *de Agricultura*, 119.

55 http://penelope.uchicago.edu/Thayer/E/Roman/Texts/Cato/De_Agricultura/G*.html. Cato, *de Agricultura*, 121.

56 Shelton, 72–74.

57 *Ibid.*, 83–84, quoting *Geoponica* 20.46.1–5.

58 *Ibid.*, 130–131.

59 Vehling, *Apicius*, 9–11.

60 *Food*, 134.

61 *Ibid.*, 137.

62 Vehling, *Apicius*, 161.

63 *Ibid.*, fn, 114–115.

64 Brothwell, *Food in Antiquity*, 48–49.

65 *Ibid.*, 52.

66 www.gmu.edu/departments/fld/classics/apicius4.html

67 Grant, *Western World*, 263.

68 www.gardenmedicinals.com

69 History Channel, *The XY Factor: The History of Sex: Ancient Civilizations*.

70 Dalby and Grainger, *Classical Cookbok*, 24.

71 *Ibid.*, 112, 46–47, 111, 129, 102.

[72] http://ancienthistory.about.com/library/bl/ bl_text_satyricon2_36.htm

[73] http://ancienthistory.about.com/library/bl/ bl_text_satyricon2_49.htm, 50.htm

[74] Shelton, *Roman Gardens*, 79.

[75] Tannahill, *Food in History*, 74–76.

[76] *Food*, 136.

[77] *Food*, 135.

[78] Lacey & Danziger, *Year 1000*, 12–13, 53.

[79] Diamond, *Guns, Germs, and Steel*, 205, 207.

[80] McNeill, *Plagues and Peoples*, 107–108.

[81] Visser, *Much Depends on Dinner*, 77.

[82] Spodek, *World History*, 152.

[83] *Food*, 129–130.

[84] Tannahill, *Food in History*, 92.

[85] Garnsey, *Food and Society in Classical Antiquity*, 68.

[86] Miller, *Spice Trade*, 25.

Third Course

[1] Phillips, *Short History of Wine*, 75.

[2] Hugh Magennis. *Anglo-Saxon Appetites*. Bodmin, Cornwall, Great Britain: MPG Books, 1999; 94.

[3] *OED*, I, 1557, 1663.

[4] Flandrin, 309–311.

[5] Flandrin, 308. Rawcliffe, *Medicine and Society*, 33. Wheaton, *Savoring the Past*, 35. Farb, 119.

[6] Flandrin, *Food*, "Seasoning, Cooking, and Dietetics in the Late Middle Ages," 318.

[7] Flandrin, *Food*, 407, 421.

[8] *Ibid.*, 316–317.

[9] *Ibid.*, 422.

[10] Flandrin, *Food*, 314.

[11] Farb, *Consuming Passions*, 121.

[12] www.ostvik.org/articles/viking_food.html.

[13] Phillips, *Wine*, 85.

[14] McGee, *On Food and Cooking*, 236.

[15] Dalby, *Flavours of Byzantium*, 65.

[16] *Ibid.*, 133–146.

[17] *Ibid.*, 147–160.

[18] *Ibid.*, 161–162.

[19] *Ibid.*, 163–169.

[20] Dalby, *Dangerous Tastes: The Story of Spices*, 86–87.

[21] Flandrin, *Food*, 189.

[22] *Ibid.*, 189.

[23] *Food in Russian History and Culture*, 29, n. 34; 20, n.21.

[24] http://www lib.usc.edu/~jnawaz/ISLAM/ PILLARS/FastFiqh.html

[25] *Fast and Feast*, 106.

[26] Achaya, *Indian Food*, 160.

[27] Barer-Stein, *You Eat What You Are*, 397.

[28] *Ibid.*, 303.

[29] Wright, *Mediterranean Feast*, 118.

[30] Roden, *Middle Eastern Food*, 234.

[31] *Ibid.*, 246–248.

[32] *Ibid.*, 250–251.

[33] *Ibid.*, 277.

[34] *Ibid.*, 305 (imam bayaldi), 302 (filling).

[35] Wright, *Mediterranean Feast*, 325.

[36] *Ibid.*, 499.

[37] Davidson, *Oxford Companion*, 523.

[38] Flandrin, *Food*, 208.

[39] Pendergrast, *Uncommon Grounds*, 4.

[40] *Ibid.*, 5–6.

[41] *Ibid.*, 12.

[42] *Ibid.*, 6.

[43] *Ibid.*, 7–18.

[44] Levenson, *Habeas Codfish*, 13.

[45] Flandrin, *Food*, 281.

[46] *Ibid.*, 275.

[47] Phillips, *Wine*, 111.

[48] Flandrin, *Food*, 117–119.

[49] Home Wine/Beer Club email.

[50] Phillips, *Wine*, 85.

[51] Chianti gained more fame in the movie *Silence of the Lambs* with Hannibal "the Cannibal" Lecter's remark about one of his victims: "I ate her liver with some fava beans and a nice Chianti."

[52] Phillips, *Wine*, 98–99.

[53] *Ibid.*, 96.

[54] *Ibid.*, 104–105.

[55] *Ibid.*, 107–111.

[56] http://www2.potsdam.edu/hansondj/ controversies/1114796842.html

[57] Lacey and Danziger, *The Year 1000*, 137.

[58] Cass, *Dancing Through History*, 41.

[59] Siberia is in remote eastern Russia. The Communists used it as a prison where they sent exiles.

[60] Quoted in Wheaton, *Savoring the Past*, 6.

[61] *Ibid.*, 7.

[62] Willan, *Great Cooks and Their Recipes*, 9.

[63] Davidson, *Oxford Companion*, 12.

[64] Beecher, *Domestic Receipt-Book*, 177.

[65] Rombauer, et al., *Joy of Cooking* (1997), 1039.

[66] Beecher, *Domestic Receipt-Book*, 118; Child, *The American Frugal Housewife*,–119; Hale, *Early American Cookery*, 78–79; Randolph, *The Virginia Housewife*, 147.

[67] Wheaton, *Savoring the Past*, 16.

[68] Elias, *Manners*, Vol. 1, 64, 153, 85, 87, 88.

[69] *Cooking Live*, 11/5/01, Elizabeth Ryan, pomologist.

[70] Woodier, *Apple Cookbook*, 42.

[71] Wright, *Mediterranean Feast*, 622.

[72] For an excellent fictitious telling of the story of this colony, see Jane Smiley's novel, *The Greenlanders*.

[73] Le Goff, *The Medieval World*, 116.

[74] http://www.crs4.it/~riccardo/Letteratura/ Decamerone/Ottava/8_03.htm
[75] Kagan, et al., *Western Heritage*, 298.
[76] Davidson, *Oxford Companion*, 367.
[77] Algar, *Classical Turkish Cooking*, 10.
[78] *Ibid.*, 11.

Fourth Course

[1] Flint, *The Imaginative Landscape of Christopher Columbus*, 4–5.
[2] Kamen, *Inquisition and Society in Spain*, 11.
[3] Krupp, *Echoes of the Ancient Skies*, 270.
[4] Coe, *America's First Cuisines*, 200.
[5] http://dsc.discovery.com/news/2009/06/08/ machu picchu spirit.html
[6] http://www.nap.edu/openbook. php?record_id=1398&page=4
[7] *Ibid.*
[8] *Ibid.*, 149.
[9] *Ibid.*, 151.
[10] Coe, *Cuisines*, 174–175.
[11] *Ibid.*, 170–171.
[12] Sokolov, *Why We Eat*, 86.
[13] Coe, *Cuisines*, 201.
[14] http://www.nap.edu/openbook. php?record_id=1398&page=23
[15] *Ibid.*, 182.
[16] http://www.nap.edu/openbook. php?record_id=1398&page=23
[17] Coe, *Cuisines*, 198.
[18] McGee, 170.
[19] http://www.nap.edu/openbook. php?record_id=1398&page=276
[20] *Ibid.*, 22
[21] *Ibid.*, 23
[22] Dor-Ner, *Columbus*, 266.
[23] Toussaint-Samat, *Food*, 711.
[24] Dor-Ner, *Columbus*, 266.
[25] *Ibid.*, 268.
[26] *Ibid.*, 266.
[27] Beck, et al., *World History*, 535.
[28] Dor-Ner, *Columbus*, 267.
[29] Toussaint-Samat, *Food*, 717.
[30] Viola and Margolis, *Seeds of Change*, 48.
[31] Dor-Ner, *Columbus*, 269.
[32] Dor-Ner, *Columbus*, 267. Toussaint-Samat, *Food*, 717.
[33] Davidson, *Oxford Companion*, 627.
[34] *Ibid.*, 628.
[35] Toussaint-Samat, *Food*, 723.
[36] Davidson, *Oxford Companion*, 627.
[37] Toussaint-Samat, *Food*, 725.
[38] http://www.conagrafoodscompany.com/corporate/ aboutus/company_history_timeline.jsp

[39] Viola and Margolis, *Seeds of Change*, 255.
[40] http://www.conagrafoodscompany.com/corporate/ aboutus/company_history_timeline.jsp
[41] http://www.nap.edu/openbook. php?record_id=1398&page=173.
[42] *OED*, 559.
[43] Fussell, *Story of Corn*, 17.
[44] Beck, et al., *World History*, 213.
[45] Sokolov, *Why We Eat*, 82.
[46] Fussell, *Corn*, 249–250.
[47] http://www.nap.edu/openbook. php?record_id=1398&page=204
[48] *Ibid.*, 205
[49] *Ibid.*, 214, 216, 218.
[50] *Ibid.*, 287.
[51] *Ibid.*, 276.
[52] *Ibid.*, 195
[53] Sokolov, *Why We Eat*, 83.
[54] *Ibid.*, 19.
[55] *Ibid.*, 14.
[56] Rain, *Vanilla*, 8.
[57] McGee, *On Food and Cooking*, 430, 432.
[58] Rain, *Vanilla*, 2.
[59] Davidson, *Oxford Companion*, 821.
[60] Rain, *Vanilla*, 73.
[61] *Ibid.*, 79.
[62] Rain, *Vanilla*, 5.
[63] Kimball, ed., *Thomas Jefferson's Cook Book*, 13.
[64] Rain, *Vanilla*, 81.
[65] *Ibid.*, 153.
[66] *Ibid.*
[67] *Ibid.*, 129.
[68] *Ibid.*, 130.
[69] *Ibid.*, 153.
[70] http://www.harpers.org/index/1986/11/26
[71] Rain, *Vanilla*, 300.
[72] http://www.harpers.org/index/1986/11/26
[73] http://www.library.northwestern.edu/govinfo/ news/2009/07/ice_cream.html
[74] Schlesinger, *Animals and Plants of the Ancient Maya*, 30–31.
[75] http://www.eric.ed.gov/ERICWebPortal/ custom/portlets/recordDetails/detailmini. jsp?_nfpb=true&_&ERICExtSearch_Sea rchValue_0=EJ431111&ERICExtSea rch_SearchType_0=no&accno=EJ431111
[76] http://www.criscenzo.com/jaguarsun/popolvuh. html
[77] Simon Martin. "Cacao in Ancient Maya Religion," in *Reconstructing Ancient Maya Diet*, ed. Christine D. White. Salt Lake City: The University of Utah Press, 1999; 156.
[78] *Ibid.*, 162–163.
[79] Martin, "Cacao," 165.

80 http://sciencereview.berkeley.edu/articles.php?issue=10&article=beerchocolate

81 David Stuart, "The Language of Chocolate: References to Cacao on Classic Maya Drinking Vessels," in *Reconstructing Ancient Maya Diet*, ed. Christine D. White. Salt Lake City: The University of Utah Press, 1999; 191.

82 *Ibid.*, 193.

83 Schlesinger, *Ancient Maya*, 56.

84 Coe, *Cuisines*, 141.

85 Schlesinger, *Animals and Plants of the Ancient Maya*, 132–134.

86 Schlesinger, *Ancient Maya*, 180.

87 *Ibid.*, 105.

88 *Ibid.*, 269.

89 Soustelle, *Daily Life Aztecs*, 96–99.

90 Coe, *Cuisines*, 98.

91 *Ibid.*, 110.

92 *Ibid.*, 111.

93 Pilcher, *¡Que Vivan Los Tamales!*, 13.

94 *Ibid.*, 12.

95 *Florentine Codex*, Book 2, Part III, 64.

96 *Ibid.*,

97 http://aces.nmsu.edu/news/1999/110299_bluecorn.html

98 Pilcher, *¡Que Vivan Los Tamales!*, 11.

99 Fussell, *Corn*, 202.

100 *Florentine Codex*, Book 2, Part III, 97.

101 *Ibid.*, 14.

102 *Ibid.*, 65.

103 *Ibid.*, 29.

104 http://www.hort.purdue.edu/newcrop/1492/amaranths.html

105 Coe and Coe, *True History of Chocolate*, 89–93.

106 http://sciencereview.berkeley.edu/articles.php?issue=10&article=beerchocolate

107 *Ibid.*, 97.

108 *Ibid.*, 98.

109 Coe, *Cuisines*, 97.

110 *Ibid.*, 99–100.

111 *Ibid.*, 100–101.

112 Pilcher, *¡Que Vivan Los Tamales!*, 18.

113 Krupp, *Echoes of the Ancient Skies*, 245.

114 Fussell, *Corn*, 200, 202.

115 http://www.accessgenealogy.com/native/tribes/pima/pimaindianhist.htm

116 http://www.nap.edu/openbook.php?record_id=1398&page=195

117 http://www.hotsauce.com/Scoville Hot Sauce Heat Scale s/78.htm

118 http://www.hotsauce.com/Scoville Hot Sauce Heat Scale s/78.htm

119 Nabhan, *Gathering the Desert*, 123–124.

120 *Ibid.*, 126.

121 *Ibid.*, 128.

122 www.press.uchicago.edu/Misc/Chicago/101363.html

123 http://cahokiamounds.org/learn/; http://cahokiamounds.org/explore/

124 Dor-Ner, *Columbus and the Age of Discovery*, 119.

125 The *Niña* was 90 feet long; compare with Zheng He's 400-foot-long ship.

126 Dor-Ner, *Columbus and the Age of Discovery*, 120.

127 *Ibid.*, 133–134.

128 *Ibid.*, 118.

129 *Ibid.*, 125.

130 No one is sure exactly which island this is.

131 *Ibid.*, 149.

Fifth Course

1 Crosby, *Columbian Exchange*, 3.

2 Silverberg, *Pueblo Revolt*, 63.

3 Coe, *America's First Cuisines*, 70–71.

4 Suzanne Austin Alchon, *A Pest in the Land: New World Epidemics in a Global Perspective*, 69, 73.

5 *Ibid.*

6 http://discovermagazine.com/2006/feb/megadeath-in-mexico

7 *Ibid.*, 53.

8 Crosby, *Columbian Exchange*, 67.

9 *Ibid.*, 106.

10 *Ibid.*, 79.

11 Coe and Coe, *Chocolate*, 216–218.

12 Bayless, *Mexican Kitchen*, 276, 286–287.

13 *NYTimes*, August 14, 2002.

14 Diana Kennedy, *Cuisines of Mexico*, 16–18.

15 Silverberg, *Pueblo Revolt*, 27.

16 Sokolov, *Why We Eat*, 88.

17 Phillips, *Wine*, 156–159.

18 Sokolov, *Why We Eat*, 84.

19 Crosby, *Exchange*, 84–87.

20 *Ibid.*, 85.

21 Ortiz, *Latin American Cooking*, 153–157.

22 Molina, *Secretos de las Brasas*, 20, 22, 26.

23 Ortiz, *Latin American Cooking*, 38–39.

24 Crosby, *Exchange*, 83.

25 Beck, et al., *World History*, 497.

26 Ortiz, *Latin American Cooking*, 215.

27 Davidson, *Oxford Companion*, 141.

28 Ortiz, *Latin American Cooking*, 333.

29 Mintz, *Sweetness*, 45–54, unless otherwise noted.

30 Phillips, *Wine*, 153.

31 McPhee, *Oranges*, 71.

32 Courtwright, *Habit*, 150.

33 www.history.ufl.edu/west1/nar1.htm

34 *Ibid.*, 50.

35 Beck, et al., *World History*, 497.

36 Davidson, *Oxford Companion*, 94, 103.

37 www.backusturner.com/demarera[sic]/history

38 McPhee, *Oranges*, quoting Samuel Pepys, 86.

39 Dor-Ner, *Columbus and Age of Discovery*, 171.

40 Crosby, *Columbian Exchange*, 199.

41 *Ibid.*, 166; all statistics except 2008.

42 http://www.nationsonline.org/oneworld/world_ population.htm

43 Crosby, *Columbian Exchange*, 191.

44 Project Gutenberg, Etext of *Don Quixote* by Miguel de Cervantes, Chapter I.

45 *Ibid.*, Chapter II.

46 Davidson, *Oxford Companion*, 494.

47 Gutenberg, *Quixote*, Chapter LIX.

48 *Ibid.*, Chapter II.

49 *Ibid.*, Chapter LIX.

50 *Ibid.*, Chapter XLIX.

51 *Ibid.*, Chapter XX.

52 Flandrin, "Seasoning, Cooking, Dietetics in the Late Middle Ages," *Food*, 313.

53 Davidson, *Oxford Companion*, 232.

54 Flandrin, "Seasoning," *Food*, 319.

55 Allen J. Grieco, "Food and Social Classes in Late Medieval and Renaissance Italy," in *Food*, ed. Flandrin, 307, 303.

56 Klapisch-Zuber, *Women, Family, and Ritual in Renaissance Italy*, 106–107.

57 Burke, *The Italian Renaissance*, 70.

58 Willan, *Great Cooks*, 23.

59 Davidson, *Oxford Companion*, 613.

60 Martino, *The Art of Cooking*, intro. Ballerini, fn 44.

61 *Ibid.*, 11, 14.

62 *Ibid.*, 5.

63 *Ibid.*, 5–6.

64 *Ibid.*, 52.

65 *Ibid.*, 69.

66 *Ibid.*, 30.

67 *Ibid.*, 49.

68 *Ibid.*, 57.

69 *Ibid.*, 68.

70 *Ibid.*, 80.

71 Terence Scully. *The Art of Cooking in the Middle Ages*. Woodbridge, England: The Boydell Press, 1995; 253.

72 Willan, *Great Cooks*, 37.

73 *Ibid.*, 39–40.

74 *Ibid.*, 40.

75 Ken Albala, *Eating Right in the Renaissance*, 12–13.

76 Albala, *Eating Right*, 1.

77 *Ibid.*, 82.

78 http://www.escholarship.org/editions/ view?docId=kt587020gg&chunk.id=fm04&toc. depth=1&toc.id=fm04&brand=ucpress

79 Albala, *Eating Right*, 88.

80 Martino, *Art of Cooking*, fn. 56.

81 *Ibid.*, 44.

82 Wheaton, *Savoring the Past*, 43.

83 Ochorowicz-Monatowa, *Polish Cookery*, throughout book; Google Translator.

84 Chamberlin, *The Bad Popes*, 167.

85 Luther, *Conversations*, 170.

86 Mayson, *Port*, 5.

87 Kagan, Osment, Turner, *Western Heritage*, 367.

88 Sass, *To the Queen's Taste*, 18.

89 *A New Booke of Cookerie.*

90 Sass, *Queen's Taste*, 26.

91 *Ibid.*, 19–20.

Sixth Course

1 Braudel, *Mediterranean*, Vol. II, 1088.

2 Bailey and Kennedy, *American Spirit*, 29.

3 Carney, *Black Rice*, 165.

4 *Ibid.*, 118–122.

5 *Ibid.*, 53.

6 Hess, *Carolina Rice Kitchen*, 93.

7 Cronon, *Changes in the Land*, 22.

8 *Ibid.*, 45, and n. 17.

9 *Ibid.*, 35–37.

10 *Ibid.*, 29, 38.

11 Nearing, *Maple Sugar Book*, 26.

12 *Ibid.*, 23–24.

13 Brillat-Savarin, *Physiology of Taste*, 78.

14 Simmons, *The First American Cookbook*, 28.

15 Kurlansky, *Cod*, 51.

16 *Ibid.*, 81.

17 "Father and I went down to camp along with Captain Gooding / And there we saw the men and boys, as thick as hasty pudding."

18 Brown, *Early American Beverages*, 40.

19 *Ibid.*, 39.

20 *Ibid.*, 67.

21 *Ibid.*, 19.

22 *Ibid.*, 17.

23 Franklin, *Autobiography*, 76–77.

24 Davidson, *Oxford Companion to Food*, 254.

25 Hutchinson, *New Pennsylvania Dutch Cookbook*, 93.

26 *Ibid.*, 150–151.

27 Hazelton, *The Swiss Cookbook*, 48.

28 http://www.lib.ksu.edu/depts/spec/rarebooks/ cookery/glasse1747.html.

29 Glasse, *Art of Cookery*, 4.

30 *Ibid.*, 5.

31 *Ibid.*, 7.

32 *Ibid.*, 6.

33 *Ibid.*, 76.

34 *Ibid.*, 24.

[35] *Ibid.*, 21.

[36] Kia, *Sweden's Regional Recipes*, 129–131.

[37] Brown, *Early American Beverages*, 20.

[38] The Americans weren't the only ones smuggling tea. By 1784, the British were paying taxes on only slightly more than one-third of the tea they consumed. The rest had entered the country illegally.

[39] Paine, *Common Sense*, 83.

[40] *Ibid.*, 86.

[41] *Ibid.*, 87.

[42] Brown, *Early American Beverages*, 22.

[43] Bailey, et al., *American Pageant*, Vol. I, 136.

[44] History Channel, "Save Our History: Valley Forge National Historical Park."

[45] Kimball, *Martha Washington Cook Book*, 18.

[46] *Ibid.*, 32–34.

[47] Phillips, *Wine*, 170.

[48] Ambrose, *Undaunted Courage*, 41.

[49] Simmons, *The First American Cookbook*, 3–4.

[50] Gutman, *Black Family*, 332–333.

[51] Simmons, *American Cookery*, 2nd ed.

[52] Election Cake, *The Boston Cooking School Cookbook*. www.bartleby.com/87/r1550.html.

[53] Hatch, *Democratization of American Christianity*, 96.

[54] Land, *New Orleans Cuisine*, 36, 29.

[55] *Ibid.*, 23.

[56] Rosenberg, *Cholera Years*, 47.

[57] Stewart, *Overland Trail*, 293.

[58] *Ibid.*, 182.

[59] *Ibid.*, 78.

[60] *Ibid.*, 79.

[61] Holliday, *The World Rushed In*, 313.

[62] West, *Growing Up with the Country*, 13.

[63] Holliday, *World Rushed*, 315, 331.

[64] Dunaway, *No Need to Knead*, 32.

[65] Pendergrast, *Uncommon Grounds*, 56–57.

[66] http://www.levistrauss.com/about/history/timeline.asp.

[67] Holliday, *World Rushed In*, 97.

[68] Shephard, *Pickled, Potted*, 216.

[69] Hurtado, *Indian Survival on the California Frontier*, 3.

Seventh Course

[1] Spodek, *World's History*, 408.

[2] Anderson, *The Food of China*, 7–8.

[3] Spodek, *World's History*, 407.

[4] Schama, *An Embarrassment of Riches*, 169.

[5] *Ibid.*, 176.

[6] *Sensible Cook*, 43.

[7] *Ibid.*, 26–127.

[8] *Ibid.*, 6–7.

[9] *Ibid.*, 66.

[10] *Ibid.*, 67.

[11] *Ibid.*, 51.

[12] Schama, *Embarrassment*, 177. Quoting Burema, L. *De voeding in Nederland von de Middeleeuwen tot de twintigste Eeuw.* Assen, 1953.

[13] Schama, *Embarrassment*, 186, 184.

[14] *Sensible Cook*, 26.

[15] Druett, *Rough Medicine*, 142.

[16] *Food for Athletes*, 48.

[17] Brennan, *Original Thai Cookbook*, 23.

[18] Druett, *Rough Medicine*, 142.

[19] Kia, *Sweden's Regional Recipes*, 112.

[20] Doub, *Tastes & Tales of Norway*, 59.

[21] Gjerde, *Peasants to Farmers*, 25.

[22] *Ibid.*, 54.

[23] Roalson and Bourret, *Norwegian Touches*, 17.

[24] Doub, *Tastes & Tales of Norway*, 68.

[25] *Ibid.*, 11.

[26] Gjerde, *Peasants*, 34–37.

[27] *Ibid.*, 126.

[28] *Ibid.*, 3.

[29] Roalson and Bourret, *Norwegian Touches*, 18.

[30] Doub, *Tastes & Tales of Norway*, 3.

[31] Gjerde, *Peasants*, 179.

[32] *Ibid.*, 139.

[33] Gaski, *Sami Culture*, 94.

[34] Glants and Toomre, *Food in Russian History and Culture*, 3.

[35] *Ibid.*, 4.

[36] http://samovars.net

[37] *LA Times Book Review*, 5/29/2005, R4.

[38] Willan, *Great Cooks and Their Recipes*, 59.

[39] Davidson, *Oxford Companion to Food*, 232.

[40] Pendergrast, *Uncommon Grounds*, 10.

[41] *Ibid.*, 15–16.

[42] Kagan, et al., *Western Heritage*, 436.

[43] Wheaton, *Savoring the Past*, 136.

[44] McGee, *On Food and Cooking*, 70.

[45] *Ibid.*, 69.

[46] *Ibid.*, 82–84.

[47] Camporesi, *Exotic Brew*, 47.

[48] Young, *Apples of Gold*, 179.

[49] Wheaton, *Savoring the Past*, 159.

[50] Young, *Apples of Gold*, 180.

[51] *Ibid.*, 174.

[52] Camporesi, *Exotic Brew*, 8.

[53] *Ibid.*, 4.

[54] *Adam's Luxury and Eve's Cookery*, 112–114.

[55] Wheaton, *Savoring the Past*, 99.

[56] Suzanne Von Drachenfels, *Art of the Table*, 49–51, 59. Young, *Apples*, 151–152, 174.

[57] Wheaton, *Savoring the Past*, 201.

[58] Camporesi, *Exotic Brew*, 37.

59 Pascal Ory, quoted in Spang, *Invention of the Restaurant*, 206.
60 Kaplan, *Bakers of Paris*, 23–24.
61 *Ibid.*, 464.
62 *Ibid.*, 66–70.
63 *Ibid.*, 215–218.
64 *Ibid.*, 470.
65 *Ibid.*, 475.
66 *Ibid.*, 464–466.
67 *Ibid.*, 101–102.
68 *Ibid.*, 106.
69 Schama, *Citizens*, 314–315.
70 http://memory.loc.gov/ammem/collections/jefferson_papers/mtjtime3a.html
71 Waters, *Chez Panisse Menu Cookbook*, 111.
72 Spang, *Restaurant*, 123–127.
73 *Ibid.*, 139.
74 *Ibid.*, 191.
75 *OED*, 1119.
76 http://www.escholarship.org/editions/view?docId=kt587020gg&chunk.id=fm04&toc.depth=1&toc.id=fm04&brand=ucpress
77 Brillat-Savarin, *The Physiology of Taste*, 51.
78 *Ibid.*, 95.
79 *Ibid.*, 311–313.
80 Willan, *Great Cooks*, 143.
81 Kelly, *Cooking for Kings*, 247.
82 *Ibid.*, 172–181.
83 *Ibid.*, 19.
84 Escoffier, *Guide*, 528.
85 Roueché, *Medical Detectives*, Vol. II, 302–305.
86 Bailey, et al., *American Pageant I*, 219.
87 Shephard, *Pickled, Potted, Canned*, 226–227.
88 Austin, 1812 *The Great Retreat*, 80.
89 *Ibid.*, 26.
90 *Ibid.*, 26.
91 *Ibid.*, 84.
92 *Ibid.*, 80.
93 *Ibid.*, 129.
94 *Ibid.*, 34.
95 *Ibid.*, 133.
96 *Ibid.*, 370.
97 *Ibid.*, 35.
98 *Ibid.*, 97.

Eighth Course
1 Gutman, *Black Family in Slavery and Freedom 1750–1925*, 336.
2 *Ibid.*, 103.
3 Fox-Genovese, *Plantation Household*, 118–119.
4 *What Mrs. Fisher Knows*, 90.
5 Fox-Genovese, *Plantation Household*, 159.
6 White, *Ar'n't I a Woman?*, 100.
7 Bailey and Kennedy, *American Spirit*, 321–322.

8 Sklar, *Catherine Beecher*, 155.
9 http://massmaple.org/history.php
10 *Underground Railroad*, 26.
11 Smith, *Blockades and Bread Riots (ms.)*, 6.
12 *Ibid.*, 21.
13 ftp://gutenberg.mirrors.tds.net/pub/gutenberg.org/4/3/6/4367/4367-h/p3.htm.
14 http://hnn.us/comments/1802.html; "Are the Media Right to Single Out William Tecumseh Sherman As the Most Reckless Civil War General of Them All?" by Dr. Michael Taylor
15 *American Spirit*, 471.
16 Florence Nightingale, *Sanitary History*, 8.
17 *Ibid.*, 7.
18 Nightingale, "Taking Food," 15.
19 Nightingale, "What Food?," 30.
20 http://www.florence-nightingale.co.uk/flo2.htm.
21 Ibid., 24.
22 *Ibid.*, 37.
23 Pryor, *Clara Barton*, 142.
24 Shange, *If I Can Cook*, 10.
25 Twain, *Roughing It*, 46–47.
26 *Ibid.*, 89.
27 Luchetti, *Home on the Range*, 56–57.
28 Twain, *Roughing It*, 292.
29 Ambrose, *Nothing Like It in the World*, 150.
30 *Ibid.*, 162–163.
31 From a *NY Times* article, quoted in Roughing It, 48.
32 Jones, *Vines in the Sun*, 17–18.
33 Martin, *The Land Looks After Us*, 91.
34 *NY Times*, June 18, 2001.
35 Atkins, *Harvest of Grief*, 30–33.
36 Labbé and Lurie, *Slaughterhouse Cases*, 50.
37 Luchetti, *Home on the Range*, 92.
38 Josephson, *Union House*, 14.
39 Williams, *Savory Suppers*, 95–96.
40 Root, *Eating in America*, 314–315.
41 Brumberg, *Fasting Girls*, 175–176.
42 Andreason and Black, *Psychiatry*, 479.
43 *Ibid.*, 480–486.
44 Thomas J. Schlereth, "Conduits and Conduct: Home Utilities in Victorian America, 1876–1915," in *American Home Life, 1880–1930*, 227.
45 Rafter, *Partial Justice*, 165.
46 Benning, *Oh, Fudge!*, 7.
47 *Ibid.*, 12.
48 Ric Burns, *New York* video.
49 www.pictureframes.co.uk/page/saint_valentine.htm.
50 Hamilton, *Mythology*, 92–100.
51 Schlereth, "Home Utilities," 233.
52 Whorton, *Crusaders*, 48.
53 Thoreau, *Walden and Other Writings*, 112.

54 *Ibid.*, 150.
55 Smith, *Peanuts*, 86–87.
56 *Ibid.*, 87.
57 Whorton, *Crusaders*, 223.
58 Pendergrast, *Coca-Cola*, 16.
59 *Ibid.*, 14–15.
60 Tedlow, *New and Improved*, 42–44.
61 Phillips, *Short History of Wine*, 282–285.
62 Jonathan Swift, "A Modest Proposal," in *Swift: Gulliver's Travels and Other Writings*, 489.
63 Gallagher, *Paddy's Lament*, 22–25.
64 www.stpatricksday.ie/cms/stpatricksday_history.html
65 Burbank, *Harvest of the Years*, 167.
66 *Castles Neuschwanstein and Hohenschwangau*, Copyright by Verlag Kienberger [no date; no page numbers]
67 http://www.muenchen-tourist.de/englisch/oktoberfest/muenchen-oktoberfest-geschichte_e_m.htm. 68 Shaw, *The World of Escoffier*, 24–27.
69 Beck, Bertholle, Child, *Mastering the Art of French Cooking*, 147.
70 Willan, *La France Gastronomique*, 28–31.
71 *Les Français et La Table*, 446–449.
72 Hazan, *The Classic Italian Cookbook*, 3.
73 *Ibid.*, 6.
74 Davidson, *Oxford Companion*, 582.
75 *Ibid.*, 800.
76 Simeti, *Pomp and Sustenance*, 89.
77 *Ibid.*, 284–293.
78 Mangione and Morreale, *La Storia*, xv.
79 *Ibid.*, 60–80.
80 http://www.mendel-museum.org/.
81 http://www.mendel-museum.org/eng/3news/road.htm.
82 Kagan, Ozment, Turner, *Western Heritage*, 823.
83 Beeton, *The Book of Household Management*, title page.
84 *Ibid.*, 259–260.
85 *Ibid.*, 590–91.
86 *Ibid.*, 242–43.

Ninth Course
1 Krishnendu Ray. *The Migrant's Table*. Philadelphia: Temple University Press, 2004; 24, 189.
2 Davidson, *Oxford Companion*, 774–775.
3 Lewicki, *West African Food*, 49.
4 *Ibid.*, 50–52.
5 *Ibid.*, 91–98.
6 *Ibid.*, 122–123.
7 *Ibid.*, 128–131.
8 *Ibid.*, 31.
9 *Ibid.*, 36–37.
10 *Ibid.*, 105.

11 Davidson, *Oxford Companion*, 57.
12 Lewicki, *West African Food*, 73.
13 *Ibid.*, 76–77.
14 *Ibid.*, 80–82.
15 *Ibid.*, 124.
16 Beck, et al., *World History*, 686.
17 Batmangli, *Silk Road Cooking*, 303; http://www.theepicentre.com/Spices/raselhanout.html.
18 Wright, *Mediterranean Feast*, 523–524.
19 http://www.globalgourmet.com/destinations/ethiopia/berbere.html; http://congocookbook.com/sauce_recipes/berbere.
20 Davidson, *Oxford Companion*, 220.
21 Roden, *Arabesque*, 30.
22 DeWitt, et al., *Flavors of Africa*, 197.
23 Hachten, *Regional African Cooking*, 125–126.
24 *Ibid.*, 114–118.
25 Hachten, *Regional African Cooking*, 217.
26 DeWitt, et al., *Flavors of Africa*, 129.
27 *Ibid.*, 9.
28 *Ibid.*, 20.
29 *Ibid.*, 69.
30 Sen, *Food Culture India*, 46.
31 *Ibid.*, 21.
32 Hamilton, *Portuguese Encounters*, 193, 202.
33 Collingham, *Curry*, 63.
34 Hamilton, *Portuguese Encounters*, 219.
35 Ray, *Migrant's Table*, 25.
36 Sen, *Food Culture India*, 117.
37 Collingham, *Curry*, 61.
38 Sen, *India*, 17–18.
39 Collingham, *Curry*, 32–33.
40 *Ibid.*, 34.
41 Chandra, *Cuisines of India*, 123–124.
42 http://economictimes.indiatimes.com/News/News_By_Industry/How_garam_masala_symbolises_Indias_culinary_tradition/articleshow/2254870.cms
43 http://www.penzeys.com/cgi-bin/penzeys/p-penzeysgarammasala.html
44 http://www.penzeys.com/cgi-bin/penzeys/p-penzeysroganjosh.html
45 http://www.penzeys.com/cgi-bin/penzeys/p-penzeysvindaloo.html
46 http://www.penzeys.com/cgi-bin/penzeys/p-penzeysbaltiseason.html
47 Achaya, *Indian Food*, 176.
48 Beeton, *Household Management*, 135–136 (#269).
49 *Ibid.*, 176–178.
50 Anderson, *Food of China*, 65.
51 *Ibid.*, 58.
52 Kurlansky, *Salt*, 35.
53 Anderson, *Food of China*, 63.
54 Chang, *Food in Chinese Culture*, 169.

55 Anderson, *Japanese Tea Ritual*, 14–15.
56 *Ibid.*, 151, 147.
57 Anderson, *Food of China*, 79.
58 Chang, 151.
59 *Ibid.*, 149.
60 Anderson, *Food of China*, 84.
61 Buell, *Turkicization*, 207.
62 *Ibid.*, 213.
63 Anderson, *Food of China*, 208–209.
64 *Ibid.*, 210–217.
65 Connor, *The Koreas*, 246–256.
66 Owen, *Indonesian Regional*, 10.
67 *Ibid.*,173–175.
68 Cordero-Fernando, *Culinary Culture of the Philippines*, 15.
69 Hoare, *Thailand*, 78.
70 Brennan, *Original Thai Cookbook*, 110–111.
71 *Ibid.*, 251.
72 Anderson, *Tea Ritual*, 57–58.
73 *Ibid.*, 150.
74 *Ibid.*, 165.
75 *Ibid.*, 166–172.
76 Mason and Caiger, *A History of Japan*, 120–121.
77 *Ibid.*, 155.
78 Beck, et al., *World History*, 720.
79 http://www.fugetsu-do.com/mochi.htm

Tenth Course

1 *A People and a Nation, Brief Edition (5th, Vol. B)*, 358.
2 Mangione and Morreale, *La Storia*, 174.
3 Diner, *Hungering for America*, 204–205.
4 Papanikolas, *Greek Odyssey*, 23.
5 *Ibid.*, 31.
6 Katatokis, et al., *Hellenic Cookery Modesto*.
7 Papanikolas, *Greek Earth*, 70–73.
8 www.agh-attorneys.com/4_lochner_wnew_york.htm.
9 http://caselaw.lp.findlaw.com/scripts/getcase.pl?court=us&vol=198&onvol=45.
10 Goodwin, *Pure Food Crusaders*, 42–46.
11 *Ibid.*, 65.
12 *Ibid.*, 221.
13 Pendergrast, *Coca-Cola*, 107–122.
14 Strenio, *Testing Trap*, 79–80.
15 Shapiro, *Perfection Salad*, 40.
16 www.biography.com/features/mother.
17 Kennedy, Randall, *Ni____r*, 8.
18 *Cooking Essentials Pro Chef*, 19–20.
19 *Ibid.*, 19.
20 Escoffier, *Guide*, ix.
21 *Ibid.*, 470.

22 Shaw, *Life and Times of Escoffier*, 52.
23 http://www.smithsonianmag.com/travel/The-Ghost-Wineries-of-Napa-Valley.html
24 Poling-Kempes, *Harvey Girls*, 238–241.
25 *Ibid.*, 39.
26 *Ibid.*, 39.
27 Coleman, *The Liners*, 183.
28 *Ibid.*, 66.
29 Archibold and McCauley, *Last Dinner*, 36.
30 *The Titanic Collection.*
31 *Slow Food*, April–June 2001, 47, 49.
32 Coleman, *Liners*, 71–81.
33 *Ibid.*, 106.
34 McClancy, *Consuming Culture*, 135.
35 Goldstein, *À La Russe*, 84.
36 Volokh, *Russian Cuisine*, 320.
37 Goldstein, *Russe*, 17–18.
38 Volokh, *Russian Cuisine*, 584–585.
39 *Ibid.*, 576–577.
40 Goldstein, *Russe*, 270.
41 Mauricio Borrero, "Communal Dining and State Cafeterias in Moscow and Petrograd, 1917–1921," in *Food in Russian History and Culture*, 163.
42 *Ibid.*, 169–170.
43 *Ibid.*, 171–172.
44 *More American Eats.*
45 Phillips, *Short History of Wine*, 303–304.
46 Jones, *Vines in the Sun*, 16.
47 Tom Wicker, *A Time to Die*, 89, 317.
48 http://www.nytimes.com/2008/05/14/nyregion/14icecream.html?_r=1
49 http://www.washingtonhistory.com/ScenesPast/images/SP_0606.pdf
50 http://www.washingtonhistory.com/ScenesPast/images/SP_0606.pdf
51 http://www.washingtonhistory.com/ScenesPast/images/SP_0606.pdf
52 http://www.washingtonhistory.com/ScenesPast/images/SP_0606.pdf
53 http://www.library.northwestern.edu/govinfo/news/2009/07/ice_cream.html
54 http://www.washingtonhistory.com/ScenesPast/images/SP_0606.pdf
55 http://www.icecreamusa.com/good_humor/history/
56 http://www.library.northwestern.edu/govinfo/news/2009/07/ice_cream.html
57 http://www.dannon.com/about.aspx
58 Goodwin, *Hollywood du Jour*, 13.
59 Leuchtenberg, *Perils of Prosperity*, 192.
60 *Ibid.*, 186.

Eleventh Course

1. Arts & Entertainment, *Biography*.
2. *U.S. Regional Cook Book*, 631.
3. Second inauguration, January 20, 1937.
4. "The Enchanted Forest," by Major John A. Porter, Q.M.C., *The Quartermaster Review*, March–April 1934.
5. Davidson, *Oxford Companion*, 153.
6. Lukacs, *American Vintage*, 105.
7. Bill Wilson letter to Dr. Carl Jung (undated); http://members.tripod.com/aainsa/frames.html
8. Philips, *Short History of Wine*, 302.
9. Smith, ed., *Oxford America*, Vol. I, 645.
10. Fussell, *The Story of Corn*, 202–203.
11. Smith, *Popped Culture*, 101–103.
12. Mendelson, *Stand Facing the Stove*, 84.
13. Edgar Rombauer, Forward to the Facsimile Edition, *The Joy of Cooking*, 1998, first page (no number).
14. Mendelson, *Stand Facing the Stove*, 96–97.
15. www.kingarthurflour.com.
16. E-mails, Bama Company to author; November 19 and 21, 2002.
17. http://www.carvel.com/about_us/history.htm
18. http://www.kraftfoodscompany.com/about/history/index.aspx
19. http://www.clevelandart.org/Kids/story/people/boiardi.html
20. http://motlc.wiesenthal.com/text/x19/xm1962.html
21. Pringle, *Food, Inc.*, 141–144.
22. http://www.navysna.org/awards/Miller.htm; http://www.history.navy.mil/faqs/faq57-4.htm; http://www.dorismiller.com; http://www.dorismiller.com/history/dorismiller/ussmiller.shtml; http://www.tsha.utexas.edu/handbook/online/articles/view/MM/fmi55.html
23. Pendergrast, *Uncommon Grounds*, 224.
24. http://www.usarmymodels.com/ARTICLES/Rations/krations.html
25. http://www.spam.com/about/history/default.aspx
26. Wyman, *Spam*, 23; http://www.spam.com/about/history/default.aspx
27. Wyman, *Spam*, 17–18, 23.
28. MacClancy, *Consuming Culture*, 47.
29. Thompson, *Canning*, 2.
30. *Ibid.*, 20.
31. *Ibid.*, 9.
32. Malgieri, *Cookies Unlimited*, 47.
33. Thompson, *Canning*, 38.
34. Daws, *Prisoners of the Japanese*, 120–121.
35. *Ibid.*, 111.
36. Andrews and Gilbert, *Over Here*, 62–63.
37. McClancy, *Consuming Culture*, 102.
38. Davidson, *Oxford Companion*, 673.
39. MacClancy, *Consuming Culture*, 47–48.
40. http://motlc.wiesenthal.com/text/x19/xm1962.html
41. McClancy, *Consuming Culture*, 340.
42. Kennedy, *Great Powers*, 362.
43. MacClancy, *Consuming Culture*, 134.
44. *More American Eats*.
45. *Finnish–American Folklore: The Legend of St. Urho*.
46. Houston, *Food Culture in the Caribbean*, 116.
47. Twain, *Roughing It*, 369.
48. *Ibid.*, 359.
49. *Ibid.*, 342, 355.
50. *Ibid.*, 354.
51. Davidson, *Oxford Companion*, 373.
52. *Ibid.*, 742.
53. http://www.spam.com/about/history/default.aspx
54. http://www.lbl.gov/Publications/Currents/Archive/Apr-21-1995.html.
55. *Suddenly Susan*.
56. *New Yorker*, January 15, 2001, 48–56.
57. Beck, et al., *World History*, 864.
58. http://www.economist.com/business/PrinterFriendly.cfm?story_id=1974103.
59. Belasco, "Food and the Counterculture," in *The Cultural Politics of Food and Eating*, Watson and Caldwell, ed., 221–222.
60. *Ibid.*, 223.
61. Smith, *Popped Culture*, 132–134.

Twelfth Course

1. http://www.bbc.co.uk/arts/books/author/david/pg3.shtml.
2. http://www.smithsonianmag.com/travel/The-Ghost-Wineries-of-Napa-Valley.html#ixzz0VjItalK9
3. http://www.goldendoor.com/escondido/faq/
4. Watson, *Golden Arches*, Intro, 23.
5. Yan, "McDonald's in Beijing," in Watson, ed., *Golden Arches*, 39.
6. Watson, "McD's in Hong Kong," in *Golden Arches*, 78.
7. *Ibid.*, "McD's Hong Kong," 89–90.
8. Yan, "McD's Beijing," in Watson, ed., *Golden Arches*, 47.
9. Watson, "McD's in Hong Kong," in *Golden Arches*, 85.
10. *Ibid.*, 36.
11. Yan, "McD's Beijing," in Watson, ed., *Golden Arches*, 74.
12. Watson, "McD's in Hong Kong," in *Golden Arches*, 93.
13. Yan, "McD's Beijing," in Watson, ed., *Golden Arches*, 61.

[14] Watson, "McD's Hong Kong," in *Golden Arches*, 90–91.

[15] *Sacramento Bee*, October 17, 2002, B1, B7.

[16] http://www.time.com/time/magazine/ article/0,9171,948969,00.html

[17] http://www.answers.com/topic/list-of-comfort-foods; *The Catholic Digest*, 1958, Vol. 23, 59.

[18] http://members.ift.org/IFT/Pubs/Newsletters/ weekly/nl_021710.htm

[19] www.mrsfields.com.

[20] From the author: that's how we made s'mores and banana boats when I was a Girl Scout.

[21] Fedoroff and Brown, *Mendel in the Kitchen*.

[22] *Ibid.*, 66.

[23] McHughen, *Pandora's Picnic Basket*, 236.

[24] *Ibid.*, 233–234.

[25] *Ibid.*, 237.

[26] http://www.cdc.gov/ncidod/dbmd/diseaseinfo/ salment_g.htm

[27] http://www.cdc.gov/mmwr/preview/mmwrhtml/ mm55d926a1.htm

[28] http://www.cdc.gov/ecoli/2009/0807.html, http:// www.washingtonpost.com/wp-dyn/content/ article/2009/08/31/AR2009083103922_pf.html

[29] http://gateway.nlm.nih.gov/MeetingAbstracts/ ma?f=102235172.html

[30] http://www.ncbi.nlm.nih.gov/pubmed/19400687

[31] http://www.law.cornell.edu/background/insane/ capacity.html

[32] http://www.cdc.gov/nccdphp/sgr/shalala.htm

[33] Heber, *L.A. Shape Diet*, 262–264.

[34] http://geography.about.com/od/ obtainpopulationdata/a/indiapopulation.htm

[35] Schlosser, *Fast Food Nation*, 3.

[36] http://foodparty.tv/2008/07/12/donut-cheeseburgers/; http://www. slashfood.com/2006/08/05/ you-got-french-fries-in-my-frosty/

[37] Heber, *What Color Is Your Diet?*, 107.

[38] *LA Times*, December 21, 2000.

[39] E-mail, October 25, 2009.

[40] Pendergrast, *Coca-Cola*, 402.

[41] *NY Times*, June 18, 2001.

[42] NBC Morning News, June 19, 2001.

[43] Food Network, *In Food Today*.

[44] www.pizzaware.com/facts.

[45] http://www.nytimes.com/2005/05/08/fashion/ sundaystyles/08age.html?pagewanted=print

[46] Saveur, "Nouvelle Schmouvelle," September/ October 2001, 15.

[47] *LA Times*, April 12, 2006, 1.

[48] *LA Times*, June 2, 2005, F1, 8, 9.

[49] Mauseth, *Botany*, 729.

[50] www.slowfood.com.

[51] *The Snail*, 12/2001, 4–5.

[52] nytimes.com/2006/01/05/science/05fish. html?pagewanted=print.

[53] nytimes.com/2006/01/04/international/ europe/04sturgeon.html?pagewanted=print.

[54] http://content.nejm.org/cgi/content/ full/362/6/485/

[55] http://www.edibleschoolyard.org/feedingfuture

[56] http://www.theatlantic.com/doc/print/201001/ school-yard-garden

[57] http://www.fns.usda.gov/tn/Healthy/ wellnesspolicy.html

[58] Schlesinger, *Animals and Plants Ancient Maya*, 44.

[59] http://globalpoverty.change.org/blog/view/ what_bill_clintons_mea_culpa_should_mean

[60] http://globalpoverty.change.org/blog/category/ natural_disasters

[61] http://news.yahoo.com/s/ap/20100616/ ap_on_bi_ge/us_gulf_oil_spill_today

[62] www.delta.com/travel/before/inflight_dining/ index.jsp.

[63] Nabhan, *Why Some Like It Hot*, 153.

[64] *LA Times*, August 18, 2005, A12.

[65] *LA Times*, September 18, 2006, F6.

[66] http://eating.health.com/2008/07/02/pomegranate-juice-packed-with-antioxidants/#more-530

[67] Fedoroff, *Mendel*, 254.

[68] http://www.nrn.com/breakingNews. aspx?id=381022

[69] Nabhan, *Why Some Like It Hot*, 119–123.

[70] http://www.nrn.com/landingPage.aspx?menu_ id=1416&coll_id=554&id=360010&utm_ source=MagnetMail&utm_ medium=email&utm_term=cucinalinda@ aol.com&utm_content=NRN-News-Marketing%20Matters%2011-20-08&utm_ campaign=Marketing%20Matters%20from%20 NRN-Online]

[71] http://www.nrn.com/landingPage.aspx?menu_ id=1416&coll_id=554&id=359834&utm_ source=MagnetMail&utm_ medium=email&utm_term=cucinalinda@ aol.com&utm_content=NRN-News-Marketing%20Matters%2011-20-08&utm_ campaign=Marketing%20Matters%20from%20 NRN-Online

[72] http://www.nrn.com/breakingNews. aspx?id=381026#ixzz0j0nPdmt5

[73] http://www.nrn.com/article. aspx?id=380480#ixzz0j0oyYbr0

[74] http://www.minyanville.com/businessmarkets/ articles/starbucks-starbucks-coffee-mcdonalds-burger-king/3/23/2010/id/27422?camp= syndication&medium=portals&from=yahoo

75 http://www.time.com/time/business/article/
0,8599,1978705,00.html

76 http://www.nrn.com/landingPage.aspx?menu_
id=1384&coll_id=654&id=374834&utm_
source=MagnetMail&utm_medium=
email&utm_term=cucinalinda@aol.com&utm_
content=NRN-News-Beverage%20Trends%20
11-12-09&utm_campaign=Holy%20atom-
izer,%20barman%21%20Mixologists%20
spray%20cocktails%20with%20aromatics

77 http://www.nytimes.com/2009/06/18/
fashion/18skinside.html?_r=1&pagewanted=print

78 http://www.nrn.com/breakingNews.
aspx?id=381030

79 http://www.nrn.com/landingPage.aspx?menu_
id=1416&coll_id=554&id=360052&utm_
source=MagnetMail&utm_medium=email&
utm_term=&utm_content=NRN-News-
Marketing%20Matters%2011-20-08&utm_
campaign=Marketing%20Matters%20from%20
NRN-Online]

80 http://www.bls.gov/oco/cg/cgs024.htm

81 Richard S. Tedlow. *New and Improved*, 1990; 196.

82 Ibid.

83 http://supermarketnews.com/profiles/
top75/2010/index.html/

84 http://www.minyanville.com/
businessmarkets/articles/organic-consumers-
manufacturers-walmart-general-mills/3/22/2010/
id/27380

85 http://newyork.grubstreet.com/2009/09/the_20_
biggest_chef_empires.html

86 http://www.joyofbaking.com/NanaimoBars.html

87 http://www.nytimes.com/2009/05/20/dining/
20united.html?th=&emc=th&pagewanted=print

88 Project Gutenberg's Etext of *Don Quixote* by
Miguel de Cervantes, Chapter XLIX.

BOOKS

Achaya, K. T. *Indian Food: a Historical Companion.* Delhi: Oxford University Press, 1994.

Albala, Ken. *Eating Right in the Renaissance.* Berkeley: University of California Press, 2002. http://ark.cdlib.org/ark:/13030/kt587020gg/

Ambrose, Stephen. *Nothing Like It in the World: The Men Who Built the Transcontinental Railroad 1863–1869.* New York: Simon & Schuster, 2000.

Amitai-Preiss, Reuven, and David O. Morgan, eds. *The Mongol Empire & its Legacy.* Leiden: Brill, 2000.

Anderson, E. N. *The Food of China.* New Haven: Yale University Press, 1988.

Anderson, Jean. *The Food of Portugal.* New York: William Morrow, an imprint of HarperCollins, 1986. Revised and updated 1994.

Andreason, Nancy C., M.D., Ph.D., and Donald W. Black, M.D. *Introductory Textbook of Psychiatry, Second Ed.* Washington, D.C.: American Psychiatric Press, 1995.

Apicius. *Cookery and Dining in Imperial Rome.* Translation by Joseph Dommers Vehling. New York: Dover Publications, Inc., 1977. Unabridged republication of the work originally published. Chicago: Walter M. Hill, 1936.

Archbold, Rick, and Dana McCauley. *Last Dinner on the Titanic: Menus and Recipes from the Great Liner.* New York: Hyperion/Madison Press, 1997.

Archestratus. *The Life of Luxury.* Translated with Introduction and Commentary by John Wilkins & Shaun Hill *[sic]*. Great Britain: Prospect Books, 1994.

Atkins, Annette. *Harvest of Grief: Grasshopper Plagues and Public Assistance in Minnesota, 1873–78.* St. Paul: Minnesota Historical Society Press, 1984.

Bayless, Rick, with Deann Groen Bayless and Jean Marie Brownson. *Rick Bayless's Mexican Kitchen.* New York: Scribner, 1996.

Benning, Lee Edwards. *Oh, Fudge!* New York: Henry Holt and Company, 1990.

Blockson, Charles L. *The Underground Railroad: First-Person Narratives of Escapes to Freedom in the North.* New York: Prentice Hall Press, 1987.

Boorstin, Daniel J. *The Discoverers: A History of Man's Search to Know His World and Himself.* New York: Vintage Books, 1983.

Bottero, Jean. *The Oldest Cuisine in the World: Cooking in Mesopotamia.* Trans. Teresa Lavender Fagan. Chicago: The University of Chicago Press, 2004.

Braudel, Fernand. *The Mediterranean and the Mediterranean World in the Age of Philip II, Vols. I and II.* Trans. Siân Reynolds. Berkeley: University of California Press, 1995.

Brenner, Joël Glenn. *The Emperors of Chocolate: Inside the Secret World of Hershey & Mars.* New York: Broadway Books, 2000.

Brenner, Leslie. *American Appetite: The Coming of Age of a National Cuisine.* New York: HarperCollins, 1999.

Brillat-Savarin, Jean-Anthelme. *The Physiology of Taste or, Meditations on Transcendental Gastronomy.* Translation by M. F. K. Fisher. Washington, D.C.: Counterpoint, 1949.

Brothwell, Don, and Patricia Brothwell. *Food in Antiquity: A survey of the diet of early peoples.* Expanded Edition. Baltimore: The Johns Hopkins University Press, 1998.

Brown, John Hull. *Early American Beverages.* Rutland, Vermont: Charles E. Tuttle Company, 1966.

Buell, Paul D. "Mongol Empire and Turkicization: The Evidence of Food and Foodways," in *The Mongol Empire & Its Legacy*, Amitai-Preiss, Reuven, and David O. Morgan, eds. Leiden: Brill, 2000.

_____ and Eugene N. Anderson. *A Soup for the Qan.* Appendix by Charles Perry. London: Kegan Paul International, 2000.

Burbank, Luther, with Wilbur Hall. *Harvest of the Years.* Boston: Houghton Mifflin Company, 1927.

Burke, Peter. *The Italian Renaissance: Culture and Society in Italy.* Princeton: Princeton University Press, 1986.

Camporesi, Piero. *Exotic Brew: The Art of Living in the Age of Enlightenment.* Trans. Christopher Woodall. Cambridge, England: Polity Press, 1994.

_____. *The Magic Harvest; Food, Folklore and Society.* Milan: Arnoldo Mondadori Editore S.p.A., 1989. Transl. Joan Krakover. Cambridge: Polity Press, 1993.

Cass, Joan. *Dancing Through History.* Englewood Cliffs, New Jersey: Prentice Hall, 1993.

Chamberlin, E. R. *The Bad Popes*. New York: Dorset Press, 1969.

Chang, K. C., Ed. *Food in Chinese Culture: Anthropological and Historical Perspectives*. New Haven: Yale University Press, 1977.

Coe, Sophie D. *America's First Cuisines*. Austin: University of Texas Press, 1994.

_____ and Michael D. Coe. *The True History of Chocolate*. London: Thames & Hudson Ltd., 1996.

Coppin, Clayton A., and Jack High. *The Politics of Purity: Harvey Washington Wiley and the Origins of Federal Food Policy*. Ann Arbor: The University of Michigan Press, 1999.

Corn, Charles. *The Scents of Eden: A Narrative of the Spice Trade*. New York: Kodansha International, 1998.

Cott, Nancy F. *The Bonds of Womanhood: "Woman's Sphere" in New England, 1780–1835*. New Haven: Yale University Press, 1977.

Courtwright, David T. *Forces of Habit: Drugs and the Making of the Modern World*. Cambridge: Harvard University Press, 2001.

Cowan, Ruth Schwartz. *More Work For Mother: The Ironies of Household Technology from the Open Hearth to the Microwave*. New York: BasicBooks a division of HarperCollins Publishers, 1983.

Cronon, William. *Changes in the Land*. New York: Hill and Wang, 1983.

_____. *Nature's Metropolis: Chicago and the Great West*. New York: W. W. Norton & Company, 1991.

Dalby, Andrew. *Dangerous Tastes: The Story of Spices*. Berkeley: University of California Press, 2000.

_____. *Flavours of Byzantium*. Devon, Great Britain: Prospect Books, 2003.

_____. *Siren Feasts: A History of Food and Gastronomy in Greece*. London: Routledge, 1996.

Daws, Gavin. *Prisoners of the Japanese: POWs of World War II in the Pacific*. New York: Quill—William Morrow, 1994.

De Sahagun, Fray Bernardino. *Florentine Codex, Book 2—The Ceremonies*. Transl. Arthur J. O. Anderson and Charles E. Dibble. Santa Fe, New Mexico: The School of American Research and The University of Utah, 1981.

De Talavera Berger, Frances, and John Parke Custis. *Sumptuous Dining in Gaslight San Francisco 1875–1915*. Garden City, New York: Doubleday & Company, Inc., 1985.

Derry, T. K. *A History of Scandinavia*. Minneapolis: University of Minnesota Press, 1979.

DeWitt, Dave, Mary Jane Wilan, and Melissa T. Stock. *Flavors of Africa Cookbook: Spicy African Cooking—From Indigenous Recipes to Those Influenced by Asian and European Settlers*. Rocklin, California: Prima Publishing, 1998.

Diamond, Jared. *Guns, Germs, and Steel*. New York: W. W. Norton & Company, 1997.

Diner, Hasia R. *Hungering for America: Italian, Irish & Jewish Foodways in the Age of Migration*. Cambridge: Harvard University Press, 2001.

Directions for Cooking By Troops. Richmond, Virginia: J. W. Randolph, 1861.

Dorris, Michael. *The Broken Cord*. New York: HarperPerennial, 1990.

Dreyer, Peter. *A Gardener Touched With Genius: The Life of Luther Burbank*. Berkeley: University of California Press, 1985.

Elias, Norbert. *The History of Manners*. Trans. by Edmund Jephcott. New York: Pantheon Books, 1978 (English translation).

Ellington, Lucien. *Japan: A Global Studies Handbook*. Santa Barbara, California: ABC Clio, 2002.

Escoffier, A. *The Complete Guide to the Art of Modern Cookery*. H. L. Cracknell and R. J. Kaufman, translators. New York: John Wiley & Sons, Inc., 1979.

Evans, Joan, Ed. *The Flowering of the Middle Ages*. New York: Barnes & Noble Books, 1998.

Fagan, Brian. *The Little Ice Age: How Climate Made History, 1300–1850*. New York: Basic Books, 2000.

Farb, Peter, and George Armelagos. *Consuming Passions: The Anthropology of Eating*. New York: Pocket Books, Washington Square Press, 1980.

Farrar, Linda. *Ancient Roman Gardens*. Phoenix Mill: Sutton Publishing Limited, 1998.

Fedoroff, Nina, and Nancy Marie Brown. *Mendel in the Kitchen: A Scientist's View of Genetically Modified Foods*. Washington, D.C.: Joseph Henry Press, an imprint of the National Academies Press, 2004.

Flandrin, Jean Louis, and Massimo Montanari, ed. *Food: A Culinary History from Antiquity to the Present*. New York: Columbia University Press, 1999.

Fox-Genovese, Elizabeth. *Within the Plantation Household: Black and White Women of the Old South*. Chapel Hill: The University of North Carolina Press, 1988.

Foy, Jessica H., and Thomas J. Schlereth, eds. *American Home Life, 1880–1930: A Social History of Spaces and Services*. Knoxville: University of Tennessee Press, 1992.

Franklin, Benjamin. *The Autobiography & Other Writings*. New York: Bantam Books, 1982.

Frazer, Sir James George. *The Illustrated Golden Bough: A Study in Magic and Religion*. Abridged by Robert K. G. Temple. Britain: The Softback Preview, 1996.

Fussell, Betty. *The Story of Corn*. New York: North Point Press; Farrar, Straus and Giroux, 1992.

Gabaccia, Donna R. *We Are What We Eat: Ethnic Food and the Making of Americans*. Cambridge: Harvard University Press, 1998.

Garcia, Sinikka Grönberg. *Suomi Specialties: Finnish Celebrations*. [no location] Penfield Press, 1998.

Garnsey, Peter. *Food and Society in Classical Antiquity*. Cambridge: The Cambridge University Press, 1999.

Gaski, Harald, ed. *Sami Culture in a New Era: The Norwegian Sami Experience*. Davvi Girji OS, 1997. Seattle: University of Washington Press, 1997.

Geertz, Clifford. *The Religion of Java*. Chicago: The University of Chicago Press, 1960.

Gin, Margaret, and Alfred E. Castle. *Regional Cooking of China*. San Francisco: 101 Productions, 1975.

Gillespie, Angus K., and Jay Mechling. *American Wildlife in Symbol and Story*. Knoxville: The University of Tennessee Press, 1987.

Gitlitz, David M., and Linda Kay Davidson. *A Drizzle of Honey: The Lives and Recipes of Spain's Secret Jews*. New York: St. Martin's Press, 1999.

Gjerde, Jon. *From Peasants to Farmers: The Migration from Balestrand, Norway, to the Upper Middle West*. Cambridge: Cambridge University Press, 1989.

Glasse, Mrs. *The Art of Cookery Made Plain and Easy*. In facsimile (1805 edition), with historical notes by Karen Hess. Bedford, Massachusetts: Applewood Books, 1997.

Goldstein, Darra. *À la Russe*. New York: Random House, 1983.

Goodwin, Lorine Swainston. *The Pure Food, Drink, and Drug Crusaders, 1879–1914*. Jefferson, North Carolina: McFarland & Company, Inc., 1999.

Gray, James. *Business Without Boundary: The Story of General Mills*. Minneapolis: University of Minnesota Press, 1954.

Gutman, Herbert G. *The Black Family in Slavery and Freedom 1750–1925*. New York: Vintage Books, 1976.

Hachten, Harva. *Best of Regional African Cooking*. New York: Hippocrene Books, 1970.

Hale, Sarah Josepha. *Early American Cookery: The "Good Housekeeper," 1841*. Mineola, New York: Dover Publications, Inc., 1996.

Hamilton, Cherie Y. *Cuisines of Portuguese Encounters*. New York: Hippocrene Books, Inc., 2008.

Hamilton, Edith. *Mythology: Timeless Tales of Gods and Heroes*. New York: Mentor Books, 1953.

Harris, Sheldon H. *Factories of Death: Japanese Biological Warfare, 1932–45, and the American Cover-up*. London: Routledge, 1994.

Hayden, Dolores. *The Grand Domestic Revolution: A History of Feminist Designs for American Homes, Neighborhoods, and Cities*. Cambridge: The MIT Press, 1981.

Hazelton, Nika Standen. *The Swiss Cookbook*. New York: Atheneum, 1967.

Henisch, Bridget Ann. *Fast and Feast: Food in Medieval Society*. University Park: The Pennsylvania State University Press, 1976.

Hess, John L., and Karen Hess. *The Taste of America*. New York: Grossman Publishers, a division of the Viking Press, 1977.

Hirtzler, Victor. *The Hotel St. Francis Cook Book*. Chicago: The Hotel Monthly Press, John Willy, Inc., 1919.

Hoare, *Thailand: A Global Studies Handbook*. Santa Barbara, California: ABC Clio, 2004.

Holliday, J. S. *The World Rushed In: The California Gold Rush Experience*. New York: Simon & Schuster, a Touchstone Book, 1981.

Houston, Lynn Marie. *Food Culture in the Caribbean*. Westport, Connecticut: Greenwood Press, 2005.

Howard, W. L. *Luther Burbank's Plant Contributions*. Berkeley: University of California, Bulletin 619, March 1945.

Hsiung, Deh-Ta. *Chinese Regional Cooking*. Secaucus, New Jersey: Chartwell Books Inc., 1979.

Hutchinson, Ruth. *The New Pennsylvania Dutch Cook Book*. New York: Harper & Row, 1985.

Jones, Idwal. *Vines in the Sun*. New York: William Morrow & Company, 1949.

Josephson, Matthew. *Union House, Union Bar: The History of the Hotel & Restaurant Employees and Bartenders International Union, AFL–CIO*. New York: Random House, 1956.

Josephy, Alvin M., Jr., ed. *America in 1492: The World of the Indian Peoples Before the Arrival of Columbus*. New York: Vintage Books, a division of Random House, Inc., 1993.

Kaplan, Steven Laurence. *The Bakers of Paris and the Bread Question 1700–1775.* Durham: Duke University Press, 1996.

Kennedy, Diana. *The Cuisines of Mexico.* New York: Harper & Row, Publishers, 1986, 1972.

_____. *Mexican Regional Cooking.* New York: HarperPerennial, a division of HarperCollins Publishers, 1978, 1984, 1990.

Kennett, Lee. *Sherman: A Soldier's Life.* New York: HarperCollins, 2001.

Kens, Paul. *Lochner v. New York: Economic Regulation on Trial.* Lawrence: The University Press of Kansas, 1998.

Kimball, Marie. *The Martha Washington Cook Book.* New York: Coward-McCann, 1940.

Klapisch-Zuber, Christiane. *Women, Family, and Ritual in Renaissance Italy.* Trans. by Lydia G. Cochrane. Chicago: The University of Chicago Press, 1985.

Klein, Herbert S. *African Slavery in Latin America and the Caribbean.* New York: Oxford University Press, 1986.

Koehler, Margaret H. *Recipes from the Portuguese of Provincetown.* Riverside, Connecticut: The Chatham Press, Inc., 1973.

Kuh, Patric. *The Last Days of Haute Cuisine: America's Culinary Revolution.* New York: The Penguin Group, Viking, 2001.

Kurlansky, Mark. *Cod: A Biography of the Fish that Changed the World.* New York: Penguin Books, 1997.

_____. *Salt, a World History.* New York: Walker and Company, 2002.

Lacey, Robert, and Danny Danziger. *The Year 1000: What Life Was Like at the Turn of the First Millennium.* Boston: Little, Brown and Company, 1999.

LaFleur, Robert André. *China: A Global Studies Handbook.* Santa Barbara, California: ABC Clio, 2003.

Lamoureux, Florence. *Indonesia: A Global Studies Handbook.* Santa Barbara, California: ABC-Clio, 2003.

Lang, George. *Hungarian Cuisine.* New York: Bonanza Books, 1971.

La Varenne. *Le Cuisinier françois. Textes présentés par Jean-Louis Flandrin, Philip et Mary Hyman. Bibliothèque bleue collection dirigée par Daniel Roche.* Paris: Montalba, 1983.

Le Goff, Jacques, ed. *The Medieval World.* London: Collins & Brown, 1990. (Originally published as *L'Uomo Medievale,* 1987, Giuseppe Laterza & Figli Spa, Roma-Bari.)

Levenstein. *Paradox of Plenty: a Social History of Eating in Modern America.* New York: Oxford University Press, 1993.

_____. *A Revolution at the Table: The Transformation of the American Diet.* New York: Oxford University Press, 1988.

Lewicki, Tadeusz, with the assistance of Marion Johnson. *West African Food in the Middle Ages.* Cambridge: Cambridge University Press, 1974.

Luchetti, Cathy. *Home on the Range: A Culinary History of the American West.* New York: Villard Books, 1993.

Lukacs, Paul. *American Vintage: The Rise of American Wine.* Boston: Houghton Mifflin Company, 2000.

Luther, Martin. Trans. Preserved Smith, Ph.D. and Herbert Percival Gallinger, Ph.D. *Conversations with Luther.* New Canaan, Connecticut: Keats Publishing, Inc., 1979.

Manchester, William. *A World Lit Only by Fire: The Medieval Mind and the Renaissance.* Boston: Little, Brown and Company, 1992.

Mangione, Jerre, and Ben Morreale. *La Storia: Five Centuries of the Italian American Experience.* New York: HarperCollins, 1992.

Mango, Cyril. *The Oxford History of Byzantium.* Oxford: Oxford University Press, 2002.

Martino of Como. *The Art of Cooking: The First Modern Cookery Book.* Ed. Luigi Ballerini; Transl. and Annotated by Jeremy Parsen. Berkeley: University of California Press, 2005.

Mason, R. H. P., and J. G. Caiger. *A History of Japan.* Tokyo: Charles E. Tuttle and Company, Inc., 1972.

McCallum, Henry D. and Frances T. *The Wire That Fenced the West.* Norman: University of Oklahoma Press, 1965.

McGee, Harold. *On Food and Cooking: The Science and Lore of the Kitchen.* New York: A Fireside Book, Simon & Schuster, 1984.

McHughen, Alan. *Pandora's Picnic Basket: The Potential and Hazards of Genetically Modified Foods.* Oxford: Oxford University Press, 2000.

McNeill, William H. *Plagues and Peoples.* New York: Anchor Books—Doubleday, 1976.

Medina, F. Xavier. *Food Culture in Spain.* Westport, Connecticut: Greenwood Press, 2005.

Mendelson, Anne. *Stand Facing the Stove.* New York: Henry Holt and Company, 1996.

Miller, J. Innes. *The Spice Trade of the Roman Empire, 29 B.C. to A.D. 641.* Oxford at the Clarendon Press, 1969.

Ministère de la Culture, Musée national des arts et traditions populaires, *Les Français et la table.* Paris: Editions de la Réunion des musées nationaux, 1985.

Mintz, Sidney. *Sweetness and Power: The Place of Sugar in Modern History.* New York: Penguin Books, 1985.

Montanari, Massimo. *The Culture of Food.* Trans. Carl Ipsen. Oxford: Blackwell Publishers Ltd., 1994.

Nabhan, Gary. *The Desert Smells Like Rain: A Naturalist in Papago Indian Country.* San Francisco: North Point Press, 1987.

_____. *Why Some Like It Hot: Food, Genes, and Cultural Diversity.* Washington: Island Press/Shearwater Books, 2004.

Nearing, Helen & Scott. *The Maple Sugar Book.* New York: Galahad Books, 1950, 1970.

Nestle, Marion. *Food Politics: How the Food Industry Influences Nutrition and Health.* Berkeley: University of California Press, 2002.

A New Booke of Cookerie. New York: Da Capo Press Inc, 1972. Facsimile of London: 1615. ("Set forth by the observation of a Traveller, I.M.")

Nightingale, Florence. *A Contribution to the Sanitary History of the British Army During the Late War with Russia.* London: John W. Parker & Son, West Strand, 1859.

_____. "Taking Food," and "What Food," in *Directions for Cooking By Troops.* Richmond, Virginia: J. W. Randolph, 1861.

Ochorowicz-Monatowa, Marja. *Polish Cookery: The Universal Cook Book.* New York: Crown Publishers, Inc., 1958.

Ortiz, Elisabeth Lambert. *The Book of Latin American Cooking.* New York: Alfred A. Knopf, 1979.

Orton, Vrest. *The American Cider Book: The Story of America's Natural Beverage.* New York: North Point Press a division of Farrar, Straus and Giroux, 1973.

Owen, Sri. *Indonesian Food and Cookery.* London: Prospect Books, 1976, 1980.

_____. *Indonesian Regional Food & Cookery.* London: Frances Lincoln, 1994.

The Compact Edition of the Oxford English Dictionary. Oxford: Oxford University Press, 1971.

Paine, Thomas. *Common Sense.* New York: Penguin Books, 1986.

Papanikolas, Helen. *A Greek Odyssey in the American West.* Lincoln: University of Nebraska Press, 1987.

Pendergrast, Mark. *Uncommon Grounds: The History of Coffee and How It Transformed Our World.* New York: Basic Books, 1999.

Phillips, Rod. *A Short History of Wine.* New York: HarperCollins Publishers, Inc., 2000.

Pilcher, Jeffrey M. *¡Que Vivan Los Tamales¡* Albuquerque: University of New Mexico Press, 1998.

Poling-Kempes, Lesley. *The Harvey Girls: Women Who Opened the West.* New York: Paragon House, 1989.

Polo, Marco. *The Travels of Marco Polo [The Venetian].* New York: Boni & Liveright, 1926. Revised from Marsden's Translation and Edited with Introduction by Manuel Komoroff.

Pyne, Stephen J. *World Fire: The Culture of Fire on Earth.* New York: Henry Holt and Company, Inc., 1995.

Rajah, Carol Selva. *Authentic Asian Ingredients.* Sydney: New Holland Publishers, 2002.

Rawcliffe, Carole. *Medicine and Society in Later Medieval England.* London: Sandpiper Books Ltd., 1999 (first published in 1995).

Read, Jan, Maite Manjón, and Hugh Johnson. *The Wine and Food of Spain.* Boston: Little, Brown and Company, 1987.

Redon, Odile, Françoise Sabban, and Silvano Serventi. *The Medieval Kitchen: Recipes from France and Italy.* Transl. by Edward Schneider. Chicago: The University of Chicago Press, 1998.

Riley-Smith, Jonathan, Ed. *The Oxford Illustrated History of the Crusades.* Oxford: Oxford University Press, 1995.

Robertson, Carol. *Portuguese Cooking.* Berkeley, California: North Atlantic Books, 1993.

Rodinson, Maxime, A. J. Arberry, and Charles Perry. *Medieval Arab Cookery.* Essays and Translations by Rodinson, Arberry, Perry. Foreword by Claudia Roden. Devon, England: Prospect Books, 2001.

Rose, H. J. *A Handbook of Greek Mythology.* New York: E. P. Dutton & Co., Inc., 1959.

Rose, Peter G., trans. and ed. *The Sensible Cook: Dutch Foodways in the Old and the New World.* Syracuse, New York: Syracuse University Press, 1989.

Roueché, Berton. *The Medical Detectives, Volume I.* New York: Washington Square Press, 1982.

_____. *The Medical Detectives, Volume II.* New York: Washington Square Press, 1986.

Saint-Ange, Mme. E. *Le Livre de Cuisine.* Paris: Librairie Larousse, 1927.

Sass, Lorna. *To the King's Taste, Richard II's Book of Feasts and recipes adapted for modern cooking* [from *The Forme of Cury*]. New York: Metropolitan Museum of Art, 1975.

Sawyer, Peter, ed. *The Oxford Illustrated History of the Vikings*. Oxford: Oxford University Press, 1997.

Schama, Simon. *The Embarrassment of Riches: An Interpretation of Dutch Culture in the Golden Age*. Berkeley: University of California Press, 1988.

_____. *Citizens: A Chronicle of the French Revolution*. New York: Alfred A. Knopf, 1989.

Schlesinger, Victoria. *Animals and Plants of the Ancient Maya*. Austin: University of Texas Press, 2001.

Schlosser, Eric. *Fast Food Nation*. New York: HarperCollins Publishers Inc., 2002.

Sen, Colleen Taylor. *Food Culture in India*. Westport, Connecticut: Greenwood Press, 2004.

Shapiro, Laura. *Perfection Salad: Women and Cooking at the Turn of the Century*. New York: Farrar, Straus & Giroux, 1986.

_____. *Something From the Oven: Reinventing Dinner in 1950s America*. New York: Viking, 2004.

Shaw, Timothy. *The World of Escoffier*. New York: Vendome, 1994.

Shephard, Sue. *Pickled, Potted, and Canned: How the Art of Food Preserving Changed the World*. New York: Simon & Schuster, 2000.

Shindler, Merrill. *American Dish: 100 Recipes from Ten Delicious Decades*. Santa Monica: Angel City Press, 1996.

Sim, Alison. *Food and Feast in Tudor England*. New York: St. Martin's Press, 1997.

Simmons, Amelia. *The First American Cookbook*. A Facsimile of "American Cookery," 1796. New York: Dover Publications, Inc., 1984 (unabridged and unaltered republication of *American Cookery* as published by Oxford University Press, New York, 1958).

Sklar, Kathryn Kish. *Catharine Beecher: A Study in American Domesticity*. New York: W. W. Norton & Company, 1976.

Smith, Andrew F. *Peanuts*. Urbana: University of Illinois Press, 2002.

_____. *Popped Culture*. Washington: Smithsonian Institution Press, 2001.

_____. *The Tomato in America*. Columbia: University of South Carolina Press, 1994.

_____, ed. *The Oxford Encyclopedia of Food and Drink in America*. New York: Oxford University Press, 2004.

Smith, Eliza. *The Compleat Housewife*. London: 1727; London, fifteenth edition, 1753; Facsimile, London: Literary Services and Production Limited; T. J. Press Ltd., 1968.

Sokolov, Raymond. *Why We Eat What We Eat: How the Encounter Between the New World and the Old Changed the Way Everyone on the Planet Eats*. New York: Summit Books, 1991.

Soustelle, Jacques. *Daily Life of the Aztecs*. Trans. Patrick O'Brian. Mineola, New York: Dover Publications, Inc., 2009.

Spang, Rebecca L. *The Invention of the Restaurant: Paris and Modern Gastronomic Culture*. Cambridge: Harvard University Press, 2000.

Spodek, Howard. *The World's History*. Upper Saddle River, New Jersey: Prentice Hall Inc., 1998.

Stewart, George. *The California Trail*. New York: McGraw-Hill Book Company, 1962.

Stewart-Gordon, Faith, and Nika Hazelton. *The Russian Tea Room Cookbook*. New York: Perigee Books (The Putnam Publishing Group), 1981.

Thoreau, Henry David. *Walden and Other Writings*. New York: Bantam Books, 1962.

Titanic: The Exhibition. Florida International Museum. Text by John P. Eaton and Charles A. Haas. Memphis, 1997.

Toland, John. *The Rising Sun: the Decline and Fall of the Japanese Empire, 1936–1945*. Toronto: Bantam Books, 1970.

Toussaint-Samat, Maguelonne. *A History of Food*. Oxford: Blackwell Publishers Ltd, 1992, 1994.

Twain, Mark. *Roughing It*. New York: New American Library, 1962.

Uccello, Antonino. *Pani e dolci di Sicilia*. Palermo: Sellerio editor, 1976.

Viola, Herman J., and Carolyn Margolis, eds. *Seeds of Change*. Washington, D.C.: Smithsonian Institution Press, 1991.

Volokh, Anne, with Mavis Manus. *The Art of Russian Cuisine*. New York: Macmillan Publishing Company, 1983.

Von Drachenfels, Suzanne. *The Art of the Table: a complete guide to table setting, table manners, and tableware*. New York: Simon & Schuster, 2000.

Washington, Booker T. *Up From Slavery*. New York: Penguin Books, 1986.

Martha Washington's Booke of Cookery and Booke of Sweetmeats. Transcribed by Karen Hess with historical notes and copious annotations. New York: Columbia University Press, 1981.

Watson, Ben. *Cider Hard and Sweet: History, Traditions, and Making Your Own*. Woodstock, Vermont: The Countryman Press, 1999.

Watson, James L. *Golden Arches East: McDonald's in East Asia*. Stanford: Stanford University Press, 1997.

West, Karen. *The Best of Polish Cooking.* New York: Weathervane Books, 1983.

What Mrs. Fisher Knows About Old Southern Cooking. Facsimile, with historical notes by Karen Hess. Bedford, Massachusetts: Applewood Books, 1995. (Mrs. Abby Fisher. San Francisco: Women's Co-operative Printing Office, 1881.)

Wheaton, Barbara Ketcham. *Savoring the Past: The French Kitchen and Table from 1300 to 1789.* University of Pennsylvania Press, 1983.

White, Deborah Gray. *Ar'n't I a Woman? Female Slaves in the Plantation South.* New York: W. W. Norton & Company, 1985.

Willan, Anne. *Great Cooks and Their Recipes.* London: Pavilion Books Limited, 1995.

_____. *La France Gastronomique.* New York: Arcade Publishing, 1991.

_____ and l'École de Cuisine La Varenne. *The La Varenne Cooking Course.* New York: William Morrow and Company, Inc., 1982.

Williams, Eric. *From Columbus to Castro: The History of the Caribbean.* New York: Vintage Books, a Division of Random House, 1970.

Williams, Susan. *Savory Suppers & Fashionable Feasts: Dining in Victorian America.* Knoxville: University of Tennessee Press, 1996.

Wilson, David Scofield and Angus Kress Gillespie. *Rooted in America: Foodlore of Popular Fruits and Vegetables.* Knoxville: The University of Tennessee Press, 1999.

Woodier, Olwen. *Apple Cookbook.* North Adams, Massachusetts: Storey Books, 2001, 1984.

Woods, L. Shelton. *Vietnam: A Global Studies Handbook.* Santa Barbara, California: ABC Clio, 2002.

Wright, Clifford A. *A Mediterranean Feast.* New York: William Morrow and Company, Inc., 1999.

Wyman, Carolyn. *Spam: A Biography.* San Diego: Harcourt Brace & Company, 1999.

Young, Carolin C. *Apples of Gold in Settings of Silver.* New York: Simon & Schuster, 2002.

Zubaida, Sami, and Richard Tapper, eds. *Culinary Cultures of the Middle East.* London: I. B. Tauris Publishers, 1994.

MAGAZINES, PERIODICALS, AND NEWSPAPERS

Cooking Light, July 2002

Los Angeles Times (LAT)

National Geographic, August 2001, "France's Magical Ice Age Art, Chauvet Cave"

New York Times (NYT)

New Yorker, January 7, 2002, "Ice Memory"

INTERNET SITES

http://www.fdrlibrary.marist.edu/psf/box3/t37o02.html: "Ten Escape From Tojo," by Commander Melvin H. McCoy, USN, and Lieutenant Colonel S. M. Mellnik, USA, as told to Lieutenant Welbourn Kelley, USNR

Diabetes: http://www.cdc.gov/nccdphp/sgr/shalala.htm; http://www.cdc.gov/nccdphp/sgr/summ.htm

Diminished Capacity Defense: http://www.law.cornell.edu/background/insane/capacity.html

Doris Miller: http://www.navysna.org/awards/Miller.htm; http://www.history.navy.mil/faqs/faq57-4.htm; http://www.dorismiller.com; http://www.dorismiller.com/history/dorismiller/ussmiller.shtml; http://www.tsha.utexas.edu/handbook/online/articles/view/MM/fmi55.html

The Edible Schoolyard: http://www.edibleschoolyard.org/missionstatement

Sherman: http://hnn.us/comments/1802.html; "Are the Media Right to Single Out William Tecumseh Sherman As the Most Reckless Civil War General of Them All?" by Dr. Michael Taylor

Siege of Leningrad: http://www.cityvision2000.com/history/900days.htm#Siege; http://motlc.wiesenthal.com/text/x19/xm1962.html

Sumeria: http://news.nationalgeographic.com/news/2001/05/0518_crescent.html

Sumerian Dictionary Project: http://news.nationalgeographic.com/news/2002/07/0723_020724_cuneiform.html

Thanksgiving Day: http://www.usus.usemb/se/Holidays/celebrate/thanksgi.html

United States Army rations: www.qmmuseum.lee.army.mil/historyweek/oct21-27.htm; www.qmmuseum.lee.army.mil/historyweek/dec2-8.htm; "The Enchanted Forest," by Major John A. Porter, Q.M.C., *The Quartermaster Review,* March-April 1934.

Pamphlet—

Castles Neuschwanstein and Hohenschwangau, Copyright by Verlag Kienberger [no date]

Index